Clinical Forensic Psychol

"Drs. Garofalo and Sijtsema have assembled an impressive collection of works from top scholars that cover a broad range of topics relevant to forensic psychology, ranging from basic research on antisocial behavior to research on risk assessment and treatment. Most impressively, the chapters are written in such a way as to provide a scholarly review of the available research that is presented in a way to be easily accessible to those without an extensive background in research methodology or forensic psychology."

—Paul J. Frick, Ph.D., *Roy Crumpler Memorial Chair, Department of Psychology, Louisiana State University, Baton Rouge*

"Brilliant book on the subject contains up-to-date information from some of the leading experts in the world. This new book is unique in that all chapters are transdisciplinary, providing the reader with a thoughtful and compelling understanding of offending. Although an introductory text, it forces even the experts in the field to think more deeply about these topics. Garofalo and Sijtsema have done a masterful job in producing an accessible yet scientifically rigorous book that should be an essential read across the various disciplines interested in a global understanding of offending."

—Eric Beauregard, Ph.D., *Professor, School of Criminology, Simon Fraser University, University Drive, Burnaby (BC), Canada*

"This book provides an excellent and comprehensive overview of forensic psychology from established scholars and practitioners in the field. It will be an excellent reference for individuals wanting to gain a broad overview of the topic and I will be recommending it to all of my students. I particularly liked the introduction to the history of forensic psychology with the focus on lack of cultural competence in the field as well as the chapter on ethics since these topics so often get neglected. In my view, this book should be the first port of call for anyone interested in getting an up-to-date grounding in this topic."

—Professor Theresa A. Gannon, D.Phil., *C.Psychol (Forensic)* | *Professor of Forensic Psychology, HCPC Registered Forensic Psychologist, Director of the Centre of Research and Education in Forensic Psychology (CORE-FP), School of Psychology, Keynes College, University of Kent, Canterbury, UK*

"This book will become the Bible of forensic mental health professionals. It has it all, in depth, and up to date. There is coverage of crime causes (e.g., biological, psychological, social), offenders' mental health (e.g., personality disorder, psychosis, ADHD), specific behaviours (e.g., sexual offending, homicide, intimate partner violence), and clinical approaches (e.g., risk assessment, prevention, treatments). The chapter authors form a who's who of worldwide experts in forensic behavior. It's a big book, but a quick read, because each chapter is superbly well written and tightly focused on exactly what we need to know. I would recommend it for forensic mental health practitioners, but also for all academics and students in clinical psychology and criminology, and for law-enforcement professionals. Anyone who wants to reduce the appalling damage of antisocial behavior will find help in this important new handbook."

"Clinical Forensic Psychology: Introductory Perspectives is simply the best introduction to this key area available and likely to remain so for some time. A comprehensive, brilliantly organised accessible review provided by the best experts in the field, A great editorial achievement that is an exceptional textbook at the same time as a desk reference of exceptional value to both students and expert practitioners."

Carlo Garofalo · Jelle J. Sijtsema
Editors

Clinical Forensic Psychology

Introductory Perspectives
on Offending

Editors
Carlo Garofalo
Department of Developmental
Psychology
Tilburg University
Tilburg, The Netherlands

Jelle J. Sijtsema
Department of Developmental
Psychology
Tilburg University
Tilburg, The Netherlands

ISBN 978-3-030-80881-5   ISBN 978-3-030-80882-2   (eBook)
https://doi.org/10.1007/978-3-030-80882-2

This Palgrave Macmillan imprint is published by the registered company Springer Nature
Switzerland AG
The registered company address is: Gewerbestrasse 11, 6330 Cham, Switzerland

To Lasse and Melissa

Foreword

The study of antisocial behavior encompasses a host of explanatory variables spanning multiple units of analysis. Invariably, our understanding of conduct problems and the individuals who perpetrate them connects to psychological phenomena, and, when considering those with severe behavioral impairments, touches on clinical forensic psychology. However, many students of crime have at best a smattering of knowledge about clinical forensic psychology. For instance, there is general understanding of ADHD, but little awareness of its subtypes. Many have general awareness of concepts such as psychosis and psychopathy, but their features are commonly juxtaposed. There is universal awareness of personality, but limited recognition of its structural foundation and the multiple, varied conditions of personality disorder. For many students and even criminologists alike, understanding of clinical forensic psychology is vague and imprecise. This book changes that.

Carlo Garofalo and Jelle J. Sijtsema's *Clinical Forensic Psychology: Introductory Perspectives on Offending* is a signal work containing contributions from experts spanning Australia, Canada, Netherlands, New Zealand, Sweden, United Kingdom, and the United States. This is one of the book's important selling points: Readers receive content directly from some of the leading experts in the world, which gives the content a richness and scholarly freshness that one does not often see in an introductory text. The focus on foundational theoretical concepts also provides the reader with the scholarly content for understanding "the story" behind conduct problems and does so by showcasing the works of seasoned scholars as well as newer scholars who are well versed in the forensic psychology tradition.

Clinical Forensic Psychology: Introductory Perspectives on Offending is organized into four parts. Part I covers theoretical and clinical models that underpin deviant behavior. Models include prevention, psychophysiology, emotion, moral development, personality, empathy, narrative roles, attachment theory, and peer effects. A unique asset is the chapters are transdisciplinary and invoke biological, cognitive, experimental, individual differences, and interpersonal perspectives rather than relying on traditional disciplinary approaches that ignore other content. Part I also shows the compelling explanatory power of specific content areas that when considered cumulatively reveal the multifaceted etiology of conduct problems. This allows the reader to ascertain the intrapersonal and interpersonal mechanisms that engender antisocial behavior.

Part II explores psychopathology and deviant behavior specifically how specific forms of psychopathology drive the propensity to have conduct problems. Again, several important content areas are provided including Antisocial Personality Disorder, Borderline Personality Disorder, Narcissistic Personality Disorder, schizophrenia, psychopathy, ADHD, substance use disorders, and intellectual disabilities. An engaging feature of the chapters is the use of a case report of a person whose symptoms instantiate a particular condition. An important takeaway from Part II is that although (with the exception of psychopathy and Antisocial Personality Disorder) many with these conditions do not engage in antisocial conduct, the condition itself does confer a significant likelihood of engaging in criminal acts. Moreover, the chapters show the nuance of psychopathology and its association with offending. For instance, readers will see that cluster B personality disorders are risk factors for offending but other personality disorders such as those that are characterized as eccentric (cluster A) and fear (cluster C) are not. Thus, simply saying someone has a personality disorder or mental illness tells us nothing about its specific and, in turn, its reach across decision-making and life domains.

Part III examines offending behaviors from a typological approach spanning aggression, juvenile offenders, adult firesetters, adult male sexual offenders, homicide offenders, and domestic violence offenders spanning those who perpetrate intimate partner violence and child maltreatment. Part III really shows the reader how the theoretical and conceptual material from the prior two parts manifests in different offending types and, very importantly, how antisocial behavior can be understood as a distribution ranging from very low (i.e., non-offending) to very high (i.e., pathological offenders). Consistent with broad social science models that convey the heterogeneity of antisocial behavior (e.g., DeLisi & Piquero, 2011; Loeber & Farrington, 1998; Moffitt, 1993), the many faces of antisocial conduct (e.g., proactive vs. reactive, direct vs. relational, intermittent vs. chronic, sexual vs. non-sexual, adult vs. youth perpetrated, specialized vs. versatile) are revealed.

Part IV spans risk assessment and treatment and includes chapters on violence risk assessment, personality assessment in forensic settings, common psychological treatment used to address criminal behavior, the Good Lives Model, Forensic Schema Therapy, and ethical issues in forensic psychology. Part IV is the pragmatic, policy part of the book, which shows the successes and the limitations of interventions to reduce conduct problems among various populations as well as the challenges of assessment in clinical and criminal justice system settings. Although devoted to risk assessment and treatment, it also shows how content areas from the first three parts of the book manifest in the mental health and judicial spheres. For instance, the chapter on the insanity defense highlights the salience of psychotic disorders where recognition of right from wrong, and thus the ability to form criminal intent, is central to whether an accused person can be prosecuted. This is a very different scenario from other constructs and conditions (e.g., aggression, psychopathy, callous-unemotional traits, and Antisocial Personality Disorder) where criminal responsibility is not an issue.

Although an introductory text, *Clinical Forensic Psychology: Introductory Perspectives on Offending* encourages even the expert reader to think more deeply about these topics. For instance, although several diagnostic entities are examined in-depth, the chapters also do a good job of showing the diversity or heterogeneity that exists within presumably discrete diagnostic conditions. To illustrate, although psychopathy encapsulates a coherent set of symptoms spanning affect, conduct, and interpersonal skills, there is also remarkable diversity among psychopathic offenders. Some are glib, showy, and engaging, others are brutally straightforward and socially indifferent. Some exhibit a range of psychiatric conditions that bear on mood and affect, others appear devoid of psychological distress. Some have lifelong contacts with the justice system, others avoid arrest but their personality functioning wreaks havoc on relationships, school, and work functioning. In the words of the editors, the various conditions herein are not monolithic entities.

Finally, the reason *Clinical Forensic Psychology: Introductory Perspectives on Offending* is such an outstanding work is owed to the brilliance of its editors. Carlo Garofalo and Jelle J. Sijtsema are versatile scholars with outstanding contributions in many content areas spanning psychopathy, emotion and emotional regulation, aggression, peer and social network effects on antisocial conduct, substance abuse, youth delinquency, normal and dark personality features, ADHD, risk assessment, sexual offending, and externalizing psychopathology. They could have written masterly on all the topics covered herein, but employed their editorial acumen to secure a global roster of experts to provide introductory perspectives on offending. In doing so, they have done clinical forensic psychology, criminology, and the social sciences an important favor. As knowledge continues to build outside the traditional criminological sphere, it is incumbent on students of antisocial and criminal activity to reach out of their wheelhouse and engage the broader literature that bears relevance to their own work.

Matt DeLisi
Ames, IA, USA

Alex R. Piquero
Miami, FL, USA

References

DeLisi, M., & Piquero, A. R. (2011). New frontiers in criminal careers research, 2000–2011: A state-of-the-art review. *Journal of Criminal Justice, 39*(4), 289–301.

Loeber, R., & Farrington, D. P. (Eds.). (1998). *Serious and violent juvenile offenders: Risk factors and successful interventions.* Sage.

Moffitt, T. E. (1993). Adolescence-limited and life-course-persistent antisocial behavior: A developmental taxonomy. *Psychological Review, 100*(4), 674–701.

Preface

Before you lies the textbook "Clinical Forensic Psychology: Introductory Perspectives on Offending". The idea for this book arose from a need to have a book that could be used to teach graduate and undergraduate courses in Forensic Psychology programs with an emphasis on mental health. Given the strong interest of many students in pursuing a clinical career, we wanted to have a book that would provide students with an introduction to Clinical Forensic Psychology in an easy to understand manner, while also offering an up-to-date overview of the various facets of this field at a level that could be useful to expert practitioners and scholars alike. Most available forensic psychology textbooks typically include a handful of chapters on "mental health" with important, yet selective and concise, reference to the psychosocial correlates of crime and offending. We thus took the task upon us to compile a book that would provide readers with a comprehensive context of the psychological and social factors that may explain offending, giving each construct of interest the space needed to be addressed thoroughly. Moreover, the book should offer knowledge about the links between mental disorders and offending, as well as the current state of affairs regarding offender assessment and treatment. The need for such a textbook is high, given that more and more universities around the world currently offer courses, majors, or (clinical) master programs in Forensic Psychology.

Because this book is written first and foremost for undergraduate and graduate students with no prior knowledge about Clinical Forensic Psychology, the book starts by introducing the reader to general theoretical explanations of antisocial behavior, before moving on to more specific topics within Clinical Forensic Psychology, such as the link between specific mental health issues and antisocial behavior, assessment, and ethical issues. At the same time, the book has also much to offer to practitioners, scientists, and people who are interested in this field of study, either approaching it for the first time (e.g., coming from a purely clinical background, or from a purely forensic/criminological background) or as seasoned experts looking for an updated collection of the mainstream topics of relevance for research and practice in this field. Each chapter is written by experts in their respective fields, provides clear definitions of the relevant psychological constructs and related biosocial correlates that are discussed, and offers ample examples from the literature and practice. Each chapter can thus also be read on its own. Moreover, when appropriate, many chapters provide additional (clinical) case material to illustrate relevant topics and help bridging the gap between theory and practice.

What is Clinical Forensic Psychology?

Clinical Forensic Psychology is a field within Clinical Psychology that centers on the study, assessment, and treatment of mental health issues in relation to offending in its broadest sense, hence bridging mental health and criminal justice systems. In so doing, it is valuable for mental health science and practice to understand those individual characteristics that pose a risk for criminal justice involvement, and it is valuable for the criminal justice system to appreciate the individual needs and risk factors that can inform trial and post-trial decision-making, including treatment and rehabilitation efforts. This field overlaps with the discipline of forensic psychiatry in some jurisdictions, which shares the same target of interest (mental health in relation to offending). Yet, Clinical Forensic Psychology integrates a medical (diagnostic) perspective with an emphasis on the dimensional nature of psychological phenomena, their interaction with the environment, and the explanatory mechanisms linking them with offending. At the same time, Clinical Forensic Psychology intersects with those areas of criminology and forensic sciences that appreciate the relevance of individual-level correlates of crime and offending, but addresses them from a purely clinical psychological angle rather than from sociological or legal ones. As such, this field offers itself with a multitude of potential connections with neighboring fields, whose integration is necessary to obtain a full appreciation of the multifarious explanations of offending.

In many countries, there is acknowledgment that mental health issues may in part explain offending behaviors and thus warrant treatment to reduce the risk of reoffending. Assessment is an important part of treatment and admission to forensic mental health care. It not only serves as an index for the level of risk, but may also provide guidance to the nature and intensity of treatment. More importantly, (risk) assessment is conducted to assist in decision-making regarding (temporal) leave and release from mental health care and/ or incarceration. Although mental health issues in essence reside within the individual, they always interact with the environment. In a very real sense, from a clinical forensic psychology point of view, offending is a product of the interaction between mental health issues and the environment. At the same time, there is much misconception about the direct links between mental health issues and offending, and often the risk of (re)offending is best predicted by considering multiple factors related to historical factors, personal(ity) factors, social factors, and compliance to treatment, as well as their inter-relations. Therefore, it is important for clinical forensic psychologists to also understand the developmental and situational perspectives of offending. While this book takes a psychological approach to understanding and explaining offending, this choice was one of scope given the clinical focus, which by no means implies that individual-level correlates of crime operate in isolation from the environment. In fact, each chapter also sheds light on the role of psychological constructs and mental health issues in specific contexts. Whether it pertains to the legal context in which child sex offending is defined, the role of peers in motivating antisocial behavior, or the role of attachment styles to caregivers early in life, each context interacts with and may shape individual characteristics that could either enhance or decrease the risk of offending.

Roadmap of the Book

The chapters are bundled in four distinct sections that are preceded by a general introductory chapter that describes the history of forensic psychology. This chapter provides insight into the development of Clinical Forensic Psychology and presents a brief introduction of many topics that are discussed in more detail in the following chapters.

Part one focuses on psychological perspectives that may explain deviant behavior and provides a solid understanding of how psychological factors come into play when explaining offending. In this section, readers learn more about the developmental, physiological, emotional, cognitive, and social underpinnings of offending. This is accomplished from a perspective that goes beyond traditional classifications of mental disorders and accounts for the natural variation of inter-individual differences in each of these domains, which in turn may explain why some individuals are more prone to offending than others. Specifically, Chapters 2 to 7 provide more information about the role of psychological constructs on offending, whereas the remaining chapters in this section focus on the role of context.

Part two zooms in on the link between mental health issues and offending, by discussing a wide range of psychopathological problems that are often observed in offenders. The first few chapters (11–13) cover personality disorders that are most prevalent in Clinical Forensic Psychology. The other chapters (14–18) discuss the wide prevalence of these psychological disorders in offender populations, but also debunk the myths that often surround the association between mental disorders and offending. Being integrated among the other sections of the book, this part does not mean to suggest a simplistic correspondence between discrete mental health conditions and offending. Rather, it offers an updated starting point on the most common forms of psychopathology that are related to an increased risk for offending and whose assessment may aid (clinical) decision-making and communication among practitioners. Such an emphasis on traditional diagnostic syndromes is also fruitful as it allows to draw from the rich streams of literature that have accumulated over the years on each of them, and of which the chapters' authors are prominent representatives. As noted across chapters, and in continuity with the previous section of the book, readers will appreciate the inevitable interconnection across mental health conditions addressed in each chapter, as well as interconnections that each has with the psychosocial factors discussed in part one.

Part three moves away from a disorder-focused approach and covers a range of behaviors and offender groups that are relevant in forensic contexts. This approach is common in correctional and forensic mental health and offers a first efficient way to allocate resources and guide subsequent personalized decision-making. The topics discussed include a focus on juvenile offenders, and other offender groups defined by specific types of offenses, each with their own set of explanatory perspectives, risk factors, and clinical and legal approaches. Although the book does not cover an exhaustive discussion of all offenses and offender groups, it includes a focus on aggressive behavior, which is at the core of many offending behaviors.

Finally, part four covers the more practical or applied aspect of Clinical Forensic Psychology by discussing risk assessment and offender treatment. This section is a must-read for students in Clinical Forensic Psychology programs, as it discusses the basics of risk assessment and common treatment approaches. In addition, this section offers the latest insights into the assessment of antisocial personality characteristics broadly defined, as well as information about the novel Forensic Schema Therapy treatment approach. This section concludes with reflections on the ethical issues that clinicians and scientists face in forensic psychology practice. As such, it provides a go-to resource for experts in need of updating their knowledge and practice skills.

In closing, with this textbook, we hope to attend to the needs of students, practitioners, and scientists who want to engage with the field of Clinical Forensic Psychology, either to develop or strengthen the clinical skills to work in forensic settings, or to complement forensic expertise with a greater attention to the needs and risks of individuals who come into contact with the criminal justice system.

Tilburg, The Netherlands   Jelle J. Sijtsema
                                                                                           Carlo Garofalo

Acknowledgments

We thank our patient wives, at times impatient babies, and problematic cats. We are grateful to Dr. Matt DeLisi and Dr. Alex Piquero, as well as to two anonymous reviewers, who supported the initiative of this book from the beginning. In addition, we are grateful to the publisher, and in particular Josie Taylor and Liam Inscoe—Jones for their confidence and continued support throughout this endeavor. And last but not least, we want to extend our gratitude to all the contributors in this book. Without them, this book would not have been possible and we are happy that they stood by us, despite all the challenges that came with the COVID-19 pandemic.

Contents

List of Tables

List of Boxes

History of Forensic Psychology

1

Jacqueline B. Helfgott and Joslyn K. Wallenborn

Key Points

- Origins of forensic psychology began in Ancient Greece and India with insanity defenses, which gained modern traction in eighteenth- and nineteenth-century Europe
- Forensic psychological research progressed in the United States and Europe in the nineteenth century with a focus on eyewitness testimony, memory recall, and practical application to the practice of law
- From the 1960s through the 2000s, forensic psychology distinguished itself academically and professionally as an established field
- Today, the scope of research and professional practice has broadened and diversified to include forensic evaluation, risk assessment, and treatment of civilly and criminally confined populations
- The future of the field will face challenges and possibilities in the assessment of diverse populations, the ethics of labeling, and technology advances

J. B. Helfgott (✉)
Department of Criminal Justice, Criminology & Forensics, Seattle University, Seattle, WA, USA
e-mail: jhelfgot@seattleu.edu

J. K. Wallenborn
Criminal Justice Division, Washington State Office of the Attorney General, Seattle, WA, USA

Introduction

This chapter begins with an overview of the historical origins, development, and milestones of the field of forensic psychology in order to provide a deeper understanding of how the field has evolved as a practice and profession, leading to examination of how modern forensic psychology has distinguished itself both academically and professionally as an established field that incorporates clinical treatment, robust research and theory, and formal standards. The definition and scope of forensic psychology will be discussed with attention to the range of disciplines and subfields in the behavioral and social sciences, interdisciplinary theories of criminal behavior, key theorists and researchers that have contributed to the development of the field, and the role and importance of forensic psychology in the study of criminal behavior and criminal justice and forensic practice. The current state of forensic psychology is examined with attention to the broad and diversified scope of research and professional practice to include forensic evaluation, risk assessment, and treatment of civilly and criminally confined populations. Historical lack of attention to race in the field of forensic psychology and the differential impacts on Black, Indigenous, and People of Color (BIPOC) within the criminal justice system is explored, followed by analysis of how criminal psychology in the media and pop culture has affected decision-making by jurors. Further, the role and importance of the practical application of forensic psychology in the criminal justice system will be examined with attention to the roles and careers offered in this field. Challenges and possibilities for the future of the field will be discussed with respect to the assessment of diverse populations, the ethics of labeling, and technological advances.

Evolution of the Field

Historical Origins

The first uses of forensic psychology can be traced back to Ancient Greece and India in which criminal insanity defenses were used for individuals who had intellectual deficits (Gutheil, 2005). Contemporary origins of forensic psychology first took root in Europe in the eighteenth and nineteenth centuries with an initial focus on insanity defenses and, later, the psychology of testimony. An early case in Britain involved an assassination attempt on King George III by James Hadfield in 1800 who shot the King at a London theater (Brigham, 1999; Moran, 1985). At trial, Hadfield successfully asserted an insanity defense by attributing his criminal behavior to a head wound suffered years earlier (Brigham, 1999). This case was significant because until this time, one had to be considered entirely out of contact with reality (as was not the case for Hadfield) to meet the standard for an insanity defense it prompted the passing of the Criminal Lunatics Act of 1800 which made indefinite confinement the standard outcome for insanity acquittals, rather than release (Brigham, 1999; Moran, 1985).

On the clinical forensic psychology frontier, French physician Phillippe Pinel introduced the novel concept of "manie sans délire," or mania without delusion, in one of the earliest conceptualizations of insanity as a moral rather than intellectual affliction (Maughs, 1941). This was significant because, historically, conceptions of insanity had been intrinsically linked with delusion, delirium, and diminished intellect (Maughs, 1941). This development paved the way for future research, diagnoses, and clinic work in psychopathy (Helfgott, 2019).

Nearly a half century later, in 1843, a shopkeeper, Daniel McNaughten, attempted to assassinate British Prime Minister Robert Peel. At trial, McNaughten had nine medical experts testify that he was insane at the time of the attack and the jury returned a verdict of not guilty by reason of insanity. This resulted in the "McNaughten Rule," which established a clearly defined legal standard for insanity defenses that remains the standard for many American courts (Finkel, 1988). These events mark milestones in the early development of forensic psychology that shaped jurisprudence and foreshadowed changes to come.

Early Development

As the end of the nineteenth century neared, J. McKeen Cattell (1895) broke ground on another forensic frontier: The psychology of testimony. In his 1893 study, Cattell asked his students to recall the weather from one week prior. Answers varied wildly, which affirmed long-held notions that eyewitness memory recall is notoriously unreliable (Cattell, 1895). Cattell (1895) highlighted the practical value and applicability of his findings to eyewitness testimony and psychological expert witnesses in courtroom settings. Joseph Jastrow, Alfred Binet, and (Louis) William Stern conducted similar experiments evaluating eyewitness accounts. Stern (1939) asserted that the expert testimony of psychologists is the "true psychological wisdom which we must strive to incorporate in responsible representatives of law…around the world" (p. 14). During this time, an early academic journal emerged, the *Journal of Forensic Psychology Practice* (1900–2016), now the *Journal of Forensic Psychology Research and Practice* (2017–present), which signaled the continued growth of forensic psychology.

As the twentieth century got underway, two rising intellectuals with divergent perspectives, Sigmund Freud and Hugo Munsterberg, both recognized the importance of the practical application of psychology to the field of law and thus attempted to integrate psychology into the legal system (Brigham, 1999; Schuller & Ogloff, 2001). In a 1906 speech, Freud (1906/1959) compellingly argued that psychology was valuable to the fact-finding process in legal proceedings when he posited, "The task of the therapist ... is the same as that of the examining magistrate. We have to uncover the hidden psychical material; and in order to do this we have invented a number of detective devices, some of which it seems that you gentlemen of the law are now about to copy from us" (Brigham, 1999, p. 108). Similarly, Munsterberg (1908) published *On the Witness Stand* (1908) to illustrate the significance of psychology to the practice of law and the decision-making processes of judges, juries, and attorneys. Munsterberg (1908) stressed, "[T]he lawyers might learn endlessly more from the psychologists" (p. 64) and that "the psychological experiment could be made helpful to the purposes of court and law" (p. 76). However, both Freud and Munsterberg had a flair for the dramatic and neither were taken very seriously in their attempts to convey the importance of psychology to law (Bartol & Bartol, 2013; Moran, 1985). Ultimately, their efforts, though harshly critiqued at the time, contributed to progressive discourse about the nascent discipline of forensic psychology and envisioned changes to come.

Legal Milestones

Despite these strides, attempts to incorporate psychology into the legal arena remained relatively isolated until the mid-century when several landmark court cases served as catalysts to greater integration of these disciplines (Schuller & Ogloff, 2001). In *Hidden v. Mutual Life Insurance Co.* (1954), the court ruled that a psychologist's testimony was admissible in a civil proceeding. That same year, Brown v. Board of Education (1954), historically significant for its racial desegregation of American schools, also contributed to the advancement of forensic psychology, as testimony was provided by psychologists for both parties, though some of their research is now considered controversial (Bartol & Bartol, 2013). Further, a "social science" brief written by psychologists was submitted to the court and cited in the momentous decision (Bartol & Bartol, 2013; Brigham, 1999; Schuller & Ogloff, 2001). However, the permissibility of expert testimony by psychologists in criminal cases remained an unresolved issue. Finally, in *Jenkins v. United States* (1962)), the court ruled that psychologists were qualified to offer expert testimony in criminal cases regarding mental disorders and that a medical degree was not necessary to do so. This decision had profound implications for the forensic psychological practice and increased the frequency of court testimony by psychologists (Bartol & Bartol, 2013; Schuller & Ogloff, 2001).

Developments—1960s Through 2000

Following these legal victories, the field of forensic psychology continued to distinguish itself both academically and professionally, firmly taking root as a legitimate and established field. Indicative of these changes, the American Psychology-Law Society was created in 1969, which marked the field's first formal professional organization, which began to hold professional conferences, publish academic journals, conduct research, and establish field standards (Grisso, 1991). In 1978, the American Board of Forensic Psychology offered a forensic psychology board certification (Otto & Heilbrun, 2002). Further, a number of scholarly journals emerged including *Criminal Justice and Behavior* (1974–present), *Law and Human Behavior* (1977–present), and *Legal and Criminological Psychology* (1996–present).

During this period, forensic psychologists also established themselves as treatment providers (Otto & Heilbrun, 2002). In 1991, standardized guidance was published by the American Academy of Forensic Psychology and the American Psychology–Law Society (Committee on Ethical Guidelines for Forensic Psychologists, 1991). On the heels of these strides, Loh (1981) declared that the field of forensic psychology had "come of age" (p. 345). Though Loh (1981) and others celebrated a century of progress, the field was not void of criticism. In a critique leveled against the evolution of forensic psychology as aimless and haphazard, Ogloff (2000) implored forensic psychologists to seize a more active role in influencing the development of law and advancing social justice.

Forensic Psychology Today

Over the past two decades, forensic psychology has indeed delivered on Ogloff's (2000) call to action: Forensic psychology has taken an active role in law and social justice initiatives both in research and practice. Forensic psychology has continued to grow rapidly and was officially recognized as a specialization within psychology by the American Psychological Association in 2001. Today, the discipline is burgeoning with intellectual capital as evidenced by the plethora of academic journals that publish progressive research and theory.

The scope of research and professional practice has broadened and diversified within the past two decades to include attention to risk assessment(McCallum & Eagle, 2015) (Chapter 25), improvement of forensic evaluation and treatment of unique populations, such as civilly committed sexually violent predators (Chapter 22), treatment of incarcerated individuals within criminal justice system, forensic neuropsychology (Cheng et al., 2019; Larrabee, 2011), the role of trauma in criminal behavior, psychopathy, and forensic mediapsychology (Luskin, 2015). Forensic psychology has also seen continued growth and shifts within legal, criminal, and police psychology, as well as victimology. Restorative justice, an alternative model of justice focusing on harm reparation through practices that include reconciliation and restoration through dialogue between victims, individuals who have committed crimes, and community members, has been recognized as an area in which the expertise and training of forensic psychologists can be particularly valuable (Noll, 2003).

Race in Forensic Psychology

One area of particular importance in any discipline that intersects with the criminal justice system is racial disproportionality. In the 1980s, psychology scholars advocated for the implementation of multicultural competence and training requirements for psychologists which resulted in the publication of the "Guidelines for Providers of Psychological Services to Ethnic, Linguistic, and Culturally Diverse Populations" (APA, 2003), and the "Guidelines on Multicultural Education, Training, Research, Practice, and Organizational Change for Psychologists" (APA, 2006) and the Council of National Psychological Associations for the Advancement of Ethnic Minority Interests (2000) developed the Guidelines for Research in Ethnic Minority Communities. Both APA guidelines were approved as APA policy and Council of the National Psychological Associations guidelines was recommended by the APA Office of Ethnic Minority Affairs and was published by, though not approved as policy of, the APA.

As has been the case in psychology generally, forensic psychology has historically shown limited focus on race. In an examination of the focus on race in forensic psychology research, Carter and Forsyth (2007) investigated the extent to which forensic psychology journals addressed issues of race in empirical articles during the period between 1998 and 2003. The researchers found that out of the total 493 empirical articles analyzed, 47.5% (234) made no mention of race or culture, 43% (212) identified the race/ethnicity of their study sample but did not address race or culture in any other section of the article, and 9.5% (47) of the articles addressed race and culture in depth. While the authors found that between 40 and 80% of published research over the past three decades in psychology as a whole across the range of subspecialties failed to report the race/ethnicity of study participants and those studies that did address race or culture, used White comparison groups, racially/culturally invalid measures, and failed to address within-group differences.

The historical lack of attention to race in the field of forensic psychology is of critical importance considering the disproportionately high representation of Black, Indigenous, and People of Color (BIPOC) within the criminal justice system (Crutchfield et al., 2010; Kovera, 2019; Krohn & Fox, 2020). These results suggest that this lack of attention to the issue of race in the history of forensic psychology has left theoretical and empirical blind spots that hinder nuanced understanding of BIPOC. In forensic psychology, the use of forensic instruments that have not been validated for BIPOC that utilize collateral data that leave open the possibility for racial bias in forensic assessment instruments and evaluations. Thus, while forensic psychology as a field has seen enormous growth, historically there have been considerable gaps between APA policy and practice where issues of race and culture are concerned that have critical implications for forensic psychology. Forensic psychologists increasingly play a role in informing legal decisions that have implications for individual liberty in criminal justice systems rooted in systemic racism.

As a result of increased attention in recent years for the need for research focusing on race and intersectionality, the APA Task Force on Re-envisioning the Multicultural Guidelines for the twenty-first century produced the report, "Multicultural Guidelines: An Ecological Approach to Context, Identity, and Intersectionality," which was developed out of a need to update the 2003 guidelines and from a "need to reconsider diversity and multicultural practice within professional psychology at a different period in time, with intersectionality as its primary purview" (APA, 2017). The 2017 guidelines call on psychologists to recognize many of the gaps such as assessment tools that are not validated with diverse populations, reliance on primarily White samples in research, and the need for culturally adapted interventions that have particular implications for forensic psychology.

Media and Pop Culture

The motivations and inner-workings of the "criminal mind" is a frequent topic of attention that has brought forensic psychology center stage. People are eager to understand the "whys" of criminal offending and despite many explanations within the body of research and theory of criminal behavior, extreme and violent criminal behavior is often culturally understood by orienting them within psychological theories and explanations. Common depictions of the psychology of criminal behavior within crime media portray mental illness, insanity defenses, and psychological histories, as well as the forensic professionals who profile, assess, investigate, and apprehend them. Rise in popularity of television shows such as *Mindhunter, Criminal Minds,* and *Law & Order,* documentaries such as *Night Stalker, American Murder,* and *Killer Inside,* films such as *Copycat, Taxi Driver, Cape Fear,* and *Silence of the Lambs,* and podcasts such as *Serial* and *Dr. Death* has cultivated public awareness of criminal psychopathology. Crime podcasts, in particular, such as *My Favorite Murder, Serial, Criminal,* and others have gained particular traction with female audiences (Boling & Hull, 2018; Moskowitz, 2020). These media depictions are important to the extent that they have the potential to influence jurors and public perceptions that may impact mental health and criminal justice-related decisions, legislation, and policy and have the potential to increase interest in forensic psychology academic programs. For example, content analysis research examining depictions of psychopathy on the television show *Dexter* emphasizes the potential of crime television to influence public perception of psychopathy (Berryessa & Goodspeed, 2019).

Much of the popularity of forensic psychology over the last 30 years can in part be attributed to media and popular culture depictions in the 1990s. The film *Silence of the Lambs* (Demme, 1991) which followed its precursor *Manhunter* (Mann, 1986), based on the novels *The Silence of the Lambs and Red Dragon* by Thomas Harris (1981, 1988) depicting the work of FBI profilers who served as consultants for the film (Jenkins, 1994), was arguably one of the most popular films in history that brought attention to the intersection of psychology, crime, and criminal justice. While the main characters in *Silence of the Lambs*—Clarice Starling (an FBI agent) and Hannibal Lecter (a forensic psychiatrist), were not forensic psychologists, *The Silence of the Lambs* popularized the use of psychological theories used by the behavioral sciences unit of the FBI, most recently depicted in the Netflix series *Mindhunter* (Kono et al., 2017–2019) based on the books *Mind Hunter: Inside the FBI's Elite Serial Crime Unit* (Douglas & Olshaker, 1996), *Crime Classification Manual (2006), and Sexual Homicide: Patterns and Motives (1992).* Other popular films and television shows that followed portrayed forensic psychologists engaged in applied work in criminal justice such, Dr. Helen Hudson in the film *Copycat* (Amiel, 1995), Dr. Tara Lewis in the TV series *Criminal Minds* (Gordon et al., 2005–2020), and Dr. Alex Cross in the film *Kiss the Girls* (Fleder, 1997).

The proliferation of media attention to forensic psychology has affected the way jurors listen to evidence and make decisions about verdicts and has influenced the views held by students interested in pursuing academic education and careers in forensic psychology. Media accounts of what forensic psychology is, what forensic psychologists do, and the roles played by forensic psychologists and other professionals such as criminal investigators and medico-legal death investigators are often confused in the media and impact students' expectations as they embark on career pathways. While raising attention to the field of forensic psychology and to subjects such as criminal psychology, psychopathy, forensic assessment, and criminal profiling, media depictions often do not reflect reality. The number of films, TV programs, memorabilia, and true crime novels depicting serial killers and profiling in the 1980s disproportionately surpassed the actual number of serial murder cases and embellished the effectiveness and role of criminal profilers in serial murder investigations (Jenkins, 1994). "Through a proliferation of forensic programs, from *Law and Order* to *C.S.I.* to *Criminal Minds*, the mass media have offered the public a haphazard education about forensic investigation. While audiences have gained greater sophistication in how crimes are solved, they have also formed erroneous ideas and expectations that can negatively affect the judicial process (Ramsland, 2009, p. 38).

Key Theories and Research

While media depictions of forensic psychologists have potentially spurred increased interest in the field of forensic psychology, the growth of the field has largely been the result of enormous growth in theory and research in the intersection of psychology, law, criminology, and criminal justice. Theoretical constructs provide orientations through which to make sense of psychological processes and behavior. Legal psychology, criminal psychology, police psychology, and victimology are the four key subfields of forensic psychology examined in this chapter. Research and theory are also discussed to provide deeper insight into each of these interdisciplinary orientations.

Legal Psychology

Legal psychology is the scientific study and practice of psychology in the legal system. Research and application of this interdisciplinary topic are valuable at all stages and all forums of the court system. The wide variety of subjects involved include family law, child custody, child testimony, competency, forensic assessment, jury psychology, interpersonal violence, eyewitness memory, and false confessions. Research, assessments, and opinions can be proffered at court through testimony or written reports. Forensic psychologists are able to provide expertise not otherwise attainable from other legal actors that can help determine need, guilt, and innocence, ultimately creating lasting impacts on people's lives.

Criminal Psychology

Criminal behavior has long captivated both scholars and society alike. Those who struggle to fathom what drives one to commit crime, violent and heinous acts especially, are fascinated by the inner-workings of the criminal mind. Considerable effort has been devoted to elucidating the motivations of criminals. Criminal psychology is the study that delves into the psychological complexities and motivations of the criminal mind and the related practices within the criminal justice system. Unraveling the criminal mind is complex work that demands the expertise of psychologists, psychiatrists, sociologists, criminology/criminal justice scholars, and others alike, which taken together, may explain some criminal behavior for some people at some time (Helfgott, 2013). Within the body of work that has been devoted to criminal psychology, there are seemingly limitless theories about criminal behavior that range from psychopathological, physiological, biological, neurological, environmental, sociological, developmental, political, and situational, to name a few. Many of these theories are complex in their own right and are often interwoven with one another. Although some have been proposed (Gottfredson & Hirschi, 1990), there is no universal theory that explains all crime. Criminal behavior is the product of chain of events influenced by an infinite possibility of variables and individual-environment interactions that can be closely examined and deliberately interrupted (Helfgott, 2008). Criminal behavior is diverse; it varies across time, culture, circumstances, and by characteristics of a person such as age, gender, location, and ability. The duality of criminal behavior is that it is both unique and universal at once.

Modern criminology was born in the mid-1700s and this period marks the early origins of the study of criminal behavior and the role of psychology in understanding the criminal mind. Classical criminology of the 1700s that located the roots of crime in free will and utilitarian motives drawing from the works of Jeremy Bentham and Cesare Beccaria shifted to positivist criminology in the 1800s and into the 1900s and the search for deterministic causes of crime (Jones, 1986). With this shift, psychologists played an increasing role in the study and treatment of criminal behavior. Recognition and evolution of the construct of psychopathy (Shipley & Arrigo, 2001a, 2001b), discourse about the demarcation of madness from badness and the law of insanity (Elliott, 1996), and early correctional reform efforts (Barnes, 1972; Foucault, 1995) laid a multidisciplinary pathway for theory, research, and practice in criminal psychology today. The psychology of crime and criminal behavior has gained increased attention over the past century. Hervey Cleckley's seminal 1941 work *The Mask of Sanity*, Krafft-Ebing (1906) *Psychopathia Sexualis*, and other work set the foundation for discourse and debate over the terminology and classification criteria for sociopathy, antisocial personality disorder, and psychopathy in editions of the American Psychiatric Association's *Diagnostic and Statistical Manual of Mental Disorders*. Later works—including Menninger's (1968) *The Crime of Punishment*; Yochelson and Samenow's (1976) *Criminal Personality*; Groth's (1979) *Men Who Rape*; Kernberg's (1984) *Severe Personality Disorders*; Meloy's (1988) *The Psychopathic Mind*; Marshall et al. (1990) *Handbook of Sexual Assault*; Raine's (1993) *The Psychopathology of Crime*; Blackburn's (1993) *Psychology of Criminal Conduct*, Johnson's (1995) *Hard Time: Understanding and Reforming the Prison*, and correctional psychology scholars including Paul Gendreau, Susan Turner, Doris MacKenzie, Ed Latessa, Frank Cullen, Patricia Van Voorhis, and others (Cullen, 2005)—were among those responsible for reviving empirical interest in psychological theories of crime that had been criticized during the anti-psychology/psychiatry movement of the 1960s and 1970s spurred by writers such as Szasz (1961) and Kittrie (1971) and the demise of the correctional rehabilitation era originating in part from Martinson's (1974) article in *The Public Interest*, "What Works?—Questions and Answers about Prison Reform." These scholars and works were instrumental in laying the foundation for increasingly sophisticated empirical research in criminal psychology and criminal behavior and growth of the field.

Psychological Theories of Crime

Criminal behavior has been of great curiosity to psychologists since the inception of psychology and continues to sustain robust interest and relevance today (Blackburn, 1993). Psychological theories offer micro-level explanations of criminal behavior that look to early psychodynamic development, information processing and cognition, and conditioning processes. In the pursuit of explaining violent and shocking crime, psychological theories have been heavily drawn upon with emphasis on personality and mental disorders. More specifically, research has applied a composite of cognitive, behavioral, and psychodynamic orientations to analyze the development of functional concepts of psychopathy and criminality (Meloy, 1988; Walters, 1990).

Psychopathy

Psychopathy (Chapter 15) is recognized as one of the most important clinical constructs in the criminal justice system (Babiak et al., 2012; Hare, 1993, 1998). Psychopathy is a unique clinical condition characterized by the "juxtaposition of affective interpersonal traits with antisocial behavior" (Hare & Neumann, 2006, p. 84) along with an inability to form human attachment and aggressive narcissism (Meloy, 1992). Early definitions of psychopathy often mischaracterized the condition as "insanity" or "psychosis," of which it is neither (Helfgott, 2019). Classic personality traits of psychopathy include superficial charm, grandiosity, pathological lying, and lack of remorse. Behavioral features of the disorder include poor behavioral controls, impulsivity, irresponsibility, and criminal versatility.

Historically, the assessment and treatment of psychopathy have been a central topic area for the field of forensic psychology given the high prevalence of psychopathy in criminal populations. Research on psychopathy has provided strong support for its association with criminal recidivism, violence, and dangerousness. *The Psychopathy Checklist-Revised (PCL-R)* (Hare, 1991, 2003) has provided a critical standardized and validated tool for the forensic assessment of psychopathy as attention has been directed to ethical issues in the use of the construct of psychopathy in criminal justice decisions in particular in using the label as applied to youth (Boccaccini et al., 2008; Jones & Cauffman, 2008) and in high stakes decisions in the criminal justice system such as capital sentencing (DeMatteo et al., 2020). The PCL-R is an unparalleled measure of psychopathy that is widely utilized throughout the criminal justice system for clinical assessment and research (Hare, 1998). Comprised of a 20-item checklist that measures the affective, interpersonal, and behavioral features of the disorder, the PCL-R is now used around the world (Sullivan & Kosson, 2006). The PCL-R has been established as a valid and reliable measure of psychopathy and a strong predictor of violent recidivism, dangerousness (Gacono, 2000; Hare, 2001, 2003; Harris et al., 1991; Hare, 1998; Hemphill et al., 1998; Hodgins, 1997; Litwack & Schlesinger, 1998; Salekin et al., 1996; Serin & Amos, 1995) and determinant of high criminogenic offender risk/needs (Simourd & Hodge, 2000).

Biological and Neuropsychological Theories

Adrian Raine's (1993, 2013) neuropsychological perspective has given new life to theories exploring the biological roots of crime (Chapter 3). Raine asserts that criminal behavior is a clinical condition based on brain scan studies of convicted murderers that reveal striking deficiencies in prefrontal cortex activity when compared to noncriminal scans. Further, Raine contends that brain imaging affirms that the roots of criminality stem from inherited genes and an individual's particular neuroanatomy, which raises important questions about culpability. However, this neuroscience is controversial, as some associate it with antiquated biological theories of the past. Early theorists who looked to biology for the explanation of criminal behavior, such as Lombroso's (1911) study of inferior atavistic traits in his 1876 book *Criminal Man*, were later critiqued as racist and obsolete. Nevertheless, researchers continue to explore the link between the brain and criminal behavior.

Behavioral Theories

Behavioral theories form a logical foundation for the explanation of criminal behavior (Chapter 10). The two behavioral theories considered here are conditioning and learning theories. Conditioning theories aver that behaviors are shaped through stimulus pairing (classical conditioning) and reinforcement and punishment (operant conditioning). Conditioning theories are rooted in the research of early behavioral theorists B. F. Skinner (operant conditioning) and Ivan Pavlov (classical conditioning). As applied to crime, these theories posit that exposure to positive and negative reinforcement will increase or decrease criminal behavior. In learning theory, criminal behavior is produced by social learning in which one's decision to commit crime is achieved through observation and association with others.

Interdisciplinary Theoretical Perspectives

Understanding the underlying causes of criminal behavior is complex and there has been recognition among scholars that explanation and prediction of criminal behavior lies in theoretical and disciplinary integration. Forensic psychological theories are an important piece in interdisciplinary theories of criminal behavior. A number of key theories in criminology rely on integrating psychological and sociological theories to explain criminal behavior including Gottfredson and Hirschi's (1990) General Theory of Crime, Sampson and Laub's (1993) Adult Social Bonds theory, and Moffitt's (1993) Adolescent-Limited and Life-Course Persistent Theory of Antisocial Behavior.

Police Psychology

Police psychology is the study and application of psychological knowledge and clinical practice to law enforcement to enhance police and public safety and well-being. The exact origins of police use of psychologists are unclear (Bartol & Bartol, 2013), however, there is documentation that German police agencies were using psychologists as early as 1919 (Viteles, 1929). The application of clinical forensic psychology in police work involves psychological screening of law enforcement candidates, fitness-for-duty assessments, and police counseling. Policing is a highly stressful occupation that can exact severe mental and physical tolls such as burnout, compassion fatigue, post-traumatic stress disorder, depression, and anxiety. For these reasons, psychologists play an integral role in police work. Going forward, police psychologists can use clinical forensic psychology to play a critical role in informing sound hiring decisions that are inclusive of diversity and reflective of the community, leading crisis intervention and de-escalation training, guiding community engagement, and providing mental health services to police personnel.

Victimology and Restorative Justice

A central role of forensic psychologists is facilitating victim healing and recovery. The experiences of crime victims are diverse and complex and can have both short- and long-term effects. Many traditional mental health therapies are utilized by forensic psychologists to help victims through this process in victim services and in restorative justice programs.

Victimology is the study of those who have experienced real or threats of physical, psychological, social, or financial harm related to an attempted or actual crime. Victimology examines how victims are socially perceived and defined, why some are more vulnerable to victimization, why victims behave in certain ways, how victims are treated within the criminal justice system, the costs and consequences of being harmed, and how victim healing can be facilitated. Application, practice, research, and training may focus on child abuse, elder abuse, intimate partner violence, mass casualty violence, workplace violence, sexual violence, stalking, hate crime, sex trafficking, prison rape, and other crime. Assessment, treatment, research, training, victim advocacy roles, crime prevention, and legislative, law, and policy change are just some of the roles victimologists fill.

Restorative justice is a model of justice that focuses on crime as harm, centralizes the victim, and works to balance victim, offender, community needs, and interests in an attempt to repair harms and restore justice. The restorative justice model of justice process is a striking shift from retributive traditions that is aligned with North American Indigenous practices (Hand et al., 2012). Restorative justice borrows concepts of reconciliation, mediation, negotiated resolution, community justice, peacemaking, and reintegrative shaming for purposes of reconciliation, closure, accountability, harm reduction, community building, and destigmatization (Noll, 2003). Restorative justice principles and practices are embedded in many forums including victim-offender mediation (Umbreit & Greenwood, 2000), prison-based encounter programs (Helfgott, et al., 2000a, 2000b, 2002; Lawrence et al., 2004; Lovell et al., 2002a, 2002b; Liebmann & Braithwaite, 1999; Swanson, 2009), and other initiatives across the criminal justice process (Van Ness & Strong, 2015).

Forensic Assessment

Forensic assessments conducted by clinical psychologists aid legal fact-finders and practitioners in decision-making processes (Chapter 25). Forensic assessment tools published and made available for widespread use in the 1990s contributed to an explosion of empirical research on forensic assessment of dangerousness. Specialized forensic assessment tools brought research and practice in the intersection of psychology and criminal justice to a new level providing a means for researchers to arrive at consensus on the construct of psychopathy and to provide criminal justice practitioners with tools to make critical risk assessment decisions at all stages of the criminal justice process. These forensic assessments included among others the *Psychopathy Checklist–Revised (PCL-R)* (Hare, 1991, 2003) and Quinsey et al.'s (1998) *Violent Offenders: Appraising and Managing Risk and the Violence Risk Appraisal Guide (VRAG)*. Forensic assessment has become one of the most common applications of psychology within legal settings and is applicable to a variety of civil and criminal legal situations such as investigation, testimony, sentencing, corrections, treatment, and reentry.

In the 1990s, a new domain of law emerged which required the use of such instruments: sexually violent predator (SVP) civil commitment laws. First enacted in Washington State in 1990 by the *Community Protection Act*, SVP laws are a unique reincarnation of old sexual psychopath law from the 1900s (Helfgott, 2008). The statutory criteria in Washington State define an SVP as "any person who has been convicted of or charged with a crime of sexual violence and who suffers from a mental abnormality or personality disorder which makes the person likely to engage in predatory acts of sexual violence if not confined in a secure facility" (RCW 71.09.020). In these cases, forensic psychologists interview and assess the respondent, submit forensic evaluations, testify at trial, and conduct annual assessments of SVPs. In the United States, 20 states, the District of Columbia, and the federal government have adopted similar statutory measures. Across the criminal justice system, forensic psychological assessment continues to be an invaluable tool in civil and criminal proceedings alike.

Academic Programs and Training

Forensic psychology has emerged as a distinct scholarly discipline with academic and training programs that have flourished in recent decades as student interest has grown and as demand has increased for forensic assessments, treatment, expert opinions, and testimony. In the 1970s, few psychology and law courses were offered (Najdowski et al., 2015). However, an increasing number of courses and degrees in forensic psychology have emerged (Fulero et al., 1999). Academic opportunities today range from certifications, courses, specializations, undergraduate, graduate, and doctoral curriculum, courses, and degrees, as well as postdoctoral specialization and continuing education. In the United States, 58 colleges and universities offer forensic psychology programs to date (National Center for Education Statistics, 2021) and forensic psychology scholarship continues to develop on the international level.

Roles and Careers in Criminal Justice and Forensic Practice

Trial Consultant

Trial consultants use psychological expertise to assist trial attorneys by preparing witnesses for trial, participating in jury selection, and identifying issues within a case. Trial consultants can assist with all types of civil and criminal proceedings.

Forensic Evaluator and Expert Witness

Forensic psychologists may be hired to provide a forensic evaluation of a party to a case and expert testimony in civil and criminal trials and other legal proceedings. Within this area of expertise, specializations include child psychology, competency, abuse, hostage or kidnapping, eyewitness accounts, false confessions, and sexually violent predators. Opposing parties in a case will typically retain experts within the same specialization but with differing opinions.

Victim Service Provider and Victim Advocate

Forensic psychologists who work as victim service providers and victim advocates assist victims with their diverse experiences and specialized needs. Navigating the criminal justice system can be challenging, especially for victims who have never done so before, may be experiencing trauma, loss, abuse, or lack of resources. Providers can support victims by accompanying them to court, providing counseling, assisting with safety planning, filling out forms and paperwork, finding shelter, transportation, and childcare, as well as providing information about their rights and protections.

Correctional Psychologist

Correctional psychologists provide counseling, treatment, and rehabilitation ser-vices to individuals incarcerated in correctional facilities, civilly committed sexually violent predators in commitment facilities, and adolescents in juvenile justice centers. Individual therapy, group therapy, relationship and family coun-seling, life skills training, crisis intervention, and release recommendations are just some of the services these positions provide. They may also offer counseling services to institutional staff as well. The rapid expansion and privatization of the US correctional system, as well as the destigmatization of mental health services over time, has created an unprecedented demand for institutional psychologists, providing many opportunities to work with this specialized population in need of services.

Police Psychologist

Police psychologists fill a variety of different roles and responsibilities that range from psychological assessments of police applicants, fitness-for-duty evaluations, evaluation of deadly force incidents, individual and group therapy, crisis inter-vention, stress management, to substance abuse treatment. Police psychologists may or not be a peace officer but must be well versed in police culture.

Criminal Profiler

Criminal profiling is a type of investigative psychology that applies psycholog-ical research and principles to the investigation of criminal behavior. Criminal profiling has been widely popularized in the media and pop culture after being formally recognized by the Federal Bureau of Investigation (FBI) in the early 1970s (Ressler et al., 1986). Criminal profiling entails classifying behavioral, cognitive, emotional, and demographic characteristics of an offender by analysis of features of crimes and crime scenes in order to focus the suspect pool more in an informed manner with the aim of identifying and apprehending a suspect (Ressler et al., 1986). Criminal profiling can be utilized for rapists, murder-ers, arsonists, burglars, bank robbers, domestic and international terrorists, mass shooters/bombers, and so on. Victim profiling is an emerging subfield aimed to prevent victimization, such as by using a typology of cyberscam victims (Whitty, 2020).

This overview of professions within forensic psychology is just a glimpse into some of the careers one can pursue. Most any application of psychology to a legal setting within the criminal justice system falls within the purview of forensic psychology, including educators, researchers, and many more.

The Future of the Field

Diverse Populations

Forensic assessment instruments must become increasingly sophisticated and must account for differences in measurement risk assessment by gender, age, culture, ability, and sexual orientation. Evaluation of female risk for violence, dangerousness, sexual offending, and recidivism remains relatively uncharted. BIPOC and female offenders possess risk factors and psychological needs distinct from their White male counterparts (the populations within which the majority of risk assessments instruments have been validated). This should be recognized by the profession in order to strive to appropriately assess risk across all groups. Differing populations will also present differently in treatment and may be more amenable to different types of treatment based on their distinct needs.

Ethics of Labeling

Increased awareness of the powerful effects that labeling has for both victims and offenders alike may prompt changes in the treatment and assessment of these individuals. Labeling can be transformative and influence the identity and behavior of individuals within the criminal justice system.

The ethics of labeling in correctional treatment settings of those who have been convicted has gained considerable attention (Willis, 2018). Labeling can have profound effects and can affect one for life. In particular, the labels "sex offender," "psychopath," and "pedophile" have the potential to harm individuals through the stigma, shame, ostracization, and humiliation these labels carry, which may lead to isolation and avoiding prosocial behavior; behaviors that are counterproductive to treatment and reintegration (Willis, 2018). Empirical evidence now shows that the "sex offender" and "pedophile" labels are associated with increased stigma compared to neutral, non-labeling language (Harris & Socia, 2016; Imhoff, 2015). Labels based on one's convictions, past behavior, or psychological characteristics may also increase recidivism (Willis, 2018).

Labeling is just one of many barriers to reentry and reintegration and has particularly negative impacts on youth (Mowen et al., 2018). Labeling that can reduce recidivism, remove stigma, encourage reintegration, and empower victims has profound implications for the future of the field. Forensic psychologists should seek increased awareness of labeling and its affects so that it may be integrated into their practice.

Technology

Technological advances and their influence in our lives are a driving force propelling the future of forensic psychology in a multitude of pivotal ways. Thus, it is imperative that forensic psychology too keeps current. For instance, information from social media sites is now being leveraged by forensic psychologists, likely due to its widespread use, wealth of personal information, and ease of accessibility. Recent research revealed that forensic psychologists now utilize social networking sites frequently in forensic mental health assessments and perceive these sites as useful sources of information about individuals to inform psycholegal evaluations, opinions, and reports (Coffey et al., 2018). This underscores ethical concerns, such as consent, accuracy, and authenticity of the information.

Traditional methods of conducting forensic psychological assessments continue to evolve with the rise of technology. Many facilities now utilize videoconferencing technology to connect forensic psychologists with incarcerated and committed individuals in order to carry out assessments and treatment. Though we are not likely to see artificial intelligence replace forensic psychologists anytime soon, forensic psychological assessments via videoconference reveal technology as a vital and evolving asset to the field.

References

American Psychological Association. (2003). Guidelines on multicultural education, training, research, practice, and organizational change for psychologists. *American Psychologist, 58*, 377–402. https://doi.org/10.1037/0003-066X.58.5.377
American Psychological Association. (2006). Guidelines and principles for accreditation of programs in professional psychology. https://www.apa.org/about/policy/accreditation-archived.pdf
American Psychological Association. (2017). Multicultural guidelines: An ecological approach to context, identity, and intersectionality. http://www.apa.org/about/policy/multicultural-guidelines.pdf
Amiel, J. (Director). (1995). *Copycat* [Film]. Warner Bros.

Babiak, P., Folino, J., Hancock, J., Hare, R. D., Logan, M., Mayer, E. L., Meloy, J. R., Häkkänen-Nyholm, H., O'Toole, M. E., Pinizzotto, A., Porter, S. Smith, S., & Woodworth, M. (July, 2012). Psychopathy: An important concept for the 21st Century. *FBI Law Enforcement Bulletin.* https://leb.fbi.gov/file-repository/archives/leb-july-2012.pdf/view

Barnes, H. E. (1972). *The story of punishment.* Montclaire, NJ: Patterson Smith.

Bartol, C. R., & Bartol, A. M. (2013). History of forensic psychology. In I. B. Weiner & R. K. Otto (Eds.), *Handbook of Forensic Psychology.* ProQuest Ebook Central.

Berryessa, C., & Goodspeed, T. (2019). The brain of Dexter Morgan: The science of psychopathy in Showtime's season 8 of Dexter. *American Journal of Criminal Justice: AJCJ, 44*(6), 962–978. https://doi.org/10.1007/s12103-019-9470-1

Blackburn, R. (1993). *The psychology of criminal conduct: Theory, research, and practice.* Wiley.

Boccaccini, M. Y., Murrie, D. C., Clark, J. W., & Cornell, D. G. (2008). Describing, diagnosing, and naming psychopathy: How do youth psychopathy labels influence jurors? *Behavioral Sciences and the Law, 26*(4), 487–510. https://doi.org/10.1002/bsl.821

Boling, K. S., & Hull, K. (2018). Undisclosed information—Serial is my favorite murder: Examining motivations in the true crime podcast audience. *Journal of Radio & Audio Media, 25*(1), 92–108. https://doi.org/10.1080/19376529.2017.1370714

Brigham, J. C. (1999). What is forensic psychology, anyway? *Law and Human Behavior, 23*(3), 273–298. https://doi.org/10.1023/A:1022304414537

Brown v. Board of Education, 347 U.S. 483 (1954).

Carter, R. T., & Forsyth, J. M. (2007). Examining race and culture in psychology journals: The case of forensic psychology. *Professional Psychology: Research and Practice, 38*(2), 133–142. https://doi.org/10.1037/0735-7028.38.2.133

Cattell, J. M. (1895). Measurements of the accuracy of recollection. *Science, 2*(49), 761–766. https://doi.org/10.1126/science.2.49.761

Cheng, J., O'Connell, M. E., & Wormith, J. S. (2019). Bridging neuropsychology and forensic psychology: Executive function overlaps with the central eight risk and need factors. *International Journal of Offender Therapy and Comparative Criminology, 63*(4), 558–573. https://doi.org/10.1177/0306624X18803818

Cleckley, H. (1941, 1976, 1988). *The mask of sanity.* Mosby.

Coffey, C. A., Batastini, A. B., & Vitacco, M. J. (2018). Clues from the digital world: A survey of clinicians' reliance on social media as collateral data in forensic evaluations. *Professional Psychology, Research and Practice, 49*(5), 345–354. https://doi.org/10.1037/pro0000206

Committee on Ethical Guidelines for Forensic Psychologists. (1991). Specialty guidelines for forensic psychologists. *Law and Human Behavior, 15*(6), 655–665. https://doi.org/10.1007/BF01065858

Council of National Psychological Associations for the Advancement of Ethnic Minority Interests. (2000). *Guidelines for research in ethnic minority communities.* https://www.apa.org/pi/oema/resources/cnpaaemi-guidelines.pdf

Crutchfield, R. D., Fernandes, A., & Martinez, J. (2010). Racial and ethnic disparity and criminal justice. How much is too much? *The Journal of Criminal Law and Criminology, 100*(3), 903–932. https://scholarlycommons.law.northwestern.edu/cgi/viewcontent.cgi?article=7366&context=jclc

Cullen, F. T. (2005). The twelve people who saved rehabilitation: How the science of criminology made a difference. *Criminology, 43*(1), 1–42. https://doi.org/10.1111/j.0011-1348.2005.00001.x

DeMatteo, D., Hart, S. D., Heilbrun, K., Boccaccini, M. T., Cunningham, M. D., Douglas, K. S., Dvoskin, J. A., Edens, J. F., Guy, L. S., Murrie, D. C., Otto, R. K., Packer, I. K., & Reidy, T. J. (2020). Death is different: Reply to Olver et al. (2020). *Psychology, Public Policy, and Law, 26*(4), 511–518. https://doi.org/10.1037/law0000285

Demme, J. (Director). (1991). *The silence of the lambs*. Strong Heart Productions.

Douglas, J. E., & Olshaker, M. (1996). *Mind hunter: Inside the FBI's elite serial crime unit*. Pocket Books.

Elliott, C. (1996). *The rules of insanity: Moral responsibility and the mentally ill offender*. State University of New York Press.

Finkel, N. (1988). *Insanity on trial*. Plenum Press.

Fleder, G. (Director). (1997). *Kiss the girls*. Rysher Entertainment: Paramount Pictures.

Foucault, M. (1995). *Discipline and punish: The birth of the prison*. Vintage (Original work published 1977).

Freud, S. (1906/1959). Psycho-analysis and the establishment of the facts in legal proceedings. In J. Strachey (Ed.), *The standard edition of the complete psychological works of Sigmund Freud* (Vol. 9, pp. 103–114). Hogarth.

Fulero, S. F., Greene, E., Hans, V., Nietzel, M. T., Small, M. A., & Wrightsman, L. S. (1999). Undergraduate education in legal psychology. *Law and Human Behavior, 23*(1), 137–153. https://doi.org/10.1023/A:1022382925188

Gacono, C. B. (Ed.). (2000). *The clinical and forensic assessment of psychopathy*. Mahwah, NJ: Erlbaum.

Gordon, M., Davis, J., Bernero, E. A., Spera, D., Mundy, C., Mirren, S., Messer, E., Barrios, J. S., Frazier, B., Bring, H., & Kershaw, G. (Executive Producers) (2005–2020). *Criminal minds*. The Mark Gordon Company, Entertainment One, Touchstone Television; CBS Television Studios.

Gottfredson, M. R., & Hirschi, T. (1990). *A general theory of crime*. Stanford University Press.

Grisso, T. (1991). A developmental history of the American Psychology-Law Society. *Law and Human Behavior, 15*(3), 213–231. https://doi.org/10.1007/BF01061710

Groth, N. A. (1979). *Men who rape: The psychology of the offender*. Plenum Press.

Gutheil, T. G., (2005). The history of forensic psychiatry. *Journal of the American Academy of Psychiatry and the Law, 33*(2) 259–262.

Hand, C. A., Hankes, J., & House, T. (2012). Restorative justice: The indigenous justice system. *Contemporary Justice Review, 15*(4), 449–467. https://doi.org/10.1080/10282580.2012.734576

Hare, R. D. (1991, 2003). *Manual for the Psychopathy Checklist–Revised*. Multi-Health Systems.

Hare, R. D. (1993). *Without conscience: The disturbing world of psychopaths among us*. Pocket Books.

Hare, R. D. (1998). Psychopaths and their nature: Implications for the mental health and criminal justice systems. In T. Millon, E. Simonsen, E. Birket-Smith, & R. D. Davis (Eds.), *Psychopathy: Antisocial, criminal, and violent behavior* (pp. 188–212). Guilford Press.

Hare, R. D. (2001). Psychopaths and their nature: Some implications for understanding human predatory violence. In A. Raine & J. Sanmartin (Eds.), *Violence and psychopathy* (pp. 5–34). Kluwer/Plenum.

Hare, R. D. (2003). *Hare Psychopathy Checklist–Revised* (2nd ed.). Multi-Health Systems.

Hare, R. D., & Neumann, C. S. (2006). The PCL-R assessment of psychopathy: Development, structural properties, and new directions. In C. J. Patrick (Ed.), *Handbook of psychopathy* (pp. 58–88). Guilford Press.

Harris, T. (1981). *Red dragon.* G. P. Putnam's Sons.

Harris, T. (1988). *The silence of the lambs.* St. Martin's Press.

Harris, G. T., Rice, M. E., & Cormier, C. A. (1991). Psychopathy and violent recidivism. *Law and Human Behavior, 15*(6), 625–637. https://doi.org/10.1007/BF01065856

Harris, A. J., & Socia, K. M. (2016). What's in a name? Evaluating the effects of the "sex offender" label on public opinions and beliefs. *Sexual Abuse, 28*(7), 660–678. https://doi.org/10.1177/1079063214564391

Helfgott, J. B., Lovell, M. L., & Lawrence, C. F. (2002). Citizens, victims, and offenders restoring justice: Accountability, healing, and hope through storytelling and dialogue. *Crime Victims Report, 6*, 3–4+.

Helfgott, J. B., Lovell, M. L., Lawrence, C. F., & Parsonage, W. H. (2000). Development of the citizens, victims, and offenders restoring justice program at the Washington state reformatory. *Criminal Justice Policy Review, 10*(3), 363–399. https://doi.org/10.1177/0887403499010003003

Helfgott, J. B., Lovell, M. L., Lawrence, C. F., & Parsonage, W. H. (2000). Results from the pilot study of the citizens, victims, and offenders restoring justice program at the Washington state reformatory. *Journal of Contemporary Criminal Justice, 16*(1), 5–31. https://doi.org/10.1080/10282580213088

Helfgott, J. B. (2008). *Criminal behavior: Theories, typologies, and criminal justice.* Sage.

Helfgott, J. B. (2013). Criminal psychology and criminal behavior. In J. B. Helfgott (Ed.), *Criminal psychology* (pp. 3–42). Praeger/ABC-CLIO.

Helfgott, J. B. (2019). *No remorse: Psychopathy and criminal justice.* Praeger/ABC-CLIO.

Hemphill, J. S., Hare, R. D., & Wong, S. (1998). Psychopathy and recidivism: A review. *Legal and Criminological Psychology, 3*(1), 139–170. https://doi.org/10.1111/j.2044-8333.1998.tb00355.x

Imhoff, R. (2015). Punitive attitudes against pedophiles or persons with sexual interest in children: does the label matter? *Archives of Sexual Behavior, 44*(1), 35–44. https://doi.org/10.1007/s10508-014-0439-3

Jenkins, P. (1994). *Using murder: The social construction of serial homicide.* Aldine de Gruyter.

Jenkins v. United States, 307 F.2d 637 (D.C. Court of Appeals, 1962).

Johnson, R. (1995). *Hard time: Understanding and reforming the prison.* Wadsworth.

Jones, D. A. (1986). *History of criminology.* Greenwood Press.

Jones, S., & Cauffman, E. (2008). Juvenile psychopathy and judicial decision making: An empirical analysis of an ethical dilemma. *Behavioral Sciences and the Law, 26*, 151–165. https://doi.org/10.1002/bsl.792

Kernberg, O. F. (1984). *Severe personality disorders: Psychotherapeutic strategies.* Yale University Press.

Kittrie, N. N. (1971). *The right to be different: Deviance and enforced therapy.* Johns Hopkins University Press.

Kono, B., Theron, C., Penhall, J., Chaffin, C., Donen, J., Fincher, D., & Miles, C. (Executive Producers) (2017–2019). *Mindhunter.* Denver and Delilah Productions; Netflix.

Kovera, M. B. (2019). Racial disparities in the criminal justice system: Prevalence, causes, and a search for solutions. *Journal of Social Issues, 75*(4), 1139–1164. https://doi.org/10.1111/josi.12355

Krafft-Ebing, R. V. (1906). *Psychopathia sexualis.* Login Brothers.

Krohn, M., & Fox, B. (2020). Causes and effects of racial disparity in the criminal justice system. *Justice Quarterly, 37*(5), 761–762. https://doi.org/10.1080/07418825.2020.1782615

Larrabee, G. J. (Ed.) (2011). *Forensic neuropsychology: A scientific approach.* Oxford University Press.

Lawrence, C. F., Lovell, M. L., & Helfgott, J. B. (2004). The moral discourse of healing: Victims and offenders for restorative justice. *Journal of Societal and Social Policy, 3*(2), 49–64.

Liebmann, M., & Braithwaite, S. (May, 1999). *Restorative justice in custodial settings: Report for the restorative justice working group in Northern Ireland.* https://restorativejustice.org.uk/sites/default/files/resources/files/Research%20into%20Restorative%20Justice%20in%20Custodial%20Settings.pdf

Litwack, T. R., & Schlesinger L. B. (1998). Dangerous risk assessments: Research, legal, and clinical considerations. In A. K. Hess & I. B. Weiner (Eds.), *Handbook of forensic psychology* (pp. 171–217). New York: Wiley.

Loh, W. D. (1981). Perspectives on psychology and law. *Journal of Applied Social Psychology, 11*(4), 314–355. https://doi.org/10.1111/j.1559-1816.1981.tb00827.x

Lombroso, C. (1911). *Criminal man.* Putnam.

Lovell, M. L., Helfgott, J. B., & Lawrence, C. F. (2002). Narrative accounts from the citizens, victims, and offenders restoring justice program at the Washington state reformatory. *Contemporary Justice Review, 5*(3), 261–272. https://doi.org/10.1080/10282580213088

Lovell, M. L., Helfgott, J. B., & Lawrence, C. F. (2002b). Citizens, victims, and offenders restoring justice: Social group work bridging the divide. In S. Henry, J. East, & C. Schmitz (Eds.), *Social work with groups.* Haworth Press.

Luskin, B. J. (2015, April 9). Forensic media psychology and a camera in every pocket! *Psychology Today.* https://www.psychologytoday.com/us/blog/the-media-psychology-effect/201504/forensic-media-psychology-and-camera-in-every-pocket

Mann, M. (1986). *Manhunter.* De Laurentiis Entertainment Group (DEG).

Marshall, W. L., Laws, D. R., & Barbaree, H. E. (Eds.). (1990). *Handbook of sexual assault: Issues, theories, and treatment of the offender.* Springer.

Martinson, R. (1974). What works?—Questions and answers about prison reform. *The Public Interest, 35,* 22–54. https://www.nationalaffairs.com/storage/app/uploads/public/58e/1a4/ba7/58e1a4ba7354b822028275.pdf

Maughs, S. (1941). A concept of psychopathy and psychopathic personality: Its evolution and historical development. *Journal of Criminal Psychopathology, 2,* 329–356.

McCallum, J., & Eagle, K. (2015). Risk assessment: A reflection on the principles of tools to help manage risk of violence in mental health. *Psychiatry, Psychology, and Law, 22*(3), 378–387. https://doi.org/10.1080/13218719.2014.959155

Meloy, J. R. (1988). *The psychopathic mind: Origins, dynamics, and treatment.* Jason Aronson.

Meloy, J. R. (1992). *Violent attachments.* Jason Aronson.

Menninger, K. (1968). *The crime of punishment.* Viking Press.

Moffitt, T. E. (1993). Adolescence-limited and life-course-persistent antisocial behavior: A developmental taxonomy. *Psychological Review, 100*(4), 674–701. https://doi.org/10.1037/0033-295X.100.4.674

Moran, R. (1985). The origin of insanity as a special verdict: The trial for treason of James Hadfield (1800). *Law & Society Review, 19*(3), 487–519. https://doi.org/10.2307/3053574

Moskowitz, P. E. (2020, May/June). *Mother Jones.* https://www.motherjones.com/media/2020/06/true-crime-podcasts-white-women/

Mowen, T. J., Brent, J. J., & Bares, K. L. (2018). How arrest impacts delinquency over time between and within individuals. *Youth Violence and Juvenile Justice, 16*(4) 358–377. https://doi.org/10.1177/1541204017712560

Munsterberg, H. (1908). *On the witness stand: Essays on psychology and crime.* The McClure Company.

Najdowski, C. J., Bottoms, B. L., Stevenson, M. C., & Veilleux, J. C. (2015). A historical review and resource guide to the scholarship of teaching and training in psychology and law and forensic psychology. *Training and Education in Professional Psychology, 9*(3), 217–228. https://doi.org/10.1037/tep0000095

National Center for Education Statistics. (2021, January 11). *College Navigator.* https://nces.ed.gov/collegenavigator/

Noll, D. E. (2003). Restorative justice: Outlining a new direction for forensic psychology. *Journal of Forensic Psychology Practice, 3*(1), 5–24. https://doi.org/10.1300/J158v03n01_02

Ogloff, J. R. P. (2000). Two steps forward and one step backward: The law and psychology movement(s) in the 20th century. *Law and Human Behavior, 24*(4), 457–483. https://doi.org/10.1023/A:1005596414203

Otto, R. K., & Heilbrun, K. (2002). The practice of forensic psychology: A look toward the future in light of the past. *The American Psychologist, 57*(1), 5–18. https://doi.org/10.1037/0003-066X.57.1.5

Quinsey, V. L., Harris, G. T., Rice, M. E., & Cormier, C. A. (1998). *Violent offenders: Appraising and managing risk.* American Psychological Association.

Raine, A. (1993). *The psychopathology of crime: Criminal behavior as a clinical disorder.* Academic Press.

Raine, A. (2013). *The anatomy of violence: The biological roots of crime* (1st ed.). Pantheon Books.

Ramsland, K. (2009). The facts about fiction: What Grissom could learn about forensic psychology. *The Journal of Psychiatry and Law, 37*(1), 37–50. https://doi.org/10.1177/009318530903700104

Ressler, R. K., Burgess, A. W., Hartman, C. R., Douglas, J. E., & McCormack, A. (1986). Murderers who rape and mutilate. *Journal of Interpersonal Violence, 1*(3), 273–287. https://doi.org/10.1177/088626086001003002

Salekin, R. T., Rogers, R., & Sewell, K. W. (1996). A review and meta-analysis of the Psychopathy Checklist and Psychopathy Checklist–Revised: Predictive validity of dangerousness. *Clinical Psychology: Science and Practice, 3*(3), 203–215. https://doi.org/10.1111/j.1468-2850.1996.tb00071.x

Sampson, R. J., & Laub, J. H. (1993). Crime in the making: Pathways and turning points through life. *Crime & Delinquency, 39*(3), 396–396. https://doi.org/10.1177/0011128793039003010

Schuller, R. A., & Ogloff, J. R. P. (2001). An introduction to psychology and law. In R. A. Schuller & J. R. P. Ogloff (Eds.), *Introduction to Psychology and Law*. ProQuest Ebook Central.

Shipley, S., & Arrigo, B. A. (2001). The confusion over psychopathy (I): Historical considerations. *International Journal of Offender Therapy and Comparative Criminology, 45*, 325–344. https://doi.org/10.1177/0306624X01453005

Shipley, S., & Arrigo, B. A. (2001). The confusion over psychopathy (II): Implications for forensic (correctional) practice. *International Journal of Offender Therapy and Comparative Criminology, 45*, 407–420. https://doi.org/10.1177/0306624X01454002

Simourd, D. J., & Hoge, R. D. (2000). Criminal psychopathy: A risk-and-need perspective. *Criminal Justice and Behavior, 27*(2), 256–272. https://doi.org/10.1177/0093854800027002007

Stern, L. W. (1939). The psychology of testimony. *Journal of Abnormal and Social Psychology, 34*(1), 3–20. https://doi.org/10.1037/h0054144

Swanson, C. (2009). *Restorative justice in a prison community: Or everything I didn't learn in kindergarten I learned in prison*. Lexington Books.

Szasz, T. S. (1961). *The myth of mental illness: Foundations of a theory of personal conduct*. Hoeber-Harper.

Umbreit, M. S., & Greenwood, J. (2000, April). *National survey of victim-offender mediation programs in the United States*. United States Office of Justice Programs. Office for Victims of Crime & Center for Restorative Justice & Peacemaking. https://www.ncjrs.gov/ovc_archives/reports/restorative_justice/restorative_justice_ascii_pdf/ncj176350.pdf

Van Ness, D., & Strong, K. H. (2015). *Restoring justice: An introduction to restorative justice* (5th ed.). Routledge, Taylor & Francis Group.

Viteles, M. S. (1929). Psychological methods in the selection of patrolmen in Europe. *Annals of the American Academy, 146*(1), 160–165. https://doi.org/10.1177/000271622914600116

Walters, G. D. (1990). *The criminal lifestyle: Patterns of serious criminal conduct*. Sage.

Washington State Community Protection Act. Wash. Laws ch. 3, § 101–1406 (1990) (Codified as Amended in Scattered Sections of Wash. Rev. Code)

Whitty, M. T. (2020). Is there a scam for everyone? Psychologically profiling cyberscam victims. *European Journal on Criminal Policy and Research, 26*(3), 399–409. https://doi.org/10.1007/s10610-020-09458-z

Willis, G. M. (2018). Why call someone by what we don't want them to be? The ethics of labeling in forensic/correctional psychology. *Psychology, Crime & Law, 24*(7), 727–743. https://doi.org/10.1080/1068316X.2017.1421640

Yochelson, S., & Samenow, S. E. (1976). *The criminal personality* (Vols. 1–3). Jason Aronson.

Part I
Underpinnings of Deviant Behavior

Antisocial Behavior Prevention: Toward a Developmental Biopsychosocial Perspective

2

René Carbonneau and Richard E. Tremblay

Key Points

- Antisocial behavior (ASB) development is an intergenerational biopsychosocial process.
- Gene-environment interactions' influence on ASB is mediated by neurobiological factors.
- The interactions between genes and environment can be additive, correlational, or interactive.
- Prenatal risk factors, epigenetic effects, and early ASB's onset point to prevention programs starting during early pregnancy with at risk families as the primary method of intervention from a developmental biopsychosocial perspective.

R. Carbonneau (✉)
Department of Pediatrics, University of Montreal, Montréal, QC, Canada
e-mail: rene.carbonneau@umontreal.ca

R. Carbonneau · R. E. Tremblay
Sainte-Justine Hospital Research Center, Montréal, QC, Canada
e-mail: richard.ernest.tremblay@umontreal.ca

Research Unit On Children's Psychosocial Maladjustment, University of Montreal, Montréal, QC, Canada

R. E. Tremblay
Departments of Pediatrics and Psychology, University of Montreal, Montréal, QC, Canada

School of Public Health, University College Dublin, Dublin, Ireland

Introduction

Antisocial behavior (ASB) emerged from half a century of longitudinal research as a developmental, biopsychosocial trait (Tremblay, 2000). According to this framework, ASB takes its roots in the interplay between nature and nurture, throughout development (Tremblay et al., 2018). Developmental theories of ASB first focused on either biological or psychosocial perspectives, which often brought scholars to view these models as competing theoretical explanations, rather than considering their potential complementarity. The biopsychosocial approach provides a comprehensive framework to integrate biological, psychological, and social perspectives.

This approach is also helpful to examine the heterogeneity inherent to the nature of ASB itself (Rutter, 2003). Indeed, across studies and disciplines (e.g., psychology, psychiatry, neurosciences, criminology, sociology), ASB has been described by a variety of different acts, at different ages, ranging from early childhood conduct problems to adult violent crimes. Broadly speaking, ASB encompasses acts that do not respect societal norms, that violate laws or the rights of others, or in the case of children, the expectations of authority figures such as parents or teachers (Frick, 1998). Despite the obvious variation between these different forms of ASB, research suggests that they reflect the same underlying dimension (McDonough-Caplan & Beauchaine, 2018). Specific causal pathways across genetic, neurobiological, and environmental factors may explain the various types of ASB, the timing of their onset in an individual's development, and their persistence or decline over time (Rutter, 2003). Throughout this chapter, ASB is examined from early childhood to adulthood, and thus refers alternately to behaviors typically related to children's disruptive behaviors, juvenile delinquency, and adult antisocial personality and offending. A brief historical overview of developmental models of ASB is first presented, followed by key findings from longitudinal studies of ASB development, before focusing on the developmental biopsychosocial framework, methods, and implications for preventive interventions and future research.

A Brief Historical Overview of Developmental Models of ASB

In the late nineteenth and early twentieth centuries, scientific, conceptual, and methodological advances led to a growing interest in the causal factors of human behavior (Anderson, 2020). An unprecedented number of studies followed, which fed a rather parallel development of distinct models, including genetic, evolutionary, and biopsychological perspectives (Fink, 1938).

Genetic Model

The *genetic model* aims to describe and understand the heritability of human behaviors and the variations leading to individual differences within the population (Walsh, 2009). After uneven contributions such as phrenological studies and genogram reports on disadvantaged families, and despite twin- and adoption-methods innovation (Rutter, 1999; Taylor, 1984), the genetic model suffered from being associated with the eugenic movement and was eventually discarded in favor of the growing influence of psychosocial theories in mid-twentieth century (Anderson, 2020).

Twin and Adoption Studies. The twin method is based on the principle that genetic mechanisms are likely to play an important role if MZ twins, who share the same genes, are more similar on a trait than DZ twins, who share only half of theirs, while both pairs share similar environments (Baker et al., 2006). From this premise, estimates of genetic, shared, and non-shared environmental influences on behavior can be drawn. The studies of ASB using twins and adoption designs (the latter based on the comparison of offspring concordance with adoptive and biological parents) substantially increased during the 1970s. As opposed to early twentieth-century studies interested in heredity as the primary determinant of ASB, this *second wave* of genetic studies aimed explicitly to disentangle genetic and environmental influences on behavior development (Taylor, 1984). Despite variations in samples characteristics, types of ASB investigated, and measures used, reviews and meta-analyses consistently showed from the early preschool years to adulthood that on average, approximately 50% of the variance in ASB is attributable to genetic effects, and a similar proportion to environmental influences (Odintsova et al., 2019; Rhee & Waldman, 2002).

Molecular Genetics. While twin and adoption studies have been the main source to estimate the influences of heritability and environment on ASB, molecular genetic studies investigate the source of genetic effects in distinct genetic polymorphisms (i.e., different forms of alleles for a given gene in a population). Candidate genes studies, based on prior empirical evidence of their biological function (e.g., serotonin and dopamine signaling genes, linked with emotion, reward, and learning processes), make up the majority of molecular genetic investigations of ASB (Gard et al., 2019). However, single polymorphisms represent a limited source of influence in regard to the total genetic variance of ASB, a polygenic trait for which the number of relevant genetic variants is likely to be large, and the effect of any specific variant, very small (Odintsova et al., 2019). There is also evidence that the nature of the genes and the strength of their influence may vary across developmental periods (Pingault et al., 2013), levels of environmental exposure, and types of ASB (Ouellet-Morin et al., 2016). In recent years, Genome Wide Association Studies (GWAS) were initiated. This promising data-driven approach uses the entire human genome to detect associations between genetic variants and traits in population samples to create polygenic scores, but has suffered so far from limited power and lack of replication (Odintsova et al., 2019).

Evolutionist Model

Originating from Darwin's theory of natural selection (1859), this approach posits that genes underlying ASB traits are in the human gene pool because they conferred an advantage to our ancestors, and endured the process of selective retention and elimination of genes across generations (Lorenz, 1966; Walsh, 2009). Traits like fearlessness, disinhibition, novelty/sensation-seeking, and aggressiveness may have been useful to succeed and dominate in hunter-gatherer bands environment, overwhelmed with concerns for resources and mate acquisition (Harris, 2009). Certain traits, like aggressiveness, may be more difficult, but not impossible to manage positively in a modern society (Lorenz, 1966). Other traits may be useful to cope with life contingencies, albeit morally undesirable (e.g., deceitfulness, cheating). Far from legitimizing ASB, the evolutionist perspective on behavior is concerned with 'why' someone behaves in a certain way, by tracing the root of his/her behavior in inherited traits that were presumably adaptive in ancestral environments (Walsh, 2009). This applies to a range of traits linked to ASB, as well as to one's capacity to control these behavioral impulses (i.e., response inhibition) and sensitivity to environmental conditions (Bjorklund & Hawley, 2014).

Biopsychological Models

The biopsychological approach started in the late nineteenth century and focuses on how different aspects of human biological systems may influence ASB, especially the brain systems, but also the hormonal system, the nervous system, and the immune system (Anderson, 2020) (Chapter 3). While tremendous progress has been accomplished since Phineas Gage's famous and first documented case of frontal lobe injury in 1848, which changed him from a kind, soft-spoken, and polite to an irritable, irresponsible, and violent man (Bigelow, 1850), the brain remains the center of interest regarding ASB. For example, a substantial body of research has shown associations between reduced brain's P300 event-related potential (a positive wave arising 300 ms after stimulus detection and linked with prefrontal activity; Downes et al., 2017) and behavioral disinhibition, including ASB in children and adults (Patrick et al., 2006). Other studies used magnetic resonance imaging to investigate both structural and functional, normal and atypical brain development, providing mutually informative references. For instance, reduced prefrontal cortex structure and function, associated with regulating social behavior and decision-making, were consistently associated with ASB (Yang & Raine, 2009). Interestingly, recent evidence shows that neuromaturation of frontal regions is sensitive to environmental risk factors such as poverty and that these effects begin in infancy (Beauchaine & Cicchetti, 2019).

Psychosocial Models

While biological models were developing, so was the psychosocial approach to ASB, and the latter benefitted from the rejection of the former in mid-twentieth century. From the post-war Mental Hygiene Movement that linked family patterns and conditions of child rearing to patterns of children's behaviors, to early longitudinal studies investigating the individual, familial and social factors associated with ASB (Rutter, 1999), the table was set for refined models of ASB development.

Social Learning Models posit that children ASB are learned through observing, modeling, and imitating others such as parents, siblings or peers, and through reinforcement within social contexts (Bandura, 1973) (Chapter 4). Bandura's work inspired others who focused more specifically on interactive processes within family or in the peer group (Chapter 10). For example, Patterson and colleagues (1991) studied social interactions within families of children referred for behavior problems and concluded that these interactions provided reinforcement for aggressive behavior, which then generalized to other settings.

Social Development Models postulate that exposure to risks factors in early development is associated with conduct problems in childhood, while prosocial factors are linked with the development of social skills (Catalano & Hawkins, 1996) (Chapter 9). The balance between these two sources of influence is hypothesized to lead either to an antisocial or prosocial lifestyle. Developmentally, an environment involving many risk factors from early childhood onwards, sequentially foster the adoption of problem behaviors, the accumulation of negative consequences (such as parent–child conflicts and school failure), and the continuity of ASB (Patterson et al., 1989). Typical risk factors across types of ASB and developmental periods may be individual (low intelligence, conduct problems), familial (poor parental supervision, harsh or inconsistent discipline, lack of positive parenting, maltreatment, parental and siblings mental health including ASB, conflicts, and separation), social (poverty, large family, delinquent peers, school and neighborhood problems), or multilevel (school difficulties). Conversely, positive parenting and involvement, constructive social interactions, school and neighborhoods offering positive opportunities are linked with prosocial behaviors and positive social bonds (Catalano & Hawkins, 1996; Patterson et al., 1989).

For over a century, alternately endorsing genetic, evolutionist, bio-systemic, social-learning or modeling arguments, biological and psychosocial perspectives have competed to explain ASB. However, following genetic and biopsychological research advances, many psychosocial approaches integrated genetic and neurobiological vulnerabilities to explain ASB (Deater-Deckard et al., 2016; Fox, 2017). As for the genetic perspective, the prolific *second wave* of studies on ASB came to the conclusion that 'the more we know about genetics of behavior, the more important the environment appears to be' (Baker et al., 2006, p.44).

An Integrative Developmental Biopsychosocial Model of ASB

Starting from the Beginning

Longitudinal studies with birth cohorts provided essential information (reviewed in: Tremblay, 2000, 2010; Tremblay et al., 2018) to understand ASB development: (1) The earliest form of ASB, physical aggression, is initiated during the first year of life; (2) it increases in frequency up to 3–4 years of age, and then decreases in frequency until adulthood; (3) a small group of individuals, mainly males, use ASB more frequently than others from early childhood to adulthood, and are likely to experience a number of negative outcomes such as school dropout, substance use, and delinquency; (4) most early risk factors of chronic trajectories are similar across measures of ASB and many originate from the prenatal period: maternal adolescent ASB, education, smoking during pregnancy, early childbearing, and depression; coercive parenting; number of siblings; family dysfunction; parental separation; and low SES; (5) these factors are consistent from preschool to adolescence; and (6) comorbidity is frequent between high trajectories of different ASB from the early preschool period onwards.

ASB Development and Its Spectrum

Developmental trajectory studies have linked ASB with early prenatal risk factors and placed its origin at the very beginning of human life, suggesting an intergenerational process. This is consistent with twin studies showing a strong genetic basis to early ASB (Lacourse et al., 2014). Therefore, to identify the mechanisms underlying trajectories of specific ASBs and their comorbidity over time, we need studies with genetically informative designs that examine the biopsychosocial aspects of their development from conception to adulthood.

A *third wave* of twin studies involves strategies that go beyond the classical twin method to investigate the combined influence of nature and nurture on behavior development (Boomsma et al., 2002). Among these, multivariate analysis of correlated phenotypes (or behaviors) examines the pattern and strength of genetic and environmental influences underlying the association between different traits. Using this method, Tuvblad and colleagues (2009) found that a common latent ASB factor (57% genetic) explained the covariance among ADHD, ODD, and CD symptoms in 9–10 years old twins. Additionally, significant unique genetic and environmental factors independently influenced each type of symptoms, supporting the idea of distinct etiological influences (and constructs). A similar pattern was found for the link between aggression and rule-breaking through a common latent factor of ASB (41–53% genetics, respectively) at age 9–10, and 14–15 (Niv et al., 2013). Furthermore, 58% of the genetic and environmental influences on this factor at age 14–15 were common with those operating at age 9–10, the remaining 42% being accounted entirely by new genetic factors. This suggests that, while genetic and environmental factors were linked with the stability of ASB between the two developmental periods, changes in behavior during the transition to adolescence may be attributed to genetic factors that emerged during puberty.

Multivariate analysis of correlated traits in twins was also used to investigate the link between ASB and potential risk factors. Novelty/sensation-seeking and impulsivity, two highly heritable risk factors of ASB (Azeredo et al., 2019), were examined in two adolescent twin samples from Australia and Texas, as potential personality endophenotypes for ASB (Mann et al., 2017). Endophenotypes are internal intermediate parts of the mechanisms linking genetic risk to a given phenotype. They can be considered as liability indices or potential mediators of the effects of genes on behavior (Kendler & Neale, 2010). Mann and colleagues found that novelty/sensation-seeking and impulsive traits shared significant proportions of genetic variance with adolescent-boys ASB, ranging overall from 47 to 65% across traits/samples. In another study, Hicks and colleagues (2007) showed that P300 amplitude and ASB in adolescent males had respective heritability estimates of 0.62 and 0.83 across cohorts/ages. The remaining variance was accounted for by non-shared environmental effects. Their association was primarily attributable to genetic effects, accounting overall for 82% of the total covariance between the two measures. Furthermore, trait disinhibition (or low self-control) was shown to mediate the observed association between P300 response and ASB, through the common genetic liability between ASB and trait disinhibition (Yancey et al., 2013).

The above studies underline the need for genetically informed etiological investigations to better understand the developmental heterogeneity and comorbidity within the ASB spectrum. They also support the idea of highly heritable, underlying transdiagnostic endophenotypes (e.g., impulsivity, emotion-regulation, self-regulation) common among ASBs, stable over time, with developmental pathways going from genotype to endophenotype (to intermediate-risk factors) and to ASB (McDonough-Caplan & Beauchaine, 2018).

Association and Interplay Between Genes and Environment

Genetic susceptibility combines in different ways with the environment to influence the development of ASB. Scarr and McCartney (1983) proposed a developmental model based on the principle that genotypic differences also affect behavior differences through their impact on the environment. This process rests on three types of 'gene-environment correlation' (rGE): a passive rGE, due to environments provided by genetically related parents; an evocative rGE, based on responses elicited in other individuals; and an active rGE, based on the different selection of environments different people make. For example, Button and colleagues (2008) showed that maternal and paternal punitive discipline shared genetic influences with adolescent ASB, suggesting passive or evocative rGE. In a similar study, investigators used the extended children-of-twins model (Boomsma et al., 2002), to examine direct, additive environmental effects, as well as passive or evocative rGE. They found that maternal criticism was primarily due to evocative rGE stemming from adolescent's ASB (Narusyte et al., 2011). Further support for this hypothesis comes from a longitudinal adoption study which observed that children at genetic risk were consistently more likely to receive negative parenting from their adoptive parents than children not at genetic risk, a robust finding across five measurement points between age 7 and 12 years (O'Connor et al., 1998). Meta-analyses of studies on child-driven genetic influence report 23 to 40% proportions of variance explained in parenting (Klahr & Burt, 2014) and 7 to 39% for family and social factors (Kendler & Baker, 2007). Consistent results in molecular genetic studies showed, for example, that preschool boys' 5-HTTLPR short variant genotype (associated with higher concentration of serotonin) affected mothers' levels of positive parenting, an effect mediated by boys' self-control, suggesting an evocative rGE (Pener-Tessler et al., 2013).

As expected, peers are also an important influence on the development of ASB (Azeredo et al., 2019) (Chapters 9 and 10). Genetically informative studies have shown that genetic and environmental factors influence deviant peer affiliation through: (1) active rGE, from preadolescence to adulthood, because antisocial children select similar peers and (2) gene-environment interaction (GxE), in younger children, as genetic influence on ASB is stronger for those having deviant peers (Brendgen, 2012). Such interactions reveal the extent to which genetic factors influence vulnerability to environmental risk. Studies also showed that genetic influences on children ASB were moderated (i.e., attenuated or exacerbated) by peer group norms (Vitaro et al., 2015) and by neighborhood characteristics, as individual genetic influence was more important for children living in wealthy neighborhoods, and shared environmental influences for those residing in disadvantaged areas (Burt et al., 2016).

Widely cited among GxE studies involving specific genetic markers, Caspi and colleagues (2002) found that exposure to childhood maltreatment predicted later ASB in male carriers of the low-activity MAOA-uVNTR allele, a marker involved in neurotransmitter metabolism. Several replication studies supported the idea of an increased vulnerability to childhood adversity in relation to ASB among male carriers of this genetic marker (Nilsson et al., 2018). Other studies on ASB examined different candidate-G × E (cGxE), notably genes associated with the dopaminergic and serotoninergic systems, or genome-wide polygenic scores, in interaction with environmental risk factors and reported significant results (Halldorsdottir & Binder, 2017). However, growing criticism underlined difficulties replicating findings, underpowered studies and consequent high false discovery rates, calling for caution regarding past cGxE findings, and for a more stringent methodological process, including replication (Nilsson et al., 2018; Odintsova et al., 2019).

Finally, the mechanisms by which interactions between environmental and genetic risks operate to influence development were recently revisited. While the classic diathesis stress model emphasizes the risk-vulnerability feature of GxE, a recent proposal pointed to the potential 'differential susceptibility' or the *plasticity* of the genetic factors involved in these interactions (Belsky et al., 2009). For example, this framework suggests that children most vulnerable to high familial adversity would be simultaneously most susceptible to benefit from low familial adversity or from supportive measures to reduce family adversity. In other words, a genetic factor that makes a child susceptible to family adversity may work both ways, i.e., 'for better and for worse' (Belsky et al., 2009).

Environmental Effects on Gene Expression: Epigenetics

The most recent chapter of the ongoing discovery regarding gene-environment influences on ASB is the study of environmental impacts on gene expression, called epigenetics. Epigenetics posit that genes can be turned on and off by environmental events through chemical signals (Szyf, 2009). The application of this approach to ASB began just over a decade ago (Tremblay & Szyf, 2010). Several studies have since shown that environments can play important roles in the development of behaviors and disorders by programming gene expression at different points during development (Cecil et al., 2018; Palumbo et al., 2018; Tremblay et al., 2018). Thus, parental behaviors can affect children's brain development,

Epigenetic effects from pregnancy →

behavior, and health, through their impact on children's gene expression programming. For example, evidence of significant hypermethylation (indexing epigenetic effects) of the glucocorticoid receptor gene NR3C1, associated with ASB, was found in children with early onset maltreatment compared to nonmaltreated children (Cicchetti & Handley, 2017). Importantly, epigenetic effects associated with prenatal and early post-natal environments impact children's neurodevelopment and predisposition to potentially long-term behavioral alterations, including impaired stress response and poor self-regulation (Palumbo et al., 2018).

A Biopsychosocial Intergenerational Perspective on the Development of ASB

mothers adolescent behaviour = risk.

Longitudinal studies of children have shown that the association between parents' and children's ASB starts early in life (Tremblay, 2010). The fact that mothers' ASB during adolescence predicted offspring chronic trajectories of ASB from preschool onwards is particularly eloquent. The sequence following mother's ASB during adolescence possibly included meeting and mating with a partner with similar problems. This phenomenon, called *assortative mating*, not only suggests similarity for ASB, but also for other mental health problems, education, ability to self-control, and values on crucial issues for children's development, such as nutrition, discipline, and lifestyle (Tremblay et al., 2018). Assortative mating leads to an interrelated set of genetic, epigenetic, and environmental conditions, originating from two lines of ancestors, from which the child will inherit his/her predispositions, and the environment in which he/she will grow up.

This is the basis from which the intergenerational transmission of ASB operates, creating a network of interrelated biopsychosocial channels that will evolve jointly throughout a child's development. Based on present knowledge, the mother of the child with ASB problems was, at the child's conception, more likely to be poor, young, depressed, with low education and behavior problems, to separate from the father, and to use coercive parenting in a dysfunctional family, exposing the child to important risks factors, including negative behavior-models. Unlikely to provide the care and education needed by a young child's brain for learning to control his/her emotions and behavior, this environment is likely to reinforce the expression of the child's inherited genetic liability and contribute to further environmental effects on gene expression (epigenetic effects). In that sense, the interrelated biopsychosocial processes that are involved in the transmission of ASB represent developmental cascades through multifactorial risks (Masten & Cicchetti, 2010), and across generations.

emotion dysregulatio

Studies reviewed above used a large variety of different methodologies (twins, adopted children, molecular genetics, epigenetics, mediation, moderation, rGE, and GxE) with specific endophenotypes and environmental measures. These studies may be combined to unravel the various pathways and to disentangle the relationships between individual and environmental risk factors to understand ASB development. For example, Davies and colleagues (2019), using a polygenic score method, showed that children with low dopamine activity displayed more ASB than their peers when faced with more destructive interparental conflicts, but they displayed fewer ASB than their peers when exposed to more constructive conflicts. While showing differential susceptibility to environmental influences— 'for better and for worse', this moderation effect was partially mediated through adolescent emotional insecurity (hypothesized to index emotion dysregulation in family context), which partially explained the greater genetic susceptibility experienced by these children. Another study showed a developmental cascade through a series of rGE where polygenic risk associated with children's impulsivity predicted poorer parental monitoring (indicating evocative rGE), which in turn predicted greater children's affiliation with substance-using peers a year and a half later (Elam et al., 2017). These results show how a developmental cascade of effects may link genotype to individual, familial, and social risk factors, to substance use.

Preventive Interventions from a Developmental Biopsychosocial Perspective

Understanding the biopsychosocial developmental mechanisms involved in ASB is interesting from a scientific perspective, but how does this complex field of research contribute to the prevention of ASB? Four interrelated themes emerge to orient preventive interventions.

First, we now know that ASB starts in early childhood and is linked with many prenatal maternal and paternal risk factors and with intergenerational genetic and epigenetic mechanisms affecting fetal development and fostering developmental cascades of deleterious influences. Indeed, children who show high ASB early on are more likely to maintain higher frequencies of these behaviors into adulthood. If the early risk factors have widespread, increasing effects, then the conclusion is that early preventive interventions should lead to widespread benefits. Therefore, preventive interventions starting during pregnancy or even earlier should be far more effective, from a behavioral and economic perspective, than treatment which

early prevention = successful

starts later in life (McDonough-Caplan & Beauchaine, 2018; Tremblay et al., 2018).

Second, as studies show multilevel risk factors operating across different developmental periods, highly disruptive children in early childhood should benefit from preventive/supportive interventions throughout childhood and adolescence.

Third, prevention programs are most successful when they target vulnerable individuals, their families and communities, struggling with a number of risk factors for developing ASB, compared to treatment applied universally (Samek & Hicks, 2014). For example, providing supportive home visitations over a two-year period to young, disadvantaged pregnant women, reduced child abuse and neglect and maternal delinquency (Olds et al., 2007) and showed, at the 19-year follow-up, a significant reduction of arrests for female offspring—mothers of the next generation (Eckenrode et al., 2010). Later on, programs targeting children's cognitive abilities and parents' disciplinary skills in socially disadvantaged children aged 3–5 years showed positive short-term (academic success) and long-term (preventing arrests and court referrals) effects (Garces et al., 2002). Social environment may also be targeted through daycare centers, schools, or neighborhoods, as their features may be improved to help reduce children ASB (Heckman et al., 2013; Jennings & Hahn-Fox, 2015).

Fourth, research provided a better understanding of the mechanisms by which environmental risk operates in regard to genetic risk and through various endo-/intermediate phenotypes, which help develop interventions tailored to children's and parents' characteristics and susceptibility for ASB (Holz et al., 2018). Moreover, recent studies reported 'gene by intervention interaction' suggesting that genetic factors may be useful in predicting which type of intervention would be most effective for a particular individual (Belsky & Ijzendoorn, 2015).

A Joint Agenda for ASB Research and Intervention: Integrated Biopsychosocial Prevention Trials

Advancing our understanding of the intergenerational mechanisms leading to ASB and improving intervention programs targeting these behaviors represent an important challenge. Therefore, large-scale and long-term intergenerational prevention programs should be designed within an experimental and longitudinal research framework. Intergenerational prevention trials should include large samples of disadvantaged, young primiparous pregnant women with low levels of education. Data collection should include genetic information, monitoring

Research need = understanding intergenerational prevention intervention in at rsk group

of epigenetic changes in parents and children, imaging of brain structure and functioning, health, cognition, language, parenting behavior, and changes in social-emotional behavior of children and in environmental factors, such as family functioning, peer relationships, school, and neighborhoods. Integrated longitudinal and experimental studies assessing the short- and long-term impacts of the preventive interventions would also advance knowledge on the biopsychosocial mechanisms involved in the development of ASB. The identification of these mechanisms should, in turn, help researchers to refine interventions. Finally, testing the differential efficacy of these interventions depending on individual biopsychosocial characteristics may enhance our understanding of 'what works for whom' (Belsky & Ijzendoorn, 2015).

Conclusion: The Developmental Biopsychosocial Model of ASB Coming of Age

In the last decades, the evolution of biological and psychosocial models of ASB, and findings from longitudinal studies from birth to adulthood converged toward an intergenerational-developmental, biopsychosocial framework to study these behaviors. We have seen that different methodologies enable us to study distinct biopsychosocial processes to advance our understanding of ASB, and enhance our ability to prevent or treat these behaviors throughout development. However, we argue that future success lies in our ability to conduct integrated biopsychosocial prevention trials within multidisciplinary longitudinal research teams. Conducted from pregnancy onwards, they should enable us to help children and their families more efficiently, in the hope that the next generation of children will suffer less from the numerous negative consequences of failing to learn to control antisocial behavior during early childhood.

References

Anderson, G. S. (2020). *Biological influences on criminal behavior* (2nd ed.). CRC Press.

Azeredo, A., Moreira, D., Figueiredo, P., & Barbosa, F. (2019). Delinquent behavior: Systematic review of genetic and environmental risk factors. *Clinical Child and Family Psychology Review, 22*(4), 502–526. https://doi.org/10.1007/s10567-019-00298-w

Baker, L. A., Bezdjian, S., & Raine, A. (2006). Behavioral genetics: The science of antisocial behavior. *Law and Contemporary Problems, 69*(1–2), 7–46.

Bandura, A. (1973). *Aggression: A social learning analysis.* Holt.

Beauchaine, T. P., & Cicchetti, D. (2019). Emotion dysregulation and emerging psychopathology: A transdiagnostic, transdisciplinary perspective. *Development and Psychopathology, 31*(3), 799–804. https://doi.org/10.1017/S0954579419000671

Belsky, J., Jonassaint, C., Pluess, M., Stanton, M., Brummett, B., & Williams, R. (2009). Vulnerability genes or plasticity genes? *Molecular Psychiatry, 14*(8), 746–754. https://doi.org/10.1038/mp.2009.44

Belsky, J., & van Ijzendoorn, M. H. (2015). What works for whom? Genetic moderation of intervention efficacy. *Development and Psychopathology, 27*(1), 1–6. https://doi.org/10.1017/S0954579414001254

Bigelow, H. J. (1850). Dr. Harlow's case of recovery from the passage of an iron bar through the head. *The American Journal of the Medical Sciences, 16*(39), 13–22.

Bjorklund, D. F., & Hawley, P. H. (2014). Aggression grows up: Looking through an evolutionary developmental lens to understand the causes and consequences of human aggression. In T. K. Shackelford & R. D. Hansen (Eds.), *The evolution of violence* (pp. 159–186). Springer.

Boomsma, D., Busjahn, A., & Peltonen, L. (2002). Classical twin studies and beyond. *Nature Reviews. Genetics, 3*(11), 872–882. https://doi.org/10.1038/nrg932

Brendgen, M. (2012). Genetics and peer relations: A review. *Journal of Research on Adolescence, 22*(3), 419–437. https://doi.org/10.1111/j.1532-7795.2012.00798.x

Button, T. M. M., Lau, J. Y. F., Maughan, B., & Eley, T. C. (2008). Parental punitive discipline, negative life events and gene environment interplay in the development of externalizing behavior. *Psychological Medicine, 38*(1), 29–39. https://doi.org/10.1017/S0033291707001328

Burt, S. A., Klump, K. L., Gorman-Smith, D., & Neiderhiser, J. M. (2016). Neighborhood disadvantage alters the origins of children's nonaggressive conduct problems. *Clinical Psychological Science, 4*(3), 511–526. https://doi.org/10.1177/2167702615618164

Caspi, A., McClay, J., Moffitt, T. E., Mill, J., Martin, J., Craig, I. W., Taylor, A., & Poulton, R. (2002). Role of genotype in the cycle of violence in maltreated children. *Science, 297*(5582), 851–854. https://doi.org/10.1126/science.1072290

Catalano, R. F., & Hawkins, J. D. (1996). The social development model: A theory of antisocial behavior. In J. D. Hawkins (Ed.), Cambridge criminology series. *Delinquency and crime: Current theories* (p. 149–197). Cambridge University Press.

Cecil, C., Walton, E., Pingault, J. B., Provençal, N., Pappa, I., Vitaro, F., Côté, S., Szyf, M., Tremblay, R. E., Tiemeier, H., Viding, E., & McCrory, E. J. (2018). DRD4 methylation as a potential biomarker for physical aggression: An epigenome-wide, cross-tissue investigation. *American Journal of Medical Genetics. Part B, Neuropsychiatric, 177*(8), 746–764. https://doi.org/10.1002/ajmg.b.32689

Cicchetti, D., & Handley, E. D. (2017). Methylation of the glucocorticoid receptor gene, nuclear receptor subfamily 3, group C, member 1 (NR3C1), in maltreated and nonmaltreated children: Associations with behavioral undercontrol, emotional lability/negativity, and externalizing and internalizing symptoms. *Development and Psychopathology, 29*(5), 1795–1806. https://doi.org/10.1017/S0954579417001407

Darwin, C. (1859). *On the origin of species*. London: John Murray, reprinted by Gryphon Editions 1987.

Davies, P., Pearson, J., Cicchetti, D., Martin, M., & Cummings, E. (2019). Emotional insecurity as a mediator of the moderating role of dopamine genes in the association between interparental conflict and youth externalizing problems. *Development and Psychopathology, 31*(3), 1111–1126. https://doi.org/10.1017/S0954579419000634

Deater-Deckard, K., Chen, N., & El Mallah, S. (2016). Gene–environment interplay in coercion. In T. J. Dishion & J. Snyder (Eds.), *The Oxford handbook of coercive relationship dynamics* (pp. 23–38). Oxford University Press.

Downes, M., Bathelt, J., & De Haan, M. (2017). Event-related potential measures of executive functioning from preschool to adolescence. *Developmental Medicine and Child Neurology, 59*(6), 581–590. https://doi.org/10.1111/dmcn.13395

Eckenrode, J., Campa, M., Luckey, D. W., Henderson, C. R., Jr., Cole, R., Kitzman, H., Anson, E., Sidora-Arcoleo, K., Powers, J., & Olds, D. (2010). Long-term effects of prenatal and infancy nurse home visitation on the life course of youths: 19-year follow-up of a randomized trial. *Archives of Pediatrics & Adolescent Medicine, 164*(1), 9–15. https://doi.org/10.1001/archpediatrics.2009.240

Elam, K. K., Chassin, L., Lemery-Chalfant, K., Pandika, D., Wang, F. L., Bountress, K., Dick, D., & Agrawal, A. (2017). Affiliation with substance-using peers: Examining gene-environment correlations among parent monitoring, polygenic risk, and children's impulsivity. *Developmental Psychobiology, 59*(5), 561–573. https://doi.org/10.1002/dev.21529

Fink, A. E. (1938). *Causes of crime: Biological theories in the United States 1800–1915.* Oxford University Press.

Frick, P. J. (1998). *Conduct disorders and severe antisocial behavior.* Springer.

Fox, B. (2017). It's nature and nurture: Integrating biology and genetics into the social learning theory of criminal behavior. *Journal of Criminal Justice, 49*, 22–31. https://doi.org/10.1016/j.jcrimjus.2017.01.003

Garces, E., Thomas, D., & Currie, J. (2002). Longer-term effects of Head Start. *The American Economic Review, 92*(4), 999–1012. http://www.jstor.org/stable/3083291

Gard, A. M., Dotterer, H. L., & Hyde, L. W. (2019). Genetic influences on antisocial behavior: Recent advances and future directions. *Current Opinion in Psychology, 27*, 46–55. https://doi.org/10.1016/j.copsyc.2018.07.013

Halldorsdottir, T., & Binder, E. B. (2017). Gene × Environment interactions: From molecular mechanisms to behavior. *Annual Review of Psychology, 68*, 215–241. https://doi.org/10.1146/annurev-psych-010416-044053

Harris, J. R. (2009). *The nurture assumption: Why children turn out the way they do* (2nd ed.). Free Press.

Heckman, J., Pinto, R., & Savelyev, P. (2013). Understanding the mechanisms through which an influential early childhood program boosted adult outcomes. *The American Economic Review, 103*(6), 2052–2086. https://doi.org/10.1257/aer.103.6.2052

Hicks, B. M., Bernat, E., Malone, S. M., Iacono, W. G., Patrick, C. J., Krueger, R. F., & McGue, M. (2007). Genes mediate the association between P3 amplitude and externalizing disorders. *Psychophysiology, 44*(1), 98–105. https://doi.org/10.1111/j.1469-8986.2006.00471.x

Holz, N. E., Zohsel, K., Laucht, M., Banaschewski, T., Hohmann, S., & Brandeis, D. (2018). Gene x environment interactions in conduct disorder: Implications for future treatments. *Neuroscience and Biobehavioral Reviews, 91*, 239–258. https://doi.org/10.1016/j.neubiorev.2016.08.017

Jennings, W. G., & Hahn Fox, B. (2015). Neighborhood risk and development of antisocial behavior. In T. P. Beauchaine & S. P. Hinshaw (Eds.), *The Oxford handbook of externalizing spectrum disorders* (pp. 313–322). Oxford University Press.

Kendler, K. S., & Baker, J. H. (2007). Genetic influences on measures of the environment: A systematic review. *Psychological Medicine, 37*(5), 615–626. https://doi.org/10.1017/S00 33291706009524

Kendler, K. S., & Neale, M. C. (2010). Endophenotype: A conceptual analysis. *Molecular Psychiatry, 15*(8), 789–797. https://doi.org/10.1038/mp.2010.8

Klahr, A. M., & Burt, S. A. (2014). Elucidating the etiology of individual differences in parenting: A meta-analysis of behavioral genetic research. *Psychological Bulletin, 140*(2), 544–586. https://doi.org/10.1037/a0034205. Epub 2013 Sep 9. PMID: 24016230.

Lacourse, E., Boivin, M., Brendgen, M., Petitclerc, A., Girard, A., Vitaro, F., Paquin, S., Ouellet-Morin, I., Dionne, G., & Tremblay, R. E. (2014). A longitudinal twin study of physical aggression during early childhood: Evidence for a developmentally dynamic genome. *Psychological Medicine, 44*(12), 2617–2627. https://doi.org/10.1017/S00332917 13003218

Lorenz, K. (1966). *On aggression*. Harcourt, Brace & World.

Mann, F. D., Engelhardt, L., Briley, D. A., Grotzinger, A. D., Patterson, M. W., Tackett, J. L., Strathan, D. B., Heath, A., Lynskey, M., Slutske, W., Martin, N. G., Tucker-Drob, E. M., & Harden, K. P. (2017). Sensation seeking and impulsive traits as personality endophenotypes for antisocial behavior: Evidence from two independent samples. *Personality and Individual Differences, 105*, 30–39. https://doi.org/10.1016/j.paid.2016.09.018

Masten, A. S., & Cicchetti, D. (2010). Developmental cascades. *Development and Psychopathology, 22*(3), 491–495. https://doi.org/10.1017/S0954579410000222

McDonough-Caplan, H. M., & Beauchaine, T. P. (2018). Conduct disorder: A neurodevelopmental perspective. In M. M. Martel (Ed.), *Developmental pathways to disruptive, impulse-control, and conduct disorders* (pp. 53–89). Academic Press.

Narusyte, J., Neiderhiser, J. M., Andershed, A. K., D'Onofrio, B. M., Reiss, D., Spotts, E., Ganiban, J., & Lichtenstein, P. (2011). Parental criticism and externalizing behavior problems in adolescents: The role of environment and genotype-environment correlation. *Journal of Abnormal Psychology, 120*(2), 365–376. https://doi.org/10.1037/a0021815

Nilsson, K. W., Åslund, C., Comasco, E., & Oreland, L. (2018). Gene-environment interaction of monoamine oxidase A in relation to antisocial behaviour: Current and future directions. *Journal of Neural Transmission, 125*(11), 1601–1626. https://doi.org/10.1007/s00702-018-1892-2

Niv, S., Tuvblad, C., Raine, A., & Baker, L. A. (2013). Aggression and rule-breaking: Heritability and stability of antisocial behavior problems in childhood and adolescence. *Journal of Criminal Justice, 41*(5), 285–291. https://doi.org/10.1016/j.jcrimjus.2013.06.014

O'Connor, T. G., Deater-Deckard, K., Fulker, D., Rutter, M., & Plomin, R. (1998). Genotype-environment correlations in late childhood and early adolescence: Antisocial behavioral problems and coercive parenting. *Developmental Psychology, 34*(5), 970–981. https://doi.org/10.1037//0012-1649.34.5.970

Odintsova, V. V., Roetman, P. J., Ip, H. F., Pool, R., Van der Laan, C. M., Tona, K. D., Vermeiren, R., & Boomsma, D. I. (2019). Genomics of human aggression: Current state of genome-wide studies and an automated systematic review tool. *Psychiatric Genetics, 29*(5), 170–190. https://doi.org/10.1097/YPG.0000000000000239

Olds, D. L., Sadler, L., & Kitzman, H. (2007). Programs for parents of infants and toddlers: Recent evidence from randomized trials. *Journal of Child Psychology and Psychiatry, 48*(3–4), 355–391. https://doi.org/10.1111/j.1469-7610.2006.01702.x

Ouellet-Morin, I., Côté, S. M., Vitaro, F., Hébert, M., Carbonneau, R., Lacourse, É., Turecki, G., & Tremblay, R. E. (2016). Effects of the MAOA gene and levels of exposure to violence on antisocial outcomes. *The British Journal of Psychiatry, 208*(1), 42–48. https://doi.org/10.1192/bjp.bp.114.162081

Palumbo, S., Mariotti, V., Iofrida, C., & Pellegrini, S. (2018). Genes and aggressive behavior: Epigenetic mechanisms underlying individual susceptibility to aversive environments. *Frontiers in Behavioral Neuroscience, 12*, 117. https://doi.org/10.3389/fnbeh.2018.00117

Patrick, C. J., Bernat, E. M., Malone, S. M., Iacono, W. G., Krueger, R. F., & McGue, M. (2006). P300 amplitude as an indicator of externalizing in adolescent males. *Psychophysiology, 43*(1), 84–92. https://doi.org/10.1111/j.1469-8986.2006.00376.x

Patterson, G. R., Capaldi, D., & Bank, L. (1991). An early starter model for predicting delinquency. In D. J. Pepler & K. H. Rubin (Eds.), *The development and treatment of childhood aggression* (pp. 139–168). Erlbaum.

Patterson, G. R., DeBaryshe, B. D., & Ramsey, E. (1989). A developmental perspective on antisocial behavior. *The American Psychologist, 44*(2), 329–335. https://doi.org/10.1037//0003-066x.44.2.329

Pener-Tessler, R., Avinun, R., Uzefovsky, F., Edelman, S., Ebstein, R. P., & Knafo, A. (2013). Boys' serotonin transporter genotype affects maternal behavior through self-control: A case of evocative gene-environment correlation. *Development and Psychopathology, 25*(1), 151–162. https://doi.org/10.1017/S095457941200096X

Pingault, J. B., Côté, S. M., Booij, L., Ouellet-Morin, I., Castellanos-Ryan, N., Vitaro, F., Turecki, G., & Tremblay, R. E. (2013). Age-dependent effect of the MAOA gene on childhood physical aggression. *Molecular Psychiatry, 18*(11), 1151–1152. https://doi.org/10.1038/mp.2012.173

Rhee, S. H., & Waldman, I. D. (2002). Genetic and environmental influences on antisocial behavior: A meta-analysis of twin and adoption studies. *Psychological Bulletin, 128*(3), 490–529.

Rutter, M. L. (1999). Psychosocial adversity and child psychopathology. *The British Journal of Psychiatry, 174*, 480–493. https://doi.org/10.1192/bjp.174.6.480

Rutter, M. (2003). Crucial paths from risk indicator to causal mechanism. In B. B. Lahey, T. E. Moffitt, & A. Caspi (Eds.), *Causes of conduct disorder and juvenile delinquency* (pp. 3–26). Guilford.

Samek, D. R., & Hicks, B. M. (2014). Externalizing disorders and environmental risk: Mechanisms of gene-environment interplay and strategies for intervention. *Clinical Practice, 11*(5), 537–547. https://doi.org/10.2217/CPR.14.47

Scarr, S., & McCartney, K. (1983). How people make their own environments: A theory of genotype greater than environment effects. *Child Development, 54*(2), 424–435. https://doi.org/10.1111/j.1467-8624.1983.tb03884.x

Szyf, M. (2009). Implications of a life-long dynamic epigenome. *Epigenomics, 1*(1), 9–12. https://doi.org/10.2217/epi.09.15

Taylor, L. (1984). *Born to crime: The genetic causes of criminal behavior.* Greenwood Press.

Tremblay, R. E. (2010). Developmental origins of disruptive behaviour problems: The "original sin" hypothesis, epigenetics and their consequences for prevention. *Journal of Child*

Psychology and Psychiatry, 51(4), 341–367. https://doi.org/10.1111/j.1469-7610.2010.02211.x

Tremblay, R. E. (2000). The development of aggressive behaviour during childhood: What have we learned in the past century? *International Journal of Behavioral Development, 24*(2), 129–141. https://doi.org/10.1080/016502500383232

Tremblay, R. E., & Szyf, M. (2010). Developmental origins of chronic physical aggression and epigenetics. *Epigenomics, 2*(4), 495–499. https://doi.org/10.2217/epi.10.40

Tremblay, R. E., Vitaro, F., & Côté, S. M. (2018). Developmental origins of chronic physical aggression: A bio-psycho-social model for the next generation of preventive interventions. *Annual Review of Psychology, 69*, 383–407. https://doi.org/10.1146/annurev-psych-010416-044030

Tuvblad, C., Zheng, M., Raine, A., & Baker, L. A. (2009). A common genetic factor explains the covariation among ADHD ODD and CD symptoms in 9–10 year old boys and girls. *Journal of Abnormal Child Psychology, 37*(2), 153–167. https://doi.org/10.1007/s10802-008-9278-9

Vitaro, F., Brendgen, M., Girard, A., Boivin, M., Dionne, G., & Tremblay, R. E. (2015). The expression of genetic risk for aggressive and non-aggressive antisocial behavior is moderated by peer group norms. *Journal of Youth and Adolescence, 44*(7), 1379–1395. https://doi.org/10.1007/s10964-015-0296-y

Yancey, J. R., Venables, N. C., Hicks, B. M., & Patrick, C. J. (2013). Evidence for a heritable brain basis to deviance-promoting deficits in self-control. *Journal of Criminal Justice, 41*(5), 309–317. https://doi.org/10.1016/j.jcrimjus.2013.06.002

Yang, Y., & Raine, A. (2009). Prefrontal structural and functional brain imaging findings in antisocial, violent, and psychopathic individuals: A meta-analysis. *Psychiatry Research, 174*(2), 81–88. https://doi.org/10.1016/j.pscychresns.2009.03.012

Walsh, A. (2009). *Biology and criminology: The biosocial synthesis.* Routledge.

Further Reading Suggestions

Belsky, J., & van Ijzendoorn, M. H. (2015). What works for whom? Genetic moderation of intervention efficacy. *Development and Psychopathology, 27*(1), 1–6. https://doi.org/10.1017/S0954579414001254

Boomsma, D., Busjahn, A., & Peltonen, L. (2002). Classical twin studies and beyond. *Nature Reviews. Genetics, 3*(11), 872–882. https://doi.org/10.1038/nrg932

Holz, N. E., Zohsel, K., Laucht, M., Banaschewski, T., Hohmann, S., & Brandeis, D. (2018). Gene x environment interactions in conduct disorder: Implications for future treatments. *Neuroscience and Biobehavioral Reviews, 91*, 239–258. https://doi.org/10.1016/j.neubiorev.2016.08.017

McDonough-Caplan, H. M., & Beauchaine, T. P. (2018). Conduct disorder: A neurodevelopmental perspective. In M. M. Martel (Ed), *Developmental pathways to disruptive, impulse-control, and conduct disorders,* pp. 53–89, London: Academic Press.

Tremblay, R. E., Vitaro, F., & Côté, S. M. (2018). Developmental Origins of Chronic Physical Aggression: A bio-psycho-social model for the next generation of preventive interventions. Annual Review of Psychology, 69, 383–407. https://doi.org/10.1146/annurev-psych-010416-044030

Cardiovascular Psychophysiology and Antisocial Behavior

3

Presley McGarry and Jill Portnoy

Key Points

- The development of antisocial behavior is a complex, multilevel process, often involving the interaction of biological and social risk factors.
- Low resting heart rate is a well-replicated risk factor for antisocial behavior.
- Research generally finds that increased respiratory sinus arrythmia (RSA) withdrawal in response to various lab tasks is associated with antisocial behavior.
- Reduced cardiac-linked sympathetic nervous system (SNS) reactivity, as indicated by pre-ejection period (PEP), is associated with general antisocial behavior, as well as antisocial personality traits, aggression, and substance abuse.
- Psychophysiological measures of autonomic nervous system (ANS) activity are more affordable and accessible than other biological measure and offer an opportunity for researchers to consider both biological and social factors to inform the future treatment and prevention of aggression and antisocial behavior.

P. McGarry (✉) · J. Portnoy
School of Criminology and Justice Studies, University of Massachusetts
Lowell, Lowell, MA, USA
e-mail: presley_mcgarry@uml.edu

J. Portnoy
e-mail: jill_portnoy@uml.edu

© The Author(s), under exclusive license to Springer Nature Switzerland AG 2022   49
C. Garofalo and J. J. Sijtsema (eds.), *Clinical Forensic Psychology*,
https://doi.org/10.1007/978-3-030-80882-2_3

Introduction

The development of antisocial behavior is a complex, multilevel process, often involving the interaction of biological and social risk factors. Several biosocial models have been developed to explain how these factors interact to contribute to the development of antisocial behavior, including the diathesis-stress model, the social push perspective, and differential susceptibility theory (Barnes & Jacobs, 2013; Barnes et al. 2020; Fox, 2017; Nedelec et al. 2017; Raine, 2013). Studies have identified biological risk factors for antisocial behavior across multiple domains, including neurology (Yang & Raine, 2009), genetics (Barnes & Jacobs, 2013; Beaver, 2008; Rhee & Waldman, 2002), and psychophysiology (Ortiz & Raine, 2004; Portnoy & Farrington, 2015). Within psychophysiology, cardiovascular psychophysiology, has been studied extensively in relation to antisocial behavior. Psychophysiology uses noninvasive measures to assess immediate psychological and emotional responses to environmental stimuli (Hugdahl, 1995). Psychophysiological measures are often recorded at rest but may also be recorded in response to experimental stimuli, such as fear conditioning or stress tasks. The purpose of this chapter is to review cardiovascular psychophysiological research into antisocial behavior with a focus on biosocial interactions. We first briefly introduce theories of biosocial interactions. We then discuss research examining heart rate, heart rate variability, and pre-ejection period in relation to antisocial behavior. We conclude by discussing directions for future research.

Theories of Biosocial Interactions

Several theories have been proposed to explain biosocial interactions. According to the diathesis-stress model, the presence of both a biological and social risk factor increases the likelihood of antisocial behavior. The risk of antisocial behavior is highest amongst those at both biological and social risk, while it is lower among those with either biological or social risk only (Barnes et al., 2020; Raine, 2013). The diathesis-stress model considers the impact of adverse social environments, but largely ignores the potential effects of especially enriching social environments. In contrast, the differential susceptibility theory and the closely related biological sensitivity to context theory argue that biological factors have different effects in adverse and enriching environments and that some children are more receptive to environmental influences than others (Belsky, 2005; Belsky et al., 2007; Boyce & Ellis, 2005; Ellis et al., 2011). The theories have largely converged to argue that children with high physiological stress reactivity *children with high stress reactivity are more susceptible to environment (for better or worse)*

will be more receptive to environmental influences—either positive or negative—than children with low reactivity (Boyce, 2016). Highly reactive children who grow up in adverse social environments will be negatively affected by that environment, while highly reactive children who grow up in especially enriching environments with be positively affected by that environment. Alternatively, the social push perspective argues that biological risk factors are more important in predicting behavior in positive social contexts, but matter little in negative social contexts, where social risk factors are more important (Barnes et al., 2020; Raine, 2013). These theories of biosocial interactions have been frequently tested in cardiovascular psychophysiological research (van Hoebroek et al., 2019).

Heart Rate and Antisocial Behavior

HR = ANS
HRV = SNS

The cardiovascular system is controlled by the parasympathetic (PNS) and sympathetic (SNS) branches of the autonomic nervous system (ANS; Berntson et al., 2017). Heart rate is a global measure of ANS activity, as it is controlled by both the PNS and SNS. Low resting heart rate has been suggested as the "best-replicated biological correlate of antisocial behavior in child and adolescent populations" (Ortiz & Raine, 2004, p. 159) and is listed in the *Diagnostic and Statistical Manual of Mental Disorders* (5th ed.; *DSM 5*; American Psychiatric Association, 2013) as a risk factor for conduct disorder. A meta-analysis of 114 reports and 115 independent effect sizes yielded a random effects summary effect size of $d = -0.20$ (SE = 0.04, $p < 0.001$) for the relationship between resting heart rate and antisocial behavior (Portnoy & Farrington, 2015). This relationship did not vary by sex, type of, or age. This relationship also did not vary by study design (prospective or longitudinal) and several recent large longitudinal studies further suggest that low heart rate may precede the onset of antisocial behavior (Latvala et al., 2015, 2016; Murray et al., 2016). While low resting heart rate is associated with multiple types of antisocial behavior, researchers have suggested that low resting heart rate may be more strongly associated with proactive (unprovoked, instrumental) aggression than reactive aggression (in response to provocation). Although limited research has supported this possibility (Raine et al., 2014), more research is needed that determines the generalizability of low resting heart rate as a risk factor for aggression sub-types.

There are several proposed explanations for the relationship between resting heart rate and antisocial behavior. The sensation seeking explanation argues that reduced ANS arousal is an unpleasant physiological state. This aversive state is

low resting HR = RISK factor.
not impacted by sex, age
precedes ATB onset.
1) low ANS is unpleasant → sensation seeking THR

thought to lead those with low resting heart rates to engage in stimulating behaviors, including antisocial behaviors, in order to increase their level of arousal to a more optimal level (Quay, 1965; Raine, 2002, 2013). Recent studies have found support for the sensation seeking explanation (Hammerton et al., 2018; Portnoy et al., 2014; Sijtsema et al., 2010). In addition, Sijtsema et al. (2013) found that affiliation with delinquent peers mediated the relationship between resting heart rate and antisocial behavior in boys, suggesting that boys with low resting heart rate may seek out stimulating peer enivironments that promote antisocial behavior. According to the alternative fearlessness explanation, low resting heart rate may reflect a relative lack of fear, which could facilitate antisocial behavior by impeding early fear conditioning to socializing punishments and reducing fear of the negative consequences of engaging in antisocial behavior (Raine, 2013). To date, studies examining resting heart rate and antisocial behavior have not found support for the fearlessness perspective (Portnoy et al., 2014; Sijtsema et al., 2010).

Both the fearlessness and sensation-seeking explanations assume a causal relationship between resting heart rate and antisocial behavior. However, a recent study using co-relative analyses found that while the relationship between internalizing behavior and high resting heart rate was causal, the relationship between externalizing behavior and low resting heart rate resulted entirely from familial confounding and was not causal (Kenneth et al., 2021). Future studies utilizing genetically-informed designs are needed to confirm these findings.

In addition to resting heart rate, researchers have also examined heart rate during stress or heart rate stress reactivity (change in heart rate from resting to stress state) in relation to antisocial behavior. A meta-analysis of nine studies found that low heart rate during stress was associated with increased antisocial behavior ($d = -0.76$, $p < 0.0001$; Ortiz & Raine, 2004). Low heart rate reactivity to stress has also been shown to be associated with higher levels of antisocial behavior, although this relationship is also moderated by social risk factors, as described below (Portnoy, Raine, Rudo-Hutt, Gao, & Monk, 2020; Sijtsema et al., 2013a). Although reduced stress reactivity may be related to the antisocial behavior through the same processes as resting heart, this mechanism is less well-understood.

Biosocial Interactions Involving Heart Rate

Several biosocial studies involving heart rate have been consistent with the diathesis-stress model of biosocial interactions. Using data from the Cambridge

[handwritten margin note: social push + r/ship between biological + social is stronger for those at low risk]

Study in Delinquent Development (CSDD), Farrington (1997, 2020) has found that low resting heart rate at age 18 years more strongly predicted future levels of antisocial behavior among boys with high levels of social risk. Similarly, several other studies found that low resting heart rate was more strongly associated with measures of antisocial behavior, including proactive aggression, psychopathy, and general antisocial behavior, among children at high levels of social risk (Gao et al., 2017; Scarpa et al., 2008; Sijtsema et al., 2013b). Alternatively, Raine and Venables (1984) found that the relationship between low resting heart rate and antisocial behavior was confined to those children from higher social classes. Relatedly, a recent study using data from the Pittsburgh Youth Study found that low resting heart rate in adolescence was associated with higher levels of adult aggression in white, but not Black males (Portnoy et al., 2020). These findings are consistent with an alternative model of biosocial interactions, the social push perspective, which argues that the relationship between biological and social factors is stronger amongst those at low social risk.

Most studies testing the differential susceptibility hypothesis have utilized measures of ANS reactivity. Of these, few studies have examined heart rate reactivity, with most using isolated measures of PNS or SNS activity. Nonetheless, the limited research examining biosocial interactions involving heart rate reactivity has tended to be more consistent with the dual-risk model, rather than differential susceptibility hypothesis (Portnoy et al., 2020; Sijtsema et al., 2013a). In general, biosocial interactions involving heart rate tend to be more consistent with the diathesis-stress model.

Heart Rate Variability

Some researchers have attempted to determine whether the relationship between heart rate and antisocial behavior is driven by increased PNS activation or rather, decreased SNS activation, as heart rate does not differentiate activation of the PNS versus the SNS. Within the ANS, the PNS and SNS can have several patterns of activation, including co-activation, reciprocal activation, or independent activation (Berntson et al., 1994). The PNS is responsible for vagally mediated heart rate, and tempers stress reactivity elicited by the SNS to induce restful behavioral states and self-regulation. The PNS lowers heart rate when sustained attention or social affiliative behaviors are adaptive (Beauchaine et al., 2008; Heponiemi et al., 2003). The SNS is responsible for cardiac contractility and for mobilizing bodily resources in response to environmental stimuli, increasing heart rate (Beauchaine et al., 2008; Heponiemi et al., 2003). Because heart rate reflects the balance of PNS and SNS activation, physiological measures have been developed to isolate PNS- and SNS-mediated cardiac activity. Respiratory sinus arrythmia (RSA) refers to the covariation of heart rate with respiration and is an index of variation in the PNS influence on heart rate. High-frequency heart rate variability (HRV) is the component of heart rate variability in the high-frequency band (~0.15–0.4 Hz) and is used as a measure of RSA (Berntson et al., 1997). Researchers tend to focus on only the high-frequency band of HRV rather than lower frequency bands, as lower frequency bands may reflect a mix of both the PNS and SNS influences (Berntson et al., 1997). Changes in RSA from resting state to challenging or stressful conditions are quantified as RSA reactivity. RSA suppression, or withdrawal, is associated with decreased PNS activity, while RSA augmentation is associated with increased PNS activity (Beauchaine, 2001).

Lower RSA is thought to be linked to higher levels of antisocial behavior through its role in top-down processes of self-regulation. Higher resting RSA and RSA reactivity have been shown to be associated with better emotion regulation (Balzarotti et al., 2017; Holzman & Bridgett, 2017). Poor emotion regulation may result in difficult temperament, poor decision-making, and problems with self-regulation, all of which may lead to poor social relationships and other decisions that lead to antisocial behavior (van Goozen, 2015). In addition, several studies found that individuals with higher resting RSA reacted less negatively to negative stimuli (Geisler et al., 2013; Del Ventura & Rhudy, 2012; Dywan et al., 2008; Palomda et al., 2000), while individuals with lower resting RSA showed increased psychological distress and poor cardiovascular recovery from stress exposure (Gouin et al., 2014; Souza et al., 2007). Resilience, or the ability to recover from stress exposure, is associated with adaptive coping skills, fewer behavioral problems, and increased pro-social behavior (Porges, 2007), leading researchers to further hypothesize that lower RSA (indicating decreased PNS activity) will be associated with higher levels of antisocial behavior.

Consistent with this, research generally finds that increased RSA withdrawal (decreased PNS activity) in response to various lab tasks is associated with antisocial behavior (Beauchaine et al., 2019; Fortunato et al, 2013; Hinnant & El-Sheikh, 2009). A meta-analysis of 37 studies and 76 effect sizes, showed that both low resting RSA and increased RSA withdrawal during behavioral tasks were associated with antisocial behavior and externalizing disorders, including ADHD, conduct disorder, substance abuse, and antisocial personality disorder (Beauchaine et al., 2019). In addition, low resting RSA and RSA withdrawal have been associated with antisocial behavior (Mezzaccapa et al., 1997; de Wied et al., 2006), aggression (Beauchaine, Hong, & Marsh, 2008; Murrary-Close et al.,

2017), psychopathic traits (Thomson et al., 2019; Wagner et al., 2015), conduct disorder (Beauchaine, Neuhaus, Brenner, & Gatzke-Kopp, 2008; de Wied et al., 2006, 2012; Mills-Koonce et al., 2015; Pang & Beauchaine, 2013), and acts of deceit (Aikins et al., 2010). Some findings, however, have been inconsistent. Several studies observed increased, rather than decreased RSA, in antisocial individuals (Dietrich et al., 2007; Scarpa et al., 2010; Wagner et al., 2018). Additionally, some studies found internalizing, but not antisocial behaviors to be associated with RSA (Fortunato et al., 2013). There are several possible explanations for these inconsistencies. First, the diverse nature of laboratory tasks used may influence results. For example, tasks that involve negative emotion inductions (e.g., sadness, threat, anger) versus positive emotion inductions have been found to produce greater effect sizes for RSA reactivity (de Wied et al., 2012; Zisner & Beauchaine, 2016). The type of antisocial behavior measured may also affect findings. As with heart rate, some studies have found that RSA differs in its relationship with reactive and proactive aggression. A study of children ages 6–13 yearsfound that reactive aggression was significantly associated with decreased resting RSA, while proactive aggression was associated with increased resting RSA (Scarpa et al., 2010). We should note, however, that reactive and proactive aggression often co-occur within individuals, making it difficult to determine unique physiological influences on these forms of aggression.

Biosocial Interactions Involving HRV

The interaction between RSA and social risk factors may also help to explain inconsistent findings. In contrast to Scarpa et al. (2010), a study of 84 college students found that higher resting RSA was associated with reactive aggression in conditions of high social adversity. Among those with low social adversity, high RSA reactivity was positively associated with reactive aggression, but negatively associated with proactive aggression (Zhang & Gao, 2015). Obradovíc et al. (2011) found that high RSA reactivity was associated with high levels of antisocial behavior among children exposed to high levels of family adversity, while high RSA reactivity was associated with low levels of antisocial behavior among children exposed to low levels of adversity. These findings are consistent with the differential susceptibility theory, which argues that high reactivity is adaptive in positive social contexts, but maladaptive in negative contexts. Other studies found that high baseline RSA buffered children against antisocial behavior problems associated with higher levels of parental marital conflict (El-Sheikh et al., 2001), parental problem drinking (El-Sheikh, 2005) and maltreatment amongst boys (Gordis et al., 2010). Several studies of RSA have been consistent with the diathesis-stress model for male but not female children, finding that low resting RSA combined with parenting risk factors increased the likelihood of antisocial behavior in boys (Dyer et al., 2016; Hinnant et al., 2013). Patterns of biosocial interactions involving RSA are mixed. Inconsistencies in findings have been partly attributed to sex differences, with interactions more consistently observed among males than females, as well as differences related to the type of social risk (van Hazeobroek et al., 2019). Nonetheless, even among boys, patterns of biosocial interactions involving RSA tend to be mixed.

Pre-Ejection Period

Pre-ejection period (PEP) is an indicator of sympathetically-driven cardiac influences (Berntson et al., 1994; Boudoulas, 1990). A shorter PEP indicates increased SNS activity, while PEP lengthening indicates lower SNS activity (Berntson et al., 1994). Several studies have indicated that lower SNS reactivity—indicated by PEP lengthening—is associated with antisocial behavior (Brenner & Beauchaine, 2011; Gao & Zhang, 2020; Hinnant et al., 2015). Attenuated cardiac-linked SNS activity has also been associated with antisocial personality traits (Sylvers et al., 2008), aggression (Babel et al., 2016), and substance abuse (Derefinko et al., 2016; Hinnant et al., 2015). However, as with RSA, there are inconsistencies among results; some studies have found increased cardiac-linked SNS activity, rather than decreased SNS activity, in antisocial individuals (Gao & Zhang, 2020; Sijtsema et al., 2015). Increased cardiac-linked SNS activity has also been associated with lower prosocial competence (Kalvin et al., 2016). These inconsistences in findings may be attributable to differences in stimulus conditions, measurement of key variables, and sampling practices (Beauchaine et al., 2001). Additionally, inconsistencies in results may also be attributable to the failure to consider interactions with environmental and social factors, as discussed below.

Lower cardiac-linked SNS activity among antisocial individuals may be due in part to the role of the SNS in the behavioral activation system (BAS). The BAS moderates appetitive motivational responses, characterized as approach and active avoidance behaviors, which aim to maximize reward and minimize punishment (Beauchaine, 2001). Increased SNS activity has been found to occur during reward conditions when the BAS is activated (Brenner et al., 2005). Several studies found that attenuated SNS activity in response to reward, indicating reduced reward reactivity, was associated with antisocial behavior (Beauchaine

[handwritten margin note: sensation seeking due to XXX + hypersensitive to reward]

et al., 2001, 2007). These findings are partly consistent with research documenting abnormal reward processing in relation to antisocial behavior, though findings in this area are mixed, with many studies documenting hyper-sensitivity to reward or an overactive BAS among antisocial individuals (Byrd et al., 2014).

Biosocial Interactions Involving PEP

[handwritten margin note: hypo vs. hyper responsivity is social risk moderated]

There is less research on biosocial interactions involving PEP and many studies have failed to observe biosocial interactions involving PEP (Alink et al., 2019; Fagan et al., 2017; Musser et al., 2018). Those studies that have observed biosocial interactions detected complex patterns of interaction effects. For instance, in a study of 8–10 year olds, Gao and Zhang (2020) found that callous–unemotional traits were associated with less PEP shortening during a reward task (indicating reward hypo-responsivity) among children with low levels of social adversity, but more PEP shortening (indicating reward hyper-responsivity) among children with high levels of social adversity. Sijtsema et al. (2015) found that prolonged experiences of stress and adversity from birth to adolescence were associated with antisocial behavior in boys with lower PEP reactivity to stress, a finding consistent with the diathesis-stress model. Among girls with higher adversity exposure, higher PEP stress recovery was associated with antisocial behavior. Overall, research into biosocial interactions involving PEP has been limited, precluding conclusions about the nature of these interactions. Though beyond the scope of the current paper, we should also note that PEP and RSA may also interact to predict antisocial behavior. Several studies have found that reciprocal pattens of SNS and PNS cardiac activity predicted antisocial behavior (Nederhof et al., 2015; Tenenbaum et al., 2018), while others found that non-reciprocal activation patterns predicted antisocial behavior (Suurland et al., 2017). Researching examining patterns of interactions involving social risk factors, as well as indicators of both PNS and SNS activity may provide the most complete understanding of the development of antisocial behavior.

Discussion

This chapter reviewed research into the cardiovascular psychophysiology of antisocial behavior. In general, research finds lower resting RSA, lower RSA withdrawal, lower resting heart rate, and PEP lengthening (indicating decreased

SNS activity) among individuals with higher levels of antisocial behaviors. However, some results are inconsistent, which may be partly explained by biosocial interactions. Several theories have been proposed to explain patterns of biosocial interactions, including the diathesis-stress model, the social push perspective, and differential susceptibility theory. While studies have demonstrated the presence of biosocial interactions, more research is needed to determine which theories best explain biosocial interactions predicting antisocial behavior. Overall, research tends to be most consistent with the diathesis-stress model, though this model has been dominant in the field for many years and other theoretical perspectives may begin to garner additional theoretical support in the future. Additionally, research has shown that different biological systems, such as the PNS and SNS, likely interact to contribute to the development of antisocial behavior. Further research should utilize measures of both branches of the ANS to explore interactions between biological systems along with social risk factors. A better understanding of biosocial interactions could have implications in the future by helping researchers to develop more targeted interventions and risk assessment tools.

There are several additional important directions for future research in this area. Interestingly, higher RSA is associated with both lower levels of antisocial behavior and lower heart rate. Lower heart rate, however, is associated with *higher* levels of antisocial behavior. More research is needed that isolates the parasympathetic and sympathetic components of heart rate in order to understand this apparent contradiction. Research examining differential correlates of reactive versus proactive aggression may also help to address this issue.

In addition, further research is needed that utilizes genetically-informed designs in order to determine whether the relationship between cardiovascular psychophysiological indices is causal. Finally, while many psychophysiological studies have tested the diathesis-stress and social push perspectives, fewer have fully tested the differential susceptibility hypothesis, which focuses on interactions involving especially enriching environments. Many biosocial studies examine the effect of a lack of social adversity, but do not test interactions involving especially positive social environments.

Conclusions

As the body of research supporting a biological basis of antisocial behavior continues to grow, it has become increasingly evident that the development of antisocial behavior is a multidimensional process that is best explained by considering both biological and social factors. Several studies have found that RSA,

PEP, and HR interact with social risk factors, including parental supervision, family size and structure, experiences of trauma, and violence exposure, to predict antisocial behavior. Additionally, the interaction of biological systems, such as the PNS and ANS, have also been found to predict antisocial behavior. Future research should incorporate multiple biomarkers and socio-contextual factors in order to gain a better understanding of the development of antisocial behavior.

Psychophysiological measures of ANS activity, including HR, HRV, and PEP, are more affordable and accessible to researchers than other biological measures, making them useful in examining the effect of PNS and SNS activity on antisocial behavior. They offer an opportunity for researchers to consider both biological and social factors to inform the future treatment and prevention of aggression and antisocial behavior. Preliminary research has shown that individual differences in autonomic arousal may predict treatment outcomes in antisocial individuals (Cornet et al., 2014). For instance, psychophysiological factors have been shown to influence the success of cognitive behavioral therapy (CBT; Cornet et al., 2014), which is already widely used in correctional settings and prevention settings. This suggests that further research using psychophysiological measures could help tailor behavioral interventions to be more successful for individuals based on their ANS activity. Future research using these tools to identify the biosocial contexts in when ANS activity is linked to behavioral problems may allow for the development of risk assessment and treatment tools that can be used to pair individuals with treatments that have the highest likelihood of success for that individual.

References

Alink, L. R., Cyr, C., & Madigan, S. (2019). The effect of maltreatment experiences on maltreating and dysfunctional parenting: A search for mechanisms. *Development and Psychopathology, 31*, 1–7.

Aikins, D. E., Martin, D. J., & Morgan, C. A., III. (2010). Decreased respiratory sinus arrhythmia in individuals with deceptive intent. *Psychophysiology, 47*, 633–636.

American Psychiatric Association. (2013). *Diagnostic and statistical manual of mental disorders (DSM-5®)*. American Psychiatric Pub.

Babel, K. A., Jambroes, T., Oostermeijer, S., van de Ven, P. M., Popma, A., Vermeiren, R. R., Theo A. H. Doreleijers & Jansen, L. M. (2016). Do post-trauma symptoms mediate the relation between neurobiological stress parameters and conduct problems in girls?. *Child and Adolescent Psychiatry and Mental Health, 10*, 1–10.

Balzarotti, S., Biassoni, F., Colombo, B., & Ciceri, M. R. (2017). Cardiac vagal control as a marker of emotion regulation in healthy adults: A review. *Biological Psychology, 130*, 54–66.

Barnes, J. C., & Jacobs, B. A. (2013). Genetic risk for violent behavior and environmental exposure to disadvantage and violent crime: The case for gene–environment interaction. *Journal of Interpersonal Violence, 28*, 92–120. https://doi.org/10.1177/0886260512448847

Barnes, J. C., Raine, A., & Farrington, D. P. (2020). The interaction of biopsychological and socio-environmental influences on criminological outcomes. *Justice Quarterly*, 1–25.

Beauchaine, T. (2001). Vagal tone, development, and Gray's motivational theory: Toward an integrated model of autonomic nervous system functioning in psychopathology. *Development and Psychopathology, 13*, 183–214.

Beauchaine, T. P., Bell, Z., Knapton, E., McDonough-Caplan, H., Shader, T., & Zisner, A. (2019). Respiratory sinus arrhythmia reactivity across empirically based structural dimensions of psychopathology: A meta-analysis. *Psychophysiology, 56*, e13329.

Beauchaine, T. P., Gatzke-Kopp, L., & Mead, H. K. (2007). Polyvagal theory and developmental psychopathology: Emotion dysregulation and conduct problems from preschool to adolescence. *Biological Psychology, 74*, 174–184.

Beauchaine, T. P., Hong, J., & Marsh, P. (2008). Sex differences in autonomic correlates of conduct problems and aggression. *Journal of the American Academy of Child & Adolescent Psychiatry, 47*, 788–796.

Beauchaine, T. P., Katkin, E. S., Strassberg, Z., & Snarr, J. (2001). Disinhibitory psychopathology in male adolescents: Discriminating conduct disorder from attention-deficit/hyperactivity disorder through concurrent assessment of multiple autonomic states. *Journal of Abnormal Psychology, 110*, 610.

Beauchaine, T. P., Neuhaus, E., Brenner, S. L., & Gatzke-Kopp, L. (2008). Ten good reasons to consider biological processes in prevention and intervention research. *Development and psychopathology, 20*, 745.

Beaver, K. (2008). *The nature and nurture of antisocial outcomes*. LFP Scholarly Publishing LLC.

Belsky, J., Bakermans-Kranenburg, M. J., & Van IJzendoorn, M. H. (2007). For better and for worse: Differential susceptibility to environmental influences. *Current Directions in Psychological Science, 16*, 300–304.

Belsky, J. (2005). Differential susceptibility to rearing influence. *Origins of the social mind: Evolutionary psychology and child development*, 139–163.

Berntson, G. G., Cacioppo, J. T., Binkley, P. F., Uchino, B. N., Quigley, K. S., & Fieldstone, A. (1994). Autonomic cardiac control. III. Psychological stress and cardiac response in autonomic space as revealed by pharmacological blockades. *Psychophysiology, 31*, 599–608.

Berntson, G. G., Quigley, K. S., Norman, G. J., & Lozano, D. L. (2017). Cardiovascular psychophysiology.

Berntson, G. G., Thomas Bigger Jr., J., Eckberg, D. L., Grossman, P., Kaufmann, P. G., Malik, M., Nagaraja, H. N., Porges, S. W., Saul, J. P., Stone, P. H., & Van Der Molen, M. W. (1997). Heart rate variability: Origins, methods, and interpretive caveats. Psychophysiology, 34, 623–648.

Boudoulas, H. (1990). Systolic time intervals. *European Heart Journal, 11*(suppl_I), 93–104.

Brenner, S. L., Beauchaine, T. P., & Sylvers, P. D. (2005). A comparison of psychophysiological and self-report measures of BAS and BIS activation. *Psychophysiology, 42*, 108–115.

Brenner, S. L., & Beauchaine, T. P. (2011). Pre-ejection period reactivity and psychiatric comorbidity prospectively predict substance use initiation among middle-schoolers: A pilot study. *Psychophysiology, 48*, 1588–1596.

Boyce, W. T. (2016). Differential susceptibility of the developing brain to contextual adversity and stress. *Neuropsychopharmacology, 41*, 142–162.

Byrd, A. L., Loeber, R., & Pardini, D. A. (2014). Antisocial behavior, psychopathic features and abnormalities in reward and punishment processing in youth. *Clinical Child and Family Psychology Review, 17*, 125–156.

Cacioppo, J. T., Tassinary, L. G., & Berntson, G. (Eds.). (2007). *Handbook of psychophysiology.* Cambridge University Press.

Cornet, L. J., de Kogel, C. H., Nijman, H. L., Raine, A., & van der Laan, P. H. (2014). Neurobiological factors as predictors of cognitive–behavioral therapy outcome in individuals with antisocial behavior: A review of the literature. *International journal of offender therapy and comparative criminology, 58*(11), 1279-1296.

Del Ventura, J. L., & Rhudy, J. L. (2012). Individual differences in respiratory sinus arrhythmia and physiological–emotional responses to pictures. *Journal of Applied Biobehavioral Research, 17*, 176–201.

Derefinko, K. J., Eisenlohr-Moul, T. A., Peters, J. R., Roberts, W., Walsh, E. C., Milich, R., & Lynam, D. R. (2016). Physiological response to reward and extinction predicts alcohol, marijuana, and cigarette use two years later. *Drug and Alcohol Dependence, 163*, S29–S36.

Dietrich, A., Riese, H., Sondeijker, F. E., Greaves-Lord, K., Ormel, J., Neeleman, J., & Rosmalen, J. G. (2007). Externalizing and internalizing problems in relation to autonomic function: A population-based study in preadolescents. *Journal of the American Academy of Child & Adolescent Psychiatry, 46*, 378–386.

de Wied, M., van Boxtel, A., Zaalberg, R., Goudena, P. P., & Matthys, W. (2006). Facial EMG responses to dynamic emotional facial expressions in boys with disruptive behavior disorders. *Journal of Psychiatric Research, 40*, 112–121.

de Wied, M., van Boxtel, A., Matthys, W., & Meeus, W. (2012). Verbal, facial and autonomic responses to empathy-eliciting film clips by disruptive male adolescents with high versus low callous-unemotional traits. *Journal of Abnormal Child Psychology, 40*, 211–223.

Dyer, W. J., Blocker, D. J., Day, R. D., & Bean, R. A. (2016). Parenting style and adolescent externalizing behaviors: The moderating role of respiratory sinus arrhythmia. *Journal of Marriage and Family, 78*, 1149–1165.

Dywan, J., Mathewson, K. J., Choma, B. L., Rosenfeld, B., & Segalowitz, S. J. (2008). Autonomic and electrophysiological correlates of emotional intensity in older and younger adults. *Psychophysiology, 45*, 389–397.

Ellis, B. J., Boyce, W. T., Belsky, J., Bakermans-Kranenburg, M. J., & Van IJzendoorn, M. H. (2011). Differential susceptibility to the environment: An evolutionary–neurodevelopmental theory. *Development and Psychopathology, 23*, 7–28.

El-Sheikh, M. (2005). The role of emotional responses and physiological reactivity in the marital conflict–child functioning link. *Journal of Child Psychology and Psychiatry, 46*, 1191–1199.

El-Sheikh, M., Harger, J., & Whitson, S. M. (2001). Exposure to interparental conflict and children's adjustment and physical health: The moderating role of vagal tone. *Child Development, 72*, 1617–1636.

Fagan, S. E., Zhang, W., & Gao, Y. (2017). Social adversity and antisocial behavior: Mediating effects of autonomic nervous system activity. *Journal of Abnormal Child Psychology, 45,* 1553–1564.

Farrington, D. P. (2020). Interactions Between Resting Heart Rate and Childhood Risk Factors in Predicting Convictions and Antisocial Personality Scores. *Crime & Delinquency,* 0011128720926108.

Farrington, D. P. (1997). The relationship between low resting heart rate and violence. In A. Raine, P. A. Brennan, D. P. Farrington, & S. A. Mednick (Eds.), *Biosocial bases of violence* (pp. 89–105). Plenum Press.

Fortunato, C. K., Gatzke-Kopp, L. M., & Ram, N. (2013). Associations between respiratory sinus arrhythmia reactivity and internalizing and externalizing symptoms are emotion specific. *Cognitive, Affective, & Behavioral Neuroscience, 13,* 238–251.

Fox, B. (2017). It's nature and nurture: Integrating biology and genetics into the social learning theory of criminal behavior. *Journal of Criminal Justice, 49,* 22–31. https://doi.org/10. 1016/j.jcrimjus.2017.01.003

Gao, Y., Huang, Y., & Li, X. (2017). Interaction between prenatal maternal stress and autonomic arousal in predicting conduct problems and psychopathic traits in children. *Journal of Psychopathology and Behavioral Assessment, 39,* 1–14.

Gao, Y., & Zhang, W. (2020). Reward processing and psychopathic traits in children. *Personality Disorders: Theory, Research, and Treatment.*

Geisler, S., & Coller, J. (2013). RNA in unexpected places: Long non-coding RNA functions in diverse cellular contexts. *Nature Reviews Molecular Cell Biology, 14,* 699–712.

Gordis, E. B., Feres, N., Olezeski, C. L., Rabkin, A. N., & Trickett, P. K. (2010). Skin conductance reactivity and respiratory sinus arrhythmia among maltreated and comparison youth: Relations with aggressive behavior. *Journal of Pediatric Psychology, 35,* 547–558.

Gouin, J. P., Deschênes, S. S., & Dugas, M. J. (2014). Respiratory sinus arrhythmia during worry forecasts stress-related increases in psychological distress. *Stress, 17,* 416–422.

Hammerton, G., Heron, J., Mahedy, L., Maughan, B., Hickman, M., & Murray, J. (2018). Low resting heart rate, sensation seeking and the course of antisocial behaviour across adolescence and young adulthood. *Psychological Medicine, 48,* 2194–2201.

Heponiemi, T., Keltikangas-Järvinen, L., Puttonen, S., & Ravaja, N. (2003). BIS/BAS sensitivity and self-rated affects during experimentally induced stress. *Personality and Individual Differences, 34,* 943–957.

Hinnant, J. B., & El-Sheikh, M. (2009). Children's externalizing and internalizing symptoms over time: The role of individual differences in patterns of RSA responding. *Journal of Abnormal Child Psychology, 37,* 1049.

Hinnant, J. B., El-Sheikh, M., Keiley, M., & Buckhalt, J. A. (2013). Marital conflict, allostatic load, and the development of children's fluid cognitive performance. *Child Development, 84,* 2003–2014.

Hinnant, J. B., Erath, S. A., & El-Sheikh, M. (2015). Harsh parenting, parasympathetic activity, and development of delinquency and substance use. *Journal of Abnormal Psychology, 124,* 137.

Holzman, J. B., & Bridgett, D. J. (2017). Heart rate variability indices as bio-markers of top-down self-regulatory mechanisms: A meta-analytic review. *Neuroscience & Biobehavioral Reviews, 74,* 233–255.

Hugdahl, K. (1995). *Psychophysiology: The mind-body perspective.* Harvard University Press.

Jennings, W. G., Piquero, A. R., & Farrington, D. P. (2013). Does resting heart rate at age 18 distinguish general and violent offending up to age 50? Findings from the Cambridge Study in Delinquent Development. *Journal of Criminal Justice, 41*, 213–219. https://doi. org/10.1016/j.jcrimjus.2013.05.003

Kalvin, C. B., Bierman, K. L., & Gatzke-Kopp, L. M. (2016). Emotional reactivity, behavior problems, and social adjustment at school entry in a high-risk sample. *Journal of Abnormal Child Psychology, 44*, 1527–1541.

Kenneth S., Kendler Sara L., Lönn Jan, Sundquist Kristina, Sundquist. (2021). The causal nature of the association between resting pulse in late adolescence and risk for internalizing and externalizing disorders: A co-relative analysis in a national male Swedish sample. *Psychological Medicine, 51*(11), 1822-1828. https://doi.org/10.1017/S00332917 20000549

Latvala, A., Kuja-Halkola, R., Almqvist, C., Larsson, H., & Lichtenstein, P. (2015). A longitudinal study of resting heart rate and violent criminality in more Than 700000 men. *JAMA Psychiatry, 72*, 971–978. https://doi.org/10.1001/jamapsychiatry.2015.1165

Latvala, A., Kuja-Halkola, R., Rück, C., D'Onofrio, B.M., Jernberg, T., Almqvist, C., Mataix-Cols, D., Larsson, H., & Lichtenstein, P. (2016). Association of resting heart rate and blood pressure in late adolescence with subsequent mental disorders: A longitudinal study of more than 1 million men in Sweden. *JAMA Psychiatry, 73*, 1268–1275.

Mills-Koonce, W. R., Wagner, N. J., Willoughby, M. T., Stifter, C., Blair, C., Granger, D. A., & Family Life Project Key Investigators. (2015). Greater fear reactivity and psychophysiological hyperactivity among infants with later conduct problems and callous-unemotional traits. *Journal of Child Psychology and Psychiatry, 56*, 147–154.

Mezzacappa, E., Tremblay, R. E., Kindlon, D., Saul, J. P., Arseneault, L., Seguin, J., Pihl, R. O., & Earls, F. (1997). Anxiety, antisocial behavior, and heart rate regulation in adolescent males. *Journal of child Psychology and Psychiatry, 38*, 457–469.

Moffitt, T. E., Caspi, A., Rutter, M., & Silva, P. A. (2001). *Sex differences in antisocial behaviour: Conduct disorder, delinquency, and violence in the Dunedin Longitudinal Study.* Cambridge University Press.

Murray-Close, D., Holterman, L. A., Breslend, N. L., & Sullivan, A. (2017). Psychophysiology of proactive and reactive relational aggression. *Biological Psychology, 130*, 77–85.

Murray, J., Hallal, P. C., Mielke, G. I., Raine, A., Wehrmeister, F. C., Anselmi, L., & Barros, F. C. (2016). Low resting heart rate is associated with violence in late adolescence: A prospective birth cohort study in Brazil. *International Journal of Epidemiology, 45*, 491–500. https://doi.org/10.1093/ije/dyv340

Musser, E. D., Lugo, Y., Ward, A. R., Tenenbaum, R. B., Morris, S., Brijmohan, N., & Martinez, J. (2018). Parent emotion expression and autonomic-linked emotion dysregulation in childhood ADHD. *Journal of Psychopathology and Behavioral Assessment, 40*, 593–605.

Nedelec, J. L., Connolly, E. J., Schwartz, J. A., & Silver, I. (2017). Biosocial criminology. In C. J. Schreck, M. J. Leiber, H. V. Miller, & K. Welch (Eds.), *Encyclopedia of juvenile delinquency and justice.* https://doi.org/10.1002/9781118524275.ejdj0111

Nederhof, E., Marceau, K., Shirtcliff, E. A., Hastings, P. D., & Oldehinkel, A. J. (2015). Autonomic and adrenocortical interactions predict mental health in late adolescence: The TRAILS study. *Journal of Abnormal Child Psychology, 43*, 847–861.

Obradović, J., Bush, N. R., & Boyce, W. T. (2011). The interactive effect of marital conflict and stress reactivity on externalizing and internalizing symptoms: The role of laboratory stressors. *Development and Psychopathology, 23,* 101–114.

Ortiz, J., & Raine, A. (2004). Heart rate level and antisocial behavior in children and adolescents: A meta-analysis. *Journal of the American Academy of Child & Adolescent Psychiatry, 43,* 154–162.

Palomba, D., Sarlo, M., Angrilli, A., Mini, A., & Stegagno, L. (2000). Cardiac responses associated with affective processing of unpleasant film stimuli. *International Journal of Psychophysiology, 36,* 45–57.

Pang, K. C., & Beauchaine, T. P. (2013). Longitudinal patterns of autonomic nervous system responding to emotion evocation among children with conduct problems and/or depression. *Developmental Psychobiology, 55,* 698–706.

Porges, S. W. (2007). The polyvagal perspective. *Biological psychology, 74,* 116–143.

Portnoy, J., Raine, A., Chen, F. R., Pardini, D., Loeber, R., & Jennings, J. R. (2014). Heart rate and antisocial behavior: The mediating role of impulsive sensation seeking. *Criminology, 52*(2), 292-311.

Portnoy, J., & Farrington, D. P. (2015). Resting heart rate and antisocial behavior: An updated systematic review and meta-analysis. *Aggression and Violent Behavior, 22,* 33–45. https://doi.org/10.1016/j.avb.2015.02.004

Portnoy, J., Jennings, J. R., Matthews, K. A., Pardini, D., & Raine, A. (2020). The relationship between resting heart rate and aggression in males is racially variant. *Aggressive Behavior, 46,* 170–180.

Portnoy, J., Raine, A., Rudo-Hutt, A. S., Gao, Y., & Monk, K. (2020). Heart rate reactivity, neighborhood disadvantage, and antisocial behavior. *Crime & Delinquency, 66,* 1392–1418

Quay, H. C. (1965). Psychopathic personality as pathological stimulation-seeking. *American Journal of Psychiatry, 122,* 180–183. https://doi.org/10.1176/ajp.122.2.180

Raine, A. (2002). Biosocial studies of antisocial and violent behavior in children and adults: A review. *Journal of Abnormal Child Psychology, 30,* 311–326.

Raine, A. (2013). *The anatomy of violence: The biological roots of crime.* Vintage.

Raine, A., Fung, A. L., Spring, V. L., Portnoy, J., & Choy, O. (2014). Low heart rate as a risk factor for child and adolescent aggressive and psychopathic behavior. *Aggressive Behavior, 40,* 290–299.

Raine, A., Venables, P. H., & Williams, M. (1990). Relationships between central and autonomic measures of arousal at age 15 years and criminality at age 24 years. *Archives of General Psychiatry, 47,* 1003–1007.

Raine, A., & Venables, P. H. (1984). Tonic heart rate level, social class and antisocial behaviour in adolescents. *Biological Psychology, 18,* 123–132.

Rhee, S. H., & Waldman, I. D. (2002). Genetic and environmental influences on antisocial behavior: A meta-analysis of twin and adoption studies. *Psychological Bulletin, 128,* 490–529.

Scarpa, A., Haden, S. C., & Tanaka, A. (2010). Being hot-tempered: Autonomic, emotional, and behavioral distinctions between childhood reactive and proactive aggression. *Biological Psychology, 84,* 488–496.

Scarpa, A., Tanaka, A., & Chiara Haden, S. (2008). Biosocial bases of reactive and proactive aggression: The roles of community violence exposure and heart rate. *Journal of Community Psychology, 36*, 969–988.

Sijtsema, J. J., Nederhof, E., Veenstra, R., Ormel, J., Oldehinkel, A. J., & Ellis, B. J. (2013). Effects of family cohesion and heart rate reactivity on aggressive/rule-breaking behavior and prosocial behavior in adolescence: The tracking adolescents' individual lives survey study. *Development and Psychopathology, 25*, 699–712.

Sijtsema, J. J., Van Roon, A. M., Groot, P. F. C., & Riese, H. (2015). Early life adversities and adolescent antisocial behavior: The role of cardiac autonomic nervous system reactivity in the TRAILS study. *Biological Psychology, 110*, 24–33.

Sijtsema, J. J., Veenstra, R., Lindenberg, S., van Roon, A. M., Verhulst, F. C., Ormel, J., & Riese, H. (2010). Mediation of sensation seeking and behavioral inhibition on the relationship between heart rate and antisocial behavior: The TRAILS study. *Journal of the American Academy of Child and Adolescent Psychiatry, 49*, 493–502. https://doi.org/10.1016/j.jaac.2010.02.005

Sijstema, J. J., Veenstra, R., Lindenberg, S., van Roon, A. M., Verhulst, F. C., Ormel, J., & Riese, H. (2013). Heart rate and antisocial behavior: Mediation and moderation by affiliation with bullies: The TRAILS study. *Journal of Adolescent Health, 52*, 102–107.

Souza, G. G. L., Mendonça-de-Souza, A. C. F., Barros, E. M., Coutinho, E. F. S., Oliveira, L., Mendlowicz, M. V., Figueira, I., & Volchan, E. (2007). Resilience and vagal tone predict cardiac recovery from acute social stress. *Stress, 10*, 368–374.

Suurland, J., Van der Heijden, K. B., Huijbregts, S. C. J., Van Goozen, S. H. M., & Swaab, H. (2017). Interaction between prenatal risk and infant parasympathetic and sympathetic stress reactivity predicts early aggression. *Biological Psychology, 128*, 98–104.

Sylvers, P., Brubaker, N., Alden, S. A., Brennan, P. A., & Lilienfeld, S. O. (2008). Differential endophenotypic markers of narcissistic and antisocial personality features: A psychophysiological investigation. *Journal of Research in Personality, 42*, 1260–1270.

Tenenbaum, R. B., Musser, E. D., Raiker, J. S., Coles, E. K., Gnagy, E. M., & Pelham, W. E. (2018). Specificity of reward sensitivity and parasympathetic-based regulation among children with attention-deficit/hyperactivity and disruptive behavior disorders. *Journal of Abnormal Child Psychology, 46*, 965–977.

Thomson, N. D., Aboutanos, M., Kiehl, K. A., Neumann, C., Galusha, C., & Fanti, K. A. (2019). Physiological reactivity in response to a fear-induced virtual reality experience: Associations with psychopathic traits. *Psychophysiology, 56*(1), e13276.

van Goozen, S. H. M. (2015). The role of early emotion impairments in the development of persistent antisocial behavior. *Child Development Perspectives, 9*, 206–210.

van Hazebroek, B. C., Wermink, H., van Domburgh, L., de Keijser, J. W., Hoeve, M., & Popma, A. (2019). Biosocial studies of antisocial behavior: A systematic review of interactions between peri/prenatal complications, psychophysiological parameters, and social risk factors. *Aggression and Violent Behavior, 47*, 169–188.

Wadsworth, M. E. J. (1976). Delinquency, pulse rates and early emotional deprivation. *British Journal of Criminology, 16*, 245–256. https://doi.org/10.1093/oxfordjournals.bjc.a046738

Wagner, C. R., & Abaied, J. L. (2015). Relational victimization and proactive versus reactive relational aggression: The moderating effects of respiratory sinus arrhythmia and skin conductance. *Aggressive Behavior, 41*, 566–579.

Wagner, N. J., Hastings, P. D., & Rubin, K. H. (2018). Callous-unemotional traits and autonomic functioning in toddlerhood interact to predict externalizing behaviors in preschool. *Journal of Abnormal Child Psychology, 46*, 1439–1450.

Yang, Y., & Raine, A. (2009). Prefrontal structural and functional brain imaging findings in antisocial, violent, and psychopathic individuals: A meta-analysis. *Psychiatry Research, 174*, 81–88. https://doi.org/10.1016/j.pscychresns.2009.03.012

Zhang, W., & Gao, Y. (2015). Interactive effects of social adversity and respiratory sinus arrhythmia activity on reactive and proactive aggression. *Psychophysiology, 52*, 1343–1350.

Zisner, A. R., & Beauchaine, T. P. (2016). Psychophysiological methods and developmental psychopathology. *Developmental Psychopathology*, 1–53.

Further Reading Suggestions

Barnes, J. C., Raine, A., & Farrington, D. P. (2020). The interaction of biopsychological and socio-environmental influences on criminological outcomes. *Justice Quarterly*, 1–25.

Beauchaine, T. P., Bell, Z., Knapton, E., McDonough-Caplan, H., Shader, T., & Zisner, A. (2019). Respiratory sinus arrhythmia reactivity across empirically based structural dimensions of psychopathology: A meta-analysis. *Psychophysiology, 56*(5), e13329.

Cacioppo, J. T., Tassinary, L. G., & Berntson, G. (Eds.). (2007). *Handbook of psychophysiology*. Cambridge University Press.

Raine, A. (2013). *The anatomy of violence: The biological roots of crime*. Pantheon Books.

van Hazebroek, B. C., Wermink, H., van Domburgh, L., de Keijser, J. W., Hoeve, M., & Popma, A. (2019). Biosocial studies of antisocial behavior: A systematic review of interactions between peri/prenatal complications, psychophysiological parameters, and social risk factors. *Aggression and Violent Behavior, 47*, 169–188.

Moral-Cognitive Delay and Distortions

4

John C. Gibbs

Key Points

- Among the factors underpinning much deviant or antisocial behavior are certain social cognitive limitations.
- These limitations include moral-cognitive delays and distortions—especially, developmental stage delay in moral judgment and self-serving distortions in social perception.
- Highly power-assertive, physically abusive, and harsh (as well as neglectful or uninvolved) parenting homes offer few if any social perspective-taking opportunities and thereby render the children at risk for these social cognitive limitations and subsequent conduct disorder.
- Treatment for antisocial individuals must include opportunities for social perspective-taking

Introduction

Among the factors underpinning much deviant or antisocial behavior are social cognitive limitations—specifically, the moral-cognitive developmental delay and self-related cognitive distortions especially evident among juvenile offenders and other antisocial individuals. It is important to note that these limitations are best construed as problematic *tendencies*, not fixed incapacities evident in all circumstances. In optimal circumstances, antisocial individuals do evidence a

J. C. Gibbs (✉)
Department of Psychology, The Ohio State University, Columbus, OH, USA
e-mail: gibbs.1@osu.edu

© The Author(s), under exclusive license to Springer Nature Switzerland AG 2022   67
C. Garofalo and J. J. Sijtsema (eds.), *Clinical Forensic Psychology*,
https://doi.org/10.1007/978-3-030-80882-2_4

potential for mature and accurate social cognition—and their potential in this regard encourages accountability and treatment. Also important to note is that their problematic tendencies reflect a complex interplay of nature and nurture. Among the risk factors for antisocial behavior, "nature" can refer to neurophysiological variables such as difficult temperament and hyperactivity. These biological factors interweave with "nurture" or environmental factors such as parental abuse and neglect, as well as background or macro conditions such as marginalized social class, negative youth culture, and economic disadvantage. Although not the focus of this chapter, these etiological factors should be kept in mind as we review the social cognitive underpinnings of antisocial behavior. Following our review, the case of the American terrorist Timothy McVeigh will be used to illustrate the key role of moral-cognitive delay and distortion in antisocial behavior.

Introduction: Social Cognitive Limitations

Among the social cognitive limitations of antisocial adolescents are moral-cognitive delays and distortions—especially, developmental stage delay in moral judgment and self-serving distortions in social perception. Although distinguishable, these limitations are interrelated (Barriga et al., 2001; Larden et al., 2006). They both point to self-centration or inadequate social perspective-taking: in particular, to a persistent and pronounced self-centered social cognition (moral-cognitive delay) that consolidates into a self-serving perception of self in relation to others in the social world (cognitive distortion). Whereas moral-cognitive delay has been identified in the context of the cognitive developmental stage approach to morality (e.g., Kohlberg, 1984; Gibbs, 2019), self-serving cognitive distortion has been studied in the context of forensic clinical psychology (e.g., Samenow, 2014).

Moral-Cognitive Delay

The cognitive developmental approach to morality (Kohlberg, 1984; Piaget, 1965/1932) emphasizes the role of moral judgment or understanding in social behavior. "Moral judgment" is conceptualized as a reasoned evaluation or decision pertaining to right and/or good social actions and values. Gibbs's (2019) neo-Kohlbergian stage conceptualization of moral judgment development derives not only from Piaget's and Kohlberg's work, but also from Flavell and colleagues' broad cognitive developmental view that "both social and nonsocial cognitive development tend to proceed from superficial appearances" or "salient features of the here-and-now" to "the construction of an inferred underlying reality" (Flavell et al., 2002, p. 181).

In this broad cognitive developmental view, moral judgment development is characterized by immature and mature levels and stages. At the immature level, moral judgment is superficial insofar as it reduces morality to the salient surface features of people, things, or actions such as pragmatic reciprocity. By adolescence, a more ideal reciprocity and profound level of moral-cognitive development typically begin to emerge across diverse cultures (Gibbs et al., 2007).

In these terms, moral-cognitive *delay* refers chiefly to the persistence of immature morality—superficial moral judgment as well as pronounced egocentric bias—into adolescence and adulthood. These two aspects of moral-cognitive delay warrant elaboration.

Superficial Moral Judgment

Superficial level moral judgment (Stages 1 and 2) reduces morality to either particular salient appearances and concrete consequences (centrations, Stage 1) or tit-for-tat exchanges of favors or blows, that is, pragmatic reciprocity (exchanges, Stage 2). Gibbs (2019) illustrated these immature stages in terms of their typical justifications for the moral value of truth and promise-keeping:

> **Stage 1, Centrations**: "You should always keep a promise, and never be a tattletale. It's a lie, and it's not nice to lie. If you made a promise to a friend, it wouldn't be nice to break it because then he won't play with you and be your friend any more. Or he'd cry and beat you up. Not only that, but you will get in trouble. Your parents will punish you if you lie or break a promise."
>
> **Stage 2, Exchanges**: "Your friend has probably done things for you and may return the favor if you help him by keeping your promise. Besides, you may like your friend, and this could be your only friend. Lies catch up with you sooner or later, and once they do and the other person finds out, they may get even. If it's parents and children, then parents should keep their promises to the children if the children have kept their promises to the parents. But if the promise is to someone you hardly, then why bother? They'll probably never know whether you kept it or not." (p. 81)

Relative to comparison peers, delinquent or conduct-disordered adolescents evidence greater use of these moral judgment stages, even after controlling for socioeconomic status, intelligence, and other correlates (Stams et al., 2006). This moral-cognitive stage delay among antisocial adolescents and adults has been found across diverse cultures (Gibbs et al., 2007).

In studies of moral-cognitive delay by area of moral value (keeping promises, helping others, respecting life, etc.), the area of greatest delay concerned the reasons offered for obeying the law. Delinquents' reasoning mainly concerned the risk of getting caught and going to jail (Gregg et al., 1994). In contrast, non-delinquents' reasons evidenced a grasp of the mutualistic bases of interpersonal relationships (Stage 3) and society (Stage 4)for example, the usual selfishness of lawbreaking such as stealing, and its ramifications in society for chaos, insecurity, and loss of trust. The mature-level stages (3 and 4) are illustrated in Gibbs (2019):

> **Stage 3, Mutualities**: "Your friend has faith in you, and you shouldn't betray that trust or hurt his feelings. After all, you'd expect him to keep his promises to you, and having a friend to share feelings with means a lot. Even if it's not a friend, honesty is still the best policy and it's just common courtesy. It's selfish to break promises, and once you make a bad impression, people won't think much of you. If it's a child and the parents don't keep promises, the children will stop believing in their parents and will start thinking that lying is all right. Even if it's someone you hardly know, you may a good relationship by showing that you care and can be trusted."
>
> **Stage 4, Systems**: "Society is based on trust and reliability, and keeping promises is necessary for the sake of social order. Honesty is a standard every-one can accept, and you wouldn't want to live in a society where you couldn't trust anyone. After all, promises have intrinsic value, and a relationship is meaningless if there is no trust. In the case of a child, parents have an obliga-tion to keep their word and provide an example of character so that the child develops a sense of responsibility. Keeping a promise is a commitment—fail-ing to keep it, even if it's to someone you hardly know, reflects on your integrity. People must be consistent and not break promises whenever they feel like it, so that they can earn others' respect, to say nothing of their own." (p. 81)

Key to moral judgment maturity or immaturity is the justification of moral values. It should be emphasized that the immature-level superficiality of delayed moral judgment pertains mainly to the *reasons* underlying moral decisions or values. The author recalls discussing moral values with Joey, a 15-year-old at a Columbus, Ohio school for juveniles with behavior problems. Joey seemed earnest and sincere as he emphatically affirmed the importance of moral values such as keeping promises, telling the truth, helping others, saving lives, not stealing, and obeying the law. "And why is it so important to obey the law or not steal?" I asked Joey. "Because [pause], like in a store, you may think no one sees you, but they could have cameras!" His other explanations were generally similar: Keeping promises to others is important because if you do not, they might find out and get even; helping others is important in case you need a favor from them later; and so forth. Could Joey be trusted to live up to his moral values in situations where his fear of observers and surveillance cameras would be less salient than his egoistic motives? Despite their evaluation of moral values as important, many antisocial juveniles are developmentally delayed in that they do not evidence much grasp of the deeper *reasons* or bases for the importance of those values and associated decisions (Gibbs et al., 2007; Stams et al., 2006; Wainryb et al., 2010).

Pronounced and Prolonged Egocentric Bias

The high salience of egocentric biases and egoistic motives in superficial moral judgment means that antisocial adolescents tend to be concerned with "getting [their] own throbbing needs [or desires] met, regardless of effects on others" (Carducci, 1980, p. 157). Relative to their non-delinquent peers, antisocial adolescents respond empathically to others less frequently and less intensely, and more frequently make self-references (Robinson et al., 2007). They tend to "complain of mistreatment if their wishes are not given priority over those of other[s]" (Beck, 1999, p. 236).

It is normal for egocentric biases to be pronounced in early childhood. It is a matter of common observation that young children tend not to decenter from their own very salient needs, desires, or impulses. With perspective-taking opportunities in the home and elsewhere, egocentric bias normally declines: "The self's welfare is still important, but at... later levels self-interest is increasingly seen in the context of the welfare of everyone in the relation" (Damon, 1977, p. 221). Highly power-assertive, physically abusive, and harsh (as well as neglectful or uninvolved) parenting homes offer few if any social perspective-taking opportunities and thereby render the children at risk for subsequent conduct disorder (Dodge, Bates, & Pettit, 1990). Accordingly, the bias of self over the welfare of others generally remains pronounced as these children move into the adolescent years.

Self-Serving Cognitive Distortions

Moral-cognitive delay relates to social cognitive distortions, i.e., inaccurate or biased ways of attending to or conferring meaning on experience. Self-serving cognitive distortions have been studied from several theoretical vantage points. In the 1950s, researchers began recognizing the role of these distortions in protecting the self from blame and disinhibiting antisocial behavior. Deviance sociologists Sykes and Matza (1957) concluded that rationalizing attitudes and beliefs "neutralize" empathic activations. In psychodynamic terms, Redl and Wineman (1957) described the "special machinery [that antisocial children have] developed in order to secure their [egoistic and impulse-gratifying] behavior against... guilt" (p. 146). Two decades later, forensic clinical psychologists Yochelson and Samenow (1976, 1977) identified criminogenic errors in the thinking of chronic offenders. Social information processing or cognitive behavioral theorists (e.g., Dodge, 1993; Kendall, 1991) viewed self-serving distortions as biased encoding and representation/interpretation tendencies. In the terminology of Bandura's (1999, 2016) cognitive social learning theory, rationalizations permit one to "disengage" one's immoral conduct from one's evaluation of self.

The Primary Cognitive Distortion: Self-Centered

The longer that pronounced egocentric bias persists through childhood, the more it tends to consolidate into a primary self-related and distorted mindset, a fundamental perception and explanation of events labeled *Self-Centered*. Self-Centered is definable as "according status to one's own views, expectations, needs, rights, immediate feelings, and desires to such an extent that the legitimate views, etc., of others (or even one's own long-term best interest) are scarcely considered or are disregarded altogether" (Gibbs, 2019, p. 183). The combination of a radically self-centered worldview with even the normal array and intensity of egoistic motives constitutes a risk factor for antisocial behavior.

Numerous clinicians working with antisocial youths have discerned a link between their antisocial or aggressive behavior and a self-centered attitude or approach to social relations. Stanton Samenow (1984; cf. Samenow, 2014) quoted a 14-year-old delinquent: "I was born with the idea that I'd do what I wanted. I always felt that rules and regulations were not for me" (p. 160). In our cognitive-behavioral group work with antisocial youth (see Potter et al., 2021, in preparation), one group member seemed to think that he had sufficiently justified having stolen a car with this explanation: "I needed to get to Cleveland." Other group members, reflecting on their shoplifting and other offenses, have recollected that their thoughts at the time concerned whether they could do what they wanted and get away successfully. The only perspective these juveniles took was their own; spontaneous references to the victims' perspectives (except perhaps to their vulnerabilities) were almost totally absent. Self-centered and other self-serving cognitive distortions correlate highly with self-reports, parent or peer ratings, and records of violent or aggressive behavior (e.g., Barriga & Gibbs, 1996; Barriga et al., 2000, 2009; Liau et al., 1998; McCrady et al., 2008; Paciello et al., 2008; Shulman et al., 2011; Wallinius et al., 2011).

Secondary Cognitive Distortions

To continue his Self-Centered attitude and antisocial behavior, the aggressor may develop protective rationalizations, or what we term *secondary* cognitive distortions. These secondary cognitive distortions protect the offender especially against two types of psychological stress that tend to be generated by their anticipated or enacted harm to others (cf. Sijtsema et al., 2019). One stress refers to the empathic distress and empathy-based guilt that may begin to be aroused by anticipated or recalled salient victim distress cues. Most of those who characteristically do salient harm to others must use protective rationalizations to neutralize incipient empathic distress and even guilt. The inverse relationship between the use of self-serving distortions and empathy for others is evident in many offenders samples (e.g., McCrady et al., 2008).

The second type of stress results from the potential inconsistency with self-concept by salient and unfair acts of harm to others (Aronson, 1992). Morality is less relevant to the self for those who engage in antisocial behavior (Aquino et al., 2007; Barriga et al., 2001). Even so, the impression of many clinicians is that, like most individuals, antisocial individuals seek to retain and maintain a "good" image (Beck, 1999; Samenow, 2014) in some sense (others are harmed only for good reason). Accordingly, highly salient, obviously unfair harm to others may contradict the good-person presentation to self and others and thereby constitutes a potential source of psychological stress from cognitive inconsistency or dissonance (Blasi, 1995; Shalvi et al., 2015; cf. Bandura, 2016).

Secondary distortions can function, then, as a perversely effective coping mechanism. Through their use, antisocial individuals can reduce the stresses of empathy and inconsistency and preserve their primary Self-Centered orientation as well as self-esteem. Higher self-esteem children with antisocial tendencies are more likely to use self-serving cognitive distortions (minimizing the harm of their aggression or blaming their victims; Menon et al., 2007). As noted, self-serving distortions relate inversely to empathy for victims and self-reported delinquency (Larden et al., 2006; McCrady et al., 2008; van Langen et al., 2014). Adolescents with high levels of self-serving distortions are more aggressive and subsequently less likely to express feelings of guilt (Paciello et al., 2008). In our typology (Barriga et al. 2001), these empathy neutralizers and protectors of self-centered attitudes and self-esteem are termed *Blaming Others, Assuming the Worst,* and *Minimizing/Mislabeling.*

Blaming Others

Generally, Blaming Others can be defined as "misattributing blame for one's harmful actions to outside sources, especially to another person, a group, or a momentary aberration (one was drunk, high, in a bad mood, etc.), or misattributing blame for one's victimization or other misfortune to innocent others" (Gibbs, 2019, p. 188). Again, antisocial individuals may use a secondary cognitive distortion such as Blaming Others to mitigate psychological stressors and thereby continue their antisocial behavior. Looking back on his burglaries and victims, one antisocial youth reflected, "If I started feeling bad, I'd say to myself, 'tough rocks for him. He should have had his house locked better and the alarm on'" (Samenow, 1984, p. 115). This youth would seem to be saying, in effect: "Upon experiencing empathy-based guilt and a threat to my self-concept for causing innocent people to suffer, I would neutralize my aversive affect by blaming my victims; they were negligent in protecting their homes and so deserved whatever happened to them." Kahn and Chambers (1991) found higher sexual recidivism rates among juvenile sex offenders who blamed their victims for the offenses than among those who did not.

Many offenders over-generalize their grievances and targets of vengeance (Wilson & Herrnstein, 1985). One of Redl and Wineman's (1957) Pioneer House children "really tried to prove that his stealing [from other House children] was all right because 'somebody swiped my own wallet two weeks ago'" (p. 150). A 16-year-old who had just fatally shot several classmates explained the violence to the school's assistant principal (who was holding him until the police arrived): "Mr. Myrick, the world has wronged me" (Lacayo, 1998). In more recent tragedies as well, accumulated—and over-generalized—grievances have been discernible in "blaming others" dynamics among individuals who commit violence in schools, workplaces, and elsewhere.

The sense that one has been *wronged* adds motive power to violent antisocial behavior. As Beck (1999) noted, an individual who has perceived himself to have been diminished in some way typically perceives that putdown to be unfair, prompting a mobilization of "his behavioral system... in preparation for counterattack" (p. 31). One must rape, steal, or kill not only to neutralize one's hurt or restore one's self-esteem but more nobly to reestablish one's rights, to correct an injustice that has been committed against one, to "get even" or "settle the score." The youth who killed to get even with the world that had wronged him was evidencing both Stage 2 tit-for-tat morality and a Blaming Others distortion to cover his highly salient, otherwise obviously unjustifiable harm to innocent others. As the earlier-noted correlational studies suggest, moral judgment delay and a tendency to externalize blame can be a deadly combination.

Assuming the Worst

A rapist who imagined that a young woman "felt uppity" and deprecated him not only evidenced a Blaming Others cognitive distortion ("it was her fault she was raped") but also an "Assuming the Worst" distortion that she specifically and deliberately meant to offend him (Groth & Birnsbaum, 1979; cf. Gannon et al., 2005). Assuming the Worst means "gratuitously attributing hostile intentions to others, considering a worst-case scenario for a social situation as if it were inevitable, or assuming that improvement is impossible in one's own or others' behavior" (Gibbs, 2019, p. 190). Dodge and colleagues (Dodge, Price, Bachorowski, & Newman, 1990) found higher levels of hostile attribution among severely reactive-aggressive juvenile offenders.

Extreme levels of Assuming the Worst can be recognized in clinical mental health populations. The psychiatric diagnosis of "delusional paranoid" is applied when individuals assume the worst regarding events and behavior irrelevant to themselves (Chapter 14). An agitated paranoid patient of Beck's interpreted the laughing of a lively group of strangers at a street corner "as a sign that they were plotting to embarrass him" (Beck, 1999, p. 28).

Like Blaming Others, Assuming the Worst distorts in part as it over-generalizes (e.g., "*every*body is against me"). Highly aggressive adolescents have frequently been found to endorse statements such as "If you back down from a fight, *every*one will think you're a coward" (Slaby & Guerra, 1988, emphasis added), and "*Every*one steals—you might as well get your share" (Gibbs et al., 2001; emphasis added). As Beck (1999) observed, "It is obviously far more painful for a person to be 'always' mistreated than mistreated on a specific occasion. The over-generalized explanation, rather than the event itself, accounts for the degree of anger" (p. 74).

Among the secondary cognitive distortions, Assuming the Worst is distinctive in that it is not only "aggressogenic" but also "*depressogenic*": Antisocial individuals often assume the worst not only about others but also about *themselves* (their capabilities, future, etc.). Barriga et al. (2000) studied not only self-serving but also self-debasing cognitive distortions (e.g., "I can never do anything right"). Self-*serving* distortion correlated more strongly with *externalizing* behavior disorders than did with internalizing behavior disorders, and self-*debasing* distortion correlated more strongly with *internalizing* disorders than it did with externalizing disorders (Barriga et al., 2000). Essentially, exaggerated *other*-blaming is *aggress*ogenic, whereas exaggerated *self*-blame is *depress*ogenic; roughly, externalizers think that every problem in their life is someone *else's* fault, whereas internalizers think that every problem in their life is *their* fault. Co-morbid (aggressive but also self-destructive) cognition was evident in some cases, i.e., self-serving cognitive distortions also correlated to some extent with internalizing behavior problems (as self-debasing distortions did to some extent with externalizing behavior problems). This self-serving-self-debasing comorbidity was accounted for mainly by Assuming the Worst (Barriga et al., 2008): Some of those who gratuitously attributed hostile intentions to others also catastrophized about their future prospects (Barriga et al., 2000; cf. Quiggle et al., 1992).

Minimizing/Mislabelling

Antisocial behavioral tendencies can be protected from inhibiting factors (empathy, inconsistency with or threat to self-concept) not only by blaming or attributing the worst of intentions to the victim but also by disparaging the victim or minimizing the victimization. The use of minimizing to protect one's positive self-concept was almost transparent in one offender's protest: "Just because I shot a couple of state troopers doesn't mean I'm a bad guy" (Samenow, 2004, p. 172). Minimizing/mislabeling is definable as "depicting antisocial behavior as causing no real harm or as being acceptable or even admirable, or referring to others with belittling or dehumanizing labels" (Gibbs, 2019, p. 192). One of our group members who had grabbed a purse dangling from a supermarket cart recalled thinking that the theft taught the purse's owner a good lesson to be more careful in the future. Vandalism is sometimes minimized as "mischief" or "a prank" (Sykes & Matza, 1957), and premeditated violent crimes as "mistakes" (Garbarino, 1999, p. 134). Slaby and Guerra (1988) found that highly aggressive adolescents were more likely to endorse statements such as "People who get beat up badly probably don't suffer a lot." Beck (1999) noted a common belief among rapists that a woman will "enjoy" being raped (p. 141; cf. McCrady et al., 2008).

Minimizing and mislabeling such as dehumanization is a staple feature of ideological "crimes of obedience" (Kelman & Hamilton, 1989). A common practice during combat training of soldiers—or, for that matter, of gang members who are to fight another gang—is to use derogatory and dehumanizing labels for the class of human beings who are to be the enemy, the out-group, so that harming or killing them will be easier. Many government torturers, to be able to continue, must frequently be reminded that their victims are "vermin" (Haritos-Fatouros, 2003; cf. Moshman, 2004, 2007; Suddendorf, 2013, p. 186)—perhaps to avoid conscious empathic recognition that their victims are human beings "with intentions and desires and projects" (Appiah, 2008, p. 145; cf. Batson, 2011, pp. 192–193).

In addition to dehumanizing their victims, glorifying or ennobling the victimizing behavior may be essential if anti-social individuals are to continue to engage in otherwise obviously immoral acts. Such distortions are not always entirely successful. Persistent guilt despite efforts to minimize or mislabel can be a factor in post-traumatic stress disorder among military combat veterans (Grossman, 1995).

One can also attempt to minimize and insulate oneself from the enormity of one's actions through their "routinization" (Kelman, 1973; Kelman & Hamilton, 1989) or "deconstruction" (Baumeister, 1991; Ward et al., 1995); i.e., selective or tunnel-vision attention to concrete details or ordinary, repetitive, and mechanical details of the offending activity. Beck's (1999) term for this cognitive strategy was *procedural thinking*. Bureaucrats serving a murderous regime, for example, "can be so focused on what they are doing—a kind of tunnel vision—that they are able to blot out the fact that they are participating in an inhuman action" (p. 18).

A Case Study

Although atypical in some respects, the infamous terrorist Timothy McVeigh—executed on May 19, 2001 for having murdered 168 innocent men, women, and children by bombing a federal building in Oklahoma City, Oklahoma—evidenced the social cognitive limitations that underpin much antisocial behavior. Study of his mindset through inspection of hundreds of hours of interviews (Michel & Herbeck, 2001) reveals a paucity of social perspective-taking as well as problematic tendencies entailing moral judgment developmental delay and self-serving cognitive distortions.

McVeigh's Moral-Cognitive Developmental Delay

McVeigh, even as a young adult, evidenced both concrete morality and pronounced egocentric bias. Eye-for-an-eye reciprocity was "a theme that became McVeigh's philosophy" (Michel & Herbeck, 2001, p. 68). His description of his philosophy—dirty for dirty, you reap what you sow, payback time—is an explicit description of the concrete tit-for-tat logic of moral judgment Stage 2. "Anyone who mistreated McVeigh—or made him think he was being mistreated—was making a formidable enemy with a long memory" (Michel & Herbeck, 2001, p. 68). Given his pronounced egocentric bias, anyone who even disagreed with McVeigh was likely to induce in McVeigh a perception of mistreatment and a motive to retaliate. His vitriol was especially aimed at agents of the U.S. government as enemies of the "gun community:" it was "time to make them all pay" (p. 168), to silence "the laughter of the bully" (p. 167). He wrote to his sister, "My whole mindset has shifted, from intellectual to... animal, Rip the bastards (*sic*) heads off and shit down their necks!" (p. 196). Indeed, to the Bureau of Alcohol, Tobacco, and Firearms, he wrote, "All you tyrannical mother fuckers will swing in the wind one day" (p. 180; see Thomaes et al., 2013).

McVeigh's Self-Serving Cognitive Distortions

Both primary (Self-Centered) and secondary (Blaming Others, Assuming the Worst, Minimizing/Mislabeling) cognitive distortions were amply evident in McVeigh's mental life.

Self-Centered

McVeigh's egocentric bias consolidated into a Self-Centered cognitive distortion. Aspects of his Self-Centered orientation suggested grandiosity or even psychopathy. In quitting college, he declared that he knew more than the teachers and that the classes were "just too boring" (Michel & Herbeck, 2001, p. 38). In the Army, he arrogantly expressed disdain for others—even officers—who seemed less knowledgeable regarding weapons and procedure manuals. Although the Army initially offered "thrills" (p. 103) and glory, McVeigh eventually became "suffocated by the repetition of ordinary life" and "restless, dissatisfied by daily life, increasingly eager to set his own rules" (pp. 122, 196). To impress his younger sister, he fabricated a military adventure. Alluding to the planned bombing, he bragged that "something big is going to happen" (p. 196). His plans were methodical, and he manipulated or intimidated others into helping him. He was convinced that "historians would call him a martyr, maybe even a hero" (p. 166). McVeigh's anticipated glory of martyrdom belied his self-presentation as a humble, selfless, sacrificial crusader. In effect, McVeigh evidenced a *false moral identity* (Moshman, 2004).

Yet McVeigh's troubled mind and feelings do not evidence the gross empathic deficits characteristic of primary psychopaths. His absence of guilt over harm to others seemed to stem from the neutralizing use of self-righteous, self-serving distortions rather than an absence of empathy. As a child, McVeigh loved animals. He cried "for days" after seeing kittens drown (Michel & Herbeck, 2001, p. 17). In another incident, he ran to his parents to gain help for an injured rabbit. He also at times evidenced an insecurity and vulnerability suggestive of the reactive offender (Dodge et al., 2006). In a rambling letter to his sister, he expressed "an urgent need for someone in the family to understand me." He even made reference to his "lawless behavior and attitude" (Michel & Herbeck, 2001, p. 145), although he quickly attributed it to a (fabricated) encounter with lawless government agents.

Blaming Others

The secondary distortions, including Blaming Others, were also thematic. In high school, McVeigh insisted that his flagging interest in academics was "the teachers' fault" (Michel & Herbeck, 2001, p. 32). His list of blameworthy agents included "crooked politicians, overzealous governmental agents, high taxes, political correctness, gun laws" (p. 2). He even blamed "American women" for "sexually shortchanging the opposite sex" (p. 114). At his trial, he sought to present a "necessity defense" to the effect that "Waco, Ruby Ridge, and other government excesses... *drove him*" to respond in kind (p. 277, emphasis added).

Assuming the Worst

Much the way highly aggressive boys point to the hostility they create as proof they were right all along about others' attitudes toward them (Lochman & Dodge, 1998), McVeigh welcomed execution as proving "that the American government was heartless and cruel" (Michel & Herbeck, 2001, p. 350). McVeigh explicitly Assumed the Worst regarding the ostensible threat from the government: "If a comet is hurtling toward the earth, and it's out past the orbit of Pluto,... it is an imminent threat." And if the U.S. government was allowed to get away with what happened at Waco and Ruby Ridge, there was an imminent threat to the lives of gun owners, McVeigh said. (Michel & Herbeck, 2001, pp. 285–286).

McVeigh saw the world as a dangerous place, necessitating constant vigilance and preparedness. He kept guns "all over" (Michel & Herbeck, 2001, p. 89) in his house and in his car because of the ever-present danger, in his mind, of attack. While in the army, he rented a storage shed where he stockpiled a hundred gallons of fresh water, food rations, guns, and other supplies in case "all hell broke loose in the world" (p. 60).

McVeigh's habitual overreaction to perceived dangers or threats may have had a heritable component. Such a possibility is suggested by his mother's subsequent commitment to a psychiatric hospital in part for paranoid delusions (an extreme level of Assuming the Worst) (Beck, 1999). McVeigh himself first noticed odd [even for him] behavior in his mother more than two years before the bombing.... She constantly pulled plugs from electrical outlets. At first, he thought she was trying to save electricity; only later did he realize she was afraid of health dangers from electromagnetic fields. (Michel & Herbeck, 2001, p. 381).

Minimizing/Mislabeling

To rationalize his crimes, McVeigh abused a military metaphor: "War means action. Hard choices. Life and death" (Michel & Herbeck, 2001, p. 212). In this hard war, he was a courageous patriot, or perhaps a Robin Hood. The innocent people he killed were, after all, "part of the evil empire" (p. 225), providing the "body count" (p. 300) he desired; the dead babies were "collateral damage" (p. 331). McVeigh saw himself as having a necessary "duty," in terms of which empathy for his victims was a sign of debilitating weakness. To his victims and their families, he minimized that death "happens every day" (p. 324). In a perverse expression of ego strength, he rejected suggestions that he show empathic distress or guilt for the victims' losses as a pathetic capitulation: "I'm not going to... curl into a fetal ball, and cry just because the victims want me to do that" (p. 325).

McVeigh also minimized empathic affect by diverting his thoughts and perceptions from the crime. His extraordinary attention to detail preparing the bomb as if it were a "science project" (Michel & Herbeck, 2001, p. 288) is suggestive of the tunnel-vision strategy described earlier. Also, after positioning and activating the bomb, he walked briskly away, wearing earplugs and not looking back at the devastation upon hearing the blast. Later, seeing on television the children among his victims "did cause him a moment's regret." His overall reaction, however, was disappointment that the effect of his bomb was not more spectacular. "'Damn,' he thought, 'the whole building didn't come down'" (Michel & Herbeck, 2001, p. 245).

Case Study Summary and Conclusion

Overall, then, McVeigh was a very self-centered, vindictive, and threatening individual, evidencing moral-cognitive delay and distortion. His morality entailed both a concrete, tit-for-tat moral judgment and a pronounced egocentric bias. Relatedly, he evidenced both primary (Self-Centered) and secondary (Blaming

Others, Minimizing-Mislabeling, Assuming the Worst) self-serving cognitive distortions. Social perspective-taking was scarcely discernible in his mental life and social behavior.

I conclude by noting a (belated) social perspective-taking opportunity afforded by Timothy McVeigh. After bragging in a rambling letter to his younger sister that "something big is going to happen," McVeigh indicated "an urgent need for someone in the family to understand me" (pp. 145, 196). No one—no family member or anyone else—met that need to understand and confront McVeigh's self-centered and troubled mind. Several years before McVeigh's execution in 2001, Oklahoma City psychiatrist Dr. John R. Smith once tried to confront McVeigh about the pain his bomb had caused others. Smith had noted how much McVeigh seemed to enjoy talking to people, and now he tried to use this quality to provoke a reaction from him. "Instead of the death penalty, Tim, they should put you in a tiny little cell," Smith said. "You wouldn't be allowed to talk to anyone, ever." McVeigh looked surprised. He stood straight up from his chair. "You'd put me in a little cell like that?" he said. "Tim, that's what you did to your victims and their families," Smith said. "They'll never be able to communicate with each other again." (p. 289).

Although Dr. Smith intervened too late to save Timothy McVeigh, Smith's social perspective-taking approach was precisely what is warranted for therapeutic work with antisocial individuals evidencing the moral-cognitive delays and distortions discussed in this chapter. Treatment for antisocial individuals (e.g., Potter et al., 2021, in preparation) must include opportunities for social perspective-taking to remedy their social cognitive risk factors of moral-cognitive delay and self-serving (as well as self-debasing) cognitive distortions.

References

Appiah, K. A. (2008). *Experiments in ethics.* Harvard University Press.
Aquino, K., Reed, A., Thau, S., & Freeman, D. (2007). A grotesque and dark beauty: How moral identity and mechanisms of moral disengagement influence cognitive and emotional reactions to war. *Journal of Experimental Social Psychology, 43,* 385–392.
Aronson, E. (1992). The theory of cognitive dissonance: The evolution and vicissitudes of an idea. In C. McGarty & S. A. Haslam (Eds.), *The message of social psychology: Perspectives on mind and society* (pp. 20–35). Cambridge.
Bandura, A. (1999). Moral disengagement in the perpetration of inhumanities. *Personality and Social Psychology Review, 3,* 193–209.
Bandura, A. (2016). *Moral disengagement: How people do harm and live with themselves.* Worth Publishers.

Barriga, A. Q., & Gibbs, J. C. (1996). Measuring cognitive distortion in antisocial youth: Development and preliminary evaluation of the *How I Think* questionnaire. *Aggressive Behavior, 22*, 333–343.

Barriga, A. Q., Hawkins, M. A., & Camelia, C. R. T. (2008). Specificity of cognitive distortions to antisocial behaviors. *Criminal Behaviour and Mental Health, 18*, 104–116.

Barriga, A. Q., Morrison, E. M., Liau, A. K., & Gibbs, J. C. (2001). Moral cognition: Explaining the gender difference in antisocial behavior. *Merrill-Palmer Quarterly, 47*, 532–562.

Barriga, A. Q., Landau, J. R., Stinson, B. L., Liau, A. K., & Gibbs, J. C. (2000). Cognitive distortion and problem behaviors in adolescents. *Criminal Justice and Behavior, 27*, 333–343.

Barriga, A. Q., Sullivan-Cosetti, M., & Gibbs, J. C. (2009). Moral cognitive correlates of empathy in juvenile delinquents. *Criminal Behaviour and Mental Health, 19*(4), 253–264.

Batson, C. D. (2011). *Altruism in humans*. Oxford University Press.

Baumeister, R. F. (1991). *Escaping the self: Alcoholism, spirituality, masochism, and other flights from the burden of selfhood*. Basic Books.

Beck, A. T. (1999). *Prisoners of hate: The cognitive basis of anger, hostility, and violence*. HarperCollins.

Blasi, A. (1995). Moral understanding and the moral personality: The process of moral integration. In W. Kurtines & J. I. Gewirtz (Eds.), *Moral development: An introduction* (pp. 229–253). Allyn & Bacon.

Carducci, D. J. (1980). Positive peer culture and assertiveness training: Complementary modalities for dealing with disturbed and disturbing adolescents in the classroom. *Behavioral Disorders, 5*, 156–162.

Damon, W. (1977). *The social world of the child*. Jossey-Bass.

Dodge, K. A. (1993). Social-cognitive mechanisms in the development of conduct disorder and depression. *Annual Review of Psychology, 44*, 559–584.

Dodge, K. A., Bates, J. E., & Pettit, G. S. (1990). Mechanisms in the cycle of violence. *Science, 250*, 1678–1685.

Dodge, K. A., Coie, J. D., & Lynam, D. (2006). Aggression and antisocial behavior in youth. In W. Damon & R. M. Lerner (Series Eds.) & N. Eisenberg (Vol. Ed.), *Handbook of child psychology: Vol. 3. Social, emotional, and personality development* (6th ed., pp. 719–788). John Wiley.

Dodge, K. A., Price, J. M., Bachorowski, J. A., & Newman, J. P. (1990). Hostile attributional biases in severely aggressive adolescents. *Journal of Abnormal Psychology, 99*, 385–392.

Flavell, J. H., Miller, P. H., & Miller, S. A. (2002). *Cognitive development* (4th ed.). Prentice Hall.

Gannon, T. A., Polaschek, D. L. L., & Ward, T. (2005). Social cognition and sex offenders. In M. McMurran & J. McGuire (Eds.), *Social problem solving and offending: Evidence, evaluation, and evolution* (pp. 223–247). John Wiley & Sons.

Garbarino, J. (1999). *Lost boys: Why our sons turn violent and how we can save them*. The Free Press.

Gibbs, J. C. (2019). *Moral development and reality: Beyond the theories of Kohlberg, Hoffman, and Haidt* (4th ed.). Oxford University Press.

Gibbs, J. C., Barriga, A. Q., & Potter, G. B. (2001). *How I Think (HIT) questionnaire*. Research Press.

Gibbs, J. C., Basinger, K. S., Grime, R. L., & Snarey, J. R. (2007). Moral judgment development across cultures: Revisiting Kohlberg's universality claims. *Developmental Review, 27*, 443–500.

Gibbs, J. C., Potter, G., & Goldstein, A. P. (1995). *The EQUIP program: Teaching youth to think and act responsibly through a peer-helping approach.* Research Press.

Gregg, V. R., Gibbs, J. C., & Basinger, K. S. (1994). Patterns of developmental delay in moral judgment by male and female delinquents. *Merrill-Palmer Quarterly, 40*, 538–553.

Grossman, D. L. (1995). *On killing: The psychological cost of learning to kill in war and society.* Little, Brown.

Groth, A. N., & Birnsbaum, J. J. (1979). *Men who rape.* Plenum.

Haritos-Fatouros, M. (2003). *The psychological origins of institutionalized torture.* Routledge.

Kahn, T., & Chambers, H. J. (1991). Assessing recidivism risk with juvenile sex offenders. *Child Welfare, 70*, 333–345.

Kelman, H. C. (1973). Violence without restraint: Reflections on the dehumanization of victims and victimizers. *Journal of Social Issues, 29*, 25–61.

Kelman, H. C., & Hamilton, V. L. (1989). *Crimes of obedience: Toward a social psychology of authority and responsibility.* Yale University Press.

Kendall, P. C. (1991). Guiding theory for therapy with children and adolescents. In P. C. Kendall (Ed.), *Child and adolescent therapy: Cognitive-behavioral procedures* (pp. 3–24). Guilford.

Kohlberg, L. (1984). *Essays on moral development: Vol. 2. The psychology of moral development.* Harper & Row.

Lacayo, R. (April 6, 1998). Toward the root of evil. *Time*, pp. 34–35.

Larden, M., Melin, L., Holst, U., & Langstrom, N. (2006). Moral judgment, cognitive distortions, and empathy in incarcerated delinquent and community control adolescents. *Psychology, Crime, and Law, 12*, 453–462.

Liau, A. K., Barriga, A., & Gibbs, J. C. (1998). Relations between self-serving cognitive distortions and overt vs. covert antisocial behavior in adolescents. *Aggressive Behavior, 24*, 335–346.

Lochman, J. E., & Dodge, K. A. (1998). Distorted perceptions in dyadic interactions of aggressive and nonaggressive boys: Effects of prior expectations, context, and peer age. *Development and Psychopathology, 10*, 495–512.

McCrady, F., Kaufman, K., Vasey, M. W., Barriga, A. Q., Devlin, R. S., & Gibbs, J. C. (2008). It's all about me: A brief report of incarcerated adolescent sex offenders' generic and sex-specific cognitive distortions. *Sexual Abuse: A Journal of Research and Treatment, 20*, 261–271.

Menon, M. [Madhavi], Tobin, D. D., Corby, B. C., Menon, M., Hodges, E. V. E., & Perry, D. G. (2007). The developmental costs of high self-esteem for antisocial children. *Child Development, 78*, 1627–1639.

Michel, L., & Herbeck, D. (2001). *American terrorist: Timothy McVeigh and the Oklahoma city bombing.* HarperCollins.

Moshman, D. (2004). False moral identity: Self-serving denial in the maintenance of moral self-conceptions. In D. Lapsley & M. Narvaez (Eds.), *Morality, self, and identity* (pp. 83–110). Lawrence Erlbaum.

Moshman, D. (2007). Us and them: Identity and genocide. *Identity: An International Journal of Theory and Research, 7*, 115–135.

Paciello, M., Fida, R., Tramontano, Lupinetti, C., & Caprara, G. V. (2008). Stability and change of moral disengagement and its impact on aggression and violence in late adolescence. *Child Development, 79*, 1288–1309.

Piaget, J. (1965). *Moral judgment of the child* (M. Gabain, Trans.). Free Press. (Original work published 1932.)

Potter, G. B., Gibbs, J. C., Robbins, M., & Langdon, P. (2021, in preparation). The *EQUIP program for high-risk adolescents: A comprehensive cognitive-behavioral program for community and residential agencies* (2nd ed.). Research Press.

Quiggle, N., Garber, J., Panak, W., & Dodge, K. A. (1992). Social information processing in aggressive and depressed children. *Child Development, 63*, 1305–1320.

Redl, F., & Wineman, D. (1957). *The aggressive child*. Free Press.

Robinson, R., Roberts, W. L., Strayer, J., & Koopman, R. (2007). Empathy and emotional responsiveness in delinquent and non-delinquent adolescents. *Social Development, 16*, 555–579.

Samenow, S. E. (1984). *Inside the criminal mind*. Random House.

Samenow, S. E. (2004). *Inside the criminal mind* (rev). Random House.

Samenow, S. E. (2014). *Inside the criminal mind* (rev. and updated ed.). Broadway Books.

Shalvi, S., Gino, F., Barkan, R., & Ayal, S. (2015). Self-serving justifications: Doing wrong and feeling moral. *Current Directions in Psychological Science, 24*, 125–130.

Shulman, E. P., Cauffman, E., Piquero, A. R., & Fagan, J. (2011). Moral disengagement among serious juvenile offenders: A longitudinal study of the relations between morally disengaged attitudes and offending. *Developmental Psychology, 47*, 1619–1632.

Sijtsema, J. J., Garofalo, C., Jansen, K., & Klimstra, T. A. (2019). Disengaging from evil: Longitudinal associations between the dark triad, moral disengagement, and antisocial behavior in adolescence. *Journal of Abnormal Child Psychology, 47*, 1351–1365.

Slaby, R. G., & Guerra, N. G. (1988). Cognitive mediators of aggression in adolescent offenders: 1 Assessment. *Developmental Psychology, 24*, 580–588.

Stams, G. J., Brugman, D., Dekovic, M., van Rosmalen, L., van der Laan, P., & Gibbs, J. C. (2006). The moral judgment of juvenile delinquents: A meta-analysis. *Journal of Abnormal Child Psychology, 34*, 697–713.

Suddendorf, T. (2013). *The gap: The science of what separates us from other animals*. Basic Books.

Sykes, G. M., & Matza, D. (1957). Techniques of neutralization: A theory of delinquency. *American Sociological Review, 22*, 664–670.

Thomaes, S., Brummelman, E., Reijntjes, A., & Bushman, B. J. (2013). When narcissus was a boy: Origins, nature, and consequences of childhood narcissism. *Child Development Perspectives, 1*, 22–26.

van Langen, M., A., M., Stams, G. J. J. M., Van Vugt, E. S., Wissink, I. B., & Asscher, J. J. (2014). *Laws, 3*, 706–720.

Wainryb, C., Komolova, M., & Florsheim, P. (2010). How violent youth offenders and typically developing adolescents construct moral agency in narratives about doing harm. In K. C. McLean & M. Pasupathi (Eds.), *Narrative development in adolescence* (pp. 185–206). Springer.

Wallinius, M., Johansson, P., Larden, M., & Dernevik, M. (2011). Self-serving cognitive distortions and antisocial behavior among adults and adolescents. *Criminal Justice and Behavior, 38*, 286–2011.

Ward, T., Hudson, S. M., & Marshall, W. L. (1995). Cognitive distortion in sex offenders: An integrative review. *Clinical Psychology Review, 17*, 470–507.

Wilson, J. Q., & Herrnstein, R. J. (1985). *Crime and human nature.* Simon & Schuster.

Yochelson, S., & Samenow, S. E. (1976). *The criminal personality: Vol. 1. A profile for change.* Jason Aronson.

Yochelson, S., & Samenow, S. E. (1977). *The criminal personality: Vol. 2. The change process.* Jason Aronson.

Suggestions for Further Reading

Bandura, A. (2016). *Moral disengagement: How people do harm and live with themselves.* Worth Publishers.

Beck, A. T. (1999). *Prisoners of hate: The cognitive basis of anger, hostility, and violence.* HarperCollins.

Gibbs, J. C. (2019). *Moral development and reality: Beyond the theories of Kohlberg, Hoffman, and Haidt* (4th ed.). Oxford University Press.

Michel, L., & Herbeck, D. (2001). *American terrorist: Timothy McVeigh and the Oklahoma City bombing.* HarperCollins.

Potter, G. B., Gibbs, J. C., Robbins, M., & Langdon, P. (2021, in preparation). The *EQUIP program for high-risk adolescents: A comprehensive cognitive-behavioral program for community and residential agencies.* (2nd ed.). Research Press.

Samenow, S. E. (2014). *Inside the criminal mind* (rev. and updated ed.). Broadway Books.

Emotion and Emotion Regulation

5

Carlo Garofalo

Key Points

The experience of negative emotions is associated with offending, and aggression in particular

The maladaptive experience of some specific emotions—such as anger and shame—is a robust correlate of aggression and offending

The maladaptive absence of some emotions—such as fear, anxiety, and guilt—is also associated with offending and aggression

Beyond emotional experience, difficulties in regulating emotions have shown consistent associations with offending and aggression

Negative emotion and emotion dysregulation can also interact, reinforcing their individual contribution to offending and aggression

Introduction

Emotion is a ubiquitous human experience and a potent driver of human behavior (Mesquita, 2016). Therefore, it is not surprising that the role emotion has featured in several theories of aggression and violent behavior (including 0), as well as antisociality more broadly. Yet, emotion has often taken a backseat in comparison to other known risk factors for antisocial behavior broadly construed, contributing to the risk of underestimating its importance when trying to explain, prevent, or intervene to reduce violence (Roberton et al., 2012). The lion's share

C. Garofalo (✉)
Department of Developmental Psychology, Tilburg University, Tilburg, The Netherlands
e-mail: c.garofalo@tilburguniversity.edu

of the literature on emotion in relation to antisociality has been devoted to the role of anger, but accumulating evidence in recent years suggests that a focus on a broader range of emotional experiences can help elucidate the nuances of the affective landscape that characterize antisocial individuals. In addition, the last decade has witnessed an increase of research suggesting that—beyond emotional *experience*—it is also the way people *regulate* emotions that explains individual differences in the propensity to engage in aggressive or otherwise antisocial behavior. The present chapter aims to summarize and harmonize these two main streams of literature. First, an overview of the role of emotion in traditional and contemporary theories in forensic psychology is presented. Then, the recent literature on emotion regulation is discussed. Finally, the chapter will address the potential interactive roles of emotion and emotion regulation, as well as their clinical implications.

Emotional Experience: Relevance for Clinical Forensic Psychology

For the purpose of this chapter, an emotion is defined as a psycho-physiological phenomenon (Frijda, 2005) that is (1) a relatively brief, event-specific, affective reaction; (2) which is functional and adaptive (that is, not inherently good or bad); and (3) involves multiple components such as an internal or external trigger, cognitive appraisal, physiological activation, an action tendency, distinctive behavioral expression, and a conscious (subjective) experience (often termed *feeling*). Importantly, all these components need not be activated for an emotion to occur (e.g., an emotional reaction that escapes conscious awareness may lack a cognitive appraisal and the subjective experience or feelings). In addition, emotional experience can be examined at the state-level (i.e., emotional reaction *at a specific moment*, such as what one is feeling *right now*) or at the trait-level, referring to the typical or habitual tendency to experience one specific or a range of emotions (e.g., trait anger and trait negative emotionality, or trait happiness and trait positive emotionality). Unless specifically noted and in the interest of simplicity, what is discussed in this chapter refers to positive/negative emotionality or specific emotions in general, that is, without referring to specific components or to state- versus trait-emotion in particular, but emphasizing in particular the subjective experience of emotions (Chapter 3). In addition, I will refer to the broad category of offending or antisociality (hence including, but not limited to, criminal behavior) as well as more specifically to aggression and violence as the most severe declension of emotion-laden offending behavior.

The relevance of emotion, and in particular negative emotions, has traditionally been an important component in theories of antisociality, and aggression in particular. Agnew's (1992, 2001) general strain theory and its subsequent reformulations are one chief example. According to this theory, life stressors (or "strains") experienced by an individual leave a mark on their affective life by increasing the tendency to experience negative emotions. In turn, this theory considers such tendencies to experience negative emotions as one of the main triggers of violent or otherwise antisocial behaviors. The preponderance of empirical evidence to date does support the link between high levels of trait negative emotionality with offending, as well as the link between low levels of positive emotionality with offending (DeLisi & Vaughn, 2014). Beyond concurrent associations drawn from cross-sectional studies and group-comparisons studies between offenders and community participants (Day, 2009; Day et al., 2020), research has also extended to showing longitudinal links between negative emotionality and later offending (e.g., Fanti & Henrich, 2010; Wang et al., 2020), as well as to concurrent associations between negative emotional arousal (i.e., state negative emotion) and aggressive behaviors (e.g., Moon et al., 2009; Twenge et al., 2001; for a review, see DeLisi & Vaughn, 2014). Negative emotions have also been linked to sexual offending in particular (Gillespie et al., 2012; Howells et al., 2004), and have been proven useful to identify subgroups of offenders with elevated levels of psychopathology (Garofalo, Velotti, Crocamo, et al., 2018). However, as will be discussed later in this chapter, a more granular perspective that appreciates the role of specific emotional experiences (and, in some cases, distinguishing between state-like and trait-like experiences) may be more advantageous. At any rate, the broader literature on negative emotions and offending retains great clinical value, as it appears that working on emotional processes is a ubiquitous characteristic of several interventions applied to reduce offending (Day, 2009; Gillespie et al., 2012; Howells et al., 2004). In addition, this broader literature on negative emotionality has set the stage for more targeted streams of literature that have focused on specific emotions, which will be discussed in the following sections. Given the sheer size of this literature, the current chapter should be considered as an introductory and non-exhaustive primer.

Anger

Anger has been defined as a "fairly specific syndrome (or network) of motoric, somatovisceral, and cognitive reactions produced by particular circumstances that are usually associated with an *urge to hurt a target* [emphasis added]" (Berkowitz,

2012, p. 322). Due to its very characteristics, the link with violence is so evident that it is not surprising that anger has traditionally been the emotion that has attracted the majority of scholarly and clinical interest in forensic psychology. Among the earliest theoretical propositions that are germane to the literature on anger was the "frustration-aggression hypothesis" initially proposed by Dollard et al. (1939) and later refined by Berkowitz (1989). According to this hypothesis, aggression is a resulting outcome of the experience that one's efforts to attain a goal are hindered or blocked (i.e., frustrated). This kind of aversive experience generates a negative affective arousal that can take the form of a fight (anger) or flight (fear) response. When anger is activated, aggression becomes the most likely behavioral response. This chain of events suggests that frustration does not necessarily lead to aggression, since aggression would only be one of the possible outcomes. However, it does posit that any form of aggression stems from frustration, indicating that frustration would represent a necessary but not sufficient pre-requisite for aggressive responses. Notably, according to the frustration-aggression hypothesis, any cognitive process related to anger and aggression occurs after the behavioral response, so that aggressive behavior is intended as purely driven by instinctive reactions not mediated by cognitive processing (Chapter 19).

Similar to the frustration-aggression hypothesis, Agnew's (1992) general strain theory conceptualizes aggression as resulting from negative affective experience—and in particular, anger—that stems from experienced strain. In this theory, that extends beyond aggression to explain criminal behavior more broadly, also the source of strain is proposed to encompass a broader array of aversive experiences, including failure to achieve goals, negative events or exposure to chronic stress, or the removal of positively valued stimuli (i.e., reinforcements or rewards). Another important addition of the general strain theory is that negative emotion, including anger, would not necessarily and directly lead to aggressive responses, but would do so only because of a lack (at least in some individuals) of adaptive coping skills. Even though this theory did not elaborate further on whether the proposed role of coping takes the form of a mediating or moderating role (or both), it did predate the later growing interest in emotion regulation processes as important correlates of aggression, both in isolation and interacting with negative emotional experiences (discussed in more details below).

Compared to the frustration-aggression hypothesis and to the general strain theory, which rose from the fields of social psychology and criminology, respectively, clinical theorizing on aggression placed relatively more emphasis on cognitive processing. Most notably, and in continuity with the previous models of aggression, Novaco (1976, 2011) proposed that aggression would stem from a reaction to aversive events (broadly construed), but that this process would be mediated by physiological arousal, cognitive processing, and behavioral disinhibition (a hypothesis partly consistent with Berkowitz's [2012] cognitive-neoassociation theory). This model had direct clinical implications in that it identified important areas of interventions to reduce aggression, in the modulation of negative physiological arousal (see also Gillespie et al., 2012), in the restructuring of cognitive processes that support the enactment of aggressive behavior, as well as in the lack of inhibition of maladaptive behavioral responses (Chapters 3 and 4).

One feature that stands out from the review of traditional models of anger and aggression is the relative separation of affective and cognitive processes that play a role in the link between anger and aggression. Anderson and Bushman (2002; see also: Allen et al., 2018; DeWall et al., 2011) have proposed an integration of previous models that goes beyond rigid dichotomies such as those between reactive vs. proactive aggression and affective vs. cognitive processes. In their General Aggression Model, they synthesized the multi-faceted and mutually related determinants of aggression divided into inputs (i.e., predisposing factors such as personal characteristics, situational characteristics, and social encounter), routes (i.e., the present internal state, characterized by affective experience, cognition, and arousal), and outcomes (i.e., from appraisal and decision processes to either thoughtful or impulsive actions). Although a detailed description of this model is well beyond the scope of the present chapter, it is worth noting how emotional experience plays a central role in the mechanisms leading to a potentially aggressive response, mutually interactive with cognitive and physiological components. The General Aggression Model places special emphasis on anger, stressing how anger—and emotion more generally—colors cognitive processing and influences behaviors, while at the same time being constantly modulated by cognitive processes as well.

More specifically, the General Aggression Model advanced five potential explanatory mechanisms for the link between anger, aggression, and violence (Allen et al., 2018; DeWall et al., 2011). First, anger can reduce inhibitions against aggression by means of cognitive beliefs that provide justification for retaliation or by interfering with higher-level cognitive processes (e.g., moral reasoning) (chapter 4). Second, anger energizes behavior by increasing physiological arousal coupled with an approach action tendency. Third, anger allows an individual to maintain an aggressive intention through several processes, such as focusing attention to provocation cues, biasing the processing of events as provoking, and facilitating the recall of provoking events that occurred in the past. Fourth, anger can be used as an information cue about the causes of an event, the culpability of a person, and ways of responding. That is, if Jelle feels angry at Carlo, he may think that because he feels angry, it must be the case that Carlo had wronged him, that he had done it on purpose, and that attacking him is the most appropriate way to react. Fifth, and lastly, anger primes aggressive thoughts, scripts, and behaviors facilitating their selection among a broader repertoire that an individual may have available.

In addition, in clinical theories, anger features prominently in many forms of personality pathology (most notably, borderline personality disorder, antisocial personality disorder and psychopathy, narcissistic personality disorder, and paranoid personality disorder) and can characterize other psychiatric syndromes (e.g., paranoid schizophrenia) with implications for violent behavior, although in different ways. For example, the strong affective arousal and lack of behavioral inhibition is what drives aggressive behavior in individuals with borderline personality disorders, whereas it is the cognitive component of anger that is more relevant in enabling aggressive behavior in the presence of paranoid ideation (McMurran & Howard, 2009; Nestor, 2002). More broadly, these different, yet anger-laden, forms of pathological externalizing, have been termed disinhibited and antagonistic externalizing, respectively. From this perspective, the former is defined by excessive physiological arousal coupled with behavioral disinhibition that lead to more reactive forms of aggression, and the latter by a more sustained experience of anger coupled with concordant cognitive processing that enables more proactive, premeditated forms of aggression (Krueger et al., 2007) (Chapter 19). Importantly, as is the case of reactive and proactive aggression, some individuals tend to show both disinhibited and antagonistic externalizing traits and behavior, most notably those with elevated levels of psychopathic traits (see Chapter 15).

Although anger has traditionally and intuitively been linked mostly with reactive forms of aggression, recent studies suggest that anger is associated with more proactive or instrumental forms of aggression as well, even though not as strongly as with reactive aggression (White & Turner, 2014). At least at the trait level, individuals who are prone to experience anger are also more likely to engage in proactive aggression (Hubbard et al., 2010). More specifically, Howard (2017; see also: McMurran & Howard, 2009) has developed a quadripartite violence typology that goes beyond the categorical distinction between reactive and proactive aggression and emphasizes how differences in motivations and differences in the subjective experience of anger may be associated with distinct types of violent behavior. This typology (summarized in Table 5.1) differentiates forms of violence in a bi-dimensional space wherein one dimension concerns the motivational valence (i.e., appetitive/offensive versus aversive/defensive, akin to proactive and

Table 5.1   Howard's (2017) quadripartite violence typology

		Offensive/appetitive (proactive)	Defensive/aversive (reactive)
Impulsive	Goal	Excitement/recreation: Inflicting harm to others to enhance positive affect	Self-protection/rage: Removing an interpersonal threat to reduce negative affect
	Affect	Positive	Negative
	Emotion(s)	Excitement, exhilaration	Fear, distress
	Anger type	*"Thrill-seeking anger"*	*"Explosive/reactive anger"*
Controlled	Goal	Self-gratification/Reward: Achieving positive outcomes or reinforcements	Revenge: Removing an interpersonal threat through a considered, premeditated action
	Affect	Positive	Negative
	Emotion(s)	Pleasant anticipation	Vengefulness
	Anger type	*"Coercive anger"*	*"Vengeful/ruminative anger"*

Note Affect refers to the subjective experience as positive (pleasant) or negative (unpleasant)

reactive, respectively) and the other dimension concerns the recruitment of deliberative self-control or the lack thereof (i.e., impulsive versus controlled). This model advances the perspective that anger may underlie or accompany several different forms of violent behavior, stressing the importance of considering that anger can be experienced negatively (i.e., as something that an individual does not want to feel) or positively (i.e., as something that an individual wants to feel). In turn, these different characteristics of the subjective experience of anger may help understand the distinct emotional routes that drive violent behavior under different circumstances.

Importantly, Howard's (2017) quadripartite violence typology converges with a recent stream of literature that goes beyond the role of negative emotions to acknowledge that also positive emotions may, in some cases, trigger externalizing behavior. This is the case of emotions like pride, exhilaration, or thrill-seeking, whereby aggression or antisocial behavior is driven by the willingness to maintain or increase positive affective experiences (Chester, 2017; Howard, 2011). Therefore, even if the trait experience of positive emotions tends to be positively related or unrelated to externalizing outcomes (DeLisi & Vaughn, 2014; Garofalo & Velotti, 2017), more theoretical and empirical work on positive emotions seems required to better elucidate their relevance for forensic psychology. Positive emotions could operate both in isolation and in combination with negative emotions (e.g., reacting with anger when one's sense of pride is threatened;) or with difficulties in modulating the experience and expression of positive emotions (e.g., as in the case of externalizing behavior for the purpose of excitement or pleasure; Chester et al., 2019; Howard, 2011).

Two general conclusive considerations are warranted. First, it is important to note that while the different theories and models described so far have focused explicitly on anger, most of them consider near-neighboring emotions belonging to the "anger family" as relevant for aggression and violence as well. That is, emotion terms like hostility, contempt, irritability, frustration, rage, fury, and the like, fit within the above theories in that they may either be associated with the experience of anger or may otherwise explain different forms of aggressive behavior depending on their characteristics (e.g., high or low level of arousal, high or low associated cognitive component). Second, most of the theories below implicitly focus on the regulation of anger and not only on its experience, at least to the extent that it is widely acknowledged that anger is not inherently maladaptive or pathological, but is an emotion that can be functional and adaptive (e.g., as a response to injustice). Thus, anger can be problematic under certain circumstances, such as if it is too easily triggered or too frequently experienced, or when associated with impairments in the regulation of anger and impulsive behavior (a topic that will be discussed later in the chapter). Notably, these impairments can be state-like, when they are triggered only under specific circumstances, or trait-like, when they are a stable and pervasive feature across time and situations. In addition, these impairments can be perceived by the individual (e.g., dysfunctional for pursuing personal goals) or only from the outside (e.g., the individual does not perceive the experience and expression of anger as problematic). Although going into details about these distinctions is not possible due to space considerations, it is important that clinicians and researchers are mindful of them when assessing the role of anger in externalizing psychopathology and aggressive behavior (for more details, see: Davey et al., 2005; McMurran & Howard, 2009; Megargee, 1984).

Beyond Anger: The Role of Other Negative Emotions

Even though the preponderance of theoretical and empirical work on emotion in forensic psychology has focused on anger, both traditional (e.g., Agnew, 1992) and more recent (e.g., DeLisi & Vaughn, 2014) theories have also emphasized that negative emotions more broadly are consequential for the development and manifestation of antisocial tendencies and aggressive behavior, including sexual offending (e.g., Baumeister & Lobbestael, 2011).

When looking at specific emotions, it is intriguing to notice how certain emotional experiences are linked with aggression or otherwise antisocial behavior not only at high levels, but also at low levels (Baumeister & Lobbestael, 2011). This is the case in particular for fear and anxiety (Blair et al., 2002). At the trait level, individuals who tend to experience these emotions more frequently and intensely are also more likely to engage in aggressive and antisocial behavior, although as stated above it remains to be ascertained whether these links are due to general distress rather than fear and anxiety specifically. At the same time, and especially at the state level, individuals who lack the normal experience of fear and anxiety (a construct often termed fearlessness) are also more prone to aggression and antisocial behavior, and especially to their most severe declensions. It is worth emphasizing that it is not the simple absence of excessive fear or anxiety that is associated with externalizing correlates. For example, an individual who does not react with extreme worry to fear- or anxiety-inducing situations will not necessarily be more prone to aggression. Rather, it is the *maladaptive* (Cardinale et al., 2020; Crego & Widiger, 2015) absence of fear and anxiety that has been linked to externalizing correlates. In other words, those individuals who lack the normal experience of fear and anxiety typically show aggressive and antisocial tendencies, along with a more general pattern of limited prosocial emotions—that is, emotions that are crucial for an adaptive socio-moral development such as guilt, shame, and sadness—and often callous affective traits (Cardinale et al., 2020) (Chapters 7 and 15). As illustrative examples, one may think of the absence of normative reactions to situations that should trigger fear or anxiety for self-preservation or for negative reinforcement, such as an immediate threat or reckless and harmful conduct against others, respectively.

It follows from the above that not only the experience but also the absence of experience of certain prosocial emotions is important to consider when assessing the affective landscape of an individual in relation to their risk for offending or re-offending. Yet, the picture is not as straightforward as it may seem, and a chief example of the complexity in these associations is represented by two similar yet distinct emotions: guilt and shame (Tangney et al., 2007). Guilt is defined as a feeling of responsibility or remorse for some wrongdoing, be it real or imagined (e.g., "I did something bad"). Shame is defined as a painful feeling arising from the awareness of something dishonorable, improper, fundamentally wrong about oneself (e.g., "I am a bad person"). Guilt has been linked with reduced levels of externalizing behaviors, to the extent that feeling guilty about one's wrongdoing inhibits continuation of the misbehavior. In contrast, even though the maladaptive absence of shame had been conceptually linked to violence and antisociality, research has shown that shame is actually positive associated with antisocial behavior, and violent recidivism in particular (Elison et al., 2014; Tangney et al., 2014; Tangney, Stuewig, & Hafez, 2011; Tangney, Stuewig, Mashek, et al., 2011; Velotti et al., 2014).

This seemingly paradoxical link between shame and aggression may be unpacked by means of an analogy between social and physical pain. The starting point consists in the perception of a (relational) devaluation (e.g., social exclusion). This type of experience, whether real or imagined, triggers the experience of emotional pain in the form of shame, although this experience may be acknowledged or not. Intriguingly, neurobiological and psychological research has linked this social pain to the same brain substrates and phenomenological experience of physical pain (Macdonald & Leary, 2005), which may explain why this emotion can be so powerful to trigger aggressive tendencies, both as immediate reactions at the moment, and as more stable and pervasive behavioral dispositions (Velotti et al., 2014).

Across the body of literature and empirical work reviewed so far, there is another potential explanatory factor for aggression that is related to emotion and shines through across the different theories and studies presented: namely, emotion regulation. This concept was somewhat implicit in some early theories (Agnew, 1992), and more explicit in others (e.g., Day, 2009; Elison et al., 2014; Gillespie et al., 2012). A more specific focus on emotion regulation in forensic psychology has only gained traction in recent years, and its main tenets and implications will be discussed in the next section.

Emotion Regulation: Discovering New Grounds

Although different definitions of the concept of emotion regulation exist, there is a general consensus that it broadly entails the processes responsible for monitoring, appraising, and modifying the experience and expression of emotions (Gross, 2013). More precisely, for the purpose of this chapter, emotion regulation is conceptualized as a multicomponent process that includes: (a) attention and awareness for emotions; (b) emotional understanding, or clarity about one's emotions; (c) acceptance of emotional experience; (d) the ability to refrain from impulsive actions when experiencing negative emotions (also known as negative urgency); (e) the ability to pursue goal-directed behavior when distressed (also known as distress tolerance); and (f) the ability to use adaptive emotion regulation strategies flexibly depending on the context and the individual's goals (Gratz & Roemer, 2004).

Regardless of the specific operationalization, most empirical evidence supports positive associations between problems in emotion regulation and aggression both prospectively across the lifespan (Scott et al., 2015; Skripkauskaite et al., 2015), and concurrently across a variety of communities, clinical, and forensic populations (Garofalo, et al., 2016; Garofalo & Velotti, 2017; Garofalo, Velotti, & Zavattini, 2018; Roberton et al., 2014, 2015). Survey and laboratory studies also suggest that both trait-like and state-dependent deficits in emotion regulation are associated with increased aggressive behavior, including sexual offending (Davidson et al., 2000; Gillespie, Brzozowski, & Mitchell, 2018; Gillespie et al., 2012; Howells et al., 2004; Roberton et al., 2012). Importantly, besides bivariate associations with aggression, emotion regulation has also shown incremental value in predicting aggression above and beyond known correlates of aggression, such as anger control, alexithymia, and impulsivity (Garofalo, Velotti, & Zavattini, 2018; Roberton et al., 2015). When looking at aggression in particular, emotion regulation difficulties have been linked with comparable strength to different components of aggression, including hostility, that is, the cognitive component that underlies some of the manifestations of aggression and antisociality (Garofalo, et al., 2016; Garofalo, Velotti, & Zavattini, 2018). Difficulties in emotion regulation are also considered a transdiagnostic marker for psychopathology, and have been linked with several forms of personality pathology, including antisocial personality disorder, sadism, and psychopathy (Dimaggio et al., 2017; Garofalo, Velotti, et al., 2018; Garofalo & Neumann, 2018; Velotti & Garofalo, 2015). Taken together, this may suggest yet another connecting link between externalizing personality pathology and aggression.

Looking at the different components of emotion regulation, research has shown rather uniform associations with aggression and externalizing psychopathology. Some components (most notably, the non-acceptance of emotions and negative urgency, that is, the inability to control impulsive behavior when experiencing negative emotions) have shown unique effects on aggression (or externalizing psychopathology) when controlling for the overlap (i.e., shared variance) among components. However, these unique effects are not always consistent across studies and should be interpreted with the caveat that it may be difficult to ascertain what remains—conceptually—in each of those components when statistically controlling for their overlap (Lynam et al., 2006). In addition, a focus on the component level may be helpful in differentiating subgroups of offenders (Day et al., 2020; Gillespie, Garofalo, & Velotti, 2018), although research has been scant in this respect. Recently, it has been suggested, on conceptual grounds, that different components of emotion regulation may be more important depending on the type of outcome under examination (e.g., reactive or proactive aggression, general antisociality). For example, negative urgency may be intuitively linked to reactive forms of aggression, whereas emotional nonacceptance or lack of emotional awareness may be more intimately linked to proactive forms of aggression, hostility, and general antisocial tendencies (Garofalo et al., 2020). Currently, these suppositions are still wanting in empirical support and will likely be subject to scrutiny in future studies.

Roberton et al. (2012) have proffered another, arguably more parsimonious, model to delineate the linkages between emotion regulation and aggression, or offending more broadly. Operating from the assumption that emotional awareness (attention to and clarity of emotional experience), emotional acceptance, and use of adaptive emotion regulation strategies are the key skills underlying successful emotion regulation, this model suggests that both the under- and the over-regulation of emotions may result in increased aggressive and antisocial tendencies, though in different ways (see also: Davey et al., 2005; Day et al., 2020; Megargee, 1966, 1984, 2011). On the one hand, the under-regulation of emotions is perhaps more intuitively connected with aggression (and in particular, impulsive or reactive forms of aggression), and has certainly attracted more extensive research attention. In particular, Roberton et al. (2012) summarized that the under-regulation of emotions may concern anger or other emotional experiences, and lead to aggression in an attempt to repair one's emotional state (i.e., feel better) or to attack the perceived source of the negative emotional experience. On the other hand, far less theoretical and empirical work has addressed the role of the over-regulation of emotions for externalizing outcomes. Yet, a review of the sparse available literature suggested that the over-regulation of emotion may indeed increase aggressive tendencies in several ways (Roberton et al., 2012). First, by contributing to a paradoxical increase—rather than a reduction—of negative affect and arousal (e.g., as in the case of emotional suppression; see also Bryant & Miron, 2003). Second, by reducing inhibitory control, for example due to losing sight of long-term goals (e.g., because all cognitive and emotional efforts are directed at down-regulating the emotion and its expression). Third, by depleting cognitive resources and in turn compromising decision-making processes or interfering with adaptive conflict resolution. Fourth, by limiting social support, since individuals who tend to over-regulate their emotions have more limited social networks , and especially connections with others who may steer one's behavior toward prosocial rather than antisocial behavioral manifestations (Chapter 10).

Emotion Regulation and Emotional Experience: Attempts at Integration

After reviewing work that has focused on emotion in general, as well as specific emotions, and on emotion regulation, it may stand to reason that emotional experience and emotion regulation do not operate in isolation to explain aggressive tendencies and antisocial behavior. Looking back at the work reviewed above on negative emotions broadly construed, as well as on anger and shame more specifically, it is also worth reiterating that emotion regulation has been posited as a possible explanatory mechanism linking the experience of emotions and aggression. This mechanism may alternatively work in terms of explaining this association (with negative emotions contributing to emotion dysregulation, which in turn contributes to aggression or antisocial behavior), or exacerbating the link between emotional experience and aggression in the presence of problems in emotion regulation. Yet, in spite of some (more or less explicit and nuanced) conceptual elaboration, very little empirical work has been devoted to examining these possibilities as well as alternative, potentially reciprocal, associations (wherein also emotion dysregulation contributes to increased levels of negative emotions). As a recent example, there is some evidence that negative emotions and emotion dysregulation interact in predicting levels of aggression in offenders (Baglivio et al., 2016; Garofalo & Velotti, 2017; Miller et al., 2012). More specifically, these studies showed that among individuals with high levels of negative emotions, the concomitant presence of high levels of emotion dysregulation strengthens the link with aggressive tendencies. This also means that better emotion regulation skills may buffer the link between negative emotions and aggression. This type of findings holds important clinical implications, in line with those described above, since targeting emotion regulation may thus prove useful to prevent the insurgence of aggression or to intervene to reduce aggression (including sexual aggression) among individuals prone to the experience of negative emotions (Gillespie et al., 2012).

A recent integrative attempt to conceptualize the complex interplay of negative emotionality and emotion regulation in relation to antisocial behavior and criminal justice system involved has been developed by DeLisi and Vaughn (2014) in their temperament-based theory. Reviewing theory and research spanning across different disciplines, these scholars put forth a comprehensive framework with two temperamental constructs—effortful control and negative emotionality—as its central tenets. Effortful control is considered a developmental precursor of emotion regulation and as such, fits nicely with the description above of the interactive roles of the *experience* and *regulation* of emotions (and associated behavioral tendencies), wherein these two components fuel and influence each other contributing to an exponentially higher risk of offending. Going beyond the explanation of offending in its various declensions, DeLisi and Vaughn's (2014) theory has the advantage of attempting to explain also the negative and aversive interactions with the criminal justice system after the first offenses have been committed. That is, it is posited that proneness to negative emotions and poor emotion regulation may explain why certain individuals respond poorly to their first contacts with law enforcement, going on to develop chronic antisocial conduct, while others (less prone to negative emotions and better able to regulate emotions) fare better, and are successful at desisting from crime. While empirical tests to support its viability are still in its infancy, it is likely that this theory will become influential and guide the next generation of forensic psychology research.

Clinical Implications

The foregoing excursus into theories and research linking the experience and regulation of emotions to offending has implications for clinical forensic practice. These can be summarized along four main lines. First, it is important to acknowledge that, while an emphasis on anger and anger management in the treatment of offenders is certainly needed, it may not be enough. Indeed, it appears evident that interventions to reduce aggression should include a broader attention to improve emotion regulation skills beyond anger and beyond those emotion regulation skills that pertain to behavioral disinhibition. It has been suggested (e.g., Davey et al., 2005; Day, 2009; Garofalo, Velotti, & Zavattini, 2018; Howells, 2004; Roberton et al., 2014) that such interventions should comprise modules aimed at strengthening the ability and motivation to: acknowledge and identify feelings; accept one's emotional experience as it unfolds; refrain from impulsive behavior when distressed; pursue goal-directed behavior even if it entails enduring some degree of stress; and be able to maintain some degree of mindfulness of the consequences of one's actions on the self and on others even when upset.

Second, to achieve this goal, and in light of the interconnectedness of these different skills, prevention and treatment modules could be directed first at enhancing self-reflection, and then at using it to further enhance the individual motivation and ability to: describe and talk about emotions, including unpleasant ones; tolerate distress as an acceptable part of the pursuit of desired goals; know and select from a broad range of emotion regulation strategies depending on individual needs and contextual demands. These goals may be achieved, for example, by exploring the nature and functionality of emotions and normalizing their experience, as well as by clarifying the difference between adaptive and maladaptive emotion regulation strategies, and recognizing the effects that these strategies have on oneself and others.

Third, when applying an emotion framework to treatments for offenders, this should not only be directed at tackling overt aggressive behaviors, but also at treating the hostile cognitive style that often accompanies them (Daffern et al., 2013). Because this hostile cognitive style has been linked to difficulties in emotion regulation, it could be tempered by improving motivations and skills pertaining to identifying, describing, and accepting one's emotional experience (Garofalo, Velotti, & Zavattini, 2018).

Fourth, it is important to stress that for these treatment efforts to be implemented, it is necessary to convince policymakers in forensic mental health care of their potential. Identifying and disseminating knowledge about potential treatment targets to reduce aggression in offenders is only the first step. Policymakers will need to ensure that treatment modules aimed at improving emotion regulation and related skills are provided to clients, while facilitating clinical research to gauge their feasibility, acceptability, and effectiveness, making sure that sufficient clinical staff with relevant training is available to deliver emotion regulation modules.

Conclusions

The present chapter took stock of the relatively recent but rapidly growing theoretical and empirical literature on the relevance of emotion and emotion regulation for clinical forensic psychology. Some key take-home messages can be delineated. One is the importance of focusing on emotional *experience* broadly, and not limited to the "usual suspect" anger and its derivatives. Another partly related point is the importance of focusing on emotion *regulation* by appreciating its multifaceted nature by going beyond the control of emotions in the sense of reducing the frequency and intensity of their experience. Against the theoretical and empirical background presented, the chapter also attempted to delineate clinical implications suggesting treatment target that could contribute to a reduction of aggression and antisocial behavior, as well as to improvements in offenders' well-being and interpersonal functioning. While work on emotion and emotion regulation represents a well-defined body of research within the field of clinical forensic psychology, it is reckoned (Smeijers et al., 2020) that the next research steps are aimed at connecting the study of emotion with knowledge on cognition, motivation, and interpersonal processes, which is imperative to elucidate their reciprocal connections.

References

Agnew, R. (1992). Foundation for a general strain theory of crime and delinquency. *Criminology, 30*(1), 47–88. https://doi.org/10.1111/j.1745-9125.1992.tb01093.x

Agnew, R. (2001). Building on the foundation of general strain theory: Specifying the types of strain most likely to lead to crime and delinquency. *Journal of Research in Crime and Delinquency, 38*(4), 319–361. https://doi.org/10.1177/0022427801038004001

Allen, J. J., Anderson, C. A., & Bushman, B. J. (2018). The general aggression model. *Current Opinion in Psychology, 19*, 75–80. https://doi.org/10.1016/j.copsyc.2017.03.034

Anderson, C. A., & Bushman, B. J. (2002). Human aggression. *Annual Review of Psychology, 53*(1), 27–51. https://doi.org/10.1146/annurev.psych.53.100901.135231

Baglivio, M. T., Wolff, K. T., DeLisi, M., Vaughn, M. G., & Piquero, A. R. (2016). Effortful control, negative emotionality, and juvenile recidivism: An empirical test of DeLisi and Vaughn's temperament-based theory of antisocial behavior. *The Journal of Forensic Psychiatry & Psychology, 27*(3), 376–403. https://doi.org/10.1080/14789949.2016.114 5720

Baumeister, R. F., & Lobbestael, J. (2011). Emotions and antisocial behavior. *Journal of Forensic Psychiatry & Psychology, 22*(5), 635–649. https://doi.org/10.1080/14789949. 2011.617535

Berkowitz, L. (1989). Frustration-aggression hypothesis: Examination and reformulation. *Psychological Bulletin, 106*(1), 59–73. https://doi.org/10.1037/0033-2909.106.1.59

Berkowitz, L. (2012). A different view of anger: The cognitive-neoassociation conception of the relation of anger to aggression. *Aggressive Behavior, 38*(4), 322–333. https://doi.org/ 10.1002/ab.21432

Blair, R. J. R., Mitchell, D. G. V., Richell, R. A., Kelly, S., Leonard, A., Newman, C., & Scott, S. K. (2002). Turning a deaf ear to fear: Impaired recognition of vocal affect in psychopathic individuals. *Journal of Abnormal Psychology, 111*(4), 682–686. https://doi. org/10.1037/0021-843x.111.4.682

Bryant, J., & Miron, D. (2003). Excitation-transfer theory. In J. Bryant, D. Roskos-Ewoldsen, & J. Cantor (Eds.), *Communication and emotion: Essays in honor of Dolf Zillmann* (pp. 31–59). Erlbaum.

Cardinale, E. M., Ryan, R. M., & Marsh, A. A. (2020). Maladaptive fearlessness: An examination of the association between subjective fear experience and antisocial behaviors linked with callous unemotional traits. *Journal of Personality Disorders*, 1–18. https://doi.org/ 10.1521/pedi_2020_34_486

Chester, D. S. (2017). The role of positive affect in aggression. *Current Directions in Psychological Science, 26*(4), 366–370. https://doi.org/10.1177/0963721417700457

Chester, D. S., DeWall, C. N., & Enjaian, B. (2019). Sadism and aggressive behavior: Inflicting pain to feel pleasure. *Personality and Social Psychology Bulletin, 45*(8), 1252–1268. https://doi.org/10.1177/0146167218816327

Crego, C., & Widiger, T. A. (2015). Psychopathy and the DSM. *Journal of Personality, 83*(6), 665–677. https://doi.org/10.1111/jopy.12115

Daffern, M., Thomas, S., Lee, S., Huband, N., McCarthy, L., Simpson, K., & Duggan, C. (2013). The impact of treatment on hostile-dominance in forensic psychiatric inpatients: Relationships between change in hostile-dominance and recidivism following release from custody. *Journal of Forensic Psychiatry & Psychology, 24*(6), 675–687. https://doi.org/10.1080/14789949.2013.834069

Davey, L., Day, A., & Howells, K. (2005). Anger, over-control and serious violent offending. *Aggression and Violent Behavior, 10*(5), 624–635. https://doi.org/10.1016/j.avb.2004.12.002

Davidson, R. J., Putnam, K. M., & Larson, C. L. (2000). Dysfunction in the neural circuitry of emotion regulation—A possible prelude to violence. *Science (New York, N.Y.), 289*(5479), 591–594. https://doi.org/10.1126/science.289.5479.591

Day, A. (2009). Offender emotion and self-regulation: Implications for offender rehabilitation programming. *Psychology, Crime & Law, 15*(2–3), 119–130. https://doi.org/10.1080/10683160802190848

Day, A., Daffern, M., Polaschek, D. L. L., Dunne, A., & Senn, A. (2020). The classification of people with a history of interpersonal violence for correctional treatment purposes: Possibilities for a schema-informed approach. *Aggression and Violent Behavior*, 101450. https://doi.org/10.1016/j.avb.2020.101450

DeLisi, M., & Vaughn, M. G. (2014). Foundation for a temperament-based theory of antisocial behavior and criminal justice system involvement. *Journal of Criminal Justice, 42*(1), 10–25. https://doi.org/10.1016/j.jcrimjus.2013.11.001

DeWall, C. N., Anderson, C. A., & Bushman, B. J. (2011). The general aggression model: Theoretical extensions to violence. *Psychology of Violence, 1*(3), 245–258. https://doi.org/10.1037/a0023842

Dimaggio, G., Popolo, R., Montano, A., Velotti, P., Perrini, F., Buonocore, L., Garofalo, C., D'Aguanno, M., & Salvatore, G. (2017). Emotion dysregulation, symptoms, and interpersonal problems as independent predictors of a broad range of personality disorders in an outpatient sample. *Psychology and Psychotherapy: Theory, Research and Practice, 90*(4), 586–599. https://doi.org/10.1111/papt.12126

Dollard, J., Miller, N. E., Doob, L. W., Mowrer, O. H., & Sears, R. R. (1939). *Frustration and Aggression*. Yale University Press.

Elison, J., Garofalo, C., & Velotti, P. (2014). Shame and aggression: Theoretical considerations. *Aggression and Violent Behavior, 19*(4), 447–453. https://doi.org/10.1016/j.avb.2014.05.002

Fanti, K. A., & Henrich, C. C. (2010). Trajectories of pure and co-occurring internalizing and externalizing problems from age 2 to age 12: Findings from the National Institute of Child Health and Human Development Study of Early Child Care. *Developmental Psychology, 46*(5), 1159–1175. https://doi.org/10.1037/a0020659

Frijda, N. H. (2005). Emotion experience. *Cognition and Emotion, 19*(4), 473–497. https://doi.org/10.1080/02699930441000346

Garofalo, C., Holden, C. J., Zeigler-Hill, V., & Velotti, P. (2016). Understanding the connection between self-esteem and aggression: The mediating role of emotion dysregulation. *Aggressive Behavior, 42*(1), 3–15. https://doi.org/10.1002/ab.21601

Garofalo, C., & Neumann, C. S. (2018). Psychopathy and emotion regulation: Taking stock and moving forward. In M. DeLisi (Ed.), *Routledge international handbook of psychopathy and crime* (pp. 76–97). Routledge.

Garofalo, C., Neumann, C. S., & Velotti, P. (2020). Psychopathy and aggression: The role of emotion dysregulation. *Journal of Interpersonal Violence*, 0886260519900946. https://doi.org/10.1177/0886260519900946

Garofalo, C., & Velotti, P. (2017). Negative emotionality and aggression in violent offenders: The moderating role of emotion dysregulation. *Journal of Criminal Justice, 51*, 9–16. https://doi.org/10.1016/j.jcrimjus.2017.05.015

Garofalo, C., Velotti, P., Callea, A., Popolo, R., Salvatore, G., Cavallo, F., & Dimaggio, G. (2018). Emotion dysregulation, impulsivity and personality disorder traits: A community sample study. *Psychiatry Research, 266*, 186–192. https://doi.org/10.1016/j.psychres.2018.05.067

Garofalo, C., Velotti, P., Crocamo, C., & Carrà, G. (2018). Single and multiple clinical syndromes in incarcerated offenders: Associations with dissociative experiences and emotionality. *International Journal of Offender Therapy and Comparative Criminology, 62*(5), 1300–1316. https://doi.org/10.1177/0306624X16682325

Garofalo, C., Velotti, P., & Zavattini, G. C. (2018). Emotion regulation and aggression: The incremental contribution of alexithymia, impulsivity, and emotion dysregulation facets. *Psychology of Violence, 8*(4), 470–483. https://doi.org/10.1037/vio0000141

Gillespie, S. M., Brzozowski, A., & Mitchell, I. J. (2018). Self-regulation and aggressive antisocial behaviour: Insights from amygdala-prefrontal and heart-brain interactions. *Psychology, Crime & Law, 24*(3), 243–257. https://doi.org/10.1080/1068316X.2017.1414816

Gillespie, S. M., Garofalo, C., & Velotti, P. (2018). Emotion regulation, mindfulness, and alexithymia: Specific or general impairments in sexual, violent, and homicide offenders? *Journal of Criminal Justice, 58*, 56–66. https://doi.org/10.1016/j.jcrimjus.2018.07.006

Gillespie, S. M., Mitchell, I. J., Fisher, D., & Beech, A. R. (2012). Treating disturbed emotional regulation in sexual offenders: The potential applications of mindful self-regulation and controlled breathing techniques. *Aggression and Violent Behavior, 17*(4), 333–343. https://doi.org/10.1016/j.avb.2012.03.005

Gratz, K. L., & Roemer, L. (2004). Multidimensional assessment of emotion regulation and dysregulation: Development, factor structure, and initial validation of the difficulties in emotion regulation scale. *Journal of Psychopathology and Behavioral Assessment, 26*(1), 41–54. https://doi.org/10.1023/b:joba.0000007455.08539.94

Gross, J. J. (2013). Emotion regulation: Taking stock and moving forward. *Emotion, 13*(3), 359–365. https://doi.org/10.1037/a0032135

Howard, R. C. (2011). The quest for excitement: A missing link between personality disorder and violence? *Journal of Forensic Psychiatry & Psychology, 22*(5), 692–705. https://doi.org/10.1080/14789949.2011.617540

Howard, R. C. (2017). Refining the construct of "anger" in relation to personality. *Journal of Behavior, 2*(3), 1013.

Howells, K. (2004). *Correctional offender rehabilitation programs: The national picture in Australia*. Criminology Research Council.

Howells, K., Day, A., & Wright, S. (2004). Affect, emotions and sex offending. *Psychology, Crime & Law, 10*(2), 179–195. https://doi.org/10.1080/10683160310001609988

Hubbard, J. A., Romano, L. J., McAuliffe, M. D., & Morrow, M. T. (2010). Anger and the reactive—Proactive aggression distinction in childhood and adolescence. In M. Potegal, G. Stemmler, & C. Spielberger (Eds.), *International handbook of anger: Constituent and concomitant biological, psychological, and social processes* (pp. 231–239). Springer. https://doi.org/10.1007/978-0-387-89676-2_14

Krueger, R. F., Markon, K. E., Patrick, C. J., Benning, S. D., & Kramer, M. D. (2007). Linking antisocial behavior, substance use, and personality: An integrative quantitative model of the adult externalizing spectrum. *Journal of Abnormal Psychology, 116*(4), 645–666. https://doi.org/10.1037/0021-843X.116.4.645

Lynam, D. R., Hoyle, R. H., & Newman, J. P. (2006). The perils of partialling: Cautionary tales from aggression and psychopathy. *Assessment, 13*(3), 328–341. https://doi.org/10.1177/1073191106290562

Macdonald, G., & Leary, M. R. (2005). Why does social exclusion hurt? The relationship between social and physical pain. *Psychological Bulletin, 131*(2), 202–223. https://doi.org/10.1037/0033-2909.131.2.202

McMurran, M., & Howard, R. (2009). *Personality, personality disorder and violence: An evidence based approach.* Wiley-Blackwell.

Megargee, E. I. (1966). Undercontrolled and overcontrolled personality types in extreme antisocial aggression. *Psychological Monographs, 80*(3), 1–29. https://doi.org/10.1037/h0093894

Megargee, E. I. (1984). Aggression and violence. In H. E. Adams & P. B. Sutker (Eds.), *Comprehensive handbook of psychopathology* (pp. 523–545). Springer US. https://doi.org/10.1007/978-1-4615-6681-6_19

Megargee, E. I. (2011). Using the algebra of aggression in forensic practice. *The British Journal of Forensic Practice, 13*(1), 4–11. https://doi.org/10.5042/bjfp.2011.0045

Mesquita, B. (2016). The legacy of Nico H. Frijda (1927–2015). *Cognition and Emotion, 30*(4), 603–608. https://doi.org/10.1080/02699931.2015.1132681

Miller, D. J., Vachon, D. D., & Aalsma, M. C. (2012). Negative affect and emotion dysregulation: Conditional relations with violence and risky sexual behavior in a sample of justice-involved adolescents. *Criminal Justice and Behavior, 39*(10), 1316–1327. https://doi.org/10.1177/0093854812448784

Moon, B., Morash, M., McCluskey, C. P., & Hwang, H.-W. (2009). A comprehensive test of general strain theory: Key strains, situational- and trait-based negative emotions, conditioning factors, and delinquency. *Journal of Research in Crime and Delinquency, 46*(2), 182–212. https://doi.org/10.1177/0022427808330873

Nestor, P. G. (2002). Mental disorder and violence: Personality dimensions and clinical features. *American Journal of Psychiatry, 159*(12), 1973–1978. https://doi.org/10.1176/appi.ajp.159.12.1973

Novaco, R. W. (1976). The functions and regulation of the arousal of anger. *The American Journal of Psychiatry, 133*(10), 1124–1128. https://doi.org/10.1176/ajp.133.10.1124

Novaco, R. W. (2011). Anger dysregulation: Driver of violent offending. *Journal of Forensic Psychiatry & Psychology, 22*(5), 650–668. https://doi.org/10.1080/14789949.2011.617536

Roberton, T., Daffern, M., & Bucks, R. S. (2012). Emotion regulation and aggression. *Aggression and Violent Behavior, 17*(1), 72–82. https://doi.org/10.1016/j.avb.2011.09.006

Roberton, T., Daffern, M., & Bucks, R. S. (2014). Maladaptive emotion regulation and aggression in adult offenders. *Psychology, Crime & Law, 20*(10), 933–954. https://doi.org/10.1080/1068316x.2014.893333

Roberton, T., Daffern, M., & Bucks, R. S. (2015). Beyond anger control: Difficulty attending to emotions also predicts aggression in offenders. *Psychology of Violence, 5*(1), 74–83. https://doi.org/10.1037/a0037214

Scott, J. P., DiLillo, D., Maldonado, R. C., & Watkins, L. E. (2015). Negative urgency and emotion regulation strategy use: Associations with displaced aggression. *Aggressive Behavior, 41*(5), 502–512. https://doi.org/10.1002/ab.21588

Skripkauskaite, S., Hawk, S. T., Branje, S. J., Koot, H. M., van Lier, P. A., & Meeus, W. (2015). Reactive and proactive aggression: Differential links with emotion regulation difficulties, maternal criticism in adolescence. *Aggressive Behavior.* https://doi.org/10.1002/ab.21583

Smeijers, D., Benbouriche, M., & Garofalo, C. (2020). The association between emotion, social information processing, and aggressive behavior: A systematic review. *European Psychologist, 25*(2), 81–91. https://doi.org/10.1027/1016-9040/a000395

Tangney, J. P., Stuewig, J., & Hafez, L. (2011). Shame, guilt and remorse: Implications for offender populations. *Journal of Forensic Psychiatry & Psychology, 22*(5), 706–723. https://doi.org/10.1080/14789949.2011.617541

Tangney, J. P., Stuewig, J., & Martinez, A. G. (2014). Two faces of shame: The roles of shame and guilt in predicting recidivism. *Psychological Science, 25*(3), 799–805. https://doi.org/10.1177/0956797613508790

Tangney, J. P., Stuewig, J., Mashek, D., & Hastings, M. (2011). Assessing jail inmates' proneness to shame and guilt: Feeling bad about the behavior or the self? *Criminal Justice and Behavior, 38*(7), 710–734. https://doi.org/10.1177/0093854811405762

Tangney, J. P., Stuewig, J., & Mashek, D. J. (2007). Moral emotions and moral behavior. *Annual Review of Psychology, 58*, 345–372. https://doi.org/10.1146/annurev.psych.56.091103.070145

Twenge, J. M., Baumeister, R. F., Tice, D. M., & Stucke, T. S. (2001). If you can't join them, beat them: Effects of social exclusion on aggressive behavior. *Journal of Personality and Social Psychology, 81*(6), 1058–1069. https://doi.org/10.1037/0022-3514.81.6.1058

Velotti, P., Elison, J., & Garofalo, C. (2014). Shame and aggression: Different trajectories and implications. *Aggression and Violent Behavior, 19*(4), 454–461. https://doi.org/10.1016/j.avb.2014.04.011

Velotti, P., & Garofalo, C. (2015). Personality styles in a non-clinical sample: The role of emotion dysregulation and impulsivity. *Personality and Individual Differences, 79*, 44–49. https://doi.org/10.1016/j.paid.2015.01.046

Wang, Y., Cao, S., Zhang, Q., & Xia, L.-X. (2020). The longitudinal relationship between angry rumination and reactive–proactive aggression and the moderation effect of consideration of future consequences-immediate. *Aggressive Behavior, 46*(6), 476–488. https://doi.org/10.1002/ab.21913

White, B. A., & Turner, K. A. (2014). Anger rumination and effortful control: Mediation effects on reactive but not proactive aggression. *Personality and Individual Differences, 56*, 186–189. https://doi.org/10.1016/j.paid.2013.08.012

Further Reading Suggestions

DeLisi, M., & Vaughn, M. G. (2014). Foundation for a temperament-based theory of antisocial behavior and criminal justice system involvement. *Journal of Criminal Justice, 42*(1), 10–25. https://doi.org/10.1016/j.jcrimjus.2013.11.001

Elison, J., Garofalo, C., & Velotti, P. (2014). Shame and aggression: Theoretical considerations. *Aggression and Violent Behavior, 19*(4), 447–453. https://doi.org/10.1016/j.avb.2014.05.002

Kring, A. M., & Sloan, D. M. (Eds.). (2010). *Emotion regulation and psychopathology: A transdiagnostic approach to etiology and treatment*. The Guilford Press.

Roberton, T., Daffern, M., & Bucks, R. S. (2012). Emotion regulation and aggression. *Aggression and Violent Behavior, 17*(1), 72–82. https://doi.org/10.1016/j.avb.2011.09.006

Smeijers, D., Benbouriche, M., & Garofalo, C. (2020). The association between emotion, social information processing, and aggressive behavior: A systematic Review. *European Psychologist, 25*(2), 81–91. https://doi.org/10.1027/1016-9040/a000395

Basic Personality and Deviant Behavior

6

Donald R. Lynam and Joshua D. Miller

Key Points

- Psychopathy, antisocial personality disorder, and narcissistic personality disorder are moderately strongly related to one another and robustly related to antisocial behavior and aggression
- These and other personality disorders can be understood as configurations of general personality traits drawn from the Five-Factor Model of personality
- Low agreeableness (i.e., antagonism) is a shared feature of psychopathy, antisocial personality disorder, and narcissistic personality disorder
- Profiles of low conscientiousness (i.e., disinhibition) similarly characterize psychopathy and antisocial personality disorder
- Low agreeableness, low conscientiousness, and some facets of neuroticism are associated with aggression and antisocial behavior.

Introduction

In this chapter, we examine the overlap among three constructs that are robustly related to antisocial behavior/aggression and to one another—psychopathy (PSY),

D. R. Lynam (✉)
Department of Psychological Sciences, Purdue University, West Lafayette, IN, USA
e-mail: dlynam@purdue.edu

J. D. Miller
Department of Psychology, University of Georgia, Athens, GA, USA
e-mail: jdmiller@uga.edu

antisocial personality disorder (ASPD), and narcissistic personality disorder (NAR). More specifically, we review the literature linking these constructs to antisocial and aggressive behavior. Following this, we decompose each construct into the trait language of the Five Factor Model (FFM), illustrate how this mapping may explain the relations among these constructs and their relations to antisocial and aggressive behavior. Next, we discuss the relative importance of the Agreeableness-Antagonism domain from the FFM to all forms of externalizing behaviors (e.g., antisocial behavior, aggression, and substance use). Finally, we end with a discussion on the ways that research on basic personality can be leveraged to better understand, assess, prevent, and intervene with ASPD, NPD, psychopathy, and deviant behavior.

Psychopathy, Antisocial Personality Disorder, and Narcissism

Psychopathy , although not an official diagnosis within the Diagnostic and Statistical Manual of Mental Disorders—5th Edition (DSM-5; APA, 2013), is a relatively prototypic personality disorder—an enduring pattern of inner experience and behavior manifest in cognition, affect, interpersonal functioning, and impulse control that is inflexible and pervasive across a broad range of personal and social situations and that leads to distress and/or impairment (Chapter 15). Cleckley's original description (1941/1988) of the psychopathic individual and Hare's (1991) refinement of it serve as the foundation for the construct as we know it today. The psychopathic individual is glib, grandiose, untruthful, conning and manipulative, callous, impulsive, irresponsible, stimulation seeking, fails to accept responsibility for their actions, and lacks guilt, empathy, and remorse. Given this description, it is not surprising that psychopathy is robustly related to antisocial behavior and aggression in adults and youth using interview—based measures like the Hare Psychopathy Checklist-Revised (PCL-R; Hare, 1991) or self-reported inventories like the Triarchic Psychopathy Measure (Patrick, 2010), Psychopathic Personality Inventory (Lilienfeld & Widows, 2005), Hare Self-report Psychopathy Scale (SRP, Paulhus et al., 2017) or the Elemental Psychopathy Assessment (EPA, Lynam et al., 2011). A number of meta-analyses have documented these relations. Across meta-analyses, total scores on the PCL-R show small to moderate relations with aggression and antisocial behavior in adults (Blais et al., 2014; Salekin et al., 1996) and juveniles (Geerlings et al., 2020). These same scores predict institutional misconduct in adults (Guy et al., 2005) and juveniles (Edens & Campbell, 2007). Finally, they predict recidivism in both adults (Salekin et al., 1996) and juveniles (Edens et al., 2006). When the PCL-R is split into its two higher-order factors, Factor 2 (e.g., impulsive and anti-social lifestyle) shows significantly larger relations to these outcomes (Leistico et al., 2008). Although fewer meta-analyses are available for self-report inventories, the two that are published show moderate relations between total scores on the inventories and a broad externalizing outcome (Miller & Lynam, 2012; Sleep et al., 2019). Although there are controversies as to whether antisocial behavior is a core part of the construct or a downstream correlate (e.g., Hare & Neumann, 2010; Neumann et al., 2015; Skeem & Cooke, 2010), there can be little doubt that interest in psychopathy among scholars and lay folks alike is driven by its intimate connect to antisociality.

Antisocial personality disorder has been an official diagnosis since the first edition of the DSM in 1952 (APA), although its criteria have changed across editions (Chapter 11). Currently, the DSM-5 describes ASPD as a pattern of disregard for and violation of the rights of others, occurring since the age of 15 years. This pattern is seen in the following: failure to conform to social norms, deceitfulness, impulsivity or failure to plan ahead, irritability and aggressiveness, reckless disregard for the safety of others, consistent irresponsibility, and lack of remorse. In many ways, ASPD is very similar to psychopathy in its core features and almost isomorphic with Factor 2 from the PCL-R. Although much was made about the asymmetry between PCL-R psychopathy and ASPD, (i.e., most psychopathic individuals receive diagnoses of ASPD, but only a small group of individuals with ASPD receive diagnoses of psychopathy; Hare, 2003), this had more to do with differences in assessment (i.e., the PCL-R using open concepts while ASPD used closed concepts) and threshold (30 of 40 points on the PCL-R versus 3 of 7 criteria for ASPD; Rogers & Rogstad, 2010).

The congruence between psychopathy and ASPD is highlighted even more in the Alternative Model of Personality Disorder (AMPD) included in DSM-5, which appears in section III on "emerging measures and models." In this section, psychopathy appears as a diagnostic specifier for ASPD. In the AMPD, personality disorders are diagnosed if seven criteria are met; the second criterion is of most interest here. For the first criterion, clinicians decide whether impairment in personality functioning (self- and interpersonal functioning) is present and to what degree. For the second criterion, the clinician decides whether the patient matches one of the six defined PD types—borderline, obsessive–compulsive, avoidant, schizotypal, antisocial, or narcissistic PD. Each PD type is defined by a number of pathological traits ranging from 2 (narcissistic) to 7 (ASPD; Borderline). The next two criteria deal with pervasiveness and stability, whereas the final three deal with alternative explanations and differential diagnoses. For

ASPD to be diagnosed, in addition to meeting all other criteria, an individual must possess at least 6 of the following traits: manipulativeness, callousness, deceitfulness, hostility, risk-taking, impulsivity, and irresponsibility. Within the AMPD, an optional specifier—with psychopathic features, is allowed for ASPD. To meet the conditions of the specifier, an individual must meet all criteria for ASPD and show the presence of three other traits—low anxiousness, low withdrawal, and high attention-seeking. This combination of traits has been referenced as Boldness or Fearless Dominance in the literature, and its centrality to psychopathy has been fiercely debated. We, ourselves, have argued that these traits are little more than window dressing, serving only to draw the eye (Lynam & Miller, 2012). What has not been up for debate, however, is the mostly adaptive nature of these traits. We have shown across multiple studies that the traits present in the psychopathy specifier of the AMPD are moderately and sometimes strongly associated with positive adjustment (e.g., absence of internalizing disorders, high extraversion, low neuroticism, absence of distress, high self-esteem) and unrelated or negatively related with other psychopathic traits (e.g., Miller et al., 2018) and negative outcomes (e.g., externalizing, aggression, antisocial behavior, delinquency, unemployment, arrest, and incarceration; Miller & Lynam, 2012; Sleep et al., 2019; Vize et al., 2016).[1] Thus, the core features of PSY and ASPD are identical. They seem only distinguished by traits that, ironically, make the psychopathic individual healthier and less antisocial than the individual with ASPD. All evidence that links PSY to antisocial behavior and aggression is evidence for the link between ASPD and these outcomes.

Narcissism describes individuals who are grandiose, entitled, require the admiration of others, and lack empathy (Chapter 13). It is studied within the official diagnostic system and outside of it. In terms of the DSM-5, it is indicated by a grandiose sense of self-importance, a preoccupation with grand fantasies, a belief oneself is special or unique, a need for admiration, a sense of entitlement, interpersonal exploitation, a lack of empathy, envy, and arrogance. Research across the last 20 years has suggested two differentiable presentations—grandiose and vulnerable (e.g., Cain et al., 2008; Miller & Campbell, 2008). On the one hand, grandiose narcissism is generally marked by arrogance, entitlement, higher self-esteem, gregariousness, aggression, perceived likability, risk taking, and a zero-sum interpersonal approach. On the other hand, vulnerable narcissism is associated with egocentrism, low self-esteem, distrust, negative affect, and social

[1] Attempts to prove the relevance of these traits to negative outcomes via interactions with other psychopathy traits (e.g., boldness x meanness) or interactions with itself (e.g., curvilinear hypotheses) have yielded little affirmative evidence (e.g., Crowe et al., 2021; Gatner et al., 2016; Vize et al., 2016; Weiss et al., 2019).

isolation. In general, grandiose and vulnerable narcissism have remarkably distinct nomological networks (Miller et al., 2011). Narcissistic personality disorder and grandiose narcissism are both much more closely related to PSY and ASPD than vulnerable narcissism, are what experts (Lynam & Widiger, 2001) and lay raters (Miller et al., 2018) think of when describing prototypical presentations of narcissism, and are more widely studied. For these reasons, when we discuss narcissism, we do not mean to be speaking of vulnerable narcissism.

Given the traits characterizing NAR (e.g., arrogance, lack of empathy, interpersonal exploitation) it is not surprising that NAR has been studied extensively in relation to aggression. A meta-analysis of the Dark Triad literature (i.e., the simultaneous study of PSY, NAR, and Machiavellianism) revealed small to moderate positive relations with aggression; it is worth noting that these relations were smaller than those observed for Dark Triad psychopathy (Vize, Lynam et al., 2018). A meta-analysis of laboratory aggression also found a small to moderate effect size for narcissism that was generally smaller than that obtained for psychopathy (Hyatt et al., 2019). In a very large, very recent meta-analysis, Du et al. (2021) found moderate effects of narcissism on general, proactive, and reactive aggression. These effects were moderated by narcissism dimension such that vulnerable narcissism was more strongly related to general and reactive aggression, whereas grandiose narcissism was more strongly related to proactive aggression.

PSY, ASPD, and NAR are substantially correlated with one another. In the meta-analysis by Vize et al., Dark Triad PSY and NAR were moderately to strongly correlated with one another (*mean r* = 0.38). In several studies (e.g., Widiger & Trull, 1998; Widiger et al., 1991), ASPD and NAR were among the most comorbid of the DSM personality disorders. Although, PSY and ASPD are not studied together very frequently, when they are, they are quite highly correlated. Collapsing across six studies, Lynam and Derefinko (2006) reported that psychopathy was most highly comorbid with ASPD followed by NPD.

A Trait Approach

PSY, ASPD, and NAR are moderately strongly related to one another and robustly related to antisocial behavior and aggression. In this section we offer a conceptualization that explains these findings and more. Specifically, we argue that these three personality disorder constructs—all personality disorders in fact—can be understood as configurations of general personality traits drawn from the Five-Factor Model of personality (FFM; McCrae & Costa, 1990). This model (Costa & McCrae, 1992), includes five higher-order factors called domains, with each domain composed of six specific facets, as descriptors of basic personality. The domains include Neuroticism (N: anxiousness, angry hostility, trait depression, self-consciousness, impulsiveness, vulnerability), Extraversion (E: warmth, gregariousness, assertiveness, activity, excitement seeking, positive emotions), Openness to Experience (O: fantasy, aesthetic, feelings, actions, ideas, values), Agreeableness (A: trust, straightforwardness, altruism, compliance, modesty, tender-mindedness), and Conscientiousness (C: competence, order, dutifulness, achievement striving, self-discipline, deliberation).

Much of our early work involved demonstrating that each personality disorder had a robust FFM profile, regardless of the method used to obtain it. The two primary methods we employed were expert ratings and meta-analyses. To obtain expert ratings, expert researchers on a given personality disorder were contacted and asked to provide ratings on each of the 30 FFM facets for a prototypic individual with that personality disorder. These ratings were checked for agreement and convergence which was always surprisingly high given that no specific individual was identified for experts to rate. Once it was clear that experts were in general agreement, the ratings were averaged across experts within a given facet, providing a general FFM description that blunted the idiosyncrasies of individual raters and brought out in bold relief the points of agreement. These final expert profiles for PSY, ASPD, and NAR (see Miller et al., 2001 for PSY; Lynam & Widiger, 2001 for ASPD and NAR) are presented in Table 6.1. A second approach to generating FFM profiles for personality disorders was an empirical one—meta-analyzing studies that reported on the relations between the FFM and the personality disorder. Collapsing across measurement instruments served the same purpose as collapsing across experts—blunting the idiosyncrasies and highlighting points of agreement. These empirical profiles are also presented in Table 6.1 (see DeCuyper et al., 2009 for ASPD; Lynam & Miller, 2015 for PSY; Miller et al., 2018 for NAR). Similarity indices, computed as zero-order correlations between columns, appear at the bottom of the table. The similarities at the bottom of the table reveal that descriptions obtained by the two methods generally converge with another. The correlations between the expert and empirical ratings range from 0.74 for PSY to 0.81 for NAR.

The Utility of the Trait Approach

There are a number of useful purposes served by conceptualizing and operationalizing personality disorders in this way. This trait approach provides a common language with which to describe, compare, and contrast each of these personality

Table 6.1 FFM profiles for PSY, ASPD, NAR, antisocial behavior, and aggression

	Psychopathy		Antisocial PD		Narcissistic PD		ASB & aggression			
	Expert	Empirical	Expert	Empirical	Expert	Empirical	ASB	AGG	Reactive	Proactive
N1 anxiety	1.47	-0.20	1.82	0.02	2.33	0.02	0.06	0.06	0.26	0.03
N2 angry hostility	3.87	0.29	4.14	0.30	4.08	0.23	0.27	0.27	0.45	0.30
N3 depression	1.40	0.04	2.45	0.14	2.42	0.03	0.16	0.16	0.27	0.11
N4 self-consciousness	1.07	-0.11	1.36	0.03	1.50	-0.03	0.05	0.04	0.11	0.00
N5 impulsiveness	4.53	0.21	4.73	0.26	3.17	0.14	0.19	0.16	0.30	0.21
N6 vulnerability	1.47	0.03	2.27	0.09	2.92	-0.01	0.13	0.11	0.25	0.08
E1 warmth	1.73	-0.22	2.14	-0.13	1.42	-0.07	-0.18	-0.16	-0.17	-0.15
E2 gregariousness	3.67	0.05	3.32	0.00	3.83	0.04	-0.03	-0.03	-0.03	0.06
E3 assertiveness	4.47	0.19	4.23	0.06	4.67	0.19	0.03	0.05	0.01	0.04
E4 activity	3.67	0.04	4.00	0.04	3.67	0.09	-0.02	-0.02	-0.06	0.00
E5 excitement seeking	4.73	0.24	4.64	0.25	4.17	0.16	0.15	0.11	0.12	0.17
E6 positive emotions	2.53	-0.19	2.86	-0.08	3.33	-0.02	-0.12	-0.12	-0.15	-0.13
O1 fantasy	3.07	0.01	3.82	0.09	3.75	0.11	0.03	0.02	0.11	0.02
O2 aesthetics	2.33	-0.05	2.36	-0.02	3.25	0.04	-0.03	-0.07	-0.07	-0.14
O3 feelings	1.80	-0.19	2.27	0.00	1.92	0.05	-0.04	-0.04	0.13	-0.09
O4 actions	4.27	0.14	4.23	0.06	4.08	0.04	0.01	-0.04	-0.06	-0.01
O5 ideas	3.53	-0.02	2.91	0.01	2.92	0.07	-0.01	0.00	-0.05	-0.08
O6 values	2.87	-0.09	3.00	-0.01	2.67	-0.01	-0.07	-0.08	-0.05	-0.06

(continued)

Table 6.1 (continued)

	Psychopathy		Antisocial PD		Narcissistic PD		ASB & aggression			
	Expert	Empirical	Expert	Empirical	Expert	Empirical	ASB	AGG	Reactive	Proactive
A1 trust	1.73	−0.29	1.45	−0.24	1.42	−0.20	−0.21	−0.21	−0.26	−0.21
A2 straightforwardness	1.13	−0.58	1.41	−0.39	1.83	−0.31	−0.31	−0.29	−0.28	−0.41
A3 altruism	1.33	−0.47	1.41	−0.25	1.00	−0.20	−0.22	−0.21	−0.21	−0.35
A4 compliance	1.33	−0.42	1.77	−0.33	1.58	−0.26	−0.32	−0.33	−0.46	−0.43
A5 modesty	1.00	−0.38	1.68	−0.15	1.08	−0.37	−0.13	−0.13	−0.11	−0.24
A6 tender-mindedness	1.27	−0.33	1.27	−0.20	1.50	−0.17	−0.14	−0.15	−0.15	−0.24
C1 competence	4.20	−0.29	2.09	−0.24	3.25	0.01	−0.17	−0.12	−0.14	−0.17
C2 order	2.60	−0.20	2.41	−0.18	2.92	−0.03	−0.08	−0.07	−0.13	−0.17
C3 dutifulness	1.20	−0.35	1.41	−0.33	2.42	−0.10	−0.22	−0.17	−0.19	−0.28
C4 achievement striving	3.07	−0.17	2.09	−0.19	3.92	0.02	−0.10	−0.06	−0.05	−0.11
C5 self-discipline	1.87	−0.24	1.81	−0.25	2.08	−0.09	−0.13	−0.09	−0.15	−0.15
C6 deliberation	1.60	−0.46	1.64	−0.37	2.25	−0.13	−0.26	−0.23	−0.29	−0.31

Similarities (zero-order rs)

(continued)

Table 6.1 (continued)

	Psychopathy		Antisocial PD		Narcissistic PD		ASB & aggression			
	Expert	Empirical	Expert	Empirical	Expert	Empirical	ASB	AGG	Reactive	Proactive
PSY expert										
PSY empirical	**0.74**						0.90	0.88	0.75	0.93
ASPD expert	0.88	0.87								
ASPD empirical	0.57	0.93	**0.79**				0.96	0.92	0.88	0.95
NAR expert	0.85	0.77	0.81	0.57						
NAR empirical	0.76	0.88	0.79	0.80	**0.81**		0.79	0.81	0.72	0.85

Within the trait profiles, Agreeableness facets are bold to highlight the consistency across the three personality disorders; Conscientiousness facets are italicized to illustrate the additional convergence between PSY and ASPD. In the ASB & Aggression columns, all correlations with absolute values greater than or equal to 0.20 are underlined

Within the similarities portion of the table, bolded correlations represent convergent correlations across methods (i.e., expert and empirical). Italicized correlations represent correlations among PSY, ASPD, and NAR in expert profiles. Underlined correlations represent correlations among PSY, ASPD, and NAR in empirical profiles disorders. This common language allows predictions to be made about comorbidity, sex differences, relations to outcomes, and so on. In terms of comorbidity or correlations among constructs, personality disorders should be comorbid to the degree that they have similar FFM profiles. Table 6.1 suggests that PSY and ASPD should be more highly comorbid (i.e., 0.88 for experts and 0.93 for empirical profiles) with one another than each is with NAR (i.e., 0.85/0.88 for experts and empirical profiles for PSY and 0.81/0.80 for ASPD), a prediction borne out empirically. These analyses were carried out for all 10 personality disorders by Lynam and Widiger (2001) who found that predictions derived based entirely on facet overlap across disorders matched quite closely the comorbidity rate observed empirically. Lynam and Derefinko (2006) compared correlations of psychopathy with the 10 DSM personality disorders predicted on the basis of facet overlap to those obtained empirically; they found very high similarity between those correlations (similarity $= 0.92$).

In addition to making predictions about the degree of overlap among personality disorders, these trait profiles offer insight into the nature of the overlap among personality disorders because the common language is used across them. Table 6.1 suggests the main reason that ASPD, PSY, and NAR overlap substantially is that each is characterized by low scores across all facets of Agreeableness-Antagonism: trust, straightforwardness, altruism, compliance, modesty, and tender-mindedness. This supposition is borne out empirically as well. Vize, Collison, and Lynam (in press) demonstrated that the overlap of PSY and NAR was reduced by 65–75% once Agreeableness was taken into account. Similarly, Vize et al. (2020), across two very large samples, demonstrated that the variance common across the Dark Triad (i.e., PSY, NAR, and Machiavellianism) was identical to Agreeableness. Although we are aware of no published studies testing this, Table 6.1 further suggests that ASPD and PSY should be more similar to one another than either is to NAR based on both being characterized as low across most facets of Conscientiousness.

Similar approaches have been used to understand the overlap of psychopathy subscales within and across inventories (Lynam & Miller, 2015; Sherman et al., 2014; Van Til et al., in press) and the overlap of grandiose and vulnerable narcissism (Miller et al., 2017). For example, using the Self-Report Psychopathy Scale, Fourth Edition (SRP-4; Paulhus et al., 2017) and two large samples (i.e., $n > 600$), Van Til et al. (in press) found that the overlap between any two pairs of the four subscales could be reduced by 73–94% by controlling for Agreeableness. Further, the latent correlation between the higher-order psychopathy factor of the SRP-4 and Agreeableness was essentially -1.0 indicating these two constructs are virtually identical.

These profiles also make predictions about other outcomes. For example, Lynam and Widiger (2007) used expert profiles of the 10 DSM personality differences and known sex differences on the 30 facets of the FFM to generate predictions about observed sex differences in the personality disorders. They found that the predictions based on the trait profiles were more similar to aggregated sex differences than any single study contributing to the aggregate. This was true for both self-reports and interview ratings for the personality disorders.

Antisocial behavior and aggression serve as an additional example. The last four columns in Table 6.1 present results from a meta-analysis on the relations between the 30 FFM facets and measures of antisocial behavior, general aggression, reactive aggression, and proactive aggression (Vize, Miller et al., 2018). Meta-analytic correlations (absolute value) equal to or higher than 0.20 are underlined. There are obvious consistencies in terms of which facets are related to these outcomes. Four of the six Agreeableness—Antagonism facets are related to all four outcomes; all six facets are related to proactive aggression. Additionally, all four outcomes are also related to angry hostility (Neuroticism) and deliberation (Conscientiousness). Reactive and proactive aggression are both also related to impulsiveness (Neuroticism). Reactive aggression has unique relations with several Neuroticism facets—anxiety, depression, and vulnerability. Based on our conceptualization, personality disorders (e.g., PSY, ASPD, and NAR) should be associated with antisocial behavior and aggression to the extent that their FFM profiles resemble the FFM profiles of these outcomes. These resemblances are seen at the bottom of the Table. In each case, the relative ordering is the same; based on profile similarity, ASPD should be the most strongly related to these outcomes, followed by PSY, followed by NAR. In fact, this is what is observed empirically.

A final advantage to this trait approach is that working from a personality model derived from basic personality science allows one to leverage basic research on that model to understand the personality disorders (Lynam & Miller, 2015). Multiple researchers study the development and continuity of FFM traits over time (e.g., Caspi et al., 2005; De Clercq & De Fruyt, 2012) and how people can change their traits (Hudson & Fraley, 2016). Others study the genetic and environmental influences on the traits (Jang et al., 2002). Still others, the processes underlying and outcomes attributable to specific domains within the FFM. For instance, Robinson and colleagues (e.g., Meier et al., 2006, 2008; Wilkowski et al., 2006) have contributed excellent basic research examining Agreeableness. Similarly, over the last decade, Roberts and colleagues have systematically studied the composition (e.g., Roberts et al., 2005) and consequences (e.g., Bogg & Roberts, 2004) of Conscientiousness. To the extent that PSY, ASPD, and NAR can be connected to this vast literature, this empirical literature can be leveraged to increase our understanding of psychopathy.

The Role of Antagonism

It should be obvious from the above discussion that Antagonism—Agreeableness is a very important trait for understanding PSY, ASPD, NAR, antisocial behavior, and aggression. We have written previously that we believe this generally understudied trait deserves much more attention than it receives in psychopathology and criminology (Lynam & Miller, 2019; Miller & Lynam, 2019). It is a basic trait that indexes one's orientation to others and is found across structural models of personality, including the interpersonal circumplex, and psychopathology. It is thought to capture an individual difference in the motivation to maintain positive social relations with others (Graziano & Eisenberg, 1997). Agreeable individuals try to maintain harmonious relations with others, while antagonistic individuals are more willing to sacrifice interpersonal harmony for other goals—wealth, status, power, etcetera. In a relative importance analysis of the FFM traits, Lynam and Miller (2019) found that Antagonism accounted for more of the explained variance than the other four FFM domains combined in psychopathy, ASPD, NPD/narcissism, and all forms of aggression and antisocial behavior. Additionally, it was the second-largest contributor, behind neuroticism, to relationship satisfaction and victimization. Recently, we have worked to identify the empirical structure of Agreeableness (Crowe et al., 2018)-Antagonism (Sleep et al., 2021) using bass-ackward analyses of comprehensive item pools.

It is noteworthy that the recently developed but increasingly prominent Hierarchical Taxonomy of Psychopathology (Kotov et al., 2017) has an "antagonistic externalizing" dimension as one of its core higher-order factors comprising, in part, ASPD, NPD, conduct disorder, and other externalizing disorders. As research on this new model of psychopathology emerges, we hope that scholars will pay more (systematic) attention to the role of this underappreciated domain that is so robustly associated with externalizing problems and interpersonal impairment.

References

American Psychiatric Association. (1952). *Diagnostic and statistical manual of mental disorders*. Author.

American Psychiatric Association. (2013). *Diagnostic and statistical manual of mental disorders* (5th ed.). American Psychiatric Publishing.

Blais, J., Solodukhin, E., & Forth, A. E. (2014). A meta-analysis exploring the relationship between psychopathy and instrumental versus reactive violence. *Criminal Justice and Behavior, 41*, 797–821.

Bogg, T., & Roberts, B. W. (2004). Conscientiousness and health-related behaviors: A meta-analysis of the leading behavioral contributors to mortality. *Psychological Bulletin, 130*, 887–919.

Cain, N. M., Pincus, A. L., & Ansell, E. B. (2008). Narcissism at the crossroads: Phenotypic description of pathological narcissism across clinical theory, social/personality psychology, and psychiatric diagnosis. *Clinical Psychology Review, 28*, 638–656.

Caspi, A., Roberts, B. W., & Shiner, R. L. (2005). Personality development: Stability and change. *Annual Review of Psychology, 56*, 453–484.

Cleckley, H. (1941/1988). *The Mask of Sanity*. Mosby.

Costa, P. T., & McCrae, R. R. (1992). *Revised NEO Personality Inventory (NEO PI-R) and the NEO Five-Factor Inventory (NEOFFI) professional manual*. Odessa, FL: Psychological Assessment Resources.

Crowe, M., Lynam, D. R., & Miller, J. D. (2018). Uncovering the structure of Agreeableness from self-report measures. *Journal of Personality, 86*, 771–787.

Crowe, M. L., Weiss, B. M., Sleep, C. E., Harris, A. M., Carter, N. T., Lynam, D. R., & Miller, J. D. (2021). Fearless Dominance/Boldness is not strongly related to externalizing behaviors: An item response-based analysis. *Assessment, 28*, 413–428.

De Clercq, B., & De Fruyt, F. (2012). A five-factor model framework for understanding childhood personality disorder antecedents. *Journal of Personality, 80*, 1534–1563.

Decuyper, M., De Pauw, S., De Fruyt, F., De Bolle, M., & De Clercq, B. J. (2009). A meta-analysis of psychopathy, antisocial PD and FFM associations. *European Journal of Personality, 23*, 531–565.

Du, T.V., Miller, J. D., & Lynam, D. R. (2021). The relation between narcissism and aggression: A meta-analysis. *Manuscript submitted for publication*.

Edens, J. F., & Campbell, J. S. (2007). Identifying youths at risk for institutional misconduct: A meta-analytic investigation of the psychopathy checklist measures. *Psychological Services, 4*, 13–27.

Edens, J. F., Campbell, J., & Weir, J. (2006). Youth psychopathy and criminal recidivism: A meta-analysis of the psychopathy checklist measures. *Law and Human Behavior, 31*, 53–75.

Gatner, D. T., Douglas, K. S., & Hart, S. D. (2016). Examining the incremental and interactive effects of boldness with meanness and disinhibition within the triarchic model of psychopathy. *Personality Disorders: Theory, Research, and Treatment, 7*, 259–268.

Geerlings, Y., Asscher, J. J., Stams, G. J. J. M., & Assink, M. (2020). The association between psychopathy and delinquency in juveniles: A three-level meta-analysis. *Aggression and Violent Behavior, 50*, 1–10.

Graziano, W. G., & Eisenberg, N. (1997). Agreeableness: A dimension of personality. In R. Hogan, J. Johnson, & S. Briggs (Eds.), *Handbook of personality psychology* (pp. 795–824). Academic Press.

Guy, L. G., Edens, J. F., Anthony, C., & Douglas, K. S. (2005). Does psychopathy predict institutional misconduct among adults? A meta-analytic investigation. *Journal of Consulting and Clinical Psychology, 73*, 1056–1064.

Hare, R. D. (1991). *Manual for the psychopathy checklist-revised*. Multi-Health Systems.

Hare, R. D. (2003). *The Hare psychopathy checklist-revised* (2nd ed.). Multi-Health Systems Inc.

Hare, R. D., & Neumann, C. S. (2010). The role of antisociality in the psychopathy construct: Comment on Skeem and Cooke (2010). *Psychological Assessment, 22*, 446–454.

Hudson, N. W., & Fraley, D. R. (2016). Changing for the better? Longitudinal associations between volitional personality change and psychological well-being. *Personality and Social Psychology Bulletin, 42*, 603–615.

Hyatt, C. S., Zeichner, A., & Miller, J. D. (2019). Laboratory aggression and personality traits: A meta-analytic review. *Psychology of Violence, 9*, 675–689.

Jang, K. L., Livesley, W. J., Angleitner, A., Riemann, R., & Vernon, P. A. (2002). Genetic and environmental influences on the covariance of facets defining the domains of the five-factor model of personality. *Personality and Individual Differences, 33*, 83–101.

Kotov, R., Krueger, R. F., Watson, D., Achenbach, T. M., Althoff, R. R., Bagby, R. M., Brown, T. A., Carpenter, W. T., Caspi, A., Clark, L. A., & Eaton, N. R. (2017). The Hierarchical Taxonomy of Psychopathology (HiTOP): A dimensional alternative to traditional nosologies. *Journal of Abnormal Psychology, 126*(4), 454–477.

Leistico, A. M., Salekin, R. T., DeCoster, J., & Rogers, R. (2008). A large-scale meta-analysis relating the Hare measures of psychopathy to antisocial conduct. *Law and Human Behavior, 32*, 28–45.

Lilienfeld, S. O., & Widows, M. R. (2005). *Psychopathic personality inventory-revised: Professional manual*. Lutz, FL: Psychological Assessment Resources Inc.

Lynam, D. R., & Derefinko, K. (2006). Psychopathy and personality. In C. J. Patrick (Ed.), *Handbook of psychopathy* (pp. 133–155). Guilford.

Lynam, D. R., Gaughan, E. T., Miller, J. D., Miller, D. J., Mullins-Sweatt, S., & Widiger, T. A. (2011). Assessing the basic traits associated with psychopathy: Development and validation of the Elemental Psychopathy Assessment. *Psychological Assessment, 23*, 108–124.

Lynam, D. R., & Miller, J. D. (2012). Fearless dominance and psychopathy: Response to Lilienfeld et al. *Personality Disorders: Theory, Research, and Treatment, 3*, 341–353.

Lynam, D. R., & Miller, J. D. (2015). Psychopathy from a basic trait perspective: The utility of a five-factor model approach. *Journal of Personality, 83*, 611–626.

Lynam, D. R., & Miller, J. D. (2019). The basic trait of antagonism: An unfortunately underappreciated construct. *Journal of Research in Personality, 81*, 118–126.

Lynam, D. R., & Widiger, T. (2001). Using the five factor model to represent the personality disorders: An expert consensus approach. *Journal of Abnormal Psychology, 110*, 401–412.

Lynam, D. R., & Widiger, T. A. (2007). Using a general model of personality to understand sex differences in the personality disorders. *Journal of Personality Disorders, 21*, 583–602.

McCrae, R. R., & Costa, P. T. (1990). *Personality in adulthood*. Guilford.

Meier, B., Robinson, M., & Wilkowski, B. M. (2006). Turning the other cheek: Agree-ableness and the regulation of aggression related primes. *Psychological Science, 17*, 136–142.

Meier, B. P., Wilkowski, B. M., & Robinson, M. D. (2008). Bringing out the agreeableness in everyone: Using a cognitive self-regulation model to reduce aggression. *Journal of Experimental Social Psychology, 44*, 1383–1387.

Miller, J. D., & Campbell, W. K. (2008). Comparing clinical and social-personality concep-tualizations of narcissism. *Journal of Personality, 76*, 449–476.

Miller, J. D., Hoffman, B. J., Gaughan, E. T., Gentile, B., Maples, J., & Keith Campbell, W. (2011). Grandiose and vulnerable narcissism: A nomological network analysis. *Journal of Personality, 79*, 1013–1042.

Miller, J. D., Lamkin, J., Maples-Keller, J. L., Sleep, C. E., & Lynam, D. R. (2018). A test of the empirical profile and coherence of the DSM-5 psychopathy specifier. *Psychological Assessment, 30*, 870–881.

Miller, J. D., & Lynam, D. R. (2012). An examination of the psychopathic personality inven-tory's nomological network: A meta-analytic review. *Personality Disorders: Theory, Research, and Treatment, 3*, 305–326.

Miller, J. D., & Lynam, D. R. (2019). *The handbook of antagonism: Conceptualizations, assessment, consequences, and treatment of the low end of agreeableness*. Elsevier.

Miller, J. D., Lynam, D. R., Hyatt, C. S., & Campbell, W. K. (2017). Controversies in narcissism. *Annual Review of Clinical Psychology, 13*, 291–315.

Miller, J. D., Lynam, D. R., Siedor, L., Crowe, M., & Campbell, W. K. (2018). Consensual lay profiles of narcissism and their connection to the five-factor narcissism inventory. *Psychological Assessment, 30*, 10–18.

Miller, J. D., Lynam, D. R., Widiger, T., & Leukefeld, C. (2001). Personality disorders as extreme variants of common personality dimensions: Can the five factor model ade-quately represent psychopathy? *Journal of Personality, 69*, 253–276.

Miller, J. D., Vize, C., Crowe, M. L., & Lynam, D. R. (2019). A critical appraisal of the dark triad literature and suggestions for moving forward. *Current Directions in Psychological Science, 28*, 353–360.

Neumann, C. S., Hare, R. D., & Pardini, D. A. (2015). Antisociality and the construct of psychopathy: Data from across the globe. *Journal of Personality, 83*, 678–692.

Patrick, C. J. (2010). *Operationalizing the triarchic conceptualization of psychopathy: Pre-liminary description of brief scales for assessment of boldness, meanness, and disinhibition* (Unpublished test manual). Florida State University, Tallahassee, FL.

Paulhus, D. L., Neumann, C., & Hare, R. D., Williams, K. M., & Hemphill J. F. (2017). *Self-report psychopathy scale 4th edition manual*. Multi-Health Systems.

Roberts, B. W., Chernyshenko, O. S., Stark, S., & Goldberg, L. R. (2005). The structure of conscientiousness: An empirical investigation based on seven major personality question-naires. *Personnel Psychology, 58*, 103–139.

Rogers, R., & Rogstad, J. E. (2010). Psychopathy and APD in non-forensic patients: Improved predictions or disparities in cut scores? *Journal of Psychopathology and Behav-ioral Assessment, 32*, 353–362.

Salekin, R. T., Rogers, R., & Sewell, K. W. (1996). A review and meta-analysis of the psychopathy checklist and psychopathy checklist-revised: Predictive validity of danger-ousness. *Clinical Psychology: Science and Practice, 3*, 203–215.

Sherman, E. D., Lynam, D. R., & Heyde, B. (2014). Agreeableness accounts for the factor structure of the Youth Psychopathic Traits Inventory. *Journal of Personality Disorders, 28*, 262–280.

Skeem, J. L., & Cooke, D. J. (2010). Is criminal behavior a central component of psychopathy? Conceptual directions for resolving the debate. *Psychological Assessment, 22*, 433–445.

Sleep, C. E., Crowe, M., Carter, N. T., Lynam, D. R., & Miller, J. D. (2021). Uncovering the structure of antagonism. *Personality Disorders: Theory, Research, and Treatment, 12*, 300-311.

Sleep, C. E., Weiss, B., Lynam, D. R., & Miller, J. D. (2019). An examination of the triarchic model of psychopathy's nomological network: A meta-analytic review. *Clinical Psychology Review, 71*, 1–26.

Van Til, K., Vize, C. E., Miller, J. D., & Lynam, D. R. (in press). Antagonism explains the higher-order factor structure of the self-report psychopathy scale, fourth edition. *Personality Disorders: Theory, Research, and Treatment.*

Vize, C. E., Collison, K. L., Crowe, M. L., Campbell, W. K., Miller, J. D., & Lynam, D. R. (2019). Using dominance analysis to decompose narcissism and its relation to aggression and externalizing outcomes. *Assessment, 26*, 260–270.

Vize, C. E., Collison, K. L., & Lynam, D. R. (in press). The importance of antagonism: Explaining similarities and differences in psychopathy and narcissism's relations with aggression and externalizing outcomes. *Journal of Personality Disorders.*

Vize, C. E., Collison, K. L., Miller, J. D., & Lynam, D. R. (2020). The "core" of the dark triad: A test of competing hypotheses. *Personality Disorders: Theory, Research, and Treatment, 11*, 91–99.

Vize, C. E., Lynam, D. R., Lamkin, J., Miller, J. D., & Pardini, D. (2016). Identifying essential features of juvenile psychopathy in the prediction of later antisocial behavior: Is there an additive, synergistic, or curvilinear role for fearless dominance? *Clinical Psychological Science, 4*, 572–590.

Vize, C. E., Lynam, D. R., Collison, K. L., & Miller, J. D. (2018). Differences among dark triad components: A meta-analytic investigation. *Personality Disorders: Theory, Research, and Treatment, 9*, 101–111.

Vize, C. E., Miller, J. D., & Lynam, D. R. (2018). FFM facets and their relations with different forms of antisocial behavior: An expanded meta-analysis. *Journal of Criminal Justice, 57*, 67–75.

Vize, C. E., Miller, J. D., & Lynam, D. R. (in press). Examining the conceptual and empirical distinctiveness of agreeableness and "dark" personality items. *Journal of Personality.*

Weiss, B., Crowe, M. L., Harris, A. M., Carter, N. T., Lynam, D. R., Watts, A. L., Lilienfeld, S. O., Skeem, J. L., & Miller, J. D. (2019). Examining hypothesized interactive and curvilinear relations between psychopathic traits and externalizing problems in an offender sample using item response-based analysis. *Journal of Abnormal Psychology, 128*, 689–699.

Widiger, T. A., Frances, A. J., Harris, M., Jacobsberg, L., Feyer, M., & Manning, D. (1991). Comorbidity among Axis II disorders. In J. Oldham (Ed.), *Axiss II: New perspectives on validity* (pp. 163–194). American Psychiatric Press.

Widiger, T. A., & Trull, T. J. (1998). Performance characteristics of the DSM-III-R personality disorder criteria sets. In T. A. Widiger, A. J. Frances, H. A. Pincus, R. Ross, M. B.

First, W. Davis, & M. Kline (Eds.), *DSM-IV sourcebook* (Vol. 4, pp. 357–373). American Psychiatric Association.

Wilkowski, B. M., Robinson, M. D., & Meier, B. P. (2006). Agreeableness and the prolonged spatial processing of antisocial and prosocial information. *Journal of Research in Personality, 40*, 1152–1168.

Suggestions for Further Reading

Lynam, D. R., & Miller, J. D. (2015). Psychopathy from a basic trait perspective: The utility of a five-factor model approach. *Journal of Personality, 83*, 611–626.

Lynam, D. R. & Miller, J. D. (2019). The basic trait of antagonism: An unfortunately underappreciated construct. *Journal of Research in Personality, 81*, 118–126.

Miller, J. D., & Lynam, D. R. (2019). *The handbook of antagonism: Conceptualizations, assessment, consequences, and treatment of the low end of agreeableness.* Elsevier.

Miller, J. D., Lynam, D. R., Hyatt, C. S., & Campbell, W. K. (2017). Controversies in narcissism. *Annual Review of Clinical Psychology, 13*, 291–315.

Vize, C. E., Miller, J. D., & Lynam, D. R. (2018). FFM facets and their relations with different forms of antisocial behavior: An expanded meta-analysis. *Journal of Criminal Justice, 57*, 67–75.

Callous-Unemotional Traits and Empathy

7

Sophie Alshukri, Kerry Lewis, and Luna C. Muñoz Centifanti

Key Points

- Callous-unemotional (CU) traits and empathy are diverse in nature and this is reflected in the methodology and measures available.
- CU traits are defined by a lack of empathy but research highlights how this is overly simplified.
- The relationship between CU traits and empathy is sensitive to the methods and context used.
- When the effort of empathy is considered, it becomes more difficult to suggest that individuals with CU traits do not possess the ability to demonstrate empathy-related processes.

Introduction

This chapter will explore the construct of callous-unemotional (CU) traits and briefly consider related behaviors. The main part of the chapter will focus on the relationship between CU traits and empathy. To provide a more thorough

S. Alshukri · K. Lewis · L. C. M. Centifanti (✉)
Primary Care and Mental Health, University of Liverpool, Liverpool, UK
e-mail: luna@centifanti.uk

S. Alshukri
e-mail: S.Alshukri@liverpool.ac.uk

K. Lewis
e-mail: Kerry.Lewis2@liverpool.ac.uk

© The Author(s), under exclusive license to Springer Nature Switzerland AG 2022   127
C. Garofalo and J. J. Sijtsema (eds.), *Clinical Forensic Psychology*,
https://doi.org/10.1007/978-3-030-80882-2_7

overview of the relationship between CU traits and empathy, different dimensions of empathy will be examined. A view of empathy as something people *do*, rather than some kind of trait people have, will also be discussed. The complex relationship between CU traits and empathy will become clear as will a need to dismiss the widely accepted notion that CU traits relate to a complete deficit in empathy.

CU Traits

Callous-unemotional (CU) traits refer to a set of affective characteristics, summarized by the DSM-5 as limited prosocial emotions (APA, 2013). These traits include a lack of remorse, empathy or concern over one's actions, and deficient affect. As such, they reflect the emotion-related aspect of psychopathy (Pisano et al., 2017) and are often seen as a gateway for progression into such aspects of adult psychopathy (Anderson & Kiehl, 2014). Psychopathy, when examined biologically, has shown an association with lesser electrical brain activity when observing emotionally evocative events (Anderson & Stanford, 2012) and reduction in physiological responsivity to emotion, both the perception and interpretation (Gordon et al., 2004; Patrick et al., 1993). Similar findings will be discussed in this chapter in relation to CU traits supporting not only this connection between CU traits and psychopathy but, more importantly to this chapter, also showing the relation of CU traits to empathy processes.

An increasing interest in CU traits has seen continued dedication to provide a range of valid questionnaires. Table 7.1 provides a summary of these measures.

Children who, over many years, have high levels of CU traits, are extremely likely to have conduct problems (Fontaine et al., 2011). If one knows that a child has CU traits, then, they can know that child's trajectory of conduct problems. The opposite is not true. If a child has high levels of conduct problems, they will not necessarily have high levels of CU traits, even if the child shows high levels of conduct problems over a number of years (Fontaine et al., 2011). This shows that conduct problems may stem from other factors, such as social contextual issues (e.g., poverty) or a lack of self-control. But when CU traits are present, society needs to consider how to disrupt their engagement in conduct problems.

As a result, CU traits have been added as a specifier for conduct disorder in the DSM-5 (APA, 2013; Frick & Moffitt, 2010), although the term "limited prosocial emotions" is used instead. CU traits help to identify and diagnose a more severe, stable pattern of behavior within youth with conduct problems (Kahn et al., 2012). Further support for this specifier comes from findings suggesting

Table 7.1 Summary of CU traits measures

Title	Authors	Population	Administered by	Format
Youth Psychopathic Traits Inventory (YPI)	Andershed et al. (2002)	Adolescent/young adult population	Academic researchers	Self-report questionnaire (subscale measures CU traits)
Antisocial Process Screening Device (APSD)	Frick and Hare (2001)	Young children/early adolescents	Health/educational professionals (e.g., psychiatrist, registered psychologist) Academic researchers	Parent, teacher, or combined report (subscale measures CU traits)
Inventory of Callous-Unemotional Traits (ICU)	Frick (2004)	Children/adolescents	Academic researchers	Self-, parent-, teacher-report questionnaire (teacher and parent report available for youth and pre-school)

that children with conduct problems and high levels of CU traits have a distinctive cognitive profile, such as lower levels of empathy (Milone et al., 2019; Rowe et al., 2010). People who lack empathy may struggle with social interactions, altruism, generosity, and regulation of aggression (Feshbach, 1975; van Dongen, 2020). They also experience poor attachment and shallow relationships with others which may impact their overall quality of life (Decety et al., 2015). A better knowledge of the relationship between CU traits and empathy is therefore vital to help understand the negative outcomes related to CU traits and to the development of successful interventions.

Empathy

A key characteristic of CU traits in children and adolescents is believed to be deficient empathy (e.g., Milone et al., 2019). Firstly, it should be noted that difficulties in empathy are not exclusively associated with CU traits. Differences in empathy are also discussed in relation to autism spectrum disorder (Harmsen, 2019) and other aspects related to psychopathy such as narcissism (Ritter et al.,

2011). Secondly, it is important to consider empathy as a complex construct that consists of related, but distinct, dimensions. For example, in a review of research and literature, 43 differing definitions of empathy were identified (Cuff et al., 2014). However, in broad terms, empathy involves an ability to be involved in aspects of, or part of, others' emotional experiences (Singer & Lamm, 2009). Empathy involves mirroring and understanding other people's emotions.

Given this intricate nature of empathy, the term "deficient empathy" may seem vague. Is the term "deficient empathy" too generalized to truly capture the relations between CU traits and this complex construct? Also, *when* do they show deficient empathy; in which contexts and under what kinds of motivation? In the next section, we will discuss the research on dimensions of empathy in relation to CU traits and discover the relationship is much more complicated than a general "deficiency" would suggest.

Affective vs Cognitive (Empathy)

Humans are social animals and employ empathy to understand another's intentions and beliefs to be able to successfully interact (Decety & Jackson, 2004; Singer & Lamm, 2009). If there is a deficit in empathic abilities, then this typically leads to unsuccessful social interactions (Fan & Han, 2008). Many researchers have argued investigating empathy as a single concept is limited in its ability to explain diverse findings. It ignores the parallel dimensions of empathy and how they represent opposing/different aspects of the complex concept. However, if CU traits are defined by a "general deficiency" in empathy, for example an overall lack of resonating with other people's feelings and being able to read other people's feelings, one may question the importance of exploring the specific dimensions of empathy. Yet, research suggests that the utility of considering different dimensions, such as cognitive and affective empathy, should not be ignored. Cognitive empathy describes the ability to take the perspective of another person to understand how they may be feeling (Davis, 1980). Affective empathy is the ability to feel or mirror another's emotional state (Blair, 2005; Jankowiak-Siuda et al., 2011; Singer & Lamm, 2009). CU traits have been found to be negatively related to both affective and cognitive dimensions (Milone et al., 2019; Pasalich et al., 2014). In contrast to a deficit model, we know that people with CU traits do not disregard other people, since they may organize and lead other people in trying to get what they want. For example, CU traits increase the tendency of youth to be involved in gangs or group delinquency and to take a leadership role within such activities (Thornton et al., 2015). So, people with CU traits may understand other people's mental states, but perhaps they use this knowledge for their own benefit or for antisocial purposes.

The distinction between deficits in cognitive and affective empathy has led to further understanding of the behavior implications that are linked to CU traits—predominantly conduct problems (Jolliffe & Farrington, 2004; Moul et al., 2018). For example, based on parent- and teacher-report, pre-school children's cognitive empathy, but not affective empathy, was related to CU traits. Furthermore, cognitive but not affective empathy has been found to mediate the association between CU traits and conduct problems (Georgiou et al., 2018). Another study on pre-teens found that lower levels of self-reported cognitive empathy were specifically related to uncaring traits associated with CU traits. Yet, lower affective empathy was found for all CU-related subscales (Centifanti et al., 2010). Similar to Georgiou and colleagues' findings, the findings indicated CU traits acted indirectly on problem behaviors (i.e., bullying) via cognitive empathy. This suggests that children with CU traits behave negatively toward others mainly because of difficulties in understanding what others are feeling (i.e., cognitive empathy) rather than because they do not *feel* others' emotions.

However, the relationships between CU traits and affective and cognitive empathy are not clear cut. Examining parent-report data of children between the ages of 3 and 13 years, associations between psychopathy-related traits and cognitive and affective empathy across the different ages were tested (Dadds et al., 2009). In contrast to the findings based on pre-school children (Georgiou et al., 2018), affective empathy deficits were related to CU traits across ages, including puberty—although only for male children. No such difficulties were found in girls with CU traits. Similar to findings with pre-school children, CU traits in both male and female participants were linked to deficits in cognitive empathy within the younger cohort of children. However, these findings provide evidence that the association is not simple. The association between CU traits and cognitive empathy deficits faded for boys who were older—where the boys appeared to have typical levels of cognitive empathetic ability (Dadds et al., 2009). Based on these findings, boys with CU traits may not be able to develop abilities to emotionally connect to others (affective empathy), but that they may learn to describe and understand others' emotions (cognitive empathy). We note that this study did not follow the same children over time, so these differences may or may not reflect *development* of empathy.

CU traits and cognitive and affective empathy have also been examined using measures that reflect what people do in real life. For example, boys aged 11–17 years old were presented with pictures of the eye regions of faces of people displaying different emotions and were asked to describe what the person was thinking or feeling (Milone et al., 2019). They found that boys with conduct problems and high levels of CU traits lacked the ability to feel compassion and concern for people who showed negative emotions, which suggests lower levels of affective empathy.

From the research above, it is clear that it is important to explore both cognitive and affective facets of empathy separately; looking at empathy as a whole hides intricate differences that exist between the two facets. However, the findings are mixed. There appears to be more, but not always consistent, support for difficulties with affective empathy as compared to cognitive empathy. Fully understanding how and when CU traits and associated outcomes relate to these dimensions of empathy requires further research.

Pain Empathy

Despite the useful insights available, there is more work needed to understand how empathy relates to CU traits. Empathy for specific emotional states is one avenue explored. One thing we know about CU traits is they are associated with a lack of concern for others and a lack of guilt when engaging in harmful behavior. One can imagine that emotions in others that signal hurt, then, might be especially hard for people with CU traits to empathize with. Thus, research has focused on the association between CU traits and empathy for pain.

Empathy for pain is measured by testing what people understand when they observe other people experiencing pain and whether they can share or mirror their feelings. This can be done by showing people facial expressions when someone is in pain or by showing people pictures of painful stimuli (e.g., a needle piercing someone's hand). Recognizing signs of distress in other people, such as pain, has been examined in adolescents with CU traits (Wolf & Muñoz Centifanti, 2014). Youths high in CU traits showed an impairment in processing negative emotions; they were less accurate in being able to "read" facial expressions of pain. The consequences of such an impairment may lead to a violent behavior in people with CU traits as they are unable to recognize and respond to other people in distress (Blair, 2001)—a dysfunction that is rooted within empathy (Frick & White, 2008). Indeed, prior research shows prisoners who have trouble understanding pain in other people are more consistently violent (Miller et al., 2013). Objective experimental methods, such as psychophysiology, have also been adopted to explore the experience of pain empathy in people with CU traits. Physiological measurement is a useful way to collect data on how the body responds to affective and aversive stimuli (Siddle, 1991). For example, if a person feels threatened or stressed, then their body will automatically respond. The sympathetic nervous system will be activated to either prepare to fight off their attacker or to get ready to run away (also known as the fight or flight response). During this time, the body releases hormones that, among other things, speed up heart rate and slow down digestion which gives their body the energy they need to respond to the threat (Berntson et al., 1991). These changes can be observed through their psychophysiology. Physiological measurements thus provide another way, in addition to self-reports, to understand how individuals with CU traits react to another person's pain. Including psychophysiology allows for triangulation of different measures in the investigation of the association between CU traits and pain empathy.

People with CU traits or psychopathic traits show deficient psychophysiological responses to their environment (Brislin et al., 2016; Fanti et al., 2016). Noise-elicited startle reflexes can be used, such that a loud noise is played while people look at an image that conveys threat, for instance. Researchers then measure how strongly people blink as a measure of startle reflex. In a sample of male and female community volunteers, noise-elicited startle reflexes have been measured while viewing violent films (Fanti et al., 2016). CU traits were associated with reduced eye-blinks (although only for those who also had high levels of impulsive aggression). These diminished startle reflexes occurred alongside lower reports of arousal in response to the film (i.e., feeling more calm when watching the clip). These findings suggest a diminished or unreactive defense system in people with CU traits when viewing others in pain as they did not physically or emotionally react to viewing others in pain.

Being numb to pain may contribute to a deficiency in being able to recognize when other people are in distress. If one fails to feel pain, then how can one recognize pain in another person? A high threshold of pain in people with psychopathic traits may be one explanation, then, for findings of low empathy. The level of pain a person can tolerate can be measured by applying gradually increasing pressure to a point on the body, such as the hand, using a pressure algometer. When the amount of pressure becomes too much for the person to withstand, they have reached their pain threshold. People with higher levels of "meanness" (a facet of psychopathy that is related to CU traits) can withstand more pain applied by a pressure algometer than people with lower levels of meanness (Brislin et al., 2016). If people high in CU are able to withstand more pain, then they may think that other people can too and thus view others' pain as less distressing. One can imagine that failing to perceive other people's pain as distressful may preclude empathy.

Overall, higher levels of CU traits are related to less accurate recognition of visual clues, and less physiological reaction, for other people's pain. CU-related traits also seem to affect the individuals' experience of pain. If one can withstand higher levels of pain, then one can disregard (and not empathize with) another's pain. In the next section, we look further into the idea that empathy is something we *do* and explore how context impacts the way people with CU traits empathize.

Modulation of Empathy

Empathy is not something that we, as humans, effortlessly do. It requires effort and thus comes with costs and the need for regulation (Hodges & Klein, 2001). Empathy can therefore be dependent on context. For example, one may express more intense empathy for a familiar person they like than for a stranger (Bucchioni et al., 2015). People can choose not to be empathetic if they feel that doing so is too taxing (Cameron et al., 2019). The cognitive effort of accurately processing emotional signals that support empathy may lead to the conclusion that being empathetic is too taxing (Cameron et al., 2019). This is true of cross-race understanding of emotions; people appear to find it easier to empathize with members of their own race (Gutsell & Inzlicht, 2012). Low levels of empathy in those with CU traits may therefore reflect a choice rather than a deficit. Rather than being unable to express any empathy at all, people with CU traits may regulate their empathetic responses differently, choosing to be more selective as to when they express empathy for others.

People with psychopathic traits, for example, do not automatically display empathetic responses toward situations involving emotion. However, they can respond in a way that shows empathy when asked to (Meffert et al., 2013). Examining brain activity, when individuals with psychopathic traits were instructed to respond empathetically, their brain activation changed. The lower activation compared to those without psychopathic traits became less prominent. People with psychopathic traits seemed to have the ability to empathize when asked to. Although CU traits were not measured here, people with traits that include CU (i.e., psychopathy) were found to be able to direct their effort toward responding in an empathetic way. If we can know which selective circumstances people with CU will respond to (without being prompted), then treatment may be possible.

The development of empathy also changes throughout childhood based on the child's upbringing. Children are more likely to exhibit empathy if their parents have encouraged them to consider other people's viewpoints, for example (Farrant et al., 2012). Lower levels of empathy in children with CU traits may therefore be due to less exposure to aspects of parenting that encourage empathy to develop. One parental factor that has been related to both empathy development and CU traits is mind-mindedness. Mind-mindedness refers to the extent to which a caregiver is attuned to, and interacts in a way that responds to a child's mind, thoughts, and feelings (Meins, 2013). The number of mind-related comments that a mother is observed to make toward their 8-month-old child had been found to be indirectly linked to levels of CU traits when children were 10 years old (Centifanti et al., 2016). In that study, empathy at 5 years of age, measured as understanding emotions (e.g., labeling, linking emotions to desires), helped to explain the indirect link between mind-related comments and CU traits. This suggests that children's empathy-related abilities are fostered by mind-related talk with their caregiver, since mind-related talk shows that the mother understands the child's thoughts and wishes and is able to verbalize them on the child's behalf. Children with CU traits may develop the ability to empathize with others, and subsequently treat others in a caring way, based on early interactions with parents.

Early interactions with parents, including the use of mind-related comments, may also affect attachment of a child to their parent. Children are likely to be more securely attached to their mothers if their mothers use mind-related comments in an appropriate manner (Meins et al., 2012). The impact of parent interaction on attachment has relevance to empathy development as more secure attachment in children is related to higher empathy (Panfile & Laible, 2012). One way in which a secure attachment was found to support empathy development was via increasing a child's emotion regulation skills. A lack of sufficient parent interaction during early childhood may therefore lead a child to have difficulties in attachment and emotion regulation, which in turn affect their empathy levels.

Since lower levels of mind-related comments have been linked to CU traits (Centifanti et al., 2016), one may expect lower empathy in children with CU traits to be related to difficulties with attachment and emotion regulation. Indeed, children with higher levels of CU traits are more likely to have insecure attachments (Pasalich et al., 2012). Furthermore, children with higher levels of CU traits show behaviors that suggest they are uncomfortable with attachment-related scenarios and use different strategies to children without CU traits to regulate this. When watching a scene from a cartoon film involving the death of the lead character's father, children with high levels of CU traits show significantly higher levels of disengagement than children with low levels of CU traits (Dadds et al.,

2016). The observed disengagement increased as the film clip intensified in emotion. This suggests that the children's disengagement was a form of emotion regulation rather than due to general distraction (Dadds et al., 2016). Thus, by disengaging from attachment-related scenes, children with CU traits attempt to manage emotions by ignoring or avoiding them. This would make sense since children with CU traits have difficulties with attachment (Pasalich et al., 2012) and emotion regulation (Wagner & Waller, 2020). The increased likelihood of insecure attachment in children with CU traits may make watching intense emotional interactions with an attachment figure more difficult to process. Thus, rather than processing it, they dampen down feelings. If this perspective is held across future research studies, then it would appear that early environmental factors, such as parent–child interactions, may have a cascading effect on the development of empathy. Further research is needed to truly understand the complex network of factors involved, but targeting parent–child interactions could be a viable option to support empathy development in children with, or at risk of developing, CU traits.

What is clear is that the development of empathy and choice to be empathetic appear to depend on context. Considering empathy as something that can be modulated introduces two new perspectives from which to examine CU traits and empathy. Firstly, a person with CU traits may appear to have low levels of empathy due to a choice not to empathize. Secondly, generally low levels of empathy that have been associated with CU traits could be due to empathy development being modulated by certain environmental factors. It is also possible that both individual and developmental modulation are playing a role in tandem. For example, CU traits may relate to lower base levels of empathy due to lack of optimal environments in which strong empathy skills could develop. A lack of strong developmental foundations may mean that empathizing requires more effort, since attachment-rejection/loss could be triggered. Individuals with high levels of CU traits may thus moderate their levels of empathy by carefully choosing the best situations in which to expend this effort. If the way people with CU traits express empathy is different due to modulation, then the argument that CU traits are related to a general deficit in empathy seems unwarranted. Any limited empathy that is found in those with CU traits can be considered a choice.

Conclusion

In sum, the path to understanding the relation between empathy and CU traits, which is crucial to understand their development and contribution to offending, is not a simple one. What *is* clear is that the complexity of empathy is not illustrated by looking at empathy as a whole, but by exploring dimensions separately. The evidence suggests there is not a consistent relationship between CU traits and empathy across people. Future research needs to look at developmental pathways of empathy, factors that modulate these pathways and how this relates to the development of CU traits over time. Also, a knowledge of when and how youths with CU traits may modulate their empathy is needed. If youths with CU traits can regulate their empathy, this may result in greater harm to other people. That is, if you can switch off feeling for someone else's pain, then you can be violent toward that person without experiencing guilt or remorse. Knowing why people with CU traits make the choice to empathize or not would arguably be a more fruitful direction to take—for research and intervention but also for preventing violence.

References

American Psychiatric Association. (2013). Conduct disorder. In *Diagnostic and statistical manual of mental disorders* (5th ed.).

Andershed, H., Kerr, M., Stattin, H., & Levander, S. (2002). Psychopathic traits in non-referred youths: A new assessment tool. In *Psychopaths: Current International Perspectives* (pp. 131–158).

Anderson, N. E., & Kiehl, K. A. (2014). Psychopathy: Developmental perspectives and their implications for treatment. *Restorative Neurology and Neuroscience, 32*(1), 103–117. https://doi.org/10.3233/RNN-139001.

Anderson, N. E., & Stanford, M. S. (2012). Demonstrating emotional processing differences in psychopathy using affective ERP modulation. *Psychophysiology, 49*, 792–806. https://doi.org/10.1111/j.1469-8986.2012.01369.x.

Berntson, G. G., Cacioppo, J. T., & Quigley, K. S. (1991). Autonomic determinism: The modes of autonomic control, the doctrine of autonomic space, and the laws of autonomic constraint. *Psychological Review, 98*(4), 459–487. https://doi.org/10.1037/0033-295X.98.4.459.

Blair, R. J. R. (2001). Neurocognitive models of aggression, the antisocial personality disorders, and psychopathy. *Journal of Neurology, Neurosurgery & Psychiatry, 71*(6), 727–731. https://doi.org/10.1136/jnnp.71.6.727.

Blair, R. J. R. (2005). Responding to the emotions of others: Dissociating forms of empathy through the study of typical and psychiatric populations. *Consciousness and Cognition, 14*, 698–718. https://doi.org/10.1016/j.concog.2005.06.004.

Brislin, S. J., Buchman-Schmitt, J. M., Joiner, T. E., & Patrick, C. J. (2016). "Do unto others"? Distinct psychopathy facets predict reduced perception and tolerance of pain. *Personality Disorders: Theory, Research, and Treatment, 7*(3), 240. https://doi.org/10.1037/per0000180.

Bucchioni, G., Lelard, T., Ahmaidi, S., Godefroy, O., Krystkowiak, P., & Mouras, H. (2015). Do we feel the same empathy for loved and hated peers? *PLoS ONE, 10*(5), e0125871. https://doi.org/10.1371/journal.pone.0125871.

Cameron, C. D., Hutcherson, C. A., Ferguson, A. M., Scheffer, J. A., Hadjiandreou, E., & Inzlicht, M. (2019). Empathy is hard work: People choose to avoid empathy because of its cognitive costs. *Journal of Experimental Psychology: General, 148*(6), 962–976. https://doi.org/10.1037/xge0000595.

Centifanti, L. C. M., Meins, E., & Fernyhough, C. (2016). Callous-unemotional traits and impulsivity: Distinct longitudinal relations with mind-mindedness and understanding of others. *Journal of Child Psychology and Psychiatry, and Allied Disciplines, 57*(1), 84–92. https://doi.org/10.1111/jcpp.12445.

Centifanti, L. C. M., Qualter, P., & Padgett, G. (2010). Empathy and bullying: Exploring the influence of callous-unemotional traits. *Child Psychiatry & Human Development, 42*(2), 183–196. https://doi.org/10.1007/s10578-010-0206-1.

Cuff, B. M. P., Brown, S. J., Taylor, L., & Howat, D. J. (2014). Empathy: A review of the concept. *Emotion Review, 8*(2), 144–153. https://doi.org/10.1177/1754073914558466.

Dadds, M. R., Hawes, D. J., Frost, A. D. J., Vassallo, S., Bunn, P., Hunter, K., & Merz, S. (2009). Learning to "talk the talk": The relationship of psychopathic traits to deficits in empathy across childhood. *Journal of Child Psychology and Psychiatry and Allied Disciplines, 50*(5), 599–606. https://doi.org/10.1111/j.1469-7610.2008.02058.x.

Dadds, M. R., Nyree, G., Godbee, M., Moul, C., Pasalich, D. S., Fink, E., & Hawes, D. J. (2016). Expression and regulation of attachment-related emotions in children with conduct problems and callous-unemotional traits. *Child Psychiatry & Human Development, 47*(4), 647–656. https://doi.org/10.1007/s10578-015-0598-z.

Davis, M. H. (1980). A multidimensional approach to individual differences in empathy. *JSAS Catalog of Selected Documents in Psychology, 10*, 1–19.

Decety, J., & Jackson, P. L. (2004). The functional architecture of human empathy. *Behavioral and Cognitive Neuroscience Reviews, 3*(2), 71–100. https://doi.org/10.1177/1534582304267187.

Decety, J., Lewis, K. L., & Cowell, J. M. (2015). Specific electrophysiological components disentangle affective sharing and empathic concern in psychopathy. *Journal of Neurophysiology, 114*, 493–504. https://doi.org/10.1152/jn.00253.2015.-Empathic.

Fan, Y., & Han, S. (2008). Temporal dynamic of neural mechanisms involved in empathy for pain: An event-related brain potential study. *Neuropsychologia, 46*, 160–173. https://doi.org/10.1016/j.neuropsychologia.2007.07.023.

Fanti, K. A., Panayiotou, G., Kyranides, M. N., & Avraamides, M. N. (2016). Startle modulation during violent films: Association with callous-unemotional traits and aggressive behavior. *Motivation and Emotion, 40*, 321–333. https://doi.org/10.1007/s11031-015-9517-7.

Feshbach, N. D. (1975). Empathy in children: Some theoretical and empirical considerations. *The Counseling Psychologist, 5*(2), 25–30.

Fontaine, N. M. G., Mccrory, E. J. P., Boivin, M., Moffitt, T. E., & Viding, E. (2011). Predictors and outcomes of joint trajectories of callous-unemotional traits and conduct problems in childhood. *Journal of Abnormal Psychology, 120*(3), 730–742. https://doi.org/10.1037/a0022620

Farrant, B. M., Devine, T. A. J., Maybery, M. T., & Fletcher, J. (2012). Empathy, perspective taking and prosocial behavior: The importance of parenting practices. *Infant and Child Development, 21*(2), 175–188. https://doi.org/10.1002/icd.740.

Frick, P. J. (2004). *The inventory of callous-unemotional traits*. The University of New Orleans.

Frick, P. J., & Hare, R. D. (2001). *Antisocial process screening device: APSD*. Multi-Health Systems.

Frick, P. J., & Moffitt, T. E. (2010). *A proposal to the DSM-V childhood disorders and the ADHD and disruptive behavior disorders work groups to include a specifier to the diagnosis of conduct disorder based on the presence of callous-unemotional traits* (pp. 1–36). American Psychiatric Association.

Frick, P. J., & White, S. F. (2008). Research review: The importance of callous-unemotional traits for developmental models of aggressive and antisocial behavior. *Journal of Child Psychology and Psychiatry, 49*(4), 359–375. https://doi.org/10.1111/j.1469-7610.2007.01862.x.

Georgiou, G., Kimonis, E. R., & Fanti, K. A. (2018). What do others feel? Cognitive empathy deficits explain the association between callous-unemotional traits and conduct problems among preschool children. *European Journal of Developmental Psychology* , 1–21. https://doi.org/10.1080/17405629.2018.1478810.

Gordon, H. L., Baird, A. A., & End, A. (2004). Functional differences among those high and low on a trait measure of psychopathy. *Biological Psychiatry, 56*, 516–521. https://doi.org/10.1016/j.biopsych.2004.06.030.

Gutsell, J. N., & Inzlicht, M. (2012). Intergroup differences in the sharing of emotive states: Neural evidence of an empathy gap. *Social Cognitive and Affective Neuroscience, 7*(5), 596–603. https://doi.org/10.1093/scan/nsr035.

Harmsen, I. E. (2019). Empathy in autism spectrum disorder. *Journal of Autism and Developmental Disorders, 49*(10), 3939–3955. https://doi.org/10.1007/s10803-019-04087-w.

Hodges, S. D., & Klein, K. J. (2001). Regulating the costs of empathy: The price of being human. *The Journal of Socio-Economics, 30*(5), 437–452.

Jankowiak-Siuda, K., Rymarczyk, K., & Grabowska, A. (2011). How we empathize with others: a neurobiological perspective. *Medical Science Monitor: International Medical Journal of Experimental and Clinical Research, 17*(1), 18–24. http://www.medscimonit.com/fulltxt.php?ICID=881324.

Jolliffe, D., & Farrington, D. P. (2004). Empathy and offending: A systematic review and meta-analysis. *Aggression and Violent Behavior, 9*, 441–476. https://doi.org/10.1016/j.avb.2003.03.001.

Kahn, R. E., Frick, P. J., Youngstrom, E. A., Findling, R. L., & Youngstrom, J. K. (2012). The effects of including a callous-unemotional specifier for the diagnosis of conduct disorder. *Journal of Child Psychology and Psychiatry, 53*(3), 271–282. https://doi.org/10.1111/j.1469-7610.2011.02463.x.

Meffert, H., Gazzola, V., den Boer, J. A., Bartels, A. A. J., & Keysers, C. (2013). Reduced spontaneous but relatively normal deliberate vicarious representations in psychopathy. *Brain, 136*(8), 2550–2562. https://doi.org/10.1093/brain/awt190.

Meins, E. (2013). Sensitive attunement to infants' internal states: Operationalizing the construct of mind-mindedness. *Attachment & Human Development, 15*(5–6), 524–544. https://doi.org/10.1080/14616734.2013.830388.

Meins, E., Fernyhough, C., de Rosnay, M., Arnott, B., Leekam, S. R., & Turner, M. (2012). Mind-mindedness as a multidimensional construct: Appropriate and non-attuned mind-related comments independently predict infant–mother attachment in a socially diverse sample. *Infancy, 17*, 393–415. https://doi.org/10.1111/j.1532-7078.2011.00087.x.

Miller, J. D., Rausher, S., Hyatt, C. S., Maples, J., & Zeichner, A. (2013). Examining the relations among pain tolerance, psychopathic traits, and violent and nonviolent antisocial behavior. *Journal of Abnormal Psychology, 123*(1), 1–9. https://doi.org/10.1037/a0035072.

Milone, A., Cerniglia, L., Cristofani, C., Inguaggiato, E., Levantini, V., Masi, G., Paciello, M., Simone, F., & Muratori, P. (2019). Empathy in youths with conduct disorder and callous-unemotional traits. *Neural Plasticity*, 1–8. https://doi.org/10.1155/2019/9638973.

Moul, C., Hawes, D. J., & Dadds, M. R. (2018). Mapping the developmental pathways of child conduct problems through the neurobiology of empathy. *Neuroscience and Biobehavioral Reviews, 91*, 34–50. https://pdf.sciencedirectassets.com/271127/1-s2.0-S0149763418X00062/1-s2.0-S0149763416300707/main.pdf?X-Amz-Security-Token=AgoJb3JpZ2luX2VjENr%2F%2F%2F%2F%2F%2F%2F%2F%2F%2FwEaCXVzLWVhc3QtMSJHMEUCIQCvUnvudAtshSKy%2FXdkMOXKQ6nFqXWMIKFnJSiMIf8nSAIgPkfZE49fkT.

Pasalich, D. S., Dadds, M. R., & Hawes, D. J. (2014). Cognitive and affective empathy in children with conduct problems: Additive and interactive effects of callous-unemotional traits and autism spectrum disorders symptoms. *Psychiatry Research, 219*(3), 625–630. https://doi.org/10.1016/j.psychres.2014.06.025.

Pasalich, D. S., Dadds, M. R., Hawes, D. J., & Brennan, J. (2012). Attachment and callous-unemotional traits in children with early-onset conduct problems. *Journal of Child Psychology and Psychiatry, and Allied Disciplines, 53*(8), 838–845. https://doi.org/10.1111/j.1469-7610.2012.02544.x.

Panfile, T., & Laible, D. (2012). Attachment security and child's empathy: The mediating role of emotion regulation. *Merrill-Palmer Quarterly, 58*(1), 1–12.

Patrick, C. J., Bradley, M. M., & Lang, P. J. (1993). Emotion in the criminal psychopath: Startle reflex modulation. *Journal of Abnormal Psychology, 102*(1), 82–92.

Pisano, S., Muratori, P., Gorga, C., Levantini, V., Iuliano, R., Catone, G., Coppola, G., Milone, A., & Masi, G. (2017). Conduct disorders and psychopathy in children and adolescents: Aetiology, clinical presentation and treatment strategies of callous-unemotional traits. *Italian Journal of Pediatrics, 43*(84), 1–11. https://doi.org/10.1186/s13052-017-0404-6.

Ritter, K., Dziobek, I., Preibler, S., Rüter, A., Vater, A., Fydrich, T., Lammer, C.-H., Heekeren, H. R., & Roepke, S. (2011). Lack of empathy in patients with narcissistic personality disorder. *Psychiatry Research, 187*(1–2), 241–247.

Rowe, R., Maughan, B., Moran, P., Ford, T., Briskman, J., & Goodman, R. (2010). The role of callous and unemotional traits in the diagnosis of conduct disorder. *Journal of Child*

Psychology and Psychiatry and Allied Disciplines, 51(6), 688–695. https://doi.org/10.1111/j.1469-7610.2009.02199.x.

Siddle, D. A. T. (1991). Orienting, habituation, and resource allocation: An associative analysis. *Psychophysiology, 28*(3), 245–259. https://doi.org/10.1111/j.1469-8986.1991.tb02190.x.

Singer, T., & Lamm, C. (2009). The social neuroscience of empathy. *Annals of the New York Academy of Sciences, 1156*(1), 81–96. https://doi.org/10.5167/uzh-25655.

Thornton, L. C., Frick, P. J., Shulman, E. P., Ray, J. V., Steinberg, L., & Cauffman, E. (2015). Callous-unemotional traits and adolescents' role in group crime. *Law and Human Behavior, 39*(4), 368.

van Dongen, J. D. M. (2020). The empathic brain of psychopaths: From social science to neuroscience in empathy. *Frontiers in Psychology, 11*(695), 1–12. https://doi.org/10.3389/fpsyg.2020.00695.

Wagner, N. J., & Waller, R. (2020). Leveraging parasympathetic nervous system activity to study risk for psychopathology: The special case of callous-unemotional traits. *Neuroscience & Biobehavioral Reviews, 118*, 175–185.

Wolf, S., & Muñoz Centifanti, L. C. (2014). Recognition of pain as another deficit in young males with high callous-unemotional traits. *Child Psychiatry & Human Development, 45*, 422–432. https://doi.org/10.1007/s10578-013-0412-8.

Further Reading

Centifanti, L. C. M., Meins, E., & Fernyhough, C. (2016). Callous-unemotional traits and impulsivity: Distinct longitudinal relations with mind-mindedness and understanding of others. *Journal of Child Psychology and Psychiatry, and Allied Disciplines, 57*(1), 84–92. https://doi.org/10.1111/jcpp.12445.

Dadds, M. R., Hawes, D. J., Frost, A. D. J., Vassallo, S., Bunn, P., Hunter, K., & Merz, S. (2009). Learning to "talk the talk": The Relationship of Psychopathic Traits to Deficits in Empathy Across Childhood. *Journal of Child Psychology and Psychiatry and Allied Disciplines, 50*(5), 599–606. https://doi.org/10.1111/j.1469-7610.2008.02058.x.

Fanti, K. A., Panayiotou, G., Kyranides, M. N., & Avraamides, M. N. (2016). Startle modulation during violent films: Association with callous-unemotional traits and aggressive behavior. *Motivation and Emotion, 40*, 321–333. https://doi.org/10.1007/s11031-015-9517-7.

Frick, P. J., Ray, J. V., Thornton, L. C., & Kahn, R. E. (2014). Annual research review: A developmental psychopathology approach to understanding callous-unemotional traits in children and adolescents with serious conduct problems. *Journal of Child Psychology and Psychiatry, 55*(6), 532–548.

Northam, J., & Dadds, M. R. (2020). Is callous always cold? A critical review of the literature of emotion and the development of callous-unemotional traits in children. *Clinical Child and Family Psychology Review, 23*(5), 1–19.

Narratives Roles of Criminal Actions

8

David Canter and Donna Youngs

Key Points

- Even forensic psychology patients have agency.
- Offenders are able to characterize their roles when committing a crime.
- The Narrative Role Questionnaire (NRQ) has reliable properties with offenders.
- The NRQ has been fruitfully used with forensic psychology patients.
- Four narrative roles have been reliably identified across different samples
  - victim, professional, hero and revenger.
- There are therapeutic implications for the narrative model of antisocial behaviour.

Introduction

Organism or Person?

In law, the person is regarded as a conscious agent making decisions in the knowledge of their consequences, referred to legally as *mens rea*, unless there are some clear indications that the person was not able to know about or was unaware of the implications of his/her actions. This is at variance with a common clinical view that the bases of deviant behaviour lie within aspects of a

D. Canter (✉)
University of Liverpool, Liverpool, UK
e-mail: dvcanter@btinternet.com

D. Youngs
Kingston University, Kingston upon Thames, UK

© The Author(s), under exclusive license to Springer Nature Switzerland AG 2022   143
C. Garofalo and J. J. Sijtsema (eds.), *Clinical Forensic Psychology*,
https://doi.org/10.1007/978-3-030-80882-2_8

person's neurology, psychophysiology, personality disturbance, cognitive distortions or learnt patterns of action. These explanations undervalue the agency at the heart of deviance, which legal processes foreground. The point here is that even people with a diagnosis of paranoid schizophrenia or other severe psychoses are not typically dangerous. It is the very small proportion of these who go on to commit violent crimes (Silverstein et al., 2015). It is therefore apparent that there is always some intention and agency involved in even the most violent of mentally disturbed individuals. It is the basis of this agency that is the focus of the present chapter.

The Narrative Perspective

A growing area of forensic research draws on the ideas that people understand their lives as unfolding narratives. These help to shape their identity and their consequent actions. Their personal storylines encapsulate their interactions with others. Given the conscious, self-aware implications of a personal narrative, it may be assumed that convicted offenders and those with a psychiatric diagnosis will not have coherent personal narratives. However, an increasing number of studies are demonstrating that is not the case.

The Narrative Roles Questionnaire

To develop the understanding of personal narratives, especially in a forensic population, it was necessary to create an effective way of assessing what those narratives are. There are two levels at which this can be done. One is in relation to a particular criminal episode. The other is by considering how a person views their life trajectory. The former is the focus of the present chapter. The latter is detailed in a number of publications (Canter, 2010; Canter & Youngs, 2012). The Narrative Roles Questionnaire (NRQ) described in detail by Youngs and Canter (2012) draws on the way any narrative may be distilled into distinct roles for the central protagonist.

Psychological Underpinnings of Narratives

One strength of the narrative perspective on criminality is that it combines major theoretical viewpoints. These include cognitive, affective and identity constructs that researchers have related to criminal behaviour. All of these are apparent in explorations of offenders' personal narratives.

Replicability of Narrative Roles

A variety of recent studies have demonstrated the replicability of the underlying set of narrative roles summarized as Victim, Hero, Professional and Revenger. This has included the recent examination of suicide notes (Grayson et al., 2020), distinguishing between people involved in riots (Wilmott and Ioannou, 2017), studies of psychopathic and personality disordered offenders (Goodlad et al., 2019) and mentally disordered offenders (Spruin et al., 2014). These results have been found also with young offenders (Ioannou et al., 2018) and female offenders (Ciesla et al., 2018).

Narrative Roles, Diagnosis and Therapeutic Implications

Having established the prevalence of various narrative roles, the emerging research is exploring the practical implications for understanding mental illness and therapeutic interventions (Spruin et al., 2014; Vaughan, 2007).

Conclusions

The exploration of criminality from the perspective of an unfolding agency that encompasses an offender's identity and relationships to others, inherent in particular criminal episodes, is proving to be a fruitful area of research. The structured methodology of the Narrative Roles Questionnaire facilitates these studies, thereby providing both a theoretical framework and a viable methodology.

Organism or Person?

There is a trend in explanations of criminality to emphasize aspects of the individual that are inherently out of their control—their genetics, biology, upbringing and culture. Within the context of psychiatric explorations, criminality may be explained as an aspect of mental illness or personality disorder, using such explanations as a defence in legal proceedings. These explanations reduce concern with the offender's intentionality. If a defendant's psychopathology or genetics are the primary "cause" of criminal actions, that individual cannot be regarded as responsible for any offending. In legal terms, they do not demonstrate *mens rea*. Within the courtroom, the conscious decision to knowingly break the law gives pride of place to a person being on trial, rather than their genetics or personality, even though these aspects of the person may be used in mitigation to indicate why the person acted out as they did. In a nutshell, often the psychological viewpoint is dominated by the individual being treated as a socio-biological organism not an active agent (discussed in more detail by Canter, 2008). As a step towards increasing an understanding of how people make criminal decisions, the emerging considerations of criminals' personal narratives provide a bridge between the law and an understanding of criminal psychology by giving emphasis to the choices offenders make; how they see themselves and their milieu, aspects under their control. Rather than emphasizing features that treat them as objects of study rather than subjects for analysis.

The Narrative Perspective

The narrative framework has well-established origins in psychology (e.g. Bruner, 1987; Crossley, 2000). Proponents of this approach draw attention to the naturally storied quality of human memory and thought, highlighting the ability of the narrative to "vivify and integrate life and make it... meaningful" (McAdams, 2001, p. 101). It offers a causal process that can inform understanding of the immediate and direct influences on specific patterns of offending action. In the criminal context, Canter (1994) was one of the first to draw on the narrative approach to show how offenders' personal storylines provide a richer understanding of the meaning of their offending than dispositional or social theories. He argued that as part of a story or narrative form, motivation and meaning necessarily become part of the intention to act; the dynamic process that is required to move the drama forward. By understanding the narrative then, we get closer to understanding the action. In this way, it is clear that the offenders' narratives can operate as what Presser (2009) calls "key instigators of action", contributing to explanations of "the neglected... here and now of crime" (p. 179).

Presser's (2009) argument is an updating of Toch's (1993) exploration of the violent men's stories he studied. Toch showed that the offending is an enactment of the narrative rather than the narrative simply being an interpretation of the context out of which the offence has emerged. Presser elaborates this viewpoint with a conceptualization "that effectively blurs the distinction between narrative and experience by suggesting that experience is always known and acted upon as it has been interpreted symbolically" (Presser, 2009, p. 184), rather than the narrative operating as a post hoc, interpretative device. Understood in this way, it becomes clear that the narrative framework has the potential to explain what Presser (2009), in her call for a narrative criminology, describes as "dynamic factors at the point of behaviour". This is an application that represents a clear development from McAdams' (1985, 2001, 2006) important work. That showed the usefulness of a narrative perspective in providing an underlying coherence to human experience over time. This was both by explaining how events have unfolded in a life story and as a psychological form for recognizing consistencies in personality and identity. Maruna (2001) draws attention to this potential for a general causal role, showing that different self-narratives are themselves implicated in whether offenders desist from crime or not. This agentic, narrative framework emphasizes the identity of deviant individuals as being embedded in their life stories and roles acted out during offences (Rowlands et al., 2019).

The Narrative Roles Questionnaire (NRQ)

Although narrative researchers expect an overall coherence over a lifetime, Presser (2009) claims that at any point in time narrative themes may change too quickly to measure. Consequently, to discern themes and related psychological meaning of particular episodes, a measure that focuses on the role experienced within an offending event may usefully encapsulate the inherent narrative that sustains and informs that event. The offending role can operate as a nonthreatening summary of a criminal narrative theme.

The focus on the description of an offender's experience of a criminal event does not require personal justification or emphasize social desirability of the response. Asking a person about the role they played during a crime, rather than an overt life-story interview, reveals the presence of narrative themes of which the individual may not be aware. The technique is particularly powerful with narrative themes that are socially unacceptable, such as greed or jealousy. The techniques may also prove useful where respondents cannot articulate the relevant themes. Offence event roles, therefore, provide a medium through which implicit narrative processes are given tangible form. They can be related to a given illegal context, capturing the quality of the agency that is underpinning the action in that event.

The offence narrative role is proposed as a distillation of an underlying story line or narrative focus. It captures the protagonist's agency and intent in relation to a specific crime event. To capture the quality of this agency, allowing the characterization of an offence narrative requires the measurement of the components of the roles. Any such measure has to draw on concepts and ideas that are meaningful to offenders and to present these in language and words used by offenders to describe their crimes.

The starting point for the development of a Narrative Roles Questionnaire (NRQ) was therefore offenders' own accounts of their experiences of committing a crime. A series of intensive, open-ended interviews were conducted with 38 offenders convicted for a variety of offence types that ranged from burglary to violence. They were asked to describe their experiences when committing a recent offence. The interviews were transcribed and subjected to a detailed content analysis to elicit core issues. This content was grouped into themes and a representative verbatim statement from the interviews selected to capture each issue.

The resulting set of 33 statements drawn from the interviews is listed in Table 8.1 (taken from Youngs & Canter, 2012). These statements capture the key descriptions of the interpretation of the event and justification of the offending actions. Respondents indicate how much each description fits their experience using a five-point Likert scale "not at all; just a little; some; a lot; very much indeed".

These statements comprised the first version of the NRQ. Other versions have been developed by other research teams to give different emphases (e.g. Ioannou et al., 2015) as well as a short-form 12 item version that also has been shown to have validity (Canter, 2021).

These statements are post-offence verbalizations. As such, they may be distorted by memory issues as well as post-offence developments such as a conviction. The issue of post-offence rewriting raises the general issue of the validity of self-reported narrative accounts. The phenomenological approach takes the stand that a person's account is their subjective perception and should be taken at face value. It does not have to be regarded as objective fact but can be taken to indicate the constructs and the individual's related perspectives. It shows how they wish to be seen, which is relevant, for example, to setting up interviews (see Youngs & Canter, 2009) and therapeutic interventions (Rowlands et al., 2019). All the narratives in personal accounts have an element of justification, but there is value in exploring the particular form the justifications take.

Table 8.1 Narrative Roles Questionnaire (NRQ) used to indicate roles criminals saw themselves as playing while committing a crime (from Youngs & Canter, 2012)

1.	I was like a professional
2.	I had to do it
3.	It was fun
4.	It was right
5.	It was interesting
6.	It was like an adventure
7.	It was routine
8.	I was in control
9.	It was exciting
10.	I was doing a job
11.	I knew what I was doing
12.	It was the only thing to do
13.	It was a mission
14.	Nothing else mattered
15.	I had power
16.	I was helpless
17.	It was my only choice
18.	I was a victim
19.	I was confused about what was happening
20.	I was looking for recognition
21.	I just wanted to get it over with
22.	I didn't care what would happen
23.	What was happening was just fate
24.	It all went to plan
25.	I couldn't stop myself
26.	It was like I wasn't part of it
27.	It was a manly thing to do
28.	For me, it was like a usual day's work
29.	I was trying to get revenge
30.	There was nothing special about what happened
31.	I was getting my own back
32.	I knew I was taking a risk
33.	I guess I always knew it was going to happen

Offence Narrative Roles

In the context of life narratives or self-stories, McAdams (1985) argues that personal myths are organized according to two themes that he terms agency and communion. Agency is concerned with power and achievement and communion with love and intimacy. These map onto the two primary psychological dimensions underpinning the differences in human functioning that have emerged across a range of areas of psychology. These include considerations of interpersonal tendency, explorations of life-story identity themes, theories of self-strivings and motivational trends. For example, Leary's (1957) consideration of interpersonal personality has two dimensions: Dominance/Submission and Love/Hate. Dimensional analyses of Schutz's (1992) widely used Fundamental Interpersonal Relations Orientation-Behavior (FIRO) theory of interpersonal tendency (e.g. Dancer & Woods, 2006) suggest that his original three dimensions of behavioural orientation may be better conceptualized as the two dimensions of Control and Openness/Inclusion. These clearly echo Leary's personality dimensions. Herman's (1996) ideas on the self, its strivings and meaning in life have two very similar motivational trends that distinguish between "S" motives, which are strivings for superiority, power and expansion, and "O" motives, which are strivings for contact and intimacy with others. All of these models of individual differences support two fundamental psychological constructs—potency and intimacy. One key challenge in developing these ideas as the basis for distinguishing particular narrative offending roles is to understand how the psychological processes of intimacy and potency may manifest in the criminal context.

Youngs and Canter (2011) argue that in criminal terms, rather than as concern with love and warm interactions with others, intimacy may be better understood as a measure of the relevance for the offender of the victim and the significance of the impact of the offending on the victim in allowing the offender to attain the objectives he/she seeks. High levels of intimacy would produce an overall approach to offending that reveal an acute awareness of the victim and an explicit desire to affect him or her. For those high on intimacy then, the criminal activity would be conceptualized by the offender as some form of interpersonal transaction with the victim.

Potency can be understood as the imposing of the offender's will rather than as productive strength and agency. High levels of potency would produce an approach to offending where offenders see themselves as taking charge, focused on maximizing gains. For those offenders high on potency, criminal activity is the conquering, or mastery, of the environment and/or victim. Violence in an attempt to control a spouse is an example of potency and intimacy. But when the violence is part of theft, as in a bank robbery, it exhibits potency but little intimacy. The emphasis on potency or intimacy can also be found within criminals' patterns of behaviour. Studies of criminal specialization, modus operandi or offending style (Canter & Fritzon, 1998; Salfati & Canter, 1999; Youngs, 2004) have consistently found support for the distinction between Instrumental/Proactive offending and Expressive/ Reactive offending (Chapter 19) as well as between an Object or Property target for this activity in contrast to a Person-focused target. These distinctions in the actual activities of offenders have parallels to variations in potency and intimacy. The focus on either property or person-focused offending patterns picks up differences in the desire and willingness to interact with others that would be produced by different levels of intimacy. Similarly, offending activities that are "instrumental" capture the tendency to dominate and take charge that is produced by high levels of potency. This distinction therefore draws attention to the different forms of sexual offences. Those against strangers in which sexual gratification is the central focus are very different from those against intimates or where violence is an important part of the crime.

There is a long tradition within literature studies that argues for a limited number of fundamental storylines in any culture. One of the most widely cited authorities on this is Frye (1957). Although Frye was at pains to emphasize that these basic stories were only to be found in fiction, real life is far more complicated. Nonetheless, there has been growing evidence, reviewed below, that a limited number of narratives underlie personal accounts of events and life stories. It is possible to show how these relate to the combinations of high and low levels of potency and high and low levels of intimacy. These four dominant themes in offenders' narratives intriguingly encapsulate a number of psychological processes.

The Revengeful Mission

When the protagonists see themselves as strong and powerful, seeking a particular impact on another person(s). This is underpinned by high criminal levels of potency and intimacy. It relates to distorted cognitions about the ends or consequences of their actions, while accepting responsibility for the means. The adoption of this role is associated with a calm, non-aroused, but negative emotional state. It can be seen as related to Frye's (1957) a Romantic Quest fundamental narrative, but in the criminal context is best described as the Revengeful Mission role.

Individual items in the NRQ, that reflect this role, help to elaborate its implications as Youngs and Canter (2012) demonstrate. Items that indicate a perception of the offending activity as having a very specific purpose (*Had to Do It*) that it was a justified response (*It Was Right*) to a wrong (*Getting Own Back; Revenge*) reveal the narrative mission of the offence. Central to this offending experience is a sense of singular commitment to and obligation in this purpose (*Only Choice; Nothing Else Mattered; Only Thing to Do*), whatever the consequences (*Didn't Care; Fate*). Taken together, these descriptions of the offending experience suggest the core Revenger role that the offender sees himself or herself as acting out.

Tragic Hero

Low levels of potency and intimacy involve the attribution of the responsibility to others as well as the dismissal of the harm done. The victim is irrelevant. Adoption of this role is associated with an aroused but not entirely negative emotional state. This accords with what Frye (1957) identifies as typical of those accounts in which the hero is brought down by the fates, a Tragedy.

The NRQ items which illustrate this depict an experience of offending as an opportunity to prove oneself (*Looking for Recognition*), to demonstrate prowess (*Manly*). They paint a picture of someone who sees himself or herself, as caught up in something highly significant (*Mission*) and overtaken by this all-encompassing assignment (*Wasn't Part of It; Couldn't Stop*). In overall terms, this covers an offending experience in which the individual sees himself or herself and the role she or he is playing as that of a Hero.

The Professional

High levels of potency but low levels of criminal intimacy are typical of an offence that is an opportunity for the protagonist to demonstrate his strength and expertise. The focus is on this mastery of the environment in pursuit of the gains sought rather than the victim or target. There are cognitive distortions produced by a combination of ignoring the victim, yet owning responsibility for the offence actions but reinterpreting the end consequences in one's own terms. The emotional state that facilitates the adoption of this role during the commission of the offence is one of calm, non-aroused, neutrality. Frye's (1957) Adventure fits this profile, indicating in the criminal context a Professional role.

The NRQ items characterize an individual who sees himself or herself as simply carrying out a task (*Doing a Job; Usual Day's Work*) and who feels a sense of satisfaction in that (e.g. *Interesting; Fun*). The items reflect a pragmatic, methodical approach to the offence (*All to Plan; Routine*). Central to this role is a keen sense of competency (e.g. *In Control; Knew What Doing*). Competency extends to an acute awareness of the potential risks associated with the activity being carried out (*Taking a Risk*). It is a role that can be readily understood as one that would emerge from an underlying life narrative of adventure (Frye uses the term "romance"). This is a story of the protagonist's victorious mastery of his or her environment as a Professional.

The Victim

Those individuals who feel they are powerless, low in potency, see themselves as suffering from what is done to them. This being a form of criminal intimacy and creates a role where the protagonist sees the offence as a consequence of helplessness at the hands of others. Within this role, responsibility is attributed to others and the offender is in an aroused, negative emotional state. The crime is interpreted by the offender as happening as a result of his confused, vulnerability and feelings of alienation from others. He sees himself as a Victim.

This offending experience is against the protagonist's will (*Wanted It Over*), out of their control (*Helpless*) and beyond their understanding (*Confused*). As captured by the key item Victim, the Victim role, in its impotency and disengagement, is consistent with Frye's broader Irony narrative (Frye, 1957). The Irony narrative is a life story underpinned by a sense that nothing makes any sense, there are no rules and nothing matters.

Table 8.2 summarizes the relationships between these four roles and the two psychological facets. That table can also be regarded as a hypothesized structure to be tested in the co-occurrences of sets of items drawn from the NRQ listed in Table 8.1. This is the structure found by Youngs and Canter (2012) from the analysis of responses from 72 convicted offenders.

Table 8.2 Relationship of fundamental psychological facet to narrative themes

Potency	Intimacy	
	High	Low
High	**Revengeful mission**	**Professional**
Low	**The victim**	**Tragic hero**

Psychological Aspects of Narratives

It is useful to specify directly the cognitive, affective and identity constructs that researchers have related to criminal behaviour which are drawn together within the narratives of offenders' roles.

Cognitive Components

Sykes and Matza (1957) propose a number of techniques of neutralization from their work on offenders' verbalizations: denial of injury, denial of responsibility, denial of the victim and condemnation of those who condemn, and an appeal to other, higher loyalties (see Chapter 4). Further, Bandura's (1990) strategies for "moral disengagement" in which criminals displace responsibility, diffuse responsibility, dehumanize the victim, assume the role of victim for oneself and distort the consequences of the action, carry narrative implications.

Maruna and Copes (2005) claim that these different neutralizations will connect with different forms of narrative. Youngs and Canter (2011) argue that those cognitions that are less focused on the impact of the crime, such as dismissing or minimizing the harm to the victim, will be part of rather different roles than cognitions that are centrally concerned with the impact. In other words, when intimacy is high and the offender is highly aware of the impact on the victim, the justificatory distortions in the interpretation of events will not minimize the harm but instead take the form of focusing on the offender's objectives. Youngs and Canter (2011) argue that low levels of potency produce a tendency to attribute the responsibility for the situation and the actions to others, for example, Sykes and Matza's (1957) denial of responsibility; Bandura's (1990) displacement of responsibility and diffusion of responsibility. In contrast, high levels of potency delineate a role within which the protagonist owns not only the actions but also the evaluation of them, refusing to submit to the judgements of others (Sykes and Matza's condemnation of the condemner or appeal to higher loyalties; Bandura's distortion of the consequences).

Items in the NRQ that minimize the impact on the victim are, for example, those that imply the action was not targeting them, "Doing a Job". The item "Getting Own Back" is also consistent with a harm minimization strategy; harm to the victim is minimized by the suggestion that they deserved it in some way. A high-intimacy concern with the impact in relation to the offender's objectives is items such as "It was a mission" and "I was looking for recognition".

Affective Components

Russell (1997) has demonstrated that emotional experience is underpinned by two major bipolar dimensions, arousal/non-arousal and pleasure/displeasure (Chapter 5). Four broad mood classes emerge from the combination of these: Elation (High Arousal, High Pleasure), Distress (High Arousal, High Displeasure), Depression (Low Arousal, High Displeasure) and Calm (Low Arousal, High Pleasure). Katz (1988) argues for the central relevance of affective states to crime. He offers in-depth descriptions of "sneaky thrills", humiliation, feelings of righteousness and cynicism as enticements to offend. Canter and Ioannou (2004) have developed this argument by considering the emotions typically associated with different types of crime.

From a narrative viewpoint, in the criminal context, a higher tendency towards intimacy will be associated with greater displeasure derived from the offending. However, in some cases, the desire for impact on others will take the form of seeking recognition rather than acting on an individual. With this lack of direct contact, an actively negative state of displeasure will not be present. Direct contact may mediate the generation of displeasure, such that displeasurable states occur only where there is direct contact with a victim. Other aspects of offending will generate some mildly positive affect. Less aroused or activated states during a crime are associated with higher levels of criminal potency where the offender is imposing his/her will. Where the offender does not feel in control, this lower potency will produce a more aroused emotional state.

The differences in the displeasure–pleasure dimension of the emotional state are revealed in items in the NRQ. There are positive descriptions (e.g. Interesting, Exciting, Fun). The items that reflect a negative mood and feelings of displeasure are "I was helpless" and "I just wanted to get it over with". The lower levels of arousal, associated with high potency, includes the NRQ items, "There was nothing special about what happened" and "It was routine". These contrast with items that reveal a more heightened emotional state during the crime, for example, "Nothing else mattered" and "I was confused about what was happening".

Identity Components

The proposition that all offending may be conceptualized as a form of interpersonal transaction, whether implicit or explicit (Canter, 1994), leads to the view that during an offence, the salient components of identity will be those that concern the offender's self-awareness relative to the victim or target of his actions.

The common theme to all potential offence identities is psychological strength and dominance. Roles will be delineated in terms of the extent to which the offender sees himself or herself as stronger rather than weaker than his or her victim, having the ability to dominate the commission of the offence.

The NRQ items that capture this aspect of offender's narratives are those that indicate a self-concept of weakness (e.g. "I was helpless") being distinct from those who see themselves as strong (e.g. "It was a manly thing to do"; "I had power"). They include self-awareness descriptions that reference how s/he might be seen by others such as an offender "looking for recognition". Items also indicate aspects of self-presentation "I was a victim" and low-intimacy in wihc others are not relevant (e.g. "I was a professional").

Replicability of Narrative Roles

A variety of studies, briefly reviewed here, have demonstrated the replicability of the underlying set of narrative roles; summarized as Victim, Hero, Professional and Revenger. This has included the recent examination by Grayson et al. (2020) who analysed 100 suicide notes (of non-offenders) using a multi-dimensional scaling (MDS) procedure. They labelled the various roles revealed within the notes: Egoistic Victim, Anomic Hero, Altruistic Professional and Fatalistic Revenger. There are implications for therapeutic interventions for people with different forms of suicidal ideation. The different emphases in the suicidal roles from those for a prisoner population indicate the ways in which the narrative framework appropriately takes on diverse foci in different contexts.

Another distinct context is the consideration of people involved in riots. Wilmott and Ioannou (2017) subjected the accounts given by 20 rioters to content analysis and MDS. They found the four themes of Professional Rioter, Revenger Rioter, Victim Rioter and Adventurer Rioter. These differences challenge the view that riots are perpetrated by a homogenous unthinking mass. This has consequences for the management of public demonstrations. A short form of the NRQ completed anonymously by people invited to take part over twitter, describing illegal acts they had carried out, also generated the fourfold narrative structure (Canter, 2021).

A study of 128 female offenders by Ciesla et al. (2018) revealed two dominant themes which they called "Avenging Angel" and "Choiceless Victim", the latter being the dominant theme. It is interesting that the Professional Role and Adventurer were not identified in this study of women criminals. This accords with many studies revealing that female offending tends to be shaped rather differently from male offending.

The relationship of risk factors to narrative roles in 23 young offenders was explored by Ioannou and her colleagues (2018). They identified three rather than four dominant narratives: "Calm Professional", "Elated Hero" and a combined theme of "Distressed Revenger" and "Depressed Victim". The small sample may have been one reason why the latter two were not differentiated, but the results broadly accord with many studies of emotional distinctions between the positively charged Professional and Hero and the negative emotions associate with revenge and being a victim initially discussed by Canter and Ioannou (2004) and more recently explored by Ioannou et al. (2017).

Narrative Roles, Diagnosis and Therapeutic Implications

Of particular note in the clinical context are narrative perspectives on people with mental disorder or diagnosed personality disorders who come into contact with the law. It may be assumed that such individuals are so cognitively incoherent that it would not be possible to identify distinct narratives. However, a growing number of studies are demonstrating that not only do they reveal clear narratives but that these elucidate the nature of their mental conditions.

Spruin et al. (2014) had 70 adult mentally disordered offenders complete the NRQ. The MDS analysis of the results revealed the same four narrative themes as in other studies.

Those with major mental illnesses were found to encounter negative criminal experiences across all crime types. Their offending was often triggered by a sense of sadness and loneliness, which they cannot control. These feelings are associated with helplessness and confusion, carrying out crimes, not really understanding why, but feeling as though it is their only option. This is reflected in a clear *Depressed Victim* theme. By contrast, patients with personality disorders displayed a moderately intense criminal experience within the *Angry Revenger* theme when committing person-centred offences. This suggests that their violent actions are driven by feelings of anger and irritation, along with the desire to seek vengeance.

In a smaller-scale study, Goodlad et al. (2019) examined the responses on the NRQ from 21 psychopathic and personality disordered offenders. Their MDS analysis also revealed the four narrative themes. Those diagnosed with borderline personality disorder were most likely to generate a "depressed victim" profile, but the sample was not large enough to indicate any other relationships between diagnosis and narrative theme.

The potential of a narrative approach for therapeutic interventions with drug addicts has been demonstrated by Rowlands et al. (2018). They showed that those who embraced more clearly agentic roles were more likely to keep away from substance abuse. This suggests that interventions that enhance their feelings of significance are likely to be of values. This study is especially fruitful in pointing to the sorts of therapeutic implications that can be garnered from working with forensic patients' views of their personal narratives and episodic role playing. The indications are that, contrary to what might be assumed, especially about people with extreme mental disorders, it is possible to explore with them how they see their lives and the roles they play when acting criminally. Helping them to reconstrue their actions in the light of more socially acceptable narratives opens a form of therapy that has been successful with offenders (Maruna, 2001), relating to the "good lives model" intervention approach (e.g. Purvis et al., 2011) (Chapter 27). The prospect indicated here is that it could also be of value with forensic patients.

Conclusions

The approach taken here recognizes diversity, against a background of a finite set of themes. These storylines are drawn from common experiences embedded within a given culture. The narrative roles derived from the primary concepts of power and intimacy capture four different emphases within a systemic model of variation, rather than discrete categories as might be implied by typological classifications. Within this thematic structure, individuals' narrative roles for any given episode reflect unique aspects of a person's cognitions, emotions and identity.

It must be emphasized that the essence of narratives is that they are dynamic, unfolding entities. The assumption is that they will change both over time and in relation to any particular context. These are not thought of as relatively stable personality aspects of an individual, like Extraversion or Openness. They are a summary of a person's experience and identity at a particular stage in their life, or during a particular episode. Future research is needed to explore how these narratives vary over the life course and in relation to different forms of criminal activity. That, of course, is not easy to carry out because offenders notoriously have disorganized kief-styles. This makes following them up over time challenging,

The Professional, Victim, Tragic Hero and Revengeful Mission roles, because they capture the intention to act that is the essential component that drives a narrative construction (rather than less immediate motivational factors and influences), get closer to understanding the processes through which action is instigated and sustained through the offence (Canter, 1994). This is the issue that Presser (2009) summarized as a question of "why this action here and now?" (p. 189). This is an application of the narrative framework to crime psychology that goes beyond work exploring post hoc interpretations of circumstances and unfolding events within offenders' life stories. It builds on the potential for the narrative perspective which recognizes redemption (as opposed to contamination) self-stories in facilitating desistance from crime (Maruna, 2001).

The key to this is enabling offenders to understand the role they are assigning themselves. Do they think of themselves, for example, as victims or heroes? By engaging with the implications of this self-reflection, they can reassess their actions and reconstruct their personal narratives with implications for how they act. Following Maruna (2001), they can reconstruct a positive view of their future in which they find ways of redeeming themselves through contributing to society. They avoid assuming that they are inevitably part of a contaminated social context in which criminality is inevitable. Many criminals' autobiographies illustrate the impact of an (often sudden) self-awareness in which they realize they are not beholden to the contamination of their criminal context and can reconstrue the possibility of acting positive roles in society. It proposes that particular narratives, operating through offence roles, act positively to drive specific criminal action patterns; and that different offending styles are underpinned by different narrative processes. Breaking free from a destructive narrative perspective and its associated criminal roles allows the offender to find new non-criminal opportunities.

The identification of different Narrative Offence Roles is a pathway to two distinct but interrelated developments for the narrative approach within forensic psychology. One explores which narratives underpin which criminal actions. Canter and Youngs (2009) offer some more detailed ideas about the action patterns that may relate to particular themes. A second considers which offenders report which narratives. This has been explored to some extent in the non-criminal context, although much of the focus of this work has been on the correlates of narrative complexity (e.g. deVries & Lehman, 1996). How the substantive content of a criminal narrative role relates to the cultural context, personal background, personality, intellectual or other psychological characteristics of an offender remains to be established. Crucially, though, this approach provides a systematic framework for putting the criminal centre stage in an offender's own story, rather than being merely an organism whose actions are to be explained by genetics, biology and social circumstances.

References

Bandura, A. (1990). Mechanisms of moral disengagement. In A. Reich (Ed.), *Origins of terrorism; psychologies, ideologies, theologies, sates of mind* (pp. 161–191). Cambridge University Press.

Bruner, J. (1987). Life as narrative. *Social Research, 54*(1), 11.

Canter, D. (1994). *Criminal shadows: The inner narratives of evil.* HarperCollins.

Canter, D. V. (2008). In the kingdom of the blind. In D. Canter & R. Zukauskiene (Eds.), *Psychology and law: Bridging the gap* (pp. 1–22). Ashgate.

Canter, D. (2010). Criminals' personal narratives. In *Cambridge handbook of forensic psychology* (pp. 791–794). Cambridge University Press.

Canter, D. (2021) *Experiments in anti-social behaviour: Ten studies for students.* Routledge (Study 6).

Canter, D., & Fritzon, K. (1998). Differentiating arsonists: A model of firesetting actions and characteristics. *Journal of Legal and Criminological Psychology, 3,* 73–96.

Canter, D., & Ioannou. . (2004). Criminal emotions experienced during crimes. *International Journal of Forensic Psychology, 1,* 71–81.

Canter, D., & Youngs, D. (2012). Narratives of criminal action and forensic psychology. *Legal and Criminal Psychology, 17,* 262–275.

Canter, D. V., & Youngs, D. E. (2009). *Investigative psychology: Offender profiling and the analysis of criminal action.* Wiley.

Ciesla, K., Ioannou, M., & Hammond, L. (2018). Women offenders' emotional experience of crime. *Journal of Investigative Psychology and Offender Profiling,* 1–15. https://doi.org/10.1002/jip.1512.

Crossley, M. L. (2000) *Introducing narrative Ppsychology: Self,trauma and the construction of meaning.* Buckingham: Open University Press.

Dancer, L. J., & Woods, S. A. (2006). Higher-order factor structures and intercorrelations of the 16PF5 and FIRO-B. *International Journal of Selection and Assessment, 14*(4), 385–391.

deVries, B., & Lehman, A. J. (1996). The complexity of personal narratives. In J. E. Birren, G. M. Kenyon, J. E. Ruth, J. J. Schroots, & T. Svensson (Eds.), *Aging and biography: Explorations in adult development* (pp. 149–166). Springer.

Frye, N. (1957). *Anatomy of criticism: Four essays.* Princeton University Press.

Goodlad, K., Ioannou, M., & Hunter, M. (2019) The criminal narrative experience of psychopathic and personality disordered offenders. *International Journal of Offender Therapy and Comparative Criminology, 62*(4), 523–542. https://doi.org/10.1177/0306624X18808433.

Grayson, S., Tzani-Pepelasi, C., Pylarinou, N.-P., Ioannou, M., & Artinopoulou, V. (2020) Examining the narrative roles in suicide notes. *Journal of Investigative Psychology and Offender Profiling*, 1–18.https://doi.org/10.1002/jip.1545.

Hermans, H. J. M. (1996). Voicing the self: From information processing to dialogical interchange. *Psychological Bulletin, 119*(1), 31–50. https://doi.org/10.1037/0033-2909.119.1.31

Ioannou, M., Canter, D., Youngs, D., & Synott, J. (2015). Offenders' crime narratives across different types of crime. *Journal of Forensic Psychology Practice, 15*, 383–400. https://doi.org/10.1080/15228932.2015.1065620

Ioannou, M., Canter, D., & Youngs, D. (2017). Criminal narrative experience: Relating emotions to offence narrative roles during crime commission. *International Journal of Offender Therapy and Comparative Criminology., 61*(14), 1531–1553.

Ioannou, M., Synnott, J., Lowe, E., & Tzani-Pepelasi, C. (2018). Applying the criminal narrative experience framework to young offenders. *International Journal of Offender Therapy and Comparative Criminology., 62*(13), 4091–4107. https://doi.org/10.1177/0306624X18774312

Katz, J. (1988). *Seductions of crime: Moral and sensual attractions in doing evil*. Basic Books.

Leary, T. (1957). *Interpersonal diagnosis of personality; a functional theory and methodology for personality evaluation*. Ronald Press.

Maruna, S. (2001). *Making good: How ex-convicts reform and rebuild their lives*. American Psychological Association Books.

Maruna,S., & Copes, H. (2005). What have we learned from five decades of neutralization research? *Crime and Justice, 32*. https://doi.org/10.1086/655355

McAdams, D. P. (1985). *Power, intimacy, and the life story: Personological inquiries into identity*. Guilford Press.

McAdams, D. P. (2001). The psychology of life stories. *Review of General Psychology, 5*(2), 100–122.

Presser, L. (2009). The narratives of offenders. *Theoretical Criminology, 13*, 177–200.

Rowlands, D., Youngs, D. E., & Canter, D. V. (2018). Exploring an agency-communion model of identity transformation in recovery from substance misuse. *Journal of Substance Use, 24*, 265–272. https://doi.org/10.1080/14659891.2018.155273

Rowlands, D., Youngs, D. E., & Canter, D. V. (2019). Themes of agency and communion and rehabilitation from substance misuse. *Drug and Alcohol Dependence, 205*(1), 107611. https://doi.org/10.1016/j.drugalcdep.2019.107611

Russell, J. (1997). How shall an emotion be called? In R. Plutchik & H. R. Conte (Eds.), *Circumplex models of personality and emotions*. American Psychological Association.

Salfati, G., & Canter, D. (1999). Differentiating stranger murders: Profiling offender characteristics from behavioral styles. *Behavioral Sciences and the Law*, 391–406.

Schutz, W. (1992). Beyond FIRO-B-3 new theory derived measures—Element B: Behaviour, element F: Feelings, element S: Self. *Psychological Reports, 70*, 915–937.

Silverstein, S. M., Del Pozzo, J., Roche, M., Boye, D., & Miskimen,T. (2015). *Schizophrenia and violence: Realities and recommendations*. Crime Psychology Review, 1(1), 21–42.

Spruin, E., Canter, D., Youngs, D., & Coulston, B. (2014). Criminal narratives of mentally disordered offenders: An exploratory study. *Journal of Forensic Psychology Practice, 14*(5), 438–455. https://doi.org/10.1080/15228932.2014.965987

Sykes, G. M., & Matza, D. (1957). Techniques of neutralisation: A theory of delinquency. *American Sociological Review, 22*, 664–673.

Toch, T. (1993). Good violence and bad violence: Self-presentations of aggressors through accounts and war stories. In R. B. Felson and J. T. Tedeschi (Eds.), *Aggression and violence: Social interactionist perspectives* (pp. 193–206). American Psychological Association.

Vaughan, B. (2007). The internal narrative of desistance. *British Journal of Criminology, 47*, 390–404. https://doi.org/10.1093/bjc/az1083

Wilmott, D., & Ioannou, M. (2017). A narrative based model of differentiating rioters. *The Howard Journal, 56*(1), 105–124. https://doi.org/10.111/hojo.12194.

Youngs, D. (2004). Personality correlates of offence style. *Journal of Investigative Psychology and Offender Profiling, 1*(1), 99–119.

Youngs, D., & Canter, D. (2009). An emerging research agenda for investigative interviewing: Hypotheses from the narrative action system. *Journal of Investigative Psychology and Offender Profiling, 6*(2), 91–99.

Youngs, D., & Canter, D. (2011). Narrative roles in criminal action: An integrative framework for differentiating offenders. *Legal and Criminological Psychology, 17*, 233–249.

Youngs, D. E., & Canter, D. V. (2012). Offenders crime narratives as revealed by the narrative roles questionnaire. *International Journal of Offender Therapy and Comparative Criminology*, 1–23. https://doi.org/10.1177/0306624X11434577.

Further Readings suggestion

Canter. D. (1994). *Criminal shadows: The inner narratives of evil.* HarperCollins

McAdams, D. P. (2006). *The redemptive self: Stories Americans live by.* Oxford University Press.

Attachment Theory and Offending

9

Gwen Adshead and Estelle Moore

Key Points

In this chapter, we set out

- some of the basic concepts that make up attachment theory
- why attachment theory is a useful paradigm in forensic psychology
- research into attachment insecurity and offending
- how understanding attachment theory helps formulate risk and plan interventions
- the influence of attachment on therapeutic relationships.

Introduction

In this chapter, we set out some of the basic concepts that make up attachment theory. We explain why attachment theory is a useful paradigm in forensic psychology with reference to published research into the relevance of attachment security and insecurity for offending risk. We set out how an understanding of attachment theory helps professionals formulate risk and plan interventions

G. Adshead (✉)
Forensic Psychiatrist and Psychotherapist, West London Trust, Broadmoor Hospital, Crowthorne, UK
e-mail: g.adshead@nhs.net

E. Moore
Consultant Clinical and Forensic Psychologist, Head of Psychological Services, West London Trust, Broadmoor Hospital, Crowthorne, UK
e-mail: Estelle.Moore@westlondon.nhs.uk

© The Author(s), under exclusive license to Springer Nature Switzerland AG 2022   163
C. Garofalo and J. J. Sijtsema (eds.), *Clinical Forensic Psychology*,
https://doi.org/10.1007/978-3-030-80882-2_9

with offenders and we remind professionals of the importance of considering the influence of attachment on therapeutic relationships.

Background

Attachment theory is a clinical and empirical approach to the study of how humans make and maintain relationships across time. Moreover, it explains how humans use those relationships to manage stress and pain, or whenever vulnerable or in need. Based on animal observation as well as studies of humans (particularly in infancy), attachment theory was developed by John Bowlby as a way to understand the dynamics of close relationships in which people care for one another (Bowlby, 1969, 1973). Attachment theory's emphasis on relationships makes it of relevance and utility in forensic settings; not only because so much violent offending arises in the context of relationships, but also because relationships are key to both the psychological treatment of offenders and the secure environments in which they are detained (Adshead & Aiyegbusi, 2014; Willmot & McMurran, 2016).

Attachment theory became a valuable research paradigm for understanding how children's relationships with their carers impact on their later emotional and intellectual development. Most of the early research in attachment theory involved the study of the attachment bond between mothers and children. This early work (Ainsworth et al., 2015; Bretherton, 1992) work found that an attachment bond builds up between a carer and child in the first 1000 days of life, and that bond can be characterised as 'secure' or 'insecure' in terms of how the infant reacted to relational stress and anxiety. Ainsworth et al., (2015: pxxxi) described three different categories of attachment bond: the secure group (B) who seemed to manage their distress by getting close to others, an avoidant (A) group who seemed to avoid closeness when distressed and an ambivalent (C) group who oscillated between seeking care and withdrawing from it. Later research by Main and Solomon (1990) described a third category of insecurity (disorganised: D) in which children seemed disorientated and frightened when separated from their carers but displayed odd and even aggressive behaviours on reunion.

The significance of the distinction between secure and insecure attachment is that children categorised as insecure (the A, C or D groups) were also children who developed emotional and behavioural problems. Prospective follow-up studies by Sroufe in Minnesota (2005, 2016) explored the stability of attachment security and insecurity in children across a thirty year time span. Three important findings emerged. First, attachment security or insecurity tended to be stable across time; insecure children tended to become insecure adolescents who tended to become insecure adults. Second, although attachment security seemed stable, it was by no means fixed; children who were insecurely attached could become securely attached if they had positive experiences of care; and children who were exposed to trauma or stress could become insecurely attached; the implication being that there was some flexibility in the attachment system in children and young people. Finally, and most importantly for forensic psychology, the Minnesota studies found an association between childhood insecurity of attachment and personality dysfunction (Sroufe et al., 2009).

Measures of attachment in adults have been developed using interview and self-report questionnaires, and these confirm that there are three categories of attachment insecurity in adults: avoidant (sometimes known as dismissing, ambivalent (also known as preoccupied) and disorganised (also known as fearful). In adults, insecure attachment is manifested in the way that adults talk about their memories of childhood attachments and in their caregiving and care eliciting behaviours with children, partners and other family members. For example, adults assessed as having insecure attachment styles were at risk of repeating those insecure attachment with romantic partners leading to marital disharmony (Hazan & Shaver, 1987).

The problem of repeating dysfunctional attachment patterns may be mediated by the capacity to *mentalise*, i.e. to think about our own minds and the minds of others. Mentalising is a psychological process that happens continuously in humans who have to live in groups and other kinds of close relationships and is valuable for making inferences about other people's minds (Allen et al., 2008; Bateman & Fonagy, 2012). Humans use mentalising skills to 'read' other people and work out if others can be trusted or mean us harm. We develop mentalising skills by developing a capacity for *self-reflection* and this develops in the context of our earliest attachments when as children we need our carers to 'read' our needs and emotions accurately.

We use mentalising skills to 'read' our own minds and this skill helps us manage our moods and the extent to which we get aroused and agitated. This may explain why people with *all* kinds of insecure attachments are over-represented in clinical groups and generally poor mental health (Bakermans-Kranenburg & van IJzendoorn, 2009). Disorganised attachment seems to be particularly associated with severe mental disorders, such as psychosis and personality disorders, especially borderline and antisocial personality disorder (BPD and ASPD). People with these diagnoses also demonstrate problems in mentalising, and Bateman and Fonagy (2012, 2016) have developed a treatment programme which has been shown to improve mentalising skills and perspective-taking (mentalisation-based therapy, or MBT).

In summary then, the human attachment system resembles the human immune system (Holmes, 2001) such that those who have secure attachments are better able to manage and survive the ordinary stress and distress that happens in close relationships that involve dependency and need. In contrast, people with insecure attachment struggle to (a) reflect on their own minds (b) understand the minds of others (c) regulate their moods and arousal in close interpersonal relationships, and (d) maintain good mental and interpersonal function. Insecurity of attachment is not a *pathology* per se, but it indicates a vulnerability that is likely to persist across a human life span.

Attachment Insecurity and Offenders

John Bowlby (1944) published an early study exploring the links between attachment insecurity and criminal rule breaking, in a study of juvenile thieves, many of whom had histories of childhood neglect and deprivation. Bowlby hypothesised that the stealing behaviour represented a dysfunctional solution to an unconscious attachment insecurity, which caused the young people to experience unresolved distress and anger (Chapter 5). Bowlby suggested that the offending had a psychological soothing function, both consciously and unconsciously, and he went on to argue that these young offenders needed a 'secure base' in therapy (Bowlby, 1984), which could address both the conscious motives for theft and the unconscious distress from the attachment insecurity.

Since then, there have been multiple studies of attachment insecurity in different groups of offenders which have commonly found high levels of attachment insecurity and very few offenders with secure attachments, compared to general populations. Studies of attachment security in offender populations include violence perpetrators in prison (Fonagy & Levinson, 2004) and forensic psychiatric hospitals (Schimmenti et al., 2014; van IJzendoorn et al., 1997), sex offenders (Smallbone & Dadds, 1998), incarcerated psychopaths (Frodi et al., 2001), stalkers in a medium secure unit (Tonin, 2004), child sex offenders (Garofalo & Bogaerts, 2019) perpetrators of intimate partner violence (Velotti et al., 2018) and parents who mistreat their children (Adshead & Bluglass, 2005). The results of so many studies have led to the conclusion that all types of attachment insecurity can be considered a risk factor for offending, typically in combination with other risk factors for violence (Ogilvie et al., 2014).

The type of attachment insecurity most often found in violent offenders is avoidant attachment (Pffaflin & Adshead, 2004; Ogilvie et al., 2014). In the general population, the prevalence of avoidant attachment is about 16%, whereas in violent offender populations, it is closer to 50–60%. Avoidant attachment may be a risk factor for offending because people who are avoidant tend to deactivate their emotions and emphasise their strength. There is also a sub-type of avoidant attachment in which vulnerability and neediness are denigrated which could also act as a risk factor in the presence of other risk factors such as psychopathy and pathological narcissism.

However, other kinds of attachment insecurity may be relevant to other kinds of violence. For example, studies of attachment insecurity in men who are violent to their intimate partners (IPV) have found high levels of preoccupied/ambivalent attachment *not* avoidant (Dutton & White, 2012; Dutton et al., 1994). Preoccupied/ambivalent attachment insecurity is associated with rapid oscillations of emotion in close relationships and struggles with interpersonal distance regulation. People with this kind of insecurity of attachment may seek care when anxious but withdraw in hostile ways if they get too close. They are also commonly diagnosed with borderline (or emotionally unstable) personality disorder, which has been reported in both victims and perpetrators of IPV.

Finally, disorganised attachment insecurity may be relevant to violence perpetration when mental illness is present. A recent study of women who killed their children when mentally ill found that many of them had disorganised attachment, with features of both avoidant and preoccupied attachment styles in addition to dissociation and other kinds of reality distorting experiences (Barone & Carone, 2020). Since most people who suffer mental illness pose no risk of violence to others, it is possible that disorganised attachment acts as a mediating factor.

Attachment Insecurity as Violence Risk Factor

Attachment insecurity is likely to be common in violent offenders because of the influence of attachment insecurity on affect dysregulation, especially painful affects like fear, anger, and shame which are often implicated in violence (Gilligan, 2003) (Chapter 5). Dysregulation may involve either deactivation and avoidance of feeling or a disorganised and hyperactive emotional response: neither of these 'strategies' enables the offender to feel soothed or contained in the long term (Mikulincer & Shaver, 2019). If a conflict with a victim arouses strong painful emotions, an avoidant attached offender may have no capacity to manage such emotions; and may become overwhelmed and terrified, panicked or angry.

Similarly, an anxiously attached offender may feel overwhelmed by both painful affects and associated arousal and may deal with that arousal by externalising their feelings in physical action, including violence to others.

Offenders with disorganised attachment may also easily feel overwhelmed and maddened by their emotions, especially those people with unresolved traumatic stress (Iyengar et al., 2014). Disorganised attachment is also associated with exposure to childhood maltreatment and adversity; both of which are known to be common in offenders, especially those convicted of severe and chronic violence. In one study, it was found that chronic severe violence perpetrators in prison had experienced high levels of childhood adversity compared to prisoners who had only committed one violent offence (Fox et al., 2015). A similar study of male prisoners in Wales (Ford et al., 2019) found that only 16% of prisoners had *no* experience of childhood adversity; and 47% had experienced very high levels of childhood adversity. People with disorganised attachment systems cannot mount an organised defence to distress, and may oscillate chaotically between hostile and helpless states of mind, which may increase the risk of violent acting out.

In states of attachment insecurity, a key risk factor is the inability to mentalise and accurately 'read' others' intentions. As the arousal grows, mentalising skills fail and violent action offers an escape and even a sense of safety or coherence of mind (Kiessling-Caver 2018). Offenders may then generate justificatory narratives in which they are the victims and were only trying to protect themselves; these narratives are often incoherent and bear little relationship with reality (Maruna & Ramsden, 2004; Youngs & Canter, 2012) (Chapter 8).

Clearly, attachment insecurity is only one risk factor for violence and it may only be a risk factor for offences that are explicitly relational. However, this accounts for high levels of violent offending, including intimate partner violence, domestic homicide and child maltreatment. In England and Wales, 46% of female victims of homicide were killed either by a partner, ex-partner or family member: people who had at some point an attachment to the victim (Office of National Statistics, 2021). Most perpetrators of child abuse are in a parental relationship with their victims (Office of National Statistics, 2016) and may rely on the relationship to make abuse possible; the majority of stalkers harass ex-partners, and in England and Wales, over one million recorded assaults take place each year which involved IPV. By contrast, violence between strangers is comparatively rare; and tends to be either instrumentally driven to obtain goods or money, or is driven by mental disorder in the perpetrator, usually a paranoid state of mind.

Attachment and Forensic Practice

In this section, we describe how an understanding of attachment theory is helpful in the assessment and treatment of offenders.

(a) Treatment for offenders with personality disorder

Attachment insecurity is commonly found in offenders diagnosed with personality disorders. Although most people with a personality disorder (PD) will not break the criminal law, a subgroup will, especially those who are either impulsive or antisocial or both. These offenders with personality disorder may benefit from a programme of interventions that support a more pro-social state of mind, which encourages mentalising and understanding other people's perspectives. Since 2012, Her Majesty's Prison and Probation Service (HMPPS, previously the national Offender Management Service) has been developing and delivering services for offenders with PD (OPD). The OPD programme is based on attachment theory (Joseph & Benefield, 2012) and explicitly sets out to help improve mentalising skills in both offenders *and the staff who work with them.*

Offenders with personality disorders who have poor mentalising skills may benefit from therapies that seek to improve mentalising (Newbury-Helps et al., 2017). In the last decade, there has been active study of the value of mentalising-based therapy (MBT) in offenders, especially those with ASPD (Bateman et al., 2013; McGauley et al., 2011). Pilot studies looked promising enough for a national treatment trial to be underway in England in which probation as usual is compared with probation plus MBT for a group of offenders with ASPD. Based on previous studies of MBT in people with BPD, those who have MBT will be better able to *mentalise* their feelings and thoughts, and experience a greater sense of agency over their minds and choices, which aids in desistance from future offending.

Vignette 1: MBT Formulation in a Man with ASPD (See Chapter 11)

As described in the vignette, Mr J's experiences embody what the word 'insecurity' really means for children. In his earliest years, he had experienced fear, rejection and neglect, which left him searching for some kind of 'home' but no means of recognising one that could bring him 'security'. Drug misuse and a violent peer group further disorganised his attachment system, and his capacity to contain himself when threatened was minimal. He could only maintain inner 'security' by being violent to others.

(b) **Attachment and forensic institutions**

The language of 'security' is used often in attachment theory, but is also used in forensic institutions that provide 'secure' care. The attachment theory paradigm connects 'security of mind' with the duty of the forensic service to provide secure safe care, whether physical, procedural or relational. Attachment theory can also help professionals understand how those who reside in a setting over long periods of time (decades rather than years for lifers, for example), may develop 'place attachment' even to environments that seem punitive, like prisons and secure hospitals. Such 'secure' environments may be the first place of safety these offenders have ever known; and 'place attachment' refers to settings where people live and operate together; and which feels like a meaningful location or 'home' (Lewicka, 2011).

Such place attachments are generally assumed to be positive; they may be located in the past, present or future and can be both private (our representations, idealisations et cetera) and public (via mutual affinity, community, or possibly shared aversion/hostility). Furthermore, the feelings associated with certain places can become defining of identity, in positive or negative ways: 'I am fortunate to be a forensic psychologist working at X hospital'; or 'I am patient in X hospital; for me it is a place of torture and I cannot wait to leave'.

Attachment to place may be especially important for prisoners or forensic patients who are likely to have had highly disrupted 'home' lives and to have insecure avoidant or disorganised attachment systems. For such men and women, the need for security and protection from others can be prolonged into adulthood because they lack the psychological capacities to soothe themselves, approach others for help with confidence, and/or build the kind of trust that allows for optimal social function and support (Fonagy et al., 2019; Garofalo & Bogaerts, 2019). They may have learned instead that it is risky to rely on others to provide basic resources, and their attachment insecurities may unconsciously influence their decisions to avoid carers, retreat from them or be ready to fight them if necessary.

In a forensic institution, residents may therefore often feel ambivalently attached to both the place and the staff (Schuengel & van IJzendoorn, 2001). Safety and security may come at the expense of lost freedom and autonomy and a sense of being both controlled and mistrusted. Studies of residents in institutions find that their sense of identity is based on how their functional and emotional needs are met in 'their' particular institution (Raymond et al., 2010). In addition, their identity may also be developed and constructed through interactions with the staff in those institutions: both the staff and the institution may have expectations of how residents should 'be'.

These studies suggest that affect related to places exists independently of other affect systems (towards objects and people), so that changes in place may have a helpful—or possibly hindering—effect on equilibrium and well-being. Research on the impact of displacement confirms that: a) continuity and discontinuity; b) feelings of belonging, and c) engagement with neighbourliness, have all been identified as closely linked to place attachment (Giuliani, 2016).

What might this mean for prisoners and patients who are transferred to and from institutions within a network of forensic care? If forensic patients form attachments to places, then sudden and unplanned changes in placement can cause affective disruption and breakdown of mentalising. Unplanned or unexpected transitions between places, especially loss of relationships with trusted staff, can cause high levels of anxiety, arousal and distress (Mutschler et al., 2019). If the prisoner or patient lacks a secure attachment model, they cannot use proximity to others to reduce distress and they cannot mentalise their own distress themselves.

Another possibility is that prisoners and patients form ambivalent attachments to places and staff that are both secure and traumatising simultaneously; like segregation units. There is evidence from the literature on solitary confinement (Shalev, 2008) that people adapt (habituate) to even the starkest settings. They will therefore require support to re-accommodate to the challenges of living in closer proximity to others after periods of comparative interpersonal isolation and/or environmentally low stimulus surroundings, like a seclusion room or segregation cell.

Forensic practitioners might consider increasing their sensitivity to how offenders might experience a change in identity if their physical environment changes, and the psychological complexities associated both kinds of change. If location changes after a long period of familiarly, to what extent is the person in agreement with the change? What preparations need to be made in readiness for the change? There may be apparently insoluble conflicts between the need to keep someone safe and the need to provide them with autonomy and choice. There are real concerns about the iatrogenic and stigmatising impacts of keeping people secluded or segregated for long periods. For example, Cavelti et al., 2012 describe how individuals come to identify with their location in a process of internalised stigmatisation: 'I am an X [place name] patient; I expect to be feared, and to remain here forever'.

(c) **Relationships with staff (See Chapter** 27)

In institutions such as prisons and secure psychiatric hospitals, a great deal of professional time and attention is paid to 'security', which is usually broken down into three modes: physical, procedural and relational security. This last aspect of security is probably the most important as it refers to the matrix of relationships that build up between those who are detained and those who have oversight of their detention and their care while detained. Relational security is therefore an aspect of forensic practice for which attachment theory is a valuable paradigm.

Relational security entails thinking about the dynamics of relationships in custodial settings, which involve disparities of power, autonomy and control; rather like parent–child relationships. These relationships can be problematic if residents and staff have experienced childhood maltreatment and have insecure attachment models of mind. Repetitions of toxic attachments can easily take place in forensic settings: although sexual boundary violations are the kind that draw attention, commoner boundary violations include rudeness, belittling behaviour, inconsistent care, neglect, staff helplessness and (more rarely) physical violence. In secure psychiatric and prison settings, abuse of detainees may reflect unresolved attachment distress in both the abused and the abusers (Adshead, 1998; Moore, 2012).

Institutions themselves can become anxious, especially when there has been past trauma. Early work by Menzies Lyth (1958) indicated that staff in organisations can be anxious if they have a difficult primary task to complete; and when staff are anxious, they can do odd things and act unprofessionally. Custodial organisations have a difficult job to do in containing people who are feared and hated in equal measure, and so they tend to operate as highly hierarchical organisations as a way of managing anxiety at a senior level. However, as we set out in Vignette 2, such hierarchical structures can also stop thinking and are unconsciously driven to reduce anxiety using measures that are controlling and not containing. In Vignette two, it seems that security concerns did not really address the impact on patients of being moved around, nor did they provide space for the staff member to process the distress they felt at moving a patient to whom they had become attached. It is essential that reflective thinking spaces are made available for professionals who work in forensic settings, as they are for other staff who work with complex care (Moore, 2012).

Vignette 1: Mentalisation-Based Therapy (MBT) for a Violent Offender with ASPD

Mr J (aged 54), was sentenced to life imprisonment for homicide when he was in his 20 s; the murder was related to a dispute about drugs. During his time in prison, he was hostile and repeatedly aggressive; which resulted in him being transferred to 15 different prisons. However, with time, he seemed to settle down and was about to be moved to a less secure prison with a view to a release programme. His mental state then deteriorated and he made a violent assault on a prison officer. He was assessed as needing treatment for ASPD in a high secure hospital.

After admission to the hospital, he expressed interest in treatment: "I just don't understand why I attacked the bloke so near to my release" he told the admission clinical team. Given his apparent motivation and willingness to try and understand himself, Mr J was referred for a range of therapies including MBT.

The MBT trained female therapist, talked about the process of engagement of Mr J in some re-telling of the story of his life to date, including the people and places of importance to him. He took some time to collaborate in the completion of pre-treatment baseline measures of attachment and his trauma history. This process revealed extensive childhood adversity: including physical abuse by his father (whose prediction 'You'll end up in jail!' was sadly fulfilled), his parents' separation, the death of his grandparents, and multiple placements in different care homes and detention centres as a result of his repetitive stealing. While in care, he was sexually abused by male and female adult carers, which left him confused, humiliated and lacking in trust.

In the formulation, the therapist set out how prison offered Mr J the security he craved; and how its potential loss (if he was released) made him fearful and hostile, leading to the attack on a member of staff he usually liked. He entered the MBT treatment phase mindful that he had sacrificed his future with others outside the walls for the safety of a predictable regime inside them; and aware of his capacity to react violently to any perceived loss of safety.

Vignette 2: An Example of Unprocessed Distress and Its Impact Within an Institution

(d) Attachment-informed assessment and intervention

Given what we have written above, we suggest that before any intervention is planned for a forensic patient/prisoner, they should have an extended assessment that pays attention to early childhood attachment experiences. This assessment (with their permission) would cover their developmental history, including early adversities, their relationships, experiences of other carers, such as foster care and how they think about their childhood and experiences of being cared for. It is vital to establish a rapport before attempting to explore the offence that has brought the person into custodial care, especially if that offence is shameful, horrific and/or involves family members.

Forensic psychologists using an attachment perspective will want to help the offender understand the meaning of the violence (and the victim) to them and then include that understanding in a collaborative plan for managing risk in future. Attachment-based assessment and formulation offer a hypothesis about who and why the victim was the target; why the offence happened at the time and place that it did; and what risk factors were operating that will need to be worked on to reduce future risk. For example, a man with a history of IPV may now be in prison on a charge of harassment and stalking his ex-partner. If he has a history of an ambivalent/preoccupied attachment, this may explain why he cannot let go of this ex-partner, and why he may see his hostility as an expression of affection and sadness. If he has an avoidant attachment and an antisocial personality disorder, he may be more paranoid about his victim and believe that she deserves being threatened for causing him pain. These different formulations carry different risks and entail different plans for managing the risk.

An individual's attachment security may affect how they talk about themselves at interview. An avoidant attachment system often manifests itself as an apparent lack of concern or memory for the past, idealising past attachment figures and deactivation of emotion. People who deactivate emotionally can present as calm or disconnected, and it is important to not mistake insecure avoidant attachment for callous remorselessness or antisocial states of mind. Similarly, people who have beaten or killed a loved one may be in a numbed state similar to trauma survivors, especially in the early days and weeks, and this can, to the uninitiated, look as if they are in a normal state of mind or don't care about what they have done. Conversely, an offender with a preoccupied attachment system may talk a lot about past and present attachments, which can sound superficially emotionally intelligent, but over time interviewers may find that it is a 'script' with little self-reflection in it and the attachments are actually incoherent and shallow.

In terms of interventions, understanding an offender's attachment insecurity may allow for anticipation of difficulties in terms of work with mental health professionals (Adams et al., 2018). Avoidant insecurely attached individuals may struggle to be aware of their feelings or put them into words (alexithymia) and they may struggle to establish trust with assessors or therapists. Ambivalently attached individuals may appear to be trusting and engaged but may abruptly disengage if they feel exposed or vulnerable during therapy. Studies of people with mental health problems who are insecurely attached suggest that they may struggle to comply with treatment regimes (e.g. Dozier, 1990) but may be able to make therapeutic gains if they can establish trust (Fonagy et al., 1996; Thomas & Jenkins, 2019).

Some offenders with insecure attachment histories may find small group work easier to start. Group work allows offenders to 'attach' to a social group, which helps reduce shame and encourages pro-social attitudes. Group therapy was first recommended for antisocial people in the 1960s because participation in a therapy group is a pro-social act in itself; and group-based interventions are traditionally offered in prisons in relation to index offences related to work and substance misuse. MBT has a group component, which is likely to be one of the factors relevant to its efficacy. Participation in such groups allows group facilitators to observe offenders' relationships with others and their capacity for mentalising and perspective-taking (Adshead, 2015).

(e) **Risk assessment (See Chapter** 25)

Psychological theories of 'repetition compulsion' and 'offense paralleling' (Daffern et al., 2010) both draw on the idea that humans tend to repeat patterns of behaviour that have meaning to them, even when those behaviours and actions are self-defeating. Given the importance of attachment security in terms of its influence on (a) interpersonal function and (b) affects regulation, we propose that an understanding of attachment security in an offender is crucial to assessing their risk to others. This may be especially true for those offenders where the violence arose in the context of a relationship disruption, and where the meaning and patterns of violence may be triggered by memories of unresolved attachment distress.

Some established risk assessment tools include attention to attachment security-related factors. The HCR-20 is an actuarial assessment tool which requires raters to assess the presence of childhood maltreatment and adversity, both of which are associated with the development of attachment insecurity. Attachment security is also relevant to the assessment of dynamics risk factors such as changes in affect and changes in interpersonal relationships (Douglas & Skeem, 2005). Dutton and Kropp (2000) discuss the use of the Propensity for Abusiveness Scale in assessing IPV perpetrators which includes an assessment of attachment style, and a study using the PCL-R in prisoners convicted of violence found a relationship between overall risk and two items which gave an indirect measure of attachment (multiple short term relationships and sexual promiscuity: Schimmenti et al., 2014).

Because attachment theory offers a relational perspective on complex violence, it may be a particularly useful paradigm for assessing risk in offenders who have targeted people for whom they have strong feelings: such as romantic partners (Dutton & Kropp, 2000; Dutton et al., 1994) and objects of obsessional attachment (McEwan et al., 2011; Tonin, 2004). In cases like these, the victim/attachment figure acts as an affect stabiliser for the perpetrator who then reacts violently if they perceive the victim to be rejecting or leaving them. Perpetrators may become highly mentally disorganised at these times, and this mental state, especially when combined with substance and alcohol misuse is extremely dangerous; and may trigger frenzied and often fatal violence.

When assessing risk, it is vital to consider the emotions that may unconsciously be affecting the mind of the risk assessor and skewing perceptions of probability (Kahneman, 2011). For example, if all my interactions with a prisoner have been warm and positive, it may be hard for me to see her as dangerous, even when other professionals have found evidence of risk. Equally, nurses who have had a conflict with a patient may see them as 'risky' because the patient expressed anger, which could be a risk factor for violence but only if other risk factors are also present. An attachment informed approach ensures that the relational origin of emotional responses is not overlooked as a source of bias (in both the offender and in staff). Using an attachment-based paradigm may also help promote collaboration between risk assessors and patients in forensic settings (Markham, 2020). For example, risk assessors would try to develop the kind of trusting therapeutic attachment that made it possible for patients/prisoners to disclose thoughts and feelings that they would know might be risky. Such an attachment is built by the assessor being open and honest in their relationship with the person being assessed and maintaining professional boundaries that are clear and consistent.

Vignette 2: Unprocessed Distress and Its Impact on Staff

A challenging series of events led to a small group of patients being moved to different wards within a forensic hospital. Senior managers were anxious that the patients were subverting security and staff were not showing discipline while middle managers were trying to resolved staffing crises, and felt that their seniors were not listening to their anxiety. Meanwhile the staff on the ward who were managing the new patients felt emotionally drained by doing extra hours to cover staff shortages, and then felt undervalued and criticised for small misdeeds (such as coming back late from break).

These anxieties in the staff team at different levels seemed to have an impact on the ward atmosphere. During a period of rising tension, two of the newly admitted patients (who did not know each other but were united in feeling unhappy about being moved to a new place) jumped into the day room area and forced the (free-standing) chairs up against the door to block staff entry.

A team of staff came together to address the situation. From an attachment perspective, the ward staff felt helpless and threatened by the direct aggression they were facing. The middle managers, hearing about this on the radio, felt both threatened and disappointed that the staff had "allowed this to happen"; and the senior managers hurried to convene the 'rescue' team who would "take the necessary action to restore order". Order was restored and the team who did so, wearing protective equipment and carrying shields, effectively opened the door and removed the patients to restrictive rooms.

Two members of this team had been involved in moving one of these patients from his previous ward, and he released a tirade of abuse at them for their actions. One of these members of staff had been the primary nurse to the patient and had worked hard to establish an alliance with him. These words of abuse, unrelenting and personal in front of all others present, were distressing for him and stayed in the staff member's mind for several days.

The next incident he attended, this staff member became aware that he had lost his confidence. He spoke to his managers who told him he had done well, that this was part of the job and that he would get over it, just as they had, with time. Unfortunately, a series of opportunities to safely share his experiences were subsequently lost as the ward's reflective practice was cancelled due to the need to carry out a planned intervention, and the next week, he was re-directed to another ward.

Conclusion

Attachment-informed practice with offenders has much in common with trauma-informed practice. Both pay attention to developmental accounts of both psychological function and the risk of offending, and both seek to explore the meaning of offending for offenders in terms of past experience. Starting from the premise of seeking to understand 'what happened to you?' provides the foundation for the potential for empathic formulation (Omer, 1997), which may resonate better than factual narratives with those who are difficult to engage. In this chapter, we have set out the rationale for using an attachment informed approach in work with offenders, which can also usefully be applied to work with staff and forensic organisations as a whole.

References

Adams, G. C., Wrath, A. J., & Meng, X. (2018). The relationship between adult attachment and mental health care utilization: A systematic review. *The Canadian Journal of Psychiatry, 63*(10), 651–660.

Adshead, G. (1998). Psychiatric staff as attachment figures: Understanding management problems in psychiatric services in the light of attachment theory. *The British Journal of Psychiatry, 172,* 64–69. https://doi.org/10.1192/bjp.172.1.64

Adshead, G. (2015). Safety in numbers: Group therapy-based index offence work in secure psychiatric care. *Psychoanalytic Psychotherapy, 29*(3), 295–310.

Adshead, G., & Aiyegbusi, A. (2014). Four pillars of security: Attachment theory and practice in forensic mental health care. In A. N. Danquah & K. Berry (Eds.), *Attachment theory in adult mental health: A guide to clinical practice* (pp. 63–77). Routledge, Taylor and Francis Group.

Adshead, G., & Bluglass, K. (2005). Attachment representations in mothers with abnormal illness behaviour by proxy. *The British Journal of Psychiatry, 187*(4), 328–333.

Ainsworth, M. D. S., Blehar, M. C., Waters, E., & Wall, S. N. (2015). *Patterns of attachment: A psychological study of the strange situation.* Psychology Press.

Allen, J. G., Fonagy, P., & Bateman, A. W. (2008). *Mentalizing in clinical practice.* American Psychiatric Publishers.

Bakermans-Kranenburg, M. J., & van IJzendoorn, M. H. (2009). The first 10,000 adult attachment interviews: Distributions of adult attachment representations in clinical and non-clinical groups. *Attachment & Human Development, 11*(3), 223–263.

Barone, L., & Carone, N. (2020). Childhood abuse and neglect experiences, Hostile-Helpless attachment, and reflective functioning in mentally ill filicidal mothers. *Attachment & Human Development*, 1–24.

Bateman, A. W., & Fonagy, P. E. (2012). *Handbook of mentalizing in mental health practice*. Oxford University Press.

Bateman, A., & Fonagy, P. (2016). *Mentalization-based treatment for personality disorders: A practical guide*. Oxford University Press.

Bateman, A., Bolton, R., & Fonagy, P. (2013). Antisocial personality disorder: A mentalizing framework. *Focus, 11*(2), 178–186.

Bowlby, J. (1944). Forty-four juvenile thieves: Their characters and home-life. *International Journal of Psycho-Analysis., 25*, 19–53.

Bowlby, J. (1969). *Attachment and Loss. Vol. 1: Attachment*. The Hogarth Press and Institute of Psycho-Analysis.

Bowlby, J. (1973). *Attachment and loss: Volume II: Separation, anxiety and anger*. The Hogarth Press and Institute of Psycho-Analysis.

Bowlby, J. (1984). *A secure base: Clinical applications of attachment theory* (Vol. 393). Taylor & Francis, 3rd edition, 2005.

Bretherton, I. (1992). The origins of attachment theory: John Bowlby and Mary Ainsworth. *Developmental Psychology, 28*(5), 759.

Cavelti, M., Kvrgic, S., Beck, E. M., Rüsch, N., & Vauth, R. (2012). Self-stigma and its relationship with insight, demoralization, and clinical outcome among people with schizophrenia spectrum disorders. *Comprehensive Psychiatry, 53*(5), 468–479.

Daffern, M., Jones, L., & Shine, J. (Eds.). (2010). *Offence paralleling behaviour: A case formulation approach to offender assessment and intervention* (Vol. 48). Wiley.

Douglas, K. S., & Skeem, J. L. (2005). Violence risk assessment: Getting specific about being dynamic. *Psychology, Public Policy, and Law, 11*(3), 347.

Dozier, M. (1990). Attachment organization and treatment use for adults with serious psychopathological disorders. *Development and Psychopathology, 2*(1), 47–60.

Dutton, D. G., & Kropp, P. R. (2000). A review of domestic violence risk instruments. *Trauma, Violence, & Abuse, 1*(2), 171–181.

Dutton, D. G., Saunders, K., Starzomski, A., & Bartholomew, K. (1994). Intimacy-anger and insecure attachment as precursors of abuse in intimate relationships 1. *Journal of Applied Social Psychology, 24*(15), 1367–1386.

Dutton, D. G., & White, K. R. (2012). Attachment insecurity and intimate partner violence. *Aggression and violent behavior, 17*(5), 475–481.

Fonagy, P., & Levinson, A. (2004). Offending and attachment: The relationship between interpersonal awareness and offending in a prison population with psychiatric disorder. *Canadian Journal of Psychoanalysis, 12*(2), 225–251.

Fonagy, P. (2003). Towards a developmental understanding of violence. *British Journal of Psychiatry., 183*, 190–192.

Fonagy, P., Leigh, T., Steele, M., Steele, H., Kennedy, R., Mattoon, G., Target, M., & Gerber, A. (1996). The relation of attachment status, psychiatric classification, and response to psychotherapy. *Journal of Consulting and Clinical Psychology, 64*(1), 22.

Fonagy, P., Luyten, P., Allison, E., & Campbell, C. (2019). Mentalizing, epistemic trust and the phenomenology of psychotherapy. *Psychopathology, 52*(2), 94–103.

Ford, K., Barton, E. R., Newbury, A., Hughes, K., Bezeczky, Z., Roderick, J., & Bellis, M. A. (2019). *The prisoner ACE survey*. University of Bangor.

Fox, B. H., Perez, N., Cass, E., Baglivio, M. T., & Epps, N. (2015). Trauma changes everything: Examining the relationship between adverse childhood experiences and serious, violent and chronic juvenile offenders. *Child Abuse & Neglect, 46*, 163–173.

Frodi, A., Dernevik, M., Sepa, A., Philipson, J., & Bragesjö, M. (2001). Current attachment representations of incarcerated offenders varying in degree of psychopathy. *Attachment & Human Development, 3*(3), 269–283.

Garofalo, C., & Bogaerts, S. (2019). Attachment and personality disorders among child molesters: The role of trust. *Sexual Abuse, 31*(1), 97–124.

George, C., Kaplan, N., & Main, M. (1996). *The adult attachment interview* (Unpublished MS). University of Berkeley. Berkeley, CA.

Gilligan, J. (2003). Shame, guilt, and violence. *Social Research: An International Quarterly, 70*(4), 1149–1180.

Giuliani, M. V. (2016). *Theory of attachment and place attachment*. In M. Bonnes, T. Lee, & M. Bonaiuto (Eds.), *Psychological theories for environmental issues* (Chapter 5). Routledge.

Grady, M. D., Levenson, J. S., & Bolder, T. (2017). Linking adverse childhood effects and attachment: A theory of etiology for sexual offending. *Trauma, Violence, & Abuse, 18*(4), 433–444.

Hazan, C., & Shaver, P. (1987). Romantic love conceptualized as an attachment process. *Journal of Personality and Social Psychology, 52*(3), 511.

Holmes, J. (2001). *The search for the secure base: Attachment theory and psychotherapy*. Psychology Press.

Iyengar, U., Kim, S., Martinez, S., Fonagy, P., & Strathearn, L. (2014). Unresolved trauma in mothers: Intergenerational effects and the role of reorganization. *Frontiers in Psychology, 5*, 966.

Joseph, N., & Benefield, N. (2012). A joint offender personality disorder pathway strategy: An outline summary. *Criminal Behaviour and Mental Health, 22*(3), 210–217.

Kahneman, D. (2011). *Thinking, fast and slow*. Macmillan.

Kiessling-Caver, A. (2018). Attachment security and violence: The role of reflective functioning capacity. *Criminology, Criminal Justice, Law & Society, 19*, 15.

Lewicka, M. (2011). Place attachment: How far have we come in the last 40 years? *Journal of Environmental Psychology, 31*, 207–230.

Main, M., & Solomon, J. (1990). Procedures for identifying infants as disorganized/disoriented during the Ainsworth Strange Situation. *Attachment in the preschool years: Theory, research, and intervention, 1*, 121–160.

Markham, S. (2020). Collaborative risk assessment in secure and forensic mental health settings in the UK. *General Psychiatry, 33*(5), e100291.

Maruna, S., & Ramsden, D. (2004). Living to tell the tale: Redemption narratives, shame management, and offender rehabilitation. In A. Lieblich, D. P. McAdams, & R. Josselson (Eds.), *The narrative study of lives. Healing plots: The narrative basis of psychotherapy* (pp. 129–149). American Psychological Association. https://doi.org/10.1037/10682-007

McEwan, T. E., Pathé, M., & Ogloff, J. R.(2011). Advances in stalking risk assessment. *Behavioral Sciences & the Law, 29*(2), 180–201.

McGauley, G., Yakeley, J., Williams, A., & Bateman, A. (2011). Attachment, mentalization and antisocial personality disorder: The possible contribution of mentalization-based treatment. *European Journal of Psychotherapy & Counselling, 13*(4), 371–393.

Menzies Lyth, I. (1988). *Containing anxiety in institutions: Selected essays* (Vol. 1). Free Association Books.

Mikulincer, M., & Shaver, P. R. (2019). Attachment orientations and emotion regulation. *Current Opinion in Psychology, 25*, 6–10.

Moore, E. (2012). Personality disorder: Its impact on staff and the role of supervision. *Advances in Psychiatric Treatment, 18*(1), 44–55.

Mutschler, C., Lichtenstein, S., Kidd, S. A., & Davidson, L. (2019). Transition experiences following psychiatric hospitalization: A systematic review of the literature. *Community Mental Health Journal, 55*(8), 1255–1274.

Newbury-Helps, J., Feigenbaum, J., & Fonagy, P. (2017). Offenders with antisocial personality disorder display more impairments in mentalizing. *Journal of Personality Disorders, 31*(2), 232–255.

Nolte, T., Campbell, C., & Fonagy, P. (2019). A mentalization-based and neuroscience-informed model of severe and persistent psychopathology. In J. Pereira, J. Goncalves, & V. Bizarri (Eds.), *The neurobiologypsychotherapy-pharmacology intervention triangle: The need for common sense in 21st century mental health* (pp. 161–186). Vernon Press.

Office of National Statistics. (2016). *Crime survey England and Wales: Abuse during childhood.* https://www.ons.gov.uk/peoplepopulationandcommunity/crimeandjustice/art icles/abuseduringchildhood/findingsfromtheyearendingmarch2016crimesurveyforenglan dandwales

Office of National Statistics. (2021). *Homicide in England and Wales: year ending March 2020.* https://www.ons.gov.uk/peoplepopulationandcommunity/crimeandjustice/articles/homicideinenglandandwales/yearendingmarch2020

Ogilvie, C. A., Newman, E., Todd, L., & Peck, D. (2014). Attachment & violent offending: A meta-analysis. *Aggression and Violent Behaviour, 19*(4), 322–339.

Omer, H. (1997). Narrative empathy. *Psychotherapy: Theory, Research, Practice, Training, 34*(1), 19–27. https://doi.org/10.1037/h0087748

Pfäfflin, F., & Adshead, G. (2004). *A matter of security: The application of attachment theory to forensic psychiatry and psychotherapy.* Jessica Kingsley.

Raymond, C. M., Brown, G., & Weber, P. (2010). The measurement of place attachment: Personal, community and environmental connections. *Journal of Environmental Psychology, 30*, 422–434.

Ross, T., & Pfäfflin, F. (2007). Attachment and interpersonal problems in a prison environment. *The Journal of Forensic Psychiatry & Psychology, 18*(1), 90–98.

Schimmenti, A., Passanisi, A., Pace, U., Manzella, S., Di Carlo, G., & Caretti, V. (2014). The relationship between attachment and psychopathy: A study with a sample of violent offenders. *Current Psychology, 33*(3), 256–270.

Schuengel, C., & van Ijzendoorn, M. H. (2001). Attachment in mental health institutions: A critical review of assumptions, clinical implications, and research strategies. *Attachment & Human Development, 3*(3), 304–323.

Shalev, S. (2008). *A sourcebook on solitary confinement.* Available at SSRN 2177495. London School of Economics.

Smallbone, S. W., & Dadds, M. R. (1998). Childhood attachment and adult attachment in incarcerated adult male sex offenders. *Journal of Interpersonal Violence, 13*(5), 555–573.

Sroufe, L. A. (2005). Attachment and development: A prospective, longitudinal study from birth to adulthood. *Attachment & Human Development, 7*, 349–376. https://doi.org/10.1080/14616730500365928

Sroufe, L. A. (2016). The place of attachment in development. *Handbook of Attachment: Theory, Research, and Clinical Applications, 3*, 997–1011.

Sroufe, L. A., Egeland, B., Carlson, E. A., & Collins, W. A. (2009). *The development of the person: The Minnesota study of risk and adaptation from birth to adulthood.* Guilford Press.

Thomas, N., & Jenkins, H. (2019). The journey from epistemic vigilance to epistemic trust: Service-users experiences of a community mentalization-based treatment programme for Anti-Social personality disorder (ASPD). *The Journal of Forensic Psychiatry & Psychology, 30*(6), 909–938.

Tonin, E. (2004). The attachment styles of stalkers. *Journal of Forensic Psychiatry & Psychology, 15*(4), 584–590.

Van Ijzendoorn, M. H., Feldbrugge, J. T. T. M., Derks, F. C. H., De Ruiter, C., Verhagen, M. F. M., Philipse, M. W. G., Van der Staak, C. P. F., & Riksen-Walraven, J. M. A. (1997). Attachment representations of personality-disordered criminal offenders. *American Journal of Orthopsychiatry, 67*(3), 449–459.

Velotti, P., Beomonte Zobel, S., Rogier, G., & Tambelli, R. (2018). Exploring relationships: A systematic review on intimate partner violence and attachment. *Frontiers in Psychology, 9*, 1166.

Willmot, P., & McMurran, M. (2016). An attachment based model of therapeutic change process in the treatment of personality disorder among male forensic inpatients. *Legal & Criminological Psychology, 21*, 390–406.

Youngs, D., & Canter, D. V. (2012). Narrative roles in criminal action: An integrative framework for differentiating offenders. *Legal and Criminological Psychology, 17*(2), 233–249.

Further Reading Suggestions

Holmes, J. (2006). *John Bowlby and attachment theory.* Routledge.

Holmes, P., & Farmfield, S. (Eds.). (2014). *The Routledge handbook of attachment theory.* Routledge.

Danquah, A., & Berry, K. (Eds.). (2014). *Attachment theory in adult mental health: A guide to clinical practice.* Routledge.

Pffaflin, F., & Adshead, G. (Eds.). (2004). *A matter of security: The application of attachment theory to forensic psychiatry and psychotherapy.* Jessica Kingsley Publishers.

Shemmings, D., & Shemmings, Y. (2011). *Understanding disorganised attachment: theory and practice for working with children and adults.* Jessica Kingsley Publishers.

Influences of Peer Relationships and Romantic Partners on Antisocial Behavior

10

Jelle J. Sijtsema

Key Points

- Social relationships are important in explaining individual differences in offending across the lifespan.
- In adolescence, offending is more likely the result of peer influence than peer selection processes.
- Processes related to group norms and social status often determine the extent to which social relationships affect individual offending.
- Serious romantic relationships are an important factor in the desistance of offending, but may also increase offending.
- For females, the negative effects of their criminal spouse seem stronger than for males.
- Individuals who committed many offenses are more likely to marry later and to marry a criminal spouse.

Introduction

Social relationships play an important role in our lives. Social ties fulfill general human needs related to belongingness, affection, and status (Baumeister & Leary, 1995). Besides providing intimacy and support, social relationships may also shape our behavior, for better or worse. In this chapter, the focus is on the

J. J. Sijtsema (✉)
Department of Developmental Psychology, Tilburg University, Tilburg, The Netherlands
e-mail: j.j.sijtsema@tilburguniversity.edu

© The Author(s), under exclusive license to Springer Nature Switzerland AG 2022   183
C. Garofalo and J. J. Sijtsema (eds.), *Clinical Forensic Psychology*,
https://doi.org/10.1007/978-3-030-80882-2_10

negative side of behavioral influence, namely the extent to which social relationships may increase the likelihood of offending or predispose to antisocial
developmental trajectories. We take a somewhat broader definition of offending
that also includes antisocial behaviors in youths, such as physical aggression and
delinquency. Studies showed that behavioral influence processes with regard to
antisocial behavior already start in kindergarten (e.g., Snyder et al., 1997, 2005)
with children mimicking the aggressive behaviors of their playmates. In adolescence, these processes become more frequent because (a) peers take up a more
prominent role in youths' lives (Hartup, 1996), (b) antisocial behavior can be
used to fulfill status needs, and (c) deviant peers may place youths on a criminal trajectory (Moffitt, 2018). It thus comes as no surprise that much research
that studies social influence processes has focused specifically on this age group.
In adulthood, social relationships often take a turn for the better, as life transitions such as marriage or cohabitation, parenthood, and employment are generally
associated with desistance from offending (Sampson & Laub, 1995). However,
there is also evidence that spouses and romantic partners may foster offending in
adulthood, suggesting that these turning points may not have the same effect on
everyone.

In the following, the role of social relationships on adolescent and adult
offending is discussed in more detail. We start by discussing several theories
that may explain the effects of social relationships on offending and then zoom
in on insights from recent empirical studies.

Theories and Mechanisms of Social Influence on Antisocial Behavior

Given the importance of social relationships, it is not surprising that those who
affiliate with each other are often similar to each other in terms of behavior,
attitudes, and preferences. Such similarity between those who frequently interact
(e.g., friends, peers, family members, spouses) is also observed with regard to
antisocial behavior (Brechwald & Prinstein, 2011; Dishion & Tipsord, 2011).
Although several theories provide an explanation for this similarity, most have
their roots in social learning theory.

Social Learning Theory

Albert Bandura's social-cognitive learning theory (1973) offers an elegant explanation for why people would copy each other's antisocial behavior. In his famous Bobo-doll experiment, Bandura not only showed that children imitated aggressive behavior once it was rewarded, but also imitated these behaviors by watching someone *else* being rewarded. This showed a learning effect through observation (observational learning) without direct reinforcement. Later adaptations of his theory have also been applied to explain criminal behavior in adolescents and adults and are at the basis of many theories and studies that examined peer relationship processes in children and adolescents.

Differential Association

Related to social learning theory, Sutherland (1947) introduced the theory of differential association to explain criminal behavior from a social perspective. According to this theory, people learn criminal behavior by interacting with others and through the subsequent exchange of values, motivations, and rationalizations that predispose to criminal behavior. Although this theory does not explain why people would offend in the first place, it does predict that through experience some people may be more inclined to offend because of social influence, in particular when influence comes from those with a higher status, and under the condition that the rewards of offending outweigh the rewards of non-offending behavior. This theory has often been used to explain how delinquent attitudes and delinquent peer association may be related to individual delinquent behavior (e.g., Janssen et al., 2016).

Deviancy Training

As opposed to more direct social influence, the concept of *deviancy training* was introduced to describe how youths may *indirectly* socially influence each other with regard to deviant behavior (Dishion & Tipsord, 2011; Dishion et al., 1994). According to this notion, antisocial behavior develops in friendship contexts indirectly through peer reinforcement processes such as deviant talk. This reinforcement occurs because youths shift in the direction of deviant attitudes and values, because they are rewarded by the peer group through for example, laughter or praise. As such, peers implicitly or explicitly promote antisocial behavior and use antisocial behavior to fit in, or to gain and maintain a central position in the peer group.

Selection Processes

Although social influence is an important factor in explaining offending, similarity in delinquency between peers is often the combined result of peer influence *and* selection processes (McPherson et al., 2001). That is, people may select with whom they affiliate because of *similarity attraction*: the notion that similarity itself is attractive. The idea that people who affiliate with each other are similar is often referred to as homophily and is usually determined by general characteristics such as gender, race, and age (McPherson et al., 2001). However, similarity attraction is also observed for antisocial behaviors (cf. Sijtsema & Lindenberg, 2018). Delinquent peers may select each other as friends because they are similar in antisocial cognitions, attitudes, and behaviors. Alternatively, people may select their friends because of *default selection*. That is, some people may not be able to establish the relationships they prefer and may settle, instead, for relationships with less preferred peers (cf. Deptula & Cohen, 2004). This mechanism has been used to explain similarity between peers on less attractive characteristics (e.g., interpersonal aggression). Overall, social selection processes may differ depending on the social rewards associated with delinquency, and these rewards may differ for different forms of delinquency and the specific social contexts in which people reside. For example, in adolescent peer groups, aggressive behaviors and rule-breaking behaviors can be differently rewarded within peer groups (Sijtsema & Lindenberg, 2018): Whereas (physical) aggression is often associated with low social status (e.g., peer rejection), rule-breaking behaviors are often associated with high social status (e.g., popularity) within peer groups. However, in groups where aggression is associated with high social status, people may be more inclined to imitate and select friends based on this behavior compared to groups in which aggression is associated with low social status (Laninga-Wijnen et al., 2017). In the next section, these processes are discussed in more detail in youth populations.

Peer Relationships and Offending in Youths

The lives of adolescents are characterized by changes. Not only do youths change physically, there are also important social and cognitive changes. Social relationships become more prominent and serve an important role in shaping youths' identity and behaviors (Hartup, 1996). As youths spend more time with their peers, away from parents and other forms of supervision, there is also more room for peer influences on delinquency. The processes through which such influences may come about have been discussed in the previous section, but in the following sections, more detail is provided on why such processes occur in adolescence and what they might look like.

Mechanisms of Social Influence

Social Network Processes

To study social influence processes, or more broadly, the effect that social relationships have on individual behavior, many scholars have employed dyadic or social network analyses to understand the working of delinquent social groups. Although not the first in his mathematical approach to explain social behavior, psychiatrist Jacob Moreno (1934) was the first who applied social network analysis to explain the increase in runaway behavior at the Hudson School for girls in upstate New York. He found that, instead of looking for explanations related to individual traits for why these girls ran away from home, the social relationships between the girls were crucial in the spreading of ideas and social influences that determined whether and when they would run away (see also Borgatti et al., 2009).

Social network analysis relies on the idea that people are connected to each other via social ties and that information, attitudes, and behaviors may spread from one actor to another actor in the network via these ties (or relationships). The spreading of attitudes and behaviors may not always be a conscious process, as group norms may dictate social behavior or attitudes in indirect ways. *Descriptive norms* are derived from behaviors and attitudes that are frequently displayed or used in a social group and as such may set a standard for normative behavior. For example, in peer groups of aggressive children, aggression is often perceived as more normative, because the majority displays this behavior (cf. Laninga-Wijnen et al., 2017). Alternatively, *injunctive norms* are derived from the behaviors and attitudes of more influential group members. Such norms may be especially influential as imitating the behaviors and attitudes of popular group members can help in attaining (and maintaining) a high social position in the group (Dijkstra et al., 2008).

In past decades, scholars have sought to quantify information from social networks by mapping networks of individuals (so-called ego networks) or by mapping all social relationships within a certain group (so-called complete networks), for example, all friendship relations within a classroom. Information about social relationships can then be connected to individual (or group) behavior, such as offending or other antisocial behaviors and attitudes. Social network analysis often accounts for the underlying social network structures. That is, to assess the actual influence network members have on each other, it is important to account for effects that relate to reciprocity (social ties are often mutual), transitivity (social networks often include smaller tightly knit clusters: 'a friend of a friend is also my friend'), and the position one has in the network (being more central—or having more connections to others—affects the degree to which individuals are influenced and influential).

Since Moreno's work, many scholars have employed social network analysis to explain delinquency and offending in youths, which has led to several relevant insights. First, researchers consistently find that delinquent youths have a tendency to select peers and peer groups that are similar in aggression and delinquency. This clustering of antisocial youths is already visible at young ages (e.g., at age 7, Witvliet et al., 2010) and continues into adolescence (Espelage et al., 2003). However, clusters of antisocial youths tend to be smaller compared to non-antisocial youths' clusters and are less stable over time (Kwon & Lease, 2009; Witvliet et al., 2010).

Second, studies using longitudinal social network analyses have teased apart social influence and selection effects, to provide more insight into whether antisocial youths select similar peers, whether youths become more similar to each other in antisocial behavior over time, or both. Work that studies cliques in adolescence (i.e., tightly connected peer groups), showed that being in a clique with aggressive peers increased individual levels of both direct and indirect forms of aggression over time (Low et al., 2013). A series of studies using stochastic-based actor models, employing the simultaneous development of social relationship and antisocial behavior, also indicated that youths become more similar to their peers with respect to aggression, delinquency, weapon carrying, and broad measures of externalizing behaviors (Gallupe et al., 2019; Sijtsema & Lindenberg, 2018). Although there is also some support for antisocial youths selecting peers who are similar in antisocial behavior, these effects were only consistently observed for delinquency as opposed to aggression and broad assessments of externalizing behavior, which may pertain to the relatively strong connection between social status and delinquency in adolescence (see following section). Third, many processes related to social selection and influence with regard to antisocial behavior are contingent upon processes related to social status. Because these processes are so fundamental to social relationships and behavioral similarity, we discuss relevant insights more extensively in the following section.

Status-Related Processes

To understand how social status may affect social influences and social selection processes with regard to offending, it is important to consider both the social and biological changes in adolescence. In her seminal work, Moffitt (1993) refers to a discrepancy between biological and social maturity, the so-called *maturity gap*. As youths develop their own identity, they strife for more autonomy and acknowledgment of their mature status (see also Agnew, 2001). However, because parents, teachers, and other authority figures may deny this autonomy by forbidding or disapproving certain 'mature' behaviors (including delinquency), these behaviors are reinforced. That is, they become more attractive as they offer a means for youths to show that they are mature and that they can make their own independent choices. Delinquent behavior can thus be a strategy to close the maturity gap. Thus, delinquency becomes more normative in adolescence and can be used as a means to gain and maintain status (cf., Hawley, 1999). It is therefore not surprising that delinquency is adopted from peers, also called *social mimicry*, and serves as an important selection criterion for new social relationships. Together with these social changes, neural changes are thought to be responsible for heightened sensitivity to social situations and to socially rewarding behaviors (Crone & Dahl, 2012; Somerville, 2013). For example, work focusing on risk behaviors, including antisocial behavior, indicated that frontal brain regions related to reward were more active in adolescents during a risk-taking task, but only when peers were present (Chein et al., 2011; Steinberg, 2008). Finally, physical maturation and increased mating competition increase the frequency of contexts in which status is salient (De Bruyn et al., 2012).

In line with these notions that emphasize the salience of social status, classrooms with a more hierarchical network structure (i.e., larger differences between the social positions of individual children) are more likely to be characterized by aggression, compared to less hierarchical groups (Ahn & Rodkin, 2014). Social influences on aggression are also more likely to be observed in cliques with many high-status peers (Pattiselanno et al., 2015), suggesting that social status is tied to antisocial behaviors in such groups and hence more likely to be adopted by others.

Gang Involvement

One context in which status-related processes are often observed are youth gangs. Gangs are deviant peer groups that are more organized and structured than regular peer groups. Although gangs differ in the extent to which they are engaged in violence and drug trafficking, gangs that are larger and gangs that consist of males or young adult offenders are more likely to engage in serious violence (Lantz, 2020).

Status processes play an important role in gangs, and hence not surprisingly, social dynamics related to offending are highly prevalent in this context. First, dynamics related to not losing face, retribution, and group honor may lead to waves of mutual gang violence, in which gang members react to the actions of members from other gangs (e.g., Papachristos, 2009; Randle & Bichler, 2017).

Second, gang members also influence each other's offending within gangs. For example, several studies have shown that gun violence and weapon carrying can easily spread through social interactions in youths (Dijkstra et al., 2010; Green et al., 2011), as peers became more similar in weapon carrying over time (Dijkstra et al., 2010, 2012). In contrast, these studies also found that youths were not more likely to select peers who carried weapons. This suggests that youths may arm themselves in response to the weapon carrying of other youths in their social network, either to feel safer or to go along with peer norms in their respective groups. Moreover, violence and non-violent offenses often dictate one's status within the gang, for example, to show off, to deserve a place within the gang, or to show who is boss (e.g., McCuish et al., 2015). Finally, youths may be pressured into joining a gang by their peers (Pitts, 2008). Interestingly, in one study, it was found that high-status gang members often are in a socially central position outside their gang as well and may thus influence others to join gangs or to commit offenses (Gallupe & Gravel, 2018).

In sum, social relationships, and in particular social influence processes, play an important role in the explanation and development of offending and related behaviors in youths. Processes of social maturation and related status dynamics are often at the source of these social influences, which play out in an extreme form in violent (youth) gangs. However, such influences are not limited to youths, but also extend to adult forensic populations. Research from the US showed that adult offenders' attitudes and beliefs about the legitimacy of the law were more likely to be negative in gang members, and especially in gangs with more criminal members, as compared to offenders with fewer ties to criminal peers (Papachristos et al., 2012). Moreover, social networks play a crucial role in pedophilic offending by spreading pornographic materials and setting norms about the justification of sexual relationships with minors (Holt et al., 2010; Houtepen et al., 2016). Finally, using statistical social network analysis, it was found that the nature of social relationships between psychiatric forensic patients residing in a high-security setting was related to social skills, impulsivity, and problem awareness (Van der Horst et al., 2010). Among others, the authors showed that socially skilled patients were more likely to influence the behavior of their fellow patients and that more impulsive patients were more likely to instrumentally use fellow patients. Similarly, among Danish inmates, prison served as a context in which peer reinforcement led to stronger ties between offenders who were already acquainted before incarceration and was associated with increased recidivism for crimes often committed in groups (e.g., theft, drug crimes) (Damm & Gorinas, 2020). Besides these studies, most research that focuses on social influence in adult populations has studied spousal relationships. Work from this field is discussed below.

Romantic and Spousal Relationships

Though the social networks of prisoners are large and dense, they consist primarily of family members and romantic partners (Bellair et al., 2018). Hence, it is not surprising that quite some studies have described the role of romantic partners or spouses on the development, persistence, and desistance of criminal behavior. In their seminal work on turning points, Sampson and Laub (1995) argued that marriage or a steady relationship would be associated with desistance a criminal path as the result of taking up more responsibility, more mature roles, and bringing higher costs with crime and its consequences. However, recent studies have shown that behavioral similarity also plays an important role when it comes to romantic partners or spouses, which may thus mitigate the positive effects of romantic relationships. Below, a brief overview of the insights from this work is presented for romantic relationships in adolescence and cohabitation and marriage relationships in adulthood.

The Role of Romantic Partners in Adolescence

Similar to non-romantic peer relationships, dating partners may exert social influence with regard to offending as well. Many studies that examined these social influence processes in adolescence have used data from the Study of Adolescent Health (Add Health), in which youths and their social relationships are followed from early adolescence into adulthood. Analyses on these data have shown that romantic partners' deviance affects the other's deviant behavior, but has a stronger effect on female involvement in minor deviance (Haynie et al., 2005). Moreover, in the same study it was found, for more serious deviance, that romantic partners' delinquency exerts a unique effect on respondents' delinquency above and beyond that of delinquent peers. Other work also showed that involvement with a delinquent romantic partner was associated to adolescents' delinquency, irrespective of friends' and parents' behavior (Lonardo et al., 2009), thus emphasizing the important role that romantic partners play in adolescence.

Interestingly, the social influence of romantic partners on offending differs for boys and girls. Whereas boys become more resistant to the antisocial influences of their romantic partners, girls become increasingly vulnerable to their partners' antisocial behaviors with age (Monahan et al., 2014). These negative social influence effects are also stronger in relatively short-term relationships, and girls in such relationships run the risk of persisting in antisocial behavior. In one study that specifically examined female offenders in adolescence, it was also found that the majority (73.6%) dated antisocial males in young adulthood, suggesting selection processes. Girls with antisocial partners also showed more continuity in violent offending from adolescence to adulthood (Oudekerk et al., 2014). Another interesting aspect is that having delinquent peers also increased the likelihood of having an antisocial romantic partner, which in turn affected the risk of offending in young adulthood (Simons et al., 2002).

The Role of Marriage and Cohabitation in Adulthood

In general, marriage, cohabitation, or involvement in stable romantic relationships have been associated with desistance from offending (Nielsen, 2018; Sampson et al., 2006). However, there are a few important nuances to this association.

First, this association depends on the criminal behavior of the romantic partner. In a study examining previously convicted men from a large birth cohort in Denmark, it was shown that marriage reduced recidivism compared to those who were not married, only when the spouse had no criminal record (Andersen et al., 2015; Van Schellen et al., 2012; Woodward et al., 2002). Furthermore, when involved with an antisocial female partner, men were more likely to be arrested at an earlier age and were more likely to persist in offending behavior (Capaldi et al., 2008). Another study among couples, of which one partner had been institutionalized during adolescence in a juvenile treatment center, showed that these influence effects are rather direct (Zoutewelle-Terovan et al., 2013): Partner's offending significantly increased the other's likelihood of offending within the same month, for both males and females. Criminal spouses may thus increase the other's risk of offending.

Second, the association depends on the stability of the romantic relationship (Capaldi et al., 2008). Although recently formed partnerships and cohabitation are also associated with reductions in offending, these reductions were not as strong as compared to marital relationships and relationships that lasted longer than a year (Gottlieb & Sugie, 2019).

Third, similar to studies in adolescence, there is some evidence that suggests that the negative effects of criminal spouses are stronger for women than men. In a study examining participants of 18 years and older from the Add Health data, it was shown that being in a relationship with a violent partner only increased the odds of violent behavior for women (Herrera et al., 2011). Moreover, some studies have also suggested that romantic relationships for female offenders may incur risk rather than mitigate risk of re-offending. For example, ex-convicted women were more likely to form relationships with antisocial partners who offered shared experiences and understanding, but at the same time, such partners also stood in the way of successful re-entry into society (Leverentz, 2016). Work that examined romantic partners in forensic psychiatric patients also emphasized these points, but showed that this applied to male and female patients, though female patients were more likely to be in a relationship with antisocial partners.

Fourth, also here, processes related to default selection may occur. Following a large sample of offenders who were tried in the Netherlands, it was found that the more criminal offenses individuals had committed, the lower their chances of marrying and, given marriage, the higher the chances of marrying a criminal partner (Van Schellen et al., 2011). Moreover, individuals born in families that are characterized by crime were found to marry at a later age as compared to other individuals (Lyngstad & Skardhamar, 2016). These studies suggest that offenders may be less attractive as romantic partners and be more likely to end up in relationships with individuals similar to them (Mulvey et al., 2020).

Conclusion

In this chapter, we showed that social relationships play an important role in offending in adolescence and adulthood. Although the social processes that underlie social influence may differ in peer relationships and romantic relationships, they sometimes interact and illustrate that people close to us are relevant drivers of our behavior. Herein lies a challenge for treatment and interventions as social roles and social dynamics are often hard to break, and approaches that focus on individual traits may miss out on explanatory factors that are in large part driven by the social environment. At the same time, the importance of social relationships also provides an opportunity: The social environment may be changed or adapted in such a way that negative social influences decrease and positive behaviors may spread. Although this is easier said than done, current efforts in this regard capitalize on the notion that by changing social norms, individual behavior may also change. An effective example of such an approach is the Finnish anti-bullying program Kiva in schools (Yang & Salmivalli, 2015), in which the status rewards associated with bullying are decreased through promoting norms suggesting that bullying is not 'nice' (*kiva* in Finnish) or cool. With regard to the role of romantic partners, treatment programs that also include partners may help in reducing offending and recidivism. However, more research is needed that examines the role of partner selection and influence in offenders and that considers the broader network in which people are embedded, both within (children, siblings) and outside the direct family (peers, schools, neighborhood). Finally, more attention should be given to studying individual differences in these social processes: Who is more at risk for negative influences and who exerts more influence over others?

Acknowledgements I want to thank Magdelena Juskaite for assisting in summarizing the available literature on romantic relationships and offending.

References

Agnew, R. (2001). Building on the foundation of general strain theory: Specifying the types of strain most likely to lead to crime and delinquency. *Journal of Research in Crime and Delinquency, 38*(4), 319–362.

Ahn, H.-J., & Rodkin, P. C. (2014). Classroom-level predictors of the social status of aggression: Friendship centralization, friendship density, teacher–student attunement, and gender. *Journal of Educational Psychology, 106*(4), 1144–1155. https://doi.org/10.1037/a0036091

Andersen, S. H., Andersen, L. H., & Skov, P. E. (2015). Effect of marriage and spousal criminality on recidivism. *Journal of Marriage and the Family, 77*(2), 496–509. https://doi.org/10.1111/jomf.12176

Bandura, A. (1973). *Aggression: A social learning analysis.* Prentice.

Baumeister, R. F., & Leary, M. R. (1995). The need to belong: Desire for interpersonal attachments as a fundamental human motivation. *Psychological Bulletin, 117*, 497–529. https://doi.org/10.1037/0033-2909.117.3.497

Bellair, P. E., Light, R., & Sutton, J. (2018). Prisoners' personal networks in the months preceding prison: A descriptive portrayal. *International Journal of Offender Therapy and Comparative Criminology.* https://doi.org/10.1177/0306624X18799575

Borgatti, S. P., Mehra, A., Brass, D. J., & Labianca, G. (2009). Network analysis in the social sciences. *Science, 323*(5916), 892–895. https://doi.org/10.1126/science.1165821

Brechwald, W. A., & Prinstein, M. J. (2011). Beyond homophily: A decade of advances in understanding peer influence processes. *Journal of Research on Adolescence, 21,* 166–179.

Capaldi, D. M., Kim, H. K., & Owen, L. D. (2008). Romantic Partners' influence on men's likelihood of arrest in early adulthood. *Criminology, 46*(2), 267–299. https://doi.org/10.1111/j.1745-9125.2008.00110.x

Chein, J., Albert, D., O'Brien, L., Uckert, K., & Steinberg, L. (2011). Peers increase adolescent risk taking by enhancing activity in the brain's reward circuitry. *Developmental Science, 14,* F1–F10. https://doi.org/10.1111/j.1467-7687.2010.01035.x

Crone, E. A., & Dahl, R. E. (2012). Understanding adolescence as a period of social-affective engagement and goal flexibility. *Nature Reviews Neuroscience, 13*(9), 636–650. https://doi.org/10.1038/nrn3313

Damm, A. P., & Gorinas, C. (2020). Prison as a criminal school: Peer effects and criminal learning behind bars. *The Journal of Law and Economics, 63*(1), 149–180. https://doi.org/10.1086/706820

De Bruyn, E. H., Cillessen, A. H. N., & Weisfeld, G. E. (2012). Dominance-popularity status, behavior, emergence sexual activity in young adolescents. *Evolutionary Psychology, 10,* 296–319.

Deptula, D. P., & Cohen, R. (2004). Aggressive, rejected, and delinquent children and adolescents: A comparison of their friendships. *Aggression and Violent Behavior, 9*(1), 75–104. https://doi.org/10.1016/s1359-1789(02)00117-9

Dijkstra, J. K., Lindenberg, S., & Veenstra, R. (2008). Beyond the class norm: Bullying behavior of popular adolescents and its relation to peer acceptance and rejection. *Journal of Abnormal Child Psychology, 36*(8), 1289–1299. https://doi.org/10.1007/s10802-008-9251-7

Dijkstra, J. K., Gest, S. D., Lindenberg, S., Veenstra, R., & Cillessen, A. H. N. (2012). Testing three explanations of the emergence of weapon carrying in peer context: The roles of aggression, victimization, and the social network. *Journal of Adolescent Health, 50,* 371–376. https://doi.org/10.1016/j.jadohealth.2011.08.010

Dijkstra, J. K., Lindenberg, S., Veenstra, R., Steglich, C., Isaacs, J., Card, N. A., & Hodges, E. V. E. (2010). Influence and selection processes in weapon carrying during adolescence: The roles of status, aggression, and vulnerability. *Criminology, 48,* 187–220.

Dishion T. J., Patterson G. R., & Griesler P. C. (1994). Peer adaptations in the development of antisocial behavior. In L. R. Huesmann (Ed.), *Aggressive behavior: Current perspectives* (pp. 61–95). Plenum Press. https://doi.org/10.1007/978-1-4757-9116-7_4

Dishion, T. J., & Tipsord, J. M. (2011). Peer contagion in child and adolescent social and emotional development. *Annual Review of Psychology, 62,* 189–214.

Espelage, D. L., Holt, M. K., & Henkel, R. R. (2003). Examination of peer-group contextual effects on aggression during early adolescence. *Child Development, 74,* 205–220. https://doi.org/10.1111/1467-8624.00531

Gallupe, O., McLevey, J., & Brown, S. (2019). Selection and influence: A meta-analysis of the association between peer and personal offending. https://doi.org/10.1007/s10940-018-9384-y

Gallupe, O., & Gravel, J. (2018). Social Network Position of gang members in schools: Implications for recruitment and gang prevention. *Justice Quarterly, 35*(3), 505–525. https://doi.org/10.1080/07418825.2017.1323114

Gottlieb, A., & Sugie, N. F. (2019). Marriage, cohabitation, and crime: Differentiating associations by partnership stage. *Justice Quarterly, 36*(3), 503–531. https://doi.org/10.1080/07418825.2018.1445275

Green, B., Horel, T., & Papachristos, A. V. (2017). Modeling Contagion through social networks to explain and predict gunshot violence in Chicago, 2006 to 2014. *JAMA Internal Medicine, 177*(3), 326–333. https://doi.org/10.1001/jamainternmed.2016.8245

Hartup, W. W. (1996). The company they keep: Friendships and their developmental significance. *Child Development, 67*, 1–13. https://doi.org/10.1111/j.1467-8624.1996.tb01714.x

Hawley, P. H. (1999). The ontogenesis of social dominance: A strategy-based evolutionary perspective. *Developmental Review, 19*(1), 97–132. https://doi.org/10.1006/drev.1998.0470

Haynie, D. L., Giordano, P. C., Manning, W. D., & Longmore, M. A. (2005). Adolescent romantic relationships and delinquency involvement. *Criminology, 43*(1), 177–210. https://doi.org/10.1111/j.0011-1348.2005.00006.x

Herrera, V. M., Wiersma, J. D., & Cleveland, H. H. (2011). Romantic partners' contribution to the continuity of male and female delinquent and violent behavior. *Journal of Research on Adolescence, 21*(3), 608–618. https://doi.org/10.1111/j.1532-7795.2010.00693.x

Holt, T. J., Blevins, K. R., & Burkert, N. (2010). Considering the pedophile subculture online. *Sexual Abuse, 22*(1), 3–24. https://doi.org/10.1177/1079063209344979

Houtepen, J. A. B. M., Sijtsema, J. J., & Bogaerts, S. (2016). Being sexually attracted to minors: Sexual development, coping, and risk factors for offending in self-identified pedophiles. *Journal of Sex & Marital Therapy, 42*(1), 48–69. https://doi.org/10.1080/0092623X.2015.1061077

Janssen, H. J., Eichelsheim, V. I., Deković, M., & Bruinsma, G. J. N. (2016). How is parenting related to adolescent delinquency? A between- and within-person analysis of the mediating role of self-control, delinquent attitudes, peer delinquency, and time spent in criminogenic settings. *European Journal of Criminology, 13*(2), 169–194. https://doi.org/10.1177/1477370815608881

Kwon, K., & Lease, A. M. (2009). Examination of the contribution of clique characteristics to children's adjustment: Clique type and perceived cohesion. *International Journal of Behavioral Development, 33*, 230–242. https://doi.org/10.1177/0165025408098023

Laninga-Wijnen, L., Harakeh, Z., Steglich, C., Dijkstra, J. K., Veenstra, R., & Vollebergh, W. (2017). The norms of popular peers moderate friendship dynamics of adolescent aggression. *Child Development, 88*(4), 1265–1283. https://doi.org/10.1111/cdev.12650

Lantz, B. (2020). Co-offending group composition and violence: The impact of sex, age, and group size on co-offending violence. *Crime & Delinquency, 66*(1), 93–122. https://doi.org/10.1177/0011128719834564

Leverentz, A. M. (2016). The love of a good man? Romantic relationships as a source of support or hindrance for female ex-offenders. *Journal of Research in Crime and Delinquency.* https://doi.org/10.1177/0022427806293323

Lonardo, R. A., Giordano, P. C., Longmore, M. A., & Manning, W. D. (2009). Parents, friends, and romantic partners: Enmeshment in deviant networks and adolescent delinquency involvement. *Journal of Youth and Adolescence, 38*(3), 367–383. https://doi.org/10.1007/s10964-008-9333-4

Low, S., Polanin, J. R., & Espelage, D. L. (2013). The role of social networks in physical and relational aggression among young adolescents. *Journal of Youth and Adolescence, 42*, 1078–1089. https://doi.org/10.1007/s10964-013-9933-5

Lyngstad, T. H., & Skardhamar, T. (2016). Family formation and crime: What role for the family network? *Advances in Life Course Research, 28*, 41–51. https://doi.org/10.1016/j.alcr.2015.09.007

van der Horst, R., Snijders, T., Völker, B., & Spreen, M. (2010). Social interaction related to the functioning of forensic psychiatric inpatients. *Journal of Forensic Psychology Practice, 10*(4), 339–359. https://doi.org/10.1080/15228932.2010.481238

McCuish, E. C., Bouchard, M., & Corrado, R. R. (2015). The search for suitable homicide co-offenders among gang members. *Journal of Contemporary Criminal Justice, 31*(3), 319–336. https://doi.org/10.1177/1043986214553375

McPherson, M., Smith-Lovin, L., & Cook, J. M. (2001). Birds of a feather: Homophily in social networks. *Annual Review of Sociology, 27*, 415–444. https://doi.org/10.1146/annurev.soc.27.1.415

Moffitt, T. E. (1993). Adolescence-limited and life-course-persistent antisocial behavior: A developmental taxonomy. *Psychological Review, 100*(4), 674–701. https://doi.org/10.1037/0033-295x.100.4.674

Moffitt, T. E. (2018). Male antisocial behaviour in adolescence and beyond. *Nature Human Behavior, 2*(3), 177–186.

Monahan, K. C., Dmitrieva, J., & Cauffman, E. (2014). Bad romance: Sex differences in the longitudinal association between romantic relationships and deviant behavior. *Journal of Research on Adolescence, 24*(1), 12–26. https://doi.org/10.1111/jora.12019

Moreno, J. L. (1934). *Who shall survive? A new approach to the problem of human interrelations* (pp. xvi, 441). Nervous and Mental Disease Publishing Co. https://doi.org/10.1037/10648-000

Mulvey, P., Larson, M., & Terpstra, B. (2020). Understanding the nature and implications of romantic relationships among criminally involved individuals with mental illness. *Justice Quarterly, 37*(4), 667–696. https://doi.org/10.1080/07418825.2019.1589556

Nielsen, A. A. (2018). How are social bonds to a romantic partner related to criminal offending? *European Journal of Criminology, 15*(3), 321–343. https://doi.org/10.1177/1477370817737234

Oudekerk, B. A., Burgers, D. E., & Reppucci, N. D. (2014). Romantic partner deviance and the continuity of violence from adolescence to adulthood among offending girls. *Journal of Research on Adolescence, 24*(1), 27–39. https://doi.org/10.1111/j.1532-7795.2012.00823.x

Papachristos, A. V. (2009). Murder by structure: Dominance relations and the social structure of gang homicide. *American Journal of Sociology, 115*(1), 74–128. https://doi.org/10.1086/597791

Papachristos, A. V., Meares, T. L., & Fagan, J. (2012). Why Do Criminals Obey The Law? The influence of legitimacy and social networks on active gun offenders. *Journal of Criminal Law & Criminology, 102*(2), 397–440.

Pattiselanno, K., Dijkstra, J. K., Steglich, C., Vollebergh, W., & Veenstra, R. (2015). Structure matters: The role of clique hierarchy in the relationship between adolescent social status and aggression and prosociality. *Journal of Youth and Adolescence, 44*, 2257–2274. https://doi.org/10.1007/s10964-015-0310-4

Pitts, J. (2008). *Reluctant gangsters: The changing face of youth crime.* Taylor & Francis.

Randle, J., & Bichler, G. (2017). Uncovering the social pecking order in gang violence. In B. LeClerc & E. U. Savona (Eds.), *Crime prevention in the 21st century: Insightful approaches for crime prevention initiatives* (pp. 165–186). Springer International Publishing. https://doi.org/10.1007/978-3-319-27793-6_12

Sampson, R. J., & Laub, J. H. (1995). *Crime in the making: pathways and turning points through life.* Harvard University Press.

Sampson, R. J., Laub, J. H., & Wimer, C. (2006). Does marriage reduce crime? A counterfactual approach to within-individual causal effects. *Criminology, 44*(3), 465–508. https://doi.org/10.1111/j.1745-9125.2006.00055.x

van Schellen, M., Apel, R., & Nieuwbeerta, P. (2012). "Because you're mine, i walk the line"? Marriage, spousal criminality, and criminal offending over the life course. *Journal of Quantitative Criminology, 28*(4), 701–723. https://doi.org/10.1007/s10940-012-9174-x

van Schellen, M., Poortman, A.-R., & Nieuwbeerta, P. (2011). Partners in crime? Criminal offending, marriage formation, and partner selection. *Journal of Research in Crime and Delinquency.* https://doi.org/10.1177/0022427811414197

Sijtsema, J. J., & Lindenberg, S. M. (2018). Peer influence in the development of adolescent antisocial behavior: Advances from dynamic social network studies. *Developmental Review, 50*, 140–154.

Simons, R. L., Stewart, E., Gordon, L. C., Conger, R. D., & Elder, G. H. (2002). A test of life-course explanations for stability and change in antisocial behavior from adolescence to young adulthood. *Criminology, 40*(2), 401–434. https://doi.org/10.1111/j.1745-9125.2002.tb00961.x

Snyder, J., Horsch, E., & Childs, J. (1997). Peer relationships of young children: Affiliative choices and the shaping of aggressive behavior. *Journal of Clinical Child Psychology, 26*(2), 145–156. https://doi.org/10.1207/s15374424jccp2602_3

Snyder, J., Schrepferman, L., Oeser, J., Patterson, G., Stoolmiller, M., Johnson, K., & Snyder, A. (2005). Deviancy training and association with deviant peers in young children: Occurrence and contribution to early-onset conduct problems. *Development and Psychopathology, 17*, 397–413. https://doi.org/10.1017/S0954579405050194

Somerville, L. (2013). The teenage brain: Sensitivity to social evaluation. *Current Directions in Psychological Science, 22*, 121–127. https://doi.org/10.1177/0963721413476512

Steinberg, L. (2008). A social neuroscience perspective on adolescent risk-taking. *Developmental Review, 28*, 78–106. https://doi.org/10.1016/j.dr.2007.08.002

Sutherland, E. H. (1947). *Principles of criminology* (4th ed., pp. vii, 643). J. B. Lippincott.

Witvliet, M., Van Lier, P. A. C., Cuijpers, P., & Koot, H. M. (2010). Change and stability in childhood clique membership, isolation from cliques, and associated child characteristics. *Journal of Clinical Child & Adolescent Psychology, 39*(1), 12–24. https://doi.org/10.1080/15374410903401161

Woodward, L. J., Fergusson, D. M., & Horwood, L. J. (2002). Deviant partner involvement and offending risk in early adulthood. *Journal of Child Psychology and Psychiatry, 43*(2), 177–190. https://doi.org/10.1111/1469-7610.00011

Yang, A., & Salmivalli, C. (2015). Effectiveness of the KiVa antibullying programme on bully-victims, bullies and victims. *Educational Research, 57*(1), 80–90. https://doi.org/10.1080/00131881.2014.983724

Zoutewelle-Terovan, M. V., van der Geest, V., Bijleveld, C., & Liefbroer, A. C. (2013). Associations in criminal behaviour for married males and females at high risk of offending. *European Journal of Criminology.* https://doi.org/10.1177/1477370813497632

Further Readings

Dishion, T. J., & Tipsord, J. M. (2011). Peer contagion in child and adolescent social and emotional development. *Annual Review of Psychology, 62,* 189–214.

van Mastrigt, S. B. (2017). Co-offending and co-offender selection. In W. Bernasco, J.-L. Van Gelder, & H. Elffers (Eds.), *The Oxford handbooks in criminology and criminal justice. The Oxford handbook of offender decision making* (pp. 338–360). Oxford University Press.

Sijtsema, J. J., & Lindenberg, S. M. (2018). Peer influence in the development of adolescent antisocial behavior: Advances from dynamic social network studies. *Developmental Review, 50,* 140–154.

Part II
Psychopathology and Deviant Behavior

Antisocial Personality Disorder

11

Jessica Yakeley

Key Points

- Antisocial personality disorder (ASPD) can be understood within an attachment framework.
- Patients with ASPD are difficult to engage in treatment but are often denied treatment as well.
- Interventions aimed at improving self-regard and promoting positive social interactions are likely more effective than interventions focused on victim-empathy.
- Service user involvement in interventions for ASPD should increase for the benefit of patients with ASPD and their (potential) victims.

Introduction

Antisocial personality disorder (ASPD) is a debilitating condition that continues to be under-diagnosed and untreated. Despite many advances in the field of personality disorders over the past two decades, with accumulating research into their aetiology, developmental trajectory and prognosis, as well as the creation of specific evidence-based psychological therapies targeted at treating underlying personality dysfunction, the field has mostly focussed on borderline personality disorder, and beliefs that people with ASPD are untreatable remain widespread.

This chapter examines the diagnosis and epidemiology of ASPD, its aetiology and conceptualisation as a disorder of attachment, the evidence base of

J. Yakeley (✉)
Portman Clinic, The Tavistock and Portman NHS Foundation Trust, London, UK
e-mail: jyakeley@tavi-port.nhs.uk

© The Author(s), under exclusive license to Springer Nature Switzerland AG 2022   203
C. Garofalo and J. J. Sijtsema (eds.), *Clinical Forensic Psychology*,
https://doi.org/10.1007/978-3-030-80882-2_11

specific therapies developed for this condition, and general principles of treating individuals with ASPD.

Diagnosis

ASPD is a particular type of personality disorder as defined by the DSM-5 (American Psychiatric Association, 2013). It is characterised as a pervasive pattern of disregard for and violation of rights of others since age 15, including failure to conform to social norms, deceitfulness, impulsivity or failure to plan ahead, irritability and aggressiveness, reckless disregard for safety of self and others, consistent irresponsibility, and lack of remorse. A diagnosis of schizophrenia or mania must be excluded as causes of antisocial behaviour. As with other personality disorders, the diagnosis cannot be made before the age of 18; however, unlike other DSM-5 defined personality disorders, to make a diagnosis of ASPD, the person must show evidence of having conduct disorder before the age of 15 years.

The diagnosis has been criticised for its focus on antisocial behaviour and criminality rather than on underlying personality structure and interpersonal deficits (Widiger & Corbitt, 1993). This reflects the historical problematic relationship and divergence of the DSM antisocial personality disorder construct with the construct of psychopathy as originally described by Cleckley (1941) and subsequently operationalised by Hare (1991) in the Psychopathy Checklist (Crego & Widiger, 2015). The DSM-5 diagnosis of ASPD does also not distinguish between those individuals with mild, moderate, or severe psychopathy, as measured on the Psychopathy Checklist-Revised (PCL-R) (Hare, 2003). Studies show that only one third of individuals with antisocial personality disorder has severe psychopathy, which carries a significantly poorer prognosis than individuals with mild to moderately psychopathic traits (Hare, 1991, 2003). However, the alternative model of personality disorders (AMPD) in Section III of the DSM-5, which incorporates two key features in the conceptualisation of personality disorders—personality impairment and the presence of maladaptive personality traits generally aligned with the five-factor model of personality disorder, which is more consistent with models of psychopathy. The AMPD operationalises ASPD with seven traits coming from the antagonism (manipulativeness, deceitfulness, callousness and hostility) and disinhibition (irresponsibility, impulsivity and risk taking) domains of the five factor model, and includes a psychopathy features specifier for ASPD characterised by three additional traits (low anxiousness, low withdrawal and attention seeking) (American Psychiatric Association, 2013).

Prevalence and Co-Morbidity

Estimates of the prevalence of ASPD in the general population vary according to the methodology and countries studied, and range from around 1% (Coid, Yang, Tyrer et al., 2006; Torgerson et al., 2001) to 6.8% (Swanson et al., 1994). All studies show that the prevalence of ASPD is consistently higher in men than in women (National Institute for Health and Clinical Excellence, 2009). The prevalence is significantly increased in criminal justice settings, representing up to 80% of the prison population (Moran, 1999; Ogloff, 2006; Singleton et al., 1998). People with ASPD are significantly more likely to commit violent crimes (Coid, Yang, Roberts et al., 2006) and the diagnosis is highly predictive of future violence, future reconviction or reincarceration upon release, and recidivism severity (Hodkins et al., 1996; Wormith et al., 2007).

ASPD carries a considerable co-morbidity with other mental disorders, particularly substance misuse (Compton et al., 2005; Robins et al., 1991), anxiety disorders (Goodwin & Hamilton, 2003) and depressive disorders (Lenzenweger et al., 2007). It is also associated with poor physical health (Byrne et al., 2013) and increased mortality, particularly at a young age, not only due to an increased risk of suicide, but also to reckless behaviour such as drug misuse and aggression (Black et al., 1996). Individuals with ASPD also exert a heavy toll on others, with negative impacts on their families and relationships with others, as well as increased involvement with social services, health and the criminal justice system. The financial burden of injury to victims, damage to property, involvement with the criminal justice system, use of healthcare facilities, lost employment, family disruption, childcare proceedings, gambling, and alcohol and substance misuse is large (Home Office & Department of Health, 2002; Myers et al., 1998; National Institute for Health and Clinical Excellence, 2009; National Research Council, 1999).

Aetiology

Although the precise aetiology of ASPD remains unknown, like most mental disorders it is considered to be a multifactorial construct with both a biological and environmental foundation. There is significant evidence that ASPD is a neurodevelopmental disorder in that it originates in childhood, has a genetic basis, shows abnormalities in brain structure and function throughout development with corresponding neurocognitive impairment, and has a relatively stable course throughout development, with impaired social, academic, or occupational functioning in adulthood (Raine, 2018).

The heritability of ASPD has been estimated as between 40 and 70% (Ferguson, 2010; Fu et al., 2002; Mason & Frick, 1994; Torgersen et al., 2008) and is more pronounced in aggressive and antisocial children with callous and unemotional traits (considered to be precursors to psychopathy in adulthood) compared to aggressive and antisocial children without such traits (Viding et al., 2005). Studies looking at genetic influences in the pathogenesis of ASPD are limited and are focussed on genetic abnormalities in antisocial and aggressive behaviours rather than samples of individuals with a diagnosis of ASPD (Basoglu et al., 2011; Merriman & Cameron, 2007; Raine, 2006). Moreover, it is unlikely that such genetic abnormalities work in isolation. Complex gene/environmental interactions are likely to operate in the development of ASPD, where adverse social experiences trigger genetic susceptibility. Antisocial behaviour in males has been linked to gene variants, but only for individuals exposed to stressful early life environments. Studies have shown that low MAO-A activity in children who had been seriously abused were more likely to have conduct disorder CD and more extreme violent behaviour than children who were not abused and also had low MAO-A activity (Caspi et al., 2000, 2002, 2004). This suggests that children who are genetically vulnerable to antisocial behaviour and also experience abuse from their caregivers are more likely to develop antisocial behaviour, which then may be exacerbated by provoking negative parental responses (National Institute for Health and Clinical Excellence, 2009).

The neurobiology of ASPD is being increasingly investigated. Neuroimaging research suggests that ASPD is linked with abnormal brain anatomy and function. MRI scans of individuals with ASPD have been shown to have significantly reduced prefrontal grey matter compared to controls (Raine et al., 2000; Yang et al., 2010), which correlated with a reduction in peripheral autonomic reactivity (evidenced by slow wave (theta) EEG activity, low resting heart rate and poor skin conductance) to aversive events in individuals with psychopathy (Raine, 2013). Given the heterogeneity of the population that fulfil criteria for a diagnosis of ASPD, particularly in relation to the presence or absence of psychopathy, some studies have distinguished between 'successful' and 'unsuccessful' psychopaths where the latter show more impulsive and risky behaviour and are incarcerated more frequently than the former group. Significant reductions in both the left and right amygdala have been noted in unsuccessful psychopaths in comparison to the successful psychopaths (Yang et al., 2010). Studies also show that offenders with ASPD and psychopathy have reduced gray matter in the prefrontal region whereas those who have ASPD without psychopathic features do not (Gregory et al., 2012) suggesting that ASPD with psychopathic features may be a separate clinical manifestation that is more neurodevelopmental in nature (Raine, 2018). Neuro-developmental abnormalities in the corpus callosum (Raine et al., 2003), and abnormalities in the symmetry of the hippocampus have also been implicated in ASPD (Raine et al., 2004), as well as enlargement of the striatum (Barkataki et al., 2006).

Raine proposes a prefrontal—amygdala—striatal model of ASPD where structural and functional abnormalities in these three structures may account for core clinical manifestations of the disorder: a lack of self-control (prefrontal), low avoidance of punishment and negative stimuli (amygdala), and a heightened sensitivity to rewarding stimuli (striatum) (Raine, 2018). Studies have also shown neurocognitive deficits in ASPD, including poor executive functions, poor facial emotion recognition and reward dominance, all of which are consistent with abnormalities in prefrontal, amygdala and striatal functioning. The prefrontal—amygdala—striatal system has also been shown to be particularly susceptible to early stress and social adversity (Tottenham & Galván 2016).

Numerous adverse environmental influences including harsh and inconsistent parenting, social adversity, poverty and associating with criminal peers are considered important causative factors for ASPD (National Institute for Health and Clinical Excellence, 2009). Several studies suggest that adverse childhood experiences (ACEs) play a significant role in the development of the disorder. Physical abuse, sexual abuse, emotional abuse and neglect in childhood, respectively, have been found to be associated with a diagnosis of ASPD in adulthood (Battle et al., 2004; De Lisi & Beauregard, 2018; Douglas et al., 2011; Farrington, 2000; Fergusson et al., 2008). However, again these studies do not distinguish between individuals with ASPD with high levels of psychopathy, and those with low levels. There is evidence to suggest that severely psychopathic adults, who would score highly on the PCL-R, experience less abuse and neglect as children than moderately psychopathic adults, which also supports evidence for a relative increase in biogenic contributions as the degree of psychopathy increases (Felthous & Saβ, 2007).

Hodgins and colleagues emphasise the importance of co-occurring anxiety in subtyping ASPD (De Brito & Hodgins, 2009). Based on studies of children and adults, they propose that around half of individuals in the ASPD population are characterised by anxiety as well as persistent antisocial behaviour and have low levels of callous unemotional traits as children and low levels of psychopathic traits as adults. This group is more likely to have experienced physical abuse as children and resort to violence as a compensatory response to underlying emotional conflict and distress. The other half have normal to low levels of anxiety and varying levels of psychopathy but include a subgroup with high levels of psychopathy. This group shows marked callous and unemotional traits as children, low levels of anxiety, more predatory (instrumental) violence and less amenability to treatment.

Based on observation and clinical work with violent offenders, including those with ASPD, many authors have emphasised the role of anxiety and other negatively experienced affects, particularly shame and humiliation, in precipitating interpersonal aggression and violence. In his work with high-security inmates, Gilligan (1996, 2002) proposed that early experiences of abuse, neglect and rejection predisposed them as adults to be sensitised to feeling ostracised, bullied or ignored, leading to unbearable feelings of shame and humiliation which need to be defended against by violent means. Within the shame literature, empirical studies have revealed the prominent role of shame and social exclusion in triggering anger and aggression, which may be seen as coping strategies, emotional regulation and evolutionary adaptations to social pain (Elison et al., 2014).

Attachment and ASPD

One hypothesis that has been proposed to explain how such adverse experiences, in conjunction with genetic precursors, may contribute to the development of ASPD is that they interfere with the normal development of attachment between the child and its caregivers (McGauley et al., 2011). Stemming from the seminal work of John Bowlby, attachment theory is a body of knowledge concerned with the emotional bonds and interactions between human beings and the psychopathological difficulties that arise when these processes are disturbed (Bowlby, 1969). It proposes that the need for significant human relationships are universal, which are established at a psychobiological level in early childhood. Attachment theory explores how these relationships are linked to caregiving and care-eliciting behaviours and used to manage fear, vulnerability and threats of loss across the lifespan.

Attachment is the normal tendency of the infant and young child to seek close proximity to its primary caregivers, usually initially the mother, for protection and a feeling of security. This develops in the first year of life to provide a safe haven and secure base for exploration, including exploration of the mind of self and others. Insecure attachment is associated with childhood trauma, separation and neglect, which disrupt the normal development of attachment and can produce long-term pathological effects including impaired affect regulation, impulse control, socialisation and mentalisation (the capacity to reflect and to think about one's own and others' mental states and to be able to interpret the actions of oneself and others as meaningful and based on intentional mental states (Bateman & Fonagy, 2019), and the development of personality difficulties and mental disorders, including ASPD, in adult life (DeKlyen & Greenberg, 2008; Kobak et al., 2006; Lyons-Ruth et al., 1987, 1993).

ASPD may thus be conceptualised as a disorder of attachment. Several studies have shown higher levels of insecure attachment in violent offenders, most of whom had a personality disorder, than in the normal population (Adshead, 2004; Bogaerts et al., 2005; Frodi et al., 2001; Levinson & Fonagy, 2004; van IJzendoorn et al., 1997). All of these studies showed an over-representation of individuals with dismissing attachment states of mind, and one study of incarcerated offenders showed that dismissive states of mind were statistically more likely in the violent prisoners compared to a matched non-violent group of patients with a personality disorder (Levinson & Fonagy, 2004). Other studies have shown that psychopathic tendencies in children have been linked with maladaptive interactive patterns in families (Dadds et al., 2012) and severe institutional deprivation (Sonuga-Barke et al., 2010). This suggests that at least in some cases apparent callous and unemotional traits exhibited in children are rooted in disrupted attachment relationships, and as such do not result in adult psychopathy but are a defence against early anxiety (Frick & Viding, 2009). A recent meta-analysis of 12 studies with a total of 1876 participants looking at the relationship between attachment styles and psychopathic traits showed a positive association between psychopathy and insecure and disorganised attachment. The strongest associations were found in forensic and prison samples (van der Zouwen et al., 2018) which is consistent with evidence that offenders, many of whom would fulfil a diagnosis of ASPD, who are detained or supervised within criminal justice systems are more likely to report having experienced disruptions in attachment due to separations, abuse and neglect from their early caregivers than in the general population (Coid, 1992; Heads, et al., 1997; Weeks & Widom, 1998).

Evidence Base for Effective Treatments for ASPD

The belief that ASPD is untreatable remains widespread and individuals with the diagnosis are frequently rejected from mental health services due to the difficulties in engaging them in treatment, their chaotic lifestyles, drug and alcohol misuse and risk of violence to themselves or others (Crawford et al., 2009; Yakeley & Williams, 2014).

The evidence base for the treatment and management of the condition is limited and only a small number of high quality treatment trials of specific psychological therapies have been conducted among people with ASPD (Gibbon et al., 2010; National Institute for Clinical Excellence, 2009). Most studies have been conducted on offenders in general rather than specifically on samples of individuals with a diagnosis of ASPD, and moreover, outcome criteria are usually restricted to the presence or absence of re-offending (National Institute for Clinical Excellence, 2009).

Following a review (Vennard et al., 1997), which gave some evidence that cognitive behavioural therapy (CBT) methods combined with training in social skills and problem solving reduced recidivism in both juvenile and adult offenders, most treatment programmes for offenders have been based on cognitive-behavioural principles. Programmes found to have the largest effect size adhere to the 'risk-needs-responsivity' (RNR) model (Andrews, 1995; Simon, 1998). These focus on risk (targeting those individuals at greatest risk of reoffending), need (focussing on dynamic criminogenic risk factors such as criminal attitudes, substance abuse and impulsivity), and responsivity (delivering interventions that maximise offender engagement in treatment).

An early review of the treatment of psychopathic and antisocial personality disorder (Dolan & Coid, 1993) concluded that the evidence base for such treatments was poor, with only a small number of studies, which were limited by poor methodology and lack of long-term follow-up. Subsequent meta-analyses have highlighted the limited evidence base for effective treatments for ASPD (Duggan et al., 2007; Gibbon et al., 2010; Warren et al., 2003) and the difficulties in comparing interventions due to differences in defining and measuring outcome; a focus on treating incarcerated offenders rather than those in the community; a focus on behavioural and symptomatic rather than structural personality change; and diagnostic inconsistencies, with most outcome studies failing to differentiate offenders with psychopathy from those without (De Brito & Hodgins, 2009). A Cochrane review of psychological interventions for ASPD (Gibbon et al., 2010) considered 11 studies, of which several looked at treatments to reduce drug or alcohol misuse in people with ASPD but few focussing on treating the disorder specifically. They found some evidence that contingency management (which provides rewards for progress in treatment) could help people with ASPD to reduce their misuse of drugs or alcohol, but no firm conclusions regarding the treatment of ASPD were found from the evidence available. There are very few studies evaluating the treatment of patients with ASPD in general mental health services, with only one published randomised controlled trial (RCT) (Davidson et al., 2009), which investigated the feasibility of carrying out a full

RCT of cognitive-behavioural therapy versus treatment as usual. A large-scale RCT evaluating mentalisation-based treatment in male offenders on community probation is currently being conducted in the UK (Fonagy et al., 2020).

There is emerging evidence for the efficacy of democratic therapeutic approaches, use peer influence as the key agent of change to help individuals acquire social skills and learn social norms for the treatment of forensic patients and offenders, including those diagnosed with ASPD. The majority of outcome studies of therapeutic communities in both health and forensic settings are hampered by poor methodology and small sample sizes but do show some improvement in interpersonal outcomes and reducing reoffending, particularly for individuals with personality disorder (Capone et al., 2016; Lees et al., 1999, 2004; Newbury, 2010; Skett & Lewis, 2019).

The evidence base for the pharmacological treatment of ASPD is equally limited. Two large meta-analyses of trials for pharmacological interventions for ASPD (National Institute for Clinical Excellence, 2009; Khalifa et al., 2010) concluded that there was no consistent evidence that supported the use of any pharmacological intervention to treat the disorder. Pharmacological interventions should be limited to the treatment of co-morbid mental disorders and not be routinely used for treating the primary traits or associated behaviours of ASPD.

Assessment of ASPD

Any treatment planning begins with a careful clinical assessment. The presence of other mental disorders such as depression or substance misuse should be identified and treated if possible. Risk should be assessed, ideally with a validated instrument such as the Historical Clinical Risk-20 (HCR-20; Webster et al., 1997) or the Violence Risk Appraisal Guide (VRAG; Harris et al., 1993). However, although the person's risk of violence to others is a primary concern, consideration of the individual's risk to self is also important because of their increased risk of suicide, which is often neglected, partly because many individuals with ASPD are ashamed to admit to any vulnerability such as suicidal ideation. Additionally, given the reckless behaviour of many of these individuals and the likelihood of head injury, neurological and neuropsychological impairments also must be excluded as these may exacerbate clinical expressions, such as physical violence.

The severity of psychopathy should be determined, preferably with the Psychopathy Checklist-Revised (PCL-R; Hare, 2003), which is a reliable and valid clinical instrument for the assessment of psychopathy. This is because patients with higher psychopathy scores are less amenable to treatment and have a poorer prognosis than those with lower scores. Moreover, psychopathic criminals have been found to be 3–5 times more violent than non-psychopathic criminals (Hare, 2003). Meloy (1988) recommends that therapy will be of no benefit and should not be offered to psychopathic patients who show any of the following features: sadistic aggressive behaviour resulting in serious injury, complete absence of remorse or justification for such behaviour, very superior or mildly mentally retarded intelligence, a historical absence of capacity to form emotional attachments, and unexpected 'atavistic' fear felt by the experienced clinician in the patient's presence.

The identification of certain personality characteristics, which are linked to the degree of psychopathy, is relevant to the treatability of patients with ASPD. These features include the degree to which the person can form emotional bonds with others, the presence of anxiety in situations which would be fear-inducing for most people, and the capacity of the person to feel guilt, remorse and empathy, all of which are compromised in more psychopathic individuals. Without a capability for attachment, any therapy that depends, either explicitly or implicitly, on the emotional relationship with the therapist will fail and may also pose a danger to the professional because a lack of empathy means that the patient with ASPD is not concerned about the impact of his aggression or violence towards the therapist. The more severe the psychopathy, the more the patient will relate to others on the basis of power rather than affection (Meloy, 1988).

Finally, current situational and environmental factors such as legal proceedings or being involved in a criminal subculture may aggravate the person's antisocial behaviours and should therefore be addressed.

Creating a Safe Treatment Setting

As well as risk assessment of the patient or offender, the safety of the setting where the treatment takes place, whether it be a high, medium or low security in-patient setting, prison, or the community, also needs to be assessed (Yakeley & Williams, 2014). In addition to considerations of physical and procedural security—for example, the walls of a prison, having panic alarms in a community setting, and policies for safeguarding vulnerable individuals—relational aspects of the treatment setting are paramount in influencing any risk posed to others by the patient or offender with ASPD. Relational security refers to a healthy emotional environment, which is created by focussing on the relationships between patients/ offenders, staff and the institution or organisation as a whole. The challenging behaviours of persons with ASPD and their unwillingness to engage in treatment can evoke negative emotional responses in professionals, at both a conscious and unconscious level, and if these are not recognised and acknowledged, they may be enacted in problematic emotional responses and behaviours. These include high staff turnover, staff sickness or burn-out, boundary violations, pathological team and institutional dynamics, and punitive attitudes towards patients such as denying leave or over-estimation of a patient's risk, attitudes which may be experienced by the individual as a repetition of their abusive experiences in childhood. The emotional reactions induced by the patient in the clinician or therapist through unconscious communications are referred to as the countertransference, a key psychoanalytic concept, and provide insights into the inner world of the patient with ASPD and the risk that they pose. Common countertransference reactions include moral outrage and beliefs that the person is untreatable; feelings of hopelessness and guilt when change does not occur; disgust; excessive fear, and its counterpart, the denial of real dangerousness; devaluation and loss of professional identity; excessively punitive and sadistic responses; and sexual excitement, which is rarely admitted, but can lead to boundary violations (Meloy & Yakeley, 2013). The availability for the staff group of supervision and reflective practice is essential in helping them think about how they are affected, both consciously and unconsciously, by the patients with whom they work.

Engagement in Treatment

Many people with ASPD associate having mental health difficulties with weakness and vulnerability and are reluctant to present for help. Those that do start therapy often attend irregularly or prematurely terminate treatment and are more likely to have poorer clinical outcomes and cause lower staff morale than those who complete the course (McMurran, 2012). Other challenges engaging patients with ASPD include their chaotic lifestyle, frequent crises, boundary violations and substance misuse. Pre-treatment strategies to enhance engagement are useful, such as psychoeducation about personality disorder, goal-based motivational interviews, and instilling beliefs about their potential for change (Dowsett & Craissati, 2008). Proactively following up patients, such as calling to remind them of appointments, is also recommended. Referrals for treatment are commonly prompted by professionals' concerns about reducing risk rather than the patient himself being motivated to change. Those who appear compliant and motivated to participate in treatment in prisons or secure forensic units may revert to antisocial behaviours once released into the community (Yakeley & Williams, 2014).

Building a positive therapeutic alliance with the patient is associated with better outcomes in therapy, whereas punitive interventions that focus on control and surveillance have been shown to increase recidivism if not combined with rehabilitative efforts (Skeem et al., 2009). The distrust that many individuals with ASPD have towards professionals stems from their childhood experiences of abuse and neglect from those who were meant to look after them. The treatment relationship should therefore be collaborative, and caring, with an authoritative, but not authoritarian, style.

Boundary violations in treatment should be anticipated given the lack of appropriate boundaries that they experienced in childhood and their resulting tendency to mistrust authority and to rebel against any rules imposed on them. At the same time, they may have their own strict code of conduct, which may be particularly evident in the hierarchical structure of gangs and criminal organisations. An important aim of treatment is to foster a sense of responsibility and awareness of appropriate boundaries in relation to others.

Specific Treatment Approaches

Because of the lack of empirical evidence for any effective treatment, services for patients or offenders specifically with a diagnosis of ASPD are limited. However, in the past decade there has been renewed interest in the psychological treatment of ASPD, and several specific evidence-based therapies, originally developed for the treatment of individuals with borderline personality disorder, have been adapted to treat those with ASPD. These therapies include cognitive behavioural therapy (Davidson et al., 2009), dialectical behaviour therapy (Linehan, 1993), schema-focussed therapy (Chakhssi et al., 2010) and mentalisation-based therapy (Bateman & Fonagy, 2019), and may be delivered in health and criminal justice settings in both individual and group formats (see Table 11.1).

A common aim of many of these therapies is enabling the patient to link their actions to their affects and internal mental states. Many individuals with ASPD find it difficult to mentalise or reflect on the contents of their own and others' minds—their emotions, thoughts and motivations; and are often paranoid and misinterpret others' intentions (Bateman et al., 2019). They also find it difficult to tolerate affects associated with vulnerability such as anxiety, shame and humiliation, which often underlie and trigger their violent behaviour. This may become evident in treatment when they feel belittled, criticised or interrupted by the therapist, or other members of a therapy group, and may lead to an aggressive response or disengagement from therapy.

Table 11.1 Psychological therapies for ASPD

Cognitive behavioural therapy (CBT)	CBT focusses on challenging and changing unhelpful cognitive distortions (e.g., thoughts, beliefs and attitudes) and behaviours, improving emotional regulation and the development of personal coping strategise that target solving current problems
Schema focussed therapy (SFT)	Focusses on challenging early maladaptive schemas by therapist's 're-parenting', encourages better regulation of narcissistic fluctuations in emotional reactivity, and promotes development of empathy and emotional intimacy with others
Dialectical behaviour therapy (DBT)	Individual and group therapy sessions incorporating cognitive behavioural principles with acceptance and mindfulness based-skills. Skills group training sessions used to promote mindfulness, emotional regulation, distress tolerance and interpersonal effectiveness
Mentalisation-based therapy (MBT)	Group and individual therapy based on attachment theory integrating psychodynamic, cognitive and relational components. Focusses on enhancing mentalisation (the ability to reflect upon one's own and others' states of mind and link these to actions and behaviours)

Some treatment programmes for offenders focus on 'victim empathy', i.e., interventions aimed at fostering awareness of and concern for the impact of their actions on others. However, because of their difficulties in empathising with other people's affective states, which may stem, at least in part, from the failure of their early caregivers to empathise with them, such interventions may be counterproductive, and those aimed at improving self-regard and promoting positive social interactions may be more effective (Bateman et al., 2019).

Finally, although most individuals with a diagnosis of ASPD are male (Dolan & Völlm, 2009), women with the disorder may also present for treatment. Such women commonly have complex needs regarding the care of their children and involvement with social services, as well as being more likely to have co-morbid borderline personality disorder and associated self-harm. For these reasons it is advisable to develop separate services for male and female patients with ASPD. Furthermore, in mixed therapy groups of both male and female patients, men may express negative and derogatory attitudes towards the women leading to disruption and disengagement of the female patients (Yakeley & Williams, 2014).

Conclusion and Future Directions

Although primarily focussed on risk to the public, there is evidence that politicians and policy makers in some countries are promoting the development of less punitive and more humane approaches to the management and rehabilitation of violent offenders, many of whom would fulfil diagnostic criteria for ASPD. Violence is not only damaging to the welfare of others, but to the perpetrators themselves, and has been recognised by the World Health Organisation as a major public health priority (Krug et al., 2012). In the UK, a large-scale government funded national programme theoretically underpinned by a developmental and attachment framework, the Offender Personality Disorder Pathway, was initiated in 2011 and is aimed at identifying, managing and treating offenders with personality disorder in prisons and probation settings.

A key aspect of the programme is the involvement of service users—ex-offenders who have benefitted from treatment—in the design, delivery, review and evaluation of services (Skett & Lewis, 2019). This is an example of a wider movement in service user involvement in criminal justice settings, which originated in prisons in the 1950s and 1960s in the US with ex-prisoners helping to rehabilitate other offenders (LeBel et al., 2015), and the more recent creation of 'forensic peer specialists', individuals who use their own experiences of the criminal justice system and mental health difficulties to engage others with psychiatric disabilities who have had contact with the criminal justice system (Adams & Lincoln, 2020). However, despite these activities, service user involvement remains less well developed in criminal justice settings than within health and social care services in both the US and UK (Barrenger et al., 2019; Jeffcote et al., 2018). Unless collaborative and concerted efforts are directed at changing negative attitudes towards people with ASPD, including the development of empirically-based therapies through methodologically robust studies despite the inherent challenges of engaging such individuals in research, people with this personality disorder will continue to be denied access to treatment and will continue to suffer and cause others to suffer.

References

Adams, W. E., & Lincoln, A. K. (2020). Forensic peer specialists: Training, employment, and lived experience. *Psychiatric Rehabilitation Journal, 43*(3), 189–196.

Adshead, G. (2004). Three degrees of security: Attachment in forensic institutions. In F. Pfafflin & G. Adshead (Eds.), *A matter of security: The application of attachment theory to forensic psychiatry and psychotherapy* (pp. 147–166). Jessica Kingsley Publishers.

American Psychiatric Association. (2013). *Diagnostic and statistical manual of mental disorders* (5th ed.). American Psychiatric Association.

Andrews, D. (1995). The psychology of criminal conduct and effective treatment. In J. McGuire (Ed.), *What works: Reducing reoffending: Guidelines from research and practice* (pp. 3–34). Wiley.

Baglivio, M. T. (2018). On cumulative childhood traumatic exposure and violence/aggression: the implications of adverse childhood experiences (ACE). In A. T. Vazsonyi, D. J. Flannery, & M. DeLisi (Eds.), *The Cambridge handbook of violent behavior and aggression* (2nd ed., pp. 467–487). Cambridge University Press.

Baglivio, M. T., Wolff, K. T., Piquero, A. R., & Epps, N. (2015). The relationship between adverse child-hood experiences (ACE) and juvenile offending trajectories in a juvenile offender sample. *Journal of Criminal Justice, 43*(3), 229–241.

Barkataki, I., Kumari, V., Das, M., Taylor, P., & Sharma, T. (2006). Volumetric structural brain abnormalities in men with schizophrenia or antisocial personality disorder. *Behavioural Brain Research, 169*(2), 239–247.

Barrenger, S. L., Hamovitch, E. K., & Rothman, M. R. (2019). Enacting lived experiences: Peer specialists with criminal justice histories. *Psychiatric Rehabilitation Journal, 42*(1), 9–16.

Basoglu, C., Oner, O., Ates, A., Algul, A., Bez, Y., & Cetin, M. (2011). Synaptosomal-associated protein 25 gene polymorphisms and antisocial personality disorder: Association with temperament and psychopathy. *Canadian Journal of Psychiatry, 56*(6), 341–347.

Bateman, A. W., & Fonagy, P. (Eds.). (2019). *Handbook of mentalizing in mental health practice* (2nd ed.). American Psychiatric Publishing.

Bateman A., Yakeley J., & Motz A. (2019). Mentalizing and antisocial personality disorder. In A. Bateman & F. Fonagy (Eds.), *Handbook of mentalizing in mental health practice* (2nd ed., pp. 335–350). American Psychiatric Publishing.

Battle, C. L., Shea, M. T., Johnson, D. M., Yen, S., Zlotnick, C., Zanarini, M. C., et al. (2004). Childhood maltreatment associated with adult personality disorders: Findings from the collaborative longitudinal personality disorders study. *Journal of Personality Disorders, 18*, 193–211.

Black, D. W., Baumgard, C. H., Bell, S. E., & Kao, C. (1996). Death rates in 71 men with antisocial personality disorder A comparison with general population mortality. *Psychosomatics, 37*, 131–136.

Blair, R. J. R. (2004). The roles of orbital frontal cortex in the modulation of antisocial behavior. *Brain and Cognition, 55*(1), 198–208.

Bogaerts, S., Vanheule, S., & Declerq, F. (2005). Recalled parental bonding, adult attachment style and personality disorders in child molesters: A comparative study. *Journal of Forensic Psychiatry and Psychology, 16*, 445–458.

Bowlby, J. (1969). *Attachment and loss* (Vol. 1). *Attachment* Basic Books.

Byrne, S. A., Cherniack, M. G., & Petry, N. M. (2013). Antisocial personality disorder is associated with receipt of physical disability benefits in substance abuse treatment patients. *Drug and Alcohol Dependence, 132*(1–2), 373–377.

Capone, G., Schroder, T., Clarke, S., & Braham, L. (2016). Outcomes of therapeutic community treatment for personality disorder. *Therapeutic Communities: THe International Journal of Therapeutic Communities, 37*(2), 84–100.

Chakhssi, F., de Ruiter, C., & Bernstein, D. (2010). Change during forensic treatment in psychopathic versus nonpsychopathic offenders. *Journal of Forensic Psychiatry and Psychology, 21*, 660–682.

Cleckley, H. (1941). *The mask of sanity*. St. Louis, MO: C.V. Mosby.

Coid, J. (1992). DSM-III diagnosis in criminal psychopaths: A way forward. *Criminal Behaviour and Mental Health, 2*, 78–94.

Coid, J., Yang, M., Tyrer, P., Roberts, A., & Ullrich, S. (2006). Prevalence and correlates of personality disorder in Great Britain. *British Journal of Psychiatry, 188*, 423–431.

Coid, J., Yang, M., Roberts, A., Ullrich, S., Moran, P., Bebbington, P., Brugha, T., Jenkins, R., Farrell, M., Lewis, G., & Singleton, N. (2006). Violence and psychiatric morbidity in a national household population - A report from the British household survey. *American Journal of Epidemiology, 164*(12), 1199–1208. https://doi.org/10.1093/aje/kwj339

Compton, W. M., Conway, K. P., Stinson, F. S., Colliver, J. D., & Grant, B. F. (2005). Prevalence, correlates, and comorbidity of DSM-IV antisocial personality syndromes and alcohol and specific drug use disorders in the United States: Results from the national epidemiologic survey on alcohol and related conditions. *The Journal of Clinical Psychiatry, 66*(6), 677–685. https://doi.org/10.4088/jcp.v66n0602

Craig, J. M., Piquero, A. R., Farrington, D. P., & Ttofi, M. M. (2017). A little early risk goes a long bad way: Adverse childhood experiences and life-course offending in the Cambridge study. *Journal of Criminal Justice, 53*, 34–45. https://doi.org/10.1016/j.jcrimjus.2017.09.005

Crawford, M. J., Sahib, L., Bratton, H., Tyrer, P., & Davidson, K. (2009) Service provision for men with antisocial personality disorder who make contact with mental health services. *Personality and Mental Health, 3*(3), 165–171. https://doi.org/10.1002/pmh.85

Crego, C., & Widiger, T. A. (2015). Psychopathy and the DSM. *Journal of Personality, 83*(6), 665–677. https://doi.org/10.1111/jopy.12115

Caspi, A., McClay, J., Moffitt, T. E., Mill, J., Martin, J., Craig, I. W., Taylor, A., & Poulton, R. (2002). Role of genotype in the cycle of violence in maltreated children. *Science, 297*(5582), 851–854.

Caspi, A., Moffitt, T. E., Morgan, J., Rutter, M., Taylor, A., Arseneault, L., Tully, L., Jacobs, C., Kim-Cohen, J., & Polo-Tomas, M. (2004). Maternal expressed emotion predicts children's antisocial behavior problems: Using monozygotic-twin differences to identify environmental effects on behavioral development. *Developmental psychology, 40*(2), 149–161.

Caspi, A., Taylor, A., Moffitt, T. E., & Plomin, R. (2000). Neighborhood deprivation affects children's mental health: Environmental risks identified in a genetic design. *Psychological Science, 11*(4), 338–342.

Dadds, M. R., Allen, J. L., Oliver, B. R., Faulkner, N., Legge, K., Moul, C., Woolgar, M., & Scott, S. (2012). Love, eye contact and the developmental origins of empathy v. psychopathy. *The British Journal of Psychiatry: The Journal of Mental Science, 200*(3), 191–196. https://doi.org/10.1192/bjp.bp.110.085720

Davidson, K. M., Tyrer, P., Tata, P., Cooke, D., Gumley, A., Ford, I., Walker, A., Bezlyak, V., Seivewright, H., Robertson, H., & Crawford, M. J. (2009). Cognitive behaviour therapy for violent men with antisocial personality disorder in the community: An exploratory randomized controlled trial. *Psychological Medicine, 39*(4), 569–577. https://doi.org/10.1017/S0033291708004066

De Brito, S. A., & Hodgins, S. (2009). Antisocial personality disorder. In M. McMurran & R. Howard (Eds.), *Personality, personality disorder and violence* (pp. 133–153). Wiley.

De Lisi, M., & Beauregard, E. (2018). Adverse childhood experiences and criminal extremity: New evidence for sexual homicide. *Journal of Forensic Sciences, 63*(2), 484–489. https://doi.org/10.1111/1556-4029.13584

DeKlyen, M., & Greenberg, M. T. (2008). Attachment and psychopathology in childhood. In J. Cassidy & P. R. Shaver (Eds.), *Handbook of attachment. Theory, research, and clinical applications* (2nd ed., pp. 647–655). The Guilford Press.

Dolan, B., & Coid, J. (1993). Summary of findings and recommendations for future research. In B. Dolan & J. Coid (Eds.), *Psychopathic and antisocial personality disorders: Treatment and research issues*. Gaskell.

Dolan, M., & Völlm, B. (2009). Antisocial personality disorder and psychopathy in women: A literature review on the reliability and validity of assessment instruments. *International Journal of Law and Psychiatry, 32*(1), 2–9.

Douglas, K., Chan, G., Gelernter, J., Arias, A. J., Anton, R. F., Poling, J., Farrer, L., & Kranzler, H. R. (2011). 5-HTTLPR as a potential moderator of the effects of adverse childhood experiences on risk of antisocial personality disorder. *Psychiatric Genetics, 21*(5), 240–248. https://doi.org/10.1097/YPG.0b013e3283457c15

Dowsett, J., & Craissati, J. (2008). *Managing personality disordered offenders in the community: A psychological approach*. Routledge.

Duggan, C., Huband, N., Smailagic, N., Ferriter, M., & Adams, C. (2007). The use of psychological treatments for people with personality disorder: A systematic review of randomized controlled trials. *Personality, 1*, 95–125. https://doi.org/10.1002/pmh.22

Elison, J., Garofalo, C., & Velotti, P. (2014). Shame and aggression: Theoretical considerations. *Aggression and Violent Behavior, 19*(4), 447–453.

Farrington, D. P. (2000). Psychosocial predictors of adult antisocial personality and adult convictions. *Behavioral Sciences & the Law, 18*(5), 605–622. https://doi.org/10.1002/1099-0798(200010)18:5%3c605::aid-bsl406%3e3.0.co;2-0

Felthous, A. R., & Saβ, H. (Eds.). (2007). *International handbook on psychopathic disorders and the law*. Wiley.

Ferguson, C. J. (2010). Genetic contributions to antisocial personality and behavior: A meta-analytic review from an evolutionary perspective. *The Journal of Social Psychology, 150*(2), 160–180. https://doi.org/10.1080/00224540903366503

Fergusson, D. M., Boden, J. M., & Horwood, L. J. (2008). Exposure to childhood sexual and physical abuse and adjustment in early adulthood. *Child Abuse & Neglect, 32*(6), 607–619. https://doi.org/10.1016/j.chiabu.2006.12.018

Fonagy, P., Yakeley, J., Gardner, T., Simes, E., McMurran, M., Moran, P., Crawford, M., Frater, A., Barrett, B., Cameron, A., Wason, J., Pilling, S., Butler, S., & Bateman, A. (2020). Mentalization for Offending Adult Males (MOAM): Study protocol for a randomized controlled trial to evaluate mentalization-based treatment for antisocial personality disorder in male offenders on community probation. *Trials, 21*(1), 1001.

Fox, B. H., Perez, N., Cass, E., Baglivio, M. T., & Epps, N. (2015). Trauma changes everything: Examining the relationship between adverse childhood experiences and serious, violent and chronic juvenile offenders. *Child Abuse & Neglect, 46*, 163–173. https://doi.org/10.1016/j.chiabu.2015.01.011

Frick, P. J., & Viding, E. (2009). Antisocial behavior from a developmental psychopathology perspective. *Development and Psychopathology, 21*(4), 1111–1131. https://doi.org/10.1017/S0954579409990071

Frodi, A., Dernevik, M., Sepa, A., Philipson, J., & Bragesjö, M. (2001). Current attachment representations of incarcerated offenders varying in degree of psychopathy. *Attachment & Human Development, 3*(3), 269–283. https://doi.org/10.1080/14616730110096889

Fu, Q., Heath, A. C., Bucholz, K. K., Nelson, E., Goldberg, J., Lyons, M. J., True, W. R., Jacob, T., Tsuang, M. T., & Eisen, S. A. (2002). Shared genetic risk of major depression, alcohol dependence, and marijuana dependence: Contribution of antisocial personality disorder in men. *Archives of General Psychiatry, 59*(12), 1125–1132. https://doi.org/10.1001/archpsyc.59.12.1125

Gibbon, S., Duggan, C., Stoffers, J., Huband, N., Völlm, B. A., Ferriter, M., & Lieb, K. (2010). Psychological interventions for antisocial personality disorder. *The Cochrane database of Systematic Reviews* (6), CD007668. https://doi.org/10.1002/14651858.CD007668.pub2

Gilligan, J. (1996). *Violence: Our deadliest epidemic and its causes.* New York: Grosset/Putnam.

Gilligan, J. (2002). *Violence: Reflections on our deadliest epidemic.* Jessica Kingsley Publishers.

Goodwin, R. D., & Hamilton, S. P. (2003). Lifetime comorbidity of antisocial personality disorder and anxiety disorders among adults in the community. *Psychiatry Research, 117*(2), 159–166. https://doi.org/10.1016/s0165-1781(02)00320-7

Gregory, S., ffytche, D., Simmons, A., Kumari, V., Howard, M., Hodgins, S., & Blackwood, N. (2012). The antisocial brain: Psychopathy matters. *Archives of General Psychiatry, 69*(9), 962–972. https://doi.org/10.1001/archgenpsychiatry.2012.222

Hare, R. D. (1991). *The Hare psychopathy checklist—Revised manual.* Multi Health Systems.

Hare, R.D. (2003) *Manual for the Hare psychopathy checklist–Revised* (2nd ed.). Multi-health Systems.

Harris, G. T., Rice, M. E., & Quinsey, V. L. (1993). Violent recidivism of mentally disordered offenders: The development of a statistical prediction instrument. *Criminal Justice and Behavior, 20*(4), 315–335. https://doi.org/10.1177/0093854893020004001

Heads, T., Taylor, P., & Leese, M. (1997). Childhood experiences of patients with schizophrenia and a history of violence: A special hospital sample. *Criminal Behaviour and Mental Health, 7*, 117–130. https://doi.org/10.1002/cbm.157

Hodgins, S., Mednick, S. A., Brennan, P. A., Schulsinger, F., & Engberg, M. (1996). Mental disorder and crime. Evidence from a Danish birth cohort. *Archives of General Psychiatry, 53*(6), 489–496. https://doi.org/10.1001/archpsyc.1996.01830060031004

Home Office & Department of Health (2002). *Managing dangerous people with severe personality disorder: Proposals for policy development.* HMSO.

Jeffcote, N., Van Gerko, K., & Nicklin, E. (2018). Meaningful service user participation in the pathway. In C. Campbell & J. Craissati (Eds.), *Managing personality disordered offenders: A pathways approach* (pp. 145–173). Oxford University Press.

Khalifa, N., Duggan, C., Stoffers, J., Huband, N., Völlm, B. A., Ferriter, M., & Lieb, K. (2010). Pharmacological interventions for antisocial personality disorder. *The Cochrane database of Systematic Reviews* (8), CD007667. https://doi.org/10.1002/14651858.CD0 07667.pub2

Kobak, R., Cassidy, J., Lyons-Ruth, K., & Ziv, Y. (2006). Attachment, stress, and psychopathology: A developmental pathways model. In D. Cicchetti & D. J. Cohen (Eds.), *Developmental psychopathology: Volume one: Theory and method* (2nd ed., pp. 333–367). Wiley.

Krug, E. G et al., (Eds.). (2002). *World report on violence and health.* Geneva: World Health Organization.

LeBel, T. P., Richie, M., & Maruna, S. (2015). Helping others as a response to reconcile a criminal past: The role of the wounded healer in prisoner reentry programs. *Criminal Justice and Behavior, 42*(1), 108–120. https://doi.org/10.1177/0093854814550029

Lees, J., Manning, N., & Rawlings, B. (1999). *Therapeutic community effectiveness: A systematic international review of therapeutic community treatment for people with personality disorders and mentally disordered offenders (CRD Report no. 17).* NHS Centre for Reviews and Dissemination, University of York.

Lees, J., Manning, N., & Rawlings, B. (2004). A culture of enquiry: Research evidence and the therapeutic community. *The Psychiatric Quarterly, 75*(3), 279–294. https://doi.org/10.1023/b:psaq.0000031797.74295.f8

Lenzenweger, M. F., Lane, M. C., Loranger, A. W., & Kessler, R. C. (2007). DSM-IV personality disorders in the National Comorbidity Survey Replication. *Biological Psychiatry, 62*(6), 553–564. https://doi.org/10.1016/j.biopsych.2006.09.019

Levinson, A., & Fonagy, P. (2004). Offending and attachment. The relationship between interpersonal awareness and offending in a prison population with psychiatric order. *Canadian Journal of Psychoanalysis, 12,* 225–251.

Linehan, M. M. (1993) *Cognitive-behavioural treatment of borderline personality disorder.* Guildford Press.

Luntz, B. K., & Widom, C. S. (1994). Antisocial personality disorder in abused and neglected children grown up. *American Journal of Psychiatry, 151*(5), 670–674.

Lyons-Ruth, K., Connell, D. B., Zoll, D., & Stahl, J. (1987). Infants at social risk: Relations among infant maltreatments, maternal behavior, and infant attachment behavior. *Development and Psychopathology, 23,* 223–232.

Lyons-Ruth, K., Alpern, L., & Repacholi, B. (1993). Disorganized infant attachment classification and maternal psychosocial problems as predictors of hostile-aggressive behavior in the preschool classroom. *Child Development, 64*(2), 572–585.

Mason, D. A., & Frick, P. (1994). The heritability of antisocial behavior: A meta-analysis of twin and adoption studies. *Journal of Psychopathology and Behavioral Assessment, 16,* 301–323.

McGauley, G., Yakeley, J., Williams, A., & Bateman, A. (2011). Attachment, mentalization and antisocial personality disorder; the possible contribution of mentalization-based treatment. *European Journal of Psychotherapy and Counselling, 13*(4), 1–22.

McMurran, M. (2012). Readiness to engage in treatments for personality disorder. *International Journal of Forensic Mental Health, 11,* 289–298.

Meloy, J. R. (1988). *The psychopathic mind: Origins, dynamics and treatment.* Jason Aronson.

Meloy, R. & Yakeley, J. (2013). Antisocial personality disorder. In G. O. Gabbard, & J. Gundersons (Eds.), *Gabbard's treatments of psychiatric disorders.* American Psychiatric Publishing.

Merriman, T., & Cameron, V. (2007). Risk-taking: Behind the warrior gene story. *Journal of the New Zealand Medical Association (Online Source), 120*(1250).

Moran, P. (1999). The epidemiology of antisocial personality disorder. *Social Psychiatry and Psychiatric Epidemiology, 34,* 231–242.

Myers, M. G., Stewart, D. G., & Brown, S. A. (1998). Progression from conduct disorder to antisocial personality disorder following treatment for adolescent substance abuse. *American Journal of Psychiatry, 155,* 479–485.

National Institute for Health and Clinical Excellence (NICE). (2009). *Antisocial personality disorder: Treatment, management and prevention. NICE Clinical Guideline 77, Full Guideline.* National Collaborating Centre for Mental Health, Commissioned by the National Institute for Health and Clinical Excellence.

National Research Council. (1999). *Pathological gambling: A critical review.* Washington Academy Press.

Newbury, M. (2010). A synthesis of outcome research at Grendon Therapeutic Community Prison. *Therapeutic Communities, 31*(4), 356–371.

Ogloff, J. R. (2006). Psychopathy/antisocial personality disorder conundrum. *Australian and New Zealand Journal of Psychiatry, 40,* 519–528.

Ogloff, J., Wong, S., & Greenwood, A. (1990). Treating criminal psychopaths in a therapeutic community program. *Behavioral Sciences & the Law, 8,* 181–190.

Pasalich, D. S., Dadds, M. R., Hawes, D. J., & Brennan, J. (2012). Attachment and callous-unemotional traits in children with early-onset conduct problems. *Journal of Child Psychology and Psychiatry, and Allied Disciplines, 53*(8), 838–845. https://doi.org/10.1111/j.1469-7610.2012.02544.x

Raine, A., Lencz, T., Bihrle, S., LaCasse, L., & Colletti, P. (2000). Reduced prefrontal gray matter volume and reduced autonomic activity in antisocial personality disorder. *Archives of General Psychiatry, 57*(2), 119–127.

Raine, A. (2006). *Crime and schizophrenia: Causes and cures.* New York: Nova Science.

Raine, A. (2013). *The anatomy of violence.* Pantheon.

Raine, A. (2018). Antisocial personality as a developmental disorder. *Annual Review of Clinical Psychology, 14,* 259–289.

Raine, A., Lencz, T., Taylor, K., Hellige, J. B., Bihrle, S., Lacasse, L., Lee, M., Ishikawa, S., & Colletti, P. (2003). Corpus callosum abnormalities in psychopathic antisocial individuals. *Archives of General Psychiatry, 60*(11), 1134–1142.

Raine, A., Ishikawa, S. S., Arce, E., Lencz, T., Knuth, K. H., Bihrle, S., LaCasse, L., & Colletti, P. (2004). Hippocampal structural asymmetry in unsuccessful psychopaths. *Biological Psychiatry, 55*(2), 185–191.

Robins, L. N., Tipp, J., & Przybeck, T. (1991). Antisocial personality. In L. N. Robins & D. A. Regier (Eds.), *Psychiatric disorders in America: The epidemiological catchment area study* (pp. 258–290). The Free Press.

Skeem, J., Polaschek, D., & Manchak, S. (2009). Appropriate treatment works but how? Rehabilitating general, psychopathic, and high risk offenders. In J. L. Skeem, K. S. Douglas, & S. L. Lilienfeld (Eds.), *Psychological science in the courtroom: Consensus and controversies* (pp. 358–384). Guilford.

Skett, S., & Lewis, C. (2019). Development of the offender personality disorder pathway: A summary of the underpinning evidence. *Probation Journal, 66*(2), 167–180.

Simon, L. M. J. (1998). Does criminal offender treatment work? *Applied Preventive Psychology, 7*, 137–159.

Singleton, N., Meltzer, H., Gatward, R., Coid, J. W., & Deasy, D. (1998). *Psychiatric morbidity among prisoners in England and Wales.* The Stationary Office.

Sonuga-Barke, E. J., Schlotz, W., & Kreppner, J. (2010). Differentiating developmental trajectories for conduct, emotion and peer problems following early deprivation. *Monographs of the Society for Research in Child Development, 75*, 102–124.

Swanson, M. C., Bland, R. C., & Newman, S. C. (1994). Epidemiology of psychiatric disorders in Edmonton. Antisocial personality disorders. *Acta Psychiatrica Scandinavica. Supplementum, 376*, 63–70.

Torgersen, S., Kringlen, E., & Cramer, V. (2001). The prevalence of personality disorders in a community sample. *Archives of General Psychiatry, 58*(6), 590–596. https://doi.org/10.1001/archpsyc.58.6.590

Torgersen, S., Czajkowski, N., Jacobson, K., Reichborn-Kjennerud, T., Røysamb, E., Neale, M. C., & Kendler, K. S. (2008). Dimensional representations of DSM-IV cluster B personality disorders in a population-based sample of Norwegian twins: A multivariate study. *Psychological Medicine, 38*(11), 1617–1625. https://doi.org/10.1017/S0033291708002924

Tottenham, N., & Galván, A. (2016). Stress and the adolescent brain: Amygdala-prefrontal cortex circuitry and ventral striatum as developmental targets. *Neuroscience and Biobehavioral Reviews, 70*, 217–227. https://doi.org/10.1016/j.neubiorev.2016.07.030

van der Zouwen, M., Hoeve, M., Hendriks, A. M., Asscher, J. J., & Stams, G. J. J. M. (2018). The association between attachment and psychopathic traits. *Aggression and Violent Behavior, 43*, 45–55.

van IJzendoorn, M. H., Feldbrugge, J. T., Derks, F. C., de Ruiter, C., Verhagen, M. F., Philipse, M. W., van der Staak, C. P., & Riksen-Walraven, J. M. (1997). Attachment representations of personality-disordered criminal offenders. *American Journal of Orthopsychiatry, 67*(3), 449–459.

Vennard, D., Sugg, D., & Hedderman, C. (1997). *Changing offenders' attitudes and behaviour: What works?* The National Criminal Justice Reference Service.

Viding, E., Blair, R. J., Moffitt, T. E., & Plomin, R. (2005). Evidence for substantial genetic risk for psychopathy in 7-year-olds. *Journal of Child Psychology and Psychiatry, and Allied Disciplines, 46*(6), 592–597. https://doi.org/10.1111/j.1469-7610.2004.00393.x

Warren, F., McGauley, G., Norton, K., Dolan, B., Preedy-Fayers, K., Pickering, A., & Geddes, J. R. (2003). *Review of treatments for severe personality disorder*. London, Home Office. http://www.homeoffice.gov.uk/rds/pdfs2/rdsolr3003.pdfhttp://www.homeoffice.gov.uk/rds/pdfs2/rdsolr3003.pdf.

Webster, C. D., Douglas, K. S., Eaves, D., & Hart, S. T. (1997). *HCR-20: Assessing risk for violence, Version 2*. Mental Health, Law and Policy Institute, Simon Fraser University.

Weeks, R., & Widom, C. S. (1998). Self-report of early childhood victimization among incarcerated adult male felons. *Journal of Interpersonal Violence, 13*, 346–361.

Wormith, J. S., Olver, M. E., Stevenson, H. E., & Girard, L. (2007). The long-term prediction of offender recidivism using diagnostic, personality, and risk/need approaches to offender assessment. *Psychological Services, 4*(4), 287–305. https://doi.org/10.1037/1541-1559.4.4.287

Wolff, K. T., & Baglivio, M. T. (2017). Adverse childhood experiences, negative emotionality, and pathways to juvenile recidivism. *Crime & Delinquency, 63*(12), 1495–1521. https://doi.org/10.1177/0011128715627469

Widiger, T. A., & Corbitt, E. M. (1993). Antisocial personality disorder: Proposals for DSM-IV. *Journal of Personality Disorders, 7*(1), 63–77. https://doi.org/10.1521/pedi.1993.7.1.63

Yang, Y., Raine, A., Colletti, P., Toga, A. W., & Narr, K. L. (2010). Morphological alterations in the prefrontal cortex and the amygdala in unsuccessful psychopaths. *Journal of Abnormal Psychology, 119*(3), 546–554.

Yakeley, J., & Williams, A. (2014). Antisocial personality disorder: New directions. *Advances in Psychiatric Treatment, 20*, 132–143.

Key Reading Suggestions

Gibbon, S., Duggan. C., Stoffers, J., Huband, N., Völlm, B. A., & Ferriter, M. (2010). *Psychological interventions for antisocial personality disorder (review)*. The Cochrane Collaboration. The Cochrane Library.

McGauley, G., Yakeley, J., Williams, A., & Bateman, A. (2011). Attachment, mentalization and antisocial personality disorder; the possible contribution of Mentalization-Based Treatment. *European Journal of Psychotherapy and Counselling, 13*(4), 1–22.

Raine, A. (2018). Antisocial personality as a developmental disorder. *Annual Review of Clinical Psychology, 14*, 259–289.

Yakeley, J., & Williams, A. (2014). Antisocial personality disorder: New directions. *Advances in Psychiatric Treatment, 20*, 132–143.

Borderline Personality Disorder Among Justice-Involved Populations

12

Madison D. Smith, Rachelle H. Kromash, Shania L. Siebert, Genevieve J. Allison, and Kelly E. Moore

Key Points

- There are likely different pathways explaining criminal justice system involvement in patients with borderline personality disorders (BPD).
- These pathways include factors such as impulsivity, emotion dysregulation, substance use, poor distress tolerance, and co-occurrence with antisocial personality disorder.
- Socialized gender attributes might explain gender differences in prevalence rates for BPD and antisocial personality disorders in the criminal justice system.
- Effective treatments for BPD in the community should be adapted to serve the specific needs of patients involved in the criminal justice system.

M. D. Smith · R. H. Kromash · S. L. Siebert · G. J. Allison · K. E. Moore (✉)
Department of Psychology, East Tennessee State University, Johnson City, TN, USA
e-mail: mooreke2@etsu.edu

M. D. Smith
e-mail: smithmd6@etsu.edu

R. H. Kromash
e-mail: kromash@etsu.edu

S. L. Siebert
e-mail: colesl@etsu.edu

G. J. Allison
e-mail: allisongj@etsu.edu

Introduction

This chapter summarizes three areas of research concerning individuals with BPD in the criminal justice system (CJS): prevalence, hypothesized mechanisms leading to arrest, and effective treatment approaches. Within these sections, we discuss the intersection of BPD psychopathology and criminal behavior, and highlight the role of co-occurring antisocial personality disorder (ASPD) and gender in understanding these relationships. We conclude with clinical implications for CJS staff who manage and treat people with BPD.

Prevalence

BPD is a psychiatric disorder characterized by severe dysphoria and mood swings, disproportionate anger and difficulty controlling anger, stress-related paranoid ideation or dissociation, feelings of emptiness, unstable self-image, impulsive behavior (e.g., reckless driving, risky sex, substance use), suicidal behavior and non-suicidal self-injury (NSSI), fears of and attempts to avoid being abandoned, and chaotic interpersonal relationships (APA, 2013). Epidemiological surveys show that prevalence rates of BPD in community samples are around 2.7% (Tomko et al., 2014). People with BPD often experience frequent crises, extensive functional impairment, and repeated hospitalizations (Skodol et al., 2002). Many people with BPD disengage or prematurely dropout of treatment (Landes et al., 2016; Stewart et al., 2019) and are described as one of the most difficult populations to work with by treatment providers (Foertsch et al., 2003).

Considering the symptom set, it is not surprising that many individuals with BPD become involved in the CJS. Prevalence rates of BPD diagnosis are exceedingly higher among justice-involved individuals compared to the general population (Bebbington et al., 2017), ranging from 15 to 29.5% (Black et al., 2007; Jordan et al., 1996; Mir et al., 2015). Studies that use symptom inventories (e.g., Personality Assessment Inventory) rather than structured diagnostic interviews find even higher rates of BPD among correctional samples, ranging from 25 to 50% (Conn et al., 2010; Drapalski et al., 2009). Moreover, a large majority of justice-involved individuals struggle with symptoms of BPD even if they do not meet the diagnostic threshold or clinically significant symptom cutoffs (Black et al., 2007).

In the community, over a third of people with BPD report a history of criminal justice involvement (Howard et al., 2008). People with clinically significant BPD symptoms report engaging in a wide range of criminal behaviors, including destruction of property, disorderly conduct, shoplifting, substance-related crimes, non-intimate assault, intimate partner violence (IPV), violent assault, and rarely murder or familicide (Sansone et al., 2011; Sansone & Sansone, 2012). Studies also show that having more BPD symptoms is associated with more lifetime criminal charges (Moore et al., 2017) and people with BPD are more likely to recidivate when compared to people with depression, anxiety disorders, or psychotic disorders (Abracen et al., 2014). Moreover, people with BPD (and those with co-occurring BPD and ASPD) have a shorter time to re-conviction compared to those without these disorders (Howard et al., 2013) (Chapter 11).

Pathways into the Criminal Justice System

There are several potential pathways related to BPD psychopathology that may explain how individuals become involved in the CJS. Although few studies have explicitly investigated mechanisms explaining CJS involvement among people with BPD (Gardner et al., 2012, 2014; Mancke et al., 2017; Moore et al., 2017; Newhill et al., 2012; Scott et al., 2014), several studies have explored engagement in illegal behaviors.

People with BPD are likely to engage in (Sijtsema et al., 2014) and be arrested for (Shorey et al., 2012; Stuart et al., 2006) IPV. Studies among women arrested for domestic violence incidents show that 27 to 29.5% meet clinically significant cutoffs for BPD (Shorey et al., 2012; Stuart et al., 2006). Other studies have shown that nearly half of participants arrested for IPV charges endorsed 4 or more BPD criteria (Ross, 2011). Aggression and violence among people with BPD are often directed toward oneself, such as with deliberate self-harm; however, externalized aggression, such as with IPV, is also common (Newhill et al., 2009; Sansone & Sansone, 2012) (Chapter 24). Aggression can be distinguished as reactive (impulsive or dysregulated), proactive (premeditated or controlled), or relational (damaging relationships as a means to harm others) (Chapter 19). People with BPD are most likely to exhibit reactive relational aggression (Banny et al., 2014; Mancke et al., 2015) toward people they are in close interpersonal relationships with (Sarkar, 2019). Most aggressive behavior among people with BPD is thought to stem from emotion dysregulation, impulsivity, threat hypersensitivity, and intense anger that occurs in the context of unstable and conflict-laden interpersonal relationships (Harford et al., 2018; Mancke et al., 2015; Newhill et al., 2012). Indeed, emotion dysregulation has been found to fully mediate the relationship between BPD symptoms and aggressive behavior in both community and clinical samples (Gardner et al., 2012; Newhill et al., 2012; Scott et al., 2014), which suggests that struggling to control behavioral impulses during times of emotional distress may increase violence toward others. Additionally, sequential mediation research has suggested that emotion dysregulation intensifies aggression through trait anger among people with BPD (Mancke et al., 2017). Moreover, both emotion dysregulation and trait anger have been linked to aggression in people with BPD symptoms (Moore et al., 2017; Scott et al., 2014). Therefore, it may be that violent behaviors prompted by dysregulated anger and impulsivity explains the high prevalence of people with BPD in the CJS.

Substance use is another mechanism through which individuals with BPD become involved in the CJS. Up to half of people with BPD have co-occurring substance use disorders (SUDs; Trull et al., 2018). Among incarcerated populations, 13 to 28% have co-occurring BPD and SUD diagnoses (Chapman & Cellucci, 2007; Grella et al., 2008; Mir et al., 2015). In a recent study, the most commonly reported SUD co-occurring with BPD was alcohol use disorder (Trull et al., 2018), which can prompt reckless behaviors during intoxication (e.g., driving under the influence, assault) and is strongly linked to legal problems (Moore et al., 2019). People with BPD also have an increased risk for injecting drugs (Adams et al., 2016). Substance use is often thought of as an emotion regulation strategy among people with BPD (Chapman & Cellucci, 2007) to mitigate the dysphoria, emptiness, and intense dysregulated emotions they experience. Indeed, violent behavior among people with BPD has sometimes been attributed to co-occurring substance use (González et al., 2016; Sarkar, 2019; van den Brink et al., 2018). Specifically, the BPD-SUD comorbidity may involve higher levels of impulsivity (Heath et al., 2017; Magd et al., 2019), fluctuations in mood (Heath et al., 2017; Martino et al., 2017), and aggression (Armenti et al., 2017; Martino et al., 2017), which can result in illegal behavior (e.g., IPV, disorderly conduct) that ends in arrest (Thomas et al., 2013). In support of this, many people with BPD report a history of substance-related crimes, such as assault and disorderly conduct related to drug use, driving while intoxicated, and public intoxication (Sansone et al., 2013).

It is also worth mentioning other, less-researched mechanisms that may explain how individuals with BPD become involved in the CJS. Interactions between life stress, poor distress tolerance, and characteristics of BPD (e.g., active passivity, difficulties problem-solving) may indirectly lead to CJS involvement. For example, people with BPD may accrue legal problems by failing to effectively navigate stressors that arise in their life, such as paying child support, appearing in court, or renewing an expired driver's license. Similarly, individuals with BPD who are on probation may struggle to cope with the significant stress of court-imposed conditions such as attending treatment and staying sober, leading to technical violations and chronic CJS involvement. Additionally, difficulties navigating interpersonal stressors post-release, such as limiting contact with antisocial or drug-using individuals, may hinder probation compliance. Given the unstable self-image and fears of abandonment people with BPD have, they often remain engaged in unhealthy relationships despite negative impacts on their well-being. Research has yet to explore these mechanisms to CJS involvement among people with BPD.

BPD and ASPD Co-occurrence

A substantial portion of justice-involved people with BPD are also diagnosed with ASPD, ranging from 36 to 91% (Black et al., 2007, 2010; Howard et al., 2013; Moore et al., 2018; Wetterborg et al., 2015). ASPD's defining traits include a pervasive pattern of neglecting or violating the rights of others beginning before the age of 15, including non-compliance with social norms or laws, deceitfulness, impulsivity, aggressiveness, recklessness, irresponsibility, and lack of remorse (APA, 2013). ASPD is highly prevalent in correctional settings (Black et al., 2010; Fazel & Danesh, 2002) and is strongly linked to recidivism (de Barros & de Pádua Serafim, 2008; Howard et al., 2013; Penson et al., 2018).

BPD and ASPD share several clinical features and correlates. Both disorders involve poor anger regulation and reckless impulsive behaviors that can lead to CJS involvement. BPD and ASPD in adulthood have been predicted from similar internalizing and externalizing problems in justice-involved youth (Krabbendam et al., 2015). In community samples, BPD and ASPD are both associated with impulsivity, alcohol use, and aggression after rejection (Hahn et al., 2016; Scott et al., 2017), which can escalate into contact with justice agencies. Indeed, individuals with BPD and ASPD both have an increased potential for violence, aggression, and law-breaking behaviors in their histories, as indicated in archival data records (de Barros & de Pádua Serafim, 2008). The co-occurrence of BPD and ASPD may be particularly problematic for criminal behavior, as research suggests that the presence of borderline traits contributes uniquely to criminal risk above and beyond ASPD (Newhill et al., 2012; Scott et al., 2017). Studies of justice-involved adolescents have shown that antisocial traits are more predictive of future crime when BPD traits are present (Penson et al., 2018), and studies of adults find that those with comorbid BPD and ASPD have more extensive forensic and substance use histories, outwardly express their anger and impulsivity, and demonstrate less control over their anger compared to either disorder alone

(Howard et al., 2008). Some research suggests that the high levels of criminal involvement among people with co-occurring BPD and ASPD may be due to particularly heightened dysregulation of anger paired with impulsivity (Howard et al., 2008; Newhill et al., 2012). Further, studies find that emotion dysregulation is a unique mechanism leading to increased violence and aggression in BPD that is not present in ASPD (Moore et al., 2017; Newhill et al., 2012; Scott et al., 2014), which may explain how BPD symptoms contribute to greater recidivism risk (Weinstein et al., 2012).

Although BPD and ASPD often co-occur, important differences have been found between individuals with BPD vs. ASPD suggesting different neurobiological origins. Some features of ASPD (i.e., lack of empathy and remorse) have been associated with dysfunctions in the paralimbic system (Muller et al., 2008), whereas BPD features (i.e., increased emotional responses) have been linked to decreased activity in the prefrontal cortex among inhibitory regions (Frankle et al., 2005). In terms of symptomology, BPD features appear to be associated with more dissociation and hyperactivity (Krabbendam et al., 2015) and inabilities to remain focused on a task, whereas ASPD features are uniquely related to sensation seeking and lack of premeditation in impulsivity (Hahn et al., 2016). Research also suggests differences in the types of crimes people with BPD vs. ASPD commit. People with ASPD are more likely to report engaging in crimes against property, whereas people with BPD report engaging in misdemeanor crimes against people (de Barros & de Pádua Serafim, 2008).

Gender Differences

Compared to the general population, gender differences in BPD rates are less prominent in the CJS, as the disorder is commonly diagnosed among justice-involved men and women. Several studies do show slightly higher prevalence rates for justice-involved women, ranging from 34.7 to 64.6% compared to 26.8 to 62.6% among men (Black et al., 2007; Conn et al., 2010; Drapalski et al., 2009). There is some evidence that women in the justice system may be more likely to be diagnosed with BPD whereas men are more likely to be diagnosed with ASPD, despite exhibiting similar symptomology (Black et al., 2007; Bohle & de Vogel, 2017). Some research suggests these disorders are overlapping, and the behaviors manifest differently due to socialized gender attributes. Specifically, women may be more likely to be diagnosed with BPD when they are not displaying "normal" gendered behaviors (i.e., argumentative, sexually promiscuous, or intense anger) that would be acceptable in males (Simmons, 1992). For instance, intense violent and criminal behavior has been attributed to BPD severity in women, while it is thought to be due to co-occurring substance use in men (Sarkar, 2019; van den Brink et al., 2018). Additionally, while experiencing trauma appears to be a common risk factor for later exhibiting BPD and ASPD, women who have experienced emotional and sexual abuse are more likely to be diagnosed with BPD, in contrast to men who have experienced physical abuse during childhood being more commonly diagnosed with ASPD (Bohle & de Vogel, 2017).

Treatment and Management of BPD in Criminal Justice Settings

Incarceration settings can be particularly difficult for individuals with BPD to adjust to, as they likely experience a great deal of invalidation from staff who are unable to meet their needs (due to lack of awareness of BPD symptoms as well as resource restrictions) and interpersonal stressors with other staff and inmates (Schrader et al., 2016). As a result, incarcerated individuals with BPD present special management concerns; they more commonly have violent interactions with staff and peers and display other disruptive behaviors (Moore et al., 2018; Walters & Crawford, 2013), and are likely to be observed for NSSI and suicide in correctional settings (Gardner et al., 2014). It is essential for justice-involved individuals with BPD to receive effective treatment to improve behavior in and outside of correctional facilities.

Dialectical behavior therapy (DBT; Linehan, 1987) is an effective treatment for BPD (Kliem et al., 2010) that has been adapted for justice-involved populations. DBT is typically delivered for one year or longer and involves weekly skills groups, individual therapy, and as needed skills coaching. DBT teaches four core skillsets including mindfulness, interpersonal skills/assertiveness training, emotion regulation, and distress tolerance. Techniques of validation, collaborative problem-solving, and contingency management are used to eliminate suicidal and other problematic behavioral patterns as well as reinforce new coping skills. Despite DBT's promise in treating BPD, there are a number of barriers to implementation in justice settings (Berzins & Trestman, 2004). To name a few, there is limited supervision for paraprofessionals that administer group therapy, prison staff are not adequately trained to enforce DBT skills outside of groups, and offering 24-hour phone coaching is nearly impossible (Nee & Farman, 2008). In addition, there are high attrition rates in DBT programs in correctional settings (Eccleston & Sorbello, 2006; Moore et al., 2016; Nee & Farman, 2008), possibly due to unpredictable sentence lengths. Various modifications have been made to the original DBT protocol to better fit correctional settings, including the development of a Corrections Modified version (DBT-CM; Shelton et al., 2011). Such modifications include adaptations to vocabulary (e.g., more "inmate friendly"), variations of examples or acronyms used in the manual (e.g., DEAR MAN changed to REAL MAN; Gee & Reed, 2013), and shortening the treatment length (Berzins & Trestman, 2004; Shelton et al., 2011). Moreover, certain adaptations of DBT have added modules that specifically focus on understanding the sequence of behaviors leading up to and surrounding crime (Berzins & Trestman, 2004). Other modifications include offering limited telephone coaching (Eccleston & Sorbello, 2006).

Tomlinson (2018) conducted a systematic literature review of DBT in correctional settings and found that DBT reduces criminogenic needs (e.g., procriminal attitudes), recidivism, borderline symptoms, rates of self-harm/suicidality, aggression, impulsivity, and disciplinary infractions. Other studies of adapted DBT for justice-involved populations show reduced substance use (Santisteban et al., 2015) and self-reported stress levels (Eccleston & Sorbello, 2006). Additionally, adapted DBT interventions have improved participants' coping beliefs, mindfulness, distress tolerance, and self-esteem (Tomlinson, 2018). Tomlinson (2018) also found that several of the 34 DBT programs included in the review adhered to different parts of the Risk-Need-Responsivity (RNR) model (Andrews et al., 2011) (Chapter 27).

In addition to DBT, Systems Training for Emotional Predictability and Problem Solving (STEPPS), developed by Black and colleagues (2013, 2015), is a 20-week group therapy that holds promise for justice-involved individuals with BPD. STEPPS has a multisystemic systems component where family members, friends, corrections officers, and other staff members participate in the treatment. This is combined with cognitive behavioral elements and skills training. For individuals with BPD and ASPD, STEPPS produced significant improvements in BPD-related symptoms, mood, negative affectivity, and significant decreases in self-harming behaviors and disciplinary infractions occurring in prison. Mentalization-based treatment (MBT) is another possible treatment. MBT is a psychodynamically oriented treatment with individual and group techniques rooted in principles pertaining to cognition, attachment, and neuropsychology (Bateman & Fonagy, 2010). It emphasizes the capacity to make sense of both oneself and others' behavior (i.e., mentalization; Bateman & Fonagy, 2010). MBT targets both controlling affect (Bateman & Fonagy, 2010) and re-instating and maintaining mentalization (Bateman & Fonagy, 2010), and is considered an effective treatment for BPD in clinical samples (Vogt & Norman, 2019). Few studies have tested MBT among justice-involved individuals with BPD (Ware et al., 2016), however, one qualitative study using a small forensic sample found that MBT helped participants process emotions and interpersonal difficulties, and assess past, present, and potential future criminal behavior. Moreover, MBT has been suggested as a potential treatment for people with BPD who have violent charges, purported to improve affect control, reality testing, and perspective taking (Adshead et al., 2013).

More research aimed at adapting evidence-based approaches for BPD within the CJS (both during incarceration and community supervision) is needed. It is also important to bear in mind that correctional staff, administrators, and treatment providers may need psychoeducation around BPD to aid with implementation efforts.

Conclusions

BPD is highly prevalent within the CJS. The emotion dysregulation, anger, impulsivity, substance use, and poor distress tolerance that individuals with BPD struggle with are likely mechanisms explaining justice system involvement, however, more mechanistic research is needed. Effective treatments for BPD, such as DBT, are highly promising for improving emotion dysregulation, impulsivity, aggression, and criminal behavior among justice-involved individuals, but are not yet implemented widely in correctional settings. Broader implementation of evidence-based treatments for BPD in the justice system will require adaptation of existing treatments to fit the unique justice-system context, and staff psychoeducation to increase awareness of BPD and its symptoms. Given the severity of BPD symptoms, it is imperative to identify which justice-involved individuals have BPD and provide effective treatments that maximize their chance of adjustment during and after incarceration.

References

Abracen, J., Langton, C. M., Loomna, J., Gallo, A., Ferguson, M., Axford, M., & Dickey, R. (2014). Mental health diagnoses and recidivism in paroled offenders. *International Journal of Offender Therapy and Comparative Criminology, 58*(7), 765–779. https://doi.org/10.1177/0306624X13485930

Adams, L. M., Stuewig, J. B., & Tangney, J. P. (2016). Relation of borderline personality features to preincarceration HIV risk behaviors of jail inmates: Evidence for gender differences? *Personality Disorders: Theory, Research, and Treatment, 7*(1), 40–49. https://doi.org/10.1037/per0000124

Adshead, G., Moore, E., Humprey, M., Wilson, C., & Tapp, J. (2013). The role of mentalizing in the management of violence. *Advances in Psychiatric Treatment, 19,* 67–76. https://doi.org/10.1192/apt.bp.110.008243

American Psychiatric Association. (2013). *Diagnostic and statistical manual of mental disorders* (5th ed.). https://doi.org/10.1176/appi.books.9780890425596.

Andrews, D. A., Bonta, J., & Wormith, J. S. (2011). The risk-need-responsivity (RNR) model: Does adding the good lives model contribute to effective crime prevention? *Criminal Justice and Behavior, 38*(7), 735–755. https://doi.org/10.1177/0093854811406356

Armenti, N. A., Snead, A. L., & Babcock, J. C. (2017). Exploring the moderating role of problematic substance use in the relations between borderline and antisocial personality features and intimate partner violence. *Violence Against Women, 24*(2), 223–240. https://doi.org/10.1177/1077801216687875

Banny, A. M., Tseng, W.-L., Murray-Close, D., Pitula, C. E., & Crick, N. R. (2014). Borderline personality features as a predictor of forms and functions of aggression during middle childhood: Examining the roles of gender and physiological reactivity. *Development and Psychopathology, 26*(3), 789–804. https://doi.org/10.1017/S095457941400039X

Bateman, A., & Fonagy, P. (2010). Mentalization based treatment for borderline personality disorder. *World Psychiatry, 9,* 11–15. https://doi.org/10.1002/j.2051-5545.2010.tb00255.x

Bebbington, P., Jakobowitz, S., McKenzie, N., Killaspy, H., Iveson, R., Duffield, G., & Kerr, M. (2017). Assessing needs for psychiatric treatment in prisoners: 1. Prevalence of disorder. *Social Psychiatry and Psychiatric Epidemiology, 52*(2), 221–229. https://doi.org/10.1007/s00127-016-1311-7.

Berzins, L. G., & Trestman, R. L. (2004). The development and implementation of dialectical behavior therapy in forensic settings. *International Journal of Forensic Mental Health, 3*(1), 93–103. https://doi.org/10.1080/14999013.2004.10471199

Black, D. W., Blum, N., McCormick, B., & Allen, J. (2013). Systems training for emotional predictability and problem solving (STEPPS) group treatment for offenders with borderline personality disorder. *The Journal of Nervous and Mental Disease, 201*(2), 124–129. https://doi.org/10.1097/NMD.0b013e31827f6435

Black, D. W., Gunter, T., Allen, J., Blum, N., Arndt, S., Wenman, G., & Sieleni, B. (2007). Borderline personality disorder in male and female offenders newly committed to prison. *Comprehensive Psychiatry, 48*(5), 400–405. https://doi.org/10.1016/j.comppsych.2007.04.006

Black, D. W., Gunter, T., Loveless, P., Allen, J., & Sieleni, B. (2010). Antisocial personality disorder in incarcerated offenders: Psychiatric comorbidity and quality of life. *Annals of Clinical Psychiatry, 22,* 113–120. http://www.antoniocasella.eu/archipsy/Black_aspd_2010.pdf.

Black, D. W., Simsek-Duran, F., Blum, N., McCormick, B., & Allen, J. (2015). Do people with borderline personality disorder complicated by antisocial personality disorder benefit from the STEPPS treatment program? *Personality and Mental Health, 10*(3), 205–215. https://doi.org/10.1002/pmh.1326

Bohle, A., & de Vogel, V. (2017). Gender differences in victimization and the relation to personality disorders in forensic psychiatry. *Journal of Aggression, Maltreatment & Trauma*, 1–19. https://doi.org/10.1080/10926771.2017.1284170.

Chapman, A. L., & Cellucci, T. (2007). The role of antisocial and borderline personality features in substance dependence among incarcerated females. *Addictive Behaviors, 32*(6), 1131–1145. https://doi.org/10.1016/j.addbeh.2006.08.001

Conn, C., Warden, R., Stuewig, J., Kim, E. H., Harty, L., Hastings, M., & Tangney, J. P. (2010). Borderline personality disorder among jail inmates: How common and how distinct? *Correctional Compendium, 35*(4), 6–13. https://www.ncbi.nlm.nih.gov/pmc/articles/PMC482 5675/.

de Barros, D. M., & de Pádua Serafim, A. (2008). Association between personality disorder and violent behavior pattern. *Forensic Science International, 179*, 19–22. https://doi.org/10.1016/j.forsciint.2008.04.013

Drapalski, A. L., Youman, K., Stuewig, J., & Tangney, J. (2009). Gender differences in jail inmates' symptoms of mental illness, treatment history and treatment seeking. *Criminal Behaviour and Mental Health, 19*(3), 193–206. https://doi.org/10.1002/cbm.733

Eccleston, L., & Sorbello, L. (2006). A structured intervention for prisoners who are at risk of self-harming. In G. G. Dear (Ed.), *Preventing suicide and other self-harm in prison* (pp. 74–87). Palgrave Macmillan.

Fazel, S., & Danesh, J. (2002). Serious mental disorder in 23,000 prisoners: A systematic review of 62 surveys. *The Lancet, 359*, 545–550. https://doi.org/10.1016/S0140-673 6(02)07740-1

Foertsch, C., Manning, S. Y., & Dimeff, L. (2003). Difficult-to-treat patients: The approach from dialectical behavior therapy. In R. L. Leahy (Ed.), *Roadblocks in cognitive-behavioral therapy: Transforming challenges into opportunities for change* (pp. 255–273). Guilford Press.

Frankle, W. G., Lombardo, I., New, A. S., Goodman, M., Talbot, P. S., Huang, Y. Y., Slifstein, M., Curry, S., Abi-Dargham, A., Laruelle, M., & Siever, L. J. (2005). Brain serotonin transporter distribution in subjects with impulsive aggressivity: A positron emission study with [C-11]McN 5652. *American Journal of Psychiatry, 162*(5), 915–923. https://doi.org/10.1176/appi.ajp.162.5.915

Gardner, K. J., Archer, J., & Jackson, S. (2012). Does maladaptive coping mediate the relationship between borderline personality traits and reactive and proactive aggression? *Aggressive Behavior,* 1–11. https://doi.org/10.1002/ab.21437.

Gardner, K. J., Dodsworth, J., & Selby, E. A. (2014). Borderline personality traits, rumination, and self-injurious behavior: An empirical test of emotional cascades model in adult male offenders. *Journal of Forensic Psychology Practice, 14*(5), 398–417. https://doi.org/10.1080/15228932.2014.962379

Gee, J., & Reed, S. (2013). The HoST programme: A pilot evaluation of modified dialectical behaviour therapy with female offenders diagnosed with borderline personality disorder. *European Journal of Psychotherapy & Counselling, 15*(3), 233–252. https://doi.org/10.1080/13642537.2013.810659

González, R. A., Igoumenou, A., Kallis, C., & Coid, J. W. (2016). Borderline personality disorder and violence in the UK population: Categorical and dimensional trait assessment. *BMC Psychiatry, 16*, 180. https://doi.org/10.1186/s12888-016-0885-7

Grella, C. E., Greenwell, L., Prendergast, M., Sacks, S., & Melnick, G. (2008). Diagnostic profiles of offenders in substance abuse treatment programs. *Behavioral Sciences & the Law, 26,* 369–388. https://doi.org/10.1002/bsl.825

Hahn, A. M., Simons, R. M., & Hahn, C. K. (2016). Five factors of impulsivity: Unique pathways to borderline and antisocial personality features and subsequent alcohol problems. *Personality and Individual Differences, 99,* 313–319. https://doi.org/10.1016/j.paid.2016.05.035

Heath, L. M., Laporte, L., Paris, J., Hamdullahpur, K., & Gill, K. J. (2017). Substance misuse is associated with increased psychiatric severity among treatment-seeking individuals with borderline personality disorder. *Journal of Personality Disorders,* 1–15. https://doi.org/10.1521/pedi_2017_31_307.

Harford, T. C., Chen, C. M., Kerridge, B. T., & Grant, B. F. (2018). Borderline personality disorder and violence toward self and others: A national study. *Journal of Personality Disorders,* 1–18. https://doi.org/10.1521/pedi_2018_32_361.

Howard, R. C., Huband N., Duggan C., & Mannion A. (2008). Exploring the link between personality disorders and criminality in a community sample. *Journal of Personality Disorders, 22,* 589–603. https://doi.org/10.1521/pedi.2008.22.6.589.

Howard, R., McCarthy, L., Huband, N., & Duggan, C. (2013). Re-offending in forensic patients released from secure care: The role of antisocial/borderline personality disorder co-morbidity, substance dependence and severe childhood conduct disorder. *Criminal Behaviour and Mental Health, 23,* 191–202. https://doi.org/10.1002/cbm.1852

Jordan, K., Schlenger, W. E., Fairbank, J. A., & Caddell, J. M. (1996). Prevalence of psychiatric disorders among incarcerated women. *Archives of General Psychiatry, 53,* 513–519. https://doi.org/10.1001/archpsyc.1996.01830060057008

Kliem, S., Kröger, C., & Kosfelder, J. (2010). Dialectical behavior therapy for borderline personality disorder: A meta-analysis using mixed-effects modeling. *Journal of Consulting and Clinical Psychology, 78*(6), 936–951. https://doi.org/10.1037/a0021015

Krabbendam, A. A., Colins, O. F., Doreleijers, T. A. H., van der Molen, E., Beekman, A. T. F., & Vermeiren, R. R. J. M. (2015). Personality disorders in previously detained adolescent females: A prospective study. *American Journal of Orthopsychiatry, 85,* 63–71. https://doi.org/10.1037/ort0000032

Landes, S. J., Chalker, S. A., & Comtois, K. A. (2016). Predicting dropout in outpatient dialectical behavior therapy with patients with borderline personality disorder receiving psychiatric disability. *Borderline Personality Disorder and Emotion Dysregulation, 3*(1), 9. https://doi.org/10.1186/s40479-016-0043-3

Linehan, M. M. (1987). Dialectical behavior therapy for borderline personality disorder: Theory and method. *Bulletin of the Menninger Clinic, 51*(3), 261–276. https://doi.org/10.1111/j.1600-0447.1994.tb05820.x

Magd, S. A., Rakhawy, M., Mamdouh, R., & Shaheen, S. (2019). Impulsivity, suicidality, and emotional dysregulation in women having borderline personality disorder with and without substance dependence. *Egyptian Journal of Psychiatry, 40*(2), 59–63. http://new.ejpsy.eg.net/text.asp?2019/40/2/59/262550.

Mancke, F., Herpertz, S. C., & Bertsch, K. (2015). Aggression in borderline personality disorder: A multidimensional model. *Personality Disorders: Theory, Research, and Treatment, 6*(3), 278–291. https://doi.org/10.1037/per0000098

Mancke, F., Herpertz, S. C., Kleindienst, N., & Bertsch, K. (2017). Emotion dysregulation and trait anger sequentially mediate the association between borderline personality disorder and aggression. *Journal of Personality Disorders, 31*(2), 256–272. https://doi.org/10.1521/pedi_2016_30_247

Martino, F., Spada, M. M., Menchetti, M., Lo Sterzo, E., Sanza, M., Tedesco, P., Trevisani, C., & Berardi, D. (2017). Substance-related and addictive disorders as mediators between borderline personality disorder and aggressive behavior. *Clinical Psychologist, 22*(2), 211–219. https://doi.org/10.1111/cp.12115

Mir, J., Kastner, S., Priebe, S., Konrad, N., Ströhle, A., & Mundt, A. (2015). Treating substance abuse is not enough: Comorbidities in consecutively admitted female prisoners. *Addictive Behaviors, 46*, 25–30. https://doi.org/10.1016/j.addbeh.2015.02.016

Moore, K. E., Folk, J. B., Boren, E. A., Tangney, J. P., Fischer, S., & Schrader, S. W. (2016). Pilot study of a brief dialectical behavior therapy skills group for jail inmates. *Psychological Services, 15*(1), 98–108. https://doi.org/10.1037/ser0000105

Moore, K. E., Gobin, R. L., McCauley, H. L., Kao, C.-W., Anthony, S. M., Kubiak, S., Zlontnick, C., & Johnson, J. E. (2018). The relation of borderline personality disorder to aggression, victimization, and institutional misconduct among prisoners. *Comprehensive Psychiatry, 84*, 15–21. https://doi.org/10.1016/j.comppsych.2018.03.007

Moore, K. E., Oberleitner, L., Pittman, B. P., Roberts, W., Verplaetse, T. L., Hacker, R. L., Peltier, M. R., & McKee, S. A. (2019). The prevalence of substance use disorders among community-based adults with legal problems in the U.S. *Addiction Research and Theory*, https://doi.org/10.1080/16066359.2019.1613524.

Moore, K. E., Tull, M. T., & Gratz, K. L. (2017). Borderline personality disorder symptoms and criminal justice system involvement: The roles of emotion-driven difficulties controlling impulsive behaviors and physical aggression. *Comprehensive Psychiatry, 76*, 26–35. https://doi.org/10.1016/j.comppsych.2017.03.008

Muller, J. L., Sommer, M., Dohnel, K., Weber, T., Schmidt-Wilcke, T., & Hajak, G. (2008). Disturbed prefrontal and temporal brain function during emotion and cognition interaction in criminal psychopathy. *Behavioral Sciences & the Law, 26*, 131–150. https://doi.org/10.1002/bsl.796

Nee, C., & Farman, S. (2008). Treatment of borderline personality disorder in prisons: Findings from the two dialectical behaviour therapy pilots in the UK. In J. C. Hagen & E. I. Jensen (Eds.), *Personality disorders: New research* (pp. 107–121). Nova Science Publishers.

Newhill, C. E., Eack, S. M., & Mulvey, E. P. (2009). Violent behavior in borderline personality. *Journal of Personality Disorders, 23*(6), 541–554.

Newhill, C. E., Eack, S. M., & Mulvey, E. P. (2012). A growth curve analysis of emotion dysregulation as a mediator for violence in individuals with and without borderline personality disorder. *Journal of Personality Disorders., 26*, 452–467. https://doi.org/10.1521/pedi.2012.26.3.452

Penson, B. N., Ruchensky, J. R., Morey, L. C., & Edens, J. F. (2018). Using the personality assessment inventory antisocial and borderline features scales to predict behavior change: A multisite longitudinal study of youthful offenders. *Assessments, 25*(7), 858–866. https://doi.org/10.1177/1073191116680292

Ross, J. M. (2011). Personality and situational correlates of self-reported reasons for intimate partner violence among women versus men referred for batterers' intervention. *Behavioral Sciences and the Law, 29*, 711–727. https://doi.org/10.1002/bsl.1004

Sansone, R. A., Lam, C., & Wiederman, M. W. (2011). The relationship between shoplifting and borderline personality symptomatology among internal medicine outpatients. *Innovations in Clinical Neuroscience, 8*(3), 12–13. https://www.ncbi.nlm.nih.gov/pmc/articles/PMC3074195/pdf/icns_8_3_12.pdf.

Sansone, R. A., & Sansone, L. A. (2012). Borderline personality and externalized aggression. *Innovations in Clinical Neuroscience, 9*(3), 23–26. https://www.ncbi.nlm.nih.gov/pmc/articles/PMC3342993/pdf/icns_9_3_23.pdf.

Sansone, R. A., Watts, D. A., & Wiederman, M. W. (2013). Borderline personality symptomatology and legal charges related to drugs. *International Journal of Psychiatry in Clinical Practice, 18*(2), 150–152. https://doi.org/10.3109/13651501.2013.847107

Santisteban, D. A., Mena, M. P., Muir, J., McCabe, B. E., Abalo, C., & Cummings, A. M. (2015). The efficacy of two adolescent substance abuse treatments and the impact of comorbid depression: Results of a small randomized controlled trial. *Psychiatric Rehabilitation Journal, 38*(1), 55–64. https://doi.org/10.1037/prj0000106

Sarkar, J. (2019). Borderline personality disorder and violence. *Australasian Psychiatry, 1–3*. https://doi.org/10.1177/1039856219878644.

Schrader, S., Moore, K. E., Folk, J., & Tangney, J. P. (2016). Borderline personality disorder among jail inmates. *American Jails, 29*, 19–22.

Scott, L. N., Stepp, S. D., & Pilkonis, P. A. (2014). Prospective associations between features of borderline personality disorder, emotion dysregulation, and aggression. *Personality Disorders, 5*(3), 278–288. https://doi.org/10.1037/per0000070

Scott, L. N., Wright, A. G. C., Beeney, J. E., Lazarus, S. A., Pilkonis, P. A., & Stepp, S. D. (2017). Borderline personality disorder symptoms and aggression: A within-person process model. *Journal of Abnormal Psychology, 126*(4), 429–440. https://doi.org/10.1037/abn0000272

Shelton, D., Kesten, K., Zhang, W., & Trestman, R. (2011). Impact of a dialectic behavior therapy—Corrections modified (DBT-CM) upon behaviorally challenged incarcerated male adolescents. *Journal of Child and Adolescent Psychiatric Nursing, 24*(2), 105–113. https://doi.org/10.1111/j.1744-6171.2011.00275.x

Shorey, R. C., Elmquist, J., Ninnemann, A., Brasfield, H., Febres, J., Rothman, E. F., Schonbrun, Y. C., Temple, J. R., & Stuart, G. L. (2012). The association between intimate partner violence perpetration, victimization, and mental health among women arrested for domestic violence. *Partner Abuse, 3*(1), 3–21. https://doi.org/10.1891/1946-6560.3.1.3

Sijtsema, J. J., Baan, L., & Bogaerts, S. (2014). Associations between dysfunctional personality traits and intimate partner violence in perpetrators and victims. *Journal of Interpersonal Violence, 29*(13), 2418–2438. https://doi.org/10.1177/0886260513520228

Simmons, D. (1992). Gender issues and borderline personality disorder: Why do females dominate the diagnosis? *Archives of Psychiatric Nursing, 6*(4), 219–223. https://doi.org/10.1016/0883-9417(92)90063-O

Skodol, A. E., Gunderson, J. G., McGlashan, T. H., Dyck, I. R., Stout, R. L., Bender, D. L., Grillo, C. M., Shea, M. T., Zanarini, M. C., Morey, L. C., Sanislow, C. A., & Oldham, J. M. (2002). Functional impairment in patients with schizotypal, borderline, avoidant, or obsessive-compulsive personality disorder. *American Journal of Psychiatry, 159,* 276–283. https://doi.org/10.1176/appi.ajp.159.2.276

Stewart, N. A. J., Wilkinson-Tough, M., & Chambers, G. N. (2019). Psychological interventions for individuals with a diagnosis of borderline personality disorder in forensic settings: A systematic review. *The Journal of Forensic Psychiatry & Psychology, 30,* 744–793. https://doi.org/10.1080/14789949.2019.1637917

Stuart, G. L., Moore, T. M., Gordon, K. C., Ramsey, S. E., & Kahler, C. W. (2006). Psychopathology in women arrested for domestic violence. *Journal of Interpersonal Violence, 21*(3), 376–389. https://doi.org/10.1177/0886260505282888

Thomas, M. D., Bennett, L. W., & Stoops, C. (2013). The treatment needs of substance abusing batterers: A comparison of men who batter their female partners. *Journal of Family Violence, 28,* 121–129. https://doi.org/10.1007/s10896-012-9479-4

Tomko, R. L., Trull, T. J., Wood, P. K., & Sher, K. J. (2014). Characteristics of borderline personality disorder in a community sample: Comorbidity, treatment utilization, and general functioning. *Journal of Personality Disorders, 28*(5), 734–750. https://doi.org/10.1521/pedi_2012_26_093

Tomlinson, M. F. (2018). A theoretical and empirical review of dialectical behavior therapy within forensic psychiatric and correctional settings worldwide. *International Journal of Forensic Mental Health, 17*(1), 72–95. https://doi.org/10.1080/14999013.2017.1416003

Trull, T. J., Freeman, L. K., Vebares, T. J., Choate, A. M., Helle, A. C., & Wycoff, A. M. (2018). Borderline personality disorder and substance use disorders: An updated review. *Borderline Personality Disorder and Emotion Dysregulation, 5*(1). https://doi.org/10.1186/s40479-018-0093-9.

van den Brink, C., Harte, J. M., & Denzel, A. D. (2018). Men and women with borderline personality disorder resident in Dutch special psychiatric units in prisons: A descriptive and comparative study. *Criminal Behaviour and Mental Health, 28*(4), 324–334. https://doi.org/10.1002/cbm.2084

Vogt, K. S., & Norman, P. (2019). Is mentalization-based therapy effective in treating the symptoms of borderline personality disorder? A systematic review. *Psychology and Psychotherapy: Theory, Research and Practice, 92,* 441–464. https://doi.org/10.1111/papt.12194

Walters, G. D., & Crawford, G. (2013). Major mental illness and violence history as predictors of institutional misconduct and recidivism: Main and interaction effects. *Law and Human Behavior, 38*(3), 238–247. https://doi.org/10.1037/lhb0000058

Ware, A., Wilson, C., Tapp, J., & Moore, E. (2016). Mentalisation-based therapy (MBT) in high secure hospital setting: Expert by experience feedback on participation. *Journal of Forensic Psychiatry & Psychology.* https://doi.org/10.1080/14789949.2016.1174725

Weinstein, Y., Gleason, M. E. J., & Oltmanns, T. F. (2012). Borderline but not antisocial personality disorder symptoms are related to self-reported partner aggression in late middle-age. *Journal of Abnormal Psychology, 121*(3), 692–698. https://doi.org/10.1037/a0028994

Wetterborg, D., Långström, N., Andersson, G., & Enebrink, P. (2015). Borderline personality disorder: Prevalence and psychiatric comorbidity among male offenders on probation in Sweden. *Comprehensive Psychiatry, 62,* 63–70. https://doi.org/10.1016/j.comppsych.2015.06.014

Narcissistic Personality Disorder and Deviant Behavior

13

Tiffany D. Russell[iD], Samantha M. Holdren, and Elsa Ronningstam

Key Points

- Individuals with pathological narcissism can have overt traits commonly associated with narcissistic personality disorder (grandiosity, arrogance), as well as discreet, vulnerable characteristics, including fragile self-esteem, avoidance, and shame.
- Pathological narcissism is characterized by fluctuation and reactivity related to life events that are experienced as threatening and/or destructive. Anger and hostility can result from this reactivity.
- People with pathological narcissism are often portrayed as unempathetic, but their empathic functioning is better described as compromised or fluctuating rather than absent.
- Aggression, violence, and criminality relate to pathological narcissistic traits in empirical studies of white-collar crime, domestic violence, physical aggression, and sexual violence.
- Special care must be taken when conducting forensic interviews with individuals suspected of having pathological narcissistic traits, as interviews devolve into power struggles when interviewees detect disrespect, contempt, or distrust.
- Instruments for forensic assessment of NPD and pathological narcissism are lacking, and practitioners should use a multitrait/multimethod approach to measuring these traits.

T. D. Russell · S. M. Holdren
Department of Psychology and Philosophy, Sam Houston State
University, Huntsville, TX, USA
e-mail: tiffdrussell@shsu.edu

S. M. Holdren
e-mail: smh100@shsu.edu

E. Ronningstam (✉)
Department of Psychiatry Harvard Medical School, McLean Hospital, Belmont, MA, USA

Introduction

Narcissistic personality disorder (NPD), as outlined in the Diagnostic and Statistical Manual, Fifth Edition (DSM-5) has been associated with insensitive,
manipulative, deceitful, and exploitative attitudes and behaviors. Nevertheless,
people with NPD can usually feel guilt and even show remorse. On a more
severe level with malignant narcissism (Kernberg, 1975, 1992), narcissism is
associated with antisocial, paranoid, and sadistic traits with more pervasive moral
and empathic aberrations. These are often combined with empowering sadistic control, callousness, and hostility. Pathological narcissistic traits can be a
factor in numerous occasional and recurrent deviant behaviors, including white
collar crime, domestic violence, physical aggression, and sexual violence (Ronningstam, 2005a; Russell & King, 2017; Stone, 2009; Zeigler-Hill et al., 2013).
Clinical characteristics of pathological narcissism can co-occur and interact with
deviant behaviors in different ways. This chapter focuses on integrating diagnostic and forensic assessment of NPD and pathological narcissism, including
narcissistic grandiosity and vulnerability. Clinical cases of NPD are presented,
including select forensic assessment scores, notable clinical interview findings,
and explanations for patients' behavior.

Narcissism: From Normal to Pathological to Malignant

Narcissism is a particularly complicated construct. It encompasses central and
important aspects of normal, healthy, and exceptional personality functioning,
as well as signifiers of pathological and exceedingly malignant features and
behaviors. As a result, people with narcissistic traits can present with a range
of functional competence. Some are high functioning, successful, proficient,
and socially well-adjusted with no notable psychiatric symptomology. These
individuals can be charismatic, humorous, and wise, and they often make exceptional leaders (Crevani & Hallin, 2017; Stone, 1998). Others have consistent
or intermittent functional impairment in work or interpersonal relationships,
with fluctuations in self-esteem, hypersensitivity, and emotional reactivity (e.g.,
Dawood et al., 2020; Ronningstam, 2016; Ronningstam & Russell, 2020). As
narcissism increases to a more severe pathological level, individuals often demonstrate intensifying social and/or functional impairment, although select areas of
competence and achievement can remain intact. Social isolation and comorbid
Axis I (depressive disorders, substance use disorder, bipolar I and II) and Axis

II disorders (borderline, antisocial, obsessive–compulsive, and avoidant personality disorders) are common in these individuals (Clemence et al., 2009; Levy et al., 2009; Simonsen & Simonsen, 2012; Stinson et al., 2008; Widiger, 2012). Independent of the level of severity, pathological narcissism can either be overtly striking and obtrusive (grandiose), or internally concealed and unnoticeable (vulnerable). The grandiose features of pathological narcissism are described in Section II of the DSM-5 as narcissistic personality disorder (NPD), and the vulnerable aspects are found in NPD's "Associated Features Supporting Diagnosis." There are ongoing discussions regarding the importance of including vulnerable features in NPD diagnoses (e.g., Dawood et al., 2020; Ronningstam & Russell, 2020), but for the purposes of this chapter, the term "pathological narcissism" refers to both grandiose and vulnerable traits which usually are present and oscillating within the same individual.

Narcissistic pathology is characterized by reactivity and fluctuation. Changes, both for the better and worse, occur in the context of life events associated with vocational, social, interpersonal, medical, or financial circumstances. Any of these can, for various reasons, be experienced as threatening or corrosive and escalate pathological traits and functioning (Ronningstam et al., 1995). These changes can be the result of fragile and conditional self-esteem, but they may also stem from wounded pride. Individuals with elevated levels of narcissism have a strong sense of superiority, and those undermining or challenging them tend to provoke intense emotional reactions (Baumeister et al., 2000; Bushman, 2018). These responses include anger, hostility, shame, and fear, as well as mood shifts that include irritability, anxiety, depression, or elation. They may be expressed openly or remain hidden and can result in deceitfulness and retaliation, including aggression, antisocial acts, and/or suicidal or parasuicidal behaviors (Ronningstam & Maltsberger, 1998). Life events can also be experienced as supportive, encouraging, or corrective, and they can stabilize self-esteem and decrease pathological functioning, particularly in interpersonal relations. Paradoxically, life events that encourage and maintain pathological, malignant narcissistic behavior may temporarily stabilize or increase self-esteem and sense of control in some individuals with severe narcissistic pathology (Ronningstam et al., 1995). For example, Mr. Brown, a married man with two children, was known for several incidences of financial theft and fraud with legal consequences. He also showed open aggressive behavior and got into fights, in particular with his wealthy father-in-law whom he deeply envied and despised. At a family gathering, the father-in-law collapsed and got acutely ill. Mr. Brown, who sat close to him, suddenly took charge, did life-rescuing CPR, ordered an ambulance, and assisted him to the emergency room. The father-in-law survived and Mr. Brown was told that he had saved his father-in-law's life. He was instantly considered "the hero of the party," which for the moment overruled his aggressivity and revengeful urges.

The term "malignant narcissism" was originally coined by Fromm (1964), who called it the "quintessence of evil." Beyond core NPD features, individuals with malignant forms of narcissism demonstrate antisocial behavior, ego-syntonic sadism, and paranoia (Kernberg, 1984). In high functioning individuals with narcissistic traits, the appearance of intermittent deviant and malignant behaviors can be confusing and misleading. Aggression is usually ego-syntonic and anchored in patterns of aggressive self-affirmation. A productive, functional person can become competitive, angry, derogating, willful, exaggerative, dishonest, and hypersensitive to criticism in situations that challenge self-esteem, competence, power, or sense of control (Maccoby, 2007). Nevertheless, people with this condition can still have capacity for group loyalty, concerns for others and feelings of guilt (Facchi et al., 2011; Goldner-Vukov, More, 2010; Kernberg, 2007, 2009; Stone, 2009). When co-occurring with antisocial or psychopathic features (Chapter 11 and 15), these individuals may be aggressive, hostile, cruel, and sadistic, and they can involve themselves in criminal and violent behaviors (Baumeister et al., 2002; Bushman, 2018; Bushman et al., 2003; Jones & Paulhus, 2010; Lambe et al., 2018; Stone, 1998).

The prevalence of NPD in community populations ranges from 0% to 6.2% (Dhawan et al., 2010), but that rate increases considerably in clinical settings where traits are found in 1.3% to 22% of patients (e.g., Grilo et al., 1998; Zimmerman et al., 2005). The overlap between psychopathic and narcissistic traits makes the prevalence of NPD in forensic populations less certain, but white-collar criminals (Blickle et al., 2006) and violent offenders with narcissistic traits report more criminal behaviors (Blackburn & Coid, 1999). Pathological narcissism accounts for a 1.2% to 11.5% increase in violence perpetration, with the greatest odds occurring in the most severe types of violence (homicide). Individuals with both psychopathic and narcissistic traits are particularly prone to violence following an insult to their ego via rejection or negative feedback ("ego threat"; Lambe et al., 2018). These violent reactions can serve to protect and enhance the individuals' self-esteem and may be driven by envy, entitlement, vengefulness, or sadism combined with severely compromised morals and empathy. This is particularly true when empathic functioning relates to exploitative ambitions or sadistic pursuits (Kernberg, 1984, 1992; Stone, 2009).

Pathological Narcissism and Empathic Functioning

Traditionally, people with pathological narcissism have been conceptualized as lacking the capacity for empathy. Conclusions from more recent empirical studies, however, have shown evidence of a compromised but not an absence of empathic ability. Empirical evidences point to a neural deficiency in emotional empathy (i.e., the ability to emotionally process and respond to someone else's emotional expression), with motivational and self-regulatory-based fluctuations causing engagement and disengagement in cognitive empathic functioning (the ability to recognize and take on another's perspective). While there is a tendency to overestimate their own emotional empathic capability, these individuals also have trouble accessing their own and others' emotions and affective states. In emotionally intense interpersonal situations, people with pathological narcissism shift from inter- to intra-subjective relationships and increasingly focus on themselves (Fan et al., 2011; Marissen et al., 2012; Nenadic et al., 2015; Ritter et al., 2011; Schulze et al., 2013).

From a pathological personality perspective, findings demonstrating compromised empathic functioning can be caused by lack of motivation or deficits in cognitive functioning or emotion regulation. The individual can see and understand others' emotions and reactions, but chooses to deliberately or automatically ignore or put aside this ability due to unwillingness to engage. Alternatively, the situation can also become too emotionally overwhelming and intolerable, which makes them unable to respond appropriately. Perceiving others' emotions can evoke overwhelming powerlessness, disgust, shame, or loss of internal control that can trigger strong, aggressive reactions or emotional and physical withdrawal. Others' empathy towards the individuals with pathological narcissism can be experienced as an overwhelming, or even dangerous, intrusion and they may or may not be aware of this deficit. They may struggle internally with oscillations between susceptible awareness of intense negative reactivity (pain, intolerance, irritability), and coexisting obliviousness or ignorance. Externally, interpersonal fluctuations are notable. These fluctuations alternate between self-motivated and skillful self-promoting engagement, aggressive rejections, emotional coldness, and dismissive avoidance. At the same time, these individuals can demonstrate a surprising capability and accuracy in reported self-awareness, as well as in their more distant perceptions and descriptions of own and others' emotional states and reactions. This is especially noticeable in situations when they intend or need to take charge and remain in control, for example in psychiatric evaluations or in psychotherapy. In other words, motivational fluctuations between engagement and disengagement, as well as interactions and fluctuations between competence and deficits in empathic processing, actively influence the empathic interactions in individuals with NPD (Baskin-Sommers et al., 2014; Glasser, 1992; Ronningstam, 2009; Tangney, 1995).

Anger and Aggression in Pathological Narcissism:

Emotional anger and aggressive behavior can be normal, justified reactions to life experiences (Chapter 19). They can also be emblematic of personality pathology, including the narcissistic. Normal, justified anger and aggression allow individuals to assert autonomy, eliminate obstacles to satisfaction, or reduce pain, threat, or frustration. Individuals with pathological narcissism are often hypervigilant to ego threats, and anger and aggression can be tools aiding regulation of self-esteem and interpersonal functioning when threats are perceived. To guard against uncomfortable fluctuations in self-esteem when questioned or challenged, individuals with narcissism may aggress to assert dominance to prevent feeling inferior.. People with pathological narcissism may also regulate interpersonal functioning with aggressive tactics, such as withholding love or support, exploitation, manipulation, and physical and/or verbal abuse (Baumeister et al., 1996, 2000; Jones & Paulhus, 2010; Lambe et al., 2018). In addition, feelings of anger with urges to retaliate or destroy may not necessarily lead to overt aggressive behavior, but can actually result in well planned and effective actions to penalize with well hidden aggressive intents.

A sometimes surprising and seemingly paradoxical aspect of pathological narcissism is the propensity for suicide. This act of self-inflicted aggression can occur "out of the blue" and unrelated to depressive disorders. Suicidal behaviors in individuals with pathological or malignant narcissism can reflect superiority and triumph over the human fear of death. It can also represent sadistic control over others in that it is retaliation, destruction of a hated object, and a way to exit uncontrollable conditions. The act of suicide equates to victory over reality and punishment for those who caused pain or humiliation (Kernberg, 1992; Ronningstam & Maltsberger, 1998).

Pathological Narcissism and Criminal Behavior

White-Collar Crime

White-collar crimes are non-violent crimes involving deception for financial gain. They are typically committed by upper-level, professional, or entrepreneurial individuals who have specialized skills and opportunities to commit fraud. Perpetrators of white-collar crime often hold positions of power or trust, such as financial officers, supervisors, managers, corporate officers, and accountants (Collins & Schmidt, 1993). Most white-collar crimes are self-serving, as gains typically further private interests; however, some may be committed to protect or enhance a corporate entity, particularly if preservation of the business is tied to the individual's identity (e.g., President or CEO; Blickle et al., 2006).

People with NPD in professional or semi-professional occupations are particularly at risk for abuse of power and white-collar crime. These behaviors are linked to narcissistic fantasies of omnipotence and the pursuit of success at any cost, and it is rare for these individuals to demonstrate feelings of guilt once caught (Bromberg, 1965). White-collar crime can be a manifestation of excessive self-confidence and assuredness, and this hubris often explains why these individuals make an error that leads to their subsequent demise. Indeed, those incarcerated for white-collar crimes have greater levels of irresponsibility, risk-taking, unreliability, hedonism, and disregard for rules relative to individuals in professional positions who have not been charged with white-collar crime (Blickle et al., 2006; Collins & Schmidt, 1993).

Case 1: Alex, 48-year-old male[1]

Alex was admitted to a forensic psychiatric unit after surviving a near lethal suicide attempt when realizing he may be charged with money laundering and fraud. Alex was a corporate officer at a large investment firm where he and 2 co-conspirators defrauded wealthy customers' money, then laundered the cash utilizing offshore bank accounts. Alex was intelligent and a natural leader, and under his guidance, the group evaded suspicion for over 3 years. During that time, he became quite wealthy and lived a lavish life with his wife and 3 children. Alex's scheme was eventually discovered by the FBI when an innocent colleague accused of theft by a client inadvertently redirected suspicion onto Alex. During initial FBI questioning at Alex's office, Alex realized he had been discovered and would likely face extensive jail time. He excused himself to use the restroom and made the drastic decision to end his life by hanging himself in the company storage room. A janitor inadvertently interrupted his suicide attempt, cut him down, then called for help. Alex regained consciousness in the emergency room where he was handcuffed to the bed. Alex was enraged and devastated. Not only had his scheme been discovered, but his suicide attempt had been thwarted, causing more shame and embarrassment. After spending two days in the hospital, Alex learned his co-conspirators had made a plea deal with the FBI in exchange for testimony against Alex.

Psychosocial History

Alex was the youngest of 5 siblings and grew up in a small town in the midwest. His father owned a hardware store, and his mother was a housewife. When Alex was 9, his father filed for bankruptcy and closed the store. Although the bankruptcy had been coming for some time, his father was private and kept the decline in business to himself. The bankruptcy came as a shock to the family. The struggles continued when his father died of lung cancer a year later. Alex's mother was overwhelmed after her husband died and Alex's two older siblings left school to provide for the family. Alex never processed these experiences. He harbored resentment and rage towards his father and pity and contempt for his mother. Alex had a strong relationship with his maternal grandfather, although he developed Alzheimer's and died when Alex was 14. His grandfather's gradual death triggered sadness, fear, and resentment in Alex. He focused his efforts on school and sports, and his intelligence and athletics earned him a scholarship at a large university where he majored in business. He earned his MBA from an Ivy League university. Alex had temporary friendships in college, but he never really felt close to anyone. His identity was comprised mainly of his accomplishments in sports and business.

After graduation, Alex was hired by a large financial firm in a different part of the country. Once Alex settled in, he decided he needed a wife. He attended singles events to find one. Alex met Kari during the first event he attended, and they married after dating for 6 months. Kari was from a wealthy, well-known family, which pleased Alex. They had the first of 3 children within the first year of marriage. Alex was a generous and reliable provider, but he kept his family at a distance by working long hours and traveling. Kari cared for the children, and Alex attended their school and sports functions when their outstanding performances allowed him to present as the proud, supportive father. His marriage went through periods of stagnation and limited intimacy. Alex could not tolerate much closeness and intimacy with Kari, and he often felt controlled, intruded upon, and angry. However, he knew it was in his best interest to maintain his self-control and be a polite, likeable spouse to his wealthy in-laws. He maintained his façade by daily controlled alcohol consumption and having extramarital affairs. Alex often reflected upon how he needed to earn more money to stay in league with Kari's family, and he envisioned financial gains far beyond his salary at his firm. He made several exploratory attempts to gain money from unwitting clients at work and found it easy. Alex increased the fraud in earnest and eventually recruited co-conspirators to maximize gains. He continued to evade suspicion by company auditors, and his successes made him more confident. He soon started taking bigger risks until he was finally discovered.

Domestic Violence

Domestic violence is the use of aggression within romantic relationships (Chapter 24). This definition is commonly called intimate partner violence (IPV), and it can include sexual aggression and coercion against a romantic partner. Although not criminal, emotional abuse and verbal aggression are also within the realm of IPV.

Most domestic abusers exhibit some type of personality disorder, including narcissistic (e.g., Craig, 2003). Individuals with NPD often interpret vague and ambivalent communications as personal attacks, and their hypersensitivity to criticism, coupled with entitlement and envy, make romantic relationships especially precarious (Miller et al., 2007). Not only does pathological narcissism contribute to the perpetration of domestic violence (Beasley & Stoltenberg, 1992; Craig, 2003; Flournoy & Wilson, 1991; Green et al., 2020), it also leads to the belief that domestic violence is normal within romantic relationships (Blinkhorn et al., 2016).

One potentially surprising aspect of domestic violence is the fact that it commonly involves female perpetrators. There is considerable evidence implicating narcissistic traits in the female perpetration of psychological (Gormley & Lopez,

---

[1] Names and details have been changed to preserve patient confidentiality.

2010), verbal (Lamkin et al., 2017), sexual (Russell et al., 2017), and physical abuse of romantic partners (Blinkhorn et al., 2015). Recent findings reveal vulnerable narcissism in females predicts physical, emotional, and sexual abuse perpetration. In men, vulnerable narcissism predicts physical and sexual abuse perpetration, and grandiose narcissism predicts emotional abuse perpetration (Green et al., 2020).

Case 2: Diana, 37-year-old female[2]

Diana presented for forensic evaluation as a step in her negotiations with the district attorney in her state. She hoped for a plea bargain for domestic violence, assault in the second degree (class B felony). Diana's charges stemmed from an altercation with her romantic partner, James. Shortly after a verbal argument with James, Diana approached him while he was watching television on the couch and struck him in the head with a cast iron skillet. James lost consciousness and had a large head wound that bled profusely. Diana left to her friend's house while James was unconscious. When he regained consciousness, James called the police and went to the hospital. He was diagnosed with a severe concussion, received numerous stiches, and stayed in the hospital for 2 days. When Diana returned home, she learned James was in the hospital. She went to see him and was detained by hospital security until police arrived. She was released on bond and James filed a restraining order against her. She was living with a friend, Nicole, at intake.

Psychosocial History

Diana was the youngest child of 3, and she had 2 older brothers, although they were not close. When she was 10, Diana's parents divorced after her father had extramarital affairs. She lived with her mother after the divorce, and Diana often felt burdened by her. Diana greatly admired her father, who worked his way up from a blue-collar trucking job to a union boss for the northwest portion of the country. Her father was known as a ruffian when he was young, and he garnered considerable respect from the local citizenry as he matured. Diana noted he "could go anywhere in town and everyone knew who he was," and he "never took 'no' for an answer." Her father also dated multiple women at a time, and she referred to him as an "unapologetic player." Diana had average intelligence, and she enjoyed several benefits in childhood thanks to her father's reputation. She admitted trying to impress her father with grades, which she earned by cheating. Her efforts were "useless," as he took little interest in scholastic accomplishments. Diana felt the only time her father was truly proud of her was when she got arrested during high school for slashing another girl's tires after an argument.

Diana's father died in a drunk driving accident when she was 19. Although her father was the intoxicated driver, Diana expressed deep, unresolved anger at the other driver. She described the funeral as having "everyone in town" in attendance and hoped to have a similar funeral when she dies.

Diana met James 2 years before the assault. He was a trucker she met at a local pool hall, and they fell immediately and passionately in love. At the time, James was married with 2 children and lived in another state, and they maintained a secret, long-distance relationship for 10 months. James eventually decided to leave his wife and move in with Diana, who initially was excited and enthusiastic about this revelation. However, after he arrived, something changed for Diana. Her passion turned into an unexpected distancing and uncontrollable repulsion. James was understanding of her negativity and chalked it up to Diana's inexperience with long-term relationships. She had only had casual relationships before meeting James, and he suspected she would adapt. However, he gradually realized something was wrong with Diana. She got angry and rejecting of him when he tried to assure her that he understood her feelings. Eventually, James became depressed, which further repulsed Diana. She provoked arguments with him followed by blaming, criticizing, and dismissing him, and she often went into deep, ruminative states where she avoided everyone. Finally, the night of the assault, Diana accused James of having an affair. The argument devolved into vicious name-calling and threats. James finally disengaged, calling Diana "a psycho." He watched television on the couch while Diana fumed in the kitchen. After a few minutes alone, she returned to physically attack James.

---

[2] Names and details have been changed to protect patient confidentiality.

Physical Aggression

There is a clear link between pathological narcissism and physical violence (e.g., Baumeister et al., 2000; 1996; Bushman, 2018). Physical violence often occurs when a person with pathological narcissism has their motives questioned or their inflated, unstable self-views attacked (Baumeister et al., 1996; Lambe et al., 2018; Stone, 2009). Pathological narcissism is a significant predictor of violence in clinical populations (Lambe et al., 2018; Schulte et al., 1994; Svindseth et al., 2008), forensic populations, and college students (e.g., Lambe et al., 2018), and pathological narcissism in adolescence predicts violent criminal behavior (i.e., fighting, assault, arson/vandalism, breaking and entering) in adulthood (Johnson et al., 2000).

Sexual Violence

There is strong and consistent evidence of a relationship between pathological narcissism and sexual aggression and coercion, which is likely due to entitlement to sexual access. Moreover, individuals with pathological narcissism or NPD are unable or unwilling to take another's perspective in sexual scenarios, become punitive when denied sex, and seek to impress others with their sexual prowess (Baumeister et al., 2002; Bushman et al., 2003; Zeigler-Hill et al., 2013). Pathological narcissistic traits predict sexual aggression and coercion in community men when it is mediated by hostile masculinity (Russell & King, 2017). These traits are mediated by hostile femininity and everyday sadism in sexually violent women (Russell et al., 2017). Moreover, male sexual offenders who use diverse tactics (verbal threats, physical aggression, forced intoxication) to assault women are more than 3 times as likely to have pathological narcissistic traits (Norton-Baker et al., 2018).

Assessment of Pathological Narcissism

Interview

Preparing and conducting an interview is often a first step in assessing factors like pathological narcissism for forensic purposes. Interviewers are cautioned not to rush into an interview with someone suspected of having high levels of narcissistic traits, as the slightest provocation can elicit non-compliance, anger, and aggression. The value of preparation before the interview cannot be overstated. Gathering collateral information from friends, family, and other known associates, as well as becoming familiar with facts and circumstances surrounding the case, are especially fruitful endeavors that should occur prior to the interview (Ackley et al., 2011). Collateral information signifying pathological narcissism may include:

- Statements that they are important and/or entitled to special treatment
- A history of degrading and demeaning staff, friends, family, and strangers
- Disparaging, dismissive remarks about romantic partners/spouses
- Indicating they have "the best" professionals at their disposal (lawyers, doctors)
- Arrogance, with pervasive "me" and "I" statements
- Insensitive, unemotional responses to emotional stimuli
- Hypersensitivity to criticism
- Incidents of "blind rage" seemingly "out of the blue"
- Hyper-competitiveness ("sore loser")
- Jealousy in multiple spheres (romantic, work, and social relationships)
- Elaborate displays of accomplishments
- Fishing for compliments with effusive descriptions of achievements
- Inability to cede control in competitive and non-competitive situations
- Oscillating states of grandiose boastfulness and vulnerable insecurity
- Periods of social withdrawal, shame, rumination, depression
- Hero worship of a parent or caregiver that seems bizarre and/or incongruent with reality
- Substance abuse and self-destructiveness
- Unnecessary lies about trivial information

While not exhaustive, the presence of this kind of collateral evidence suggests the interviewer may encounter pathological narcissism during an interview (e.g., Ackley et al., 2011; Pincus & Roche, 2012; Ronningstam, 2005a, 2005b).

When pathological narcissism is known or anticipated, steps to reduce provocation during the interview are recommended. It is crucial for the interviewer to recognize their own likely reactions to dismissiveness, condescension, or verbal abuse. Defensiveness in the face of narcissistic reactance often results in an unproductive power struggle. The interviewer's alternative is to allow the interviewee to feel appreciated, respected, and in control of the interview by taking a curious, validating stance. The interviewer should be confident (but not confrontational), professional (but not strict), and well informed about the case (but not accusatory). It is helpful to use honorifics or surnames when addressing the individual. Expressing appreciation and regret for the schedule disruption allows the interviewee to feel important and understood. While it is helpful and often telling to occasionally return to previously covered topics ("I apologize, I forgot to ask something earlier..."), it is vital to maintain control of facial expressions and limit pointed follow-up questions when dishonesty is uncovered. Above all, patience is paramount for gaining necessary information. Losing patience in the interview can rupture rapport and disturb the validity of subsequent assessment efforts (Ackley et al., 2011; Ronningstam, 2012).

Instruments

There is a dearth of assessment instruments measuring the full range of narcissism as presented in this chapter. There are even fewer that an expert witness can use in their court testimony due to current legal standards requiring an instrument to be scientifically rigorous, generally accepted, and widely used in the field of clinical psychology. The instruments acceptable for forensic use often assess grandiose NPD exclusively, and practitioners are left to measure vulnerable traits on avoidance, depression, anxiety, and obsessive–compulsive personality disorder scales. One barrier for assessment of pathological narcissism is the prevalence of self-report instruments for personality disorders. Patients with narcissistic traits tend to have poor insight into their own personality functioning (Miller et al., 2008), which causes a divergence between self- and informant-reported traits on narcissism scales (Miller et al., 2005). Another barrier is the overlap of pathological narcissism with psychopathy, sadism, Machiavellianism, and borderline personality disorder (Buckels et al., 2013; Miller et al., 2010; Paulhus & Williams, 2002). These personalities appear to share a common "dark" core of similar traits like callousness and manipulativeness, but few clinical evaluations account for this shared variance and parse out features that are specific to pathological narcissism. The Minnesota Multiphasic Personality Inventory-II, Restructured Form (MMPI-2-RF), Millon Clinical Multiaxial Inventory-IV (MCMI-IV), and Personality Assessment Inventory (PAI) are self-report instruments commonly used in forensic psychology that measure grandiose forms of narcissism.

An alternative to self-report instruments is a structured or semi-structured clinical interview. There are drawbacks to these, as well. Truthfulness and insight are necessities for accurate interviews, and neither can be assumed in evaluation of pathological narcissism or NPD. This problem is exacerbated by the lack of validity scales in diagnostic interviews to assess under/over reporting and inconsistent responding. Interviews are also time consuming and require more expertise than self-report instruments. Clinicians could administer a self-report instrument, then conduct an interview assessing only specific personality disorders indicated by scale elevations (Watson & Bagby, 2012), but patient lack of insight can still cause a type II error (i.e., false negative) if they underreport at the outset. The Structured Clinical Interview for DSM-5 (SCID-5) includes a scientifically valid clinical interview assessing grandiose narcissism that is available for use in forensic settings.

We recommend forensic clinicians overcome these limitations by collecting thorough collateral information, watching for the signs detailed in the forensic interview section above, and using a multitrait/multimethod approach for arriving at a diagnosis. Robust assessment from multiple angles (collateral, self-reports, informant-reports, and structured/semi-structured/unstructured interview data) will yield the most accurate results when a firm diagnosis of pathological narcissism or NPD is necessary. When a case requires determination of pathological narcissistic behaviors and corollaries, the field's movement towards a dimensional model of personality (the Alternative Model of Personality Disorders; AMPD) shows considerable promise. The AMPD can be found in Section III of the DSM-5, and a large body of empirical evidence has amassed since its inception (Hopwood et al., 2019). The AMPD appears ready for forensic use, and the body of literature is broad and consistent enough to meet legal standards (Mulay & Waugh, 2019).

The DSM-5 AMPD diagnostic criteria for NPD aims to broaden the construct to successfully capture the clinical presentation of pathological narcissism. To meet these criteria, an individual must have impairment in two of four domains: identity, self-direction, empathy, or intimacy. Within NPD, impairment in identity often translates to exaggerated self-appraisal, either inflated or deflated, or fluctuating between the extremes. Impairment in self-direction can include setting of unreasonably high personal standards to view oneself as exceptional, or too low because of a sense of entitlement, a lack of awareness of one's motivations, and goal setting with the aim of gaining approval by others. Deficits in empathy can involve a poor ability to recognize or identify with the needs and feelings of others, being excessively sensitive to others' reactions only when perceived as relevant to the self, and over- or underestimating one's own effect on others. Intimacy issues in NPD individuals can manifest in largely superficial relationships that exist to regulate self-esteem, marked by little genuine interest in others' experiences and an emphasis placed on personal gain. The pathological personality traits of grandiosity and attention seeking must both be present for a diagnosis of NPD using the DSM-5 AMPD diagnostic criteria. The Personality Inventory for DSM-5 (PID-5; Krueger et al., 2012), a self-report inventory developed in conjunction with the DSM-5 AMPD, can be used to aid in the assessment of NPD and other personality psychopathology.

Alex's Forensic Assessment

Collateral Information

Information from the referral was corroborated with Alex's colleagues and wife. Alex had a prominent shrine in his office, including numerous trophies, degrees, and plaques. Kari revealed that she knew about Alex's affairs, but he was so cold towards her, she did not confront him for fear he would want a divorce. Kari worried about Alex's hidden, controlled, but significant alcohol use for the last few years, but when she approached him about it, he would minimize or refute it. He never struck the children, but he criticized and demeaned them for seemingly no reason several times

Colleagues provided similar information. They described meetings as "the Alex show," in which he "constantly steals the spotlight" and "regales us with his greatness." Four secretaries quit in the last 2 years because Alex found them not measuring up to his standards and harshly criticized them. Alex was described as competitive, vengeful, and unpredictable.

Forensic Interview

When the female clinician arrived with a male intern, Alex refused to let the intern participate. He allowed him to observe after the clinician asked permission and indicated the case was "a rare learning experience." Alex agreed, stating he was indeed an interesting person and it was unlikely they would meet many others like him

When discussing his home life, Alex regularly downplayed his wife's intelligence and ability to maintain a proper household. He reported only staying in the marriage because it would be an inconvenience to get a divorce and he did not want to lose his affiliation to her prominent family. He also did not want to abandon his children like his father had abandoned him. Alex denied any recent sexual contact with Kari, indicating her body did not attract him. He reported an ongoing sexual relationship with another woman but denied deeper feelings for her. Alex spoke glowingly about his children's accomplishments. He suspected they were "devastated" by his arrest and missed his cheering at their sporting events; however, he had not spoken to them since his arrest.

Alex denied committing any crimes. He believed the FBI officers were "too stupid to understand complicated financial transactions." Alex stated his co-conspirators and the colleague who "ratted to the FBI" were simply jealous of his success and station in life. Alex's face flushed and he was noticeably angry when discussing these colleagues. Alex reminded the clinician about his Ivy League education three times during the interview

When asked why he attempted suicide, Alex said he wanted to protect his reputation, retaliate against his coworkers, and escape losing his job and going to jail. He reportedly felt trapped and suicide seemed reasonable. He admitted considerable shame and guilt about "the incident" since it would have left his children fatherless. He denied the likelihood of acting on suicidal urges in the future. Since his admission on the unit, Alex refused all family visits, and he stated he "felt too bad" about the arrest and suicide attempt.

Assessments

Alex completed the Minnesota Multiphasic Personality Inventory-II-Restructured Form (MMPI-2-RF; Ben-Porath & Tellegen, 2011) and the Structured Clinical Interview for DSM-5 Personality Disorders (SCID-5-PD; First et al., 2016).

MMPI-2-RF

Alex's response pattern suggests minor underreporting and an attempt to present himself in a positive light (L-r = 65). This pattern also represents a history of traditional family values, which is consistent with reports. The test administration appears valid, but some interpretive caution is warranted.

Alex had a scale elevation representing the tendency to externalize and act out (controlled substance use, crime; BXD = 71). He may be at risk for treatment non-compliance, and interventions should target development of self-control. He also reported impulsivity, aggression, mood instability, and risk-taking (RC9 = 74; ACT = 67). This pattern is consistent with pathological narcissism. Alex endorsed being prone to anger, irritability, and problems controlling his temper (ANP = 73).

Alex reported emotional distress with demoralization, low positive emotions, helplessness, and/or pessimism (EID = 65). He can be self-critical and hypervigilant to others' criticism (RC7 = 70; NEG-r = 66). Low emotions appear associated with anhedonia and social disengagement (RC2 = 65). Alex reported considerable cynicism about others, including distrust in their motives (RC3 = 68). He endorsed suicidality and should undergo regular suicide risk assessment (SUI = 79). Suicidality may have occurred when he felt unable to cope with his current difficulties (NFC = 68).

Alex reported conflicted family relationships and feeling unsupported by family (FML = 79). This suggests strong underlying negative feelings towards some family members (wife, in-laws), and he may blame them for his current troubles. Interpersonally, Alex endorsed being a leader, with strong opinions and assertive qualities (IPP = 34). Others may view him as domineering, and he likely utilizes instrumental aggression to meet his needs (AGGR-r = 74; Ben-Porath, 2012).

PID-5

Severe Dysfunction of the following Personality Trait Facets: Attention Seeking (2.63), Callousness (2.07), Deceitfulness (2.50), Grandiosity (3.00), Manipulativeness (3.00), Rigid Perfectionism (2.10), Suspiciousness (2.14).

Moderate Dysfunction of the following Personality Trait Facets: Hostility (1.90), Irresponsibility (1.00), Perseveration (1.00), Risk Taking (1.00).

Personality Trait Domain: Severe dysfunction within Antagonism (8.20; consists of Manipulativeness, Deceitfulness, and Grandiosity).

SCID-5-PD

Principal Personality Disorder Diagnosis: Narcissistic Personality Disorder (8/9 criteria; 16/18 on dimension).

Other notable personality characteristics:

Antisocial (4/7 + 2 conduct symptoms; 9/14 on dimension).

Avoidant (3/7, 6/14 on dimension).

Diana's Forensic Assessment

Collateral Information

Collateral information was corroborated with James (former partner) and Nicole (friend). James was somewhat uncooperative and indicated he was returning to his state of origin soon. He indicated Diana was "self-centered" and "crazy" when she did not get her way. He recounted a time when his children visited, and Diana was cold and aloof with him and his children.

James eventually took the children and stayed at a hotel after an argument with a jealous, enraged Diana. James reported Diana was jealous and extremely critical, and he was satisfied with his decision to leave.

Nicole reported Diana as "a diva." She indicated her social media is "filled with sexy selfies," and Diana often believes everyone likes and envies her. Nicole stated Diana lies about "weird stuff" like age, height, and "even what she had for dinner." She often presents as "the life of the party," but becomes petulant if people do not cooperate with her suggestions. Nicole reported Diana has an "all about me" attitude that is frustrating. Conversations usually revolve around Diana, even if they originally had nothing to do with her. Diana also talks about her father like he was perfect, even though "everyone knows he was drinking and womanizing." Diana tends to hold a grudge and develops "uncontrolled rage" when someone says something critical about her. Diana is prone to "disappear" and "tries to make everyone worry if she is okay" by not responding to messages or phone calls. Nicole often believes Diana has problematic drinking habits and uses too much cocaine.

Forensic Interview
Diana presented dressed like she was going to a party, including full makeup, styled hair, and revealing clothing. She was occasionally expansive and tangential. Diana seemed to flirt with the male clinician and female intern. She was easy to anger and verbally lashed out at the intern when she unintentionally interrupted her ("Can you let me finish? Thanks a bunch, student").

When describing the referral event, Diana claimed James has "done all this for attention" and she did not hurt him badly. She stated the argument was James's fault, and she was simply trying to defend herself. Diana was reportedly afraid of James that evening because he was yelling. Contrary to evidence (pool of blood on the couch), Diana reported hitting James in the kitchen when he aggressively charged her. When confronted with the evidence, Diana suggested James had planted it to make her look bad. Diana acknowledged feeling repulsion towards James, but she could not explain why she felt this way. No matter how much she tried, she was unable to feel love for him when he was affectionate. Diana suspected she had been "wrapped up in lust" when they first met, but she did not realize who James really was until he moved into her house. She described "giving up everything" for James, and he paid her back by having her

arrested. Diana indicated the charges were "the hardest thing [she's] ever
gone through" and she felt "so depressed about everything."

Assessments

Diana completed the Minnesota Multiphasic Personality Inventory-II-
Restructured Form (MMPI-2-RF) the Structured Clinical Interview for
DSM-5 Personality Disorders (SCID-5-PD).

MMPI-2-RF

Diana's scores were very similar to Alex's, with a few differences. Diana
did not have elevations on any validity scale. She reported some unusual
thoughts and perceptions, and she may experience disorganized and unrealistic thinking (RC8 = 66). She also endorsed more severe antisocial
behavior than Alex, indicating she likely has trouble conforming to societal
norms and often challenges authority figures (RC4 = 74). Unlike Alex,
Diana did not endorse ineffectualness (NFC = 39). Diana reported head
pain (HPC = 65) and cognitive complaints (COG = 65), suggesting she
may somaticize when distressed. She endorsed rule-breaking behavior as a
juvenile, indicating distrust and conflictual early relationships (JCP = 67).
Diana reported uncontrolled physical aggression, suggestive of abusiveness
and rage (AGG = 69; Ben-Porath, 2012).

PID-5

Severe Dysfunction of the following Personality Trait Facets: Attention
Seeking (2.50), Distractibility (2.56), Grandiosity (3.00), Hostility (2.70),
Impulsivity (2.50), Irresponsibility (2.43), Manipulativeness (2.00), Rigid
Perfectionism (2.50).

Moderate Dysfunction of the following Personality Trait Facets: Anxiousness (1.22), Callousness (1.14), Deceitfulness (1.50), Eccentricity
(1.00), Restricted Affectivity (1.14), Risk Taking (1.50), Suspiciousness
(1.43), Withdrawal (1.60).

Personality Trait Domain: Moderate dysfunction within Antagonism
(6.50; consists of Manipulativeness, Deceitfulness, and Grandiosity).

SCID-5-PD

Principal Personality Disorder Diagnosis: Narcissistic Personality Disorder
(8/9 criteria; 16/18 on dimension).

Other notable personality characteristics:
Antisocial (5/7 + 5 conduct symptoms; 10/14 on dimension).

Histrionic (subclinical, 4/8 symptoms; 8/16 on dimension).

Treatment Considerations

Individuals with narcissistic personality disorder often resist engagement in treatment. They can experience psychotherapy as intrusive or threatening, especially if it treatment goals focus on problems related to their deviant behavior. Consequently, they tend to compartmentalize and provide "dosages" of information to the therapist, hold on to their own hidden agendas, and use a range of strategies to protect self-esteem and avoid intolerable affects. They also tend to avoid or refuse to discuss issues that in any way challenge their sense of control or unfold essential demeaning or embarrassing aspects of themselves. It is important to apply a flexible treatment approach, adjusted to the individual patient's functioning, motivation, and degree of self-awareness. Similarly, it is pivotal to invite the patient's curiosity and encourage a collaborative exploration of relevant problems. Psychoeducation about personality functioning, especially the cause and function of deviant behavior in the context of pathological narcissism and NPD is important. The choice of modality specifically adjusted to treatment of NPD (i.e., Mentalization-Based Therapy (MBT), Transference-Focused Therapy (TFP), Dialectical Behavioral Therapy (DBT), or Schema-Focused Therapy) will depend on the patient's motivation, reflective ability, and direction towards change.

Conclusion

Pathological narcissism is a complicated construct that can frustrate the clinical picture in forensic settings. As is demonstrated by the example cases, insight into narcissistic personality functioning is generally quite poor, and individuals can oscillate between grandiose expansiveness and ruminative vulnerability. Both cases had the potential for violence, yet only Diana was arrested for violent behavior. Alex's violence was directed at himself, and it was swift and decisive. Indeed, Alex only survived by happenstance. Both cases involved adverse childhood experiences, contempt for a parent, and manipulative, dismissive behavior towards family, friends, and romantic partners. Both were also described as arrogant and boastful by collateral contacts, and this grandiosity was evident to everyone but Alex and Diana.

Narcissistic vulnerability was also apparent in both cases. Both abused alcohol to cope with their internal states, and Diana also abused cocaine. When James was empathetic and affectionate towards Diana, it felt like an unwelcome intrusion, and she became overwhelmed. Her automatic reaction was repulsion and dismissive distancing. Diana also exhibited blind rage when James called her "a psycho," and she responded with an act of domestic violence. Alex became similarly dismissive with Kari, and he eventually shut her out by having extramarital affairs.

The forensic interview in these cases demonstrates the care that must be taken with assessing pathological narcissism. It is an exercise in futility to directly challenge an interviewee with pathological narcissism. As with treatment of NPD, respect, patience, and preparation should be a priority. Interviewers must recognize the countertransference they will almost certainly feel in the interview and collecting robust collateral information is paramount before beginning.

The assessment of pathological narcissism is still developing. NPD was a latecomer to the DSM, and the field is still catching up. Forensic assessment batteries should include a structured or semi-structured interview, along with self- and informant-reports whenever possible. The AMPD is rapidly evolving, and acceptance of this dimensional model by the field seems probable. Practitioners should prepare for this change and familiarize themselves with the literature.

References

Ackley, C.N., Mack, S.M., Beyer, K., & Erdberg, P. (2011). The narcissistic personality. In *investigative and forensic interviewing: A personality-focused approach* (pp. 9–42). Taylor & Francis Group.

Baskin-Sommers, A., Krusemark, E., & Ronningstam, E. (2014). Empathy in narcissistic personality disorder: From clinical and empirical perspectives. In *personality disorders: theory, research, and treatment* (Vol. 5, Issue 3, pp. 323–333). American Psychological Association. https://doi.org/10.1037/per0000061

Baumeister, R. F., Bushman, B. J., & Campbell, W. (2000). Self-Esteem, narcissism, and aggression: Does violence result from low self-esteem or from threatened egotism. *Current Directions in Psychological Science, 9*(1), 26–29.

Baumeister, R. F., Catanese, K. R., & Wallace, H. M. (2002). Conquest by force: A narcissistic reactance theory of rape and sexual coercion. *Review of General Psychology, 6*(1), 92–135. https://doi.org/10.1037/1089-2680.6.1.92

Baumeister, R. F., Smart, L., & Boden, J. M. (1996). Relation of threatened egotism to violence and aggression: The dark side of high self-esteem. *Psychological Review, 103*(1), 5. https://doi.org/10.1037/0033-295X.103.1.5

Beasley, R., & Stoltenberg, C. D. (1992). Personality characteristics of male spouse abusers. *Professional Psychology: Research and Practice, 23*(4), 310–317. https://doi.org/10.1037/0735-7028.23.4.310

Ben-Porath, Y. S. (2012). *Interpreting the MMPI-2-RF*. University of Minnesota Press.

Ben-Porath, Y. S., & Tellegen, A. (2011). *Minnesota Multiphasic personality inventory-2-restructured form: Manual for administration, scoring, and interpretation*. University of Minnesota Press.

Blackburn, R., & Coid, J. W. (1999). Empirical clusters of DSM-III personality disorders in violent offenders. *Journal of Personality Disorders, 13*(1), 18–34. https://doi.org/10.1521/pedi.1999.13.1.18

Blickle, G., Schlegel, A., Fassbender, P., & Klein, U. (2006). Some personality correlates of business white-collar crime. *Applied Psychology, 55*(2), 220–233. https://doi.org/10.1111/j.1464-0597.2006.00226.x

Blinkhorn, V., Lyons, M., & Almond, L. (2015). The ultimate femme fatale? Narcissism predicts serious and aggressive sexually coercive behaviour in females. *Personality and Individual Differences, 87*, 219–223. https://doi.org/10.1016/j.paid.2015.08.001

Blinkhorn, V., Lyons, M., & Almond, L. (2016). Drop the bad attitude! Narcissism predicts acceptance of violent behaviour. *Personality and Individual Differences, 98*, 157–161. https://doi.org/10.1016/j.paid.2016.04.025

Bromberg, W. (1965). Crime and the Mind. In *Social work* (Issue 1). Macmillan Co. https://doi.org/10.1093/sw/12.1.117

Buckels, E. E., Jones, D. N., & Paulhus, D. L. (2013). Behavioral confirmation of everyday sadism. *Psychological Science, 24*(11), 2201–2209. https://doi.org/10.1177/0956797613490749

Bushman, B. J. (2018). Narcissism, fame seeking, and mass shootings. *American Behavioral Scientist, 62*(2), 229–241. https://doi.org/10.1177/0002764217739660

Bushman, B. J., Bonacci, A. M., van Dijk, M., & Baumeister, R. F. (2003). Narcissism, sexual refusal, and aggression: Testing a narcissistic reactance model of sexual coercion. *Journal of Personality and Social Psychology, 84*(5), 1027–1040. https://doi.org/10.1037/0022-3514.84.5.1027

Clemence, A. J., Perry, J. C., & Plakun, E. M. (2009). Narcissistic and borderline personality disorders in a sample of treatment refractory patients. *Psychiatric Annals, 39*(4), 175–184. https://doi.org/10.3928/00485713-20090401-05

Collins, J. M., & Schmidt, F. L. (1993). Personality, integrity, and white collar crime: A construct validity study. *Personnel Psychology, 46*(2), 311.

Craig, R. J. (2003). Use of the millon clinical multiaxial inventory in the psychological assessment of domestic violence: A review. *Aggression and Violent Behavior, 8*, 235–243. https://doi.org/10.1016/S1359-1789(01)00058-1

Crevani, L., & Hallin, A. (2017). Performative narcissism: When organizations are made successful, admirable, and unique through narcissistic work. *Management Learning, 48*(4), 431–452. https://doi.org/10.1177/1350507617692295

Dawood, S., Wu, L. Z., Bliton, C. F., & Pincus, A. L. (2020). Narcissistic and histrionic personality disorders. In C. W. Lejuez & K. L. Gratz (Eds.), *The Cambridge handbook of personality disorders* (pp. 277–291). Cambridge University Press.

Dhawan, N., Kunik, M.E., Oldham, J., & Coverdale, J. (2010). Prevalence and treatment of narcissistic personality disorder in the community: A systematic review. In *comprehensive psychiatry* (Vol. 51, Issue 4, pp. 333–339). W.B. Saunders. https://doi.org/10.1016/j.com ppsych.2009.09.003

Facchi, L., Gattoni, T., Cemmi, C., & Stratico, E. (2011). Murder and madness: A case study of the criminogenesis and psychodynamics of a dual murder. *International Journal of Offender Therapy and Comparative Criminology, 55*(5), 799–815. https://doi.org/10. 1177/0306624X10371299

Fan, Y., Wonneberger, C., Enzi, B., De Greck, M., Ulrich, C., Tempelmann, C., Bogerts, B., Doering, S., & Northoff, G. (2011). The narcissistic self and its psychological and neural correlates: An exploratory fMRI study. *Psychological Medicine, 41*(8), 1641–1650. https:// doi.org/10.1017/S003329171000228X

First, M., Williams, J., Benjamin, L., & Spitzer, R. (2016). *Structured clinical interview for dsm-5 personality disorders: SCID-5-PD*. American Psychiatric Association Publishing.

Flournoy, P. S., & Wilson, G. L. (1991). Assessment of MMPI profiles of male batterers. *Violence and Victims, 6*(4), 309–320. https://doi.org/10.1891/0886-6708.6.4.309

Fromm, E. (1964). *The heart of man*. Harper and Row.

Glasser, M. (1992). Problems in the psychoanalysis of certain narcissistic disorders. *International Journal of Psycho-Analysis, 73*, 493–503.

Goldner-Vukov, M., & More, L. J. (2010). Malignant narcissism: From fairy tales to harsh reality. *Psychiatria Danubina, 22*(3), 392–405.

Gormley, B., & Lopez, F. G. (2010). Psychological abuse perpetration in college dating relationships: Contributions of gender, stress, and adult attachment orientations. *Journal of Interpersonal Violence, 25*(2), 204–218. https://doi.org/10.1177/0886260509334404

Green, A., MacLean, R., & Charles, K. (2020). Unmasking gender differences in narcissism within intimate partner violence. *Personality and Individual Differences, 167*, 110247. https://doi.org/10.1016/j.paid.2020.110247

Grilo, C. M., McGlashan, T. H., Quinlan, D. M., Walker, M. L., Greenfeld, D., & Edell, W. S. (1998). Frequency of personality disorders in two age cohorts of psychiatric inpatients. *American Journal of Psychiatry, 155*(1), 140–142. https://doi.org/10.1176/ajp.155.1.140

Hopwood, C. J., Mulay, A. L., & Waugh, M. H. (2019). The DSM-5 alternative model for personality disorders: Integrating multiple paradigms of personality assessment. In *The DSM-5 alternative model for personality disorders: Integrating multiple paradigms of personality assessment*. Routledge/Taylor & Francis Group.https://doi.org/10.4324/978 1315205076

Johnson, J. G., Cohen, P., Smailes, E., Kasen, S., Oldham, J. M., Skodol, A. E., & Brook, J. S. (2000). Adolescent personality disorders associated with violence and criminal behavior during adolescence and early adulthood. *American Journal of Psychiatry, 157*(9), 1406–1412. https://doi.org/10.1176/appi.ajp.157.9.1406

Jones, D. N., & Paulhus, D. L. (2010). Different provocations trigger aggression in narcissists and psychopaths. *Social Psychological and Personality Science, 1*(1), 12–18. https://doi. org/10.1177/1948550609347591

Kernberg, O. F. (1975). *Borderline conditions and pathological narcissism*. Aronson.

Kernberg, O. F. (1984). *Severe personality disorders.* Yale University Press.

Kernberg, O. F. (1992). *Aggression in personality disorders and perversions.* Yale University Press.

Kernberg, O. F. (2007). The almost untreatable narcissistic patient. *Journal of American Psychoanalytic Association, 55*(2), 503–539. https://doi.org/10.1177/00030651070550020701

Kernberg, O. F. (2009). The concept of death drive: A clinical perspective. *International Journal of Psychoanalysis, 90*(5), 1009–1023. https://doi.org/10.1111/j.1745-8315.2009.00187.x

Krueger, R. F., Derringer, J., Markon, K. E., Watson, D., & Skodol, A. E. (2012). Initial construction of a maladaptive personality trait model and inventory for DSM-5. *Psychological Medicine, 42*, 1879–1890. https://doi.org/10.1017/S0033291711002674

Lambe, S., Hamilton-Giachritsis, C., Garner, E., & Walker, J. (2018). The Role of narcissism in aggression and violence: A systematic review. *Trauma, Violence, & Abuse, 19*(2), 209–230. https://doi.org/10.1177/1524838016650190

Lamkin, J., Lavner, J. A., & Shaffer, A. (2017). Narcissism and observed communication in couples. *Personality and Individual Differences, 105*224–228. https://doi.org/10.1016/j.paid.2016.09.046

Levy, K. N., Chauhan, P., Clarkin, J. F., Wasserman, R. H., & Reynoso, J. S. (2009). Narcissistic pathology: Empirical approaches. *Psychiatric Annals, 39*(4), 203–213. https://doi.org/10.3928/00485713-20090401-03

Maccoby, M. (2007). *Narcissistic leaders: Who succeeds and who fails.* Harvard Business School Press.

Marissen, M. A. E., Deen, M. L., & Franken, I. H. A. (2012). Disturbed emotion recognition in patients with narcissistic personality disorder. *Psychiatry Research, 198*(2), 269–273. https://doi.org/10.1016/j.psychres.2011.12.042

Miller, J. D., Campbell, W. K., & Pilkonis, P. A. (2007). Narcissistic personality disorder: Relations with distress and functional impairment. *Comprehensive Psychiatry, 48*(2), 170–177. https://doi.org/10.1016/j.comppsych.2006.10.003

Miller, J. D., Campbell, W. K., Pilkonis, P. A., & Morse, J. Q. (2008). Assessment procedures for narcissistic personality disorder: A comparison of the personality diagnostic questionnaire-4 and best-estimate clinical judgments. *Assessment, 15*(4), 483–492. https://doi.org/10.1177/1073191108319022

Miller, J. D., Dir, A., Gentile, B., Wilson, L., Pryor, L. R., & Campbell, W. K. (2010). Searching for a vulnerable dark triad: Comparing factor 2 psychopathy, vulnerable narcissism, and borderline personality disorder. *Journal of Personality, 78*(5), 1529–1564. https://doi.org/10.1111/j.1467-6494.2010.00660.x

Miller, J. D., Pilkonis, P. A., & Clifton, A. (2005). Self- and other-reports of traits from the five-factor model: Relations to personality disorder. *Journal of Personality Disorders, 19*(4), 400–419. https://doi.org/10.1521/pedi.2005.19.4.400

Mulay, A.L., & Waugh, M.H. (2019). Forensic applications of the AMPD and case illustration. In *The DSM-5 alternative model for personality disorders: Integrating multiple paradigms of personality assessment* (pp. 209–220). Routledge. https://doi.org/10.4324/9781315205076

Nenadic, I., Güllmar, D., Dietzek, M., Langbein, K., Steinke, J., & Gaser, C. (2015). Brain structure in narcissistic personality disorder: A VBM and DTI pilot study. *Psychiatry*

Research—Neuroimaging, 231(2), 184–186. https://doi.org/10.1016/j.pscychresns.2014. 11.001

Norton-Baker, M., Russell, T. D., & King, A. R. (2018). "He seemed so normal": Single tactic perpetrators of sexual violence are similar to non-violent men using the DSM-5's hybrid personality disorder model. *Personality and Individual Differences, 123*, 241–246. https:// doi.org/10.1016/j.paid.2017.11.032

Paulhus, D. L., & Williams, K. M. (2002). The dark triad of personality: Narcissism, machiavellianism, and psychopathy. *Journal of Research in Personality, 36*(6), 556–563. https:// doi.org/10.1016/S0092-6566(02)00505-6

Pincus, A.L., & Roche, M.J. (2012). Narcissistic grandiosity and narcissistic vulnerability. In *The handbook of narcissism and narcissistic personality disorder: Theoretical approaches, empirical findings, and treatments* (pp. 31–40). John Wiley and Sons. https://doi.org/10. 1002/9781118093108.ch4

Ritter, K., Dziobek, I., Preißler, S., Rüter, A., Vater, A., Fydrich, T., Lammers, C. H., Heekeren, H. R., & Roepke, S. (2011). Lack of empathy in patients with narcissistic personality disorder. *Psychiatry Research, 187*(1–2), 241–247. https://doi.org/10.1016/j.psychres.2010. 09.013

Ronningstam, E. (2005). *Identifying and understand the narcissistic personality.* Oxford University Press.

Ronningstam, E. (2005). Narcissistic personality disorder: A review. In M. Maj, H. S. Akiskal, J. E. Mezzich & A. Okasha (Eds.), *Evidence and experience in psychiatry: Volume 8 personality disorders* (pp. 277–327). Wiley.

Ronningstam, E. (2009). *Narcissistic personality disorder* In P. H. Blaney & T. Millon (Eds.). Oxford University Press.

Ronningstam, E. (2012). Alliance building and narcissistic personality disorder. *Journal of Clinical Psychology, 68*(8), 943–953. https://doi.org/10.1002/jclp.21898

Ronningstam, E. (2016). New insights into narcissistic personality disorder. *Psychiatric Times, 33*(2).

Ronningstam, E., Gunderson, J., & Lyons, M. (1995). Changes in pathological narcissism. *American Journal of Psychiatry, 152*(2), 253–257. https://doi.org/10.1176/ajp.152.2.253

Ronningstam, E., & Maltsberger, J. T. (1998). Pathological narcissism and sudden suicide-related collapse. *Suicide and Life-Threatening Behavior, 28*(3), 261–271. https://doi.org/ 10.1111/j.1943-278X.1998.tb00856.x

Ronningstam, E., & Russell, T. (2020). Beyond nucleus diagnostic conceptualizations: Commentary on narcissistic and histrionic personality disorders. In *The cambridge handbook of personality disorders* (pp. 296–299). Cambridge University Press. https://doi.org/10. 1017/9781108333931.051

Russell, T. D., Doan, C. M., & King, A. R. (2017). Sexually violent women: The PID-5, everyday sadism, and adversarial sexual attitudes predict female sexual aggression and coercion against male victims. *Personality and Individual Differences, 111*, 242–249. https://doi.org/10.1016/j.paid.2017.02.019

Russell, T. D., & King, A. R. (2017). Distrustful, conventional, entitled, and dysregulated: PID-5 personality facets predict hostile masculinity and sexual violence in community men. *Journal of Interpersonal Violence, 35*(3–4), 707–730. https://doi.org/10.1177/088 6260517689887

Schulte, H. M., Hall, M. J., & Crosby, R. (1994). Violence in patients with narcissistic personality pathology: Observations of a clinical series. *American Journal of Psychotherapy,
48*(4), 610–623. https://doi.org/10.1176/appi.psychotherapy.1994.48.4.610

Schulze, L., Dziobek, I., Vater, A., Heekeren, H. R., Bajbouj, M., Renneberg, B., Heuser,
I., & Roepke, S. (2013). Gray matter abnormalities in patients with narcissistic personality
disorder. *Journal of Psychiatric Research, 47*(10), 1363–1369. https://doi.org/10.1016/j.
jpsychires.2013.05.017

Simonsen, S., & Simonsen, E. (2012). Comorbidity between narcissistic personality isorder
and axis I diagnoses. In *The handbook of narcissism and narcissistic personality disorder:
Theoretical approaches, empirical findings, and treatments* (pp. 237–247). John Wiley and
Sons. https://doi.org/10.1002/9781118093108.ch21

Stinson, F. S., Dawson, D. A., Goldstein, R. B., Chou, S. P., Huang, B., Smith, S. M., Ruan, W.
J., Pulay, A. J., Saha, T. D., Pickering, R. P., & Grant, B. F. (2008). Prevalence, correlates,
disability, and comorbidity of DSM-IV narcissistic personality disorder: Results from
the wave 2 national epidemiologic survey on alcohol and related conditions. *Journal of
Clinical Psychiatry, 69*(7), 1033–1045. https://doi.org/10.4088/JCP.v69n0701

Stone, M. H. (1998). Normal narcissism: An etiological and ethological perspective. In E. Ronningstam (Ed.), *Disorders of narcissism: Diagnostic, clinical, and empirical implications*
(pp. 7–28). American Psychiatric Association.

Stone, M. H. (2009). *The anatomy of evil*. Prometheus Books.

Svindseth, M. F., Nøttestad, J., Wallin, J., Roaldset, J., & Dahl, A. A. (2008). Narcissism in
patients admitted to psychiatric acute wards: Its relation to violence, suicidality and other
psychopathology. *BMC Psychiatry, 8*(1), 1–11. https://doi.org/10.1186/1471-244X-8-13

Tangney, J. P. (1995). Recent advances in the empirical study of shame and guilt. *American
Behavioral Scientist, 38*(8), 1132–1145. https://doi.org/10.1177/0002764295038008008

Watson, C., & Bagby, R.M. (2012). Assessment of narcissistic personality disorder. In *The
handbook of narcissism and narcissistic personality disorder: Theoretical approaches,
empirical findings, and treatments* (pp. 117–132). John Wiley and Sons. https://doi.org/
10.1002/9781118093108.ch10

Widiger, T.A. (2012). The comorbidity of narcissistic personality disorder with other DSM-IV
personality disorders. In *The handbook of narcissism and narcissistic personality disorder:
Theoretical approaches, empirical findings, and treatments* (pp. 248–260). John Wiley and
Sons. https://doi.org/10.1002/9781118093108.ch22

Zeigler-Hill, V., Enjaian, B., & Essa, L. (2013). The role of narcissistic personality features
in sexual aggression. *Journal of Social and Clinical Psychology, 32*(2), 186–199. https://
doi.org/10.1521/jscp.2013.32.2.186

Zimmerman, M., Rothschild, L., & Chelminski, I. (2005). The prevalence of DSM-IV personality disorders in psychiatric outpatients. *American Journal of Psychiatry, 162*(10),
1911–1918. https://doi.org/10.1176/appi.ajp.162.10.1911

Further Readings

Ackley, C. N., Mack, S. M., Beyer, K., & Erdberg, P. (2011). The narcissistic personality.
In *Investigative and forensic interviewing: A personality-focused approach* (pp. 9–42).
Taylor & Francis Group.

Crevani, L., & Hallin, A. (2017). Performative narcissism: When organizations are made successful, admirable, and unique through narcissistic work. *Management Learning, 48*(4), 431–452. https://doi.org/10.1177/1350507617692295

Lambe, S., Hamilton-Giachritsis, C., Garner, E., & Walker, J. (2018). The role of narcissism in aggression and violence: A systematic review. *Trauma, Violence, & Abuse, 19*(2), 209–230. https://doi.org/10.1177/1524838016650190

Mulay, A.L., & Waugh, M.H. (2019). Forensic applications of the AMPD and case illustration. In *The DSM-5 alternative model for personality disorders: Integrating multiple paradigms of personality assessment* (pp. 209–220). Routledge. https://doi.org/10.4324/978131520 5076

Ronningstam, E. (2005). *Identifying and understand the narcissistic personality.* Oxford University Press.

Ronningstam, E., & Maltsberger, J. T. (1998). Pathological narcissism and sudden suicide-related collapse. *Suicide and Life-Threatening Behavior, 28*(3), 261–271.

Schizophrenia Spectrum, Other Psychotic Disorders and Violence

14

Zhaorong Song, Rhiannon Corcoran, and Steven M. Gillespie

Key Points

- Schizophrenia and other primary psychotic disorders are characterized by a collection of positive (e.g., hallucinations, delusions, disordered thoughts) and negative (e.g., lack of motivation or enthusiasm) symptoms
- The presence of schizophrenia or other psychotic disorders is associated with an increased risk for violence compared with the general population
- Risk factors for violence in psychosis include:

  o The presence of specific symptoms including paranoid ideation
  o Comorbid substance abuse
  o Comorbidity with other disorders (e.g., psychopathy)
  o Impairments in theory of mind/mentalization
  o Poor insight into illness

- Treatments to minimize violent behaviors include pharmacological and cognitive behavioral approaches

Z. Song (✉) · R. Corcoran · S. M. Gillespie
Institute of Population Health, University of Liverpool, Liverpool, UK
e-mail: zhaorong.song@liverpool.ac.uk

R. Corcoran
e-mail: corcoran@liverpool.ac.uk

S. M. Gillespie
e-mail: steven.gillespie@liverpool.ac.uk

© The Author(s), under exclusive license to Springer Nature Switzerland AG 2022   269
C. Garofalo and J. J. Sijtsema (eds.), *Clinical Forensic Psychology*,
https://doi.org/10.1007/978-3-030-80882-2_14

Introduction

We will begin this chapter by briefly describing the symptoms of schizophrenia and other primary psychotic disorders and existing frameworks for diagnosing these disorders. We will then summarize research showing that the presence of schizophrenia or other psychotic disorders is associated with an increased risk of violence. Next, we will discuss specific risk factors that might be driving this association. These risk factors include specific psychotic symptoms (e.g., paranoid ideation), substance abuse, comorbidity with other disorders (e.g., psychopathy), impaired theory of mind/mentalization, and poor insight into illness. At the end of this chapter, we will briefly talk about different treatments for different potential risk factors to minimize violent behaviors.

Schizophrenia or Other Primary Psychotic Disorders

Mental health conditions are mainly classified under two diagnostic manuals: the International Classification of Diseases, currently at its eleventh edition (ICD-11; WHO, 2019) and the Diagnostic and Statistical Manual of Mental Disorders, at its fifth version (DSM-5; APA, 2013). Both diagnostic classifications have been the subject of clinical controversies. It is argued that ICD-11 is more frequently used for clinical utility and diagnosis, while DSM-5 is more valued for diagnostic validity and research (Stein et al., 2013). ICD-11 is also more widely used by other health workers and organizations beyond mental health professionals (Biedermann & Fleischhacker, 2016). For this reason, we will be using ICD-11 to introduce schizophrenia and other psychotic disorders in this chapter. According to ICD-11, schizophrenia spectrum disorders (SSDs) and other psychotic disorders are defined by significant impairments in reality testing and alterations in behavior that broadly manifest in two types of symptoms: positive and negative. Positive symptoms and signs include delusions (i.e., fixed beliefs that are not amenable to change in light of conflicting evidence), hallucinations (i.e., perception-like experiences that occur without an external stimulus, for example, voice hearing in the absence of voices that are heard by others), disorganized thinking, which typically manifests as disorganized speech (i.e., a severe disruption of verbal communication in which ideas shift rapidly and incoherently from one topic to another), and grossly disorganized behavior (i.e., behavior that is inappropriate for the situation or ineffective in attaining goals, often with specific motor disturbances). Negative symptoms and signs include blunted or flat affect, avolition and apathy (i.e., lack of interest, enthusiasm or motivation to complete goal-directed activities), and psychomotor disturbances such as catatonia (i.e., disturbances that may alternate between extremes such as hyperkinesis and stupor, or automatic obedience and negativism).

Although SSDs and other psychotic disorders are recognized, diagnosable disorders according to diagnostic frameworks (e.g., using the ICD-11), evidence suggests that these disorders actually lie on a continuum that ranges from healthy and well-functioning to severe symptoms that have debilitating effects on everyday life (Cochrane et al., 2012; Nelson et al., 2013). Consistent with this model, symptoms of psychotic disorders are a relatively common experience even among healthy functioning individuals with no history of mental illness. According to such dimensional accounts that place psychosis on a continuum, all individuals lie somewhere on the psychosis spectrum. This includes individuals who present with schizotypal personality traits (or, in extremis, schizotypal personality disorder), with schizotypy commonly considered to represent subclinical manifestations of the same biological and psychological factors that characterize schizophrenia and other psychoses (Cochrane et al., 2012; Meehl, 1962).

Schizophrenia

Schizophrenia is characterized by disturbances in multiple mental modalities, and the presence of both positive and negative symptoms. Patients with schizophrenia often present with persistent delusions, persistent hallucinations, thought disorder, and experiences of influence, passivity, or control. For a patient to receive an ICD-11 diagnosis of schizophrenia, symptoms must have persisted for at least one month. They must not be better explained by another health condition (e.g., a brain tumor) and must not be due to the effects of a substance (e.g., recreational drug use, medication) on the central nervous system (e.g., corticosteroids), including the effects of withdrawal (e.g., alcohol withdrawal). Unlike ICD-10, ICD-11 has omitted all schizophrenia subtypes (e.g., paranoid, hebephrenic, catatonia) and de-emphasizes first-rank symptoms (i.e., auditory hallucinations, thought broadcast, thought insertion, thought withdrawal, and delusional perception) due to a lack of longitudinal stability and clinical utility (Gaebel et al., 2017; Nordgaard et al., 2008; Schneider, 1959).

Other Primary Psychotic Disorders

According to ICD-11, other primary psychotic disorders include schizoaffective disorder, acute and transient psychotic disorder (ATPD), schizotypal disorder, and delusional disorder (WHO, 2019).

Schizoaffective disorder is an episodic disorder in which the diagnostic requirements of schizophrenia and a manic (e.g., elevated mood, increase in the quality and speed of physical and mental activity), mixed, or moderate or severe depressive (e.g., depressed mood, loss of interest, reduced energy) episode are met within the same episode of illness, either simultaneously or within a few days of each other.

Acute and transient psychotic disorder is characterized by acute onset of psychotic symptoms that emerge without a prodrome (i.e., an early sign or symptom indicating the onset of a disease) and reach their maximal severity within two weeks. Symptoms typically change rapidly, both in nature and intensity, from day to day, or even within a single day.

Schizotypal disorder is characterized by an enduring pattern (i.e., characteristic of the person's functioning over a period of at least several years) of eccentricities in behavior, appearance and speech, accompanied by cognitive and perceptual distortions, unusual beliefs, and discomfort with—and often reduced capacity for—interpersonal relationships. Symptoms of schizotypal disorder include constricted or inappropriate affect and anhedonia (negative schizotypy).

Delusional disorder is characterized by the development of a delusion or set of related delusions that persist for at least three months (usually much longer), which occur in the absence of a depressive, manic, or mixed mood episode. Other characteristic symptoms of schizophrenia (e.g., persistent auditory hallucinations, disorganized thinking, negative symptoms) are not present, although various forms of perceptual disturbances (e.g., hallucinations, misidentifications of persons) thematically related to the delusion are still consistent with the diagnosis. Apart from actions and attitudes directly related to the delusion or delusional system, affect, speech, and behaviors are typically unaffected.

Recent studies have shown an association between experience of psychosis and negative outcomes such as poor physical health (Moreno et al., 2013) and early mortality (Fazel et al., 2014). In this chapter, we will focus specifically on interpersonal violence perpetrated by individuals with schizophrenia or other psychotic disorders. In the below section, we will provide a brief definition of violence and distinguish between two types of aggression, reactive and proactive (Chapter 19). These types of aggression are differentially motivated but both linked with the presence of schizophrenia and other psychotic disorders according to research.

Definition of Violence

Violence is defined as "the expression of hostility and rage with the intent to injure or damage people or property through physical force" (VandenBos, 2007). Some studies use a more restrictive definition of violence and limit their inclusion criteria based on history of severe physical violence such as assaults using a weapon. Some studies use broader definitions that include threats and minor assaults, while others include a wide range of behaviors from destructive acts to severe violence resulting in injury to others or death.

Violence and aggression appear to lie on the same continuum of intensity, injury, and illegality (Marcus, 2007) and these terms are often used interchangeably, both sharing the intention of harm to others (Large & Nielssen, 2011). Aggression is heterogeneous and typically understood as either reactive or proactive in nature (Ross & Babcock, 2009).

Reactive aggression, also known as hostile, impulsive, unplanned, expressive, affective or hot-blooded aggression (Ramírez & Andreu, 2006), is perpetrated in response to provocation and is associated with high arousal and anger. Proactive aggression, also called instrumental, planned, predatory, premediated, or cold-blooded aggression (Ramírez & Andreu, 2006), is enacted without provocation and is usually premediated. For instance, proactive aggression and violence may serve as a means to dominate others or may be motivated by perceived benefits such as money or drugs. Measures of the tendency towards reactive and proactive aggression are highly correlated (Walters, 2005), making it difficult to distinguish purely reactively and proactively aggressive individuals. Frequent reactive aggression is associated with poor emotion regulation and impairments of executive function, while proactive aggression is associated with callous-unemotional traits such as lack of empathy, guilt and shallow affect (Frick & Viding, 2009).

The issues around definition and measurement have posed difficulties for researchers looking to understand the causes and correlates of violence (Bo et al., 2011). Moving forward, it is important for future research to adopt and operationalize a unified, agreed upon definition of violence. In the sections that follow, we will consider the multiple psychosis-related factors that are associated with a tendency to be more violent, and highlight explanatory accounts for this increased risk. These include the presence of specific psychotic symptoms, comorbid conditions, substance misuse, and impairments in socio-cognitive functioning.

Risk Factors for Violence in Psychosis

Psychotic Symptoms

Individuals with schizophrenia are four to six times more likely to commit violent crime compared to the generally healthy population (Kooyman et al., 2007; Senior et al., 2020). In a Swedish national cohort study (Chang et al., 2015), it was reported that people with psychosis released from prison showed an increased risk of recidivism (i.e., repeat violent offence), while a UK study found that approximately 14% of patients with first-episode psychosis were violent within 12 months following early interventions service entry (Winsper et al., 2013).

Research suggests an association between specific psychotic symptoms and violence (Bo et al., 2011). One meta-analysis examined whether violence is associated with psychotic disorder via specific symptoms or through comorbid substance abuse/disorder (Coid et al., 2016). It was found that violence is most strongly associated with paranoid ideation (i.e., symptoms dominated by paranoid or persecutory delusions, usually accompanied by hallucinations). Furthermore, this meta-analysis demonstrated that other associations between violence and psychosis were explained by comorbid substance abuse or other disorders.

It is thought that the association between paranoid delusions and violence is often prompted by associated emotional responses such as anger (Lamsma & Harte, 2015). Anger appears to constitute the main drive to violence and mediates the association between paranoid delusions and violence (Coid et al., 2018; Ullrich et al., 2018) (Chapter 5). Moreover, impulsivity also plays a role in the association between psychosis and violence (Moulin et al., 2018), suggesting that the interaction between impulsivity and positive psychotic symptoms has an impact on the risk of violent behaviors.

Substance Abuse

According to ICD-11, disorders due to substance use and addictive behaviors are "mental and behavioral disorders that develop as a result of the use of predominantly psychoactive substances, including medications, or specific repetitive rewarding and reinforcing behaviors" (see Chapter 17 and 23). The prevalence of substance use disorders is approximately three to four times greater than that for psychosis (Saha et al., 2005). Substance abuse is also highly prevalent among patients with schizophrenia and is frequently established at first presentation (Mullen, 2009).

Although a modest association between violence and psychosis has been well documented, a robust body of evidence suggests that this association is increased in the context of substance abuse comorbidity (Elbogen & Johnson, 2009; Van Dorn et al., 2012). For example, in a longitudinal study (Fazel, Långström, et al., 2009), it was found that schizophrenia patients with comorbid substance use issues were three times more likely to commit violent offences than schizophrenic patients without substance abuse. However, the finding that schizophrenia without substance abuse is associated with an increased risk for violence has been challenged in a systematic review and meta-analysis (Fazel, Gulati, et al., 2009), which showed that psychotic disorders did not account for any additional risk of violence compared with individuals with diagnoses of substance use disorders alone. It is suggested that a third factor (e.g., personality traits/social conditions) might mediate the association between psychotic disorders, substance abuse and violence (Mullen, 2006).

Overall, the above findings strongly suggest that substance abuse in patients with schizophrenia elevates the risk of violence. It is suggested that clinical practice as well as risk assessments in forensic settings should target the presence of substance misuse to reduce the risk of violence in patients with psychosis in the future.

Comorbidity with Other Disorders

It has been found that comorbid personality pathology (e.g., antisocial personality disorder/psychopathy) could increase the risk of violence in psychosis (Bo et al., 2011; Lamsma & Harte, 2015). According to the DSM-5, antisocial personality disorder (ASPD) is characterized by a lack of empathy, impulsivity, disregard for societal norms, deceitfulness and remorselessness (Chapter 11). Although psychopathy shares some behavioral features with ASPD, psychopathy can be readily differentiated from ASPD on the basis of core personality features including callousness, a lack of remorse or guilt, and the ability to manipulate or deceive others for personal gain (Hervé, 2007) (Chapter 15). However, it should be noted that although most psychopaths would also meet the criteria for ASPD, only a small proportion of all people with ASPD would also meet the criteria for psychopathy.

Both ASPD and psychopathy are associated with criminality and specifically with violent crime (Alm et al., 1996; Sedgwick et al., 2017). In relation to antisocial traits, patients with early onset psychosis tend to have higher rates of ASPD than individuals with adult-onset, and these patients also tend to have increased levels of aggressiveness (Huber et al., 2016). Thus, assessing for antisocial traits in prodromal patients may have important practical implications for predicting violence. Furthermore, it has been found that aggressive schizophrenia patients tend to have higher psychopathy scores than non-aggressive schizophrenia patients (Nolan et al., 1999; Rasmussen et al., 1995). Elevated levels of violence in patients with comorbid psychopathy or ASPD with schizophrenia may reflect increased impulsivity, a common feature of both ASPD and psychopathic personality that has been linked with violence perpetration (Volavka, 2014).

We have highlighted above that both ASPD and psychopathic personality are associated with an increased risk for violence in patients with schizophrenia. In patients who develop comorbid schizophrenia and ASPD/psychopathy, whether antisocial behaviors (associated with a diagnosis of ASPD/psychopathy) occur prior to the onset of psychosis may be an important factor when attempting to discriminate developmental trajectories of the occurrence of violence (Bo et al., 2011; Huber et al., 2016; Lamsma & Harte, 2015). It seems that violence in schizophrenia is mostly explained by ASPD/psychopathic traits if antisocial behaviors appear before the onset of psychotic illness. In contrast, violence is thought to be primarily a consequence of paranoid psychotic symptoms in patients without comorbid ASPD/psychopathy.

Theory of Mind/Mentalization

Theory of mind, also known as mentalization, is defined as the ability to attribute internal states such as emotions, intentions, and beliefs to others (Gallese & Sinigaglia, 2011; Premack & Woodruff, 1978). When people try to understand and predict why others do the things they do and what they might do next, it is possible to entertain a false belief—a representation of another's mental state that turns out to be incorrect (Wimmer & Perner, 1983).

There are many tests to assess theory of mind in adults including the *Movie for the Assessment of Social Cognition* (MASC; Dziobek et al., 2006) and the *Reading the Mind in the Eyes Test* (RMET; Baron-Cohen et al., 2001). In the MASC, participants watch a series of film clips showing a group of friends interacting and are asked to judge the characters' feelings, thoughts and intentions. In the

RMET, participants are asked to infer the mental state of a person just from photographs of that person's eye region. The MASC and the RMET are clearly very different, but both are argued to test the construct of theory of mind and can be used in healthy adult and clinical samples.

Many studies, beginning in the mid 1990's and continuing to this day, have found impairments in theory of mind ability in schizophrenia patients using a variety of tasks (Corcoran et al., 1995; Frith, 2004; Frith & Corcoran, 1996). These impairments in representing mental states may result in a bias when monitoring the thoughts and intentions of others that can underpin persecutory ideation (Doody et al., 1998). Thus, impairments in theory of mind may underpin the delusional symptoms that are associated with violence (Bo et al., 2011). However, paradoxical associations between mentalizing ability and violence in schizophrenia have also been found. For example, it has been shown that the likelihood for violence among patients with schizophrenia increases with both cognitive-mental-state understanding and hostility towards others, but decreases with better recognition of faux-pas, that is, a test that requires one to have the ability to understand and recognize situations when someone says something inappropriate. Poorer performance on faux-pas recognition in violent than non-violent patients with paranoid schizophrenia may suggest that violent patients have impaired moral reasoning and affective empathy (Abu-Akel & Abushua'leh, 2004). The failed faux pas recognition task may also suggest that affective empathy acts to inhibit violence and aggression (Tangney, 1991). Although seemingly paradoxical, the finding that violence increases with cognitive mental state understanding suggests that the ability to infer others' cognitive mental states may contribute to deceptive and manipulative tendencies that are essential for acts of proactive aggression. The hypothesis that theory of mind may allow one to deceive and manipulate others has received some support in a sample of boys with conduct problems and psychopathic tendencies (Gillespie et al., 2018) and in patients with schizophrenia (Bo et al., 2015).

In line with these suggestions, it is argued that the relationship between theory of mind and schizophrenia might also depend on the presence of other personality disorders such as psychopathy. A recent study found that psychopathic tendencies in patients with schizophrenia were associated with lower metacognitive abilities, whereas better metacognitive abilities were found in schizophrenia patients with extreme levels of psychopathy (Abu-Akel et al., 2015). These seemingly paradoxical findings might suggest that patients with schizophrenia and co-occurring psychopathic tendencies are better able to manipulate and extort their victims for personal gain. In another study that asked non-clinical participants to infer the mental states of a group of actors interacting over a series of video clips, increasing psychopathic tendencies were associated with better mentalizing ability in participants who also showed more frequent positive psychotic experiences (Gillespie et al., 2017). Similar results were also found in a sample of incarcerated adolescent boys where better theory of mind ability (assessed using the RMET) was associated with co-occurring psychopathic traits and schizotypal symptoms (Gillespie et al., 2020).

The above studies suggest that psychopathic patients with schizophrenia may have intact cognitive empathic abilities (i.e., the ability to represent the internal mental state of the other) (Chapter 7). Nonetheless, these individuals may still show impairments in affective empathy (i.e., the ability to feel what another is feeling) that are considered a defining feature of psychopathic personality (Blair, 2007). In relation to psychopathy, impairments in affective empathy can be considered to play a role in aggressive and violent behaviors (Blair, 2007) and studies have shown that individuals with psychopathy show a blunted affective response when viewing others in distress (Decety et al., 2013). However, the ways in which affective empathic abilities are affected in individuals with comorbid psychopathy and schizophrenia is not well understood.

Taken together, existing research does not allow for clear conclusions to be reached about the role of theory of mind in the relationship between schizophrenia and violence. Comorbid conditions (e.g., psychopathy) may also play a role in this relationship. Nonetheless, the importance of distinguishing between violence related to schizophrenia and to antisocial traits should not be neglected.

Poor Insight into Illness

Insight into illness is a contested topic but it can be defined as an individual's awareness and understanding of their mental health difficulties (Amador & David, 1998) (see also Chapter 25). Although not associated exclusively with psychosis, poor insight is a core feature of psychotic experience. The prevalence of lack of insight is between 50 and 80% among patients with schizophrenia (Amador & Gorman, 1998). Inadequate insight has been regarded as a risk factor for violence in individuals with psychosis. For instance, denial of understanding the illness or the need for psychiatric care may induce violent behaviors through non-adherence to treatment (Bjørkly, 2006). In addition to traditional understanding of clinical insight (i.e., the awareness of having a mental disorder), the concept has been expanded to include cognitive insight (i.e., a patient's current capacity to evaluate their anomalous experiences and atypical interpretations of events) (Beck et al., 2004).

Several studies have found a positive relationship between poor clinical insight and violence in psychosis (Ekinci & Ekinci, 2013; Soyka et al., 2007). However, conflicting evidence (i.e., no relationship between insight and violence) has also been reported (Köşger et al., 2015; Umut et al., 2012). One potential reason behind the contradictory findings is the choice of measurement tool of insight. One systematic review (Smith et al., 2020) found that there tends to be a positive relationship between poor insight and violence in psychotic individuals in all studies using the *Scale to Assess Unawareness in Mental Disorder* (SUMD; Amador et al., 1993) whereas insight measured by the *Beck Cognitive Insight Scale* (BCIS; Beck et al., 2004) does not appear to be correlated with violence. The contrasting pattern of results emphasizes the importance of using carefully chosen measurement tools, and highlights differences between cognitive insights relative to clinical insight. These results suggest that the insight dimensions should be more clearly defined and measured in future studies.

Treatment

Due to the complex etiology of violent behaviors in psychosis, it is difficult to tailor particular treatments to meet the specific needs of offenders with an SSD with specific risk factors for violence. Nonetheless, there is some evidence that attest to the potential effectiveness of some methods. For example, pharmacoepidemiologic work that has shown that violent crime has reduced significantly in those with psychosis receiving treatment compared to those who were not (Tracy & Gaughran, 2017). Current treatment of violence in schizophrenia relies on antipsychotics and mood stabilizers, with clozapine showing particular efficacy for reducing violence, perhaps because this medication is associated with improvements across several symptoms of psychosis, particularly in treatment resistant schizophrenia (Buchanan, 1995; Volavka & Citrome, 2008).

However, as this chapter states, many incidents of aggressive behaviors in those with psychoses appear to be driven primarily by comorbid factors. For instance, when violent behaviors are caused by drug-induced psychoses, the focus of treatment should be on substance dependance if the intention is to delay reoffending (Igoumenou et al., 2015). Psychological treatments such as cognitive behavioral therapy (CBT), motivational interviewing, family therapies as well as group-based therapies all appear to be effective.

As for violent behaviors that are associated with mentalizing abilities, mentalization-based therapy (MBT) offers a useful adjunct in addition to pharmacotherapy for psychosis (Brent, 2009), with the goal being to re-establish an attachment relationship with the patient and improve awareness of the self and others.

CBT, motivational interviewing, psychosocial education, and social skills training have all been successful in teaching patients to cope with their symptoms and make changes in health-related behaviors (Baier, 2010; Lysaker et al., 2013). A meta-analysis reported that individual treatments such as psychoeducation and cognitive behavior therapy exert a small, at best marginal, impact on insight (Pijnenborg et al., 2013). It is hence suggested that treatment will likely require multiple components if it is to deal with the factors that promote poor insight.

Overall, aggressive behaviors in psychosis are etiologically complex as they may be caused by numerous interacting risk factors. It is suggested that in addition to antipsychotic medication (e.g., clozapine), adjunctive treatments are also required when risk factors other than psychotic symptoms are detected.

Conclusion

There is substantial evidence demonstrating the relationship between violence and psychosis. However, understanding the foundations and evaluating the risk of violent behavior in psychosis is complex. Violence in the context of psychosis may be associated with various inter-related factors: psychotic symptoms, substance abuse, comorbid ASPD/psychopathy, mentalization, and diminished clinical insight. To improve research, knowledge and clinical practice aimed at reducing the risk of violence in those with psychosis, these risk factors need to be considered together and the associations between them thoroughly examined with a view to targeting therapeutic interventions at the most fundamental of these psychosis-related attributes.

References

Abu-Akel, A., & Abushua'leh, K. (2004, July). 'Theory of mind' in violent and nonviolent patients with paranoid schizophrenia [Article]. *Schizophrenia Research, 69*(1), 45–53. https://doi.org/10.1016/s0920-9964(03)00049-5. (Schizophrenia Research).

Abu-Akel, A., Heinke, D., Gillespie, S. M., Mitchell, I. J., & Bo, S. (2015). Metacognitive impairments in schizophrenia are arrested at extreme levels of psychopathy: The cut-off effect [Article]. *Journal of Abnormal Psychology, 124*(4), 1102–1109. https://doi.org/10.1037/abn0000096. (Journal of Abnormal Psychology).

Alm, P. O., Klinteberg, B., Humble, K., Leppert, J., Sörensen, S., Thorell, L. H., Lidberg, L., & Oreland, L. (1996). Psychopathy, platelet MAO activity and criminality among former juvenile delinquents. *Acta Psychiatrica Scandinavica, 94*(2), 105–111.

Amador, X. F., & David, A. S. (1998). *Insight and psychosis.* Oxford University Press.

Amador, X. F., & Gorman, J. M. (1998). Psychopathologic domains and insight in schizophrenia. *Psychiatric Clinics of North America, 21*(1), 27–42.

Amador, X. F., Strauss, D. H., Yale, S. A., Flaum, M. M., Endicott, J., & Gorman, J. M. (1993, June). Assessment of insight in psychosis. *Am J Psychiatry, 150*(6), 873–879. https://doi.org/10.1176/ajp.150.6.873

American Psychiatric Association. (2013). Anxiety disorders. In *Diagnostic and statistical manual of mental disorders* (5th ed.).

Baier, M. (2010, August 1). Insight in Schizophrenia: A review. *Current Psychiatry Reports, 12*(4), 356–361. https://doi.org/10.1007/s11920-010-0125-7

Baron-Cohen, S., Wheelwright, S., Hill, J., Raste, Y., & Plumb, I. (2001, Febrauary). The "Reading the Mind in the Eyes" Test revised version: A study with normal adults, and adults with Asperger syndrome or high-functioning autism. *J Child Psychol Psychiatry, 42*(2), 241–251.

Beck, A. T., Baruch, E., Balter, J. M., Steer, R. A., & Warman, D. M. (2004, June 1). A new instrument for measuring insight: The Beck Cognitive Insight Scale. *Schizophrenia Research, 68*(2), 319–329. https://doi.org/10.1016/S0920-9964(03)00189-0

Biedermann, F., & Fleischhacker, W. (2016). Psychotic disorders in DSM-5 and ICD-11. *CNS Spectrums, 21*(4), 349–354.

Bjørkly, S. (2006, July 1). Empirical evidence of a relationship between insight and risk of violence in the mentally ill—A review of the literature. *Aggression and Violent Behavior, 11*(4), 414–423. https://doi.org/10.1016/j.avb.2006.01.006

Blair, R. J. R. (2007). Empathic dysfunction in psychopathic individuals. *Empathy in Mental Illness, 1*, 3–16.

Bo, S., Abu-Akel, A., Kongerslev, M., Haahr, U. H., & Simonsen, E. (2011, July 1). Risk factors for violence among patients with schizophrenia. *Clinical Psychology Review, 31*(5), 711–726. https://doi.org/10.1016/j.cpr.2011.03.002

Bo, S., Kongerslev, M., Dimaggio, G., Lysaker, P. H., & Abu-Akel, A. (2015, Febrayary 28). Metacognition and general functioning in patients with schizophrenia and a history of criminal behavior. *Psychiatry Res, 225*(3), 247–253. https://doi.org/10.1016/j.psychres.2014.12.034

Brent, B. (2009). Mentalization-based psychodynamic psychotherapy for psychosis. *Journal of Clinical Psychology, 65*(8), 803–814.

Buchanan, R. W. (1995). Clozapine: Efficacy and safety. *Schizophrenia Bulletin, 21*(4), 579–591.

Chang, Z., Larsson, H., Lichtenstein, P., & Fazel, S. (2015). Psychiatric disorders and violent reoffending: A national cohort study of convicted prisoners in Sweden. *The Lancet Psychiatry, 2*(10), 891–900.

Cochrane, M., Petch, I., & Pickering, A. D. (2012). Aspects of cognitive functioning in schizotypy and schizophrenia: Evidence for a continuum model. *Psychiatry Research, 196*(2–3), 230–234. https://doi.org/10.1016/j.psychres.2012.02.010

Coid, J. W., Kallis, C., Doyle, M., Shaw, J., & Ullrich, S. (2018). Shifts in positive and negative psychotic symptoms and anger: Effects on violence. *Psychological Medicine, 48*(14), 2428–2438. https://doi.org/10.1017/S0033291718000077

Coid, J. W., Ullrich, S., Bebbington, P., Fazel, S., & Keers, R. (2016). Paranoid ideation and violence: Meta-analysis of individual subject data of 7 population surveys. *Schizophrenia Bulletin, 42*(4), 907–915.

Corcoran, R., Mercer, G., & Frith, C. D. (1995, September 1). Schizophrenia, symptomatology and social inference: Investigating "theory of mind" in people with schizophrenia. *Schizophrenia Research, 17*(1), 5–13. https://doi.org/10.1016/0920-9964(95)00024-G

Decety, J., Skelly, L. R., & Kiehl, K. A. (2013). Brain response to empathy-eliciting scenarios involving pain in incarcerated individuals with psychopathy. *JAMA Psychiatry, 70*(6), 638–645.

Doody, G. A., Johnstone, E. C., Sanderson, T. L., Owens, D. G., & Muir, W. J. (1998, August). "Pfropfschizophrenie" revisited: Schizophrenia in people with mild learning disability. *British Journal of Psychiatry, 173*, 145–153. https://doi.org/10.1192/bjp.173.2.145

Dziobek, I., Fleck, S., Kalbe, E., Rogers, K., Hassenstab, J., Brand, M., Kessler, J., Woike, J. K., Wolf, O. T., & Convit, A. (2006, July 1). Introducing MASC: A movie for the assessment of social cognition. *Journal of Autism and Developmental Disorders, 36*(5), 623–636. https://doi.org/10.1007/s10803-006-0107-0

Ekinci, O., & Ekinci, A. (2013, Apr). Association between insight, cognitive insight, positive symptoms and violence in patients with schizophrenia. *Nord J Psychiatry, 67*(2), 116–123. https://doi.org/10.3109/08039488.2012.687767

Elbogen, E. B., & Johnson, S. C. (2009). The intricate link between violence and mental disorder: Results From the national epidemiologic survey on alcohol and related conditions. *Archives of General Psychiatry, 66*(2), 152–161. https://doi.org/10.1001/archgenpsychiatry.2008.537

Fazel, S., Gulati, G., Linsell, L., Geddes, J. R., & Grann, M. (2009). Schizophrenia and violence: Systematic review and meta-analysis. *PLOS Medicine, 6*(8), e1000120. https://doi.org/10.1371/journal.pmed.1000120

Fazel, S., Långström, N., Hjern, A., Grann, M., & Lichtenstein, P. (2009). Schizophrenia, substance abuse, and violent crime. *JAMA, 301*(19), 2016–2023. https://doi.org/10.1001/jama.2009.675

Fazel, S., Wolf, A., Palm, C., & Lichtenstein, P. (2014, June). Violent crime, suicide, and premature mortality in patients with schizophrenia and related disorders: a 38-year total population study in Sweden. *Lancet Psychiatry, 1*(1), 44–54. https://doi.org/10.1016/s2215-0366(14)70223-8

Frick, P. J., & Viding, E. (2009, Fall). Antisocial behavior from a developmental psychopathology perspective. *Dev Psychopathol, 21*(4), 1111–1131. https://doi.org/10.1017/s0954579409990071

Frith, C. D. (2004, April). Schizophrenia and theory of mind. *Psychol Med, 34*(3), 385–389. https://doi.org/10.1017/s0033291703001326

Frith, C. D., & Corcoran, R. (1996). Exploring 'theory of mind' in people with schizophrenia. *Psychological Medicine, 26*(3), 521–530.

Gaebel, W., Zielasek, J., & Reed, G. M. (2017, April 30). Mental and behavioural disorders in the ICD-11: Concepts, methodologies, and current status. *Psychiatr Pol, 51*(2), 169–195. https://doi.org/10.12740/pp/69660. (Zaburzenia psychiczne i behawioralne w ICD-11: koncepcje, metodologie oraz obecny status).

Gallese, V., & Sinigaglia, C. (2011, Nov). What is so special about embodied simulation? *Trends Cogn Science, 15*(11), 512–519. https://doi.org/10.1016/j.tics.2011.09.003

Gillespie, S. M., Kongerslev, M. T., Bo, S., & Abu-Akel, A. M. (2020, May 31). Schizotypy and psychopathic tendencies interactively improve misattribution of affect in boys with conduct problems. *European Child & Adolescent Psychiatry*. https://doi.org/10.1007/s00787-020-01567-8

Gillespie, S. M., Kongerslev, M. T., Sharp, C., Bo, S., & Abu-Akel, A. M. (2018). Does affective theory of mind contribute to proactive aggression in boys with conduct problems and psychopathic tendencies? [Article]. *Child Psychiatry and Human Development, 49*(6), 906–916. https://doi.org/10.1007/s10578-018-0806-8. (Child Psychiatry and Human Development).

Gillespie, S. M., Mitchell, I. J., & Abu-Akel, A. M. (2017, July). Autistic traits and positive psychotic experiences modulate the association of psychopathic tendencies with theory of mind in opposite directions [Article]. *Scientific Reports, 7*, 9. https://doi.org/10.1038/s41598-017-06995-2. (Scientific Reports).

Hare, R. D. (2003). The psychopathy checklist–Revised.

Hervé, H. (2007). Psychopathic subtypes: Historical and contemporary perspectives. *The psychopath: Theory, research, and practice* (pp. 431–460).

Huber, C. G., Hochstrasser, L., Meister, K., Schimmelmann, B. G., & Lambert, M. (2016, August 1). Evidence for an agitated-aggressive syndrome in early-onset psychosis correlated with antisocial personality disorder, forensic history, and substance use disorder. *Schizophrenia Research, 175*(1), 198–203. https://doi.org/10.1016/j.schres.2016.04.027

Igoumenou, A., Kallis, C., & Coid, J. (2015). Treatment of psychosis in prisons and violent recidivism. *Bjpsych Open, 1*(2), 149–157. https://doi.org/10.1192/bjpo.bp.115.000257

Kooyman, I., Dean, K., Harvey, S., & Walsh, E. (2007). Outcomes of public concern in schizophrenia. *British Journal of Psychiatry, 191*(S50), s29–s36. https://doi.org/10.1192/bjp.191.50.s29

Köşger, F., Eşsizoğlu, A., Sönmez, İ., Güleç, G., Genek, M., & Akarsu, Ö. (2015, Summer). The relationship between violence and clinical features, insight and cognitive functions in patients with schizophrenia. *Turkish Journal of Psychiatry, 27*(2), 1–7. (Şizofrenide Şiddet Davranışının Klinik Özellikler, İçgörü ve Bilişsel İşlevler ile İlişkisi).

Lamsma, J., & Harte, J. M. (2015, September 1). Violence in psychosis: Conceptualizing its causal relationship with risk factors. *Aggression and Violent Behavior, 24*, 75–82. https://doi.org/10.1016/j.avb.2015.05.003

Large, M. M., & Nielssen, O. (2011, Febrauary 1). Violence in first-episode psychosis: A systematic review and meta-analysis. *Schizophrenia Research, 125*(2), 209–220. https://doi.org/10.1016/j.schres.2010.11.026

Lysaker, P. H., Vohs, J., Hillis, J. D., Kukla, M., Popolo, R., Salvatore, G., & Dimaggio, G. (2013). Poor insight into schizophrenia: contributing factors, consequences and emerging treatment approaches. *Expert Review of Neurotherapeutics, 13*(7), 785–793.

Marcus, R. F. (2007). Prevalence of Aggression and Violence in Adolescence. In R. F. Marcus (Ed.), *Aggression and Violence in adolescence* (pp. 8–34). Cambridge University Press. https://doi.org/10.1017/CBO9780511611292.002

Meehl, P. E. (1962). Schizotaxia, schizotypy, schizophrenia. *American Psychologist, 17*(12), 827–838.

Moreno, C., Nuevo, R., Chatterji, S., Verdes, E., Arango, C., & Ayuso-Mateos, J. L. (2013). Psychotic symptoms are associated with physical health problems independently of a mental disorder diagnosis: results from the WHO World Health Survey. *World Psychiatry, 12*(3), 251–257. https://doi.org/10.1002/wps.20070

Moulin, V., Golay, P., Palix, J., Baumann, P. S., Gholamrezaeec, M. M., Azzola, A., Gasser, J., Do, K. Q., Alamedae, L., & Conus, P. (2018). Impulsivity in early psychosis: A complex link with violent behaviour and a target for intervention. *European Psychiatry, 49*, 30–36. https://doi.org/10.1016/j.eurpsy.2017.12.003

Mullen, P. E. (2006). Schizophrenia and violence: From correlations to preventive strategies. *Advances in Psychiatric Treatment, 12*(4), 239–248. https://doi.org/10.1192/apt.12.4.239

Mullen, P. E. (2009). Facing up to unpalatable evidence for the sake of our patients. *PLOS Medicine, 6*(8), e1000112. https://doi.org/10.1371/journal.pmed.1000112

Nelson, M. T., Seal, M. L., Pantelis, C., & Phillips, L. J. (2013, March 1). Evidence of a dimensional relationship between schizotypy and schizophrenia: A systematic review. *Neuroscience & Biobehavioral Reviews, 37*(3), 317–327. https://doi.org/10.1016/j.neubiorev.2013.01.004

Nolan, K. A., Volavka, J., Mohr, P., & Czobor, P. (1999, June 1). Psychopathy and violent behavior among patients with schizophrenia or schizoaffective Disorder. *Psychiatric Services, 50*(6), 787–792. https://doi.org/10.1176/ps.50.6.787

Nordgaard, J., Arnfred, S. M., Handest, P., & Parnas, J. (2008). The diagnostic status of first-rank symptoms. *Schizophrenia Bulletin, 34*(1), 137–154. https://doi.org/10.1093/schbul/sbm044

Pijnenborg, G. H. M., van Donkersgoed, R. J. M., David, A. S., & Aleman, A. (2013, 2013/03/01/). Changes in insight during treatment for psychotic disorders: A meta-analysis. *Schizophrenia Research, 144*(1), 109–117. https://doi.org/10.1016/j.schres.2012.11.018

Premack, D., & Woodruff, G. (1978). Does the chimpanzee have a theory of mind? *Behavioral and Brain Sciences, 1*(4), 515–526. https://doi.org/10.1017/S0140525X00076512

Ramírez, J. M., & Andreu, J. M. (2006, Janauary 1). Aggression, and some related psychological constructs (anger, hostility, and impulsivity) Some comments from a research project. *Neuroscience & Biobehavioral Reviews, 30*(3), 276–291. https://doi.org/10.1016/j.neubiorev.2005.04.015

Rasmussen, K., Levander, S., & Sletvold, H. (1995). Aggressive and non-aggressive schizophrenics: Symptom profile and neuropsychological differences. *Psychology, Crime and Law, 2*(2), 119–129.

Ross, J. M., & Babcock, J. C. (2009, November 1). Proactive and reactive violence among intimate partner violent men diagnosed with antisocial and borderline personality disorder. *Journal of Family Violence, 24*(8), 607–617. https://doi.org/10.1007/s10896-009-9259-y

Saha, S., Chant, D., Welham, J., & McGrath, J. (2005). A systematic review of the prevalence of schizophrenia. *PLOS Medicine, 2*(5), e141. https://doi.org/10.1371/journal.pmed.002 0141

Sariaslan, A., Arseneault, L., Larsson, H., Lichtenstein, P., & Fazel, S. (2020). Risk of subjection to violence and perpetration of violence in persons with psychiatric disorders in Sweden. *JAMA Psychiatry, 77*(4), 359–367. https://doi.org/10.1001/jamapsychiatry. 2019.4275

Schneider, K. (1959). *Clinical psychopathology.* (MW hamilton, Trans.).

Sedgwick, O., Young, S., Baumeister, D., Greer, B., Das, M., & Kumari, V. (2017, December). Neuropsychology and emotion processing in violent individuals with antisocial personality disorder or schizophrenia: The same or different? A systematic review and meta-analysis [Review]. *Australian and New Zealand Journal of Psychiatry, 51*(12), 1178–1197. https://doi.org/10.1177/0004867417731525. (Australian and New Zealand Journal of Psychiatry).

Senior, M., Fazel, S., & Tsiachristas, A. (2020, Febrauary 1). The economic impact of violence perpetration in severe mental illness: A retrospective, prevalence-based analysis in England and Wales. *The Lancet Public Health, 5*(2), e99-e106. https://doi.org/10.1016/ S2468-2667(19)30245-2

Smith, K. J., Macpherson, G., O'Rourke, S., & Kelly, C. (2020, March 3). The relationship between insight and violence in psychosis: A systematic literature review. *The Journal of Forensic Psychiatry & Psychology, 31*(2), 183–221. https://doi.org/10.1080/14789949. 2019.1706760

Soyka, M., Graz, C., Bottlender, R., Dirschedl, P., & Schoech, H. (2007, August 1). Clinical correlates of later violence and criminal offences in schizophrenia. *Schizophrenia Research, 94*(1), 89–98. https://doi.org/10.1016/j.schres.2007.03.027

Stein, D. J., Lund, C., & Nesse, R. M. (2013). Classification systems in psychiatry: Diagnosis and global mental health in the era of DSM-5 and ICD-11. *Current Opinion in Psychiatry, 26*(5), 493–497. https://doi.org/10.1097/YCO.0b013e3283642dfd

Tangney, J. P. (1991). Moral affect: The good, the bad, and the ugly. *Journal of Personality and Social Psychology, 61*(4), 598.

Tracy, D. K., & Gaughran, F. (2017). Effects, adherence, and risk. *Care of the mentally disordered offender in the community,* 149.

Ullrich, S., Keers, R., Shaw, J., Doyle, M., & Coid, J. W. (2018). Acting on delusions: The role of negative affect in the pathway towards serious violence. *The Journal of Forensic Psychiatry & Psychology, 29*(5), 691–704.

Umut, G., Altun, Z. O., Danismant, B. S., Kucukparlak, I., & Karamustafalioglu, N. (2012). Relationship between treatment adherence, insight and violence among schizophrenia inpatients in a training hospital sample. *Dusunen Adam, the Journal of Psychiatry and Neurological Sciences, 25*(3), 212–220.

Van Dorn, R., Volavka, J., & Johnson, N. (2012, March). Mental disorder and violence: Is there a relationship beyond substance use? *Social Psychiatry Psychiatric Epidemiology, 47*(3), 487–503. https://doi.org/10.1007/s00127-011-0356-x

VandenBos, G. R. (2007). *APA dictionary of psychology.* American Psychological Association.

Volavka, J. (2014, 2014/03/01). Comorbid personality disorders and violent behavior in psychotic patients. *Psychiatric Quarterly, 85*(1), 65–78. https://doi.org/10.1007/s11126-013-9273-3

Volavka, J., & Citrome, L. (2008). Heterogeneity of violence in schizophrenia and implications for long-term treatment. *International Journal of Clinical Practice, 62*(8), 1237–1245.

Walters, G. D. (2005). Proactive and Reactive Aggression: A Lifestyle View. In *Psychology of aggression.* (pp. 29–43). Nova Science Publishers.

Wimmer, H., & Perner, J. (1983). Beliefs about beliefs: Representation and constraining function of wrong beliefs in young children's understanding of deception. *Cognition, 13*(1), 103–128. https://doi.org/10.1016/0010-0277(83)90004-5

Winsper, C., Singh, S. P., Marwaha, S., Amos, T., Lester, H., Everard, L., Jones, P., Fowler, D., Marshall, M., & Lewis, S. (2013). Pathways to violent behavior during first-episode psychosis: Areport from the UK National EDEN Study. *JAMA Psychiatry, 70*(12), 1287–1293.

World Health Organization. (2019). 2A85.5 Mantle cell lymphoma. In *International statistical classification of diseases and related health problems* (11th ed.).

Recommended Reading

Bo, S., Abu-Akel, A., Kongerslev, M., Haahr, U. H., & Simonsen, E. (2011). Risk factors for violence among patients with schizophrenia. *Clinical Psychology Review, 31*(5), 711–726.

Fazel, S., Gulati, G., Linsell, L., Geddes, J. R., & Grann, M. (2009). Schizophrenia and violence: Systematic review and meta-analysis. *PLOS Medicine, 6*(8), e1000120.

Lamsma, J., & Harte, J. M. (2015). Violence in psychosis: Conceptualizing its causal relationship with risk factors. *Aggression and Violent Behavior, 24*, 75–82.

Smith, K. J., Macpherson, G., O'Rourke, S., & Kelly, C. (2020). The relationship between insight and violence in psychosis: A systematic literature review. *The Journal of Forensic Psychiatry & Psychology, 31*(2), 183–221.

Ullrich, S., Keers, R., Shaw, J., Doyle, M., & Coid, J. W. (2018). Acting on delusions: The role of negative affect in the pathway towards serious violence. *The Journal of Forensic Psychiatry & Psychology, 29*(5), 691–704.

Psychopathy

15

Matt DeLisi

Key Points

- Psychopathy is a personality disorder with affective, interpersonal, lifestyle, and behavioral features that are associated with conduct problems across the life span.
- Psychopathy has a gradient effect on criminal careers such that offenders who are most psychopathic generally have the most severe, violent, and extensive offending careers.
- Psychopathy is consistently related to the most violent forms of crime, such as homicide and sexual aggression and various features of the disorder, such as impaired or absent empathy, facilitate the ability to violently victimize others.
- Psychopathic individuals involved in the criminal justice system and various correctional clients, such as probationers, parolees, and inmates exhibit less compliance with court orders and engage in more misconduct.
- The American serial murderer Ted Bundy who killed dozens of victims exemplified psychopathy in terms of his social ability to procure victims, various characterological features, and lifelong antisocial conduct.

Introduction

The present chapter addresses psychopathy in its implications for offending. First, a section on psychopathy and its association with serious criminal careers

M. DeLisi (✉)
Department of Sociology and Criminal Justice, Iowa State University, Ames, IA, USA
e-mail: delisi@iastate.edu

© The Author(s), under exclusive license to Springer Nature Switzerland AG 2022   287
C. Garofalo and J. J. Sijtsema (eds.), *Clinical Forensic Psychology*,
https://doi.org/10.1007/978-3-030-80882-2_15

highlights research on serious, violent, and chronic offending trajectories among children, adolescents, and adults drawing on research from multiple nations. Next, a section on psychopathy and its association with homicide highlights the linkages between psychopathy and various forms of homicide offending including sexual homicide, serial homicide, multi-offender homicide, and other specifications of lethal violence based on scientific studies from multiple nations. Then, a section on psychopathy and its association with sexual offending synthesizes research on the association between psychopathy and various forms of sexual offending and aggression including rape, child molestation, and diverse forms of sexual coercion. Finally, a section on psychopathy among arrestees, inmates, and correctional clients explicates research on the prevalence and manifestations of psychopathy among offenders in the criminal justice system spanning law enforcement, judicial, and correctional domains. To guide the chapter, the case study of Ted Bundy is presented: The infamous serial sexual homicide offender articulates his floridly psychopathic features as seen in his life history, criminal career, and interactions with criminal justice practitioners.

Psychopathy

Of all the forms of psychopathology that have associations with externalizing symptoms, psychopathy is the nonpareil correlate of antisocial behavior. A personality disorder with a generally coherent constellation of affective characteristics, interpersonal style, lifestyle deficits, and behavioral tendencies, psychopathy typifies an individual who exhibits conduct problems across life (DeLisi, 2009, 2016; Hare, 1996, 1999; Karpman, 1941; Meloy, 1988) and consequently generally suffers from impaired functioning in social, educational, and work domains. Although there is idiosyncrasy in every disorder, the following is the general, modal profile of the psychopathic person. In the affective realm, psychopathic individuals have reduced conscience and tend to experience little and at times virtually no forms of self-conscious, self-inhibiting emotions, such as fear, anxiety, embarrassment, remorse, or guilt. In this regard, prototypical psychopaths, such as Ted Bundy who is profiled below, appear "clean" and psychologically unencumbered by other forms of psychological distress, such as anxiety and depression. Psychopathic persons are also rational and are cognizant of their behavior. In this regard, they are very different than another legal term—psychotic—that typifies people with severe mental illness who are unable to appreciate the wrongfulness or illegality of their behavior. Although psychopathic and psychotic seem similar, they are different.

Case Study: Ted Bundy

In terms of media coverage, public fascination, and his central role in the commercialization of criminal justice from the 1970s to the present, Ted Bundy is arguably the most culturally impactful criminal offender in American history. Although only Bundy knew the precise number of persons he killed, the usually accepted range is 30 to 100 homicide victims over a homicide career that likely began during his early adolescence around age 14 years and culminated in a series of murders in Florida that resulted in his execution in January 1989. All of Bundy's official known victims were females, and Bundy's signature crimes involved rape, sodomy, and strangulation that would fatally asphyxiate his victims. Floridly sadistic, Bundy was also a necrophile who decapitated some of his victims in order to later engage in sexual activity with the victim's head (for biographical details and extensive autobiographical insights, see, Michaud & Aynesworth, 1999, 2000; Rule, 1980).

Another reason for Bundy's infamy is the textbook collection of psychopathic traits that he exuded. Bundy was intelligent and superficially affable, and he used this charm to approach women who he wanted to sexually violate. A master of manipulation who would often use disguise or ruse, Bundy presented himself as a harmless "normal guy" whom women did not feel could harm them. Rather quickly, however, Bundy would incapacitate women with a blow to the head usually with a tire iron, then abduct, rape, and murder them. Handsome and glib, Bundy projected a façade of erudition and accomplishment and was a law student at the time of his ultimate capture. However, beneath this veneer Bundy was less successful. He did not complete university until age 26, never completed his legal training, and was a generally bad student with excessive truancy. He led a parasitic orientation living on stolen property and credit and did not achieve conventional measures of socioeconomic success, such as owning a home. His lifestyle was peripatetic and involved thousands of miles of driving mostly across the western United States to hunt and murder victims. By his own admission, the latter years of Bundy's life were dominated by one instrumental goal: to sexually abuse and murder.

Emotionally, Bundy exhibited zero remorse for his conduct and until his deathbed confessions to law enforcement and media contacts (which itself was a grandiose act of manipulation to delay his execution), and behaved as if he bore no responsibility for his crimes. At his trial, Bundy acted as his own attorney and at times called witnesses to describe his Florida murders so that he could relive the experiences in open court. Despite a later onset arrest record, there is evidence in Bundy's life history of disturbing and conflicted behavior relating to sexual aggression as well as lifelong involvement in theft, burglary, voyeurism, and other series of felonies that accompanied his sexual homicides. During his 1970s killing spree, Bundy demonstrated a tenacious refusal to comply with the criminal justice system involving multiple escapes from custody and was a wanted fugitive when he was ultimately apprehended in Florida.

Perhaps more than any other criminal offender, Ted Bundy wore the psychopathic mask that Cleckley originally conceptualized. With charm, guile, and subterfuge, Bundy was able to largely hide his homicidal and sadistic impulses and engage in versatile crimes often at a stunning rate, sometimes murdering more than one victim in a single day. He was the quintessential psychopath.

Although often caricaturized as being completely devoid of emotion, psychopathy, like any forensic feature, denotes heterogeneity in the presentation of its core features. The emotional life of psychopaths is generally dysphoric and is pervaded by anger, hostility, contempt, spitefulness, uncaring, callousness, and feelings of persecution (see, Hicks & Patrick, 2006; Kosson et al., 2020) (Chapter 5). During forensic interviews, psychopathic offenders reported to the current author that they experienced a sense of rage, hostility, and rejection throughout life even though they were uncertain about the origin of their negative emotionality. Given the emotional regulation deficits that psychopathic persons exhibit (Garofalo et al., 2018, 2019, 2020), these emotions serve as kindling for interpersonal conflict, interpersonal disputes, and aggression. Moreover, like other psychological conditions, psychopathy can be comorbid with other personality disorders, substance use disorders, mood disorders, and other psychopathology. Referring to the aforementioned forensic interview, the interviewee with psychopathy informed me that although he did not consider himself to have any emotion until very late in life, the constant anger and motivation to hurt others before they hurt him caused a sense of unease that substance use helped to mollify.

Against this affective profile, psychopathy drives an interpersonal style that is extremely self-interested to the point where the effects of one's conduct on others are nearly completely discounted. This is seen most vividly in the case of serious violent offenders like Ted Bundy whose desire for violence and sexual gratification was superordinated to the victim's right to life. In less extreme examples, psychopathic offenders exhibit an unapologetic sense of irresponsibility or remorselessness that is most clear in courtroom behavior where they are often unmoved by the victimization they created (Edens et al., 2013). In mundane interaction patterns, psychopathic persons tend to objectify, dominate, and manipulate others. They are insincere, manipulative, and controlling and often use lying and other deception to achieve their goals. Importantly, the psychopathic individual's interpersonal style varies and ranges from a highly extroverted, insincere, charming, and ingratiating one to a brutishly direct, overpowering one. To illustrate, some psychopathic offenders will articulate outlandish stories to explain their behavior and putatively absolve them of responsibility, whereas others will honestly describe their crimes in cold, methodical, emotionless terms (DeLisi et al., 2021; Hare, 1999; Kiehl, 2014). These latter examples reveal how the various affective and interpersonal features of psychopathy interrelate.

The typical lifestyle and behavioral repertoire of psychopathic individuals is one of deviance and declension. Although there is some evidence of non-criminal psychopathy, its empirical support is remarkably limited (Benning et al., 2018; Coid et al., 2009; Lilienfeld et al., 2015) compared to research on psychopathic criminals. However, it is important to recognize that psychopathic features exist on a continuum where an individual can be low or high scoring on a measure of psychopathic traits even if that individual is mostly prosocial and does not engage in crime. This means that some traits or symptoms of psychopathy, such as impulsivity, irresponsibility, lying, a tendency to externalize blame, and self-control problems appear in the general population and are fully consistent with considerations of criminal psychopathy.

Conversely, the evidence that psychopathy is intimately related to antisocial behavior, and some even argue that it is effectively partially comprised by antisocial behavior (cf. Cleckley, 1941; Crego & Widiger, 2016; DeLisi, 2016; Hare & Neumann, 2010; Skeem & Cooke, 2010), is overwhelming. It is important to recognize that antisocial behavior is a broad concept and encompasses more than criminal acts. Antisocial behavior can also relate to early emerging and persistent conduct that can be construed as being dissocial in the sense of disregarding others' rights. Predating actual delinquent behavior that will result in law enforcement and judicial intervention, psychopaths evince early emerging self-regulation problems where they repeatedly compromise and challenge relationships with their siblings, parents, peers, and teachers. These fledgling psychopathic features include impulsivity, hyperactivity, cruelty, defiance, and willful refusal to comply with the most basic behavioral expectations of society. For example, in my research experiences, a career criminal, the small group of 5–10% of offenders who account for more than half of the crime in a population along with the majority of serious violent felonies, such as murder, rape, kidnapping, and armed robbery (Blumstein et al., 1986; Wolfgang et al., 1972), had the following written about him during his adolescence:

> The youth is thoroughly immersed in an antisocial pattern and likes it. He simply has no interest in conforming his behavior or obeying the rules of any kind in this or any setting.

That anecdote is not an isolated incident, but instead shows the usual antisocial development seen in psychopathy during adolescence (for meta-analytic review, see Geerlings et al., 2019). The following sections document research on psychopathy and antisocial conduct in several content areas including its association with serious criminal careers, associations with homicide and sexual offending, and the relevance of psychopathy among arrestees, inmates, and correctional clients.

Psychopathy and Criminal Careers

There is great variance in juvenile delinquency. Whereas some youth abstain entirely from antisocial conduct, the large bulk of the population experiments with deviance during adolescence and then reforms, and a small minority who engage in pathological offending across life (Moffitt, 1993, 2018). An international array of studies from Barbados and Grenada (Boduszek et al., 2019), Canada (Corrado et al., 2015; McCuish et al., 2015), Europe (Carabellese et al., 2019; Lehmann et al., 2019), and the United States (DeLisi et al., 2014; Vaughn & DeLisi, 2008; Vaughn et al., 2008) among other nations indicate that psychopathy is positively associated with earlier starting, more severe, violent, and versatile offending careers, and generally more adverse childhood experiences. Sadly, the most serious delinquents are significantly likely to suffer from various forms of abuse, neglect, and other trauma exposures (Baglivio et al., 2014; Fox et al., 2015; Trulson et al., 2016). The latter point is significant because it supports the notion that psychopathy has both a biological/neurological and an environmental etiological or causal basis. During the criminal career, psychopathy innervates virtually every form of deviance, criminal offending, and criminal justice system contact and shows moderate to strong convergent validity with concepts that relate to pathological offending, such as career criminality or life-course-persistent offending.

Early signs of psychopathy manifest in more severe criminal careers decades later. In one study, for instance, DeLisi et al. (2020) compared federal offenders at midlife who met criteria for fledgling psychopathy during their youth, that is, had diagnostic history for Oppositional Defiant Disorder, Conduct Disorder, and ADHD to those who did not. At midlife, fledgling psychopathy was significantly correlated with cannabis, cocaine, opiate, and alcohol dependence, several criminal lifestyle factors including gunshot wounds, stab wounds, gang activity, traumatic brain injury, and Intermittent Explosive Disorder, and Antisocial and Paranoid Personality Disorders. Fledgling psychopaths also initiated their delinquent career 12 years earlier than offenders who were not fledgling psychopaths and had more extensive, violent, and versatile criminal careers punctuated by recurrent failure with the criminal justice system (e.g., parole revocation, probation revocation, and prison terms).

When considering criminal careers, it is important to recognize that official records represent a mere fraction of the actual offending that is occurring and most criminal offenses, even those as serious as murder do not result in arrest. This is particularly true when crimes are perpetrated in remote locations without official social controls. For instance, Ted Bundy was able to avoid arrest for most of his life until the final years of his criminal career, but self-reports and other data indicate a lifetime of versatile offending suggesting that he enjoyed a clandestine criminal career before it unfolded into an official one. Indeed, one study of a nationally representative panel of adolescents and young adults found that psychopathic personality features predicted higher probabilities of arrest, placement on probation, and prison sentences and also predicted higher self-reported delinquency (Beaver et al., 2017). Thus, psychopathy is a driver of antisocial conduct across developmental periods (e.g., adolescence through adulthood) in life.

Psychopathy and Homicide

An important finding from research on criminal careers is that a small subgroup of offenders usually dubbed career criminals (DeLisi, 2001, 2005; Hare et al., 1988; Wolfgang et al., 1972), are responsible for not only the preponderance of antisocial conduct in the population, but is also over involvement in the most serious forms of crime including murder. As such, since persistent criminal behavior is infused with psychopathy, this also means that psychopathy has a disproportionate association with homicide offending as well (Chapter 23).

When examining various forms of homicide, the role of psychopathic features is clear when considering the motivation and various affective and behavioral features of homicide offenders. Because most homicides are the result of interpersonal disputes between intimates, family, and acquaintances, issue of emotional and behavioral regulation is paramount. As such, a condition that is pervaded with impulsivity, poor behavioral control, and grandiosity that would respond very unfavorably to a slight or affront would seem to be significantly associated with lethal violence (James et al., 2020; Porter & Woodworth, 2007; Rodre et al., 2019). Many homicides also arise from other criminal activity that is instrumental in nature, such as murdering a victim during an armed robbery or as an adjunct of deviant sexual activity, such as sexual homicide . Indeed, recent research substantiates that killings that involve instrumental or sexual motivation involve offenders who are much more psychopathic than less severe homicides (Rodre et al., 2019). Similarly, Porter et al. (2003) found that nearly 85% of sexual homicide offenders were moderate to highly psychopathic and their killings were more violent, sadistic, and gratuitous than those committed by non-psychopathic killers. For example, more than 82% of psychopathic murderers displayed some form of sadistic behavior during their killings compared to just over half of murders by non-psychopaths.

These findings raise important qualitative considerations. It is one thing for psychopathy to be associated with homicide offending, but it is perhaps more revealing that higher levels of psychopathy are related to more violent, sadistic, gratuitous, and shocking murders. In this way, psychopathy influences lethal violence both qualitatively and quantitatively. From a comprehensive perspective, meta-analytic research confirms that psychopathy and homicide are intertwined. For example, in their review of 22 studies, 29 unique samples, and over 2,600 homicide offenders, Fox and DeLisi (2019) reported a large effect size ($r = 0.68$) between psychopathy and homicide. Effects were even larger as the form of homicide became more pathological and violent, such as sexual, sadistic, serial, and multi-offender homicide.

Psychopathy and Sexual Offending

When considering the following mixture of traits, such as stimulation seeking, grandiosity, callousness, entitlement, and the primacy of one's wants and desires at the expense of anyone else, it is easy to see that psychopathy would be associated with sexual aggression and sexual deviance (Chapter 22). Indeed, in a recent study, Methot-Jones et al. (2019) found that psychopathic features were significantly associated with sexist and violent attitudes toward women and these effects were also linked to dehumanization. In other words, psychopathic men were more likely to dehumanize women and see them as instrumental sexual objects to be exploited and used to satiate their sexual urges.

A multitude of studies using diverse data sources indicates the broadband associations between psychopathy and sexual offending. For instance, based on data from the Incarcerated Serious and Violent Young Offenders Study in Canada, Cale et al. (2015) compared the prevalence of psychopathy among various serious juvenile offenders whose delinquent careers were characterized as serious, chronic, violent, or sexual. They found that juvenile sex offenders were far and away the most psychopathic with nearly two-thirds scoring in the moderate to clinically high-psychopathy range on the Psychopathy Checklist Youth Version (PCL: YV). In contrast, among those who did not have a sexual offense on their record, just 27.4% scored 25 or higher. In their study, the prevalence of clinical psychopathy is at least two times higher among youth who perpetrate sexual offenses as opposed to nonsexual violent offenses.

Based on data from convicted rapists involuntarily admitted to a Dutch forensic psychiatric hospital between 1975 and 1996, Hildebrand et al. (2004) examined the effects of psychopathy on sexual and other forms of reoffending after release. On average, the offenders were followed up between 12 and 24 years later. Psychopathy was significantly predictive of sexual recidivism, nonsexual violent recidivism, total violent recidivism (including sexual), and general recidivism. In addition, psychopathic rapists with paraphilic disorders, such as pedophilia or sexual sadism, were the most likely to reoffend sexually compared to psychopathic offenders without paraphilic disorders. Other studies similarly found that psychopathy is significantly associated with the extent and severity of violence that is inflicted during sexual assaults (Cardona et al., 2020) particularly among psychopathic offenders that also present with paraphilic disorders (van Bommel et al., 2018) suggesting they enjoy inflicting pain, suffering, and humiliation during the course of sexual violence.

Overall, meta-analytic data confirms the psychopathy-sexual aggression linkage. Based on a review of 20 studies including 5,239 participants, a significant association between psychopathy and sexual recidivism was reported (Hawes et al., 2013). It was also reported that high-psychopathy scores coupled with high sexual deviance were a particularly dangerous combination in terms of likelihood of sexual reoffending. Across seven studies in their meta-analysis, the high-psychopathy-high sexual deviance offenders were upwards of 15 times more likely to sexually reoffend. Importantly, psychopathy was also significantly predictive of violent recidivism not including sexual recidivism and a total recidivism measure. Moreover, meta-analyses of persistent sexual offending similarly showed that psychopathic features are a significant, moderately strong predictor of sexual recidivism (Hanson & Morton-Bourgon, 2005).

Psychopathy and Correctional Clients

Given the extensive role of psychopathy in serious offending, the downstream implication is that the criminal justice system will contain far more psychopathic persons than is found in conventional society (Coid et al., 2009; Hare,

1996). Compared to conventional society, the prevalence of psychopathy among arrestees, probationers, parolees, and prisoners is significantly higher and when one considers the most extreme civil and criminal populations, such as civilly committed sexual violent predators and condemned prisoners, psychopathy is endemic. Also, given the inextricable link between psychopathy and the most extensive offending careers, which can involve decades of arrest, prosecution, and correctional interventions, it stands to reason that the criminal justice system would have a higher prevalence of psychopathy compared to the general population.

There is substantial evidence that psychopathy is a primary causal factor in assaults, sexual assaults, and murders occurring in correctional facilities (Gray et al., 2019; Thomson et al., 2019, 2020). Recently, Thomson and colleagues (2020) found that affective, interpersonal, and antisocial features of psychopathy were significantly correlated with perpetrating prison violence. In their study of prison homicides, Reidy and Sorensen (2017) documented behavioral histories that are consistent with psychopathic career criminals in terms of their high level of violence. To illustrate, an offender whose instant offenses included four counts of first-degree murder, fatally bludgeoned another inmate after his confinement. That murder prompted an out-of-state correctional transfer. After arriving at the new facility, the inmate fatally strangled his cellmate.

Psychopaths also fare poorly in treatment regimes designed to mollify their violent conduct. In their study of sexual offenders followed up to nearly 19 years after release to the community, Sewall and Olver (2019) reported the prevalence of non-completion of sex offender treatment was five times higher among high-psychopathy versus low-psychopathy offenders. Various psychopathic features were also significantly correlated with therapeutic progress and therapeutic change.

The reasons for noncompliance, misconduct, and recidivism among psychopathic offenders are perhaps expected given their core characteristics. At a physiological level, psychopathy is marked by dysfunction in the autonomic responses to fear, which explains their seeming imperviousness to punishment or processes that would recruit emotional fear to modify behavior (see, Hare, 1965a, 1965b, 1966). Thus, physiologically and psychologically, psychopaths experience very little fear and the emotions that stem from it, namely anxiety, apprehension, shame, guilt, or remorse which results in an inability to learn from experiences. At the behavioral level, a parallel inability is seen in reluctance or refusal to reform one's conduct to comply with behavioral norms. The life history of constant conflict with authority figures, whether these concern parents, teachers, or criminal justice personnel, thus squares directly with noncompliance with probation or parole.

The current author has 25 years of experiences working with criminal defendants in a variety of roles as practitioner, as clinician, as researcher, and perhaps most importantly, as observer. To be clear, most criminal offenders are not profoundly psychopathic; however, that does not vitiate another truth, which is that psychopathic traits including impulsivity, irresponsibility, blame externalization, lying, stimulation seeking, self-regulation problems, and antisocial versatility occur in abundance among the criminal population.

Conclusion

Psychopathy is perhaps the most important form of psychopathology for understanding involvement in the most severe, violent, and recalcitrant forms of antisocial conduct. The most severe prototypes of offending spanning career criminality, homicide offending, and sexual offending are replete with evidence that psychopathy is a primary determinant, and infamous offenders, such as Ted Bundy profiled herein instantiate the disorder. Despite the empirical heft of the extant psychopathy literature, it continues to be a critical research area and new insights into its etiology, its emotional complexity, and its responsiveness to behavioral interventions are essential for informing prevention and justice system interventions to mitigate the effects of psychopathy.

References

Baglivio, M. T., Epps, N., Swartz, K., Huq, M. S., Sheer, A., & Hardt, N. S. (2014). The prevalence of adverse childhood experiences (ACE) in the lives of juvenile offenders. *Journal of Juvenile Justice, 3*(2).

Beaver, K. M., Boutwell, B. B., Barnes, J. C., Vaughn, M. G., & DeLisi, M. (2017). The association between psychopathic personality traits and criminal justice outcomes: Results from a nationally representative sample of males and females. *Crime & Delinquency, 63*(6), 708–730.

Benning, S. D., Venables, N. C., & Hall, J. R. (2018). Successful psychopathy. In C. J. Patrick (ed.), *Handbook of psychopathy, second edition* (pp. 585–608). The Guilford Press.

Blumstein, A., Cohen, J., Roth, J. A., & Visher, C. A. (Eds.). (1986). *Criminal careers and "career criminals."* National Academy Press.

Boduszek, D., Debowska, A., Willmott, D., Jones, A. D., DeLisi, M., & Kirkman, G. (2019). Is female psychopathy linked with child abuse? An empirical investigation using a person-centered approach. *Journal of Child Sexual Abuse, 28*(6), 708–725.

Cale, J., Lussier, P., McCuish, E., & Corrado, R. (2015). The prevalence of psychopathic personality disturbances among incarcerated youth: Comparing serious, chronic, violent and sex offenders. *Journal of Criminal Justice, 43*(4), 337–344.

Carabellese, F., Felthous, A. R., Mandarelli, G., Montalbò, D., Tegola, D. L., Rossetto, I., Franconi, F., & Catanesi, R. (2019). Psychopathy in Italian female murderers. *Behavioral Sciences & the Law, 37*(5), 602–613.

Cardona, N., Berman, A. K., Sims-Knight, J. E., & Knight, R. A. (2020). Covariates of the severity of aggression in sexual crimes: Psychopathy and Borderline characteristics. *Sexual Abuse, 32*(2), 154–178.

Cleckley, H. (1941). *The mask of sanity: An attempt to clarify some issues about the so-called psychopathic personality.* Mosby.

Coid, J., Yang, M., Ullrich, S., Roberts, A., & Hare, R. D. (2009). Prevalence and correlates of psychopathic traits in the household population of Great Britain. *International Journal of Law and Psychiatry, 32*(2), 65–73.

Corrado, R. R., DeLisi, M., Hart, S. D., & McCuish, E. C. (2015). Can the causal mechanisms underlying chronic, serious, and violent offending trajectories be elucidated using the psychopathy construct. *Journal of Criminal Justice, 43*(4), 251–261.

Crego, C., & Widiger, T. A. (2016). Cleckley's psychopaths: Revisited. *Journal of Abnormal Psychology, 125*(1), 75–87.

DeLisi, M. (2001). Extreme career criminals. *American Journal of Criminal Justice, 25*(2), 239–252.

DeLisi, M. (2005). *Career criminals in society.* Sage.

DeLisi, M. (2009). Psychopathy is the unified theory of crime. *Youth Violence and Juvenile Justice, 7*(3), 256–273.

DeLisi, M. (2016). *Psychopathy as unified theory of crime.* Palgrave Macmillan.

DeLisi, M., Dansby, T., Peters, D. J., Vaughn, M. G., Shook, J. J., & Hochstetler, A. (2014). Fledgling psychopathic features and pathological delinquency: New evidence. *American Journal of Criminal Justice, 39*(3), 411–424.

DeLisi, M., Drury, A. J., & Elbert, M. J. (2020). Fledgling psychopaths at midlife: Forensic features, criminal careers, and coextensive psychopathology. *Forensic Science International: Mind and Law, 1*, 100006.

DeLisi, M., Drury, A. J., & Elbert, M. J. (2021). Psychopathy and pathological violence in a criminal career: A forensic case report. *Aggression and Violent Behavior, 60*, 101521.

Edens, J. F., Davis, K. M., Fernandez Smith, K., & Guy, L. S. (2013). No sympathy for the devil: Attributing psychopathic traits to capital murderers also predicts support for executing them. *Personality Disorders: Theory, Research, and Treatment, 4*(2), 175–181.

Fox, B., & DeLisi, M. (2019). Psychopathic killers: A meta-analytic review of the psychopathy-homicide nexus. *Aggression and Violent Behavior, 44*, 67–79.

Fox, B. H., Perez, N., Cass, E., Baglivio, M. T., & Epps, N. (2015). Trauma changes everything: Examining the relationship between adverse childhood experiences and serious, violent and chronic juvenile offenders. *Child Abuse & Neglect, 46*, 163–173.

Garofalo, C., Neumann, C. S., & Velotti, P. (2018). Difficulties in emotion regulation and psychopathic traits in violent offenders. *Journal of Criminal Justice, 57*, 116–125.

Garofalo, C., Neumann, C. S., & Velotti, P. (2020). Psychopathy and aggression: The role of emotion dysregulation. *Journal of Interpersonal Violence.* https://doi.org/10.1177/0886260519900946

Garofalo, C., Neumann, C. S., Zeigler-Hill, V., & Meloy, J. R. (2019). Spiteful and contemptuous: A new look at the emotional experiences related to psychopathy. *Personality Disorders: Theory, Research, and Treatment, 10*(2), 173–184.

Geerlings, Y., Asscher, J. J., Stams, G. J. J., & Assink, M. (2019). The association between psychopathy and delinquency in juveniles: A three-level meta-analysis. *Aggression and Violent Behavior*, 101342.

Gray, N. S., Blumenthal, S., Shuker, R., Wood, H., Fonagy, P., & Snowden, R. J. (2019). The triarchic model of psychopathy and antisocial behavior: Results from an offender population with personality disorder. *Journal of Interpersonal Violence*. https://doi.org/10.1177/0886260519853404

Hanson, R. K., & Morton-Bourgon, K. E. (2005). The characteristics of persistent sexual offenders: A meta-analysis of recidivism studies. *Journal of Consulting and Clinical Psychology, 73*(6), 1154–1163.

Hare, R. D. (1965a). Psychopathy, fear arousal and anticipated pain. *Psychological Reports, 16*(2), 499–502.

Hare, R. D. (1965b). Temporal gradient of fear arousal in psychopaths. *Journal of Abnormal Psychology, 70*(6), 442–445.

Hare, R. D. (1966). Psychopathy and choice of immediate versus delayed punishment. *Journal of Abnormal Psychology, 71*(1), 25–29.

Hare, R. D. (1996). Psychopathy: A clinical construct whose time has come. *Criminal Justice and Behavior, 23*(1), 25–54.

Hare, R. D. (1999). *Without conscience: The disturbing world of the psychopaths among us.* The Guilford Press.

Hare, R. D., McPherson, L. M., & Forth, A. E. (1988). Male psychopaths and their criminal careers. *Journal of Consulting and Clinical Psychology, 56*(5), 710–714.

Hare, R. D., & Neumann, C. S. (2010). The role of antisociality in the psychopathy construct: Comment on Skeem and Cooke (2010). *Psychological Assessment, 22*(2), 446–454.

Hawes, S. W., Boccaccini, M. T., & Murrie, D. C. (2013). Psychopathy and the combination of psychopathy and sexual deviance as predictors of sexual recidivism: Meta-analytic findings using the Psychopathy Checklist—Revised. *Psychological Assessment, 25*(1), 233–243.

Hicks, B. M., & Patrick, C. J. (2006). Psychopathy and negative emotionality: Analyses of suppressor effects reveal distinct relations with emotional distress, fearfulness, and anger-hostility. *Journal of Abnormal Psychology, 115*(2), 276–287.

Hildebrand, M., De Ruiter, C., & de Vogel, V. (2004). Psychopathy and sexual deviance in treated rapists: Association with sexual and nonsexual recidivism. *Sexual Abuse: A Journal of Research and Treatment, 16*(1), 1–24.

James, J., Higgs, T., & Langevin, S. (2020). Reactive and proactive aggression in sexual homicide offenders. *Journal of Criminal Justice*, 101728.

Karpman, B. (1941). On the need of separating psychopathy into two distinct clinical types: The symptomatic and the idiopathic. *Journal of Criminal Psychopathology, 3*, 112–137.

Kiehl, K. A. (2014). *The psychopath whisperer: The science of those without conscience.* Crown Publishers.

Kosson, D. S., Garofalo, C., McBride, C. K., & Velotti, P. (2020). Get mad: Chronic anger expression and psychopathic traits in three independent samples. *Journal of Criminal Justice, 67*, 101672.

Lehmann, R. J. B., Neumann, C. S., Hare, R. D., Biedermann, J., Dahle, K. P., & Mokros, A. (2019). A latent profile analysis of violent offenders based on PCL-R factor scores: Criminogenic needs and recidivism risk. *Frontiers in Psychiatry, 10*, 627.

Lilienfeld, S. O., Watts, A. L., & Smith, S. F. (2015). Successful psychopathy: A scientific status report. *Current Directions in Psychological Science, 24*(4), 298–303.

McCuish, E. C., Corrado, R. R., Hart, S. D., & DeLisi, M. (2015). The role of symptoms of psychopathy in persistent violence over the criminal career into full adulthood. *Journal of Criminal Justice, 43*(4), 345–356.

Meloy, J. R. (1988). *The psychopathic mind: Origins, dynamics, and treatment*. Rowman & Littlefield.

Methot-Jones, T., Book, A., & Gauthier, N. Y. (2019). Less than human: Psychopathy, dehumanization, and sexist and violent attitudes towards women. *Personality and Individual Differences, 149*, 250–260.

Michaud, S. G., & Aynesworth, H. (1999). *The only living witness: The true story of serial sex killer ted bundy*. Authorlink.

Michaud, S. G., & Aynesworth, H. (2000). *Ted Bundy: Conversations with a killer*. Authorlink.

Moffitt, T. E. (1993). Adolescence-limited and life-course-persistent antisocial behavior: A developmental taxonomy. *Psychological Review, 100*(4), 674–701.

Moffitt, T. E. (2018). Male antisocial behaviour in adolescence and beyond. *Nature Human Behaviour, 2*(3), 177–186.

Porter, S., & Woodworth, M. (2007). "I'm sorry I did it… but he started it": A comparison of the official and self-reported homicide descriptions of psychopaths and non-psychopaths. *Law and Human Behavior, 31*(1), 91–107.

Porter, S., Woodworth, M., Earle, J., Drugge, J., & Boer, D. (2003). Characteristics of sexual homicide committed by psychopathic and non-psychopathic offenders. *Law and Human Behavior, 27*, 459–470.

Reidy, T. J., & Sorensen, J. R. (2017). Prison homicides: A multidimensional comparison of perpetrators and victims. *Journal of Forensic Psychology Research and Practice, 17*(2), 99–116.

Rodre, S., Hedlund, J., Liljeberg, J., Kristiansson, M., Masterman, T., & Sturup, J. (2019). Psychopathy-associated personality traits influence crime-scene behavior in male homicide offenders. *Nordic Journal of Psychiatry, 73*(8), 471–474.

Rule, A. (1980). *The stranger beside me*. W.W. Norton & Company.

Sewall, L. A., & Olver, M. E. (2019). Psychopathy and treatment outcome: Results from a sexual violence reduction program. *Personality Disorders: Theory, Research, and Treatment, 10*(1), 59–69.

Skeem, J. L., & Cooke, D. J. (2010). Is criminal behavior a central component of psychopathy? Conceptual directions for resolving the debate. *Psychological Assessment, 22*(2), 433–445.

Thomson, N. D., Moeller, F. G., Amstadter, A. B., Svikis, D., Perera, R. A., & Bjork, J. M. (2020). The impact of parental incarceration on psychopathy, crime, and prison violence in women. *International Journal of Offender Therapy and Comparative Criminology*. https://doi.org/10.1177/0306624X20904695

Thomson, N. D., Vassileva, J., Kiehl, K. A., Reidy, D., Aboutanos, M., McDougle, R., & DeLisi, M. (2019). Which features of psychopathy and impulsivity matter most for prison violence? New evidence among female prisoners. *International Journal of Law and Psychiatry, 64*, 26–33.

Trulson, C. R., Haerle, D. R., Caudill, J. W., & DeLisi, M. (2016). *Lost causes: Blended sentencing, second chances, and the Texas youth commission.* University of Texas Press.

van Bommel, R., Uzieblo, K., Bogaerts, S., & Garofalo, C. (2018). Psychopathic traits and deviant sexual interests: The moderating role of gender. *International Journal of Forensic Mental Health, 17*(3), 256–271.

Vaughn, M. G., & DeLisi, M. (2008). Were Wolfgang's chronic offenders psychopaths? On the convergent validity between psychopathy and career criminality. *Journal of Criminal Justice, 36*(1), 33–42.

Vaughn, M. G., Howard, M. O., & DeLisi, M. (2008). Psychopathic personality traits and delinquent careers: An empirical examination. *International Journal of Law and Psychiatry, 31*(5), 407–416.

Wolfgang, M. E., Figlio, R. M., & Sellin, T. (1972). *Delinquency in a birth cohort.* University of Chicago Press.

Suggested Further Readings

The following works include insights from authors who have extensive research, practitioner, and clinician experiences working with the most violent and pathological offenders.

DeLisi, M. (2016). *Psychopathy as unified theory of crime.* Palgrave Macmillan. The thesis is that psychopathy can explain conduct problems from early childhood through adulthood and that it is the best and thus "unified" theory of crime.

Hare, R. D. (1999). *Without conscience: The disturbing world of the psychopaths among us.* The Guilford Press. The most-cited and foremost psychopathy scholar in the world and the creator of the most widely-used psychopathy instruments, this works takes his psychological research to a public audience.

Kiehl, K. A. (2015). *The psychopath whisperer: The science of those without conscience.* Broadway Books. A renowned neuroimaging scholar who scans the brains of psychopathic offenders, this work does a great job of presenting scholarly information in a popular press way.

Meloy, J. R. (1988). *The psychopathic mind: Origins, dynamics, and treatment.* Rowman & Littlefield. This work contains brilliant and unparalleled insights into the psychological functioning and emotional life of psychopaths from a forensic psychologist with extensive experience with serious offenders.

Salekin, R. T., & Lynam, D. R. (Eds.). (2011). *Handbook of child and adolescent psychopathy.* The Guilford Press. This edited volume contains contributions from a worldwide cast of scholars who focus on psychopathic features among youth.

Attention-Deficit/Hyperactivity Disorder (ADHD) and Offending

16

Susan Young and Kelly Cocallis

Key Points

- ADHD is a common condition in the CJS population, but it is often unrecognized and consequently untreated.
- The presentation of ADHD in the CJS population is often complicated by the presence of other conditions. This results in cumulative vulnerability, making both diagnosis and treatment more complex.
- The prevalence of ADHD in the CJS population does not appear to differ by gender, contrary to general population studies.
- The risk of criminality is increased for individuals with ADHD, especially when comorbid with oppositional defiant disorder, conduct disorder, substance use disorder, and/or antisocial personality disorder.
- ADHD symptoms can have a significant adverse impact on a person's ability to effectively navigate the complexity of the CJS, which in turn, may result in negative sanctions.
- The approach to the treatment of ADHD is the same as for the general population (using a combination of both pharmacological and non-pharmacological interventions). Working with the CJS population, however, presents challenges, including the potential for diversion or misuse of medication.

S. Young (✉)
Psychology Services Limited, London, UK
e-mail: psychltd@aol.com

K. Cocallis
Northumbria Healthcare NHS Foundation Trust, Newcastle upon Tyne, UK

- ADHD treatment is associated with reduced rates of criminality and improvements in cognitive functioning and quality of life. This emphasizes the value of recognizing and diagnosing ADHD in the CJS population.

Introduction

Attention-deficit/hyperactivity disorder (ADHD) is a common neurodevelopmental disorder characterized by pervasive and persistent difficulties in attention, hyperactivity, and impulsivity that are associated with functional impairments in activities of daily living. ADHD is heterogeneous in presentation with three diagnostic nomenclatures: predominantly inattentive, predominantly hyperactive-impulsive, and combined type (American Psychiatric Association, 2013). Individuals presenting as inattentive often find it difficult to focus on details and sustain attention. They avoid or dislike tasks requiring sustained mental effort and make careless mistakes. They may be disorganized, easily distracted, and forgetful. They may lose or misplace things. Individuals presenting as hyperactive-impulsive are often restless and fidgety. They find it hard to settle down and get on with activities quietly on their own. They are 'always on the go'. They are often impatient, struggling to wait their turn or wait in line. They often interrupt other people and talk excessively. Those with a combined presentation often have difficulties across both domains.

Previously, ADHD was considered a childhood disorder, however, it is now accepted to be a lifespan condition. Over the natural course of the disorder, symptoms are documented to change, with behavioral symptoms of hyperactivity and impulsivity becoming more subtle as children grow into adulthood (e.g., adults present with restlessness rather than motoric hyperactivity). In around one-third of cases, symptoms remit with age; however, around two-thirds of children with ADHD will continue to suffer with symptoms that cause them functional impairments in adulthood (Faraone et al., 2006).

Studies have shown that there is no single cause of ADHD. Several genes linked to brain chemicals have been implicated (e.g., dopamine and serotonin systems), in addition to environmental factors that can also effect brain development (e.g., exposure to alcohol, nicotine, illicit substance use, high blood pressure and maternal stress during pregnancy, pre-term birth, low birth weight, birth trauma, and early deprivation) (Thapar et al., 2011). Environmental effects are understood to be modified by genetic factors.

International studies have consistently reported disproportionately higher rates of ADHD among youth and adult offenders. The present chapter starts by discussing the prevalence and gender differences rates of ADHD. Further, the chapter addresses diagnostic issues of ADHD in the criminal justice system (CJS), as well as frequent comorbidities. Next, risk factors for antisocial behavior among individuals with ADHD are elucidated, along with specific vulnerabilities that characterize these individuals in the CJS. Finally, treatment considerations for individuals with ADHD who offend are presented.

Prevalence

The worldwide prevalence of ADHD in the general population is estimated to fall between 5–7% in children and adolescents, and 2–4% in adults (Polanczyk et al., 2007; Simon et al., 2009; Thomas et al., 2015; Willcutt, 2012). International studies, by contrast, have demonstrated disproportionately higher rates of ADHD among youth and adult offenders. Prevalence rates vary across studies, most likely reflecting differences in the diagnostic tools and the criteria applied, sample characteristics, information source, and judicial practices (e.g., diversion). Nevertheless, two publications reporting meta-analyses of (1) adult prisoners and (2) participants living in detention with ADHD (both assessed by clinical interview) found similar pooled prevalence rates of 25.5% and 26.7%, respectively (Baggio et al., 2018; Young, Moss, et al., 2015).

With respect to youths, a meta-analysis of young people with ADHD (10–19 years) reported a pooled prevalence of 17% (Beaudry et al., 2021), corresponding to a ten-fold increase in the prevalence of ADHD for those in the CJS. It has been proposed that the increased prevalence rates of young people and adults with ADHD in the CJS are due to their deficits in executive dysfunction which in turn put them at greater risk of being apprehended (Young & Thome, 2011).

Gender Differences

ADHD has traditionally been perceived as a male childhood disorder. Rates of ADHD in community samples fall at around a 3-1 ratio of boys to girls (Willcutt, 2012), yet there is growing evidence that suggests ADHD symptoms are as common in females as males (Corbisiero et al., 2017). It may be that girls experience later onset of impairment or work harder to compensate for or hide their symptoms in an effort to meet parent and/or teacher expectations. This may result in reduced youth female referrals to clinical services (Young, Gudjonsson, et al., 2018). Nevertheless, the gender ratio of ADHD within the general population narrows as individuals' transition from childhood to adulthood (Cortese et al., 2016), perhaps reflecting increased contact with healthcare professionals compared to their male peers at that age (Bramham et al., 2012).

There is sparse extant research focusing on females with ADHD in the CJS and sample sizes are small, limiting representativeness and thus generalizability. Nevertheless, in contrast with general population studies reporting large gender disparities in favor of males (particularly in childhood), the prevalence of ADHD in the CJS does not appear to significantly differ between genders (Baggio et al., 2018; Young, Moss, et al., 2015). Various explanations have been proposed to explain this discrepancy. If this indicates a true narrowing in gender differences, the protective factors that typically keep females out of the CJS are absent (or overshadowed). Alternatively, females with ADHD may experience more risk factors; for example, ADHD and comorbid conduct disorder may confer greater risk for females than for males.

Diagnosing ADHD in the Criminal Justice System

Research suggests that ADHD is often underdiagnosed or misdiagnosed in offenders. A prison study reported only 18.8% of the individuals diagnosed with ADHD as part of the research protocol had been identified by a health professional previously (Young et al., 2016). Another study reported only two of the 30 prisoners diagnosed with ADHD had been diagnosed in childhood (Eme, 2013). A high rate of under-identification has also been found within probation settings (Young et al., 2014). There may be several explanations, including the fact that many offenders have underprivileged backgrounds, experience disruption to their education, or have poor access to health care.

Identifying offenders with ADHD may be further complicated by high rates of comorbidity in this population leading to misdiagnosis (Young & Thome, 2011). Symptoms of impulsivity, restlessness, oppositionality, and irritability may be perceived to be 'bad behavior' rather than recognized to be symptoms of a treatable condition (Scott et al., 2016). Furthermore, there may be systemic problems that impede accurate diagnosis, such as limited resources, restricted activities, lack of awareness and staff expertise, transfer between prisons, and inadequate continuance of medical records (Young, Adamou, et al., 2011).

Given the high comorbidity of ADHD with other symptoms and disorders in the offender population, a detailed developmental and psychiatric history needs to be undertaken and careful consideration of differential diagnosis. The assessment needs to focus on both the externalizing behavioral presentation (e.g., restlessness and poor impulse control) and the cognitive presentation of the offender (e.g., ability to focus and sustain attention), the latter being often overlooked among offenders of both genders (Young, Gudjonsson, et al., 2018). Moreover, the diagnostic process may also be complicated by a lack of childhood informants and/or collateral information to support self-reported information. Young, Gudjonsson, et al. (2018) provide detailed information regarding the assessment process (including appropriate instruments to assess ADHD in the offender population).

Comorbidity

Psychiatric comorbidity is common in offender populations, but this seems to be substantially greater in those with ADHD. A meta-analysis of comorbid psychiatric disorders in prisoners found that adult offenders with ADHD had significantly higher rates of a history of conduct disorder, substance use, depression, anxiety, and personality disorder compared with offenders without ADHD (Young, Sedgwick, et al., 2015). Higher rates of traumatic brain injury, intellectual disability, communication disorders, and autism spectrum disorder (ASD) have also been reported (McCarthy et al., 2016; Young, González, Fridman, et al., 2018; Young, González, Mullens, et al., 2018). Indeed, 96% of prisoners with ADHD have one or more comorbid conditions and this more complex presentation is likely to augment their vulnerability within the CJS (Einarsson et al., 2009).

ADHD and Risk of Antisocial and Criminal Behavior

The risk of criminality is likely to vary across the life course (Chapter 2). Moffitt's (1993) developmental taxonomy theory proposes two distinct groups of offenders: a 'life-course persistent' group who engage in antisocial behavior early in life and become life-long offenders and a larger 'adolescence-limited' group who engage in antisocial behavior during adolescent years only. ADHD is thought to be a predictor of the life-course persistent group. Thus, ADHD may be a more prominent predictor for criminality in adult populations comparative to youth populations, where youth delinquency is arguably the rule rather than the exception.

Retz and Rosler (2009) propose a theoretical framework consisting of two pathways to explain the relationship between ADHD and antisocial behavior. The first pathway is for those with early onset conduct disorder who go on to develop antisocial personality disorder (Chapter 11). It is proposed that this developmental subtype is more frequently associated with impulsive aggression as a reaction to a situation, rather than premeditated-proactive aggression. The second pathway is for those without comorbid conduct disorder. It is proposed that this developmental subtype is more associated with social problems and rule breaking behaviors (e.g. traffic infractions) but the rate of general delinquency is not elevated. Within this framework, substance use disorders (Chapter 17) are understood to be an important mediator of ADHD-related antisocial behavior. Supporting this notion, studies have found the association between ADHD symptoms and criminality are reduced or no longer present after adjusting for lifetime substance use disorders (Román-Ithier et al., 2017).

Gudjonsson and colleagues (Gudjonsson et al., 2014) attempted to disentangle the relationship between ADHD, comorbid factors, and criminality among young people. In their study, ADHD contributed 8.2% and 8.8% to the variance in nonviolent and violent behavior, respectively, although these effects were largely mediated by conduct disorder, substance use, and association with delinquent peers. The study was a national epidemiological study of 11,388 students and 5.2% self-reported ADHD. The authors acknowledge that the direct effect of ADHD on offending may be greater in clinically diagnosed samples. Other studies have also demonstrated an absence of association between ADHD and criminal behavior when controlling for externalizing comorbid conditions such as conduct disorder and antisocial personality disorder (Grieger & Hosser, 2012).

In contrast, ADHD has been found to independently increase risk of criminality (Sibley et al., 2011). This association corresponds with Gottfredson and Hirschi's (1990) general theory of crime which understands criminal behavior to be a consequence of low self-control. Diminished or delayed self-control is a core deficit in individuals with ADHD. Other research highlights how ADHD symptoms may increase susceptibility to social and environmental risk factors, thereby further increasing risk of antisocial and criminal behavior. During adolescence, young people are thought to develop a focus on peer relationships and it is common for young people with ADHD to experience peer rejection, which has been found to predict subsequent delinquency (Mrug et al., 2012). Indeed, young people with ADHD may engage with dysfunctional peer groups to gain a social network and sense of 'belonging'. Moreover, they may be more compliant than their non-ADHD peers and thus more susceptible to peer influence, regardless of whether positive or negative (Chapter 10). In the latter case, if associating with criminal peers, this may increase the risk of antisocial behavior (Gudjonsson et al., 2008).

School and educational difficulties may also be a risk factor. Research has found that that low educational attainment more than doubles the odds of past arrest and longitudinal studies report an association between policies aimed to increase educational attainment and reductions in overall crime at population level. ADHD symptoms and executive functioning deficits are understood to hinder the ability to focus on classroom tasks, complete homework, meet course deadlines, and successfully interact with peers and teachers. Many require remedial support, having to retake exams and repeat academic years. They have higher rates of school drop-out, suspension/expulsion, and lower grade/qualification attainment (de Zeeuw et al., 2017; Polderman et al., 2010).

The interaction between biological, psychological, and environmental variables can be understood within the framework of general strain theory (Agnew et al., 2002) which explains crime as a conditioned response to strain, particularly for individuals with low self-control. Research that has examined the link between ADHD and strain found when equivalent on the level of strain, those with high ADHD scores were more likely to engage in criminal behavior comparative to those with low ADHD scores (Johnson & Kercher, 2007).

Hence, the relationship between ADHD and the course of antisocial behavior and criminality is complex. There are several different theoretical approaches which may overlap. Epidemiological research is needed to test out these theoretical frameworks within the context of ADHD adopting a longitudinal design (with long-term follow-up periods into adulthood) in order to disentangle predicting factors from associated factors.

Vulnerabilities of People with ADHD in the Criminal Justice System

There are several ways in which individuals with ADHD may be vulnerable at different stages of the CJS. There is evidence supporting that young people with ADHD are substantially younger at first arrest and conviction, compared with their peers, and persist in their antisocial behavior resulting in significantly higher rates of recidivism (Mohr-Jensen & Steinhausen, 2016; Philipp-Wiegmann et al., 2018; Young, Wells, et al., 2011).

When questioned by the police, it is well documented that youths are more susceptible than adults to yield to interrogative pressure and compliance. Hence, in the UK, youths are entitled to have an 'appropriate adult' present to assist communication during police interviews. Typically, this is a parent. However, ADHD is a heritable disorder; 20–50% parents of children with ADHD have ADHD themselves, perhaps undiagnosed (Kooij et al., 2010; Starck et al., 2016), which in turn may compromise their capacity to provide the level of support required.

Research has indicated that individuals with ADHD are no more susceptible to suggestions than their non-ADHD peers. Nevertheless, when put under interrogative pressure they appear to engage in a coping strategy of disproportionately responding with "don't know" answers (even to questions which people commonly provide correct responses) (Gudjonsson & Young, 2021; Gudjonsson et al., 2007). This response style may give the impression that they are being uncooperative and/or evasive. Gudjonsson and Young (2021) suggest this may be due to lack of confidence in their memory. By contrast, individuals with ADHD may be at greater risk of complying with the requests of others (Gudjonsson et al., 2008). This is typically motivated by a desire to please others and/or to avoid conflict and confrontation and may be associated with low self-esteem and anxiety (Gudjonsson et al., 2002).

A growing body of research has identified a high susceptibility for individuals with ADHD to make a false confession (Gudjonsson, 2018; Gudjonsson et al., 2016). The risk has been reported to be up to three times higher in prisoners with ADHD compared with non-ADHD prisoners (Gudjonsson et al., 2008, 2019). The relationship may be mediated by conduct disorder (Gudjonsson et al., 2016, 2019), but when adjusting for this comorbidity, ADHD symptoms of hyperactivity/impulsivity seem to drive the association (Gudjonsson et al., 2019). There may be many reasons a person might make a false confession (Gudjonsson, 2018). These include contextual factors (e.g., associating with delinquent peers, protecting someone else); situational factors (e.g., detention in police custody, interrogative pressure), and/or personal factors (e.g., withdrawal from substances, intellectual limitations). In the case of people with ADHD, a strong motivating factor may be the desire to avoid sustained police questioning and leave the police station due to their symptoms of restlessness, poor concentration, and impulsiveness.

ADHD has been associated with difficulty in acclimatizing to detention in custodial settings. Examination of police records has found that ADHD significantly contributes to increased demands being made on police staff (after controlling for conduct disorder and duration of time in custody) (Young et al., 2013). Prison records document an eight-fold increase in aggressive incidents, and a six-fold increase when controlling for antisocial personality disorder (Young et al., 2009). Aggressive behavioral incidents have also been observed in forensic mental health settings (Young et al., 2003; Young, Misch, et al., 2011). The underlying mechanisms for this association are likely to be hyperactivity/impulsivity, emotional distress and dysregulation (González et al., 2016) and the outcome may hinder the individual's progress in custodial settings (e.g., receiving adjudications and extended tariffs). When moving 'beyond the gates' and into the community, cognitive, emotional, and behavioral difficulties associated with ADHD may continue to impede progress and limit the offenders' ability to engage meaningfully in the rehabilitation process (Young et al., 2014).

Impact of Treatment on Outcome

Pharmacological interventions are the most commonly provided treatments for adults with ADHD. Both stimulant and non-stimulant medications have been associated with reducing core ADHD symptoms and improving functional outcomes (e.g., better quality of life, reducing crime) (Chen et al., 2014; Ginsberg & Lindefors, 2012; Ginsberg et al., 2012).

The efficacy of treatment with ADHD medication has been associated with a large reduction in the crime rate in Sweden. Using national registry data, the study investigated 25,656 individuals diagnosed with ADHD, their periods of treatment with medication and criminal convictions. It was found that over a three-year period, criminal conviction rates significantly reduced by 32% for men and 41% for women when individuals were being treated with ADHD medication compared with non-medication periods. This association was irrespective of type of crime. When repeating the methodology for use of selective serotonin reuptake inhibitor (SSRI) medication, no significant association with criminal conviction rates was found (Lichtenstein et al., 2012). Hence the apparent 'treatment' effect was only established for ADHD medication.

Further evidence comes from another Swedish study, which employed a similar methodology to examine the relationship between various psychotropic medications and violent reoffending in 22,275 individuals released from prison in 2005–2010. It was found that those taking psychostimulant medication were 43% less likely to commit a violent offense during medication periods compared to non-medication periods. Dispensed antipsychotics and medications used to treat addictions were associated with a risk difference of 40% and 36% fewer violent reoffenses, respectively. Antidepressants and antiepileptics were not associated with rates of violent reoffending. The authors noted adherence issues to pre-scribed psychostimulant medication in the register and considered the reduction in violent reoffending may have been greater, had strict adherence to medication protocols been observed (Chang et al., 2016).

The use of stimulants within offender populations is contentious however (Pilkinton & Pilkinton, 2014) due to the risk of misuse to gain a euphorigenic effect (a 'high') and the potential for diversion. Furthermore, the strict dispensary procedures required for these controlled medications often complicate and bur-dens internal resources. Non-stimulant preparations may minimize some of these risks (Young, Gudjonsson, et al., 2018).

Multimodal interventions that combine medication and psychological inter-ventions are likely to be effective in targeting a broader range of outcomes and reducing functional impairments. Indeed, they have demonstrated stronger effect sizes than medication or psychological intervention alone (Arnold et al., 2015; Shaw et al., 2012). R&R2ADHD is a 15-session cognitive behavioral group program that aims to build pro-social competence (Young & Ross, 2007). R&R2ADHD is a newer version of the Reasoning & Rehabilitation program, adapted for specific use with young people and adults with ADHD. Consist-ing of core modules that address executive dysfunction, emotional dysregulation, social problem-solving, critical and moral reasoning, and comorbid symptoms, the program is considered suitable for offenders with ADHD, irrespective of age or gender. A randomized controlled trial conducted in the Icelandic community comparing those receiving the program with those receiving treatment as usual reported a significantly greater reduction for clinician-rated and self-rated ADHD symptoms; the treatment effect was maintained at three-month follow-up. Out-comes of anxiety, depression, and quality of life were significantly improved follow-up (Emilsson et al., 2011; Young et al., 2017; Young, Khondoker, et al., 2015). A study conducted in Denmark found similar results post-treatment and at three-month follow-up (Ramboll & The National Board of Social Services, 2020). Outcomes in the longer term (at 6- and 12-months post-treatment) were investigated by comparing the sample with matched controls drawn from Danish registers. Completion of R&R2ADHD was associated with increased employment and education rates and decreased use of cash benefits and social services. After six months, there was an increase in visits to the hospital emergency room, which may reflect increased insight, self-care, and personal locus of control.

Conclusion and Recommendations

ADHD is highly prevalent in offender populations, yet for many the diagnosis has been missed or misdiagnosed. These individuals are unable to access appropriate treatment and rehabilitation. Identifying this subgroup of the population, who present with complex mental health needs, is not just a matter of conferring health gain for the individual. There are also clear advantages for the custodial system itself and, more broadly, for society associated with increased productivity, decreased resource utilization, and reduced rates of reoffending.

The challenge therefore is to prevent ADHD being an overlooked diagnosis which means that those employed within the CJS need to improve awareness and understanding about ADHD and associated problems in order for them to better 'flag' the condition. This will require training within every component of the CJS in order to ensure continuity of care within its complex structure. Current best practice recommendations for effective identification and treatment of prisoners and youth offenders with ADHD are provided in an expert consensus report (Young, Gudjonsson, et al., 2018). Nevertheless, more research is needed, especially to investigate early predictors of antisocial behavior, delinquency, and youth offending in young people with ADHD. Early diagnosis may mean that early interventions can be put in place that might interrupt, or even prevent, the antisocial trajectory and pathway to crime that lies in wait for some individuals with ADHD.

References

Agnew, R., Brezina, T., Wright, J., & Cullen, F. (2002). Strain, personality traits, and delinquency: Extending general strain theory. *Criminology, 40*, 43–72. https://doi.org/10.1111/j.1745-9125.2002.tb00949.x

American Psychiatric Association. (2013). *Diagnostic and statistical manual of mental disorders: DSM-5™* (5th ed.). American Psychiatric Publishing. https://doi.org/10.1176/appi.books.9780890425596

Arnold, L. E., Hodgkins, P., Caci, H., Kahle, J., & Young, S. (2015). Effect of treatment modality on long-term outcomes in attention-deficit/hyperactivity disorder: A systematic review. *PloS One, 10*(2), e0116407. https://doi.org/10.1371/journal.pone.0116407

Baggio, S., Fructuoso, A., Guimaraes, M., Fois, E., Golay, D., Heller, P., Perroud, N., Aubry, C., Young, S., Delessert, D., Gétaz, L., Tran, N. T., & Wolff, H. (2018). Prevalence of attention deficit hyperactivity disorder in detention settings: A systematic review and meta-analysis. *Frontiers in Psychiatry, 9*, 331.

Beaudry, G., Yu, R., Långström, N., & Fazel, S. (2021). An updated systematic review and meta-regression analysis: Mental disorders among adolescents in juvenile detention and correctional facilities. *Journal of the American Academy of Child and Adolescent Psychiatry, 60*(1), 46–60. https://doi.org/10.1016/j.jaac.2020.01.015

Bramham, J., Murphy, D. G., Xenitidis, K., Asherson, P., Hopkin, G., & Young, S. (2012). Adults with attention deficit hyperactivity disorder: An investigation of age-related differences in behavioural symptoms, neuropsychological function and co-morbidity. *Psychological Medicine, 42*(10), 2225–2234. https://doi.org/10.1017/S0033291712000219

Chang, Z., Lichtenstein, P., Långström, N., Larsson, H., & Fazel, S. (2016). Association between prescription of major psychotropic medications and violent reoffending after prison release. *Jama, 316*(17), 1798–1807. https://doi.org/10.1001/jama.2016.15380

Chen, Q., Sjölander, A., Runeson, B., D'Onofrio, B., M., Lichtenstein, P., & Larsson, H. (2014). Drug treatment for attention-deficit/hyperactivity disorder and suicidal behaviour: Register based study. *BMJ, 348*, g3769. https://doi.org/10.1136/bmj.g3769

Corbisiero, S., Hartmann-Schorro, R., Riecher-Rössler, A., & Stieglitz, R. (2017). Screening for adult attention-deficit/hyperactivity disorder in a psychiatric outpatient population with specific focus on sex differences. *Frontiers in Psychiatry, 8*, 115. https://doi.org/10.3389/fpsyt.2017.00115

Cortese, S., Faraone, S. V., Bernardi, S., Wang, S., & Blanco, C. (2016). Gender differences in adult attention-deficit/hyperactivity disorder: Results from the National Epidemiologic Survey on Alcohol and Related Conditions (NESARC). *The Journal of Clinical Psychiatry, 77*(4), 421. https://doi.org/10.4088/JCP.14m09630

de Zeeuw, E. L., van Beijsterveldt, C. E. M., Ehli, E. A., de Geus, E. J. C., & Boomsma, D. I. (2017). Attention deficit hyperactivity disorder symptoms and low educational achievement: Evidence supporting a causal hypothesis. *Behavior Genetics, 47*(3), 278–289. https://doi.org/10.1007/s10519-017-9836-4

Einarsson, E., Sigurdsson, J. F., Gudjonsson, G. H., Newton, A. K., & Bragason, O. O. (2009). Screening for attention-deficit hyperactivity disorder and co-morbid mental disorders among prison inmates. *Nordic Journal of Psychiatry, 63*(5), 361–367. https://doi.org/10.1080/08039480902759184

Eme, R. (2013). Attention-deficit/hyperactivity disorder and criminal behavior. *International Journal of Sociology, 1*(2), 29–36.

Emilsson, B., Gudjonsson, G., Sigurdsson, J. F., Baldursson, G., Einarsson, E., Olafsdottir, H., & Young, S. (2011). Cognitive behaviour therapy in medication-treated adults with ADHD and persistent Symptoms: A randomized controlled trial. *BMC Psychiatry, 11*(1), 116. https://doi.org/10.1186/1471-244X-11-116

Faraone, S. V., Biederman, J., & Mick, E. (2006). The age-dependent decline of attention deficit hyperactivity disorder: A meta-analysis of follow-up studies. *Psychological Medicine, 36*(2), 159–165. https://doi.org/10.1017/S003329170500471X

Ginsberg, Y., Hirvikoski, T., Grann, M., & Lindefors, N. (2012). Long-term functional outcome in adult prison inmates with ADHD receiving OROS-methylphenidate. *European Archives of Psychiatry and Clinical Neuroscience, 262*(8), 705–724. https://doi.org/10.1007/s00406-012-0317-8

Ginsberg, Y., & Lindefors, N. (2012). Methylphenidate treatment of adult male prison inmates with attention-deficit hyperactivity disorder: Randomised double-blind placebo-controlled trial with open-label extension. *British Journal of Psychiatry, 200*(1), 68–73. https://doi.org/10.1192/bjp.bp.111.092940

González, R. A., Gudjonsson, G. H., Wells, J., & Young, S. (2016). The role of emotional distress and ADHD on institutional behavioral disturbance and recidivism among offenders. *Journal of Attention Disorders, 20*(4), 368–378. https://doi.org/10.1177/108705471 3493322

Gottfredson, M. R., & Hirschi, T. (1990). *A general theory of crime*. Stanford University Press.

Grieger, L., & Hosser, D. (2012). Attention deficit hyperactivity disorder does not predict criminal recidivism in young adult offenders: Results from a prospective study. *International Journal of Law and Psychiatry, 35*(1), 27–34. https://doi.org/10.1016/j.ijlp.2011.11.005

Gudjonsson, G., Sigurdsson, J., Bragason, O., Newton, A., & Einarsson, E. (2008). Interrogative suggestibility, compliance and false confessions among prisoners and their relationship with attention deficit hyperactivity disorder (ADHD) symptoms. *Psychological Medicine, 38*(7), 1037–1044. https://doi.org/10.1017/S0033291708002882

Gudjonsson, G. H. (2018). *The psychology of false confessions: Forty years of science and practice*. Wiley. https://doi.org/10.1002/9781119315636

Gudjonsson, G. H., Gonzalez, R., & Young, S. (2019). The risk of making false confessions: The role of developmental disorders, conduct disorder, psychiatric symptoms, and compliance. *Journal of Attention Disorders*. https://doi.org/10.1177/1087054719833169

Gudjonsson, G. H., Sigurdsson, J. F., Sigfusdottir, I. D., Asgeirsdottir, B. B., González, R. A., & Young, S. (2016). A national epidemiological study investigating risk factors for police interrogation and false confession among juveniles and young persons. *Social Psychiatry and Psychiatric Epidemiology, 51*(3), 359–367. https://doi.org/10.1007/s00127-015-1145-8

Gudjonsson, G. H., Sigurdsson, J. F., Sigfusdottir, I. D., & Young, S. (2014). A national epidemiological study of offending and its relationship with ADHD symptoms and associated risk factors. *Journal of Attention Disorders, 18*(1), 3–13. https://doi.org/10.1177/108705 4712437584

Gudjonsson, G. H., Young, S., & Bramham, J. (2007). Interrogative suggestibility in adults diagnosed with attention-deficit hyperativity disorder (ADHD): A potential vulnerability during police questioning. *Personality and Individual Differences, 43*(4), 737–745. https://doi.org/10.1016/j.paid.2007.01.014

Gudjonsson, G., Sigurdsson, J., Brynjólfsdóttir, B., & Hreinsdóttir, H. (2002). The relationship of compliance with anxiety, self-esteem, paranoid thinking and anger. *Psychology, Crime and Law, 8*, 145–153. https://doi.org/10.1080/10683160208415003

Gudjonsson, G., & Young, S. (2021). An investigation of 'don't know' and 'direct explanation' response styles on the Gudjonsson Suggestibility Scale: A comparison of three different vulnerable adult groups. *Personality and Individual Differences, 168*, 110385. https://doi.org/10.1016/j.paid.2020.110385

Johnson, M. C., & Kercher, G. A. (2007). ADHD, strain, and criminal behavior: A test of general strain theory. *Null, 28*(2), 131–152. https://doi.org/10.1080/01639620601130992

Kooij, S. J. J., Bejerot, S., Blackwell, A., Caci, H., Casas-Brugué, M., Carpentier, P. J., Edvinsson, D., Fayyad, J., Foeken, K., Fitzgerald, M., Gaillac, V., Ginsberg, Y., Henry, C., Krause, J., Lensing, M. B., Manor, I., Niederhofer, H., Nunes-Filipe, C., Ohlmeier, M. D., … Asherson, P. (2010). European consensus statement on diagnosis and treatment of adult ADHD: The European Network Adult ADHD. *BMC Psychiatry, 10*(1), 67. https://doi.org/10.1186/1471-244X-10-67

Lichtenstein, P., Halldner, L., Zetterqvist, J., Sjölander, A., Serlachius, E., Fazel, S., Långström, N., & Larsson, H. (2012). Medication for attention deficit-hyperactivity disorder and criminality. *The New England Journal of Medicine, 367*(21), 2006–2014. https://doi.org/10.1056/NEJMoa1203241

McCarthy, J., Chaplin, E., Underwood, L., Forrester, A., Hayward, H., Sabet, J., Young, S., Asherson, P., Mills, R., & Murphy, D. (2016). Characteristics of prisoners with neurodevelopmental disorders and difficulties. *Journal of Intellectual Disability Research, 60*(3), 201–206. https://doi.org/10.1111/jir.12237

Moffitt, T. E. (1993). Adolescence-limited and life-course-persistent antisocial behavior: A developmental taxonomy. *Psychological Review, 100*(4), 674–701.

Mohr-Jensen, C., & Steinhausen, H. (2016). A meta-analysis and systematic review of the risks associated with childhood attention-deficit hyperactivity disorder on long-term outcome of arrests, convictions, and incarcerations. *Clinical Psychology Review, 48*, 32–42. https://doi.org/10.1016/j.cpr.2016.05.002

Mrug, S., Molina, B. S., Hoza, B., Gerdes, A. C., Hinshaw, S. P., Hechtman, L., & Arnold, L. E. (2012). Peer rejection and friendships in children with attention-deficit/hyperactivity disorder: Contributions to long-term outcomes. *Journal of Abnormal Child Psychology, 40*(6), 1013–1026. https://doi.org/10.1007/s10802-012-9610-2

Philipp-Wiegmann, F., Rösler, M., Clasen, O., Zinnow, T., Retz-Junginger, P., & Retz, W. (2018). ADHD modulates the course of delinquency: A 15-year follow-up study of young incarcerated man. *European Archives of Psychiatry and Clinical Neuroscience, 268*(4), 391–399. https://doi.org/10.1007/s00406-017-0816-8

Pilkinton, P. D., & Pilkinton, J. C. (2014). Prescribing in prison: Minimizing psychotropic drug diversion in correctional practice. *Journal of Correctional Health Care, 20*(2), 95–104. https://doi.org/10.1177/1078345813518629

Polanczyk, G., de Lima, M. S., Horta, B. L., Biederman, J., & Rohde, L. A. (2007). The worldwide prevalence of ADHD: A systematic review and metaregression analysis. *The American Journal of Psychiatry, 164*(6), 942–948. http://doi.org/164/6/942

Polderman, T. J., Boomsma, D. I., Bartels, M., Verhulst, F. C., & Huizink, A. C. (2010). A systematic review of prospective studies on attention problems and academic achievement. *Acta Psychiatrica Scandinavica, 122*(4), 271–284. https://doi.org/10.1111/j.1600-0447.2010.01568.x

Ramboll and The National Board of Social Services. (2020). *Better help for young people and adults with ADHD and corresponding difficulties: Final evaluation report.* https://www.psychology-services.uk.com/danish-report-on-r-r2-adhd. Accessed 23 April 2020.

Retz, W., & Rösler, M. (2009). The relation of ADHD and violent aggression: What can we learn from epidemiological and genetic studies? *International Journal of Law and Psychiatry; Aggression, Science, and the Law: New Insights from Neuroscience, 32*(4), 235–243. https://doi.org/10.1016/j.ijlp.2009.04.006

Román-Ithier, J. C., González, R. A., Vélez-Pastrana, M. C., González-Tejera, G. M., & Albizu-García, C. E. (2017). Attention deficit hyperactivity disorder symptoms, type of offending and recidivism in a prison population: The role of substance dependence. *Criminal Behaviour and Mental Health, 27*(5), 443–456. https://doi.org/10.1002/cbm.2009

Scott, D. A., Gignac, M., Kronfli, R. N., Ocana, A., & Lorberg, G. W. (2016). Expert opinion and recommendations for the management of attention-deficit/hyperactivity disorder in correctional facilities. *Journal of Correctional Health Care, 22*(1), 46–61. https://doi.org/10.1177/1078345815618392

Shaw, M., Hodgkins, P., Caci, H., Young, S., Kahle, J., Woods, A. G., & Arnold, L. E. (2012). A systematic review and analysis of long-term outcomes in attention deficit hyperactivity disorder: Effects of treatment and non-treatment. *BMC Medicine, 10*, 99–99. https://doi.org/10.1186/1741-7015-10-99

Sibley, M. H., Pelham, W. E., Molina, B. S. G., Gnagy, E. M., Waschbusch, D. A., Biswas, A., MacLean, M. G., Babinski, D. E., & Karch, K. M. (2011). The delinquency outcomes of boys with ADHD with and without comorbidity. *Journal of Abnormal Child Psychology, 39*(1), 21–32. https://doi.org/10.1007/s10802-010-9443-9

Simon, V., Czobor, P., Bálint, S., Mészáros, A., & Bitter, I. (2009). Prevalence and correlates of adult attention-deficit hyperactivity disorder: meta-analysis. *The British Journal of Psychiatry: The Journal of Mental Science, 194*(3), 204–211. https://doi.org/10.1192/bjp.bp.107.048827

Starck, M., Grünwald, J., & Schlarb, A. A. (2016). Occurrence of ADHD in parents of ADHD children in a clinical sample. *Neuropsychiatric Disease and Treatment, 12*, 581–588. https://doi.org/10.2147/NDT.S100238

Thapar, A., Cooper, M., Jefferies, R., & Stergiakouli, E. (2011). What causes attention deficit hyperactivity disorder? *Archives of Disease in Childhood, 97*, 260–265. https://doi.org/10.1136/archdischild-2011-300482

Thomas, R., Sanders, S., Doust, J., Beller, E., & Glasziou, P. (2015). Prevalence of attention-deficit/hyperactivity disorder: A systematic review and meta-analysis. *Pediatrics, 135*(4), 994. https://doi.org/10.1542/peds.2014-3482

Willcutt, E. G. (2012). The prevalence of DSM-IV attention-deficit/hyperactivity disorder: A meta-analytic review. *Neurotherapeutics, 9*(3), 490–499. https://doi.org/10.1007/s13311-012-0135-8

Young, S., Emilsson, B., Sigurdsson, J. F., Khondoker, M., Philipp-Wiegmann, F., Baldursson, G., Olafsdottir, H., & Gudjonsson, G. (2017). A randomized controlled trial reporting functional outcomes of cognitive-behavioural therapy in medication-treated adults with ADHD and comorbid psychopathology. *European Archives of Psychiatry and Clinical Neuroscience, 267*(3), 267–276. https://doi.org/10.1007/s00406-016-0735-0

Young, S., González, R. A., Fridman, M., Hodgkins, P., Kim, K., & Gudjonsson, G. H. (2018). Health-related quality of life in prisoners with attention-deficit hyperactivity disorder and head injury. *BMC Psychiatry, 18*(1), 209. https://doi.org/10.1186/s12888-018-1785-9

Young, S., González, R. A., Mullens, H., Mutch, L., Malet-Lambert, I., & Gudjonsson, G. H. (2018). Neurodevelopmental disorders in prison inmates: Comorbidity and combined associations with psychiatric symptoms and behavioural disturbance. *Psychiatry Research, 261*, 109–115. https://doi.org/10.1016/j.psychres.2017.12.036

Young, S., Gonzalez, R. A., Mutch, L., Mallet-Lambert, I., O'Rourke, L., Hickey, N., Asherson, P., & Gudjonsson, G. H. (2016). Diagnostic accuracy of a brief screening tool for attention deficit hyperactivity disorder in UK prison inmates. *Psychological Medicine, 46*(7), 1449–1458. https://doi.org/10.1017/S0033291716000039

Young, S., Goodwin, E. J., Sedgwick, O., & Gudjonsson, G. H. (2013). The effectiveness of police custody assessments in identifying suspects with intellectual disabilities and attention deficit hyperactivity disorder. *BMC Medicine, 11*(1), 248. https://doi.org/10.1186/1741-7015-11-248

Young, S., Gudjonsson, G., Ball, S., & Lam, J. (2003). Attention Deficit Hyperactivity Disorder (ADHD) in personality disordered offenders and the association with disruptive behavioural problems. *Journal of Forensic Psychiatry and Psychology, 14*, 491–505. https://doi.org/10.1080/14789940310001615461

Young, S., Gudjonsson, G., Chitsabesan, P., Colley, B., Farrag, E., Forrester, A., Hollingdale, J., Kim, K., Lewis, A., Maginn, S., Mason, P., Ryan, S., Smith, J., Woodhouse, E., & Asherson, P. (2018). Identification and treatment of offenders with attention-deficit/hyperactivity disorder in the prison population: A practical approach based upon expert consensus. *BMC Psychiatry, 18*(1), 281. https://doi.org/10.1186/s12888-018-1858-9

Young, S., Gudjonsson, G. H., Goodwin, E. J., Jotangia, A., Farooq, R., Haddrick, D., & Adamou, M. (2014). Beyond the gates: Identifying and managing offenders with attention deficit hyperactivity disorder in community probation services. *AIMS Public Health, 1*(1), 33–42. https://doi.org/10.3934/publichealth.2014.1.33

Young, S., Gudjonsson, G. H., Wells, J., Asherson, P., Theobald, D., Oliver, B., Scott, C., & Mooney, A. (2009). Attention deficit hyperactivity disorder and critical incidents in a Scottish prison population. *Personality and Individual Differences, 46*(3), 265–269. https://doi.org/10.1016/j.paid.2008.10.003

Young, S., Khondoker, M., Emilsson, B., Sigurdsson, J. F., Philipp-Wiegmann, F., Baldursson, G., Olafsdottir, H., & Gudjonsson, G. (2015). Cognitive-behavioural therapy in medication-treated adults with attention-deficit/hyperactivity disorder and co-morbid psychopathology: A randomized controlled trial using multi-level analysis. *Psychological Medicine, 45*(13), 2793–2804. https://doi.org/10.1017/S0033291715000756

Young, S., Misch, P., Collins, P., & Gudjonsson, G. (2011). Predictors of institutional behavioural disturbance and offending in the community among young offenders. *The Journal of Forensic Psychiatry & Psychology, 22*(1), 72–86. https://doi.org/10.1080/14789949.2010.495991

Young, S., Moss, D., Sedgwick, O., Fridman, M., & Hodgkins, P. (2015). A meta-analysis of the prevalence of attention deficit hyperactivity disorder in incarcerated populations. *Psychological Medicine, 45*(2), 247–258. https://doi.org/10.1017/S0033291714000762

Young, S., Sedgwick, O., Fridman, M., Gudjonsson, G., Hodgkins, P., Lantigua, M., & González, R. A. (2015). Co-morbid psychiatric disorders among incarcerated ADHD populations: A meta-analysis. *Psychological Medicine, 45*(12), 2499–2510. https://doi.org/10.1017/S0033291715000598

Young, S., & Thome, J. (2011). ADHD and offenders. *The World Journal of Biological Psychiatry: The Official Journal of the World Federation of Societies of Biological Psychiatry, 12 Suppl 1*, 124–128. https://doi.org/10.3109/15622975.2011.600319

Young, S., Wells, J., & Gudjonsson, G. H. (2011). Predictors of offending among prisoners: The role of attention-deficit hyperactivity disorder and substance use. *Journal of Psychopharmacology, 25*(11), 1524–1532. https://doi.org/10.1177/0269881110370502

Young, S. J., Adamou, M., Bolea, B., Gudjonsson, G., Müller, U., Pitts, M., Thome, J., & Asherson, P. (2011). The identification and management of ADHD offenders within the criminal justice system: A consensus statement from the UK Adult ADHD Network and criminal justice agencies. *BMC Psychiatry, 11*(1), 32. https://doi.org/10.1186/1471-244X-11-32

Young, S. J., & Ross, R. R. (2007). *R&R2 for youths and adults with ADHD: A prosocial competence training program.* Cognitive Centre of Canada.

Suggested Further Reading

Chang, Z., Lichtenstein, P., Långström, N., Larsson, H., & Fazel, S. (2016). Association between prescription of major psychotropic medications and violent reoffending after prison release. *JAMA, 316*(17), 1798–1807. https://doi.org/10.1001/jama.2016.15380

Gudjonsson, G. H., Sigurdsson, J. F., Sigfusdottir, I. D., Asgeirsdottir, B. B., González, R. A., & Young, S. (2016). A national epidemiological study investigating risk factors for police interrogation and false confession among juveniles and young persons. *Social Psychiatry and Psychiatric Epidemiology, 51*(3), 359–367. https://doi.org/10.1007/s00127-015-1145-8

Young, S., Goodwin, E. J., Sedgwick, O., & Gudjonsson, G. H. (2013). The effectiveness of police custody assessments in identifying suspects with intellectual disabilities and attention deficit hyperactivity disorder. *BMC Medicine, 11*(1), 248. https://doi.org/10.1186/1741-7015-11-248

Young, S., Gudjonsson, G., Chitsabesan, P., Colley, B., Farrag, E., Forrester, A., Hollingdale, J., Kim, K., Lewis, A., Maginn, S., Mason, P., Ryan, S., Smith, J., Woodhouse, E., & Asherson, P. (2018). Identification and treatment of offenders with attention-deficit/hyperactivity disorder in the prison population: A practical approach based upon expert consensus. *BMC Psychiatry, 18*(1), 281. https://doi.org/10.1186/s12888-018-1858-9

Young, S., Moss, D., Sedgwick, O., Fridman, M., & Hodgkins, P. (2015). A meta-analysis of the prevalence of attention deficit hyperactivity disorder in incarcerated populations. *Psychological Medicine, 45*(2), 247–258. https://doi.org/10.1017/S0033291714000762

Substance Use, Abuse, and Disorder Within Forensic Psychiatry

17

Malin Hildebrand Karlén

Key Points

- Substance use problems and psychiatric symptoms are intertwined factors in forensic psychiatric care and increase risk for (violent) crimes.
- The co-occurrence between substance use disorder (SUD) and other psychiatric disorders is complex and can take different forms and directions.
- Motivation, opportunity, and capability are important components that promote addiction as well as the maintenance and severity of addictive behaviors.
- Working on motivation (e.g., using Motivational Interviewing) and flexibly adapt to the patient's cognitive and emotional functioning is crucial to assess SUD and devise intervention strategies in forensic settings.

Introduction

Substance use, abuse, and disorder (here: SU/SA/SUD) is one of the most important risk factors for committing violent crimes and is represented in several of the

M. Hildebrand Karlén (✉)
Department of Psychology, University of Gothenburg, Gothenburg, Sweden
e-mail: malin.karlen@psy.gu.se

Department of Psychiatry and Neurochemistry, Centre of Ethics, Law and Mental Health (CELAM), Institute of Neuroscience and Physiology, The Sahlgrenska Academy at University of Gothenburg, Gothenburg, Sweden

The National Board of Forensic Medicine, Department for Forensic Psychiatry, Hisings Backa, Sweden

C. Garofalo and J. J. Sijtsema (eds.), *Clinical Forensic Psychology*,
https://doi.org/10.1007/978-3-030-80882-2_17

most commonly used risk assessment instruments (e.g., HCR-20: Douglas et al., 2013; LSI-R; Andrews & Bonta, 1995). In combination with severe mental disorder, research has also shown that these factors create a negative synergy which in turn make the affected violent offenders harder to treat (Fazel et al., 2009; Pickard & Fazel, 2009). Since relapse in SUD increases the risk of relapse in violent crime after release from forensic psychiatric care, it is vital important to correctly recognize, assess, and treat SUD within this context.

The present chapter covers three main areas. First, the different kinds of psychiatric co-morbidity that research has shown relevant to forensic psychiatric care are outlined, and when applicable, how this can relate to SUD characteristics. Second, an outline is given of how to assess SUD in this group, and third, what kinds of SUD-treatment options research has indicated suitable in this patient-group.

SUD and Psychiatric Co-Morbidity

Persons with serious mental disorders are more at risk for developing SUD, and have more difficulty to recover from this, for several reasons. Psychiatric co-morbidity can impair ability to benefit from generalized treatment models for SUD, making it important to account for psychiatric profile within SUD-treatment (NIDA, 2014; SAMHSA, 2020). In the present section, different types of psychiatric co-morbidity with relevance for assessment and treatment within forensic psychiatric care are summarized.

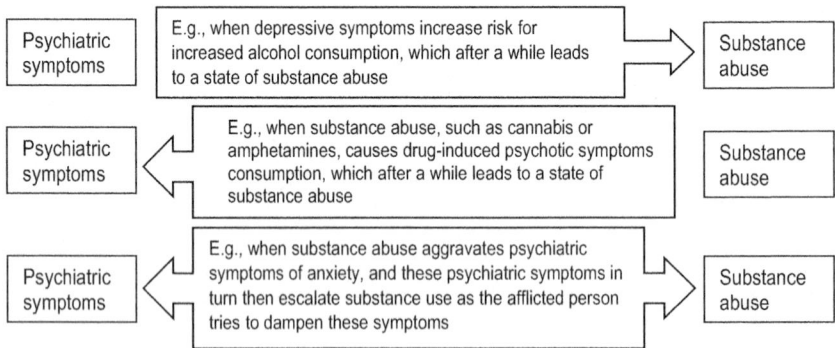

Fig. 1 Examples of how substance abuse can create, maintain, and act in synergy with psychiatric symptoms

Different Kinds of Co-Morbid Psychiatric Diagnoses Relevant to Forensic Psychiatric Care

Regarding SUD among forensic patients, the most frequent psychiatric comorbidities are personality disorders and schizophrenia (Dittman, 1996). First, regarding schizophrenia, lifetime SUD prevalence has been estimated to 55% (Kerner, 2015), and for persons with severe psychotic disorders, the risk of SUD has been shown elevated approximately 4 times (both regarding heavy and recreational use of alcohol and cannabis, see Hartz et al., 2014). Substance abuse by persons with schizophrenia increases risk of violent behavior, may worsen disease course and decrease medication adherence (SAMHSA, 2020).

Second, personality disorders and SUD is also a common profile in forensic psychiatric care (often also combined with some kind of psychotic disorder). The personality disorder/SUD-combination has been related to greater symptom load, to higher SUD-treatment dropout and greater likelihood of other psychiatric disorders (SAMHSA, 2020). Regarding borderline personality disorder (BPD), SUD is common (Chapter 12). Approx. 45% of persons with BPD have a current SUD and approx. 75% have a lifetime prevalence of SUD (Trull et al., 2018). Regarding antisocial personality disorder (ASPD) and SUD, this group has shown higher rates of aggression, impulsivity, and psychopathic traits than persons with only SUD (Alcorn et al., 2013) (Chapter 11). In treatment, due to the stigma surrounding ASPD, it is important to work with a positive and empathetic attitude but also to stand firm in enforcing structure, rules, and boundaries of the therapeutic relationship (SAMHSA, 2020).

Third, for persons with affective disorders, persons with bipolar disorder type 1 have a lifetime prevalence of 65% for SUD, and this combination is related to more severe symptomatology, worse treatment outcomes, and greater suicide risk (SAMHSA, 2020). Also, severe depressive episodes (e.g., major depressive disorder) can include hallucinations and delusional negative perceptions of the self (e.g., as being all-evil). This state can be relevant to forensic psychiatric care when, for example, a person has attempted extended suicide where he/she has harmed others before trying to commit suicide. Persons with SUD and co-morbid depression usually display a higher symptom load, more suicidal ideation, and more additional forms of psychiatric co-morbidity. This group typically use a variety of drugs (incl. cannabis), despite that it may worsen their depressive state (Bahorik et al., 2018, cited in SAMHSA, 2020).

Fourth, persons with post-traumatic stress disorder (PTSD) and SUD can come into contact with forensic psychiatric care by, for example, being violent toward others based on delusional experience. This group often use substances to dampen anxiety (e.g., opiates, benzodiazepines), which with developing SUD, often blunts their emotional response. In treatment of persons with PTSD, or other forms of severe anxiety disorders, it is important that the person is able to manage their emotional reactions to engage in treatment. This could be managed by, for example, being especially observant when difficult issues have been addressed and if needed, then take short breaks.

Fifth, ADHD and SUD in combination has shown an elevated risk of several kinds of psychiatric co-morbidity (e.g., other developmental disorders, bipolar disorder, depression, personality disorders), and due to its neurodevelopmental aspects, could be relevant to forensic psychiatric care (Chapter 16). ADHD could complicate SUD-treatment due to the diagnosis' core characteristics hyperactivity and attention difficulties, resulting in problem to engage in therapy and sticking to long-term goals (Crunelle et al., 2018). Hence, treatment needs to accommodate for these characteristics (e.g., using shorter sessions and/or more short breaks, more help in structuring the day, etc.).

Summary. Several types of psychiatric problem profiles are relevant to consider and may have a substantial—but qualitatively very different—impact, on SUD assessment and treatment within forensic psychiatric care. Some types of psychiatric problems are more obvious in this setting (e.g., schizophrenia, antisocial personality disorder), but the impact of other kinds of problems (e.g., developmental disabilities of various kinds, trauma history) can be more difficult to discern but are important to consider to adapt treatment accurately. Therefore, it is important to perform an exploratory and nuanced assessment of the persons psychiatric characteristics and level of functioning before treatment is initiated.

How to Assess SUD Within Psychiatric Co-Morbid Populations

It is important to recognize that addiction is a matter of degree, not a matter of 'present or not present', and that two aspects can illustrate the degree of addiction: the strength of the motivational forces in operation and the extent of harm that is involved (see West, 2013). According to West (2013) there are three main components that promote addiction and the maintenance of addictive behaviors:

motivation, opportunity, and *capability*. These individual and contextual components act upon the strength and the severity of addiction and are areas that should be assessed in each case. Since the forensic patient group is heterogenous and more often than not has multiple psychiatric problems in addition to SU/SA/SUD, it is central that the assessment of the aspects of addiction outlined above is indeed exploratory (i.e., not at the outset focused on confirming the existence of a specific problem).

Within psychological assessment, multiple methods should be utilized (i.e., combining information from self-report, tests, observation, life-history data from records) to illustrate different aspects and consequences of the problems (see Bornstein, 2017 for an example of a general multi-method assessment structure). To prevent bias-driven assessments, this is especially important for the assessment of SUD among co-morbid patient groups. Many of the psychiatric diagnoses usually involved overlap symptomatically, and using a broad assessment focus (including functional interactions between psychiatric symptomatology and SUD), has been recommended (see Johns, 1997). The following areas have been emphasized for assessing SA/SUD among violent offenders with psychiatric co-morbidity (Johns, 1997): pre-existing psychopathology (e.g., schizophrenia, ASPD), type of substance used (e.g., alcohol, sedatives, stimulants), availability of alcohol/drugs, pattern of use, which effects that have been/still are desired, which behaviors that are related to acute/delayed substance effects for the person (for details, see Johns, 1997). According to SAMHSA's guidelines for screening and assessment of co-occurring disorders in the justice system (2019), there are certain problems that assessors need to be especially aware of with this group and try to accommodate for.

How to Enhance Assessment Accuracy and Treatment Matching

Several factors have been suggested to enhance accuracy of the obtained information in screening and assessment of SUD and co-morbid psychiatric disorders (SAMHSA, 2019). First, to obtain information from several independent sources and construct a time line, it is important to understand how the substance use and psychiatric problems have developed, how they have interacted in the past as well as how they are interacting now. On such a time line should be noted: (a) important aspects of the psychiatric disorder (e.g., first onset, periods of heighted symptom load, longer periods of less symptomatology, etc.), (b) important aspects of the SU history (e.g., first onset of drug use, drug use history in chronological order, longer drug-free periods, eventual drug-induced psychosis), and, most important for an integrated assessment, (c) analyze potential synergy between these two time lines. An example of this is an increased drug use of perhaps a certain kind of drug in periods of more severe psychiatric symptomatology, and less drug use in general (or other kinds of drug use patterns) in periods of less pronounced psychiatric problems. This information helps the assessor as well as the patient to understand psychological mechanisms increasing risk for drug use which is of importance to therapy, or how to attenuate them with appropriate psychopharmacological interventions. In other words, such an approach illustrates the internal and contextual motivational mechanisms aggravating SUD for the person in question.

To consider level of functioning (i.e., both cognitive and emotional) is another general important factor within assessment of this patient group. This could be done by psychologically adapting language and behavior, or adjusting the pace of introducing new elements in treatment, to the patient's cognitive level and emotional capacities. Related to these factors is the importance of building good rapport and establish a working relationship before initiating assessment. Motivational interviewing technique (MI) can be an effective model to work from with forensic groups (see Tafrate & Luther, 2014), although it should be noted that interventions often need to be adapted to match the patient's level of cognitive and emotional functioning. The core interventions of MI are to express empathy, avoid confrontation, support self-efficacy, and encourage behavior change (Miller & Rollnick, 2013), as well as to discover how SU/SA/SUD are at odds with life goals and offer alternative strategies to rehearse. Hence, the strategies within MI could be utilized to diminish the influence of dynamic risk factors and to work with the patient in discovering synergies between how the persons psychiatric problems and substance use pattern interact with his/her internal and external context in escalating risk for violent acts (see Tafrate et al., 2014).

Fact Square

Regarding assessment as preceding treatment matching for groups with SUD within the justice system, the following areas of information are important to consider (SAMHSA, 2019)

1. Consider criminal risk level and criminogenic needs and their respective contribution to increasing risk for recidivism—as well as be careful to not mix persons with low risk/low need with higher risk/need persons (see Chapter 27).

2. History of psychiatric problems, including SUD, and their previous treatment

3. Include how the psychiatric and substance use problems affect level of functioning and how these factors are related, as well as having interacted in the past to increase risk for committing crime

4. If there is a functional impairment as a consequence of the psychiatric problem profile that could affect the person's ability to take part in the treatment, both psychologically (e.g., ability to engage in the material) and practically (e.g., treatment is given at a venue the person due to his/her psychiatric or substance use problems cannot easily access, etc.)

5. How to help the client engage in prosocial activities, education and/or vocational training programs, cognitive restructuring (i.e., away from criminal attitudes), and if present, help with communicating with family and adjusting social context

For an accurate treatment matching, it is important to make a specific and nuanced assessment of risk factors for SUD relapse. Marlatt and Gordon's (1985, see also Marlatt, 1996) general classification of risk situations can be a useful guideline, with differentiating between intrapersonal and interpersonal risk factors. Examples of intrapersonal factors are *negative emotional states* (e.g., anxiety, depression, helplessness, boredom, disappointment and insecurity), *negative physical states* (e.g., pain, sleep disturbance, muscle tension), and positive emotional states (e.g., good mood, feeling of success). Examples of interpersonal factors are conflict with others (e.g., critique, quarreling, feeling offended) and social pressure (e.g., other criticizing the person for not drinking, worry about being left out of the social group). For patients in forensic psychiatric care, both intrapersonal and interpersonal factors are often relevant to map out as closely as possible, since it illustrates risk situations for SUD relapse and offers insights of what to include in treatment. It should be noted that such mapping often requires complementary information (i.e., other sources than self-report), since deficits of meta-cognitive abilities as well as social cognition and memory are common in this patient group.

How to Treat SUD Within Forensic Psychiatric Populations

As previously noted, relapse in substance use after in-patient forensic psychiatric care is common and constitutes a major risk factor for criminal re-offending. Despite this, there is a common misconception that the forced abstinence during the hospital stay is enough to 'handle' the substance use problem (i.e., that SU no longer constitutes a problem after this period) (see also Schaefer et al., 2011 for a summary). Addiction is much more complicated than just the physiological adaptation and, hence, other aspects than just a long period of abstinence also need to be addressed during forensic psychiatric care. According to SAMHSA (2020), distinguishing features for SUD-treatment among persons with psychiatric co-morbidity within the justice-system in general include: (a) that the staff is trained in and experienced in treating both SUD and mental disorders; (b) that both disorders are treated as 'primary'; (c) that the treatments are integrated as far as possible; and (d) that treatment is comprehensive, flexible, and individualized as well as having a long-term focus (see also Eagle et al., 2019). It is also important to keep the treatment flexible and individualized, which entails continually working with the patient's current level of motivation to engage in integrated SUD/dual disorder treatment (see Mueser et al., 2003).

Detection: To Recognize Who Needs Treatment

That patients do not have access to alcohol or drugs during secure forensic psychiatric hospitals can lead to problems regarding detection of patients who need treatment for SUD as well as decrease their motivation to enter treatment (Schaefer et al., 2011). Who needs SUD-treatment is often clear from their psychiatric history, but suggestions have been made that engaging in certain behaviors during in-patient care, termed substance use paralleling behaviors, can be observed as markers for continuing problems to cope with the same kind of situations and emotions that previously had preceded substance use (Schaefer et al., 2011). Such substance use paralleling behaviors have helped meet the needs that were previously met through substance use, and could therefore be informative for treatment providers when working to increase the patient's motivation to enter treatment.

Examples of such types or behaviors are the following. Use of (a) other accessible substances (e.g., coffee, cigarettes, food, or medication abuse such as seeking extra medication to alter mental state rather than to alleviate experienced psychiatric symptoms), (b) engaging in similar behaviors (e.g., rolling cigarettes as similar to rolling joints), (c) engage in activities that alter state of consciousness (e.g., training hard). Shaefer et al. (2011) found that the motivations for substance use reported by forensic psychiatric in-patients were to have used drugs to escape from situations, to relieve boredom, to feel happier, to increase social confidence, and in addition, as self-medication, physical stimulation, to enhance creativity and experimentation. The relevance of these kinds of factors to maintaining SUD is confirmed by their presence in theories on addiction as summarized by West (2013).

General Treatment Interventions: Dual Disorder Treatment in Forensic Psychiatric Care

When creating addiction treatment units within forensic psychiatric hospitals (with the ultimate aim of reducing recidivism), an important focus has been the balance between treating co-morbid mental disorders and treating the addiction. In fact, McKeown et al. (1996) described their approach when conducting SUD-treatment within forensic psychiatric care as having more similarities with how a dual disorder units approach treatment than how addiction units do: by continuingly and simultaneously treating patients' mental disorders and the SUD. Regarding dual disorder treatment, it is important to note that the outcomes of sequential treatment (i.e., to treat either the SUD or psychiatric disorder first and the other afterward) have been equally poor as the outcomes of parallel treatment (i.e., that the person participates in two different treatments in parallel, typically provided by two service providers). This is because neither approach addresses the intertwined nature of SUD and psychiatric disorder (SAMHSA, 2019). This has also been shown for different kinds of psychiatric symptoms relevant to forensic psychiatry, such as psychosis (e.g., De Witte et al., 2014). According to a recent literature review of how addiction treatment should be managed within forensic psychiatric care (Eagle et al., 2019), an integrated treatment model is still what current studies on forensic psychiatric co-morbid populations recommend. However, more nuanced research is still largely lacking on how efficient different kinds of SUD-treatment methods are for patients with co-morbid disorders within the context of forensic psychiatric care. Until reliable evidence within this specific context is available, the focus in this part of the chapter is on general treatment factors that need consideration within integrated SUD/psychiatric disorder treatment given in in-patient forensic hospital care. Also, examples are given of more explorative methods which has been shown efficient in some initial studies in the forensic psychiatric care context.

Adapting Evidence-Based Treatment to Subgroups and Individual Factors

The heterogeneity of persons with SUD in forensic psychiatric care, both regarding psychiatric profiles, types of SA/SUD, and person-related factors (e.g., intellectual and affective functioning, motivational stage), makes standardized programs more problematic to use (see Eagle et al., 2019). Persons with SUD are in general considered a difficult group to treat therapeutically due to inclinations toward extreme emotional reactions, high co-morbidity rate, and difficulties regarding motivation and engaging in treatment—and forensic psychiatric patients with substance use in particular since they tend to even more often evade treatment (van der Kraan et al., 2014).

Within the forensic psychiatric SUD-population, subgroups have been identified, distinguishing patients with SU as a primary criminogenic risk factor (20% of their sample with SU directly connected to their crime/-s) from those with SU as a secondary risk factor (remaining 80%) (van der Kraan et al., 2014). In the first subgroup, primary treatment focus should be lifestyle variables related to their social network and user habits. This subgroup was characterized by a deeply rooted SU (i.e., young age at SU onset in this group) and had more SU-relapses during in-patient forensic treatment, despite a comparatively higher level of insight. In the second subgroup, focus on increasing level of insight was considered more important, since SU was often trivialized within this group. More insight in SU mechanisms has an effect on treatment motivation, an important influence on treatment effectiveness. van der Kraan et al. (2014) concluded that since these patients differed in important aspects, the respective groups might benefit from different treatment approaches focused on each group's specific needs. Other studies have found other subgroups among the 'triply troubled' (see Eriksson et al., 2013), and indicated the need to adapt treatment accordingly. Other factors indicating adaptation of treatment within the forensic psychiatric population to subgroups is risk of recidivism. Proper adaptation of intervention intensity and duration has been shown to be of important to reduce risk of recidivism, and subgroups with higher risk of recidivism need a higher treatment intensity (Andrews et al., 2006).

A basic, but useful, model for treatment goal-selection is the rehabilitation/habilitation-continuum. For some individuals (or subgroups), the primary goal of treatment should be rehabilitation, to re-establish a level of functioning that the person has previously had. A rehabilitation goal often requires that the patient has an intellectual functioning within approx. normal range and no severe and/or permanent cognitive disabilities, as well as enough affective stability to be able to visualize oneself in future scenarios, make action plans based on these in interaction with one's own characteristics and have a reasonable chance of following such plans even if under moderate affective load. If the person does not have these capacities, treatment must be adapted to accommodate for these issues (e.g., Glassmire et al., 2007), since several types of SUD-treatment methods then cannot be utilized (primarily those building in insight, see Glassmire et al., 2007). However, some aspects of such treatments can be incorporated in a treatment with a principal goal of habilitation with more focus on concrete skill-building and how to best utilize external support to prevent relapse. A goal of habilitation is then utilized when it is clear that the person does not (at least within the foreseeable future) have the cognitive capacity (e.g., intellectual disability, relatively low neuropsychiatric functioning level/has suffered brain damage, severe positive or negative cognitive symptoms of psychosis) or emotional management capacity (e.g., severe PTSD and severe borderline PD) to be able to recover lost capacities. Instead, an external support framework needs to be created for the person in important areas for him/her to be able to manage everyday life.

In sum, as in all SUD-treatments a vital first step to understanding what goal is reasonable to attain for the person in question, based on his/her psychiatric co-morbid profile, severity/complexity of SU/SA/SUD, and motivation. To increase motivation, it is important that the person is as closely involved in goal selection as possible, and that they perceive the goals as relevant, concrete, and clear throughout treatment. Goal negotiation/selection is a process during which an important treatment alliance is built and information gained regarding the state of the persons motivation, as well as ambivalence, toward participating in treatment. Hence, it is central that the person knows *why* it is so important that they should pursue treatment. Without patient involvement in this process, the risk of him/her developing an attitude of just following through the motions to keep everyone happy and to get out sooner is decreased (see SAMHSA, 2020).

Forensic Care Context-Factors of Importance for Treatment

One of the most important factors is whether there is a general treatment alliance between the staff at the clinic and the patient, which due to the mandatory context of forensic psychiatric care can be more difficult to create (i.e., the person has not voluntarily entered the treatment setting which can increase resistance). Initiating motivational interventions to make the person aware what help is available and presenting options that could be of interest for the patient. During this phase, it is important to clearly communicate the level of choice to the patient, something that is especially important within a forensic psychiatric care context. Treatment may in fact be mandatory before release from hospital, but even so, it is important to give the patient as much time as possible to enter treatment on their own terms to diminish the compulsive aspect of care as far as possible (see Tafrate et al., 2014). One of the central tenets of MI-based SUD-treatment is not to confront the person, since this evokes resistance, but rather to engage the person by evoking interest and helping him/her see the relevance and importance of treatment. To state the current circumstances of the restrictions and mandatory aspects of SUD-treatment within the forensic contest in a matter-of-fact manner can be done without a confronting attitude.

Working with motivation in early stages. Motivation is an important predictor of treatment outcome and justice-involved persons display high treatment dropout rates (see SAMHSA, 2019 for a summary). To be aware of the patient's current 'stage' within the dynamic changes of motivation, to monitor interest to engage in treatment is important to adapt treatment interventions accurately (Miller & Rollnick, 2013). However, for patients within forensic psychiatric care specifically, a considerable subgroup seems to need a treatment focus on increasing insight into how SU creates problems in their lives (see van der Kraan et al., 2014). Hence, treatment interventions for a considerable portion of this patient group should include active work with the initial motivational stages within the Prochaska, DiClemente, and Norcross model (1992). The model's initial stages entail *precontemplation, contemplation,* and the *initial preparation,* during which the patient is engaged in communication with the purpose of increasing his/her awareness of how SU/SUD is related to problems in his/her life. For example, that the lower inhibitions and more anxiety that SU/SUD brings into his/her life increases risk for him/her to act violent toward others and thorough this stands in the way of the person's own goals (e.g., to get a job). Even within forensic groups, research has shown that it is not necessary for patients initially to be motivated to provide effective interventions (NIDA, 2014), but for the patient to become more motivated to engage in treatment, it is necessary to provide motivational interventions continually with its intensity and degree adapted to the persons cognitive and affective characteristics as well as their current motivational level (see Tafrate et al., 2019; Mueser et al., 2003). To assess motivational level, standardized rating scales recommended for persons with co-morbid psychiatric problems can be used (e.g., *Substance Abuse Treatment Scale* (SATS; McHugo et al., 1995, recommended by SAMHSA, 2019). Given the success of the motivational framework for dual disorder treatment in other clinical settings (and the promise shown in many of the studies reviewed here), it is one intervention that deserves the allocation of sufficient resources on several levels of care provided, as well as to develop its evidence base within offender SUD-treatments where serious mental disorder is prevalent.

Examples of SUD-Treatment Methods Used Among Forensic Psychiatric Patients

Despite the group's psychiatric profile heterogeneity, many factors on the 'menu' of educational modules presented in previous research of forensic psychiatric patients treated for addiction/psychiatric co-morbidity (Eagle et al., 2019; McKeown et al., 1996) are similar to those recommended for dual disorder patient groups today (SAMHSA, 2019, 2020). Such modules can then be adapted to how the person is situated in relation to the rehabilitation/habilitation continuum, in other words: how to incorporate and adapt degrees of external support depending on the degree of the person's own lack of internal control.

Examples of these areas that often require interventions (both in practice and regarding psychoeducation) are social skills, increasing self-awareness (incl. meta-cognitive faculties), learning techniques for relaxation, problem solving, anger management and coping with stress as well as how to assert oneself in a flexible manner. Another example of a basic cognitive skills program is the *Reasoning & Rehabilitation program* (R&R; Cullen et al., 2012), which was shown to be effective in lowering the degree of violence and SU after 12 months post-treatment among male in-patients with both a psychotic disorder and a history of violence. This program follows a protocol and is highly structured, with the aim to increase social problem-solving skills and change styles of thinking. The eight core modules of R&R are: problem solving, assertiveness skills, social skills, negotiation skills, creative thinking, emotion management, values reasoning, and critical reasoning.

The *Relapse Prevention* program is a standardized treatment model that has been studied among forensic patients with a history of SA and severe mental disorder (Ritchie et al., 2011). The areas focused on in *Relapse prevention* are education on the effects and consequences of alcohol/drug-use, strengthening motivation to maintain behavioral change, identifying high-risk situations (incl. cues and triggers that maintain substance use), developing an individualized plan for coping (incl. avoidance and exposure strategies for handling high-risk situations for relapse), how to cope with triggers (incl. thoughts, feelings and situations), a support when implementing lifestyle changes to develop rewarding alternatives. It is important to note that even though this treatment was given in a group setting, individualized plans were made and video recordings of role-playing depicting rehearsal of the strategies were utilized so that the patients could observe themselves and reflect. Hence, these aspects illustrate how individualization and making the treatment more concrete can be employed, making the material easier to grasp for the patients, even within a 'standardized' treatment framework. This is also emphasized by Ritchie et al. (2011), stating that dual disorder treatment in forensic populations should be integrated by targeting substance use disorder, mental illness and offending behavior simultaneously, while targeting identified high-risk situations and developing personalized coping strategies and plans that follow the individual through the care system. However, it should also be noted that other studies have suggested that outcome studies on more educational and generalized programs targeting substance use relapse given in a group setting among forensic psychiatric patients have not been successful (e.g., showing no effect on objective tests such as urinalysis, see Milosevic et al., 2018). This suggests a greater emphasis for this group on motivational enhancement (due to this factor's major importance in substance use interventions, see DiClemente et al., 2008), and also to offer more support to prevent relapse (e.g., using booster sessions after concluded treatment). Examples of general dual disorder treatment models that SAMHSA (2020) presents for the forensic patient group that address the above requested motivational aspect, is *Integrated Dual Disorder Treatment* (IDDT, e.g., Mueser et al., 2003). This treatment model has been adapted to both an inpatient and outpatient setting. Another recommended treatment model (SAMHSA, 2020) is the *Risk-Need-Responsivity* model (see Andrews et al., 1990), which also has been argued to work well integrated with motivational interviewing for forensic groups (Tafrate et al., 2014).

Other evidence-based treatment interventions have been adapted specifically to forensic groups, such as *Forensic Assertive Community Treatment* (FACT). Building on the assertive community treatment model (ACT), FACT is adapted to persons involved in the justice system who have severe mental disorder and SU. The ACT-model has been modified to address criminogenic risks (i.e., likelihood to engage in future illegal behavior) and needs (i.e., factors such as SUD, lack of employment or livable wage that increase likelihood of re-offense). The target patient group for this kind of treatment should have a medium to high criminogenic risk as determined by validated risk assessment tools (see SAMHSA, PEP19-FACT-BR). Another example of a treatment program especially developed for forensic patients with SA and cognitive impairment is *Substance Abuse and Mental Illness program* (SAMI), which builds theoretically on a stages of change approach (see Glassmire et al., 2007).

Conclusions

For persons within forensic psychiatric care, SU/SA/SUD is an important risk factor for committing violent crimes, as well as worsening psychiatric symptoms. Therefore, both aspects, the substance use problems and the psychiatric problem profile, need to be explicitly addressed within forensic psychiatric care treatment to obtain better results regarding relapse. To treat SUD within this psychiatrically heterogenous patient group, a person-oriented approach is required when integrating treatment of SUD and the person's psychiatric problem profile. A flexible approach is needed when working with this patient group, working actively with enhancing the patient's motivation, adapting treatment interventions to his/her current level of motivation and cognitive and emotional functioning. As treatment progresses and the patient becomes more stable, treatment goals can be altered to accommodate the patient's cognitive and emotional development, while still maintaining focus on increasing patient awareness on how SUD and psychiatric problems interact in increasing the risk for him/her to commit violent crimes.

References

Alcorn, J. L., Gowin, J. L., Green, C. E., Swann, A. C., Moeller, F. G., & Lane, S. D. (2013). Aggression, impulsivity and psychopathic traits in combined antisocial personality disorder and substance use disorder. *Journal of Neuropsychiatry and Clinical Neuroscience, 25*, 229–232. https://doi.org/10.1176/appi.neuropsych.12030060

Andrews, D. A., & Bonta, J. (1995). *The level of service inventory–revised*. Toronto, Canada: Multi-Health Systems.

Andrews, D. A., Bonta, J., & Hoge, R. D. (1990). Classification for effective rehabilitation: Rediscovering psychology. *Criminal Justice and Behavior, 17*, 19–52.

Andrews, D. A, Bonta, J., & Wormith, J. S. (2006). The recent past and near future of risk and/or need assessment. *Crime & Delinquency, 52*, 7-27. https://doi.org/10.1177/001112 8705281756

Bornstein, R. F. (2017). Evidence-based psychological assessment. *Journal of Personality Assessment, 99*(4), 435–445. https://doi.org/10.1080/00223891.2016.1236343

Crunelle, C. L., van den Brink, W., Moggi, F., Konstenius, M., Franck, J., Levin, F. R., van de Glind, G., Demetrovics, Z., Coetzee, C., Luderer, M., & Schellekens, A. (2018). International consensus statement on screening, diagnosis and treatment of substance use disorder patients with comorbid attention deficit/hyperactivity disorder. ICASA consensus group Mathys, F. *European Addiction Research, 24*, 43–51. https://doi.org/10.1159/000487767

Cullen, A. E., Clarke, A. Y., Kuipers, E., Hodgins, S., Dean, K., & Fahy, T. (2012). A multisite randomized trial of a cognitive skills program for male mentally disordered offenders: Violence and antisocial behavior outcomes. *Journal of Consulting and Clinical Psychology, 80*, 1114–1120. https://doi.org/10.1037/a0030291

De Witte, N. A., Crunelle, C. L., Sabbe, B., Moggi, F., & Dom, G. (2014). Treatment for outpatients with comorbid schizophrenia and substance use disorders: A review. *European Addiction Research, 20*, 105–114. https://doi.org/10.1159/000355267

DiClemente, C. C., Nidecker, M., & Bellack, A. S. (2008). Motivation and the stages of change among individuals with severe mental illness and substance abuse disorders. *Journal of Substance Abuse Treatment, 34*, 25–35. https://doi.org/10.1016/j.jsat.2006.12.034

Dittmann, V. (1996). Substance abuse, mental disorders and crime: Comorbidity and multiaxial assessment in forensic psychiatry. *European Addiction Research, 2*, 3-10.

Douglas, K. S., Hart, S. D., Webster, C. D., & Belfrage, H. (2013). *HCR-20V3: Assessing risk of violence—User guide.* Burnaby, BC, Canada: Mental Health, Law, and Policy Institute, Simon Fraser University.

Eagle, K., Ma, T., & Sinclair, B. (2019). Integrated substance use rehabilitation in a secure forensic facility. *Journal of Forensic Practice, 21*, 50–60. https://doi.org/10.1108/JFP-09-2018-0037

European Monitoring Centre for Drugs and Drug Addiction/EMCDDA. (2017). *Health and social responses to drug problems: A European guide.* Publications Office of the European Union. https://doi.org/10.2810/244934

Eriksson, A., Alm, C., Palmstierna, T., Berman, A. H., Kristiansson, M., & Gumpert, C. H. (2013). Offenders with mental health problems and substance misuse: Cluster analysis based on the Addiction Severity Index version 6 (ASI-6). *Mental Health and Substance Use: Dual Diagnosis, 6*, 15–28.

Fazel, S., Bains, P., & Doll, H. (2006). Substance abuse and dependence in prisoners: A systematic review. *Addiction, 101*, 181–191. https://doi.org/10.1111/j.1360-0443.2006.01316.x

Fazel, S., Långström, N., Hjern, A., Grann, M., & Lichtenstein, P. (2009). Schizophrenia, substance abuse, and violent crime. *Journal of the American Medical Association, 301*, 2016–2023. https://doi.org/10.1001/jama.2010.1097

Glassmire, D. M., Welsh, R. K., & Clevenger, J. K. (2007). The development of a substance abuse treatment program for forensic patients with cognitive impairment. *Journal of Addictions and Offender Counseling, 27*, 66–81.

Hare, R. D. (2003). *The Hare psychopathy checklist —revised* (2nd ed). Multi-Health Systems.

Hartz, S. M., Pato, C. N., Medeiros, H., Cavazos-Rehg, P., Sobell, J. L., Knowles, J. A., Bierut, L. J., & Pato, M. T. (2014). Genomic Psychiatry Cohort Consortium. Comorbidity of severe psychotic disorders with measures of substance use. *JAMA Psychiatry, 71*(3), 248–54. https://doi.org/10.1001/jamapsychiatry.2013.3726

Johns, A. (1997). Substance misuse: A primary risk and a major problem of comorbidity. *International Review of Psychiatry, 9*, 233–241. https://doi.org/10.1080/09540269775448

Kerner, B. (2015). Comorbid substance use disorders in schizophrenia: A latent class approach. *Psychiatry Research*, *225*, 395–401. https://doi.org/10.1016/j.psychres.2014.12.006

Marlatt, G. A., & Gordon, J. R., (1985). *Relapse prevention: Maintenance strategies in the treatment of addictive behaviors*. Guilford Press.

Marlatt, G. A. (1996). Taxonomy of high-risk situations for alcohol relapse: Evolution and development of a cognitive-behavioral model. *Addiction*, *91*, 37–49.

McHugo, G. J., Drake, R. E., Burton, H. L., & Ackerson, T. H. (1995). A scale for assessing the stage of substance abuse treatment in persons with severe mental illness. *Journal of Nervous and Mental Disease*, *183*(12), 762–767. https://doi.org/10.1097/00005053-199512000-00006

McKeown, O., Forshaw, D. M., McGauley, G., Fitzpatrick, J., & Roscoe, J. (1996). Forensic addictive behaviours unit: A case study (part I). *Journal of Substance Misuse*, *1*(1), 27–31. https://doi.org/10.3109/14659899609094716

Miller, W. R., & Rollnick, S. (2013). *Motivational interviewing: Helping people change* (3rd ed.). Guilford Press.

Milosevic, A., Ahmed, A. G., Adamson, D., Michel, S. F., Rodrigues, N., & Seto, M. C. (2018). Evaluation of a substance use treatment program for forensic psychiatric inpatients, *Journal of Substance Use*, *23*, 640–647. https://doi.org/10.1080/14659891.2018.1489006

Mueser, K. T., Noordsy, D. L., Drake, R. E., & Fox, L. (2003). *Integrated treatment for dual disorders: A guide to effective practice*. New York: Guilford Publications, Inc

National Institute of Drug Abuse. (2014). *Principles of drug abuse treatment for criminal justice populations: A research-based guide* (NIH: Publication No. 11-5316).

Pickard, H., & Fazel, S. (2009). Substance abuse as a factor for violence in mental illness: Some implications for forensic psychiatric practice and clinical ethics. *Current Opinion in Psychiatry*, *26*, 349–354. https://doi.org/10.1097/YCO.0b013e328361e798

Prochaska, J. O., DiClemente, C. C., & Norcross, J. C. (1992). In search of how people change: Applications to addictive behaviors. *American Psychologist*, *47*, 1102–1114. https://doi.org/10.1037/0003-066X.47.9.1102

Ritchie, G., Weldon, S., Freeman, L., MacPherson, G., & Davies, K. (2011). Outcomes of a drug and alcohol relapse prevention program in a population of mentally disordered offenders. *British Journal of Forensic Practice*, *13*, 32–43. https://doi.org/10.5042/bjfp.2011.004832

Schaefer, R., Daffern, M., & Ferguson, A. M. (2011). The prevalence and manifestation of substance use paralleling behaviours in a secure forensic psychiatric hospital. *Mental Health and Substance Use: Dual Diagnosis*, *4*, 327–339. https://doi.org/10.1080/17523281.2011.598464

Substance Abuse and Mental Health Services Administration. (2020). *Substance use disorder treatment for people with co-occurring disorders*. Treatment Improvement Protocol (TIP) Series, No. 42. SAMHSA Publication No. PEP20-02-01-004. Rockville, MD: Substance Abuse and Mental Health Services Administration.

Tafrate, R. J., & Luther, J. D. (2014). Integrating motivational interviewing with forensic CBT. In R. Chip Tafrate & D. Mitchell (Eds.), *Forensic CBT: A Handbook for Clinical Practice* (pp. 411–435). https://doi.org/10.1002/9781118589878.ch20

Tafrate, R. C., Hogan, T., & Mitchell, D. (2019). Integrating motivational interviewing with risk-need-responsivity-based practice in community corrections: Collaboratively focusing on what matters most. In D. L. L. Polaschek, A. Day & C. R. Hollin (Eds.), *The Wiley International Handbook of Correctional Psychology* (1st ed.). John Wiley & Sons Ltd.

Tafrate, R. C., Mitchell, D., & Novaco, R. (2014). Forensic CBT: Five recommendations for clinical practice and five topics in need of more attention. In R. Tafrate, & D. Mitchell (Eds.), *Forensic CBT: A handbook for clinical practice*(pp. 473–486). Chichester, UK: Wiley.

Trull, T. J., Freeman, L. K., Vebares, T. J., Choate, A. M., Helle, A. C., & Wycoff, A. M. (2018). Borderline personality disorder and substance use disorders: An updated review. *Borderline Personality Disorder and Emotion Dysregulation, 5*(15). https://doi.org/10.1186/s40479-018-0093-9

van der Kraan, J., Verkes, R. J., Goethals, K., Vissers, A., Brazil, I., & Bulten, E. (2014). Substance use disorders in forensic psychiatric patients. *International Journal of Law and Psychiatry, 37*, 155–159. https://doi.org/10.1016/j.ijlp.2013.11.009

West, R. (2013). *Models of addiction.* EMCDDA INSIGHTS. European Monitoring Centre for Drugs and Drug Addiction. Luxembourg: Publications Office of the European Union. https://doi.org/10.2810/99994

Further Reading

De Witte, N. A., Crunelle, C. L., Sabbe, B., Moggi, F., & Dom, G. (2014). Treatment for outpatients with comorbid schizophrenia and substance use disorders: A review. *European Addiction Research, 20*, 105–114. https://doi.org/10.1159/000355267

Eagle, K., Ma, T., & Sinclair, B. (2019). Integrated substance use rehabilitation in a secure forensic facility. *Journal of Forensic Practice, 21*, 50–60. https://doi.org/10.1108/JFP-09-2018-0037

Fazel, S., Långström, N., Hjern, A., Grann, M., & Lichtenstein, P. (2009). Schizophrenia, substance abuse, and violent crime. *Journal of the American Medical Association, 301*, 2016–2023. https://doi.org/10.1001/jama.2010.1097

Pickard, H., & Fazel, S. (2009). Substance abuse as a factor for violence in mental illness: Some implications for forensic psychiatric practice and clinical ethics. *Current Opinion in Psychiatry, 26*, 349–354. https://doi.org/10.1097/YCO.0b013e328361e798

West, R. (2013). *Models of addiction.* EMCDDA INSIGHTS. European Monitoring Centre for Drugs and Drug Addiction, Luxembourg: Publications Office of the European Union. https://doi.org/10.2810/99994

Offenders with Intellectual and Developmental Disabilities

18

John L. Taylor

Key Points

- The relationship between IQ and offending is curvilinear, with negative associations at very low and very high levels of IQ
- the prevalence of intellectual disabilities in forensic populations vary widely depending on location, assessment, and sampling methods
- recidivism rates among offenders with intellectual disabilities are comparable or lower than those of offenders without intellectual disabilities
- autism spectrum disorder is frequently comorbid with intellectual disabilities, and is not linked with an increase in offending rates
- therapeutic interventions for sexual offenses, aggression, firesetting and alcohol-related offending require adaptations to target patients with intellectual disabilities.

Introduction

The present chapter begins by outlining historical perspectives on and the relationship between intellectual disability and offending behaviour along with the impact on policies for the care and treatment of people in this population.

J. L. Taylor (✉)
Northumbria University Newcastle, Newcstle upon Tyne, UK
e-mail: john.taylor@cntw.nhs.uk

Cumbria, Northumberland, Tyne & Wear NHS Foundation Trust,
Newcastle upon Tyne, UK

© The Author(s), under exclusive license to Springer Nature Switzerland AG 2022   339
C. Garofalo and J. J. Sijtsema (eds.), *Clinical Forensic Psychology*,
https://doi.org/10.1007/978-3-030-80882-2_18

Next, the chapter describes the prevalence of intellectual disabilities among offenders and the influence of intellectual disabilities for recidivism. Further, the relationship between offending behaviour and autism spectrum disorder is presented. Finally, the chapter describes in detail therapeutic approaches for treatment of offenders with intellectual disabilities, across different types of offending behaviour.

Historical Associations Between Intellectual Functioning and Offending Behaviour

In the nineteenth century, a causal association between low intelligence and criminality was suggested by key figures at that time (Scheerenberger, 1983). The presumed association between low intelligence and crime persisted well into the twentieth century. Terman (1911), a pioneer of psychometric testing, wrote that: '[t]here is no investigator who denies the fearful role of mental deficiency in the production of vice, crime and delinquency… not all criminals are feeble minded but all feeble minded are at least potential criminals' (p. 11).

Setting aside this historical association, it would seem that after controlling for socio-economic status there is a clear relationship between offending behaviour and lower intellectual functioning (e.g. Farrington, 1995; Goodman et al., 1995; Moffit et al., 1991). When studies are extended to include people with IQs below 80–85, however, the relationship does not appear to be simple. For example, Mears and Cochran (2013) reported data from the National Longitudinal Survey of Youth project in the US that indicated that the relationship between IQ and offending is curvilinear with lower IQs (<85) associated with lower levels of offending. The notion that intellectual disability (ID) is a significant risk factor for offending behaviour has been robustly critiqued (e.g. Lindsay & Dernevik, 2013; Taylor & Lindsay, 2018), but nonetheless this misattribution continues to be made. A recent example was provided by a study by Nixon et al. (2017) who used a data-linking approach to investigate the rates of commission and victimisation of offending behaviour in Victoria, Australia. They compared over 2,000 people with ID and criminal charge histories with more than 4,000 non-ID offenders. It was reported that people with ID were twice as likely to have had a criminal charge against them when compared to the non-disabled group. This finding would appear to support that ID is associated with higher rates of offending. However, as the authors included people with ID who had been *charged* with an offence and compared these data to non-disabled people in the community who had been *convicted* they were clearly not comparing like-with-like.

The assumed historical association between criminality and ID resulted in tens of thousands of people with ID being subjected to lifelong segregation in isolated asylums and colonies during the early-mid-twentieth century. Despite the influence of the deinstitutionalisation movement during the late twentieth century, the linkage of ID with delinquent behaviour continues to have an impact on the care and treatment of people with ID. For example, UK government data show that a disproportionate number of people with intellectual disabilities (7.7%) are compulsorily detained in hospitals under the Mental Health Act 1983 in England due to 'abnormally aggressive' or 'seriously irresponsible' behaviour (Health & Social Care Information Centre, 2014). Further, the median length of stay for male inpatients with ID in National Health Service hospitals in England and Wales was five times greater (at 31 months) than that (5.8 months) for non-disabled male mental health inpatients (Care Quality Commission, 2011). The situation was even worse for female inpatients with ID; their median length of stay was 11 times longer than for non-disabled women mental health inpatients (31 months and 2.5 months respectively).

Prevalence and Recidivism

It is unclear whether people with ID commit more crime than those without disabilities or whether the nature and frequency of offending by people with ID differs from that committed by offenders in the general population. The ambiguity concerning these issues is due in large part to methodological problems in prevalence studies in this area (Hayes, 2018). A major source of variation of prevalence of offending reported across studies is the location of the study (community, prison-remand, prison-sentenced, hospital—high/medium/low secure) which can result in sampling bias and filtering effects. For example, as people with mild/borderline ID progress through the different stages of criminal justice system their cognitive impairments are more likely to be recognised resulting in them being clinically evaluated and diverted to health and social care services. The inclusion criteria used in prevalence studies also vary or are not clear and this can affect the rates obtained—particularly if people with borderline intelligence (IQ 70–85) are included. Further, the method used to identify ID (standardised IQ test vs. screening test vs. educational history vs. clinical assessment) can have a significant impact.

These methodological issues are well illustrated in the research literature concerning the prevalence of offenders with intellectual disabilities in prisons compared with the approximately 2% we would expect to see in the general population (assuming a normal distribution). Crocker et al. (2007) assessed pre-trial prisoners in Montreal, Canada using selected sub-scales of a standardised ability measure and reported that 18.9% were in the ID range. Søndenaa et al. (2008) used an IQ screening assessment with a sample of prisoners in Norway and found that 10.8% fell in the ID range; while Fazel et al. (2008) reviewed 10 high quality studies of prevalence of ID in prisons (remand and sentenced) conducted between 1988 and 1997 in five common law countries and reported rates of between 0 and 2.9%. These findings contrast starkly with a study of prisoners by Holland and Persson (2011) in Victoria, Australia in which they found a prevalence of less than 1.3% using the Wechsler Adult Intelligence Scale. Furthermore, the results of a study of 389 remand prisoners in Scotland indicated that less than 0.5% of those assessed had an ID (Davidson et al., 1995). It is thus difficult to reconcile these findings and not conclude that the location, assessment and sampling methods account, in large part, for the variance observed.

Studies of recidivism rates for offenders with ID are affected by similar methodological problems. The rates reported tend to be high but vary significantly depending on research setting, procedures and definitions of re-offending used (Linhorst et al., 2003). For example, Lund (1990) found a re-offending rate of 67–72% in a follow-up study involving 155 Danish offenders with ID who had been detained on statutory orders—while Klimecki et al. (1994) reported a re-offending rate of 41.3% for 75 released prisoners with ID in Victoria, Australia. Linhorst et al. (2003) reported that 25% of 252 offenders with developmental disabilities who completed a case management community programme were re-arrested within a six-month period following case closure; 43% of those who dropped out of the programme were re-arrested during the same period.

Due to the lack of controlled studies involving ID and non-disabled offenders it is difficult to make direct comparisons of recidivism rates. There is some suggestion, however, that recidivism rates for offenders with ID are similar or even lower compared to those for populations of general offenders. Gray et al. (2007), for example, conducted a two year follow-up of 145 offenders with ID and 996 non-disabled offenders, all discharged from independent sector hospitals in the UK. The ID group had a lower rate of reconviction for violent offences after two years (4.8%) than the non-disabled group (11.2%). This trend held also true for general offences (9.7% and 18.7% for the respective groups).

Offenders with Autism Spectrum Disorders

Autistic spectrum disorders (ASD) and ID often co-occur. It has been estimated that 40–60% of people with ASD also have ID (McKenzie et al., 2016). ASD are a group of pervasive neurodevelopmental disorders characterised by impairments in social interaction, social communication and social imagination. Asperger's syndrome is a less severe form of autism without significant intellectual impairment.

Several UK studies have reported elevated prevalence of ASD in secure hospital populations (Hare et al., 1999; Scragg & Shah, 1994) and in prison (Hawes, 2003). Studies involving young offenders have also indicated high rates of ASD in this population in Sweden (Siponmaa et al., 2001) and Japan (Kumagami & Matsuura, 2009). Despite the apparent overrepresentation of people with ASD in criminal justice and secure hospital settings, research in other settings, and in community studies in particular, suggests that people with ASD offend not more frequently than the general population. A Danish study found that people with ASD offended at a significantly lower rate than those in a typically developing control group (Mouridsen et al., 2008). In Austria, Hippler et al. (2010) reported that a group of people with Asperger's syndrome offended at the same rate (under 2%) compared with a general population sample.

The crimes carried out by people with ASD are varied. Freckelton (2009), in a review of court decisions, found that people with ASD disproportionately committed arson, computer, stalking and sexual offences. It has been proposed that a different pattern of offending by people with ASD reflects specific deficits such as sensory preoccupations, poor social awareness, lack of understanding of others' feelings and deficits in theory of mind. Thus offences involving sexual interest (non-contact sex offending), stalking, firesetting and violent offences motivated by a lack of interpersonal understanding may be more common in this group. In a UK study comparing the offending behaviour of 47 people with ASD and 230 with IDD referred to community and secure services, Lindsay et al. (2014) did not, however, find that the offending behaviour of the ASD group reflected any of these patterns.

In a systematic review of 22 studies concerning people with ASD in the criminal justice system, King and Murphy (2014) concluded that evidence available indicates that people with ASD are not over-represented in the criminal justice system, do not commit more crime or different types of offenses than others.

In summary, there is a good deal of variability in the findings of studies that have considered rates of offending associated with ASD that is likely related to differences in the methodologies utilised, practices across jurisdictions, diagnostic criteria applied, and populations sampled. It would appear, however, that in general people with ASD (especially childhood autism and atypical autism) commit crime at a lower rate than people in the general population, and those with Asperger's syndrome offend at about the same rate as those in the general population. The limited research available currently does not indicate that people with ASD are more likely to commit certain types of crime compared with non-ASD or ID offenders. Despite the restricted evidence available, there is work going on to develop assessment, formulation and management approaches especially designed for offenders with ASD (see Gomez et al., 2018 for an overview).

Therapeutic Interventions

Sex Offender Attitudes and Behaviour

In the ID field, multi-component sex offender treatment programmes (SOTP) have been adapted and used as the basis for a number of group evaluations. These include the influential Sex Offender Treatment Services Collaborative (SOTSEC-ID) programme (Heaton & Murphy, 2013; Murphy et al., 2010). Murphy et al. (2010) conducted a treatment study involving 46 male sex offenders with ID who were living in community and/or secure settings in the UK. They found that sexual knowledge, victim empathy and cognitive distortions improved significantly following treatment, however, only treatment gains on sexual knowledge and cognitive distortion measures were maintained at 6-month follow-up.

In an extension of this study, involving a long term follow-up of 34 of the men who had completed SOTSEC-ID treatment, Heaton and Murphy (2013) reported that the improvements in sexual knowledge, empathy and cognitive distortions that occurred during treatment were maintained at follow-up. Thirty-two per cent (11/34) of the treated men had shown further sexually harmful behaviour, albeit of lesser severity than their original behaviours. Just seven of these 11 men were interviewed by the police and only two of the seven were convicted, an overall recidivism rate of 6%.

Lindsay et al. (2013) reported a 20-year follow-up of male sexual offenders, male non-sexual offenders and female offenders seen in community forensic ID services. All but a small number of participants continued to have unrestricted access to the community throughout the follow-up period during which time 16% of the sex offender cohort was reported to have carried out further sexually harmful behaviours. Lindsay et al. (2013) also recorded the number of incidents perpetrated by the recidivists over the follow-up period and found there was a 70% reduction in the number of incidents committed when comparing figures from two years prior to the referral and up to 20 years after referral.

Cohen and Harvey (2016) conducted a systematic review of 10 studies, published between 2006 and 2013 men with ID and harmful sexual behaviour who received adapted group CBT-based interventions in either community or secure settings, including prisons. There was evidence of pre- to post-treatment improvements on measures of sexual knowledge, victim empathy and cognitive distortions that were generally maintained at follow-up. The mean recidivism rate recorded across all 10 studies was 7.8% (although two studies did not record recidivism and the follow-up periods were short in some studies). All studies lacked control conditions thus limiting any conclusions that could be drawn about the efficacy of these interventions. In further reviews of psychological interventions of sex offenders with ID, Jones and Chaplin (2017) and Marotta (2017) reported findings and conclusions that were very similar to those of Cohen and Harvey.

Treatment for harmful sexual behaviour by adults with ID has developed significantly since the beginning of the twenty-first century. Comprehensive cognitive-behavioural approaches have been developed that address cognitive distortions, victim empathy, problem-solving, and promotion of social and self-regulation skills. However, more efficacy research is required that includes controlled designs, better definitions of ID and longer follow-up periods. At present, treatment for men with intellectual disabilities who display sexually aggressive behaviour can only be regarded as 'promising' (Lindsay et al., 2018).

Aggression and Violence

Taylor and colleagues have evaluated individual cognitive-behavioural anger treatment with detained patients with ID and significant histories of violence in a linked series of studies (Taylor & Novaco et al., 2002, 2004, 2005). Taylor and Novaco (2005) describe the 18-session treatment protocol in detail. It includes a six-session psycho-educational and motivational preparatory phase; followed by a 12-session treatment phase based on individual formulation of each participant's anger problems and needs, following the classical cognitive-behavioural stages of cognitive preparation, skills acquisition, skills rehearsal and then practice in vivo. These studies showed significant improvements on self-reported measures of anger disposition, reactivity and imaginal provocation following intervention in the treatment groups compared with scores for the control groups, and these differences were maintained for up to four-months following treatment.

The impact of these interventions on aggressive and violent behaviour has been investigated empirically on only a few occasions. Allan et al. (2001) and Lindsay et al. (2003) reported reductions in violence following a group intervention in case series of six women and six men respectively with violence convictions living in the community. In a larger study involving 47 people with ID and histories of aggression, Lindsay et al. (2004) showed that following a community group anger intervention 14% of participants had been aggressive during follow-up, compared with 45% of people in a control condition. Novaco and Taylor (2015) described an evaluation of the impact of the cognitive behavioural anger treatment described earlier (Taylor et al., 2005) on violent behaviour by 50 offenders with ID living in secure forensic hospital settings. Violence incident data were collected retrospectively from hospital case notes over a 24-month period. The total number of physical attacks against staff and patients fell from 319 in the12-months before treatment to 153 in the 12-month period following treatment. This 52% reduction in physical assaults was associated with measured reductions in anger over the course of treatment as indexed by several anger measures validated for use with this population.

In summary, there is an emerging research evidence base that cognitive behavioural anger interventions can be effective in the treatment of offenders with intellectual disabilities and histories of aggression and violence in terms of improvements on self-report and informant anger dependent measures that are associated with significant reductions in the number of violent incidents recorded following treatment.

Interventions for Firesetting Behaviour

It has been shown that firesetting accounts for only a small proportion of those referred to intellectual disability services due to offending and antisocial behaviour (O'Brien et al., 2010), the proportion of people in secure intellectual disability services with histories of firesetting is significant. Hogue et al. (2006) found that just over 21% of those detained in low/medium secure services in a UK study sample had an index offence of arson.

The research literature concerning treatment of firesetters with ID is limited, but promising. Rice and Chaplin (1979) and Clare et al. (1992) reported early studies incorporating skills-based interventions that appeared helpful in working with firesetters with intellectual disabilities. Hall et al. (2005) described the delivery of a 16-session group cognitive-behavioural approach to six male patients with ID and histories of fire-setting detained in a UK specialist NHS medium secure unit. Unfortunately, outcome data were not provided although most group participants were reported to have responded positively to the intervention in terms of their clinical presentations.

Taylor and Thorne et al. (2004) reported on a case series of four detained men with ID and convictions for arson offences who received a cognitive-behavioural, 40-session group-based intervention that involved work on offence cycles, education about the costs associated with setting fires, training of skills to enhance future coping with emotional problems associated with previous firesetting behaviour, and work on personalised plans to prevent relapse. The treatment successfully engaged these patients, all of whom completed the programme delivered over a period of four months. In a further series of case studies on six women with mild-borderline ID and histories of firesetting, Taylor et al. (2006) employed the same group intervention and found that scores on measures related to fire treatment targets improved following the intervention. All but one of the treatment group participants had been discharged to community placements at two year follow-up and there had been no reports of participants setting any fires or engaging in fire risk-related behaviour.

Using the same assessment and treatment approach as that used by Taylor and colleagues above, Taylor and Thorne et al. (2002) reported the outcomes for 14 men and women with ID and arson convictions. Following treatment, significant improvements were found on all fire-specific, anger, self-esteem and depression study measures. Finally, Taylor (2014) reported on a follow-up of 24 firesetters with ID who had completed a specialist group treatment programme. No arrests or convictions for firesetting behaviour had been recorded at four to 13 years post-treatment follow-up.

The results of these small and methodologically limited studies provide some limited encouragement and guidance to practitioners concerning the utility of group-based interventions for firesetting behaviour by people with intellectual disabilities.

Alcohol-Related Offending

Several studies conducted in Australia have reported very high levels of alcohol use and/or abuse among convicted offenders with ID (Hayes, 1996; Hayes & Carmody, 1990; Klimecki et al., 1994; McGillivray & Moore, 2001), suggesting that there is a clear association between the use of alcohol and offending behaviour in people with ID as has been found in non-ID offender populations. Studies in Ontario, Canada (Lunsky et al., 2011; Raina & Lunsky, 2010) however found much weaker associations between alcohol and substance misuse and offending behaviour in offenders with ID.

In the UK, Lindsay et al. (2013) carried out a 20-year follow-up of over 300 offenders with ID in a community forensic service. Similar to the studies in Ontario, Canada they found relatively low rates of previous alcohol problems associated with their offending behaviour. Study participants also reported relatively low rates of current alcohol problems. In a larger UK study involving 477 adults referred to services over a period of 12 months due to offending or offending-like behaviour, just 6% had an index offence involving alcohol or substance abuse.

Many offenders with ID who go through an alcohol treatment programme will also require a (concurrent) anger treatment intervention or emotional control treatment programme (see above). Alcohol treatment and anger programmes can share many components and cross-reference each other to good effect if they are well co-ordinated. Alcohol treatment will also commonly include components from social problem-solving and other offence-related programs. For example, where appropriate an alcohol abuse programme will address appropriate social and relationship skills. These adjunct components can be targeted at specific clients either in individual or group-based interventions so that the intervention is tailored and reflexive to the needs of the client(s).

Lindsay et al. (2014) developed a comprehensive 12-session programme for alcohol-related violence in offenders with ID that includes both group and individual components. Lindsay and colleagues described the programme's use in a range of community, residential and hospital settings. Early sessions are aimed at advancing knowledge on alcohol using procedures including games and quizzes. The sessions then progress to look at the effects that alcohol has on the body and brain, how the body metabolises alcohol and how long it takes for this process to occur. The relative costs of alcoholic and non-alcoholic drinks and the relative strengths of different beverages are discussed, and subsequent quizzes assess the extent of engagement and knowledge gain.

As the programme continues, sessions begin to assess the risk of alcohol misuse with exercises and discussions on its relationship to violence, conflict, money problems and stress. The theme of sensible drinking is developed with further exercises on reviewing safe limits, strategies for sensible drinking and asking for non-alcoholic drinks in a bar. The program can then become individualised so that each person can consider the effects of alcohol in relation to their own aims and goals over the next few months and years. Depending on the individual, the effect of alcohol on criminal behaviours such as violence, theft, inappropriate sexual behaviour can be reviewed. The final relapse prevention phase will include individual targets and ways of avoiding risk, and developing self-efficacy. Lindsay et al. (2014) set-out four case studies that illustrate the successful completion of their programme, with improvements on measures of alcohol knowledge, anxiety and depression along with reduced levels of alcohol consumption maintained at one-year follow-up.

In summary, it is not clear to what extent people with ID use or abuse alcohol compared with the general population, or the strength of the association of alcohol use/misuse with offending behaviour in this group. It would seem, however, that a significant number of people with ID who engage in, or at risk of offending behaviour do have difficulties with alcohol use. To date there has very little concerted effort at developing effective interventions to help offenders with ID to address their alcohol (and substance) misuse. This is surely an area requiring and worthy of urgent attention in future.

Conclusions

It remains unclear whether people with intellectual disabilities are over- or under-represented in offender populations, or whether offending is more prevalent among people with intellectual disabilities than the general population. There is a need for more rigorous research involving offenders with ID vs. non-ID offenders vs. non-offenders with ID in order to make direct comparisons of prevalence. This same requirement applies to recidivism studies, although some limited comparative research indicates that rates of re-offending are no higher and maybe lower among offenders with ID compared with non-ID offender groups.

Over the last 20 years or so there have been some significant developments in the treatment of offenders with ID based on interventions using cognitive behavioural approaches. The most significant treatment innovations have been in the field of anger treatment where programmes have been evaluated in a number of controlled studies. The raft of positive outcomes indicate that anger treatment can be incorporated into the general management of violent and aggressive offenders with intellectual disabilities with some confidence.

The second main area of development has been in the use of cognitive behavioural approaches with sex offenders with ID. There have been a number of, albeit methodologically weak studies, producing encouraging results, particularly in terms of potential harm reduction effects. The methodological weaknesses of these studies mean that the results should be viewed with caution.

In terms of interventions for firesetting behaviour and alcohol-related offending by people with ID, there have been a small number of studies and concerning cognitive behavioural programmes which have provided promising outcomes and guidance for practitioners. However, controlled evaluations of these interventions are certainly required. Some attention has started to be given to service-level interventions to ensure that detained offenders with ID are discharged from secure settings in a timely and safe manner.

For the future, larger, more powerful and better-designed controlled trials are needed to show if the effects of treatment interventions obtained to date can be replicated, and longer-term follow-up would help to evaluate the impact of psychological treatment gains on reducing future offending behaviour. A range of process issues including optimum length of treatment, the systematic involvement of carers, and relative costs require further investigation also.

References

Allan, R., Lindsay, W. R., Macleod, F., & Smith, A. H. W. (2001). Treatment of women with intellectual disabilities who have been involved with the criminal justice system for reasons of aggression. *Journal of Applied Research in Intellectual Disabilities, 14,* 340–347.

Care Quality Commission. (2011). *Count me in 2010: Results of the 2010 national census of inpatients and patients on supervised community treatment in mental health and learning disability services in England and Wales.* Care Quality Commission.

Clare, I. C. H., Murphy, G. H., Cox, D., & Chaplin, E. H. (1992). Assessment and treatment of firesetting: A single case investigation using a cognitive behavioural model. *Criminal Behaviour & Mental Health, 2,* 253–268.

Cohen, G., & Harvey, J. (2016). The use of psychological interventions for adult male sex offenders with a learning disability: A systematic review. *Journal of Sexual Aggression, 22,* 206–223.

Crocker, A. J., Cote, G., Toupin, J., & St-Onge, B. (2007). Rate and characteristics of men with an intellectual disability in pre-trial detention. *Journal of Intellectual and Developmental Disabilities, 32,* 143–152.

Davidson, M., Humphreys, M. S., Johnstone, E. C., & Owens, D. G. (1995). Prevalence of psychiatric morbidity among remand prisoners in Scotland. *British Journal of Psychiatry, 167,* 548–554.

Farrington, D. P. (1995). The development of offending and antisocial behaviour from childhood: Key findings from the Cambridge study in delinquent development. *Journal of Child Psychology & Psychiatry, 36,* 929–964.

Fazel, S., Xenitidis, K., & Powell, J. (2008). The prevalence of intellectual disabilities among 12,000 prisoners: A systematic review. *International Journal of Law and Psychiatry, 31,* 369–373.

Freckelton, I., & List, D. (2009). Asperger's disorder, criminal responsibility and criminal culpability. *Psychiatry, Psychology and Law, 16*(1), 16–40.

Gomez de la Cuesta, G., Taylor, J. L., & Breckon, S. (2018). Assessment and treatment of offenders with autistic spectrum disorders. In W. R. Lindsay & J. L Taylor (Eds.), *The*

Wiley handbook on offenders with intellectual and developmental disabilities: Research, training and practice (pp. 365–383). Wiley-Blackwell.

Goodman, R., Simonoff, E., & Stevenson, J. (1995). The impact of child IQ, parent IQ and sibling IQ on child and behaviour deviance scores. *Journal of Child Psychology & Psychiatry, 36*, 409–425.

Gray, N. S., Fitzgerald, S., Taylor, J., MacCulloch, M., & Snowden, R. (2007). Predicting future reconviction in offenders with intellectual disabilities: The predictive efficacy of the VRAG, PCL-SV and the HCR-20. *Psychological Assessment, 19*, 474–79.

Hall, I., Clayton, P., & Johnson, P. (2005). In T. Riding, C. Swann, & B. Swann (Eds.), *The handbook of forensic learning disabilities* (pp. 51–72). Radcliffe Publishing.

Hanson, R. K., & Thornton, D. (1999). *Static-99: improving actuarial risk assessments for sex offenders.* (User report 1999–02). Department of the Solicitor General of Canada.

Hare, D., Gould, J., Mills, R., & Wing, L. (1999). *A preliminary study of individuals with autistic spectrum disorders in three special hospitals in England.* Kent: Centre for Social and Communication Disorders: The National Autistic Society.

Hawes, V. (2003). Developmental disorders in prisoners volunteering for DSPD assessment. In C. Dale & L. Storey (Eds.), *The 2nd International conference on the care and treatment of offenders with learning disabilities, Preston.* UK.

Hayes, S. C. (1996). *People with an intellectual disability and criminal justice system: Two rural courts.* (Research Report Number 5). New South Wales Law Reform Commission.

Hayes, S. (2018). Criminal behavior and intellectual and developmental disabilities. In W. R. Lindsay & J. L Taylor (Eds.), *The Wiley handbook on offenders with intellectual and developmental disabilities: Research, training and practice* (pp. 21–37). Wiley-Blackwell.

Hayes, S. C., & Carmody, J. (1990). Helping those imprisoned for alcohol related crimes. In J. Vernon (Ed.), *Alcohol and crime: Proceedings of a conference held 4–6 April 1989* (pp. 179–186). Australian Institute of Criminology.

Health and Social Care Information Centre. (2014). *Inpatients formally detained in hospitals under the Mental Health Act 1983, and patients subject to community treatment: Annual report, England, 2013/14.* Health and Social Care Information Centre.

Heaton, K. M., & Murphy, G. H. (2013). Men with intellectual disabilities who have attended sex offender treatment groups: A follow-up. *Journal of Applied Research in Intellectual Disabilities, 26*, 489–500.

Heddell, F. (1980). *Accident of birth: Aspects of mental handicap.* British Broadcasting Corporation.

Hippler, K., Viding, E., Klicpera, C., & Happe, F. (2010). No increase in criminal convictions in Hans Asperger's original cohort. *Journal of Autism and Developmental Disorders, 40*(6), 774–780.

Holland, S., & Persson, P. (2011). Intellectual disability in the Victorian prison system: Characteristics of prisoners with an intellectual disability released from prison in 2003–2006. *Psychology, Crime and Law, 17*, 25–41.

Hogue, T., Steptoe, L., Taylor, J. L., Lindsay, W. R., Mooney, P., Pinkney, L., Johnston, S., Smith, A. H. W., & O'Brien, G. (2006). A comparison of offenders with intellectual disability across three levels of security. *Criminal Behaviour and Mental Health, 16*, 13–28.

Jones, E., & Chaplin, E. (2017). A systematic review of the effectiveness of psychological approaches in the treatment of sex offenders with intellectual disabilities. *Journal of Applied Research in Intellectual Disabilities.* https://doi.org/10.1111/jar.12345

King, C., & Murphy, G. H. (2014). A systematic review of people with autism spectrum disorder and the criminal justice system. *Journal of Autism and Developmental Disorders, 44*, 2717–2733.

Klimecki, M. R., Jenkinson, J., & Wilson, L. (1994). A study of recidivism among offenders with intellectual disability. *Australia & New Zealand Journal of Developmental Disabilities (journal of Intellectual & Developmental Disabilities), 19*, 209–219.

Kumagami, T., & Matsuura, N. (2009). Prevalence of pervasive developmental disorder in juvenile court cases in Japan. *The Journal of Forensic Psychiatry & Psychology, 20*(6), 974–987.

Lindsay, W. R., Allan, R., Macleod, F., Smart, N., & Smith, A. H. W. (2003). Long term treatment and management of violent tendencies of men with intellectual disabilities convicted of assault. *Mental Retardation, 41*, 47–56.

Lindsay, W. R., Allan, R., Parry, C., Macleod, F., Cottrell, J., Overend, H., & Smith, A. H. W. (2004). Anger and aggression in people with intellectual disabilities: Treatment and follow-up of consecutive referrals and a waiting list comparison. *Clinical Psychology & Psychotherapy, 11*, 225–264.

Lindsay and Dernevik. (2013). Risk and offenders with intellectual disabilities. *Criminal Behaviour and Mental Health, 23*, 151–157.

Lindsay, W. R., Smith, K. J., Tinsley, S., Macer, J., & Miller, S. (2014). A programme for alcohol related violence for offenders with intellectual disability. *Journal of Intellectual Disability and Offending Behaviour, 5*, 107–119.

Lindsay, W. R., Steptoe, L., Wallace, L., Haut, F., & Brewster, E. (2013). An evaluation and 20 year follow up of recidivism in a community intellectual disability service. *Criminal Behaviour and Mental Health, 23*, 138–149.

Lindsay, W. R., Taylor, J. L. & Murphy, G. H. (2018). The treatment and management of sex offenders. In W. R. Lindsay & J. L Taylor (Eds.), *The Wiley handbook on offenders with intellectual and developmental disabilities: Research, training and practice* (pp. 229–247). Wiley-Blackwell.

Linhorst, D. M., McCutchen, T. A., & Bennett, L. (2003). Recidivism among offenders with developmental disabilities participating in a case management programme. *Research in Developmental Disabilities, 24*, 210–230.

Lund, J. (1990). Mentally retarded criminal offenders in Denmark. *British Journal of Psychiatry, 156*, 726–731.

Lunsky, Y., Gracey, C., Koegl, C., Bradley, E., Durbin, J., & Raina, P. (2011). The clinical profile and service needs of psychiatric inpatients with intellectual disabilities and forensic involvement. *Psychology Crime and Law, 17*, 9–25.

Marotta, P. L. (2017). A systematic review of behavioral health interventions for sex offenders with intellectual disabilities. *Sexual Abuse, 29*, 148–185.

McGillivray, J. A., & Moore, M. R. (2001). Substance use by offenders with mild intellectual disability. *Journal of Intellectual & Developmental Disability, 26*, 297–310.

McKenzie, K., Milton, M., Smith, G., & Ouellette-Kuntz, H. (2016). *Systematic Review of the Prevalence and Incidence of Intellectual Disabilities: Current Trends and Issues, 3*, 104–115.

Mears, D. P., & Cochran, J. C. (2013). What is the effect of IQ on offending? *Criminal Justice and Behavior, 40*, 1280–1300.

Moffit, T. E., Gabrielli, W. F., Mednick, S. A., & Schulsinger, F. (1991). Socio-economic status, IQ and delinquency. *Journal of Abnormal Psychology, 90*, 152–157.

Mouridsen, S. E., Rich, B., Isager, T., & Nedergaard, N. J. (2008). Pervasive developmental disorders and criminal behaviour: A case control study. *International Journal of Offender Therapy and Comparative Criminology, 52*(2), 196–205.

Murphy, G. H., Sinclair, N., Hays, S.-J. (SOTSEC-ID). (2010). Effectiveness of group cognitive-behavioural treatment for men with intellectual disabilities at risk of sexual offending. *Journal of Applied Research in Intellectual Disabilities, 26*, 537–551.

NHS England. (2015). *Building the right support: A national plan to develop community services and close inpatient facilities for people with a learning disability and/or autism who display behaviour that challenges, including those with a mental health condition.* Available at https://www.england.nhs.uk/wp-content/uploads/2015/10/ld-nat-imp-plan-oct15.pdf

Nixon, M., Thomas, S., Daffern, M., & Ogloff, J. (2017). Estimating the risk of crime and victimisation in people with intellectual disability: A data-linkage study. *Social Psychiatry and Psychiatric Epidemiology, 52*. https://doi.org/10.1007/s00127-017-1371-3

Novaco, R. W., & Taylor, J. L. (2015). Reduction of assualtive behaviour following anger treatment of forensic hospital patients with intellectual disabilities. *Behaviour Research and Therapy, 65*, 52–59.

O'Brien, G., Taylor, J. L., Lindsay, W. R., Holland, A. J., Carson, D., Steptoe, L., et al. (2010). A multi-centre study of adults with learning disabilities referred to services for antisocial or offending behaviour: Demographic, individual, offending and service characteristics. *Journal of Learning Disabilities and Offending Behaviour, 1*(2), 5–15.

Raina, P., & Lunsky, Y. (2010). A comparison study of adults with intellectual disability and psychiatric disorder with and without forensic involvement. *Research in Developmental Disabilities, 31*, 218–223.

Rice, M. E., & Chaplin, T. C. (1979). Social skills training for hospitalised male arsonists. *Journal of Behaviour Therapy & Experimental Psychiatry, 10*, 105–108.

Scheerenberger, R. C. (1983). *A history of mental retardation.* Brooks.

Scragg, P., & Shah, A. (1994). Prevalence of asperger's syndrome in a secure hospital. *British Journal of Psychiatry, 165*(5), 679–682.

Seguin, E. (1846). *Traitement moral, hygiène et éducation des idiots et des autres enfants arriérés.* J.B. Bailliere.

Siponmaa, L., Kristiansson, M., Jonson, C., Nyden, A., & Gillberg, C. (2001). Juvenile and young adult mentally disordered offenders: The role of child neuropsychiatric disorders. *Journal of the American Academy of Psychiatry and the Law, 29*(4), 420–426.

Søndenaa, E., Rasmussen, K., Palmstierna, T, & Nøttestad J. (2008). The prevalence and nature of intellectual disability in Norwegian prisons. *Journal of Research in Intellectual Disabilities, 53*, 1129–1137.

Taylor, J. L. (2014). Roots, referrals, risks and remedies for offenders with intellectual disabilities. Paper presented to 'A Risky Business' BPS conference, October, 2014, University of Manchester, UK.

Taylor, J. L. (2019, September 18). *Developing discharge pathways for detained patients with intellectual disabilities.* Paper presented at the Forensic Dual Diagnosis Speciality Service Conference, Toronto, ON, Canada.

Taylor, J. L. & Lindsay, W. R. (2018). Offenders with intellectual and developmental disabilities: Future directions for research and development. In W. R. Lindsay & J. L Taylor (Eds.), *The Wiley handbook on offenders with intellectual and developmental disabilities: Research, training and practice* (pp. 453–471). Wiley-Blackwell.

Taylor, J. L., & Novaco, R. W. (2005). *Anger treatment for people with developmental disabilities: A theory, evidence and manual based approach.* Wiley.

Taylor, J. L., Novaco, R. W., Gillmer, B. T., Robertson, A., & Thorne, I. (2005). Individual cognitive-behavioural anger treatment for people with mild-borderline intellectual disabilities and histories of aggression: A controlled trial. *British Journal of Clinical Psychology, 44,* 367–382.

Taylor, J. L., Novaco, R. W., Gillmer, B., & Thorne, I. (2002). Cognitive-behavioural treatment of anger intensity among offenders with intellectual disabilities. *Journal of Applied Research in Intellectual Disabilities, 15,* 151–165.

Taylor, J. L., Novaco, R. W., Guinan, C., & Street, N. (2004). Development of an imaginal provocation test to evaluate treatment for anger problems in people with intellectual disabilities. *Clinical Psychology & Psychotherapy, 11,* 233–246.

Taylor, J. L., Robertson, A., Thorne, I., Belshaw, T., & Watson, A. (2006). Responses of female firesetters with mild and borderline intellectual disabilities to a group-based intervention. *Journal of Applied Research in Intellectual Disabilities, 19,* 179–190.

Taylor, J. L., Thorne, I., Robertson, A., & Avery, G. (2002). Evaluation of a group intervention for convicted arsonists with mild and borderline intellectual disabilities. *Criminal Behaviour and Mental Health, 12,* 282–293.

Taylor, J. L., Thorne, I., & Slavkin, M. (2004). Treatment of firesetters. In W. R. Lindsay, J. L. Taylor, & P. Sturmey (Eds.), *Offenders with developmental disabilities* (pp. 221–240). Wiley.

Terman, L. (1911). *The measurement of intelligence.* Houghton Mifflin.

Additional Reading

Lindsay, W. R. (2009). *The treatment of sex offenders with developmental disabilities: A practice workbook..* Wiley-Blackwell.

Lindsay, W. R., & Taylor, J. L. (2018). Assessment and treatment of alcohol related violence. In W. R. Lindsay & J. L Taylor (Eds.), *The Wiley handbook on offenders with intellectual and developmental disabilities: Research, training and practice* (pp. 289–307). Wiley-Blackwell.

Taylor, J. L., & Thorne, I. (2018). The assessment and treatment of fire setting behaviour. In W. R. Lindsay & J. L Taylor (Eds.), *The Wiley handbook on offenders with intellectual and developmental disabilities: Research, training and practice* (pp. 272–288). Wiley-Blackwell.

Part III
Offending Behaviors

Forms and Functions of Aggression

19

Morsal Khouwaga Yusoufzai and Jill Lobbestael

Key Points

- Aggression is any behavior directed toward another individual that is carried out with the proximate intent to cause harm. Additionally, the perpetrator must believe that the behavior will harm the target and that the target is motivated to avoid the behavior.
- Often a distinction is made between reactive (RA) and proactive (PA) aggression, which have differential psychological correlates. RA is hot-blooded, impulsive, and in retaliation to a perceived provocation, whereas PA is cold-blooded, deliberate, and has a goal other than harming the victim.
- Men are more likely to engage in direct forms of aggression, specifically physical aggression, than women. Women are more likely to engage in indirect forms of aggression.
- Three lifetime trajectories are found for physical aggression: stable low incidence, desisting moderate incidence, and stable high incidence. Two trajectories are found for indirect aggression: stable low incidence, and increasing high incidence.
- Many studies use the Reactive Proactive Aggression Questionnaire to measure aggression through self-report, or the Competitive Reaction Time Task to measure aggression behaviorally.

M. Khouwaga Yusoufzai (✉) · J. Lobbestael
Department of Clinical Psychological Science, Maastricht University, Maastricht,
The Netherlands
e-mail: k.yusoufzai@maastrichtuniversity.nl

© The Author(s), under exclusive license to Springer Nature Switzerland AG 2022   357
C. Garofalo and J. J. Sijtsema (eds.), *Clinical Forensic Psychology*,
https://doi.org/10.1007/978-3-030-80882-2_19

Introduction

The current chapter provides a description of aggression; its forms and functions; and its occurrence, correlates, and assessment. We start by outlining the definition of aggression, along with its further categorization into subtypes. Then, historical trends, sex differences, and lifetime trajectories are explained. Next, differential correlates of the reactive and proactive subtypes of aggression are outlined. These differential correlates support the utility of these subtypes of aggression, and lead to suggestions for concrete applications in clinical settings. Finally, methods of assessing aggression are described.

What Is Aggression?

The word "aggression" brings a number of images to mind; an angry face, a person hitting another person, or teenagers purposefully slamming their door or trashing their room after an argument with a parent. Aggression has many forms and functions, though academics typically define it as follows:

> Any behavior directed toward another individual that is carried out with the proximate (immediate) intent to cause harm. In addition, the perpetrator must believe that the behavior will harm the target and that the target is motivated to avoid the behavior. (Bushman & Anderson, 2001, p. 274)

In line with this definition, the current chapter focuses on interpersonal aggression. Aggression is a specific behavior that is part of the broader category of antisocial behavior. While all instances of aggression fall under antisocial behavior, not all instances of antisocial behavior are categorized as aggression. Violence is also part of the taxonomy of antisocial behavior, which is typically described as a specific form of aggression with extreme harm as its goal (Anderson & Bushman, 2002).

Then, there is the matter of categorizing specific forms of aggression. Usually, aggression is classified according to one of three dimensions: (i) direct or indirect, (ii) the manner in which it is expressed, and (iii) the motivation for the aggression.

Indirect aggression refers to covert forms of aggressive behavior where personal harm is inflicted via indirect means, such as damaging someone's social status or excluding someone (Björkqvist et al., 1992). Hence, the perpetrator is likely to avoid counter-aggression and to remain unidentified if possible. In contrast, direct aggression is visible and straightforward, and the perpetrator is easily identified (Salmivalli et al., 2000), for example when insulting another person in a confrontation. The categorization of aggression subtypes based on their expression forms includes verbal (harming another person through language), relational (harming another person's social relationships), and physical aggression (harming another person physically). Property destruction is another expression form of aggression, albeit not interpersonal.

In most scientific literature however, aggression is commonly classified according to its motivation, leading to the differentiation between reactive and proactive aggression. Reactive aggression (RA) refers to a hot-blooded and impulsive form of aggression that occurs in retaliation to perceived provocation. Other words used to describe this type of aggression include hostile or defensive aggression. This form of aggression has theoretical roots in the frustration–aggression model (originally posited by Dollard et al., 1939; later reformulated by Berkowitz, 1989), which states that any form of negative affect—and especially frustration—can activate anger-related feelings and thoughts, and will eventually lead to some tendency to aggress. Proactive aggression (PA) refers to a cold-blooded and premeditated form of aggression where the perpetrator has a goal other than harming the victim, such as obtaining resources or status. This form of aggression is also referred to as instrumental or offensive aggression. The distinction between RA and PA has been a topic of debate in aggression research. Specifically, it is sometimes seen as an outdated classification that is not particularly useful (Bushman & Anderson, 2001), because of the high overlap between the two forms of aggression: many aggressive behaviors are characterized by elements of both RA and PA. Furthermore, studies show considerable correlations between the two (see also Merk et al., 2005). Additionally, individuals are often found to show either predominantly RA or a combination of RA and PA: individuals engaging exclusively in PA are rare (Crapanzano et al., 2010; Lynam et al., 2006; Stickle et al., 2012). Nonetheless, clear differences between correlates of RA and PA demonstrate that these aggression subtypes do comprise distinct dimensions of aggression (see also Crick & Dodge, 1996; Poulin & Boivin, 2000; Raine et al., 2006), proving that both concepts are theoretically, scientifically, and most important, clinically, meaningful (see section "Differential Correlates of Reactive and Proactive Aggression").

Prevalence

To gain insight into the prevalence of aggression, we can look at historical trends in aggression. Extensive research (Pinker, 2011) has demonstrated a persistent decline in human violence in the last two millenia. This trend is supported by a large number of data sets, from homicide rates to socially sanctioned forms of violence such as slavery and cruelty to animals, to organized conflicts such as wars, genocides, and terrorist attacks. Although this perspective has drawn much criticism, with some pointing out a negligence of violence rates against women and girls (True, 2014), flaws in statistical methods (Cirillo & Taleb, 2016), and a Western-centric perspective (Micale & Dwyer, 2018), there is broad consensus regarding the decline in violence among historians and political scientists.

A second area of interest regarding aggression prevalence is that of sex differences. Typically, one may assume that men are more aggressive than women, though this has not been uniformly supported by data. One robust finding though is that men tend to engage more in direct forms of aggression compared to women, especially when it comes to physical aggression (Archer, 2004). Another difference, albeit less robust and smaller in size, is that proportionately, women tend to engage more in indirect forms of aggression than men (Archer, 2004; Card et al., 2008; Smith et al., 2009). The latter difference has been demonstrated across cultures in adolescents in Finland, Israel, Italy, and Poland (Österman et al., 1998).

A third indication of aggression prevalence can be found by looking at the lifetime trajectory of aggression. Generally, longitudinal studies have found three types of physical aggression trajectories. The first being an absence or low incidence of physical aggression starting in early toddlerhood, persisting through childhood and into adolescence (Campbell et al., 2006). The second trajectory reflects a moderate level of aggression starting in early toddlerhood, which usually desists in childhood and adolescence (Côté, 2007). The third trajectory shows stable high physical aggression incidences starting in early toddlerhood. The most prevalent developmental trajectory is one of declining use of physical aggression, with most children following either the moderate trajectory (occasional use of physical aggression in toddlerhood to infrequent use by age 11) or the low trajectory (infrequent use during toddlerhood to virtually no use by age 11) (Côté, 2007). Physical aggression seems to peak in toddlerhood, being part of most children's behavioral repertoire to at least some extent, after which occurrence declines (Côté, 2007; Nærde et al., 2014). A consistent minority of children, however, fall into the third category of stable and high incidence of physical aggression (Brame et al., 2001; Campbell et al., 2006; Cleverley et al., 2012; Côté, 2007; Maughan et al., 2000). Notably, boys are overrepresented in the high-stable physical aggression trajectory, whereas girls are more likely to follow the low-desisting trajectory (Cleverley et al., 2012).

For indirect aggression, studies found that development generally follows one of two trajectories starting between age 4 and 8: either a low and stable trajectory, or a high and increasing trajectory (Côté, 2007; Underwood et al., 2009; Vaillancourt et al., 2007). A slight majority of children seem to follow the low trajectory. Some studies also found a third trajectory of indirect aggression with a small minority (4.6–6.5%) falling into the most aggressive group, also starting in early childhood (4–8 years) and displaying indirect aggression into adolescence (Cleverley et al., 2012; Orpinas et al., 2015). Additionally, more girls than boys followed the high trajectory versus the low trajectory, although this sex gap closed in adulthood (Archer, 2000). Taken together, the developmental trajectory of physical aggression will show in most cases either a low stable or moderate desisting incidence, with a minority showing a high stable incidence, whereas differences in indirect aggression trajectories seem to be more evenly divided between low stable versus high increasing incidence.

Differential Correlates of Reactive and Proactive Aggression

It has become evident that multiple causal factors are involved in aggression: from biological factors such as genetic polymorphisms and abnormalities in brain function and -structure (Raine, 2008) (Chapter 3), to environmental factors such as malnutrition early in life (Liu et al., 2004), and exposure to aggression through television (Huesmann et al., 2003; though this is heavily debated—see also Bushman & Huesmann, 2006; Ferguson & Kilburn, 2009). Other causal factors in aggression include exposure through family violence (Litrownik et al., 2003), and interactions between genetic factors and social experiences (Provencal et al., 2015). Unfortunately, the two most widely recognized theoretical frameworks of aggression (i.e., the General Aggression Model [Anderson & Bushman, 2002], and the I^3 model of aggression [Slotter & Finkel, 2011]) do not provide specific information about the unique causes of RA and PA (see e.g., Ferguson & Dyck, 2012; Hsieh & Chen, 2017), and have been criticized for being too broad. Therefore, the current chapter provides an overview of the *correlates* of each subtype, as these have been the topic of extensive research. By shedding light on the differential correlates of RA versus PA, their dissociation and therefore their probable separate emergence, is stressed. Reviewing the literature, we can conclude that differences between RA and PA have been found in at least six different areas, which we outline below.

Regulation of Behavior, Emotion, and the Self

RA occurs in retaliation to perceived provocation and is characterized by a "hot" emotional state. In line with this definition, studies have repeatedly linked RA to deficits in the regulation of behavior and emotion. One study using parent-reports of clinically referred children found that when controlling for PA, RA was uniquely associated with poor self-regulation, which refers to the ability to control and change responses according to one's goals, often in an effortful manner (White et al., 2013). Another study using self-reports of detained girls found RA to be uniquely associated with poorly regulated emotion when controlling for PA (Marsee & Frick, 2007). Yet another study using self-reports of adolescent boys found RA to be uniquely associated with impulsivity when controlling for PA (Raine et al., 2006). Although studies have demonstrated that PA is also related to deficits in behavior and emotion regulation (e.g., Garofalo et al., 2020; Orobio de Castro et al., 2005; Zhang et al., 2017), support for this link is considerably less robust. In summary, consistent with its theoretical definition, RA seems to be characterized by poor behavioral-, emotion-, and self-regulation, whereas this does not seem to be a distinct characteristic of PA.

Psychopathology

Differences between RA and PA are found in general domains as well as specific forms of psychopathology. On the one hand, RA has been linked repeatedly to internalizing problems. For example, in one study that used parent- and teacher-reports of toddlers it was found that RA was uniquely associated with negative emotionality when controlling for PA (Vitaro et al., 2006). This finding is further supported by research in young adults, where self-reported RA was more strongly correlated to trait neuroticism, a personality feature implying stability and negative affectivity, as compared to self-reported PA (Miller & Lynam, 2006). Furthermore, a study using self-reports of adolescent boys, found that RA was uniquely associated with social anxiety when controlling for PA (Raine et al., 2006).

On the other hand, PA has repeatedly been linked to externalizing problems. For example, based on teacher-reports it was found that 12-year-old boys' PA uniquely predicted oppositional defiant disorder and conduct disorder problems (assessed by a structured interview) and self-reported delinquency at age 15 when controlling for RA (Vitaro et al., 1998). In another study of young adults, it was found that both self-reported RA and PA correlated significantly with violent crime and property crime, however, PA was more strongly related to substance use and property crime (Miller & Lynam, 2006). Moreover, in a longitudinal study using self-reports of adolescent males PA was found to be uniquely associated with adult binge drinking and indicators of antisocial behavior, such as violence and delinquency when controlling for RA (Fite et al., 2010).

Another difference between the aggression subtypes is found in their association with psychopathic traits, a personality constellation characterized by affective, interpersonal, and behavioral characteristics, such as shallow emotions, pathological lying, and impulsivity (Hare, 1996). One study using self-reports of detained adolescent girls found PA to be uniquely associated with callous-unemotional traits—a set of developmental precursor traits of adult psychopathy including lack of empathy and guilt, use of others for own gain—when controlling for RA (Marsee & Frick, 2007). Although psychopathy has been linked more often to PA than to RA (e.g., Cima & Raine, 2009), a review of the literature has demonstrated that both forms of aggression are in fact related to psychopathy (Blais et al., 2014). Interestingly, sub-characteristics of psychopathy have been demonstrated to be differentially related to the aggression subtypes. Specifically, the fearlessness and alienation characteristics of psychopathy are more strongly related to RA than to PA (Cima & Raine, 2009). The finding concerning the fearlessness characteristic seems surprising considering that PA is often associated with cold-bloodedness, and thus would be expected to be accompanied by a lack of strong emotions including fear. However, the tendency of the reactive aggressor to respond to a provocation is proposed as a possible explanation: here, a certain level of fearlessness is required, whereas PA can be planned and executed in such a way that there is nothing to fear by the aggressor. Taken together, although psychopathy is related to both PA and RA, dimensions of psychopathy seem to be differentially related to the aggression subtypes. Furthermore, RA is associated with internalizing problems such as anxiety and negative emotionality, whereas this association has not been found for PA. PA is (at least more strongly) associated with externalizing problems, such as delinquency and violence.

Cognitive Biases

Cognitive biases are often mentioned as contributing factors in aggression. For example, the Social Information Processing (SIP) model (Crick & Dodge, 1994) states that an aggressive person tends to make mistakes at one or more steps in the way they process social information, leading to aggression. Here, RA is explained as being caused in part by a deficit in the earlier stages of a person's SIP, specifically a hostile attribution bias. This bias refers to an aggressor's tendency to interpret the intentions of others as hostile under ambiguous circumstances (Milich & Dodge, 1984). For example, someone bumping into the aggressor in a busy street would be viewed by the aggressor as having been intentionally harmful, whereas someone without this particular bias would not think twice about it. The link between RA and a hostile attribution bias has been empirically validated repeatedly, in child samples using teacher-reports (Orobio de Castro et al., 2005), adult patient and non-patient samples using self-reports (Lobbestael et al., 2013), and prison samples using self-reports (Walters, 2007).

PA, however, seems to be associated with a deficit in the later stages of SIP, specifically in outcome expectancies of aggression. Someone with this deficit in outcome expectancies would be more likely to expect aggression to have some sort of favorable outcome (whether monetary, social, or otherwise). Accordingly, positive outcome expectancies for aggression have been linked to PA in a number of studies. A teacher report study found that primarily proactively aggressive children evaluated verbally and physically aggressive acts and their consequences as being significantly more positive than children who were not primarily proactively aggressive (Crick & Dodge, 1996). The latter was supported by another study of incarcerated adolescents, in which staff-reported PA was uniquely associated with positive outcome expectancies for aggression when controlling for RA (Smithmyer et al., 2000). Lastly, a study of incarcerated adults using self-reports of criminal cognition found that the proactive criminal thinking subscale of this measure predicted self-reported positive outcome expectancies for crime, which was measured by asking participants to rate a crime they had committed with respect to anticipated outcomes (Walters, 2007).

Taken together, the distinction between RA and PA is further supported by studies showing a clear difference in their association with deficits in distinct stages of SIP. RA is associated with a hostile attribution bias, whereas PA is associated with positive outcome expectancies for aggression.

Social Adjustment

Social adjustment refers to the ability to cope with the standards, demands, and restrictions of a society, and the ability to engage in satisfying interactions and relationships. One meta-analytic review of 42 studies of child samples found RA to be more strongly related to most indices of social adjustment than PA (Card & Little, 2006). Specifically, RA was more strongly related to low prosocial behavior, high peer rejection (being disliked by peers), and high peer victim-ization (being the target of peers' aggression). Another study in children using teacher-, parent-, peer-, and self-reports found RA, but not PA, to be consistently related to poor social skills (McAuliffe et al., 2006). In summary, RA seems to be characterized by more problems in social adjustment than PA.

Brain Function

Although relatively few studies have examined brain function in relation to RA and PA, some differences between the aggression subtypes in this area have been found. For example, one study of university students found brain stimulation in the right dorsolateral prefrontal cortex (a brain area implicated in emotional and cognitive processes generating avoidance motivation) to be associated with reductions in behaviorally measured PA, but not RA, in men (Dambacher et al., 2015). Another study of children found teacher-reported RA, but not PA, to be associated with a heightened hypothalamic pituitary adrenal axis (i.e., the central stress response system in the brain) reactivity (Lopez-Duran et al., 2009).

Genetic Influences

Similar to brain research, studies examining RA and PA specific genetic con-tributions are scarce. Nonetheless, some differences between the subtypes have been found. One study compared the contribution of genes to teacher-reported physical aggression in child twin pairs, and found distinct genetic effects (albeit small) to account for the variance in RA and PA (Brendgen et al., 2006; see also Waltes et al., 2016). A longitudinal study using parent-reports in a sample of twins found that continuity in RA across assessment points was mainly due to genetic and nonshared environmental influences (such as continuous exposure to harsh and threatening environments), whereas continuity in PA was mostly due to genetic influences (Tuvblad et al., 2009). Furthermore, the latter study revealed unique genetic variance for each aggression subtype during the later assessment in mid-adolescence, which indicates that the genetic distinction between RA and PA becomes more important as children develop. Further research is needed to fully elucidate the role of genes in RA and PA.

In summary, RA is characterized by a hostile emotional state with deficient behavior, poor emotion regulation, and co-occurring poor social adjustment and internalizing symptoms such as anxiety. PA, however, is characterized by less

Table 19.1 Correlates of reactive and proactive aggression

Reactive aggression	Proactive aggression
Poor self-regulation	Oppositional defiant disorder
Poor emotion-regulation	Conduct disorder
Impulsivity	Delinquency
Negative emotionality	Substance use
Neuroticism	Property crime
Social anxiety	Binge drinking
Hostile attribution bias	Antisocial behavior
Peer rejection	Callous-unemotional traits
Peer victimization	Positive outcome expectancies
Poor social skills	
Overactive hypothalamic–pituitary–adrenal axis response to stress	

Note This table provides an overview of the study findings mentioned in the current chapter regarding the differential characteristics of reactive (RA) and proactive aggression (PA). Characteristics that are more strongly correlated with RA as opposed to PA are placed under RA, and vice versa

prominent emotionality, a cold-blooded goal-oriented state, and positive outcome expectancies for aggression, co-occurring with externalizing behaviors such as delinquency. Table 19.1 provides a summary of the findings discussed in relation to correlates of RA and PA.

Clinical Relevance

Prevention and intervention efforts could benefit from the abovementioned findings by consciously targeting the specific characteristics and deficiencies implicated in either type of aggression, and by identifying at-risk children early in life. When treating a primarily reactively aggressive person for example, treatment could target cognitive biases, as was done in an earlier study demonstrating that intervention focused on altering hostile attributions was effective for reactively aggressive boys (Hudley & Graham, 1993). Furthermore, in light of the link between RA and social maladjustment, intervention efforts could target social skills in this subsample of aggressive individuals. Considering that exclusive use of PA is rare, interventions in proactively aggressive subsamples should target both aggression types: in addition to a focus on e.g., hostile attributions, operant techniques could be used where rewards are used as motivation, considering the positive outcome expectancies related to PA (see also Merk et al., 2005). If treatment of proactively aggressive subsamples is focused on RA-related corre-lates only, not all underlying causes are addressed, leaving lost opportunities in therapy. As research in this area progresses, and causal factors in both aggression subtypes are identified, intervention efforts can thus be tailored accordingly.

Assessment

The majority of studies use self-reports to assess RA and PA. One of the most often used questionnaires is the Reactive Proactive Aggression Questionnaire (RPQ; Raine et al., 2006), where participants are asked to rate the frequency of items like *"Gotten angry when others threatened you"* and *"Hit others to defend yourself"* to assess their general level of RA, and *"Yelled at others so they would do things for you"* or *"Had fights with others to show who was on top"* for PA. Lit-tle et al. (2003) developed a questionnaire that additionally distinguishes between *forms* of aggression, providing the opportunity to assess overt and relational forms of aggression. In addition to a self-report version, an informant report version of this questionnaire was developed. In participants with known past incidents of aggression, the Impulsive/Premeditated Aggression Scale (IPAS; Stanford et al., 2003) can be used to determine the impulsive versus premeditated nature of these aggressive incidents. Although questionnaires like these have the clear advantage of being short and quick to administer and posing few ethical challenges, they cannot circumvent underreporting of aggression. Underreporting aggression can emerge either because aggression is socially unacceptable and therefore prone to elicit socially desirable responses, or due to lack of insight. Informant reports have the added disadvantage of a lack of insight into the motives behind the observable behavior. In response to these drawbacks of self-report and informant report measures, many studies rely instead on behavioral measures of aggres-sion. These behavioral paradigms (see also Box 19.1) are based on providing participants with the opportunity to negatively impact an alleged opponent, e.g., by subtracting points from a competitive score in the Point Subtraction Aggres-sion Paradigm (Cherek, 1981) or by exposure to aversive food in the Hot Sauce Aggression Paradigm (Lieberman et al., 1999). One of the most often-used behav-ioral aggression paradigms is the Competitive Reaction Time Task (CRTT, see e.g., Bushman & Baumeister, 1998; Warburton & Bushman, 2019), a variant of the Taylor Aggression Paradigm (TAP, Taylor, 1967). The CRTT requires participants to compete against another fictitious participant in a computerized online reaction-time task. Participants are instructed to react as fast as possible in response to a visual signal, and, by doing so, avoid getting punished by the opponent: when losing a trial, participants hear an unpleasant noise. Prior to each reaction trial, participants are requested to determine the volume and duration of the sound that the opponent will be confronted with when losing a trial. A recent psychometric study (Lobbestael et al., in press) evidenced that the 30-trials CRTT version can reliably differentiate between the assessment of RA and PA. Specifically, RA can be assessed by adding all trial scores (i.e., both duration and intensity) subsequent to the first time the participant received aversive feedback (i.e., after the 7th trial), while PA can best be operationalized through the sum of all trial scores prior to this first aversive feedback. Behavioral measures of aggression come with specific drawbacks, however. One major criticism of behavioral aggression paradigms concerns their limited generalization to behavior in the real world, as they often are not likely to cause real harm to another person. Other criticisms include distance between victim and aggressor (this tends to be smaller in real instances of aggression), lack of insight into participant motives during tasks, and cover stories used to disguise the real purpose of studies (for a review, see Ritter & Eslea, 2005). Nonetheless, these paradigms are continually improved to be more ecologically valid, and are a promising area of aggression research.

Box 19.1 Behavioral measures in aggression research

Different measures have been used to examine behavioral aggression in addition to the Competitive Reaction Time Task discussed in section "Assessment". Considering the ethical constraints that are necessarily a part of experimental studies in this area of human behavior, these tasks do not come without weaknesses. Regardless, the following tasks have repeatedly demonstrated positive associations with other measures of aggression, such as trait and state questionnaires, and act as useful instruments in aggression research.

Point Subtraction Aggression Paradigm (Cherek, 1981)

This measure consists of a computer task where participants can earn money (usually a few cents) by pressing a specific button, typically 100 times. However, they can also deduct the same amount of money from another supposed participant playing the same game in a different room. During the task, participants cannot only see their running total, but also when their opponent has deducted money from their pot. In reality, there is no opponent, as it is a predetermined program participants are playing against. The frequency with which money is deducted from the supposed opponent is used as an indicator of aggression. One variation of this task includes a third button which participants can use to protect their total from subtraction for a certain amount of time, allowing researchers to examine to what extent participants are willing to sacrifice using this button for their own gain in order to keep deducting money from their opponent.

Hot Sauce Aggression Paradigm (Lieberman et al., 1999)
Here, participants are instructed to determine the amount of hot sauce that will be consumed by another specified person who doesn't like spicy foods, and who has provoked the participant beforehand in one way or another (for example, by insulting the worldview of the participant) as part of the experiment. The amount of hot sauce participants administer is then used as an indicator of aggression.

Voodoo Doll Task (DeWall et al., 2013)
In this task, participants are presented with the opportunity to inflict harm on a doll that represents another person by stabbing it with pins. Often times the doll represents someone in the participant's life, or a person involved in the experiment, who has provoked the participant in some way. This task is not only used in laboratory studies with an actual doll and needles, but also in a computer-based paradigm using an image of the doll. The word "voodoo" is not used when participants receive instructions for this task. The frequency with which participants stab the doll is used as an indicator of aggression. Some studies also include the location of the stabbing as an additional measure of aggression.

Summary

Regarding the prevalence of aggression, historical trends suggest a visible decline in violence. Furthermore, sex differences in aggression prevalence are found between men and women: men are more likely to engage in direct forms of aggression, whereas women are more likely to engage in indirect forms of aggression. Lastly, three lifetime trajectories are found for physical aggression: stable low incidence, desisting moderate incidence, and stable high incidence. Two trajectories are found for indirect aggression: stable low incidence, and increasing high incidence.

Different categorizations of aggression include direct versus indirect aggression, and distinctions between verbal, relational, and physical aggression. Current literature shows that RA and PA subtypes are related to different characteristics in multiple areas. RA is characterized by a hostile emotional state with deficient behavior and emotion regulation, and co-occurring poor social adjustment and internalizing problems. In contrast, PA is characterized by less prominent emotionality, a cold-blooded goal-oriented state, and positive outcome expectancies for aggression, co-occurring with externalizing problems. This bimodal motivational distinction is thus valid and clinically meaningful.

Finally, the RPQ is one of the most used self-report measures of aggression. The CRTT is one of the most used behavioral measures of aggression. Both the RPQ and the CRTT are empirically validated and reliable, although the CRTT and behavioral measures in general circumvent the challenge of underreporting in aggression research.

References

Anderson, C. A., & Bushman, B. J. (2002). Human aggression. *Annual Review of Psychology, 53*, 27–51.

Archer, J. (2000). Sex differences in aggression between heterosexual partners: A meta-analytic review. *Psychological Bulletin, 126*(5), 651–680. https://doi.org/10.1037/0033-2909.126.5.651

Archer, J. (2004). Sex differences in aggression in real-world settings: A meta-analytic review. *Review of General Psychology, 8*(4), 291–322.

Berkowitz, L. (1989). Frustration-aggression hypothesis: Examination and reformulation. *Psychological Bulletin, 106*(1), 59.

Björkqvist, K., Lagerspetz, K. M., & Kaukiainen, A. (1992). Do girls manipulate and boys fight? Developmental trends in regard to direct and indirect aggression. *Aggressive Behavior, 18*(2), 117–127.

Blais, J., Solodukhin, E., & Forth, A. E. (2014). A meta-analysis exploring the relationship between psychopathy and instrumental versus reactive violence. *Criminal Justice and Behavior, 41*(7), 797–821.

Brame, B., Nagin, D. S., & Tremblay, R. E. (2001). Developmental trajectories of physical aggression from school entry to late adolescence. *The Journal of Child Psychology and Psychiatry and Allied Disciplines, 42*(4), 503–512.

Brendgen, M., Vitaro, F., Boivin, M., Dionne, G., & Pérusse, D. (2006). Examining genetic and environmental effects on reactive versus proactive aggression. *Developmental Psychology, 42*(6), 1299.

Bushman, B. J., & Anderson, C. A. (2001). Is it time to pull the plug on hostile versus instrumental aggression dichotomy? *Psychological Review, 108*(1), 273–279.

Bushman, B. J., & Baumeister, R. F. (1998). Threatened egotism, narcissism, self-esteem, and direct and displaced aggression: Does self-love or self-hate lead to violence? *Journal of Personality and Social Psychology, 75*(1), 219.

Bushman, B. J., & Huesmann, L. R. (2006). Short-term and long-term effects of violent media on aggression in children and adults. *Archives of Pediatrics & Adolescent Medicine, 160*(4), 348–352.

Campbell, S. B., Spieker, S., Burchinal, M., Poe, M. D., & Network, N. E. C. C. R. (2006). Trajectories of aggression from toddlerhood to age 9 predict academic and social functioning through age 12. *Journal of Child Psychology and Psychiatry, 47*(8), 791–800. https://doi.org/10.1111/j.1469-7610.2006.01636.x

Card, N. A., & Little, T. D. (2006). Proactive and reactive aggression in childhood and adolescence: A meta-analysis of differential relations with psychosocial adjustment. *International Journal of Behavioral Development, 30*(5), 466–480.

Card, N. A., Stucky, B. D., Sawalani, G. M., & Little, T. D. (2008). Direct and indirect aggression during childhood and adolescence: A meta-analytic review of gender differences, intercorrelations, and relations to maladjustment. *Child Development, 79*(5), 1185–1229.

Cherek, D. R. (1981). Effects of smoking different doses of nicotine on human aggressive behavior. *Psychopharmacology (berl), 75*(4), 339–345.

Cima, M., & Raine, A. (2009). Distinct characteristics of psychopathy relate to different subtypes of aggression. *Personality and Individual Differences, 47*(8), 835–840.

Cirillo, P., & Taleb, N. N. (2016). *The decline of violent conflicts: What do the data really say?* In Nobel Foundation Symposium 161: The Causes of Peace (pp. 1–26): Nobel Foundation.

Cleverley, K., Szatmari, P., Vaillancourt, T., Boyle, M., & Lipman, E. (2012). Developmental trajectories of physical and indirect aggression from late childhood to adolescence: Sex differences and outcomes in emerging adulthood. *Journal of the American Academy of Child & Adolescent Psychiatry, 51*(10), 1037–1051.

Côté, S. M. (2007). Sex differences in physical and indirect aggression: A developmental perspective. *European Journal on Criminal Policy and Research, 13*(3–4), 183–200. https://doi.org/10.1007/s10610-007-9046-3

Crapanzano, A. M., Frick, P. J., & Terranova, A. M. (2010). Patterns of physical and relational aggression in a school-based sample of boys and girls. *Journal of Abnormal Child Psychology, 38*(4), 433–445.

Crick, & Dodge, K. A. . (1996). Social information-processing mechanisms in reactive and proactive aggression. *Child Development, 67*, 993–1002.

Crick, N. R., & Dodge, K. A. (1994). A review and reformulation of social information-processing mechanisms in children's social adjustment. *Psychological Bulletin, 115*(1), 74–101. https://doi.org/10.1037//0033-2909.115.1.74

Crick, N. R., & Dodge, K. A. (1996). Social information-processing mechanisms in reactive and proactive aggression. *Child Development, 67*(3), 993–1002.

Dambacher, F., Schuhmann, T., Lobbestael, J., Arntz, A., Brugman, S., & Sack, A. T. (2015). Reducing proactive aggression through non-invasive brain stimulation. *Social Cognitive and Affective Neuroscience, 10*(10), 1303–1309. https://doi.org/10.1093/scan/nsv018

DeWall, C. N., Finkel, E. J., Lambert, N. M., Slotter, E. B., Bodenhausen, G. V., Pond, R. S., Jr., & Fincham, F. D. (2013). The voodoo doll task: Introducing and validating a novel method for studying aggressive inclinations. *Aggressive Behavior, 39*(6), 419–439.

Dollard, J., Miller, N. E., Doob, L. W., Mowrer, O. H., & Sears, R. R. (1939). *Frustration and aggression.*

Farrington, D. P. (1989). Early predictors of adolescent aggression and adult violence. *Violence and Victims, 4*(2), 79–100.

Ferguson, C. J., & Dyck, D. (2012). Paradigm change in aggression research: The time has come to retire the General Aggression Model. *Aggression and Violent Behavior, 17*(3), 220–228.

Ferguson, C. J., & Kilburn, J. (2009). The public health risks of media violence: A meta-analytic review. *The Journal of Pediatrics, 154*(5), 759–763.

Fite, P. J., Raine, A., Stouthamer-Loeber, M., Loeber, R., & Pardini, D. A. (2010). Reactive and proactive aggression in adolescent males: Examining differential outcomes 10 years later in early adulthood. *Criminal Justice and Behavior, 37*(2), 141–157.

Frick, P. J., & White, S. F. (2008). Research review: The importance of callous-unemotional traits for developmental models of aggressive and antisocial behavior. *Journal of Child Psychology and Psychiatry, 49*(4), 359–375.

Garofalo, C., Neumann, C. S., & Velotti, P. (2020). Psychopathy and aggression: The role of emotion dysregulation. *Journal of Interpersonal Violence*, 0886260519900946.

Hare, R. D. (1996). Psychopathy: A clinical construct whose time has come. *Criminal Justice and Behavior, 23*(1), 25–54.

Herrenkohl, T. I., McMorris, B. J., Catalano, R. F., Abbott, R. D., Hemphill, S. A., & Toumbourou, J. W. (2007). Risk factors for violence and relational aggression in adolescence. *Journal of Interpersonal Violence, 22*(4), 386–405.

Hsieh, I.-J., & Chen, Y. Y. (2017). Determinants of aggressive behavior: Interactive effects of emotional regulation and inhibitory control. *PLoS One, 12*(4), e0175651.

Hudley, C., & Graham, S. (1993). An attributional intervention to reduce peer-directed aggression among African-American boys. *Child Development, 64*(1), 124–138.

Huesmann, L. R., Moise-Titus, J., Podolski, C.-L., & Eron, L. D. (2003). Longitudinal relations between children's exposure to TV violence and their aggressive and violent behavior in young adulthood: 1977–1992. *Developmental Psychology, 39*(2), 201–221. https://doi.org/10.1037/0012-1649.39.2.201

Lieberman, J. D., Solomon, S., Greenberg, J., & McGregor, H. A. (1999). A hot new way to measure aggression: Hot sauce allocation. *Aggressive Behavior, 25*(5), 331–348.

Litrownik, A. J., Newton, R., Hunter, W. M., English, D., & Everson, M. D. (2003). Exposure to family violence in young at-risk children: A longitudinal look at the effects of victimization and witnessed physical and psychological aggression. *Journal of Family Violence, 18*(1), 59–73.

Little, T. D., Henrich, C. C., Jones, S. M., & Hawley, P. H. (2003). Disentangling the "whys" from the "whats" of aggressive behaviour. *International Journal of Behavioral Development, 27*(2), 122–133.

Liu, J., Raine, A., Venables, P. H., & Mednick, S. A. (2004). Malnutrition at age 3 tears and externalizing behavior problems at ages 8, 11, and 17 years. *American Journal of Psychiatry, 161*(11), 2005–2013.

Lobbestael, J., Cima, M., & Arntz, A. (2013). The relationship between adult reactive and proactive aggression, hostile interpretation bias, and antisocial personality disorder. *Journal of Personality Disorders, 27*(1), 53–66. https://doi.org/10.1521/pedi.2013.27.1.53

Lobbestael, J., Emmerling, F., Brugman, S., Broers, N., Sack, A. T., Schuhmann, T., . . . Arntz, A. Towards a more valid assessment of behavioral aggression: An open source platform and an empirically derived scoring method for using the Competitive Reaction Time Task (CRTT). *Assessment*.

Lopez-Duran, N. L., Olson, S. L., Hajal, N. J., Felt, B. T., & Vazquez, D. M. (2009). Hypothalamic pituitary adrenal axis functioning in reactive and proactive aggression in children. *Journal of Abnormal Child Psychology, 37*(2), 169–182. https://doi.org/10.1007/s10802-008-9263-3

Lynam, D. R., Hoyle, R. H., & Newman, J. P. (2006). The perils of partialling: Cautionary tales from aggression and psychopathy. *Assessment, 13*(3), 328–341.

Marsee, M. A., & Frick, P. J. (2007). Exploring the cognitive and emotional correlates to proactive and reactive aggression in a sample of detained girls. *Journal of Abnormal Child Psychology, 35*(6), 969–981.

Maughan, B., Pickles, A., Rowe, R., Costello, E. J., & Angold, A. (2000). Developmental trajectories of aggressive and non-aggressive conduct problems. *Journal of Quantitative Criminology, 16*(2), 199–221.

McAuliffe, M. D., Hubbard, J. A., Rubin, R. M., Morrow, M. T., & Dearing, K. F. (2006). Reactive and proactive aggression: Stability of constructs and relations to correlates. *The Journal of Genetic Psychology, 167*(4), 365–382.

Merk, W., Orobio de Castro, B., Koops, W., & Matthys, W. (2005). The distinction between reactive and proactive aggression: Utility for theory, diagnosis and treatment? *European Journal of Developmental Psychology, 2*(2), 197–220.

Micale, M. S., & Dwyer, P. (2018). History, violence, and Steven Pinker. *Historical Reflections, 44*(1), 1–5. https://doi.org/10.3167/hrrh.2018.440102

Milich, R., & Dodge, K. A. (1984). Social information processing in child psychiatric populations. *Journal of Abnormal Child Psychology, 12*(3), 471–489. https://doi.org/10.1007/BF00910660

Miller, J. D., & Lynam, D. R. (2006). Reactive and proactive aggression: Similarities and differences. *Personality and Individual Differences, 41*(8), 1469–1480. https://doi.org/10.1016/j.paid.2006.06.004

Nærde, A., Ogden, T., Janson, H., & Zachrisson, H. D. (2014). Normative development of physical aggression from 8 to 26 months. *Developmental Psychology, 50*(6), 1710.

Orobio de Castro, B., Merk, W., Koops, W., Veerman, J. W., & Bosch, J. D. (2005). Emotions in social information processing and their relations with reactive and proactive aggression in referred aggressive boys. *Journal of Clinical Child and Adolescent Psychology, 34*(1), 105–116.

Orpinas, P., McNicholas, C., & Nahapetyan, L. (2015). Gender differences in trajectories of relational aggression perpetration and victimization from middle to high school. *Aggressive Behavior, 41*(5), 401–412. https://doi.org/10.1002/ab.21563

Österman, K., Björkqvist, K., Lagerspetz, K., Kaukiainen, A., Landau, S. F., Fracczek, A., & Caprara, G. V. (1998). *Cross-Cultural Evidence of Female Indirect Aggression., 24*, 1–8.

Pavlov, K. A., Chistiakov, D. A., & Chekhonin, V. P. (2012). Genetic determinants of aggression and impulsivity in humans. *Journal of Applied Genetics, 53*(1), 61–82. https://doi.org/10.1007/s13353-011-0069-6

Pinker, S. (2011). *The better angels of our nature: The decline of violence in history and its causes*. Penguin.

Poulin, F., & Boivin, M. (2000). Reactive and proactive aggression: Evidence of a two-factor model. *Psychological Assessment, 12*(2), 115–122. https://doi.org/10.1037/1040-3590.12. 2.115

Provencal, N., Booij, L., & Tremblay, R. E. (2015). The developmental origins of chronic physical aggression: Biological pathways triggered by early life adversity. *Journal of Experimental Biology, 218*, 123–133. https://doi.org/10.1242/jeb.111401

Raine, A. (2008). From genes to brain to antisocial behavior. *Current Directions in Psychological Science, 17*(5), 323–328.

Raine, A., Dodge, K., Loeber, R., Gatzke-Kopp, L., Lynam, D., Reynolds, C., & Liu, J. (2006). The reactive-proactive aggression questionnaire: Differential correlates of reactive and proactive aggression in adolescent boys. *Aggressive Behavior, 32*(2), 159–171.

Ritter, D., & Eslea, M. (2005). Hot sauce, toy guns, and graffiti: A critical account of current laboratory aggression paradigms. *Aggressive Behavior: Official Journal of the International Society for Research on Aggression, 31*(5), 407–419.

Salmivalli, C., Kaukiainen, A., & Lagerspetz, K. (2000). Aggression and sociometric status among peers: Do gender and type of aggression matter? *Scandinavian Journal of Psychology, 41*(1), 17–24.

Slotter, E. B., & Finkel, E. J. (2011). I^3 theory: Instigating, impelling, and inhibiting factors in aggression. In *Human aggression and violence: Causes, manifestations, and consequences.* (pp. 35–52). American Psychological Association.

Smith, R. L., Rose, A. J., & Schwartz-Mette, R. A. (2009). Relational and overt aggression in childhood and adolescence: Clarifying mean-level gender differences and associations with peer acceptance. *Social Development, 19*(2), 243–269. https://doi.org/10.1111/j.1467-9507.2009.00541.x

Smithmyer, C. M., Hubbard, J. A., & Simons, R. F. (2000). Proactive and reactive aggression in delinquent adolescents: Relations to aggression outcome expectancies. *Journal of Clinical Child and Adolescent Psychology, 29*(1), 86–93.

Stanford, M. S., Houston, R. J., Villemarette-Pittman, N. R., & Greve, K. W. (2003). Premeditated aggression: Clinical assessment and cognitive psychophysiology. *Personality and Individual Differences, 34*(5), 773–781.

Stickle, T. R., Marini, V. A., & Thomas, J. N. (2012). Gender differences in psychopathic traits, types, and correlates of aggression among adjudicated youth. *Journal of Abnormal Child Psychology, 40*(4), 513–525.

Taylor, S. P. (1967). Aggressive behavior and physiological arousal as a function of provocation and the tendency to inhibit aggression. *Journal of Personality, 35*(2), 297–310.

Tremblay, R. E. (2016). The development of aggressive behaviour during childhood: What have we learned in the past century? *International Journal of Behavioral Development, 24*(2), 129–141. https://doi.org/10.1080/016502500383232

True, J. (2014). Are war and violence really in decline? *Australian Journal of International Affairs, 68*(5), 487–494. https://doi.org/10.1080/10357718.2014.947354

Tuvblad, C., Raine, A., Zheng, M., & Baker, L. A. (2009). Genetic and environmental stability differs in reactive and proactive aggression. *Aggressive Behavior, 35*(6), 437–452. https://doi.org/10.1002/ab.20319

Underwood, M. K., Beron, K. J., & Rosen, L. H. (2009). Continuity and change in social and physical aggression from middle childhood through early adolescence. *Aggressive Behavior, 35*(5), 357–375. https://doi.org/10.1002/ab.20313

Vaillancourt, T., Miller, J. L., Fagbemi, J., Cote, S., & Tremblay, R. E. (2007). Trajectories and predictors of indirect aggression: Results from a nationally representative longitudinal study of Canadian children aged 2–10. *Aggressive Behavior, 33*(4), 314–326. https://doi.org/10.1002/ab.20202

Vitaro, F., Barker, E. D., Boivin, M., Brendgen, M., & Tremblay, R. E. (2006). Do early difficult temperament and harsh parenting differentially predict reactive and proactive aggression? *Journal of Abnormal Child Psychology, 34*(5), 685–695. https://doi.org/10.1007/s10802-006-9055-6

Vitaro, F., Gendreau, P. L., Tremblay, R. E., & Oligny, P. (1998). Reactive and proactive aggression differentially predict later conduct problems. *The Journal of Child Psychology and Psychiatry and Allied Disciplines, 39*(3), 377–385.

Walters, G. D. (2007). Measuring proactive and reactive criminal thinking with the PICTS. *Journal of Interpersonal Violence, 22*(4), 371–385.

Waltes, R., Chiocchetti, A. G., & Freitag, C. M. (2016). The neurobiological basis of human aggression: A review on genetic and epigenetic mechanisms. *American Journal of Medical Genetics Part B: Neuropsychiatric Genetics, 171*(5), 650–675.

Warburton, W. A., & Bushman, B. J. (2019). The competitive reaction time task: The development and scientific utility of a flexible laboratory aggression paradigm. *Aggressive Behavior, 45*(4), 389–396.

White, B. A., Jarrett, M. A., & Ollendick, T. H. (2013). Self-regulation deficits explain the link between reactive aggression and internalizing and externalizing behavior problems in children. *Journal of Psychopathology and Behavioral Assessment, 35*(1), 1–9.

Woodworth, M., & Porter, S. (2002). In cold blood: Characteristics of criminal homicides as a function of psychopathy. *Journal of Abnormal Psychology, 111*(3), 436.

Zhang, Z., Wang, Q., Liu, X., Song, P., & Yang, B. (2017). Differences in inhibitory control between impulsive and premeditated aggression in juvenile inmates. *Frontiers in Human Neuroscience, 11*, 373.

Further Reading

Anderson, C. A., & Bushman, B. J. (2002). Human aggression. *Annual Review of Psychology, 53*, 27–51.

Bushman, B. J., & Anderson, C. A. (2001). Is it time to pull the plug on hostile versus instrumental aggression dichotomy? *Psychological Review, 108*(1), 273–279.

Cima, M., & Raine, A. (2009). Distinct characteristics of psychopathy relate to different subtypes of aggression. *Personality and Individual Differences, 47*(8), 835–840.

Ferguson, C. J., & Dyck, D. (2012). Paradigm change in aggression research: The time has come to retire the General Aggression Model. *Aggression and Violent Behavior, 17*(3), 220–228. https://doi.org/10.1016/j.avb.2012.02.007

Pinker, S. (2011). *The better angels of our nature: The decline of violence in history and its causes.* Penguin.

Poulin, F., & Boivin, M. (2000). Reactive and proactive aggression: Evidence of a two-factor model. *Psychological Assessment, 12*(2), 115–122. https://doi.org/10.1037/1040-3590.12.2.115

Juvenile Offenders

20

Michael G. Vaughn, Leslie J. Sattler, and Katherine J. Holzer

Key Points

- Rates of mental health disorders among juvenile offenders are much higher than among the general population of youth.
- The continued evolution of assessment among juvenile offenders necessarily focuses on a combination of risk and needs.
- Effective intervention for juvenile offenders involves creating a system of care that is community-based and matches identified needs and level of motivation.
- To serve juvenile offenders future research needs a deeper understanding of subthreshold psychiatric symptoms and their correlates with attention to variation by gender and racial and ethnic differences.

M. G. Vaughn (✉)
School of Social Work, SLU Health Criminology Research Consortium, Saint Louis University, St. Louis, MO, USA
e-mail: michael.vaughn@slu.edu

L. J. Sattler
School of Social Work, Bridgewater State University, Bridgewater, MA, USA
e-mail: lsattler@bridgew.edu

K. J. Holzer
Washington University in St. Louis, St. Louis, MO, USA
e-mail: kholzer@wustl.edu

C. Garofalo and J. J. Sijtsema (eds.), *Clinical Forensic Psychology*,
https://doi.org/10.1007/978-3-030-80882-2_20

Introduction

Although it is relatively normal, especially for male youth, to engage in some law breaking during adolescence, juvenile offenders are those youths who are processed in juvenile courts for generally more serious and/or chronic delinquent acts. It is important to note that the numbers of juvenile arrests, at least in the United States, has been in decline since the mid-1990s (Puzzanchera, 2019). Despite these declines, there are still a substantial number of youths who encounter the juvenile justice system and have myriad needs. The goal of the present chapter is to focus on the major issues that these youths and practitioners face in achieving beneficial outcomes. Given the high rates of mental health problems in this population, we begin with a brief review of the *psychopathology of juvenile offenders*. Next, we turn to the pivotal issues surrounding the proper *assessment* of these youths while also pointing out limitations with respect to minority populations. Assessment can help us identify needs and risk, which facilitates the proper matching of these characteristics to treatment. We discuss *treatment and treatment effectiveness* within the context of evidence-informed decision making pointing out the challenge of diagnostic labeling, access, implementation of best practices, and empirical evaluation of interventions. A strong balance to treatment is prevention. As such, we consider the extent to which there is *a role for prevention* with respect to juvenile offending. The first task for prevention is diversion, which was a core component in the development of juvenile courts. Juvenile diversion programs were implemented to navigate juvenile offenders away from formal juvenile court involvement and connect them with alternative services in the community (Development Services Group, 2017a). The services or interventions offered through these programs vary and may include therapeutic intervention, behavioral modification strategies, community service, and/or forms of restitution to victims or the community. The next stage of prevention relies on employing risk and protective factor frameworks to identify those variables that are associated with mental health and behavioral problems in these youth. These variables typically present themselves earlier in the life course during childhood. Finally, we consider some of the *future clinical research needs* that accompany the study of juvenile offenders. These needs include a finer grained investigation of psychiatric symptoms and their correlates, heterogeneity across jurisdictions (and indeed nations), and a deeper understanding of gender differences in psychopathology and their relationship to current and future behaviors.

Case Study
John is a sixteen and a half-year-old Caucasian male from a working-class family of four. His commitment to the state juvenile justice system stemmed from larceny and possession of heroin charges. As with most youth in this state system, he entered secure detention on his arrest and transferred to a secure assessment program from the courthouse on the day of his commitment. The assessment process involved a 45-day stay, during which time John participated in a biopsychosocial assessment of his current functioning. For this assessment, clinicians gathered relevant family, educational, occupational, developmental, and health data and screened for substance use and mental health concerns. The substance use and mood screening results indicated further assessment; thus, John participated in the self-administered Global Appraisal of Individual Needs (GAIN) inventory and clinicians then evaluated him using protocols established by the Diagnostic and Statistical Manual of Mental Disorders, Fifth Edition. He received a diagnosis of polysubstance addiction and generalized anxiety disorder. He moved to a short-term community-based residential treatment center to begin intervention to reduce his substance use and work with his family to improve communication and trust. His treatment included individual therapy once a week, daily group therapy (Cognitive behavior-based relapse prevention, adventure-based group treatment, and Dialectical Behavior Therapy skills group), weekly family therapy, and medication assessment/management from a psychiatrist. Educationally, John performed at grade level but was behind in his coursework. Due to his substance addiction and need for individualized education tailored at allowing John to catch up on his work, the program enrolled him in a community-based recovery focused high school that he attended during the day returning to the program in the evenings. John completed his treatment in six months and was discharged home to his family. His aftercare plan consisted of continued enrollment in the recovery high school, daily recovery groups at the high school, and weekly individual therapy sessions. He remained in the community and under supervision by the juvenile justice department until his discharge at age eighteen.

Psychopathology of Juvenile Offenders

The prevalence rates of mental disorders among youths in the criminal justice system are found to be consistently higher than those for adolescents in the general population (Schubert & Mulvey, 2014; Vaughn et al., 2015). It is estimated that about 50–70% of criminal-justice-involved youth have at least one mental disorder (Colins et al., 2010; Fazel et al., 2008; Kazdin, 2000; Teplin et al.,

2002) compared with 16.5% of general population of youths (Whitney & Peterson, 2019). The difference in prevalence rates between juvenile offenders and adolescents in the community varies based on type of disorder with the largest disparities found for conduct disorder and psychotic illness (Beaudry et al., 2020).

Within the juvenile justice population, the prevalence of mental disorders appears to differ significantly by gender. A consistent finding among studies into the mental health of this population is the higher rates of mental disorders in females compared to males (Beaudry et al., 2020; Fazel et al., 2008; Holzer et al., 2018; Skowyra & Cocozza, 2007; Teplin et al., 2003; Wasserman et al., 2002). Specifically, it is estimated that approximately three-quarters of females and two-thirds of males in juvenile justice facilities meet criteria for at least one mental disorder (Developmental Services Group, 2017b; Underwood & Washington, 2016). Females also have higher rates of co-occurring disorders with 57% of females and 46% of males in this population meeting criteria for at least two psychiatric disorders (Teplin et al., 2013). A recent systematic review of 47 studies from 1966 to 2019 on the prevalence of mental disorders in juvenile offenders in 19 countries (Beaudry et al., 2020) computed the pooled prevalence estimates of a variety of mental disorders stratified by gender. The most common disorders among female adolescents were conduct disorder (59%), major depression (25.8%), posttraumatic stress disorder (PTSD) (18.2%), and attention deficit hyperactivity disorder (ADHD) (17.5%) (Chapter 16). Among male offenders, the most frequently diagnosed disorders were conduct disorder (61.7%), ADHD (17.3%), and major depression (10.1%).

The psychopathology of juvenile offenders has also been shown to differ by race. Baglivio and colleagues (2017) found that Black males and females in juvenile justice residential programs were 40–54% more likely to be diagnosed with a conduct disorder than Whites. Black and Hispanic males were 40% less likely to be diagnosed with ADHD than White males. Similarly, Vaughn et al. (2008) found that Black juvenile offenders report lower levels of mental disorders and substance use than Whites, however they demonstrated higher levels of delinquency. Further, an investigation by Lee and colleagues (2017) revealed that White youth in residential placement had significantly higher scores on a mental health measure compared to their Black and Hispanic peers. Using data on justice-involved youth from the National Survey on Drug Use and Health, Holzer et al. (2018) found that Black females were less likely to be diagnosed with major depression than White or Hispanic female offenders. Importantly, multiple studies (Baglivio et al., 2017; Dalton et al., 2009; Lee et al., 2017; Rawal et al., 2004) reveal that despite controlling for differences in psychopathology, Black youths are significantly less likely to be referred to and use mental health services than White youths in juvenile justice facilities. Variations in the psychopathology and treatment of juvenile offenders based on sex and race warrant the need for prevention and intervention efforts to acknowledge and accommodate these differences.

Assessment

The role of assessment in juvenile justice has evolved over the decades from an emphasis on violence prevention to the systematic prediction of risk currently used (Borum & Verhaagen, 2006; Lyons, 2016). This evolution is promising in that the principles of the risk-needs-responsivity framework guide the assessment process (RNR; Andrews & Bonta, 2010) (Chapter 27). However, questions remain about the role of the assessment process in the disproportionate rates of juvenile justice involvement experienced by youth of color (disproportionate minority contact [DMC]; Development Services Group Inc [DSG], 2015; Mendel, 2014).

The RNR framework aims to estimate the risk of recidivism, the specific factors or needs targeted for intervention, and identification of the responsivity to treatment. Risk factors include static factors that are unchangeable via intervention, dynamic factors amenable to treatment, and criminogenic and non-criminogenic factors (DSG, 2015; Hilterman et al., 2016). The RNR model suggests that interventions should match an individual's level of risk, targeting those factors that are associated with delinquency, and tailored to the characteristics that enhance an individual's responsivity to treatment.

Assessment is a comprehensive process of gathering data via self-report screening scales, practitioner administered assessment instruments, and review of existing records. Considered best practice is the structured professional judgment approach that relies on practitioner selection of specific tools necessary to measure risk (DSG, 2015; Lyons, 2016; Poortinga et al., 2009; Vizard, 2013). Tools typically include brief screening scales that detect issues needing in-depth assessment and comprehensive instruments that identify general delinquency and personality characteristics, risk of engaging in specific behaviors, risk levels for specific populations of juveniles, and measures of psychopathology.[1]

---

[1] Screening and assessment tools include the Massachusetts Youth Screening Instrument II ([MAYSI-II]; Grisso & Barnum, 2000) Youth Assessment Screening Instrument (Orbis Partners, 2007), Youth Level of Service/Case Management Inventory ([YLS/CMI], Bechtel et al., 2007), Minnesota Multiphasic Personality Inventory-Adolescent Scale ([MMPI-A] Williams et al., 1992), Structure of Assessment of Violence Risk in Youth ([SAVRY], Borum et al., 2002), Substance Abuse Subtle Screening Inventory for Adolescents-2 (Miller & Lazowski,

Assessment plays a vital role in the legal decisions concerning diversion, adjudication, the disposition to community-based or residential care, and treatment planning; the individual's stage of involvement in the juvenile justice system dictating the process. For example, assessment tools measuring general delinquency inform diversion decisions, whereas those used for disposition hearings measure specific risk behaviors and identify treatment readiness. However, limitations to assessment include the validity of measures for use across populations, to predict risk and recidivism, and to assess treatment readiness. For instance, screening tools such as the MAYSI and YLS/CMI lack research support with youth from underrepresented groups (Campbell et al., 2018; Coker et al., 2014). Likewise, the JI-R and JSOAP-II are often used to assess risk yet do not reliably predict recidivism, especially among different types of offending behaviors (Olver & Stockdale, 2017; Semel, 2016; Wijetunga et al., 2018). Last, these tools are ineffective when used in isolation to predict risk, and many do not adequately measure treatment readiness (Mossiere & Serin, 2014; Semel, 2016).

Underlying the limitations of assessment is the existence of DMC (Thompson & McGrath, 2012 as cited in DSG, 2015). Black, Hispanic, and Native American youth have higher rates of arrest and experience more involvement in the juvenile justice system than their white peers, yet many of these youths reside in communities of concentrated disadvantage (Puzzanchera & Hockenberry, 2008; Sickmund et al., 2011). Decades of sociological research demonstrate that structural factors of oppression influence the segregation of underrepresented groups into communities replete with factors that contribute to crime (Sampson et al., 1997; Sharkey & Sampson, 2010). Perhaps, for youth of color, existing criminogenic factors do not accurately measure their risk. Instead, these factors reflect the disparities inherent in the systems that reinforce segregation (National Research Council, 2013). If this is true, the existing assessment process may inadvertently fuel DMC. For example, the measurement of past offending behavior as a static risk factor may not accurately reflect risk; instead, it may reflect the disparities in the legal system (DSG, 2015).

2001), Juvenile Sex Offender Assessment Protocol-II ([JSOAP], Prentky & Righthand, 2003), Estimate of Risk of Adolescent Sexual Offense Recidivism ([ERASOR], Worling & Curwen, 2001), Jesness Inventory-Revised ([JI-R], Jesness, 2004), and the Hare Psychopathology Checklist Youth Version (Forth et al., 2003).

Treatment & Treatment Effectiveness

Assessments identify the potential risk of recidivism, but also inform decisions regarding the type of treatment setting most likely to be effective. Placing juveniles in the least restrictive environment is a priority as youth experience abuse, worse rates of recidivism, and inadequate care when placed in secure settings, with more significant adverse effects for youth with a history of trauma or mental illness (Mendel, 2011, 2014). These adverse outcomes, combined with research on brain development, prompted a shift in the juvenile justice system from a punitive orientation to one of rehabilitation (Mendel, 2014; Perelman & Clements, 2009). The result is a continuum of treatment settings ranging from living at home, community-based day treatment and shelter care, intensive supervision programs, specialized foster care, group homes, residential treatment centers, wilderness programs, detention centers, and secure confinement facilities. These settings vary in the length of time in placement, level of supervision, and type of treatment provided (DSG, 2014; Mendell, 2011). This continuum of care aligns with the RNR framework (Mendall, 2014) by providing youth the level of care that matches their level of risk.

Treatment interventions target criminogenic needs and range from techniques addressing family functioning to individual mental health and behavioral needs. Interventions include name brand evidence-based practices (EBP) and generic versions of existing EBPs modified by individual treatment settings (Howell & Lipsey, 2012; Lipsey, 2018). Such generic interventions adapted to the individual treatment setting consist of cognitive and behavioral approaches delivered within a comprehensive program of care that addresses behavior and builds skills (Pederson et al., 2020; Underwood et al., 2015). Brand name EBP that have demonstrated effectiveness with juvenile offenders include Multi-Systemic Therapy ([MST; Henggeler et al., 2009]; Dixon et al., 2015; Dopp et al., 2018), Functional Family Therapy ([FFT; Sexton & Alexander, 1999]; Boxer et al., 2017; Gottfredson et al., 2018), and cognitive-behavioral interventions including Cognitive Behavioral Therapy ([CBT; Beck, 2011]; Jewell et al., 2015; Mpofu et al., 2018), Dialectical Behavior Therapy ([DBT; Linehan, 1993]; Banks & Gibbons, 2016; Walden et al., 2019), Aggression Replacement Therapy ([ART; Goldstein et al., 1998]; Kaya & Buzlu, 2016; Knoth et al., 2020) and social training programs such as LifeSkills (Botvin & Kantor, 2000).

The most widely implemented programs are FFT and MST. FFT is a family-centered model used primarily with teenagers at risk for or presenting with delinquency and behavior disorders (Underwood et al., 2015). There are three phases: engagement and motivation, behavior change, and generalization (Sexton & Alexander, 1999). Objectives for the engagement phase include developing alliances, minimizing hopelessness, reducing dropout potential, increasing motivation for change, and developing a family focus. In the behavior change phase, therapists help the clients to develop and implement change plans and build relational skills. In the final phase, generalization, clients work on maintain change, preventing relapses and coordinating community resources to support change. MST is an intensive, multi-modal, family-based approach that has been found to primarily be effective with juveniles who have behavioral and emotional problems (Underwood et al., 2015). In this model, empirically-based treatment approaches are integrated into an ecological framework that addresses risk factors across family, peer, school, and community contexts (Henggeler, 1999). The interventions are typically adapted from problem-focused treatments that have empirical literature supporting their efficacy. Interventions usually employed in MST include cognitive behavior therapies (Kendall & Braswell, 1993), structural family therapy (Minuchin, 1974), and strategic family therapy (Haley, 1976). When appropriate, psychopharmacological treatment is combined with psychosocial intervention.

Questions regarding treatment effectiveness stem from diagnostic labeling, accessibility, implementation of EBP, and evaluation of interventions. Diagnostic labels of psychopathology assigned to juveniles may bias placement decisions resulting in youth mandated to secure settings wherein public safety is the priority over treatment (Lyons, 2016). For example, researchers have found that judges perceive youth with psychopathic traits as dangerous and therefore, requiring more restrictive placements than treatment-focused institutions (Jones & Cauffman, 2008). These decisions reinforce DMC as behavior-related disorders are assessed to youth of color more frequently than white youth (Baglivio et al., 2017; Liang et al., 2016). Also, for juveniles placed in rehabilitative settings, many do not receive services, or the delivery is ineffective, as seen with EBP (Henggeler & Schoenwalk, 2011; Lipsey, 2018; Welsh & Greenwood, 2015). Relatively few treatment programs implement EBP with fidelity due to a lack of resources to ensure adequately trained staff or fund the related expenditures (Fixsen et al., 2009; Liddle, 2014). As for programs offering generic interventions, the lack of consensus regarding evaluation protocols limits understanding of their effectiveness (Dodge & Mandel, 2012; Greenwood & Welsh, 2012; Lipsey, 2018).

Addressing the issue of effectiveness requires a reconceptualization of treatment. One solution involves creating a system of care where behavior is described instead of labeled, is community-based, the juvenile justice system plays a minimal role, and the treatment context matches identified needs and level of motivation. In such a system, relationships between providers and youth take the forefront, and the emphasis is not on behavioral compliance but on developing skills and enhancing an internal locus of control (Lyons, 2016; Mathys, 2017; Underwood & Washington, 2016). Furthermore, there is a need to validate the use of EBP *and* the generic versions of EBP by evaluating not fidelity to a specific model, but those aspects of an intervention that are necessary and sufficient to bring about change (Dodge & Mandell, 2012: Howell & Lipsey, 2012; Liddle, 2014). Doing so supports a better alignment between the intervention and the youth in care, considers the community context in which the offending behavior occurs and matches the resources of the existing treatment setting (Dodge & Mandell, 2012; Lipsey, 2018).

A Role for Prevention?

The juvenile justice system was originally intended as a rehabilitative and preventive approach to diverting youth from the punitive adult system (Garascia, 2005). Following an increase in violent delinquency in the 1980s and 1990s there appears to have been a shift from the rehabilitative/medicalization model to a more punitive and criminalization approach to crime among youth. Recently, however, research has demonstrated that, for the majority of juvenile offenders, long-term confinement causes more harm than benefit and often leads to re-offending, while community-based alternatives have been shown to reduce re-offending (Mendel, 2011, 2014). Juvenile courts appear to be shifting as a result of these findings towards the original rehabilitative paradigm, with public opinion following suit. As the juvenile justice system has evolved, so too have public mental health services for youth. In the 1990s, many states experienced a decline in the availability of these services and turned to the juvenile corrections system to fill the void. Meanwhile, researchers have identified a number of risk factors related to mental disorders in the juvenile offender population that should be incorporated into prevention efforts of both psychopathology and delinquency. These risk factors fall into a variety of domains: individual, peer, family, school, and community factors. With respect to individual factors, studies suggest that approximately 35–50 percent of juvenile referrals to mental health clinics present a history of severe antisocial and aggressive behavior patterns (Rogers et al., 1997). The onset of these patterns is often early in life and they have been found to correspond with later mental illness (Underwood et al., 2006). Research into the developmental processes of conduct disorder suggests that certain risk factors in early childhood and preschool years precede even early conduct problems, including difficult or fearless temperament, poor emotional regulation, hyperactivity/impulsivity/attention problems, and showing no remorse (Frick, 2012). Abusing substances, engaging in sex, and stealing in early adolescence are also risk factors. Biological factors related to mental disorders include head injury, exposure to environmental toxins, impairment of the central nervous system, and genetic predisposition (Cellini, 2000; DeLisi & Vaughn, 2015).

Environmental risk factors include a variety of family issues such as difficult parent–child relationships, family conflict, neglect, minimal discipline, absent fathers, lack of affection, sexual abuse, parental substance abuse, and sexual abuse (Farrington, 1998, Henggeler, 1999, Patterson et al., 1992). Community risk factors include living in an urban area, school dropout, high crime rates, drug use, and increased opportunity for participation in delinquent behaviors (Murray & Farrington, 2010; Pyle et al., 2019). Without targeted prevention efforts, individuals with any of the above risk factors may develop further mental health problems and engage in delinquent behaviors.

To address the high levels of mental disorders among juvenile offenders and research suggesting that these youth have a greater risk of re-offending, Underwood and Washington (2016) recommend a number of best practices for the juvenile justice system to employ in response to the mental health needs of this population. First, any measures should be collaborative with child welfare, child protection, and education agencies. To reduce, or possibly prevent, the risk of further exacerbation of the youth's mental health difficulties, systems need to implement diversion programs and community-based intervention programs. Finally, the thoughtful and comprehensive education of juvenile justice system personnel on the nature of mental health problems in youth is critical to the efficient and effective deployment of these practices. These education initiatives should be informed by existing evidence and tailored based on the needs and resources of the facility and jurisdiction.

Future Clinical Research Needs

Though recent research has made meaningful progress in the prevention and intervention of mental illness among juvenile offenders, the results of these studies have highlighted critical gaps in our understanding of the psychopathology of juvenile offenders that offer important implications for future research. Although we now have an idea of the prevalence of mental disorders among justice-involved youth due to increased attention towards the mental health of juvenile offenders and subsequent meta-analyses, the majority of these estimates are based on formal diagnoses rather than symptoms and severity level. This information is crucial to reaching a deeper understanding of the level of need in juvenile justice centers. Examining the prevalence of subthreshold psychiatric symptoms and their correlates will provide a more accurate picture of the need and which groups to target for preventive programs.

Additional concerns with regard to the accuracy of prevalence estimates are the important differences at both the facility and jurisdiction level. There are a variety of juvenile justice settings with distinct features that could uniquely impact the mental health of justice-involved youth. Researchers have noted the insufficient regard for the type of facility where juveniles are detained in prevalence investigations (Beaudry et al., 2020). Facility characteristics—short term or long term, pretrial or post-sentencing, high or low security—may be associated with heterogeneity in prevalence estimates and type of mental illness. Any potential differences between settings will have important practice and policy implications and must be considered when developing facility-specific mental health programs. Future research should also examine how differences at the jurisdictional level may be relevant to mental health and the related policies and practices. The availability and effectiveness of psychiatric services, who they detain, and the prison culture within each jurisdiction are important variables to consider and report in future studies investigating the mental health of juvenile offenders.

There appear to be important gender differences in the prevalence of mental disorders among juvenile offenders. Substantial prior research indicates that mental health disorders are more persistent and associated with worse outcomes in female delinquents compared to males (Abram et al., 2014; Grande et al., 2012; Holzer et al., 2018; Teplin et al., 2002; Van Damme et al., 2014). These differences combined with the unique adversities females face when entering the system and historical focus of research on males only (Ehrmann et al., 2019), necessitate a greater understanding of the psychiatric comorbidity and associated risk factors in justice-involved female youth. Even among males, the primary focus has been on White males with only recent attention given to Black youth. Completely absent from investigations are other minority groups, like American Indians, a particularly relevant section of the population given their high rates of co-occurring disorders (Wasserman et al., 2010). This inattention coupled with the existence of behavioral health disparities among non-delinquent youth highlights the need for examination of racial and ethnic differences in disorder prevalence.

Conclusion

Juvenile offenders are notable for their co-extensive psychopathology and broad psychosocial needs. These youths require comprehensive assessments to facilitate matching interventions that fit their risk profile. While there does exist many evidence-informed treatment packages, the delivery of these intervention protocols is complex requiring careful execution and attention to extant gender and racial and ethnic differences. Front end diversion away from juvenile facilities along with community-based childhood prevention programing can reduce the need for deep-end services for juvenile offenders who evince lower levels of violence risk. To be sure, there is a subset of juvenile offenders with severe behavioral issues and criminogenic propensity for which close surveillance is warranted. This close surveillance should not exclude treatment opportunities as they arise. Juvenile offenders would benefit from greater research on finer grained symptoms and their behavioral correlates for youth with differing sociodemographic backgrounds, systematic attention to facility-based program implementation and fidelity, and ongoing testing of effects for these programs.

References

Aalsma, M. C., Schwartz, K., & Perkins, A. J. (2014). A statewide collaboration to initiate mental health screening and assess services for detained youths in Indiana. *American Journal of Public Health, 104*(10), e82–e88.

Abram, K. M., Choe, J. Y., Washburn, J. J., Teplin, L. A., King, D. C., Dulcan, M. K., & Bassett, E. D. (2014). *Suicidal thoughts and behaviors among detained youth.* US Department of Justice, Office of Justice Programs, Office of Juvenile Justice and Delinquency Prevention.

Andrews, D. A., & Bonta, J. (2010). Rehabilitating criminal justice policy and practice. *Psychology, Public Policy, and Law, 16*(1), 39.

Baglivio, M. T., Wolff, K. T., Piquero, A. R., Greenwald, M. A., & Epps, N. (2017). Racial/ethnic disproportionality in psychiatric diagnoses and treatment in a sample of serious juvenile offenders. *Journal of Youth and Adolescence, 46*(7), 1424–1451.

Banks, B. P., & Gibbons, M. M. (2016). Dialectical behavior therapy techniques for counseling incarcerated female adolescents: A case illustration. *Journal of Addictions & Offender Counseling, 37*(1), 49–62.

Beaudry, G., Yu, R., Långström, N., & Seena, F. (2020). Mental disorders among adolescents in juvenile detention and correctional facilities: An updated systematic review and meta-regression analysis. *Journal of the American Academy of Child & Adolescent Psychiatry.* https://doi.org/10.1016/j.jaac.2020.01.015

Bechtel, K., Lowenkamp, C. T., & Latessa, E. (2007). Assessing the risk of re-offending for juvenile offenders using the Youth Level of Service/Case Management Inventory. *Journal of Offender Rehabilitation, 45*(3–4), 85–108.

Beck, J. S. (2011). Cognitive-behavioral therapy. *Clinical Textbook of Addictive Disorders,* 491, 474–501.

Borum, R., Bartel, P., & Forth, A. (2002). *Manual for the structured assessment for violence risk in youth (SAVRY): Consultation version.* University of South Florida, Florida Mental Health Institute.

Borum, R., & Verhaagen, D. A. (2006). *Assessing and managing violence risk in juveniles.* Guilford Press.

Botvin, G. J., & Kantor, L. W. (2000). Preventing alcohol and tobacco use through life skills training: Theory, methods, and empirical findings. *Alcohol Research & Health, 24*(4), 250.

Boxer, P., Docherty, M., Ostermann, M., Kubik, J., & Veysey, B. (2017). Effectiveness of Multi-systemic Therapy for gang-involved youth offenders: One year follow-up analysis of recidivism outcomes. *Children and Youth Services Review, 73*, 107–112.

Campbell, C., Papp, J., Barnes, A., Onifade, E., & Anderson, V. (2018). Risk assessment and juvenile justice: An interaction between risk, race, and gender. *Criminology & Public Policy, 17*(3), 525–545.

Cellini, H. R. (2000). Mental health concerns of adjudicated adolescents. *Offender Programs Report, 4*(2), 17–32.

Coker, K. L., Wernsman, J., Ikpe, U. N., Brooks, J. S., Bushell, L. L., & Kahn, B. A. (2014). Using the Massachusetts youth screening instrument–version 2 on a community sample of african american and latino/a juvenile offenders to identify mental health and substance abuse treatment needs. *Criminal Justice and Behavior, 41*(4), 492–511.

Colins, O., Vermeiren, R., Vreugdenhil, C., van den Brink, W., Doreleijers, T., & Broekaert, E. (2010). Psychiatric disorders in detained male adolescents: A systematic literature review. *The Canadian Journal of Psychiatry, 55*(4), 255–263.

Dalton, R. F., Evans, L. J., Cruise, K. R., Feinstein, R. A., & Kendrick, R. F. (2009). Race differences in mental health service access in a secure male juvenile justice facility. *Journal of Offender Rehabilitation, 48*(3), 194–209.

DeLisi, M., & Vaughn, M. G. (2015). *The Routledge International Handbook of Biosocial Criminology.* Routledge.

Development Services Group, Inc. (2014). *"Alternatives to Detention and Confinement." Literature review.* Washington, D.C. Office of Juvenile Justice and Delinquency Prevention. https://www.ojjdp.gov/mpg/litreviews/AlternativesToDetentionandConfinement.pdf

Development Services Group, Inc. (2017a). *"Diversion Programs." Literature review.* Office of Juvenile Justice and Delinquency Prevention. https://www.ojjdp.gov/mpg/litreviews/Diversion_Programs.pdf

Development Services Group, Inc. (2017b). *Intersection between mental health and the juvenile justice system.* Office of Juvenile Justice and Delinquency Prevention. https://www.ojjdp.gov/mpg/litreviews/Intersection-Mental-Health-Juvenile-Justice.pdf

Development Services Group, Inc., & United States of America. (2015). *Model Programs Guide Literature Review: Risk/Needs Assessments for Youths.*

Dixon, L., Dopp, A. R., Borduin, C. M., & Brown, C. E. (2015). Evidence-based treatments for juvenile sexual offenders: Review and recommendations. *Journal of Aggression, Conflict and Peace Research.*

Dodge, K. A., & Mandel, A. D. (2012). Building evidence for evidence-based policy making. *Criminology & Public Policy, 11*(3), 525.

Dopp, A. R., Coen, A. S., Smith, A. B., Reno, J., Bernstein, D. H., Kerns, S. E., & Altschul, D. (2018). Economic impact of the statewide implementation of an evidence-based treatment: Multi-systemic therapy in New Mexico. *Behavior Therapy, 49*(4), 551–566.

Ehrmann, S., Hyland, N., & Puzzanchera, P. (2019). *Juvenile justice statistics national report series bulletin: Girls in the juvenile justice system.* U.S. Department of Justice. https://ojjdp.ojp.gov/sites/g/files/xyckuh176/files/pubs/251486.pdf

Farrington, D. P. (1998). Predictors, causes, and correlates of male youth violence. *Crime and Justice, 24,* 421–475.

Fazel, S., Doll, H., & Långström, N. (2008). Mental disorders among adolescents in juvenile detention and correctional facilities: A systematic review and metaregression analysis of 25 surveys. *Journal of the American Academy of Child & Adolescent Psychiatry, 47*(9), 1010–1019.

Fixsen, D. L., Blase, K. A., Naoom, S. F., & Wallace, F. (2009). Core implementation components. *Research on Social Work Practice, 19*(5), 531–540.

Forth, A. E., Kosson, D. S., & Hare, R. D. (2003). *Hare psychopathy checklist: Youth version.* Multi-Health Systems.

Frick, P. J. (2012). Developmental pathways to conduct disorder: Implications for future directions in research, assessment, and treatment. *Journal of Clinical Child & Adolescent Psychology, 41*(3), 378–389.

Garascia, J. A. (2005). The price we are willing to pay for punitive justice in the juvenile detention system: Mentally ill delinquents and their disproportionate share of the burden. *Indiana Law Journal, 80,* 489–515.

Goldstein, A. P., Glick, B., & Gibbs, J. C. (1998). *Aggression replacement training: A comprehensive intervention for aggressive youth.* Research Press.

Gottfredson, D. C., Kearley, B., Thornberry, T. P., Slothower, M., Devlin, D., & Fader, J. J. (2018). Scaling-up evidence-based programs using a public funding stream: A randomized trial of functional family therapy for court-involved youth. *Prevention Science, 19*(7), 939–953.

Grande, T. L., Hallman, J. M., Underwood, L. A., Warren, K. M., & Rehfuss, M. (2012). Treating detained juveniles: Measuring mental health traits and gender differences. *Review of European Studies, 4,* 14–23.

Greenwood, P. W., & Welsh, B. C. (2012). Promoting evidence-based practice in delinquency prevention at the state level: Principles, progress, and policy directions. *Criminology & Public Policy, 11*(3), 493–513.

Grisso, T., & Barnum, R. (2000). *Massachusetts Youth screening instrument, second version (MAYSI-2): User's manual and technical report.* University of Massachusetts, Medical School, Department of Psychiatry.

Haley, J. (1976). *Problem solving therapy.* Jossey-Bass.

Henggeler, S. W. (1999). Multisystemic therapy: An overview of clinical procedures, outcomes, and policy implications. *Child Psychology and Psychiatry Review, 4*(1), 2–10.

Henggeler, S. W., & Schoenwald, S. K. (2011). Evidence-based interventions for juvenile offenders and juvenile justice policies that support them and commentaries. *Social Policy Report, 25*(1), 1–28.

Henggeler, S. W., Schoenwald, S. K., Borduin, C. M., Rowland, M. D., & Cunningham, P. B. (2009). *Multi-systemic therapy for antisocial behavior in children and adolescents.* Guilford Press.

Hilterman, E. L., Bongers, I., Nicholls, T. L., & Van Nieuwenhuizen, C. (2016). Identifying gender specific risk/need areas for male and female juvenile offenders: Factor analyses with the Structured Assessment of Violence Risk in Youth (SAVRY). *Law and Human Behavior, 40*(1), 82.

Holzer, K. J., Oh, S., Salas-Wright, C. P., Vaughn, M. G., & Landess, J. (2018). Gender differences in the trends and correlates of major depressive episodes among juvenile offenders in the United States. *Comprehensive Psychiatry, 80,* 72–80.

Howell, J. C., & Lipsey, M. W. (2012). Research based guidelines for juvenile justice programs. *Justice Research and Policy, 14*(1), 17–34.

Jesness, C. F. (2004). *The Jesness Inventory-Revised*. Multi-health Systems.

Jewell, J. D., Malone, M. D., Rose, P., Sturgeon, D., & Owens, S. (2015). A multiyear follow-up study examining the effectiveness of a cognitive behavioral group therapy program on the recidivism of juveniles on probation. *International Journal of Offender Therapy and Comparative Criminology, 59*(3), 259–272.

Jones, S., & Cauffman, Ph. D, E. (2008). Juvenile psychopathy and judicial decision making: An empirical analysis of an ethical dilemma. *Behavioral Sciences & the Law, 26*(2), 151–165.

Kaya, F., & Buzlu, S. (2016). Effects of aggression replacement training on problem solving, anger and aggressive behaviour among adolescents with criminal attempts in Turkey: A quasi-experimental study. *Archives of Psychiatric Nursing, 30*(6), 729–735.

Kazdin, A. E. (2000). Adolescent development, mental disorders, and decision making of delinquent youths. In T. Grisso & R. G. Schwartz (Eds.), *Youth on trial: A developmental perspective on juvenile justice* (pp. 33–65). University of Chicago Press.

Kendall, P. C., & Braswell, L. (1993). *Cognitive-behavioral therapy for impulsive children* (2nd ed.). Guilford Press.

Knoth, L., Page, W. & He, L., (2020). *Washington state's aggression replacement training for juvenile court youth*. Juvenile Justice Update, Winter, Civic Research Institute.

Lee, L. H., Goodkind, S., & Shook, J. J. (2017). Racial/ethnic disparities in prior mental health service use among incarcerated adolescents. *Children and Youth Services Review, 78,* 23–31.

Liang, J., Matheson, B. E., & Douglas, J. M. (2016). Mental health diagnostic considerations in racial/ethnic minority youth. *Journal of child and family studies, 25*(6), 1926–1940.

Liddle, H. A. (2014). Adapting and implementing an evidence-based treatment with justice-involved adolescents: The example of multidimensional family therapy. *Family Process, 53*(3), 516–528.

Linehan, M. M. (1993). *Skills training manual for treating borderline personality disorder*. Guilford Press.

Lipsey, M. W. (2018). Effective use of the large body of research on the effectiveness of programs for juvenile offenders and the failure of the model programs approach. *Criminology & Public Policy, 17*(1), 189–198.

Lyons, C. L. (2016). The role of the child and adolescent psychiatrist in the adjudicatory assessment. *Child and Adolescent Psychiatric Clinics, 25*(1), 61–69.

Mathys, C. (2017). Effective components of interventions in juvenile justice facilities: How to take care of delinquent youths? *Children and Youth Services Review, 73,* 319–327.

Mendel, R. A. (2011). *No place for kids: The case for reducing juvenile incarceration*. The Annie E. Casey Foundation.

Mendel, R. A. (2014). *Juvenile detention alternatives initiative progress report 2014.* Annie E. Casey Foundation.

Miller, F. G., & Lazowski, L. E. (2001). *The adolescent substance abuse subtle screening inventory-A2 (SASSI-A2) manual.* SASSI Institute.

Minuchin, S. (1974). *Families and family therapy.* Harvard University Press.

Mossière, A., & Serin, R. (2014). A critique of models and measures of treatment readiness in offenders. *Aggression and Violent Behavior, 19*(4), 383–389.

Mpofu, E., Athanasou, J. A., Rafe, C., & Belshaw, S. H. (2018). Cognitive-behavioral therapy efficacy for reducing recidivism rates of moderate-and high-risk sexual offenders: A scoping systematic literature review. *International Journal of Offender Therapy and Comparative Criminology, 62*(1), 170–186.

Murray, J., & Farrington, D. P. (2010). Risk factors for conduct disorder and delinquency: Key findings from longitudinal studies. *The Canadian Journal of Psychiatry, 55*(10), 633–642.

National Research Council. (2013). *Reforming juvenile justice: A developmental approach.* National Academies Press.

Olver, M. E., & Stockdale, K. C. (2017). Convergent and predictive validity of the Jesness Inventory in a sample of juvenile offenders. *Assessment, 24*(7), 865–884.

Orbis Partners, Inc. (2007). *Youth Assessment & Screening Inventory: Administration Guide.* Author.

Patterson, G. R., Reid, J. B., & Dishion, T. J. (1992). *A social interactional approach: Antisocial boys.* Oregon Social Learning Center & Castilian Publishing Company.

Pederson, C. A., Fite, P. J., Weigand, P. D., Myers, H., & Housman, L. (2020). Implementation of a behavioral intervention in a juvenile detention center: Do individual characteristics matter? *International Journal of Offender Therapy and Comparative Criminology, 64*(1), 83–99.

Perelman, A. M., & Clements, C. B. (2009). Beliefs about what works in juvenile rehabilitation: The influence of attitudes on support for "get tough" and evidence-based interventions. *Criminal Justice and Behavior, 36*(2), 184–197.

Poortinga, E., Newman, S. S., Negendank, C. E., & Benedek, E. P. (2009). *Juvenile Sexual Offenders: Epidemiology, Risk Assessment, and Treatment* (Sex Offenders: Identification, Risk Assessment, Treatment, and Legal Issues, 221).

Prentky, R., & Righthand, S. (2003). *Juvenile sex offender assessment protocol-II (J-SOAP-II) manual.* US Department of Justice, Office of Justice Programs, Office of Juvenile Justice and Delinquency Prevention.

Puzzanchera, C. (2019). *Arrests of juveniles in 2018 reached lowest level in nearly 4 decades.* Office of Justice Programs. https://www.ncjrs.gov/App/Publications/abstract.aspx?ID=277732

Puzzanchera, C., & Hockenberry, S. (2008). *National disproportionate minority contact databook.* National Center for Juvenile Justice. http://www.ojjdp.gov/ojstatbb/dmcdb

Pyle, N., Flower, A., Williams, J., & Fall, A. M. (2019). Social risk factors of institutionalized juvenile offenders: A systematic review. *Adolescent Research Review,* 1–14.

Rawal, P., Romansky, J., Jenuwine, M., & Lyons, J. S. (2004). Racial differences in the mental health needs and service utilization of youth in the juvenile justice system. *The Journal of Behavioral Health Services & Research, 31*(3), 242–254.

Rogers, R., Johansen, J., Chang, J. J., & Salekin, R. T. (1997). Predictors of adolescent psychopathy: Oppositional and conduct-disordered symptoms. *Journal of the American Academy of Psychiatry and the Law Online, 25*(3), 261–271.

Sampson, R. J., Raudenbush, S. W., & Earls, F. (1997). Neighborhoods and violent crime: A multilevel study of collective efficacy. *Science, 277*(5328), 918–924.

Schubert, C. A., & Mulvey, E. P. (2014). *Behavioral health problems, treatment, and outcomes in serious youthful offenders.* US Department of Justice, Office of Justice Programs, Office of Juvenile Justice and Delinquency Prevention. https://ojjdp.ojp.gov/sites/g/files/xyckuh 176/files/pubs/242440.pdf

Semel, R. A. (2016). Incorporating the Jesness Inventory-Revised (JI-R) in a Best-Practice Model of Juvenile Delinquency Assessments. *Journal of Forensic Psychology Practice, 16*(1), 1–23.

Sexton, T. L., & Alexander, J. F. (1999). *Functional family therapy: Principles of clinical intervention, assessment, and implementation.* RCH Enterprises.

Sharkey, P., & Sampson, R. J. (2010). Destination effects: Residential mobility and trajectories of adolescent violence in a stratified metropolis. *Criminology, 48*(3), 639–681.

Sickmund, M., Sladky, T. J., Kang, W., & Puzzanchera, C. (2011). *Easy access to the census of juveniles in residential placement.* Retrieved February 14, 2013.

Skowyra, K. R., & Cocozza, J. J. (2007). *Blueprint for change: A comprehensive model for the identification and treatment of youth with mental health needs in contact with the juvenile justice system.* Policy Research Associates, Inc. https://www.ncmhjj.com/wp-content/upl oads/2013/07/2007_Blueprint-for-Change-Full-Report.pdf

Teplin, L. A., Abram, K. M., McClelland, G. M., & Dulcan, M. K. (2003). Comorbid psychiatric disorders in youth in juvenile detention. *Archives of General Psychiatry, 60*(11), 1097–1108.

Teplin, L. A., Abram, K. M., McClelland, G. M., Dulcan, M. K., & Mericle, A. A. (2002). Psychiatric disorders in youth in juvenile detention. *Archives of General Psychiatry, 59*(12), 1133–1143.

Teplin, L. A., Abram, K. M., Washburn, J. J., Welty, L. J., Hershfield, J. A. & Duncan, M. K. (2013). *The Northwestern Juvenile Project: Overview.* Juvenile Justice Bulletin. U.S. Department of Justice, Office of Justice Programs, Office of Juvenile Justice and Delinquency Prevention. https://ojjdp.ojp.gov/sites/g/files/xyckuh176/files/pubs/234522. pdf

Underwood, L. A., Dailey, F. L., Merino, C., & Crump, Y. (2015). Results from a multi-modal program evaluation of a four year statewide juvenile sex offender treatment and reentry program. *Journal of Prison Education and Reentry, 2*(2), 19–32.

Underwood, L. A., Phillips, A., Von Dresner, K., & Knight, P. D. (2006). Critical factors in mental health programming for juveniles in corrections facilities. *International Journal of Behavioral Consultation and Therapy, 2*(1), 107–140.

Underwood, L. A., & Washington, A. (2016). Mental illness and juvenile offenders. *International Journal of Environmental Research and Public Health, 13*(2), 228.

Van Damme, L., Colins, O. F., & Vanderplasschen, W. (2014). Gender differences in psychiatric disorders and clusters of self-esteem among detained adolescents. *Psychiatry Research, 220*(3), 991–997.

Vaughn, M. G., Salas-Wright, C. P., DeLisi, M., Maynard, B. R., & Boutwell, B. (2015). Prevalence and correlates of psychiatric disorders among former juvenile detainees in the United States. *Comprehensive Psychiatry, 59,* 107–116.

Vaughn, M. G., Wallace, J. M., Jr., Davis, L. E., Fernandes, G. T., & Howard, M. O. (2008). Variations in mental health problems, substance use, and delinquency between African American and Caucasian juvenile offenders: Implications for reentry services. *International Journal of Offender Therapy and Comparative Criminology, 52*(3), 311–329.

Vizard, E. (2013). Practitioner Review: The victims and juvenile perpetrators of child sexual abuse–assessment and intervention. *Journal of Child Psychology and Psychiatry, 54*(5), 503–515.

Walden, A. L., Stancil, N., & Verona, E. (2019). Reaching underserved youth: A pilot implementation of a skills-based intervention in short-term juvenile detention. *Journal of Prevention & Intervention in the Community, 47*(2), 90–103.

Wasserman, G. A., McReynolds, L. S., Lucas, C. P., Fisher, P., & Santos, L. (2002). The voice DISC-IV with incarcerated male youths: Prevalence of disorder. *Journal of the American Academy of Child & Adolescent Psychiatry, 41*(3), 314–321.

Wasserman, G. A., McReynolds, L. S., Schwalbe, C. S., Keating, J. M., & Jones, S. A. (2010). Psychiatric disorder, comorbidity, and suicidal behavior in juvenile justice youth. *Criminal Justice and Behavior, 37*(12), 1361–1376.

Welsh, B. C., & Greenwood, P. W. (2015). Making it happen: State progress in implementing evidence-based programs for delinquent youth. *Youth Violence and Juvenile Justice, 13*(3), 243–257.

Whitney, D. G., & Peterson, M. D. (2019). US national and state-level prevalence of mental health disorders and disparities of mental health care use in children. *JAMA Pediatrics, 173*(4), 389–391.

Wijetunga, C., Martinez, R., Rosenfeld, B., & Cruise, K. (2018). The influence of age and sexual drive on the predictive validity of the juvenile sex offender assessment protocol–revised. *International Journal of Offender Therapy and Comparative Criminology, 62*(1), 150–169.

Williams, C. L., Butcher, J. N., Ben-Porath, Y. S., & Graham, J. R. (1992). *MMPI-A content scales: Assessing psychopathology in adolescents.*

Worling, J. R., & Curwen, T. (2001). Estimate of risk of adolescent sexual offense recidivism (ERASOR; Version 2.0). *Juveniles and Children Who Sexually Abuse: Frameworks for Assessment, 2,* 372–397.

Further Reading

Beaudry, G., Yu, R., Långström, N., & Seena Fazel, F. (2020). Mental disorders among adolescents in juvenile detention and correctional facilities: An updated systematic review and meta-regression analysis. *Journal of the American Academy of Child & Adolescent Psychiatry.* https://doi.org/10.1016/j.jaac.2020.01.015

Gottfredson, D. C., Kearley, B., Thornberry, T. P., Slothower, M., Devlin, D., & Fader, J. J. (2018). Scaling-up evidence-based programs using a public funding stream: A randomized trial of functional family therapy for court-involved youth. *Prevention Science, 19*(7), 939–953.

Lipsey, M. W. (2018). Effective use of the large body of research on the effectiveness of programs for juvenile offenders and the failure of the model programs approach. *Criminology & Public Policy, 17*(1), 189–198.

Sanders, W. B. (2018). *Juvenile offenders for a thousand years: Selected readings from Anglo-Saxon times to 1900.* UNC Press Books.

Whitney, D. G., & Peterson, M. D. (2019). US national and state-level prevalence of mental health disorders and disparities of mental health care use in children. *JAMA Pediatrics, 173*(4), 389–391.

Adult Perpetrated Firesetting

21

Nichola Tyler⊙ and Magali-Fleur Barnoux⊙

Key Points

- Deliberate firesetting is frequently encountered by clinicians working in forensic mental health settings.
- The Multi-Trajectory Theory of Adult Firesetting (M-TTAF) represents the latest contemporary theory of adult firesetting to guide assessment and treatment of this behaviour.
- Individuals who set fires can be distinguished from non-firesetting individuals based on key clinical features (i.e., potential criminogenic needs).
- Rather than being directly causal, psychopathology is hypothesised to exacerbate pre-existing psychological vulnerabilities, increasing the risk of firesetting in certain contexts.
- A number of emerging firesetting specific risk assessment tools and intervention programmes are showing promising results, though much more research is needed.

N. Tyler (✉)
School of Psychology, Victoria University of Wellington, Wellington, New Zealand
e-mail: Nichola.Tyler@vuw.ac.nz

M.-F. Barnoux
Tizard Centre, Division of the Study of Law, Society and Social Justice, University of Kent, Canterbury, UK
e-mail: M.Barnoux@kent.ac.uk

Introduction

Deliberate firesetting by adults, is increasingly recognised as a significant international issue that has a considerable impact on the physical, psychological, and economic wellbeing of society. This chapter will first introduce key terminology and then outline the prevalence and incidence of this behaviour. An overview of contemporary theoretical explanations for deliberate firesetting will be provided followed by a discussion of demographic, developmental, and clinical features of individuals who set deliberate fires. Consideration is given to the role of psychopathology in the aetiology of firesetting, including disorders where firesetting is detailed as a specific symptom (e.g., pyromania) and other psychopathological conditions identified as prevalent among those who set fires. Finally, the chapter will conclude with a discussion on current approaches to assessment and treatment.

Terminology

Historically, the terms *arson, pyromania,* and *firesetting* have been used interchangeably, however, these are conceptually very different. *Arson* is a legal term that refers to a criminal offence involving the unlawful damage or destruction of property by fire, either recklessly or with intent (Gannon & Pina, 2010). *Pyromania* is a psychiatric disorder within the International Classification of Diseases (ICD-10; WHO, 2019) and the Diagnostic and Statistical Manual of Mental Disorders 5 (DSM-5; American Psychiatric Association, 2013) of which firesetting is a primary symptom. *Firesetting* is currently the preferred term in the literature and is used to describe all acts of intentionally set fires regardless of the individual's legal or medical status (Dickens & Sugarman, 2012; Gannon & Pina, 2010). Throughout this chapter, the term *firesetting* will be used unless referring to studies or research which specifically include individuals convicted of *arson* or diagnosed with *pyromania.*

Prevalence

Statistics published by fire and emergency services indicate that tens of thousands of fires are intentionally lit in the UK, USA, Australia, and New Zealand every year (Campbell, 2017; Fire and Emergency New Zealand, 2019; Home Office, 2017; Smith et al., 2014). These fires are responsible for significant amounts human, property, environmental, economical, and societal harm. Despite the large numbers of deliberate fires, it is unclear how prevalent firesetting is as a behaviour, with little research directly examining this in the general population. Research examining data collected within the National Epidemiological Survey of Alcohol and Related Conditions (NESARC) in the US, found that approximately 1% of adults reported a lifetime history of deliberate firesetting with 38% of these individuals reporting having engaged in firesetting past 15 years of age (Blanco et al., 2010; Vaughn et al., 2010). Whilst these findings indicate that a minority of people engage in deliberate firesetting, methodological limitations associated with the survey limit conclusions regarding the prevalence of this behaviour (e.g., lack of question specificity, risk of socially desirable responding with face-to-face data collection). Research with community samples in the UK, which sought to improve on the methodology of the NESARC, suggests that between 11% and 17.8% of adults report having intentionally set a fire over the age of 10 years for either antisocial or fire interest purposes (Barrowcliffe & Gannon, 2015, 2016; Gannon & Barrowcliffe, 2012).

Historically, firesetting has been suggested to be over-represented among individuals with mental health issues and/or intellectual and developmental disabilities (IDD) (Henry & Chaplin, 2016; Tyler & Gannon, 2012) (Chapter 18). Research from the UK, Europe, and Scandinavia suggests that between 10 and 14% of individuals in forensic mental health services have a lifetime history of intentional firesetting (Coid et al., 2001; Fazel & Grann, 2002; Hollin et al., 2013; Repo et al., 1997). In samples of individuals with an IDD, the prevalence of firesetting has largely been estimated from unrepresentative samples and varies from 0.4% to 66.6%, depending on the recruitment and sampling strategy (Alexander et al., 2015; Burns et al., 2003; Ritchie & Huff, 1999). Despite an increased prevalence, there is insufficient evidence to support a direct association between mental health or IDD and firesetting (Henry & Chaplin, 2016; Tyler & Gannon, 2012).

Theoretical Explanations

There has been some attempt to apply single factor theories to explain firesetting (e.g., psychodynamic theory, social learning theory, displaced aggression, biological theory, and communication), however, there is a distinct lack of comprehensive multi-factor theories for firesetting compared to other types of offending (e.g., sexual offending and violent offending). Fineman's Dynamic Behaviour Theory (Fineman, 1980, 1995) and Jackson et al.'s (1987) functional analytic theory represent two early developments in the literature. Fineman's Dynamic Behaviour Theory hypothesises that firesetting is the result of an inter-action between factors that predispose an individual to engage in maladaptive behaviours, developmental experiences that reinforce firesetting as a normative behaviour, immediate environmental and contextual factors that support firesetting as an appropriate response (e.g., triggering event, crisis or trauma; cognition and affect), and internal and external perpetuating factors (e.g., reinforcers). Similarly, Jackson et al.'s (1987) functional analytic theory of recidivistic arson hypothe-sises that repeat firesetting results from a complex interaction between distal (i.e., psychosocial disadvantage, dissatisfaction with life and self, ineffective social skills, previous fire experiences) and proximal antecedents (i.e., triggering events, increased negative affect) and positive (i.e., gaining attention, power, influence over peers) and negative (i.e., punishment, and intense supervision) behavioural reinforcers.

A key strength of both Fineman's and Jackson et al.'s multi-factor theories, is that they integrate established psychological theory (e.g., social learning theory, dynamic behaviour, functional analysis principles) , empirical research, and clin-ical experience to provide overarching explanations of firesetting. However, both theories have been criticised for failing to include (a) a wide range of risk fac-tors to account for myriad motivations associated with firesetting, (b) a detailed explanation of how various risk factors may interact to produce firesetting, and (c) factors that may be associated with desistance from firesetting (Gannon et al., 2012). Further, both theories draw heavily on literature using male psychiatric samples and lack empirical validation across other populations.

More recently, the Multi-Trajectory Theory of Adult Firesetting (M-TTAF; Gannon et al., 2012) was developed using a theory knitting approach (Kalmar & Sternberg, 1988) to address the issues associated with previous theories and pro-vide a comprehensive overarching framework to explain adult firesetting. The resulting framework is a two-tiered multi-factor theory, describing the aetiology of firesetting (tier one) and five prototypical trajectories to firesetting (tier two).

Tier one of the M-TTAF hypothesises that *developmental factors and expe-riences* (e.g., caregiver experiences; social skills; learning about the forms and functions of fire; biological and cultural influences ; see Chapters 3 and 9) predispose individuals to developing a range of *psychological vulnerabilities* (e.g., inappropriate interests, attitudes, and associations with fire; cognitive rules about when and how to use fire; attitudes supportive of offending; self and emotional-regulation issues; interpersonal difficulties) which put them at risk of firesetting. Psychological vulnerabilities are suggested to be primed by *proxi-mal factors/triggers* (i.e., life events; contextual factors; internal affect/cognition;

cultural and biological influences) making these more chronic (i.e., *critical risk factors*), which in turn increase the risk of firesetting. *Moderating factors* (i.e., mental health and self-esteem) are hypothesised to be protective or exacerbate pre-existing psychological vulnerabilities. Tier two of the M-TTAF outlines five prototypical trajectories to firesetting that are characterised by their unique combination of psychological vulnerabilities and critical risk factors in tier one: *antisocial, grievance, fire interest, emotionally expressive/need for recognition*, and *multifaceted* (see Table 21.1 for case descriptions).

Whilst the M-TTAF represents the latest comprehensive theory of firesetting, the framework is limited by inherent weaknesses in the extant literature and the paucity of research on risk factors for firesetting and various subgroups (e.g., females, IDD). Further, the mechanisms by which psychological vulnerabilities/critical risk factors influence deliberate firesetting are yet to be empirically tested. Thus, the M-TTAF is likely to require further refining and evaluation as new knowledge is generated.

Characteristics of Adults Who Set Fires

The majority of research has focused on either describing those who set fires or distinguishing them from non-firesetting individuals on various demographic and background factors. Research suggests firesetting is predominantly a male perpetrated crime, with gender ratios around 6:1 male to female (Gannon & Pina, 2010). However, women who set fires appear to be over-represented in forensic mental health samples, with ratios reported as low as 1.5:1 males to females, depending on the sample and setting (Enayati et al., 2008; Hollin et al., 2013; Swinton & Ahmed, 2001). Further, research suggests that women who set fires have significantly higher rates of firesetting incidents on record and are significantly more likely to be reconvicted of arson on discharge than their male counterparts (Hollin et al., 2013; Tyler et al., 2015; Wyatt et al., 2019).

Adults who set fires are frequently reported to lack intimate relationships (Dickens et al., 2009; Rice & Harris, 1991; Rix, 1994), come from low socioeconomic backgrounds (Rice & Harris, 1991; Ritchie & Huff, 1999), have poor educational attainment (Anwar et al., 2011; Räsänen et al., 1996), and have a history of unemployment (Anwar et al., 2011; Rice & Harris, 1991). Difficult developmental contexts are reportedly common including histories of abuse and parental substance abuse (Alexander et al., 2015; Dickens et al., 2007; Jayaraman & Frazer, 2006; Repo et al., 1997; Root et al., 2008). A history of previous

Table 21.1 Case descriptions of the M-TTAF trajectories adapted from Gannon et al. (2012)

Trajectory	Case description
Antisocial	General antisocial lifestyle (e.g., presence of antisocial peers, antisocial personality traits, attitudes, and beliefs that support general offending, long and diverse criminal history). Fire is often used out of convenience as part of antisocial or criminal pursuits. Individuals likely have a cognitive script that fire is the best way to get rid of evidence as well as poor impulse control and problem solving. Likely motivators include boredom, vandalism, crime concealment, financial gain, and retribution
Grievance	Poor self-regulation particularly in relation to feelings of anger, hostility, and aggressive responding. Likely to have poor interpersonal skills, issues with anger rumination, and a cognitive script for using fire as a powerful messenger. Likely motivators include revenge and retribution
Fire interest	Inappropriate interest or fascination with fire, attitudes/beliefs that support firesetting (e.g., firesetting as normal, fire is controllable), highly impulsive, and have a script around using fire to cope with/manage negative affect. Likely motivators include fire interest, thrill/sensation seeking, stress or boredom
Emotionally expressive/ Need for recognition	This trajectory reflects two subgroups who both have primary risk factors associated with poor interpersonal skills (e.g., intimacy, communication, social interactions), poor problem solving, and cognitive scripts around fire as a powerful messenger (e.g., to draw attention to emotional needs) and as a coping mechanism. Emotionally expressive individuals have additional risk factors of poor coping and emotional regulation and likely motivators include cry for help, self-harm, and suicide. Need for recognition individuals are likely to have additional risk factors associated with narcissistic personality traits, and a surplus in self-regulation. Their likely motivator is need for recognition
Multi-faceted	A unique combination of risk factors that reflect both an intrinsic interest/fascination with fire and entrenched offense-supportive attitudes. Also likely to have issues with anger, hostility, rumination, poor problem solving, impulsivity, and communication. For these individuals, fire is their preferred "tool" for solving a range of different problems and therefore likely hold various cognitive scripts around how and when fire should be used as well as multiple motivations for firesetting

antisocial behaviour and criminal convictions, including firesetting, has also been frequently identified in adults who set fires (Hill et al., 1982; Rice & Harris, 1996; Soothill et al., 2004) with research suggesting that firesetting adults are criminally versatile (Ducat, Ogloff, et al., 2013).

Clinical Features

Psychopathology

The relationship between firesetting and psychopathology is complex. Several psychiatric conditions have been proposed over the years, which have listed fire-setting as a core symptom (e.g., conduct disorder in youth; pyromania in adults) (Nanayakkara et al., 2014). Research has also sought to examine the prevalence and relationship between firesetting and a range of other mental health conditions, so as to understand the contribution of psychopathology to the aetiology of firesetting. Due to these complexities, it is important to distinguish between adult psychiatric conditions where firesetting is a primary symptom and those conditions that have been found to be associated with firesetting.

Pyromania. Pyromania is classified within the *Disruptive, Impulse-Control and Conduct Disorders* section of the DSM-5 (APA, 2013) and the *Habit and Impulse Disorders* section of the ICD-10 (WHO, 2019). Unlike conduct disorder in youth, intentional firesetting is the sole behavioural symptom for pyromania. Under the DSM-5, the diagnostic criteria for pyromania are comprised of four clusters of positive symptoms and two clusters of exclusionary criteria. Positive symptoms include (a) multiple episodes of deliberate and purposeful firesetting, (b) tension or affective arousal before setting a fire, (c) fascination, interest, curiosity, or attraction to fire, fire paraphernalia, its uses or consequences, and (d) experiencing pleasure, gratification, or relief when setting, witnessing the effects of, or participating in the aftermath of a fire. Exclusionary criteria include (e) fires set for monetary gain, an expression of socio-political ideology, to conceal a crime, as an expression of anger or revenge, to improve one's living circumstances, or in response to delusions or hallucinations, and (f) the firesetting is better explained by conduct disorder, a manic episode, or antisocial personality disorder (APA, 2013). Symptoms under the ICD-10 are broadly similar to those specified in the DSM-5, although the exclusion criteria vary and include *"firesetting by or in (a) adult dissocial personality disorder, (b) alcohol or psychoactive substance intoxication, (c) as the reason for observation for suspected mental disorder, (d) conduct disorders, (e) organic mental disorders, or (f) schizophrenia"* (WHO, 2019).

Although deliberate firesetting is the essential behavioural feature of pyromania, due to the strict diagnostic criteria, diagnoses of the condition are rare. Research examining the prevalence of pyromania has either found no *true* cases (Leong, 1992; Prins et al., 1985; Rice & Harris, 1991; Ritchie & Huff, 1999) or reported very small estimates in psychiatric samples, ranging from 3 to 10% (Grant et al., 2005; Lindberg et al., 2005; Lejoyeux et al., 2002; McElroy et al., 1992). It is therefore unsurprising that the DSM-5 states that primary diagnoses of pyromania are very rare (APA, 2013). Given the rarity of pyromania, it has been suggested that firesetting may be better explained by other psychopathology (Gannon & Pina, 2010; Nanayakkara et al., 2014).

General psychopathology. Early writings implied a direct link between fireset-ting and poor mental health. However, research suggests that whilst mental health issues and/or IDD may be factors related to firesetting for some, most individuals who set fires do not have a mental illness, personality disorder, or IDD (Henry & Chaplin, 2016; Tyler & Gannon, 2012). Although the majority of adults who set fires do not have a mental illness or IDD, research indicates increased rates of psychopathology and contact with mental health services (Ducat, Ogloff, et al., 2013).

Several mental and behavioural disorders have been identified as being comor-bid with firesetting including schizophrenia, mood disorders, personality disorder, IDD, and substance dependence (Gannon & Pina, 2010; Nanayakkara et al., 2014; Tyler & Gannon, 2012). Studies that have compared firesetting and non-firesetting samples (both general population and other offending groups) have found signifi-cantly higher rates of schizophrenia, psychosis, borderline personality traits, drug dependence, major depression, IDD, and antisocial personality disorder (Anwar et al., 2011; Ó Ciardha, Alleyne et al., 2015). These findings suggest that a range of psychopathology are commonly identified in individuals who set fires and that such issues are more prevalent among those who set fires than both non-firesetting offending groups and the general population. However, whilst these findings sug-gest a possible association between mental health and/or IDD and firesetting, it does not suggest that firesetting is caused by these conditions (McEwan & Ducat, 2016). Contemporary theories of firesetting suggest that mental health and/or IDD may in fact be indirectly associated with firesetting behaviour, interacting with and reflecting other pre-existing psychological vulnerabilities and making these more chronic (Gannon et al., 2012). It is therefore important to formulate the role that psychopathology plays in an individual's firesetting alongside other psychological factors.

Psychological Characteristics

There has been limited research exploring the psychological characteristics of individuals who set fires, with the majority of existing studies using small and highly selected samples (e.g., those residing in prisons or forensic mental health settings). However, the extant literature suggests that individuals who set fires are characterised by low levels of assertiveness and poor communication skills (Jackson et al., 1987), low self-esteem (Jackson et al., 1987; Räsänen et al., 1996), high impulsivity (Dolan et al., 2002; Räsänen et al., 1996), poor interpersonal skills (Jackson et al., 1987; Rice & Chaplin, 1979), and difficulties with initiating and maintaining relationships (Dickens et al., 2007; Rice & Harris, 1991; Ritchie & Huff, 1999). More recently, research has focused on identifying psychological characteristics that are able to distinguish those who set fires from non-firesetting individuals. Gannon et al. (2013) examined the treatment needs of 68 imprisoned males with a history of firesetting and compared these to a matched control group of 68 non-firesetting imprisoned males. Compared to the non-firesetting controls, participants with a history of firesetting reported significantly higher levels of anger arousal and cognition (i.e., rumination), identification with fire, and serious fire interest. They also reported a more externalised locus of control, lower levels of self-esteem, and poorer fire safety awareness. These findings suggest that adults who set fires have a distinct set of psychological needs that should be targeted as part of prevention and intervention efforts.

Motivations

Multiple motive-based classification systems for firesetting have been proposed in the literature. Commonly identified motivations include anger or revenge, fire interest or "pyromaniac tendencies", stimulation (e.g., excitement, boredom), crime concealment, profit, financial reward or insurance fraud, attention seeking/cry for help, suicide or self-harm, and as a result of psychotic symptoms (Dickens & Sugarman, 2012; Gannon & Pina, 2010) (see also Chapter 8). Although the prevalence of motives vary across studies depending on the sample, setting, and the way in which datapoints are defined and coded, anger and revenge have consistently been identified as one of the most prevalent motives for firesetting, with estimates of around 33% (Rix, 1994). These findings suggest that people set fires for a variety of different reasons.

Risk Factors for Reoffending

As noted earlier, individuals who set deliberate fires often engage in a range of antisocial and offending behaviours (Ducat, McEwan, et al., 2013; Dickens et al., 2009). Thus, unsurprisingly, research suggests that this group are highly likely to reoffend (Ducat et al., 2015; Edwards & Grace, 2014; Rice & Harris, 1996). Individuals who set fires are more likely to reoffend with either a violent or non-violent offence than with fire (Ducat et al., 2015; Edwards & Grace, 2014; Rice & Harris, 1996) with estimations of firesetting reoffending ranging between 4 and 16% (Ducat et al., 2015; Edwards & Grace, 2014; Rice & Harris, 1996).

Little research has examined risk factors associated with deliberate firesetting. Most studies involve retrospective file reviews comparing factors which distinguish firesetting and non-firesetting individuals and "one-time" and repeat firesetting. Factors that have been consistently associated with repeat firesetting include an expressed interest in fire/explosives (Rice & Harris, 1996; Tyler et al., 2015), history of relationship problems (Dickens et al., 2009; Rice & Harris, 1996), the presence of a mental illness (Dickens et al., 2009; Ducat et al., 2015; Lindberg et al., 2005), a history of childhood firesetting (Rice & Harris, 1996), medication non-compliance (Ritchie & Huff, 1999; Wyatt et al., 2019), and social isolation (Repo & Virkkunen, 1997; Wyatt et al., 2019).

Clinical Applications: Assessment and Treatment of Firesetting

There is a lack of validated assessment and intervention protocols for deliberate firesetting. As a result, there has been little guiding information for clinicians to inform case formulation and treatment planning for those who set fires. Given that fire-specific interests, associations, and attitudes appear to be important psychological factors associated with firesetting, some attention has been given to developing measures to assess these constructs. These include the *Fire-setting Assessment Schedule* (FAS; Murphy & Clare, 1996), *Fire Setting Scale* (FSS; Gannon & Barrowcliffe, 2012), *Fire Proclivity Scale* (FPS; Gannon & Barrowcliffe, 2012), and *Four Factor Fire Scales* (FFFS; Ó Ciardha, Barnoux et al., 2015, Ó Ciardha et al., 2016). Although validation studies for the above measures are limited, the latter three measures have been found to discriminate between firesetting and non-firesetting adults; representing potentially helpful aids for experienced clinicians to inform assessment and treatment.

In the absence of a validated risk assessment tool for firesetting, several frameworks have been developed to guide the collection of clinical information to inform firesetting risk assessment and treatment planning: *Pathological Fire-setters Interview* (Taylor et al., 2004), *St Andrew's Fire and Arson Risk Instrument* (SAFARI; Long et al., 2014), and the *Northgate Firesetter Risk Assessment* (Taylor & Thorne, 2005). These frameworks aim to provide clinicians with a helpful guide to factors associated with firesetting to identify relevant risk and treatment needs. However, the ability of these frameworks to predict future firesetting has yet to be assessed.

There has been little focus on developing and evaluating specialist interventions for firesetting (see also Chapter 29). Most published evaluations represent small single cohort studies (e.g., Annesley et al., 2017; Taylor et al., 2002, 2006). More recently, two specialist interventions underpinned by the M-TTAF were developed: *the Firesetting Intervention Programme for Prisoners* (FIPP; Gannon, 2012) and *the Firesetting Intervention Programme for Mentally Disordered Offenders* (FIP-MO; Gannon & Lockerbie, 2011). The FIPP and FIP-MO are semi-structured interventions that target the psychological vulnerabilities associated with firesetting. Both interventions have been subject to quasi-experimental multisite evaluations with participants who attended the interventions demonstrating larger improvements pre-post treatment, relative to a treatment as usual comparison group, across the majority of treatment targets. Whilst the FIPP and FIP-MO evaluations represent emerging evidence regarding "what works" in firesetting treatment, research is still required to establish their suitability for subgroups with complex needs (i.e., IDD), the effectiveness of the interventions in reducing reoffending, and to understand any potential unintended effects associated with partial or non-completion of the programmes.

Conclusions

Whilst there have been significant advancements in our understanding of adult firesetting in recent years, more research is required to further our understanding of aetiology and approaches to assessment and treatment. For example, little is known about the relationship between cultural factors and fire misuse, gender-specific factors, or the needs of individuals with IDD. In addition, research on factors that influence the maintenance and desistance process for fire setting will aid the construction of valid and reliable risk assessment tools and ensure individualised treatment approaches are evidence-led. This will also ensure that treatment efforts evolve to meet the needs of individuals who have set fires regardless of the treatment setting.

References

Alexander, R. T., Chester, V., Green, F. N., Gunaratna, I., & Hoare, S. (2015). Arson or fire setting in offenders with intellectual disability: Clinical characteristics, forensic histories, and treatment outcomes. *Journal of Intellectual and Developmental Disability, 40*(2), 189–197. https://doi.org/10.3109/13668250.2014.998182

American Psychiatric Association. (2013). *Diagnostic and statistical manual of mental disorders* (5th ed.).

Annesley, P., Davison, L., Colley, C., Gilley, L., & Thomson, L. (2017). Developing and evaluating interventions for women firesetters in high secure mental health care. *Journal of Forensic Practice, 19*(1), 59–76. https://doi.org/10.1108/JFP-12-2015-0054

Anwar, S., Långström, N., Grann, M., & Fazel, S. (2011). Is arson the crime most strongly associated with psychosis?—A national case-control study of arson risk in schizophrenia and other psychoses. *Schizophrenia Bulletin, 37*(3), 580–586. https://doi.org/10.1093/sch bul/sbp098

Barrowcliffe, E. R., & Gannon, T. A. (2015). The characteristics of un-apprehended firesetters living in the UK community. *Psychology, Crime and Law, 21*(9), 836–853. https://doi.org/10.1080/1068316X.2015.1054385

Barrowcliffe, E. R., & Gannon, T. A. (2016). Comparing the psychological characteristics of un-apprehended firesetters and non-firesetters living in the UK. *Psychology, Crime and Law, 22*(4), 382–404. https://doi.org/10.1080/1068316X.2015.1111365

Blanco, C., Alegria, A. A., Petry, N. M., Grant, J., Blair Simpson, H., Liu, S.-M., Grant, B. F., & Hasin, D. (2010). Prevalence and correlates of firesetting in the US: Results from the National Epidemiologic Survey on Alcohol and Related Conditions (NESARC). *Journal of Clinical Psychiatry, 71*(9), 1218–1225. https://doi.org/10.4088/JCP.08m04812gry

Burns, M., Bird, D., Leach, C., & Higgins, K. (2003). Anger management training: The effects of a structured programme on the self-reported anger experience of forensic inpatients with learning disability. *Journal of Psychiatric and Mental Health Nursing, 10*(5), 569–577. https://doi.org/10.1046/j.1365-2850.2003.00653.x

Campbell, R. (2017). *Intentional Fires*. National Fire Protection Association. http://www.nfpa.org/news-and-research/fire-statistics-and-reports/fire-statistics/fire-causes/arson-and-juvenile-firesetting/intentional-fires

Coid, J., Kahtan, N., Gault, S., Cook, A., & Jarman, B. (2001). Medium secure forensic psychiatry services: Comparison of seven English health regions. *British Journal of Psychiatry, 178*, 55–61. https://doi.org/10.1192/bjp.178.1.55

Dickens, G., & Sugarman, P. (2012). Adult firesetters: Prevalence characteristics and psychopathology. In G. L. Dickens, P. A. Sugarman, & T. A. Gannon (Eds.), *Firesetting and Mental Health* (pp. 3–27). RCPsych.

Dickens, G., Sugarman, P., Ahmad, F., Edgar, S., Hofberg, K., & Tewari, S. (2007). Gender differences amongst adult arsonists at psychiatric assessment. *Medicine, Science and the Law, 47*, 233–238. https://doi.org/10.1258/rsmmsl.47.3.233

Dickens, G., Sugarman, P., Edgar, S., Hofberg, K., Tewari, S., & Ahmad, F. (2009). Recidivim and dangerousness in arsonists. *Journal of Forensic Psychiatry & Psychology, 20*(5), 621–639. https://doi.org/10.1080/14789940903174006

Dolan, M., Millington, J., & Park, I. (2002). Personality and neuropsychological function in violent, sexual and arson offenders. *Medicine, Science and the Law, 42*(1), 34–43. https://doi.org/10.1177/002580240204200107

Ducat, L., McEwan, T. E., & Ogloff, J. R. P. (2013). Comparing the characteristics of firesetting and non-firesetting offenders: Are firesetters a special case? *Journal of Forensic Psychiatry and Psychology, 24*(5), 549–569. https://doi.org/10.1080/14789949.2013.821514

Ducat, L., McEwan, T. E., & Ogloff, J. R. P. (2015). An investigation of firesetting recidivism: Factors related to repeat offending. *Legal and Criminological Psychology, 2091*, 1–18. https://doi.org/10.1111/lcrp.12052

Ducat, L., Ogloff, J. R. P., & McEwan, T. E. (2013). Mental illness and psychiatric treatment amongst firesetters, other offenders, and the general community. *Australian and New Zealand Journal of Psychiatry, 47*(10), 945–953. https://doi.org/10.1177/0004867413492223

Edwards, M. J., & Grace, R. C. (2014). The development of an actuarial model for arson recidivism. *Psychiatry, Psychology and Law, 21*(2), 218–230. https://doi.org/10.1080/13218719.2013.803277

Enayati, J., Grann, M., Lubbe, S., & Fazel, S. (2008). Psychiatric morbidity in arsonists referred for forensic assessment in Sweden. *The Journal of Forensic Psychiatry and Psychology, 19*(2), 139–147. https://doi.org/10.1080/14789940701789500

Fazel, S., & Grann, M. (2002). Older criminals: A descriptive study of psychiatrically examined offenders in Sweden. *International Journal of Geriatric Psychiatry, 17*, 907–913. https://doi.org/10.1002/gps.715

Fineman, K. R. (1980). Firesetting in childhood and adolescence. Child psychiatry: Contributions to diagnosis, treatment and research. *Psychiatric Clinics of North America, 3*(3), 483–500.

Fineman, K. R. (1995). A model for the qualitative analysis of child and fire deviant behavior. *American Journal of Forensic Psychology, 13*(1), 31–60.

Fire and Emergency New Zealand. (2019). *Data on deliberately lit fire incidents by fire type and cause.*

Gannon, T. (2012). *The Firesetting Intervention Programme for Prisoners (FIPP).* University of Kent.

Gannon, T. A., & Barrowcliffe, E. (2012). Firesetting in the general population: The development and validation of the Fire Setting and Fire Proclivity Scales. *Legal and Criminological Psychology, 17*(1), 105–122. https://doi.org/10.1348/135532510X523203

Gannon, T. A., & Lockerbie, L. (2011). *Firesetting Intervention Programme for Mentally Disordered Offenders (FIP-MO) Version 1.0.* CORE-FP, University of Kent and Kent Forensic Psychiatry Services, NHS.

Gannon, T. A., Ó Ciardha, C., Barnoux, M. F. L., Tyler, N., Alleyne, E. K. A., & Mozova, K. (2013). Male imprisoned firesetters have different characteristics than other imprisoned offenders and require specialist treatment. *Psychiatry: Interpersonal and Biological Processes, 76*(4) 349–364. https://doi.org/10.1521/psyc.2013.76.4.349

Gannon, T. A., Ó Ciardha, C., Doley, R. M., & Alleyne, E. (2012). The multi-trajectory theory of adult firesetting (M-TTAF). *Aggression and Violent Behavior, 17*, 107–121. https://doi.org/10.1016/j.avb.2011.08.001

Gannon, T. A., & Pina, A. (2010). Firesetting: Psychopathology, theory and treatment. *Aggression and Violent Behavior, 15*, 224–238. https://doi.org/10.1016/j.avb.2010.01.001

Grant, J. E., Levine, L., Kim, D., & Potenza, M. D. (2005). Impulse control disorders in adult psychiatric inpatients. *American Journal of Psychiatry, 162*(11), 2184–2188. https://doi.org/10.1176/appi.ajp.162.11.2184

Henry, J., & Chaplin, E. (2016). Assessment and treatment of deliberate firesetters with intellectual disability. In R. M. Doley, G. L. Dickens, & T. A. Gannon (Eds.), *The psychology of arson: A practical guide to understanding and managing deliberate firesetters* (pp. 55–67). Routledge.

Hill, R. W., Langevin, R., Paitich, D., Handy, L., Russon, A., & Wilkinson, L. (1982). Is arson an aggressive act or property offense? *Canadian Journal of Psychiatry, 27*, 648–654.

Hollin, C. R., Davies, S., Duggan, C., Huband, N., McCarthy, L., & Clarke, M. (2013). Patients with a history of arson admitted to medium security: Characteristics on admission and follow up post-discharge. *Medicine, Science and the Law, 53*(3), 154–160. https://doi.org/10.1258/msl.2012.012056

Home Office. (2017). *Fire Statistics: Deliberate fires attended.* https://www.gov.uk/government/statistical-data-sets/fire-statistics-data-tables#deliberate-fires

Jackson, H. F., Hope, S., & Glass, C. (1987). A functional analysis of recidivistic arson. *British Journal of Clinical Psychology, 26*, 175–185. https://doi.org/10.1111/j.2044-8260.1987.tb01345.x

Jayaraman, A., & Frazer, J. (2006). Arson: A growing inferno. *Medicine, Science and the Law, 46*, 295–300. https://doi.org/10.1258/rsmmsl.46.4.295

Kalmar, D. A., & Sternberg, R. J. (1988). Theory knitting: An integrative approach to theory development. *Philosophical Psychology, 1*, 153–170. https://doi.org/10.1080/09515088808572934

Lejoyeux, M., Arbaretaz, M., McLoughlin, M., & Adès, J. (2002). Impulse control disorders and depression. *Journal of Nervous and Mental Disease, 190*(5), 310–314.

Lindberg, N., Holi, M. M., Tani, P., & Virkkunen, M. (2005). Looking for pyromania: Characteristics of a consecutive sample of Finnish male criminals with histories of recidivist fire-setting between 1973 and 1993. *BMC Psychiatry, 5*(47), 1–5. https://doi.org/10.1186/1471-244X-5-47

Leong, G. B. (1992). A psychiatric study of persons charged with arson. *Journal of Forensic Science, 37*(5), 1319–1326.

Long, C. G., Banyard, E., Fulton, B., & Hollin, C. R. (2014). Developing an assessment of fire-setting to guide treatment in secure settings: The St Andrew's fire and arson risk instrument (SAFARI). *Behavioural and Cognitive Psychotherapy, 42*(5), 617–628. https://doi.org/10.1017/S1352465813000477

McElroy, S. L., Hudson, J. I., Pope, H. G., Keck, P. E., & Aizley, H. G. (1992). The DSM-III impulse control disorders not elsewhere classified: Clinical characteristics and relationship to other psychiatric disorders. *American Journal of Psychiatry, 149*(3), 318–326.

McEwan, T. E., & Ducat, L. (2016). The role of mental disorder in firesetting behaviour. In R. M. Doley, G. L. Dickens, & T. A. Gannon (Eds.), *The psychology of arson: A practical guide to understanding and managing deliberate firesetters* (pp. 211–227). Routledge.

Murphy, G. H., & Clare, I. C. H. (1996). Analysis of motivation in people with mild learning disabilities (mental handicap) who set fires. *Psychology, Crime and Law, 2*, 153–164. https://doi.org/10.1080/10683169608409774

Nanyakkara, V., Ogloff, J. R. P., & Thomas, S. D. M. (2014). From haystacks to hospitals: An evolving understanding of mental disorder and firesetting. *International Journal of Forensic Mental Health, 14*(1), 66–75. https://doi.org/10.1080/14999013.2014.974086

Ó Ciardha, C., Alleyne, E. K. A., Tyler, N., Barnoux, M. F. L., Mozova, K., & Gannon, T. A. (2015). Examining the psychopathology of incarcerated male firesetters using the Millon Clinical Multiaxial Inventory-III. *Psychology, Crime and Law, 21*(6), 606–616. https://doi.org/10.1080/1068316X.2015.1008478

Ó Ciardha, C., Barnoux, M. F. L., Alleyne, E. K. A., Tyler, N., Mozova, K., & Gannon, T. A. (2015). Multiple factors in the assessment of firesetters' fire interest and attitudes. *Legal and Criminological Psychology, 20*, 37–47. https://doi.org/10.1111/lcrp.12065

Ó Ciardha, C., Tyler, N., & Gannon, T. A. (2016). A practical guide to assessing adult firesetters' fire-specific treatment needs using the Four Factor Fire Scales. *Psychiatry: Interpersonal and Biological Processes, 78*(4), 293–304. https://doi.org/10.1080/003 32747.2015.1061310

Prins, H., Tennent, G., & Trick, K. (1985). Motives for arson (fire raising). *Medicine, Science and the Law, 25*(4), 275–278.

Räsänen, P., Puumalainen, T., Janhonen, S., & Väisänen, E. (1996). Fire-setting from the viewpoint of an arsonist. *Journal of Psychosocial Nursing, 34*(3), 16–21.

Repo, E., & Virkkunen, M. (1997). Outcomes in a sample of Finnish fire setters. *Journal of Forensic Psychiatry & Psychology, 8*(1), 127–137.

Repo, E., Virkkunen, M., Rawlings, R., & Linnoila, M. (1997). Criminal and psychiatric histories of Finnish arsonists. *Acta Psychiatrica Scandinavia, 95*, 318–323. https://doi.org/10.1111/j.1600-0447.1997.tb09638.x

Rice, M. E., & Chaplin, T. (1979). Social skills training for hospitalized male arsonists. *Journal of Behavior Therapy and Experimental Psychiatry, 10*, 105–108. https://doi.org/10.1016/0005-7916(79)90083-1

Rice, M. E., & Harris, G. T. (1991). Firesetters admitted to a maximum security psychiatric institution. *Journal of Interpersonal Violence, 6*, 461–475. https://doi.org/10.1177/088626 091006004005

Rice, M. E., & Harris, G. T. (1996). Predicting the recidivism of mentally disordered firesetters. *Journal of Interpersonal Violence, 11*(3), 364–375. https://doi.org/10.1177/088626096011 003004

Ritchie, E. C., & Huff, T. G. (1999). Psychiatric aspects of arsonists. *Journal of Forensic Science, 44*(4), 733–740.

Rix, K. J. B. (1994). A psychiatric study of adult arsonists. *Medicine, Science and the Law, 34*, 21–24. https://doi.org/10.1177/002580249403400104

Root, C., Mackay, S., Henderson, J., Del Bove, G., & Warling, D. (2008). The link between maltreatment and juvenile firesetting: Correlates and underlying mechanisms. *Child Abuse & Neglect, 32*(2), 161–176. https://doi.org/10.1016/j.chiabu.2007.07.004

Smith, R. G., Jorna, P., Sweeney, J, & Fuller, G. (2014). *Counting the costs of crime in Australia: A 2011 estimate* (Australian Institute of Criminology: Research and public Policy Series 129). http://www.aic.gov.au/media_library/publications/rpp/129/rpp129.pdf

Soothill, K., Ackerley, E., & Francis, B. (2004). The criminal careers of arsonists. *Medicine, Science and the Law, 44*(1), 27–40. https://doi.org/10.1258/rsmmsl.44.1.27

Swinton, M., & Ahmed, A. (2001). Arsonists in maximum security: Mental state at time of firesetting and relationship between mental disorder and pattern of behaviour. *Medicine, Science, and the Law, 41*(1), 51–57. https://doi.org/10.1177/002580240104100110

Taylor, J. L., & Thorne, I. (2005). *Northgate firesetter risk assessment*. Unpublished Manual, Gosforth: Northgate and Prudhoe NHS Trust.

Taylor, J. L., Robertson, A., Thorne, I., Belshaw, T., & Watson, A. (2006). Responses of female fire-setters with mild and borderline intellectual disabilities to a group intervention. *Journal of Applied Research in Intellectual Disabilities, 19*(2), 179–190. https://doi.org/10.1111/j.1468-3148.2005.00260.x

Taylor, J. L., Thorne, I., & Slavkin, M. (2004). Treatment of firesetters. In. W. R. Lindsay, J. L. Taylor, & P. Sturmey (Eds.), *Offenders with Developmental Disabilities* (pp. 221–240). Wiley.

Taylor, J. L., Thorne, I., Robertson, A., & Avery, G. (2002). Evaluation of a group intervention for convicted arsonists with mild and borderline intellectual disabilities. *Criminal Behavior and Mental Health, 12*, 282–293. https://doi.org/10.1002/cbm.506

Tyler, N., & Gannon, T. A. (2012). Explanation of firesetting in mentally disordered offenders: A review of the literature. *Psychiatry: Interpersonal and Biological Processes, 175*(3), 150–169. https://doi.org/10.1521/psyc.2012.75.2.150

Tyler, N., Gannon, T. A., Dickens, G. L., & Lockerbie, L. (2015). Characteristics that predict firesetting in male and female mentally disordered offenders. *Psychology, Crime and Law, 21*(8), 776–797. https://doi.org/10.1080/1068316X.2015.1054382

Vaughn, M. G., Qiang, F., DeLisi, M., Wright, J. P., Beaver, K. M., Perron, B. E., & Howard, M. O. (2010). Prevalence and correlates of fire-setting in the United States: Results from the National Epidemiological Survey on alcohol and related conditions. *Comprehensive Psychiatry, 5*, 217–223. https://doi.org/10.1016/j.comppsych.2009.06.002

WHO. (2019). *Pathological Fire-Setting (Pyromania)*. Retrieved July 8, 2020, from ICD-10 Version: 2016 https://icd.who.int/browse10/2016/en#/F63.1

Wyatt, B., Gannon, T. A., McEwan, T., Lockerbie, L., & O'Connor, A. (2019). Mentally disordered firesetters: An examination of risk factors. *Psychiatry: Interpersonal and Biological Processes, 82*(1), 27–41. https://doi.org/10.1080/00332747.2018.1534520

Further Readings

Dickens, G., Sugarman, P., Edgar, S., Hofberg, K., Tewari, S., & Ahmad, F. (2009). Recidivim and dangerousness in arsonists. *Journal of Forensic Psychiatry & Psychology, 20*(5), 621–639. https://doi.org/10.1080/14789940903174006

Gannon, T. A., Ó Ciardha, C., Barnoux, M. F. L., Tyler, N., Mozova, K., & Alleyne, E. K. A. (2013). Male imprisoned firesetters have different characteristics to other imprisoned offenders and require specialist treatment. *Psychiatry: Interpersonal and Biological Processes, 76*(4), 349–364. https://doi.org/10.1521/psyc.2013.76.4.349

Gannon, T. A., Ó Ciardha, C., Doley, R. M., & Alleyne, E. (2012). The multi-trajectory theory of adult firesetting (M-TTAF). *Aggression and Violent Behavior, 17*, 107–121. https://doi.org/10.1016/j.avb.2011.08.001

Ó Ciardha, C., Tyler, N., & Gannon, T. A. (2016). A practical guide to assessing adult firesetters' fire-specific treatment needs using the Four Factor Fire Scales. *Psychiatry: Interpersonal and Biological Processes, 78*(4), 293–304. https://doi.org/10.1080/003 32747.2015.1061310

Tyler, N., Gannon, T. A., Lockerbie, L., & Ó Ciardha, C. (2018). An evaluation of a specialist firesetting treatment programme for male and female mentally disordered offenders (FIP-MO). *Clinical Psychology and Psychotherapy, 25*(3), 388–400. https://doi.org/10.1002/cpp.2172

Adult Male Contact Sexual Offenders: Challenges in Classification and Theoretical Perspectives

22

Mirthe G. C. Noteborn

Key Points

- Male sexual contact offenders constitute a heterogeneous population that varies in (offending) behavior, individual characteristics, risk factors, and re-offending risk.
- Child sexual abusers are largely classified based on sexual preference for children (exclusively or not), level of social competency, and relationship to the victim(s).
- Men who sexually offend against adults are mainly classified based on offending motivation, amount of aggression used, and relationship to the victim(s).
- Classification typologies are user-friendly, but often limited by cross-classifications and legal definitions of offending that are state- and time-specific.
- Other classifications include those based on risk assessment or multifactorial models, both with their merits and limitations.
- A step forward may be found in a developmental life-course perspective aimed at explaining sexual offending via between- and within-person differences and changes.

Introduction

Adult male contact sexual offenders are often regarded as a homogeneous group with extremely high recidivism rates and low treatment success (e.g., Levenson et al., 2007). However, researchers and clinicians have indicated that sexual offenders constitute a heterogeneous population that varies in (offending) behavior, individual characteristics (e.g., psychological problems, motivation), risk

M. G. C. Noteborn (✉)
Department of Developmental Psychology, Tilburg University, Tilburg, The Netherlands
e-mail: m.g.c.noteborn@tilburguniversity.edu

© The Author(s), under exclusive license to Springer Nature Switzerland AG 2022   415
C. Garofalo and J. J. Sijtsema (eds.), *Clinical Forensic Psychology*,
https://doi.org/10.1007/978-3-030-80882-2_22

factors, and re-offending risk (e.g., Mathews & Collin-Vézina, 2019). Classification systems and explanatory theories can be used to simplify and explain the heterogeneity of the sex offender population, assist in practical decision-making related to the type and duration of the intervention(s), and risk assessment instruments/management and risk of recidivism (e.g., Thornton, 2020).

This chapter provides a glance into the current classification and theoretical perspectives of adult male contact sexual offenders. Classifications and theoretical perspectives will be reviewed by looking at four important criteria for clinical forensic practice and sexual offenders. For one, classifications and theories should have a certain level of *practicality and user-friendliness* for the clinical field. Among researchers and clinicians, there should thus be a clear understanding of what the category or theory entails, indicating a certain level of simplicity (see also Thornton, 2020; Ward et al., 2006). Additionally, it should account for the heterogeneity of the sexual offender population by explaining, accounting for, and validating differences between sexual offenders (*validity in differences*). Moreover, as forensic practice's primary goal is to manage (sexual) offending behavior, classifications and theories should be *helpful in treatment* and should be able to assist in *the prediction of recidivism* (see also Thornton, 2020).

First, I will review several examples of the most commonly known and researched classifications in the sexual offending literature.[1] Pros and cons of the classifications types will be discussed, focusing on the four criteria mentioned above (for a more extensive review of classifications of sexual offenders see Thornton, 2020). Second, multifactorial theories about adult male contact sexual offenders are discussed by focusing on general limitations. Finally, directions for future research are mentioned from a developmental life-course perspective.

Classification of Adult Male Contact Sexual Offenders

In the following section, classification systems based on (1) offense and offender characteristics and (2) risk assessment will be discussed, addressing their strengths and weaknesses.

---

[1] The current chapter describes the classifications in terms of offense and offender characteristics and risk assessment. However, other categorizations of the classification systems have been mentioned, such as clinical descriptions, demographic clusters, psychometric profiles, and theory-driven groups (Bickley & Beech, 2001) or first–fourth-generation classification systems (Cale, 2018).

Classification Based on Offense and Offender Characteristics

The type of offense classification is based most often on the victim's age (i.e., children vs. adults). The term rapist[2,3] often refers to a person who has sexually assaulted an adult, whereas a person who has sexually abused a child is often labeled a *child sexual abuser*. Research has indicated that men who offend against adult women differ from men who offend against children based on the kind of offense supportive attitudes and coping strategy, the level of social competence, and a history of antisocial behavior (e.g., Cale, 2015; Feelgood et al., 2005; Sigre-Leiros et al., 2015). Moreover, men who abuse children are often older and show fewer externalizing behaviors than men who sexually offend against adults (Gannon & Ward, 2008; Whitaker et al., 2008). At the same time, men who rape are more likely to abuse alcohol and to be diagnosed with an (antisocial) personality disorder (e.g., Langstorm et al., 2004).

Adult Men Who Sexually Offended Against Children

Men who sexually abuse children are often described as having low social and emotional functioning (e.g., developmental immaturity, poor social skills, problems with adult relationships), and social incompetence (e.g., low self-image, feelings of being inadequate and loneliness, fear of intimacy in adult relationships, depression, and anxiety) (Allan et al., 2007; Beech, 1998; Bumby & Hansen, 1997; Maniglio, 2012). Additionally, a history of sexual victimization in childhood is prevalent in men who sexually abuse children (Jespersen et al., 2009).

Men who sexually assault children are often classified based on the degree of their sexual preference for children (exclusively or not). As having a pedophilic disorder is a strong predictor of sexual recidivism (Hanson & Bussiere, 1998), the

---

[2] Terminology and definitions on (contact) sexual offenses (e.g., rape, (child) sexual abuse/assault) can differ significantly across legal frameworks, policymaking, social norms, and research. While the current chapter will touch upon some aspects of this issue, it is beyond the current chapter's scope to address this in more detail. For suggested reading, see Mathews and Collin-Vézina (2019).

[3] Many scientific journals are currently moving away from using terms that define the perpetrator and refer to the offense rather than the offender, e.g., men who rape vs. rapist. However, I have chosen to use rapists and child sexual abusers in this paragraph in keeping with previously cited research. Throughout the rest of the chapter, a reference toward the offense will be used (e.g., men who sexually offend against children /adults).

foremost distinction is based on having a pedophilic disorder or not. Pedophilia is described by the *Diagnostic and Statistical Manual of Mental Disorders* (5th ed; DSM–5; American Psychiatric Association, 2013) as "Over a period of at least six months recurrent, intense sexually arousing fantasies, sexual urges, or behaviors involving sexual activity with a prepubescent child or children (generally age 13 or younger). [...] The individual is at least age 16 years and at least five years older than the aforementioned child or children" (p. 697; American Psychiatric Association, 2013). To be diagnosed with a pedophilic disorder, the sexual urges and fantasies have to cause clinically significant distress or impairment in social, occupational, or other functioning areas, or the person has to have acted on these urges. The latter means that someone can have a pedophilic disorder without having acted on these feelings. Hence, this person can have a pedophilic disorder without abusing children. In turn, someone can be convicted of having molested a child without having recurrent sexual urges, fantasies, or behaviors that would indicate a pedophilic disorder's diagnosis. Thus, merely the existence of isolated instances of child sexual abuse does not warrant the diagnosis of pedophilia. Seto (2008) estimated that approximately half (40–50%) of the men who sexually abuse children are diagnosed with a pedophilic disorder.

Additionally, men who sexually abuse children are often classified based on:

(1) The degree to which the sexual behavior is fixated (also called preferential; primary sexual preference for children of a certain age) or the basis for psychological needs (regressed or situational; abuse in case of stress or psychological problems, while being primarily attracted to adults) (Groth & Birnbaum, 1978; Groth et al., 1982);

(2) A multidimensional axis system in which the offender is classified on the degree of fixation on children and the level of social competency on one axis, and the amount of contact, the relationship with the victim, the injury conflicted on the victim, and the level of sadistic interest on another axis (Massachusetts Treatment Center Child Molester Classification System (MCT:CM3)) (Knight et al., 1989; Knight & King, 2012; Knight & Prentky, 1990);

(3) The relationship with the victim (e.g., intra- (incest and sibling sexual abuse; Loinaz et al., 2019) or extra-familiar victim).

See Table 22.1 for an overview and explanation of these classifications.

Table 22.1 Overview of adult male contact sexual offender classifications systems

Classification category	Reason of classification		Example classification	Short explanation
Offence and offender characteristic	Men who offend against children	Degree of sexual preference / fixation	1	Pedophilic disorder	Classification based on having the DSM-IV diagnosis of pedophilic disorder or not.Focus is on "Over a period of at least 6 months recurrent, intense sexually arousing fantasies, sexual urges, **or** behaviors" p. 697
			2	Fixated or situational offender	Fixated offender • Primarily social and sexual preference for children certain age • Prefer male victims • Lack peer-age relationships • Often diagnosed pedophilic disorder Situational offender • Primarily attracted to adults • Prefer female victims • Abuse under stress or psychological problems • Often under influence during offence
		Multilevel classification		Massachusetts Treatment Center Child Molester Classification System (MCT:CM3)	Two multidimensional axes; separate axis I and II typology resulting in 24 types

(continued)

Table 22.1 (continued)

Classification category	Reason of classification	Example classification	Short explanation
			• Axis I: The degree of fixation on children (high/low) and the level of social competence (SC; high/low). 4 types: high fixation, low SC (type 0), high fixation, high SC (type 1), low fixation, low SC (type 2), low fixation, high SC (type 3) • Axis II: Amount of contact (high/low), relationship with victim (interpersonal/narcissistic), injury conflicted on victim (high/low) and sadistic interest (SI; high/low). 6 types: high amount of inter-personal (type 1) or narcissistic (type 2) contact; low amount of contact, low physical injury and low SI (type 3) or high SI (type 4); low amount of contact, high physical injury and low SI (type 5) or high SI (type 6)
	Relationship with the victim	Intra- and extra-familiar victim	Intra-familiar • ↓ Antisocial behavior, sexual deviance, offence supportive beliefs • ↑ History of childhood difficulties Extra-familiar • ↓ Age • ↑ Denial and minimization, risk for reoffending
Men who offend against adults	Motivation for offending	1 Groth and Birnbaum (1978)'s rape typology	Motivation and amount of aggression

(continued)

Table 22.1 (continued)

Classification category	Reason of classification	Example classification	Short explanation	
			• Power assertive	Impulsive, to confirm virility and dominance. ↑ aggression.
			• Power reassurance	Overcome insecurities related to women and poor social skill. +/− aggression
			• Anger retaliation	Revenge and power. ↑ aggression
			• Anger excitation / sadistic	Planned eroticized sadistic aggression
			• Opportunistic (Hazelwood, 1987)	In conjunction with other crimes. Rape was not the main reason for offence +/− aggression
		2 Massachusetts Treatment Center Rape Classification System (MTC:R3)	Multilevel classification based on 4 primary motivation including 9 types	
			• Opportunistic: ↑ or ↓ SC (1 & 2)	Impulsive, unplanned, predatory act seeking gratification
			• Pervasively angery (3)	Undifferentiated anger in different domains
			• Sexual: + Sadistic Overt (4), Muted (5) − Sadistic ↑ SC (6), ↓ SC (7)	Prolonged sexual / sadistic fantasies - Aggression, mixture of sexual arousal, distorted cognitions, inadequate sexuality and masculine self-image
			• Vindictive: ↑ SC (8), ↓ SC (9)	Women are focal point of anger, ↓ impulsivity

(continued)

Table 22.1 (continued)

Classification category	Reason of classification	Example classification	Short explanation
	Relationship with the victim	Stranger vs. acquaintance rape	Difference based on the notion that the offender "knows" the victim before the offence. Sometimes defined as known 24 hours before the offence
			• Most sexual offences are against acquaintances · Stranger victims is ↑ risk for reoffending
Risk assessment	Risk level		Based on the final judgment of the risk assessment the offender is classified. For instance, low, medium, or high risk
	Dynamic risk factors		Statistical analyses created typologies based on dynamic risk factors, crimingenic needs and the accumulation of dynamic risk factors

Note. DSM-IV = Diagnostic and Statistical Manual of Mental Disorders, 5th Edition (American Psychiatric Association, 2013), SC=social competence, SI=sadistic interest

Adult Men Who Sexually Offend Against Adults

Despite the heterogeneity, men who sexually offend against adults are generally characterized by low social economic status, poor education, maltreatment in childhood, and psychopathic traits (e.g., Bard et al., 1987; Olver & Wong, 2006; Vess et al., 2004). In terms of criminal history, men who abuse adults are often compared to violent offenders as they are both characterized by a more extensive criminal record pertaining to non-sexual offenses (e.g., Simon, 2000; Smallbone et al., 2003).

Previous work has classified men who sexually offend against adults into several typologies mainly based on offending motivation. Groth and Birnbaum (1978) developed such a typology based on motivation for the offense in combination with the amount of aggression displayed, resulting in four different types of men who rape: (1) power assertive type (i.e., *antisocial rapist*)—impulsive, sexual offense to confirm virility and dominance by using aggressive methods; (2) *power reassurance*—overcome insecurity concerning women and poor social skills by displaying dominant behavior; (3) *anger retaliation* type (also called the aggressive aim rapist)—revenge and power; and (4) *anger excitation* or *sadistic*—expresses planned eroticized sadistic aggression. Later on, Hazelwood (1987) added a fifth type, named *opportunistic rapist*—abuses due to opportunity while committing another offense.

Similar to men who sexually offend against children, there is also a multi-dimensional typology classifying men who sexually offend against adults based on four main motivations for offending, (1) opportunistic, (2) pervasively angry, (3) sexually sadistic/gratification, or (4) vindictive (the Massachusetts Treatment Center Rape Classification System (MTC:R3 Knight & Prentky, 1990; Prentky et al., 1985).

Additionally, men who sexually offend against adults can be classified based on their relationship with the victim. The most used classification is based on stranger vs. acquaintance rape (e.g., date rape, intimate partner rape).[4] The term acquaintance is often defined as a victim with *any degree of familiarity* with the perpetrator (Koss et al., 1988) or based on the notion that the victim and perpetrator *know* each other (Benson et al., 1992). However, as these definitions

---

[4] Having a stranger victim is also a risk factor for men who sexually abuse children (Helmus & Thornton, 2015).

are ambiguous, some research refers to sexual assault involving assailants known for more than 24 hours (Stermac et al., 2004). The prevalence of acquaintance rape is about 60–80% of all rape cases (for an overview, see Lopez et al., 2019). Sexual assault of a stranger or an unknown victim is seen as a risk factor for re-offending (e.g., Helmus & Thornton, 2015).

Pros and cons. The *practicality and user-friendliness* of the classification based on offense type are mixed. Classifying sexual offenders based on the victim's age or the victim's relationship can be considered user-friendly. This type of classification is often straightforward—it is often based on index offense—and therefore widely used in clinical and research practice. However, there is also criticism on this use as the multidimensional models (e.g., MCT:CM 3 and MCT:R3) are considered too complicated for clinical practice (e.g., Knight & King, 2012).

When looking at the *validity* of several classifications, as indicated above, some differences between the categories have been found, indicating that there is some truth in these classifications. However, the primary source of criticism when considering the validation of the classifications is twofold. First, research has indicated a crossover effect between categories (e.g., Heil et al., 2003). For instance, some offenders have both child and adult victims, known and unknown victims, or committed both sexual and non-sexual crimes (for an overview, see Saramago et al., 2020). Moreover, many classifications are based on the nature and characteristics of a particular sexual offense, usually, the offense for which the person is currently incarcerated/arrested (i.e., the index offense) rather than taking into account crossover offenses and victim characteristics over a more extended period (Cale, 2018).

The second point of criticism is based on the legal definition of sexual offending, as sexual offenders are often classified after being convicted of a crime (i.e., incarcerated samples). Whether someone is a sexual offender is determined in the first place by the definition of the law, such as the definition of statutory rape (i.e., sexual contact with a person under the age of consent is illegal regardless of whether both parties freely consented), the age of consent (the age from which someone is deemed capable of consenting to sexual contact), what is considered "consent," and the minimum age of criminal responsibility. The differences in laws between countries or states complicate the definition and classification based on offense type as sexual offender populations differ between countries.

An example of how differences in legal definitions of sexual offending can vary between countries/states is given in Textbox 1.

Textbox 1

Laws and legislation concerning sexual offenses and offenders can differ considerably across countries. For instance, the age of consent is often clearly prescribed by law. However, in some countries, the age of consent is not defined. However, sexual contact outside wedlock is illegal, or may differ depending on marital status or indicate contradicting laws and regulations (e.g., in Indonesia age of consent is 15 for girls, who can marry at 16, whereas children are defined as 18 years or younger by law; for a discussion see Wismayanti et al., 2019). Additionally, same-sex contact is often treated differently—in some countries, same-sex intercourse is per definition considered illegal, or the age of consent differs between same-sex and opposite-sex sexual contact.

Furthermore, some countries do not use gender-neutral language in the statutory rape law, whereby the perpetrator and victim can only be male and female, respectively (e.g., Morocco; Moroccan Penal Code Art. 486). The difference in the minimum age of criminal responsibility (MCAR) also differs significantly across countries. In some Islamic societies, such as Iran, criminal responsibility is linked to the age of maturity or puberty. According to Sharia law, it is nine years for girls and 15 years for boys. In Europe, the age of criminal responsibility ranges from ten (e.g., Switzerland; Loi fédérale régissant la condition pénale des mineurs Art. 3.1) to 16 (e.g., Portugal; the Portuguese penal code art. 19).

The combination of the age of consent and the MCAR provides another challenge: the age of consent and MCAR are often close in age. This resulted that in some countries, sexual activity between consenting adolescents close in age is criminalized and can be considered an act of statutory rape. For this reason, some countries implemented the so-called Romeo and Juliet laws, also called the close-in-age exception, to avoid criminalizing sexual activity between consenting adolescents close in age. In some geographical areas, however, these exceptions are limited to sexual activities of the opposite sex (e.g., Texas; Tex. Penal Code § 21.11). Furthermore, age of consent and MCAR also contribute to the debate about including hebephilic disorder (sexual attraction to children age 11–14 years (early pubertal children)) in the diagnostic manual. While some researchers argue that the inclusion of this additional age category would result in increased diagnostic reliability, others argue that defining something as a disorder when it is considered acceptable in some countries as indicated by the age of consent seems to be a form of social control and would not increase psychiatric credibility (see Blanchard, 2013; Green, 2010).

Case Example

To illustrate the differences in defining a sexual offender and its problems in the definition of sexual offending and the classification systems, the following case is presented, including several alternative scenarios. Possible outcomes in 5 different countries/states are illustrated below.

It is hereby important to note that the following examples are used for illustrative purposes only and do not include exemptions in the law or personal/situational circumstances.

Daniel H. (49) was arrested for having sexual contact with Anna (12). Both Daniel H. and Anna state that the sexual contact was consensual. Is Daniel in this context considered a sexual offender? Or if Daniel (16) and Anna (13) were close in age? Moreover, would it differ if Anna was, in fact, Arno, who was in a same-sex relationship with Daniel?

Country/State	Sexual offender	
	Daniel (49) and Anna (12) / Daniel (49) and Arno (12), same-sex relationship	Daniel (16) and Anna (13) /Daniel (16) and Arno (13), same-sex relationship
The Netherlands	No. The age of consent is 12, making sexual contact with Anna or Arno not a criminal offence per se. No exemption to same-sex relationship.	No. Age of consent is 12, MCAR is also 12. The Netherlands also has a close-in-age exemption (at the discretion of the prosection). No differences for same-sex relationships.
Chile	Yes. The age of consent is 14, making sexual contact with Anna a criminal offence whether the relationship was mutual or not. In same sex the age of consent is higher, namely 18, making sexual contact with Arno also a criminal offense.	Yes/No, Chile has a close-in-age exemption. However, this age gap can be a maximum of 2–3 years depending on the sexual crime. MCAR is 18 and can be lowered to 14 in certain cases. Therefore Daniel would be considered a sexual offender in the heterosexual relationship. However, for same-sex relationships the age of consent is 18 making Daniel and Arno both under the age of consent.
United Kingdom (England and Wales)	Yes. The age of consent is 16, making sexual contact with Anna/Arno a criminal offence whether the relationship was mutual or not. No exception to same-sex relationship.	Yes, the United Kingdom has no close-in-age exemption. The minimal age of criminal responsibility is 10 years old.
Texas, US	Yes. The age of consent is 17, making sexual contact with Anna/Arno a criminal offence whether the relationship was mutual or not. While made invalid by the Supreme court, Texas Penal code still states: "A person commits an offense if he engages in deviate sexual intercourse with another individual of the same sex".	Yes, Texas has a close-in-age exemption, however the age differences is maximum 3 years and it only applies to couples of the opposite sex. MCAR is said to be 15. However, between the age of 10–15 years a judge can decide that you were liable and charge the person with the offence.

	Sexual offender	
Country/State	Daniel (49) and Anna (12) / Daniel (49) and Arno (12), same-sex relationship	Daniel (16) and Anna (13) /Daniel (16) and Arno (13), same-sex relationship
Iran	Yes, both could be considered punishable. Sexual contact outside the marriage is illegal. Legal age for marriage is 13 for girls. Marriage at younger age is possible with guardian's permission. Assuming Daniel and Anna are not married with permission, Daniel and Anna both could be punished for the sexual contact as MCAR is 9 years for girls Iran's Islamic law considers same-sex relationships a crime punishable by the death penalty.	It depends on Daniel and Anna's marital status. Sexual contact outside the marriage is illegal. When Daniel and Anna are married sexual contact is permitted as girls can legally marry at the age of 13. The minimum age of criminal responsibility is 9 for girls and 15 for boys under Sharia law, so both could be held accountable in case the two are not married. Same-sex relationships are a criminal offence.

Note. These examples were chosen to illustrate a point and do not take other factors into account

The Netherlands; Criminal code §245, §247, §486

Texas: Texas Penal Code §8.07, § 21.02, § 21.06, §21.11

Iran: Iranian Civil Code §1041; Islamic Penal Code 1991; see also Mousavi et al. (2012)

Chile: Chilean Penal Code §363; Law 20.084 §3; see also Ahumada (2009)

United Kingdom: Children and Young Persons Act 1933, Section 50; Sexual Offences Act 2003

When considering the *treatment use* of classifications based on offense and offender characteristics, classifications are sometimes used to indicate placement in treatment facilities, intervention groups, and supervision (e.g., specific treatments for child sexual abusers). However, classifications based on offense and offender characteristics fail to provide specific treatment needs and thereby complicate effective risk management partly due to their often simplistic nature and heterogeneity of the offender population. (Ward & Carter, 2019).

Additionally, several classifications have failed to *predict recidivism* (Camilleri & Quinsey, 2008). For instance, the multidimensional axis typologies of Knight and colleagues have been empirically validated (e.g., Loomans et al., 2001; Schaaf et al., 2019, but see also Barbaree et al., 1994), but have been criticized, also by the authors themselves, because of their limited treatment relevance and predictive ability (e.g., Camilleri & Quinsey, 2008). The limited predictive ability of some of these typologies may in part be due to the complexity of some of the typologies (e.g., MCT-CM3), crossover effects, and legal complexities.

Classification Based on Risk Level and Dynamic Risk Factors

An additional way of classifying offenders is the use of risk assessment. Risk assessment instruments can be used to identify the risk of re-occurrence of the same criminal behavior. There are currently two widely accepted approaches to assess recidivism risk for (sexual) re-offending: (1) actuarial risk assessment and (2) structured professional judgment (SPJ) (Chapter 25). An example of an actuarial risk assessment instrument commonly used to assess a sexual offenders' recidivism risk is the STATIC-99(R)/2002[5] (Hanson & Thornton, 2000/2003). The Static comprises 10—primarily static—risk factors based on empirical research in combination with rules for aggregating the relevant information, a numerical score is obtained. The evaluator can come to a numerical prediction of the risk based on included outcome tables and norms. Examples of risk factors include age at release from the index sex offense, criminal history (e.g., prior non-sexual violent or sexual offenses), and several items, including victim characteristics (stranger, unrelated, male).

SPJ instruments, such as the second version of the Sexual Violence Risk–20 (SVR-20 V2; Boer et al., 2018), comprise risk factors (e.g., sexual deviation, escalation in sexual offending, extreme minimization/denial of sexual offending, attitudes that support or condone sexual offending, negative attitude toward supervision/intervention) that are supported by scientific literature to lead to an increased risk in re-offending. Instead of relying on statistical estimates, total scores and norm/percentile tables are used as guidelines for evaluators to decide about the offenders' risk level (Hart et al., 2017).

The two ways of using risk assessment instruments in classifying male contact sexual offenders are somewhat equivocal to the two assessment methods. The first way to use risk assessment in the classification of sexual offenders is by using the total risk level. That is, based on the assessed level of risk for re-offending, the sexual offender can be classified as, for instance, low, medium, or high risk. The second way is focused on classifications based on dynamic risk

---

[5] To assess recidivism risk, the STATIC can be used in combination with the STABLE (Fernandez et al., 2012) and the ACUTE (Hanson & Harris, 2012). In short, the STABLE measures 13 dynamic risk factors and gives information that can also be used for risk management and treatment goals. The ACUTE consists of seven acute dynamic risk factors that can change in a relatively short time.

factors and criminogenic needs and the accumulation of dynamic risk factors—
which is more in line with using an SPJ method. Several studies have attempted
to create such typologies using statistical methods, resulting in typologies such
as a "high-needs group," a "moderate-needs group," and a "low-needs/high-denial
group and/or sexually deviant group" (Beech, 1998; Martínez-Catena et al., 2017;
Seto & Fernandez, 2011).

Risk level pros and cons. This classification can be considered user-friendly.
Most clinicians who work with sexual offenders are experienced in working with
risk assessment instruments or can obtain a risk assessment of the offender (*practicality* and *user-friendliness*). Considering *treatment use*, classification based on
risk level can help clinicians indicate the level and intensity of treatment needed.
For instance, research has indicated that providing long, intense treatment to low-
risk offenders increases the risk of re-offending (see Andrews & Bonta, 2010;
Bonta & Andrews,2017; Risk principle of the Risk Need Responsivity Model)
(Chapter 27). However, classification based on risk level alone neither specifies
the interplay between the risk factors underneath the risk level nor the specific
treatment needs related to the sexual re-offending behavior and the offender.
Risk levels are developed to predict a person's chance of committing the same
offense again; however, they fail to explain why the offender committed the
crimes or what the offender needs to refrain from re-offending (e.g., the Need
and Responsivity Principles form the RNR model; see Ward & Carter, 2019).

Classification based on risk level helps inform practitioners who are most
likely to re-offend and provide a probability of re-offending within a specific
period (Ward & Carter, 2019). However, whereas research has indicated that
risk levels predict recidivism—which is logical as these risk levels are based
on recidivism data—risk levels used in different risk assessment instruments can
have a different meaning. For example, a high-risk level (score four or higher) as
indicated by the STATIC-99R[6] indicates an estimated chance of 27.3 to 48.5%
of re-offending within ten years. However, the same risk level (high; score +
20 and higher) using the Sex Offender Risk Appraisal Guide (SORAG; Quinsey et al., 2006) indicates a probability of re-offending of 80–100% in the same
period. Therefore, it could also be necessary to specify the risk assessment tool

---

[6] Table of the Static-99R used: Observed and estimated ten-year sexual recidivism rates for
Static-99R: High Risk/need Sample. Supplemental Recidivism Rate Tables for Static-99R and
Static-2002R (2015) obtained from www.Static-99.org. Table of the SORAG used from Mac-
Donald, D. K. (2017). Using the Sex Offender Risk Appraisal Guide (SORAG). Retrieved on
March 16, 2021, from http://dustinkmacdonald.com/using-sex-offender-risk-appraisal-guide-
sorag/.

used to determine the classified risk level and re-offending probability (*predicting recidivism*).

Dynamic risk factors pros and cons. In terms of *practicality and user-friendliness*, classifications based on dynamic risk factors are similar to those for risk level. Additionally, dynamic risk factors are part of risk assessment and *risk of recidivism*. Some researchers argue that the classification based on dynamic risk factors works in treatment settings when treatment adheres to the risk-need-responsivity principle (e.g., Martínez-Catena et al., 2017). More precisely, classifications based on dynamic risk factors assess the risk level, which is often used to determine treatment intensity and the need principle, indicating which factors need to be targeted in treatment (RNR-model, see criticism risk level). However, the description of a single risk factor often includes several components of that risk factor (see Ward & Carter, 2019), leaving room for differences between offenders who may seem similar at first sight (*validity in differences*). For instance, the item Sexual Deviance of the STABLE (Fernandez et al., 2012) includes deviant behaviors, deviant victims, and a range of interests and activities. Different offenders could thus end up having the same score on this item.

Multifactorial Models of Adult Male Contact Sexual Offending

In the next section, the major multifactorial models of adult male contact sexual offending will be reviewed. Multifactorial models, also called Level I theories, consider multiple factors in creating a comprehensive account of what causes sexual offending and how certain factors may lead to sexual offending (e.g., Ward et al., 2006). These models will be reviewed by linking general criticism to the four aspects mentioned before: practicality and user-friendliness, explanation and differences between offenders, treatment use, and predictive validity. A full review of these explanatory models and their criticism is beyond the scope of this chapter. However, a brief overview is provided in Table 22.2. Interested readers are referred to Ward and colleagues (2006) who provided an in-depth evaluation and explanation of several of the mentioned theories separately.

The first multifactorial models of child sexual abuse and adult sexual abuse are Finkelhor's (1984) Precondition Model of child sexual abuse and Malamuth and colleagues' (1986, 1996) Confluence model of sexual aggression, respectively. These models were followed by Marshall and Barbaree's (1990) Integrated Theory and Hall and Hirschman's (1992) Quadripartite Model, which aimed to explain sexual offending against children and adults. After evaluating the

Table 22.2 Short overview of multifactorial theories of adult male contact sexual offending

	Short explanation
Sexual offences against children	
Finkelhor's (1984) Preconditions model	Includes four preconditions occurring in sequential order containing four etiological factors: (1) the motivation to sexually abuse and includes 3 of the etiological factors—emotional congruence with children, being sexually aroused by children, and blockage of sexual gratification and sexual fulfillment in more socially approved ways, (2) overcoming internal inhibitors and contains the fourth etiological factors, disinhibition including trait factors (e.g., personality) and state factors (intoxication, stress, cognitive distortions), (3) overcoming external barriers (e.g., lack of parental control) and (4) overcoming resistance by the child (e.g., seeking vulnerable child, using force, manipulation). The four conditions have to be met before sexual abuse will occur
Ward and Siegert's (2002) Pathway model	Five different pathways to sexually abusing a child. These pathways have at the core four clusters of distinct but interacting psychological problems (i.e., intimacy and social skill deficits, distorted sexual scripts, emotional dysregulation, and cognitive distortions). In each pathway, all the clusters are present however differ in degree. The five pathways are (1) Intimacy deficits, (2) Deviant sexual scripts, (3) Emotional dysregulation, (4) Antisocial cognitions, and (5) Multiple dysfunctional mechanisms
Sexual offences against adults	
Malamuth and colleagues (1986, 1996) Confluence model of sexual aggression	An evolutionary and feminist sociocultural approach explains sexual offending and uses ultimate and proximate causes of sexual offending. Men and women have evolutionary different mating strategies. It is a small investment for men to produce offspring (minutes); however, he is never certain that the offspring is his. For women, the investment is longer and the number of offspring lower, resulting in choosing partners based on genetic quality and commitment to parenting. As a result, Malamuth indicated two pathways that converge to produce sexually aggressive behavior: (1) sexual promiscuity (i.e., a preference for impersonal sex with many partners) and (2) hostile masculinity—the use of hostile, dominating, and controlling characteristics to have sexual contact (and other interactions with women) based on the fear and anger resulting from the mating strategy of women. As proximate elements, there are four central elements in Malamuths theory, (1) sexual aggression results from a convergence of risk factors, (2) that predict aggression against woman and not other men, (3) and other coercive and dominating behaviors towards women, and (4) factors beyond the evolutionary factors are important in explaining the occurrence of sexually aggressive behavior (e.g., situational factors, child abuse, parental relationship)

(continued)

Table 22.2 (continued)

	Short explanation
Sexual offences against both children/adults	
Marshall and Barbaree's (1990) Integrated theory	Sexual abuse occurs as a sequence of a number of interacting distal and proximal factors. Developmentally adverse events in early life (e.g., poor or harsh parenting, abuse) result in distorted internal working models of relationship, particularly regarding sex and aggression. These in turn will cause poor social relationship and self-regulation skills. These experiences in early childhood result in several difficulties and vulnerabilities in adolescence leaving the offender illequiped to deal with challanges of adolescence (e.g., dealing with the increase in hormons; resulting in an increase in aggressive and sexual impulses) resulting in greater chance of a disturbed sexual development, low self-esteem etc. These vulnerabilities interact with more transient situational factors that remove the offenders inhibition to sexually offend (e.g., intoxication, stress, presence of a potential victim)
Hall and Hirschman's (1991, 1992) Quadripartite model	Based on four so-called primary motivational precursors: 3 state factors (1) physical sexual arousal (e.g., pedophilia,violent sexual fantasies), (2) inaccurate cognitions that justify sexual aggression (e.g., cognitive distortions, offense supportive beliefs), (3) affective dyscontrol, and one trait factors (4) developmental personality problems (e.g., antisocial personality traits). Whereas all factors are seen as precursors for offending, one factor seems as predominant. Situational factors (e.g., encountering a child alone) function as an activator of the primary factors above the individual's threshold for offending, subsequently increasing the intensity of the other factors. Each of the four factors can be used to identify a particular type of offender, thereby including a male contact sexual offender classification system
Ward and Beech's (2006, 2016) Integrated theory	Four sets of factors converge to cause sexual offending. Biological factors (genetics and brain development) interact with ecological niche factors (e.g., social and cultural environment, personal circumstances, physical environment), resulting in the different neuropsychological factors (motivation/emotion, action selection and control, perception and memory). Together, these factors generate clinical problems related to sexual offending (deviant arousal, offense-related thoughts and fantasies, negative and positive emotional states, and social difficulties. These factors are mediated by the personal agency (i.e., intentional mental states). The consequence of the sexual abuse functions to maintain the cycle as mentioned above

(continued)

Table 22.2 (continued)

	Short explanation
Seto's (2008, 2019) Motivation-facilitation model	Indicates three primary motivations for sexual offending (paraphilia's, high sex drive, and intense mating effort). As only being motivated to offend does not always result in offending behavior (e.g., due to high levels of self-control), facilitation factors may lower the inhibiting factors (e.g., alcohol a state factor, antisocial personality as a state factor). However, Seto argues that even if motivation and facilitation factors are present, sexual offenses cannot occur without situational factors to create opportunities to act (e.g., seeking vulnerable victims). The interaction of motivation, facilitation, and situation leads to sexual offending

strengths and weaknesses of the theories mentioned above concerning child sexual abuse, Ward and Siegert (2002) developed the Pathways Model of child sexual abuse. Building on these theories, Ward and Beech (2006, 2016) developed the Integrated Theory of Sexual Offending (ITSO), a broad theoretical framework through which sexual offending can be understood, including aspects of etiology, biology, and neurology. Not long after the ITSO, Seto (2008, 2019) established the Motivation-Facilitation Model (MFM) of Sexual Offending, focusing on motivations for offending with state and trait factors that facilitate acting upon these motivations.

Taking a close look at these multidimensional theories, it becomes clear that (most of) these models attempt to account for some variation in sexual offenders with different offending motivations. However, the central focus of these theories is on the sexual aspect or motivation of the crime. Because these theories focus primarily on sexual aspects, they are not suitable for offenders who commit sexual offenses out of a mere antisocial motivation. Additionally, in these theories, crossover effects are not always considered and explained by the models, making them most suitable for index offenses explanation instead of explaining more general offense patterns. Similar to classifications, legal definitions concerning sexual offenses differ across countries, which make cross-country validation difficult (*validity in differences*). That is, if theories are built on or developed for specific classifications of offenders, the process of crossover effects and legal definitions becomes circular (see Bickley & Beech, 2001). In terms of *user-friendliness and practicality*, a certain level of simplicity is needed for a theory to be used in daily practice. Whereas some of the listed theories explain offending behavior in a relatively straightforward manner (e.g., Finkelhor's Precondition Model), others include too many factors and conditions to be considered user-friendly (e.g., Hall & Hirschman's Quadripartite Model; Ward et al., 2006). Although these multidimensional models are based on single-factor theories (e.g., Level II theories; theories aimed at understanding individual factors that contribute to sexual offending behavior such as sexual deviance, social skill deficits), the definition of these single-factor theories is not always straightforward. An important example is the term 'cognitive distortions', which is often used in sexual offending literature (Chapter 4). This term is often criticized for its vagueness and broad formulation (e.g., Ó Ciardha & Gannon, 2011), as is illustrated by the fact that distorted sexual scripts (Ward Pathway Model), inaccurate cognitions that justify sexual aggression (Hall & Hirschman's Quadripartite model), and offense-related thoughts and fantasies (Ward & Beech's Integrated theory), all fall under the umbrella of *cognitive distortions*. Additionally, the term may also include justifications, excuses, denial, minimization, and rationalizations concerning antisocial behavior (see Ó Ciardha & Gannon, 2011). Although efforts have been made to provide more clarity regarding this term (i.e., Ó Ciardha & Ward, 2013), there is not one single clear definition used by researchers and clinicians that defines *cognitive distortions*. The lack of clarity regarding such terminology can make communication between clinicians complex (*practicality* and *user-friendliness*).

Considering *treatment use*, these multifactorial models explain offending behavior and are partly developed to help treat sexual offenders. Multifactorial models can help clinicians understand the offense patterns and *causal* factors leading up to the offense (see criticism *predicting recidivism*). Such knowledge is vital for effective practice as it informs clinicians what to target in treatment and how. That is, theories can inform clinicians about different treatment strategies for different motivations, pathways, and offending factors. However, an essential criticism often offered is the vagueness of these theories describing processes and their lack of conceptual clarity (see Ward et al., 2006). This may limit treatment effectiveness as it could be unclear what should be the target of treatment (*treatment use;* see Maruna & Mann, 2006).

Considering the *risk of recidivism*, multidimensional models consist of several single-factor theories considered to be involved in the sexual offending process and are often included in risk assessment instruments. For example, all theories include the single-factor theory of deviant sexual interest, which is considered one of the strongest predictors of sexual recidivism (Hanson & Morton-Bourgon, 2005). However, caution is warranted as formal tests of these theories are challenging. When theories are tested (level I or II), conclusions are often based on cross-sectional correlational designs, making causal interference and predictive conclusions limited (i.e., temporal precedence; McMillan et al., 2008). Additionally, the number of study participants, that is, sexual offenders, is often limited. Against popular belief, the rate of adult male contact sexual offending is - comperatively - low. This low rate of offending in combination with the heterogeneity of sexual offenders makes generalizability difficult. Moreover, most studies are conducted in clinical or legal settings, which leads to an overrepresentation of more serious offenders (e.g., Lussier, 2017; *predicting recidivism*).

Future Steps in Classification and Theory of Adult Male Contact Sexual Offending

Several researchers state that using a more developmental life-course approach to classification and theory could solve several of the aforementioned problems of current classifications and/or theories (e.g., Cale, 2018; Lussier & Blokland, 2017; Seto, 2018). Current perspectives on male contact sexual offending mainly focus on differences across individuals (i.e., between-person differences). In contrast, the developmental life-course (DLC) perspective aims at explaining sexual offending by looking at both these between-person and within-individual differences, such as a person's ability to change their offending behavior over time. The DLC approach thereby focuses on the onset and duration of offending, turning points and life events, and the time of desistance from offending. Moreover, it focuses on longitudinal patterns of individual criminal behavior (Lussier, 2017), which requires longitudinal data from birth cohorts. Although this is challenging (e.g., a significant time investment, clear definitions of single factors that might contribute to the several stages of offending behavior, questionnaire development of certain factors; Lussier & Blokland, 2017), it would eliminate biases related to the use of incarcerated and clinical samples and limit temporal precedence. The advantages of such a longitudinal approach include more precise predictions about recidivism (*predicting recidivism*) and avoiding the implicit bias that sexual offenders are lifelong offenders with a relatively high chance of re-offending (e.g., Spaan et al., 2020; *predict recidivism*).

Whereas multidimensional models using a DLC perspective are still in its infancy, some steps have been taken in the direction of life-course typologies. A life-course typology often used in the general criminal literature is Moffitt's dual taxonomy. Moffit distinguishes two offending pathways, a life-course-persistent offending pathway and an adolescence-limited offending pathway (Moffitt, 1993) (Chapter 2). In the sexual offending literature, there is some evidence for early onset and late-onset antisocial trajectories in men who sexually assault women, whereas most men who sexually assault children engage in minimal offending across the life span and are more associated with late-onset offending trajectories (*predicting recidivism*; e.g., Cale, 2015; Cale et al., 2009; Francis et al., 2014).

Furthermore, crossover effects could be lowered because more general criminal trajectories are often included in typologies based on a more life-course approach (e.g., Spaan et al., 2020). However, it has to be noted that life-course typologies using populations from different countries suffer from similar difficulties with the definition of the law and sexual offender populations across countries as the aforementioned classification and multifactorial approaches (*validity in differences;* see Spaan et al., 2020). Considering treatment use, a within-person approach may entail a more prominent focus in treating patients' individual needs and values related to the onset, desistance, or handling specific turning points in their life.

Conclusion

Despite the merits of using a DLC model for classification and theory, this approach will not solve all the listed challenges faced by current classifications and theories. For instance, the fact that offender samples are generally small, sexual offender populations can change—among others—across jurisdictions and geographical locations, and the fact that definitions of level II theories are sometimes not clear does not disappear when using a DLC approach. More priority in research, law, and policymaking regarding universal definitions of (contact) sexual offenses and the concepts of risk factors (Level II theories) would provide an essential basis for clear classifications and theories' development. One theory can never explain all forms and motivations for adult male contact sexual offending while still being straightforward and specific at the same time. Future research and clinical practice should thus examine a DLC approach in terms of practicality and user-friendliness and its ability to explain and account for differences between offenders, treatment use, and predicting recidivism.

References

Ahumada, C. (2009). Statutory rape law in Chile: For or against adolescents. *Journal of Politics & Law, 2*(2), 94–108. https://www.ccsenet.org/journal/index.php/jpl/article/view/2311

Allan, M., Grace, R. C., Rutherford, B., & Hudson, S. M. (2007). Psychometric assessment of dynamic risk factors for child molesters. *Sexual Abuse: A Journal of Research and Treatment, 19*(4), 347–367. https://doi.org/10.1177/107906320701900402

American Psychiatric Association. (2013). *Diagnostic and statistical manual of mental disorders* (5th ed.). American Psychiatric Association. https://doi.org/10.1176/appi.books.978 0890425596

Andrews, D. A. & Bonta, J. (2010). *The Psychology of Criminal Conduct* (5th ed.). Anderson Publishing Co.

Barbaree, H. E., Seto, M. C., Serin, R. C., Amos, N. L., & Preston, D. L. (1994). Comparisons between sexual and nonsexual rapist subtypes: Sexual arousal to rape, offense precursors, and offense characteristics. *Criminal Justice and Behavior, 21*(1), 95–114. https://doi.org/10.1177/0093854894021001007

Bard, L. A., Carter, D. L., Cerce, D. D., Knight, R. A., Rosenberg, R., & Schneider, B. (1987). A descriptive study of rapists and child molesters: Developmental, clinical, and criminal characteristics. *Behavioral Sciences & the Law, 5*(2), 203–220. https://doi.org/10.1002/bsl.2370050211

Beech, A. R. (1998). A psychometric typology of child abusers. *International Journal of Offender Therapy and Comparative Criminology, 42*(4), 319–339. https://doi.org/10.1177/0306624X9804200405

Benson, D., Charlton, C., & Goodhart, F. (1992). Acquaintance rape on campus: A literature review. *Journal of American College Health, 40*(4), 157–165. https://doi.org/10.1080/07448481.1992.9936277

Bickley, J., & Beech, A. R. (2001). Classifying child abusers: Its relevance to theory and clinical practice. *International Journal of Offender Therapy and Comparative Criminology, 45*(1), 51–69. https://doi.org/10.1177/0306624X01451004

Blanchard, R. (2013). A dissenting opinion on DSM-5 pedophilic disorder. *Archives of Sexual Behavior, 42*(5), 675–678. https://doi.org/10.1007/s10508-013-0117-x

Boer, D. P., Hart, S. D., Kropp, P. R., & Webster, C. D. (2018). *Manual for Version 2 of the Sexual Violence Risk-20: Structured professional guidelines for assessing and managing risk of sexual violence.* Psychological Assessment Resources.

Bonta, J., & Andrews, D. A. (2017). *The psychology of criminal conduct.* Routledge.

Bumby, K. M., & Hansen, D. J. (1997). Intimacy deficits, fear of intimacy, and loneliness among sexual offenders. *Criminal Justice and Behavior, 24*(3), 315–331. https://doi.org/10.1177/0093854897024003001

Cale, J. (2015). Antisocial trajectories in youth and the onset of adult criminal careers in sexual offenders of children and women. In A. Blokland & P. Lucier (Eds.), *Sex offenders: A criminal career approach* (pp. 143–170). Wiley. https://doi.org/10.1002/9781118314630.ch7

Cale, J. (2018). Classification of perpetrators of sexual offences: An overview of three generations of research and development. In P. Lussier & E. Beauregard (Eds.), *Sexual offending a criminological perspective* (pp. 326–348). Routledge.

Cale, J., Lussier, P., & Proulx, J. (2009). Heterogeneity in antisocial trajectories in youth of adult sexual aggressors of women: An examination of initiation, persistence, escalation, and aggravation. *Sexual Abuse, 21*(2), 223–248. https://doi.org/10.1177/1079063209333134

Camilleri, J. A., & Quinsey, V. L. (2008). Pedophilia: Assessment and treatment. In D. R. Laws & W. O'Donohue (Eds.), *Sexual deviance: Theory, assessment, and treatment* (pp. 183–212). Guilford Press.

Feelgood, S., Cortoni, F., & Thompson, A. (2005). Sexual coping, general coping and cognitive distortions in incarcerated rapists and child molesters. *Journal of Sexual Aggression, 11*(2), 157–170. https://doi.org/10.1080/13552600500073657

Fernandez, Y., Harris, A. J. R., Hanson, R. K., & Sparks, J. (2012). *Stable-2007 Coding Manual: Revised*. Her Majesty The Queen in Right of Canada.

Finkelhor, D. (1984). *Child sexual abuse: New theory and research*. Free Press.

Francis, B., Harris, D. A., Wallace, S., Knight, R. A., & Soothill, K. (2014). Sexual and general offending trajectories of men referred for civil commitment. *Sexual Abuse, 26*(4), 311–329. https://doi.org/10.1177/1079063213492341

Gannon, T. A., & Ward, T. (2008). Rape: Psychopathology and theory. In D. R. Laws & W. O'Donohue (Eds.), *Sexual deviance: Theory, assessment, and treatment* (Vol. 2, pp. 336–355). Guilford Press. https://doi.org/10.1016/j.cpr.2008.02.005

Green, R. (2010). Sexual preference for 14-year-olds as a mental disorder: You can't be serious!!. *Archives of sexual behavior, 39*(3), 585–586. https://doi.org/10.1007/s10508-010-9602-7

Groth, A. N., & Birnbaum, A. H. (1978). Adult Sexual Orientation and Attraction to Underage Persons. *Archives of Sexual Behavior, 7*(3), 175–181. http://doi.org/10.1007/BF01542377

Groth, A. N., Hobson, W. F., & Gary, T. S. (1982). The child molester: Clinical observations. *Journal of Social Work & Human Sexuality, 1*(1–2), 129–144. https://doi.org/10.1300/J29 1v01n01_08

Hall, G. C. N., & Hirschman, R. (1991). Toward a theory of sexual aggression: A quadripartite model. *Journal of Consulting and Clinical Psychology, 59*(5), 662–669. https://doi.org/10.1037/0022-006X.59.5.662

Hall, G. C. N., & Hirschman, R. (1992). Sexual aggression against children: A conceptual perspective of etiology. *Criminal Justice and Behavior, 19*(1), 8–23. https://doi.org/10.1177/0093854892019001003

Hanson, R. K., & Bussiere, M. T. (1998). Predicting relapse: A meta-analysis of sexual offender recidivism studies. *Journal of Consulting and Clinical Psychology, 66*(2), 348–362. https://doi.org/10.1037/0022-006X.66.2.348

Hanson, R. K., & Harris, A. J. R. (2012). *ACUTE-2007 Coding Manual*. Her Majesty The Queen in Right of Canada.

Hanson, R. K., & Morton-Bourgon, K. E. (2005). The characteristics of persistent sexual offenders: A Meta-analysis of recidivism studies. *Journal of Consulting and Clinical Psychology, 73*(6), 1154–1163. https://doi.org/10.1037/0022-006X.73.6.1154

Hanson, R. K., & Thornton, D. (2003). *Notes on the development of Static-2002* (User Report 2003-01). Department of the Solicitor General of Canada.

Hart, S. D., Douglas, K. S., & Guy, L. S. (2017). The structured professional judgement approach to violence risk assessment: Origins, nature, and advances. In D. P. Boer, A. R. Beech, T. Ward, L. A. Craig, M. Rettenberger, L. E. Marshall, & W. L. Marshall (Eds.), *The Wiley handbook on the theories, assessment, and treatment of sexual offending* (p. 643–666). Wiley Blackwell. https://doi.org/10.1002/9781118574003.wattso030

Hazelwood, R. R. (1987). Analyzing the rape and profiling the offender. In R. R. Hazelwood, & A. W. Burgess (Eds.), *Practical aspects of rape investigation: A multidisciplinary approach* (pp. 169–199). Elsevier. https://doi.org/10.1201/9781315316369-7

Heil, P., Ahlmeyer, S., & Simons, D. (2003). Crossover sexual offenses. *Sexual Abuse: Journal of Research and Treatment, 15*(4), 221–236. https://doi.org/10.1177/107906320301500401

Helmus, L. M., & Thornton, D. (2015). Stability and predictive and incremental accuracy of the individual items of the Static-99R and Static-2002R in predicting sexual recidivism: A meta-analysis. *Criminal Justice and Behaviour, 42*, 917–937. https://doi.org/10.1177/0093854814568891

Jespersen, A. F., Lalumière, M. L., & Seto, M. C. (2009). Sexual abuse history among adult sex offenders and non-sex offenders: A meta-analysis. *Child Abuse & Neglect, 33*, 179–192. https://doi.org/10.1016/j.chiabu.2008.07.004

Knight, R. A., & King, M. W. (2012). Typologies for child molesters: The generation of a new structural model. In B. K. Schwartz (Ed.), *The Sex offender: Current trends in policy and treatment practice, Vol. 7* (pp. 5-1–5-33). Civic Research Institute, Inc.

Knight, R. A., & Prentky, R. A. (1990). *Classifying sexual offenders: The development and corroboration of taxonomic models.* In W. L. Marshall, D. R. Laws, & H. E. Barbaree (Eds.), *Applied clinical psychology. Handbook of sexual assault: Issues, theories, and treatment of the offender* (pp. 23–52). Plenum Press.

Knight, R. A., Warren, J. I., Reboussin, R., & Soley, B. J. (1989). Predicting rapist type from crime-scene variables. *Criminal Justice and Behavior, 25*(1), 46–80. https://doi.org/10.1177/0093854898025001004

Koss, M. P., Dinero, T. E., Seibel, C. A., & Cox, S. L. (1988). Stranger and acquaintance rape: Are there differences in the victim's experience? *Psychology of Women Quarterly, 12*(1), 1–24. https://doi.org/10.1111/j.1471-6402.1988.tb00924.x

Långström, N., Sjöstedt, G., & Grann, M. (2004). Psychiatric disorders and recidivism in sexual offenders. *Sexual Abuse: A Journal of Research and Treatment, 16*(2), 139–150. https://doi.org/10.1023/B:SEBU.0000023062.56389.ed

Levenson, J. S., Brannon, Y. N., Fortney, T., & Baker, J. (2007). Public perceptions about sex offenders and community protection policies. *Analyses of Social Issues and Public Policy, 7*(1), 137–161. https://doi.org/10.1111/j.1530-2415.2007.00119.x

Loinaz, I., Bigas, N., & de Sousa, A. M. (2019). Comparing intra and extra-familial child sexual abuse in a forensic context. *Psicothema, 31*(3), 271–276. https://doi.org/10.7334/psicothema2018351

Looman, J., Gauthier, C., & Boer, D. (2001). Replication of the Massachusetts Treatment Center child molester typology in a Canadian sample. *Journal of Interpersonal Violence, 16*(8), 753–767. https://doi.org/10.1177/088626001016008002

Lopez, E. C., Koss, M. P., & Kennon, K. (2019). Acquaintance rape. *The Encyclopedia of Women and Crime*, 1–8. https://doi.org/10.1002/9781118929803

Lussier, P. (2017). Juvenile sex offending through a developmental life course criminology perspective: An agenda for policy and research. *Sexual Abuse: A Journal of Research and Treatment, 29*(1), 51–80. https://doi.org/10.1177/1079063215580966

Lussier, P., & Blockland, A. A. J. (2017). A developmental life-course perspective of juvenile and adult sexual offending. In T. Sanders (Ed.), *The Oxford Handbook of Sex Offenses and Sex Offenders* (pp. 242–269). Oxford Handbooks. https://doi.org/10.1093/oxfordhb/9780190213633.013.12

MacDonald, D. K. (2017). *Using the Sex Offender Risk Appraisal Guide (SORAG)*. Retrieved on March 5, 2021 from http://dustinkmacdonald.com/using-sex-offender-risk-appraisal-guide-sorag/

Malamuth, N. M. (1986). Predictors of naturalistic sexual aggression. *Journal of Personality and Social Psychology, 50*(5), 953–962. https://doi.org/10.1037/0022-3514.50.5.953

Malamuth, N. M. (1996). The confluence model of sexual aggression: Feminist and evolutionary perspectives. In D. M. Buss & N. M. Malamuth (Eds.), *Sex, power, conflict: Evolutionary and feminist perspectives* (pp. 269–295). Oxford University Press.

Maniglio, R. (2012). The role of parent–child bonding, attachment, and interpersonal problems in the development of deviant sexual fantasies in sexual offenders. *Trauma, Violence, & Abuse, 13*(2), 83–96. https://doi.org/10.1177/1524838012440337

Marshall, W. L., & Barbaree, H. E. (1990). An integrated theory of the etiology of sexual offending. In *Handbook of sexual assault* (pp. 257–275). Springer. https://doi.org/10.1007/978-1-4899-0915-2_15

Martínez-Catena, A., Redondo, S., Frerich, N., & Beech, A. R. (2017). A dynamic risk factors–based typology of sexual offenders. *International Journal of Offender Therapy and Comparative Criminology, 61*(14), 1623–1647. https://doi.org/10.1177/0306624X16629399

Maruna, S., & Mann, R. E. (2006). A fundamental attribution error? Rethinking cognitive distortions. *Legal and Criminological Psychology, 11*(2), 155–177. https://doi.org/10.1348/135532506X114608

Mathews, B., & Collin-Vézina, D. (2019). Child Sexual Abuse: Towards a Conceptual Model and Definition. *Trauma, Violence, & Abuse, 20*(2), 131–148. https://doi.org/10.1177/1524838017738726

McMillan, D., Hastings, R. P., Salter, D. C., & Skuse, D. H. (2008). Developmental risk factor research and sexual offending against children: A review of some methodological issues. *Archives of Sexual Behavior, 37*(6), 877–890. https://doi.org/10.1007/s10508-007-9193-0

Moffitt, T. (1993). Adolescence-limited and life-course-persistent antisocial behavior: A developmental taxonomy. *Psychological Review, 100*(4), 674–701. https://doi.org/10.1037/0033-295X.100.4.674

Mousavi, S., Shapiee, R., & Nordin, R. (2012). Child offenders in Iran: Legal analysis on the age of criminal responsibility and sentencing. *International Journal of West Asian Studies, 4*(1), 31–48. https://doi.org/10.5895/IJWAS2012.03

Ó Ciardha, C., & Gannon, T. A. (2011). The cognitive distortions of child molesters are in need of treatment. *Journal of Sexual Aggression, 17*(2), 130–141. https://doi.org/10.1080/13552600.2011.580573

Ó Ciardha, C., & Ward, T. (2013). Theories of cognitive distortions in sexual offending: What the current research tells us. *Trauma, Violence, & Abuse, 14*(1), 5–21. https://doi.org/10.1177/1524838012467856

Olver, M., & Wong, S. (2006). Psychopathy, sexual deviance and recidivism among sex offenders. *Sexual Abuse: A Journal of Research and Treatment, 18*(1), 65–81. https://doi.org/10.1177/107906320601800105

Prentky, R., Cohen, M., & Seghorn, T. (1985). Development of a rational taxonomy for the classification of rapists: The Massachusetts treatment center system. *Bulletin of the American Academy of Psychiatry and the Law, 13*(1), 39–70.

Quinsey, V. L., Harris, G. T., Rice, M. E., & Cormier, C. A. (2006). *The law and public policy. Violent offenders: Appraising and managing risk* (2nd ed.). American Psychological Association. https://doi.org/10.1037/11367-000

Saramago, M. A., Cardoso, J., & Leal, I. (2020). Victim crossover index offending patterns and predictors in a Portuguese sample. *Sexual Abuse, 32*(1), 101–124. https://doi.org/10.1177/1079063218800472

Schaaf, S., Jeglic, E. L., Calkins, C., Raymaekers, L., & Leguizamo, A. (2019). Examining ethno-racial related differences in child molester typology: An MTC:CM3 approach. *Journal of Interpersonal Violence, 34*(8), 1683–1702. https://doi.org/10.1177/0886260516653550

Seto, M. C. (2008). Pedophilia and sexual offending against children: Theory, assessment, and intervention. *American Psychological Association.* https://doi.org/10.1037/11639-000

Seto, M. C. (2018). *Explaining sexual offending against children.* In M. C Seto, *Pedophilia and sexual offending against children: Theory, assessment, and intervention* (pp. 85–111). American Psychological Association. https://doi.org/10.1037/0000107-005

Seto, M. C. (2019). The motivation-facilitation model of sexual offending. *Sexual Abuse, 31*(1), 3–24. https://doi.org/10.1177/1079063217720919

Seto, M. C., & Fernandez, Y. M. (2011). Dynamic risk groups among adult male sexual offenders. *Sexual Abuse, 23*(4), 494–507. https://doi.org/10.1177/1079063211403162

Sigre-Leirós, V., Carvalho, J., & Nobre, P. (2015). Cognitive schemas and sexual offending: Differences between rapists, pedophilic and nonpedophilic child molesters, and nonsexual offenders. *Child Abuse & Neglect, 40*, 81–92. https://doi.org/10.1016/j.chiabu.2014.10.003

Simon, L. M. (2000). An examination of the assumptions of specialization, mental disorder, and dangerousness in sex offenders. *Behavioral Sciences & the Law, 18*(2–3), 275–308. https://doi.org/10.1002/1099-0798(200003/06)18:2/3%3c275::AID-BSL393%3e3.0.CO;2-G

Smallbone, S. W., Wheaton, J., & Hourigan, D. (2003). Trait empathy and criminal versatility in sexual offenders. *Sexual Abuse: A Journal of Research and Treatment, 15*(1), 49–60. https://doi.org/10.1023/A:1020615807663

Spaan, P., Blokland, A., De Blander, R., Robert, L., Maes, E., Blom, M., & Wartna, B. (2020). Differentiating individuals convicted of sexual offenses: A two-country latent class analysis. *Sexual Abuse, 32*(4), 423–451. https://doi.org/10.1177/1079063219893370

Stermac, L., Del Bove, G., & Addison, M. (2004). Stranger and acquaintance sexual assault of adult males. *Journal of Interpersonal Violence, 19*(8), 901–915. https://doi.org/10.1177/0886260504266887

Thornton, D. (2007). *Scoring Guide for the Risk Matrix 2000.9/SVC: February 2007 Version.* http://www.bhamlive1.bham.ac.uk/Documents/college-les/psych/RM2000 scoringinstructions.pdf

Thornton, D. (2020). Sexual offending and classification. *Aggression and Violent Behavior, 59*(2), 101436. https://doi.org/10.1016/j.avb.2020.101436

Vess, J., Murphy, C., & Arkowitz, S. (2004). Clinical and demographic differences between sexually violent predators and other commitment types in a state forensic hospital. *Journal of Forensic Psychiatry & Psychology, 15*(4), 669–681. https://doi.org/10.1080/147899404 10001731795

Ward, T., & Beech, A. (2006). An integrated theory of sexual offending. *Aggression and Violent Behavior, 11*(1), 44–63. https://doi.org/10.1016/j.avb.2005.05.002

Ward, T., & Beech, A. (2016). The integrated theory of sexual offending–revised: A multifield perspective. *The Wiley Handbook on the Theories, Assessment and Treatment of Sexual Offending*, 123–137. https://doi.org/10.1002/9781118574003.wattso006

Ward, T., & Carter, E. (2019). The classification of offending and crime related problems: A functional perspective. *Psychology, Crime & Law, 25*(6), 542–560. https://doi.org/10. 1080/1068316X.2018.1557182

Ward, T., Polaschek, D. L., & Beech, A. R. (2006). *Theories of sexual offending* (Vol. 21). Wiley. https://doi.org/10.1002/9780470713648

Ward, T., & Siegert, R. J. (2002). Toward a comprehensive theory of child sexual abuse: A theory knitting perspective. *Psychology, Crime and Law, 8*(4), 319–351. https://doi.org/ 10.1080/10683160208401823

Whitaker, D. J., Le, B., Hanson, R. K., Baker, C. K., McMahon, P. M., Ryan, G., Klein, A., & Rice, D. D. (2008). Risk factors for the perpetration of child sexual abuse: A review and meta-analysis. *Child Abuse & Neglect, 32*(5), 529–548. https://doi.org/10.1016/j.chiabu. 2007.08.005

Wismayanti, Y. F., O'Leary, P., Tilbury, C., & Tjoe, Y. (2019). Child sexual abuse in Indonesia: A systematic review of literature, law and policy. *Child Abuse & Neglect, 95*, 104034. https://doi.org/10.1016/j.chiabu.2019.104034

Suggested Reading

Lussier, P., & Blockland, A. A. J. (2017). A developmental life-course perspective of juvenile and adult sexual offending. In T. Sanders (Ed.), *The Oxford Handbook of Sex Offenses and Sex Offenders* (pp. 242–269). Oxford Handbooks. https://doi.org/10.1093/oxfordhb/ 9780190213633.013.12

Mathews, B., & Collin-Vézina, D. (2019). Child sexual abuse: Towards a conceptual model and definition. *Trauma, Violence, & Abuse, 20*(2), 131–148. https://doi.org/10.1177/152 4838017738726

Thornton, D. (2020). Sexual offending and classification. *Aggression and Violent Behavior, 101436*,. https://doi.org/10.1016/j.avb.2020.101436

Ward, T., Polaschek, D. L., & Beech, A. R. (2006). *Theories of sexual offending* (Vol. 21). Wiley. https://doi.org/10.1002/9780470713648

Homicide and Mental Disorder

23

Pauline G. M. Aarten and Marieke C. A. Liem

Case study

On 10 March 2010, a 12-year-old girl named Millie disappeared from her home in the Netherlands. Her mother had talked to her on the phone just before her disappearance. She hung up the phone by stating to her mother: 'I have to go, there is a man at the door.' When her parents got home, Millie was gone. Her parents reported her missing that same day. Six days later the police found her body buried in the garden of her 26-year-old neighbor Sander, a police officer. He lured her into his home with an excuse where he sexually assaulted her and strangled her. Society was shocked that a neighbor, a police officer who holds a legitimate position within society, was able to commit such a crime. Soon after his confession to the police, which led them to the body of the young girl, his surrounding claimed he suffered from mental health issues. His mentor from high school stated that he was suicidal and cut his arms with raisers: 'You forget a thousand students, but you don't forget him', his mentor explained. An ex-girlfriend claimed he was sexually disturbed and violent in bed (Nu.nl, 2010)

P. G. M. Aarten (✉) · M. C. A. Liem
Institute of Security and Global Affairs, Leiden University, The Hague, The Netherlands
e-mail: p.g.m.aarten@fgga.leidenuniv.nl

M. C. A. Liem
e-mail: m.c.a.liem@fgga.leidenuniv.nl

Key points

- Individuals with a mental disorder seem to run a higher risk of becoming an offender or victim of homicide compared to the general population but the proportion of violence of this group is small.
- Substance abuse seems to play a role in the relationship between mental disorder and homicide.
- A causal relationship between mental disorder and homicide cannot be determined, mostly because of the limitations of scholarly research.

Introduction

Homicides are crimes that concern the most severe types of violence. The killing of one human being by another has far-reaching consequences. Not only is there a loss of a life, but also there are long-lasting (mental health) consequences for the family of the victim, including, but not limited to, posttraumatic stress disorder and depression (Kaltman & Bonanno, 2003; Miller, 2009; Zinzow et al., 2009). It is also seen as a public health threat to society: (high rates of) violence can generate fear among community members which not only affects members' mental health but it can also affect community cohesion and vitality (Pridemore, 2003).

Yet, homicide also interests us. The need to understand the nature and causes of homicide, as well as ways of preventing it, has led to a considerable body of research that has focused on international comparisons of homicide, types of homicides, and the risk factors associated with homicide offending and victimization (for a detailed overview see: Brookman et al., 2017; Liem & Pridemore, 2012).

The relationship between homicide and mental disorders has also received considerable scholarly attention (see, e.g., Large & Nielssen, 2008; Large et al., 2009; Mulvey, 1994; Shaw et al., 2006; Wilcox, 1985). This is partly driven by a flawed perception that individuals with a mental disorder are unequivocally dangerous and not in control of their own behavior (Angermeyer & Dietrich, 2006). In other words, from this perspective individuals with a mental disorder are thought to be more likely to resort to violent behavior. While this idea started in the nineteenth century (Howitt, 1998) this assumption still perseveres today. When, what we perceive to be, a random act of violence occurs we are quick to label the offender as 'crazy' or 'insane,' and just like that we implicitly connect homicide with mental disorders. In the case study presented at the start of this chapter, the offender's surrounding was quick to claim that he had mental health issues. The media used their stories to paint a picture of an offender with severe psychological issues that *led* him to kill a young innocent girl (Nu.nl, 2010).

Yet, research evidence suggests that very few homicides are committed by those with a mental disorder (e.g., Erb et al., 2001; Liem & Vinkers, 2012; Schanda et al., 2006; Simpson et al., 2004; Swinson et al., 2011). In this light, the extent to which homicide is *causally related* to a mental disorder becomes an even more pressing question, especially when looking at ways of preventing homicide. What role do mental disorders play in leading up to a homicide? What do we actually know about the (causal) relationship between mental disorders and homicide? In seeking answers to these questions, we will critically review the vast body of research in this chapter that has examined the potential relationship between homicide and mental disorders. We start by clarifying the key terms in this chapter: homicide and mental disorder.

Defining Homicide and Mental Disorders

With regard to the term homicide, it should be noted that we are using the social-scientific term 'homicide' here, rather than legal terms such as murder (killing another human being with malice aforethought) and manslaughter (not involving malice aforethought). Here, we define intentional homicide as unlawful death purposefully inflicted on an individual by another individual (UNODC, 2019a).

A mental disorder is also subject to different definitions and the research evidence presented in this chapter does not adhere to one definition. For example, some studies adhere to the ICD classification of mental and behavioral disorders by the World Health Organization (e.g., Crump et al., 2013; Golenkov et al., 2011; Hiroeh et al., 2001; Shaw et al., 2006) while other studies relied on the DSM-classification of a mental disorder (e.g., Eronen et al., 1996; Joyal et al., 2004; Putkonen et al., 2004). And yet other studies relied on psychiatric assessments found in court files disallowing any transparency with regard to how clinical judgments about the presence of a mental disorder in a homicide offender were made (e.g., Swinson et al., 2011). Each definition comes with a different assessment of determining the presence of a (specific) mental disorder (Andrews et al., 1999). Furthermore, assessments can also differ because clinical judgments are made by psychologists and psychiatrists who have followed a different training which is also subject to change over the years (Häkkänen & Laajasalo, 2006; Minero et al., 2017). In this chapter, therefore, we refrain from choosing a single definition as the goal of this chapter is to present the research evidence of the relationship between homicide and mental disorders.

The Bigger Picture: General Homicide Rates

Before we describe the research evidence on homicide and mental disorders, let us first turn to the general homicide rates. This will help to better understand and interpret the potentially contributing role of mental disorders in homicide offenders and victims. We use the rate of homicide victims per 100.000 inhabitants so we are able to compare countries with different population sizes with one another.

The United Nations Office on Drugs and Crimes (UNODC) estimated that worldwide in the year 2017 6.1 individuals per 100.000 inhabitants fell victim to homicide. Large regional differences in homicide rates exist: Where the Americas reported a homicide rate of 17.2 victims per 100.000 inhabitants, Africa reported a rate of 13 victims per 100.000 inhabitants, and Asia, Europe, and Oceania reported a rate of 3 victims or less per 100.000 inhabitants in 2017 (UNODC, 2019a). Nevertheless, Europe, North America, and Australia have witnessed a drop in their homicide rates in the past decades (LaFree et al., 2015; Tuttle et al., 2018; UNODC, 2019a; Weiss et al., 2016). In Europe, the average homicide rate has decreased by 37% since 1990 with countries such as Norway, Italy, Spain, the Netherlands, Greece, and Germany reporting a homicide rate of less than 1 victim per 100.000 inhabitants in 2018 (Lappi-Seppälä & Lethi, 2014). This homicide drop is not a universal, but rather a Western phenomenon (LaFree et al., 2015). Countries in Central and South America, in contrast, have shown a rise in homicide rates since the 1980s, a consequence of the local drug markets, firearm availability, and social inequalities (Briceno-León et al., 2008). In a country-level study of homicide rates since the 1950, LaFree and colleagues found that around 1980, the median national homicide rate of Central and South America was below 10 victims per 100.000 inhabitants, but in 2010 this number had doubled (LaFree et al., 2015). This number seems to have risen ever since. According to the UNODC homicide statistics, Venezuela, Honduras, and El Salvador had one of highest homicide rates in 2018 with 30 victims and higher per 100.000 inhabitants (UNODC, 2019b).

Research Evidence on Homicide and Mental Disorders

The evidence to date suggests that few homicides are committed by those with a mental disorder. However, individuals with a mental disorder run a higher risk of becoming an offender or victim of homicide compared with members of the general public (Crump et al., 2013; Nielssen & Large, 2010). These two findings require further clarification.

Prevalence and Incidence[1] of Mental Disorders in Homicide Offenders

Only a few studies have examined the prevalence and incidence of mental disorders in homicide offenders. These studies were largely conducted in Western countries, including but not limited to Canada, England and Wales, Finland, Sweden, and the Netherlands. The countries that have studied the relationship between homicide and mental disorders vary in their approaches on how they examined the role of mental disorders in homicide. Some focused on a specific mental disorder (e.g., Large et al., 2009; Swinson et al., 2011), while others studied the relationship between mental disorder and homicide in general (e.g., Liem & Vinkers, 2012). Mental disorders that are most commonly found in homicide offenders, and most widely studied, are schizophrenia and other types of psychotic disorders as well as personality disorders (Häkkänen & Laajasalo, 2006; Nielssen & Large, 2010; Schanda et al., 2006). Furthermore, the homicide populations differed between studies, where some studies focused on homicide suspects and other studies on convicted offenders (Cote & Hodgins, 1992; Liem & Vinkers, 2012; Nielssen & Large, 2010). For this reason, we have decided to use the more general term *homicide offenders* and specify the population and type of mental disorder when applicable in the presentation of a specific study. This means that there are variations in how studies examined the prevalence and incidence of mental disorders in homicide offenders. These variations also affect the conclusions drawn on the prevalence of mental disorders in homicide offenders, which we will discuss later on in this chapter.

Keeping in mind that each study used a different methodology and data collection techniques, the research evidence suggests that studies based on Western samples have found that one or more mental disorders are present in 5–21% of

---

[1] Prevalence refers to the percentage or proportion of homicide offenders who were diagnosed with a mental disorder and incidence refers to the rate per 100.000 inhabitants.

homicide offenders (Cote & Hodgins, 1992; Eronen et al., 1996; Fazel & Grann, 2004; Large et al., 2009; Meehan et al., 2006; Nielssen & Large, 2010; Schanda et al., 2006; Shaw et al., 2006; Swinson et al., 2011). The incidence of mental disorders among homicide offenders is between 0.05 and 0.35 per 100.000 inhabitants. The large difference in prevalence and incidence cannot only be explained by the variations in study design and focus on (type of) mental disorder, but there is evidence suggesting that homicide rates committed by an individual with a mental disorder are related to the total homicide rates of each country.

To illustrate, Swinson and colleagues (2011) examined rates of mental disorders in convicted homicide offenders in England and Wales in the period 1997–2006. Based on psychiatric reports, contacts with psychiatric services, diminished responsibility verdicts, and hospital disposal, the researchers concluded that 4% of the homicide offenders were diagnosed with schizophrenia and 6% with psychosis at the time of the offense. With an overall homicide rate of 1.28 per 100.000 inhabitants, the homicide rate of individuals diagnosed with psychosis was 0.07, and for individuals diagnosed with schizophrenia the homicide rate was 0.08. Other countries with similar low rates in homicides committed by individuals with a mental disorder and total homicides were Austria, Germany, the Netherlands, and New Zealand (Erb et al., 2001; Liem & Vinkers, 2012; Schanda et al., 2006; Simpson et al., 2004). On the other hand, Golenkov and colleagues (2011) examined the rates of mental disorders in homicide suspects in Chuvash Republic of the Russian Federation, a region in Russia with a high total homicide rate of 12.4 victims per 100.000 inhabitants. They examined pre-trial psychiatric assessments and all legal proceedings of all suspects charged with homicide in the period 1981–2010. The researchers found the rate of schizophrenia in their sample to be 0.35 per 100.000 inhabitants, which is a much higher rate compared with the countries mentioned above. The reason for such elevated rates can most likely be found in the fact that both mental disorder and homicide have etiological factors in common, such as substance abuse, relative and absolute deprivation, and weapon availability (Large et al., 2009). This relationship, however, does not find full (academic) support as will be further discussed in Box 23.1.

Besides the fact that only a small group of homicide offenders are diagnosed with a mental disorder, research evidence suggests that individuals diagnosed with a mental disorder have a 10–20 times greater risk of committing homicide compared with the general population (Erb et al., 2001; Eronen et al., 1996; Fazel & Grann, 2004; Fazel Gulati, et al. 2009; Fazel Langström, et al., 2009; Gotlieb et al., 1987; Joyal et al., 2004; Large et al., 2009; Putkonen et al., 2004;

Schanda et al., 2006). To illustrate, it is estimated that less than 1% of the population has a schizophrenic disorder, but of all homicide offenders, between 5 and 20% are diagnosed with schizophrenia (Fazel & Grann, 2004; Nielssen & Large, 2010). Furthermore, in a systematic review on homicide rates during the first episode of psychosis and after treatment, Nielssen and Large (2010) concluded that individuals diagnosed with psychosis also ran a higher risk of committing homicide compared with the general population, particularly if they did not receive treatment. Based on 10 Western studies,[2] they found that approximately 4 in 10 homicides were committed by individuals with a psychosis before treatment. This number reduced to 1 in approximately 10.000 individuals diagnosed with psychosis who committed homicide after treatment (similar results were also found by Shaw et al., 2006). In other words, the rate of homicide in individuals diagnosed with psychosis before treatment was 15 times higher than when individuals received treatment for their diagnosed psychosis.

Box 23.1 The debate surrounding the relationship between homicide rates committed by the mentally ill and overall homicide rates

In 1983, Jeremy Coid, a forensic psychiatrist, examined existing literature to determine the epidemiology of abnormal homicides and homicide-suicides. He defined abnormal homicides as homicides by individuals who were examined and diagnosed with a mental disorder soon after the offense or homicides by individuals who were deemed insane or who had diminished responsibility according to the court. Based on 12 studies, he formulated an epidemiological law to explain why abnormal homicides follow different patterns than homicides committed by 'normal' offenders. Coid (1983) found a fixed homicide rate of approximately 0.13 individuals diagnosed with a mental disorder per 100.000 inhabitants, regardless of the country. He concluded that homicide rates of individuals diagnosed with a mental disorder were similar across countries and unrelated to their total homicide rates since he found. Based on his findings he argued that most of these homicides were due to the illness itself. His 'law' has found empirical support in other scholarly research (Gudjonsson & Petursson, 1982; Shaw, 1999; Simpson et al., 2004; Taylor & Gunn, 1999)

However, there are two major issues with Coid's study. First, Coid's research was flawed, as he did not report the criteria used to include and

---

[2] Included countries were: England and Wales (2 studies), Canada, Germany, United States, Finland, Australia, New Zealand, and Israel.

exclude studies, there was no statistical evidence to support his findings and the results were confounded by heterogeneous definitions of mental disorder (see also Coid, 2009a, 2009b; Large et al., 2009). Second, while some studies have found support for his laws, lately, other studies have not. In a systematic literature review on the rate of schizophrenia in homicide, Large and colleagues (2009) found that the number of homicides per capita committed by those diagnosed with schizophrenia was positively associated with the total homicide rate in every country (see also Fazel & Grann, 2004; Wilcox, 1985). This begs the question that if it is not the illness itself, what are the factors that mediate or interact with the illness, thereby increasing an individuals' likelihood of committing or becoming a victim of homicide?

Prevalence and Incidence of Mental Disorders in Homicide Victims

In addition to being associated with increased risks of homicide offending, individuals diagnosed with a mental disorder are also at an increased risk of homicide victimization. However, similar to the research on homicide offenders, the same methodological variations apply in the research on mental disorder and homicide victims, with one important difference. While research on homicide offenders included various populations, research on homicide victims mainly concerned population-based studies.

Two of the most recent population-based studies in England and Wales and in Sweden have shown that between 6 and 22% of the individuals with a mental disorder become a victim of a homicide (Crump et al., 2013; Rodway et al., 2014). Furthermore, individuals with a mental disorder run a 2–6 times higher risk of becoming a victim of homicide compared with the general population (Crump et al., 2013; Hillard et al., 1985; Hiroeh et al., 2001; Ruschena et al., 1998). In a nationwide cohort study of the entire population in Sweden in the period 2001–2008, researchers examined homicidal death of the entire population (Crump et al., 2013). They concluded that the general homicide rates were 1.1 per 100.000 inhabitants, but for individuals with a mental disorder the homicide rate was 2.8 per 100.000 and 0.9 among those without a mental disorder. More specifically, after adjusting for the sociodemographic confounders sex and age, the risk of homicidal death was sevenfold among individuals diagnosed with a personality disorder, fivefold among individuals diagnosed with schizophrenia, and threefold among individuals diagnosed with depression or anxiety disorders. In a national study of all confirmed homicides in England and Wales in the period from 2003 to 2005, researchers reached a similar conclusion: individuals diagnosed with a mental disorder had an increased risk of becoming a victim of homicide compared with the general population (Rodway et al., 2014). The increased risk of being a victim is possibly related to the individual's social environment, their use of alcohol or drugs, or the people found in their proximity such as being a patient in a mental health institute and coming into contact with other patients with a history of violence.

Co-morbidity

The rate of mental disorders in homicide offenders and victims is relatively low. In addition, the prevalence and incidence of mental disorders among homicide offenders and victims alone cannot determine causality. To what extent can we state that homicide is the result of a mental disorder? As the risk of homicide is higher in individuals diagnosed with a mental disorder compared with the general public, the fact remains that the vast majority of individuals do not commit or become a victim of homicide. Why do some individuals run a higher risk of becoming a homicide offender or victim? The research evidence suggests that the presence of two or more mental disorders increases the risk of committing or becoming a victim of homicide.

One of the most robust findings is that the presence of substance abuse together with another mental disorder increases the likelihood of homicide. Many of the studies described above found that alcohol and/or drugs abuse increased the risk of committing homicide among individuals with one of the major mental disorders such as schizophrenia, psychosis, depression, and personality disorders (Eronen et al., 1996; Fazel Gulati et al., 2009; Fazel Langström, et al., 2009; Fazel & Grann, 2004; Joyal et al., 2004; Laajasalo & Häkkänen, 2005; Meehan et al., 2006; Putkonen et al., 2004; Swinson et al., 2011). In a study on homicide rates of individuals with a mental disorder in England and Wales, an increase in the prevalence of psychosis and schizophrenia among homicide offenders in the period 1997–2006 was found (Swinson et al., 2011). The most likely explanation was the use of substances at the time of offense as the researchers also found an increase in substance abuse in their sample. In their study in New South Wales, Australia, Nielssen, and colleagues (2007) found that 73% of the homicide offenders diagnosed with a mental disorder were also diagnosed with a substance abuse disorder.

There are also indications that substance abuse plays a role in the association between homicidal death and mental disorder (Crump et al., 2013; Rodway et al., 2014). In a Swedish nationwide cohort study, the risk of homicidal death was higher among individuals diagnosed with a mental disorder who also abused substances compared with individuals who did not (Crump et al., 2013). However, this increased risk was not found for all types of mental disorder they examined, and for this reason, the observed association between mental disorder and homicidal death could not be fully explained by comorbid substance abuse (Crump et al., 2013, p. 3). The lack of studies done in this area inhibits us from further unraveling how substance abuse can increase the risk of homicidal death in individuals diagnosed with a mental disorder.

The Methodological Limitations of the Research Evidence on Homicide and Mental Disorder

The relationship between mental disorder and homicide is more complex than meets the eye and so far, we have only discussed the tip of the iceberg with regard to understanding this relationship. However, the design and operationalizations of the abovementioned scholarly research have inhibited scholars to draw any conclusions about the causality of this relationship. Here we will discuss three main limitations.

First, there is heterogeneity in how studies define and operationalize mental disorder. As described at the start of this chapter, some studies focused on mental disorders in general, whereas other studies focused on a specific mental disorder, such as schizophrenia and psychosis. Homicide is also susceptible to different definitions, with some studies including attempted homicide, or focusing on homicide suspects versus convicted homicide offenders (Cote & Hodgins, 1992; Liem & Vinkers, 2012; Nielssen & Large, 2010). In addition, in most studies, researchers relied on clinical diagnoses to describe their population, but this can affect the rate of the diagnosed mental disorder because these studies vary in the threshold they use for determining a psychiatric diagnosis (Golenkov et al., 2016). The lack of a clear definition and operationalization does not allow for strong statements about the causal relationship between mental disorder—in general or related to specific disorders—and homicide.

Second, most, if not all, of the studies remain descriptive and retrospective. Descriptive research has the limitation that the focus of the research relies solely on describing a phenomenon and not explaining the phenomenon. Many studies have focused on describing rates of mental disorder in homicide offenders. Retrospective research focuses on collecting data by retrospectively asking respondents about their past. While it has the advantage of being able to study rare events, its main limitation is that it can never be determined with certainty whether, and to what extent, mental disorder played a role in the commission of the offense. Prospective research with a representative control sample of non-violent individuals diagnosed with a mental disorder can give us more insight into the causal link between mental disorder and homicide. However, such research designs are difficult to achieve in this specific population.

Third, the geographical focus of many studies is limited. Some studies focused on a region or city within a country (e.g., Erb et al., 2001; Golenkov et al., 2011; Nielssen et al., 2007). The studies that examined representative samples of homicide offenders and victims diagnosed with a mental disorder have mainly been conducted in countries with generally low homicide rates. For example, the systematic review by Large and colleagues (2009) discussed 18 studies of which 17 came from Western Europe, Australia, and East Asia that have (low) homicide rates of about 2.3 per 100.000 inhabitants. Only a handful of studies have examined mental disorder and homicide in countries with homicide rates higher than 10 per 100.000 inhabitants (see, e.g., Golenkov et al., 2011). However, these studies often focused on a specific region or date from a while ago. The findings presented in this chapter thus apply mainly to countries with a low homicide rate and it is unclear what the relationship between mental disorder and homicide entails in countries with higher homicide rates.

Homicide and Mental Disorder: A Complex Relationship

To conclude, the finding that individuals with a mental disorder run a higher risk of becoming an offender or victim of homicide compared to the general population confirms the existence of a relationship between mental disorder and homicide. However, the perception that mental disorder is causally related to homicidal violence has not found support in the still evolving research evidence. This conclusion is important to challenge the stigma and discrimination against individuals with a mental disorder; those with a mental disorder are not all dangerous and that they are just as vulnerable of becoming a victim of homicide besides solely being viewed as the aggressor. The overall message is that within the group of individuals with a mental disorder, there is a specific group that are at a higher risk of committing or becoming a victim of homicide, where certain mental disorders and the co-morbidity with substance abuse warrants closer attention. This could be a fruitful starting point for more research to lay bare the complex relationship between mental disorder and homicide. (Chapter 28).

While causality on macro-levels (population levels) cannot be determined, this question is of great importance at the individual level, particularly in a legal setting. Here, forensic psychiatrists and psychologists seek to answer the question to what extent a mental disorder has contributed to an individual committing violent crime, including homicide. The degree to which mental disorder has played a contributing role in turn influences the degree to which the accused can be held accountable for his or her behavior. This question was also raised in the trial of Sander, the homicide offender in our case study. Psychologists and psychiatrists determined that his drug addiction combined with his personality disorder most likely lowered the obstacle for the offender to kill the young girl. They concluded that Sander was diminished responsible for the crime.

We would like to end this chapter with three final suggestions that we hope future scholars will take at heart. First, we know little about the substantive relationship between mental disorder and homicide. Most of the studies presented in this chapter concentrated on finding a statistical relationship between mental disorders and homicide. This kind of information does not inform us on the mechanisms underlying homicide. From a public health perspective, we have learned that violence in general and homicide specifically is the result of a complex interaction of underlying risk factors that increase the risk of becoming an offender or victim of violence (see also Krug et al., 2002; Thornicroft, 2020). There is some research evidence that specific mental disorders are related to specific crime scene and victim characteristics (see Häkkänen & Laajasalo, 2006; Minero et al., 2017) which needs further exploration.

Secondly, we have outlined that explanatory and predictive research is extremely difficult to conduct, as it requires prospective research instead of retrospective studies. This knowledge is essential to be able to work on prevention, to treat homicide offenders with a mental disorder effectively, and to predict recidivism.

Finally, there is a need for more research that systematically studies the relationship between mental disorder and homicide by using standardized approaches of diagnosing mental disorder in offenders suspected of homicide. This way, we are able to get more (accurate) figures on the prevalence of mental disorder in homicide perpetration and victimization. Together with a standardized inventory of other risk factors that might contribute to the commission of the homicide, it will allow us to further unravel the complex relationship between mental disorder and homicide. This information will not only help us understand to what extent a mental disorder plays a role in homicide, but also on how to shape policies to prevent victimization as well as decreasing recidivism risk through treatment.

References

Andrews, G., Slade, T., & Peters, L. (1999). Classification in psychiatry: ICD-10 versus DSM-IV. *British Journal of Psychiatry, 174*, 3–5.

Angermeyer, M. C., & Dietrich, S. (2006). Public beliefs about and attitudes towards people with mental illnes: A review of population studies. *Acta Psychiatrica Scandinavica, 113*(3), 163–179.

Briceno-León, R., Villaveces, A., & Concha-Eastman, A. (2008). Understanding the uneven distribution of incidence of homicide in Latin America. *International Journal of Epidemiology, 37*(4), 751–757. https://academic.oup.com/ije/article/37/4/751/742442

Brookman, F., Maguire, E. R., & Maguire, M. (2017). *The handbook of homicide*. Wiley-Blackwell.

Coid, J. (1983). The epidemiology of abnormal homicide and murder followed by suicide. *Psychological Medicine, 13*, 855–860.

Coid, J. (2009a). Correspondence: The epidemiology of abnormal homicide and murder followed by suicide. *Psychol Med, 39*, 700–701.

Coid, J. (2009b). Homicide due to mental disorder. *British Journal of Psychiatry, 194*(2), 185–186.

Cote, G., & Hodgins, S. (1992). The prevalence of major mental disorders among homicide offenders. *International Journal of Law and Psychiatry, 15*, 89–99.

Crump, C., Sundquist, K., Winkleby, M. A., & Sundquist, J. (2013). Mental disorders and vulnerability to homicidal death: Swedish nationwide cohort study. *BMJ, 346*. https://doi.org/10.1136/bmj.f557

Erb, M., Hodgins, S., Freese, R., Müller-Isberner, R., & Jöckel, D. (2001). Homicide and schizophrenia: Maybe treatment does have a preventive effect. *Criminal Behavior and Mental Health, 11*, 6–26.

Eronen, M., Hakola, P., & Tiihonen, J. (1996). Mental disorders and homicidal behavior in Finland. *Archives of General Psychiatry, 53*, 497–501.

Fazel, S., & Grann, M. (2004). Psychiatric morbidity among homicide offenders: A Swedish population study. *American Journal of Psychiatry, 163*, 1397–1403.

Fazel, S., Gulati, G., Linsell, L., Geddes, J. R., & Grann, M. (2009). Schizophrenia and violence: Systematic review and meta-analysis. *PLoS Med, 6*, e1000120.

Fazel, S., Langström, N., Hjern, A., Grann, M., & Lichtenstein, P. (2009). Schizophrenia, substance abuse, and violent crime. *JAMA, 301*, 2016–2023.

Golenkov, A., Large, M., Nielssen, O., & Tsymbalova, A. (2011). Characteristics of homicide offenders with schizophrenia from the Russian Federation. *Schizophrenic Research, 133*, 232–237.

Golenkov, A., Large, M., Nielssen, O., & Tsymbalova, A. (2016). Homicide and mental disorder in a region with a high homicide rate. *Asian Journal of Psychiatry, 23*, 87–92.

Gotlieb, P., Cabrielsen, G., & Kramp, P. (1987). Psychotic homicide in Copenhagen from 1959 to 1983. *Acta Psychiatrica Scandinavica, 76*, 285–292.

Gudjonsson, G. H., & Petursson, H. (1982). Some criminological and psychiatric aspects of homicide in Iceland. *Medicine, Science and the Law, 22*(2), 91–98.

Häkkänen, H., & Laajasalo, T. (2006). Homicide crime scene behaviors in a Finnish sample of mentally ill offenders. *Homicide Studies, 10*(1), 33–54.

Hillard, J. R., Zung, W. W., Ramm, D., Holland, J. M., & Johnson, M. (1985). Accidental and homicidal death in a psychiatric emergency room population. *Hospital & Community Psychiatry, 36*, 640–643.

Hiroeh, U., Appleby, L., Mortensen, P. B., & Dunn, G. (2001). Death by homicide, suicide, and other unnatural causes in people with mental illness: A population-based study. *Lancet, 358*, 2110–2112.

Howitt, D. (1998). *Crime, the media and the law*. Wiley.

Joyal, C. C., Putkonen, A., Paavola, P., & Tiihonen, J. (2004). Characteristics and circumstances of homicidal acts committed by offenders with schizophrenia. *Psychological Medicine, 34*, 433–442.

Kaltman, S., & Bonanno, G. A. (2003). Trauma and bereavement: Examining the impact of sudden and violent deaths. *Journal of Anxiety Disorders, 17*, 131–147.

Krug, E. G., Dahlberg, L. L., Mercy, J. A., Zwi, A. B., & Lozano, R. (2002). World report on violence and health. *The Lancet, 360*, 1083–1088.

LaFree, G., Curtis, K., & McDowall, D. (2015). How effective are our "better angels"? Assessing country-level declines in homicide since 1950. *European Journal of Criminology, 12*(4), 482–504.

Lappi-Seppälä, T., & Lethi, M. (2014). Cross-comparative perspectives on global homicide trends. *Crime and Justice, 43*(1), 135–230.

Large, M., & Nielssen, O. (2008). Evidence for a relationship between the duration of untreated psychosis and the proportion of psychotic homicides prior to treatment. *Social Psychiatry & Psychiatric Epidemiology, 43*, 37–44.

Large, M., Smith, G., & Nielssen, O. (2009). The relationship between the rate of homicide by those with schizophrenia and the overall homicide rate: A systematic review and meta-analysis. *Schizophrenia Research, 112*, 123–129.

Laajasalo, T., & Häkkänen, H. (2005). Offence and offender characteristics among two groups of Finnish homicide offenders with schizophrenia: Comparison of early-and late-start offenders. *Journal of Forensic Psychiatry and Psychology, 16*(1), 41–59.

Liem, M. C. A., & Pridemore, W. A. (2012). *Handbook of European homicide research: Patterns, explanations, and country studies*. Springer.

Liem, M., & Vinkers, D. J. (2012). Levensdelicten door verdachten met een psychotische stoornis in Nederland. *Tijdschrift Voor Psychiatrie, 54*(6), 509–516.

Meehan, J., Flynn, S., & Hunt, I. M. (2006). Perpetrators of homicide with schizophrenia: A national clinical survey in England and Wales. *Psychiatric Services, 57*, 1648–1651.

Miller, L. (2009). I. Family survivors of homicide: Symptoms, syndromes, and reaction patterns. *American Journal of Family Therapy, 37*, 67–79.

Minero, V. A., Barker, E., & Bedford, R. (2017). Method of homicide and severe mental illness: A systematic review. *Aggression and Violent Behavior, 37*, 52–62.

Mulvey, E. P. (1994). Assessing the evidence of a link between mental illness and violence. *Hospital & Community Psychiatry, 45*, 663–668.

Nielssen, O., & Large, M. (2010). Rates of homicide during the first episode of psychosis and after treatment: A systematic review and meta-analysis. *Schizophrenia Bulletin, 36*(4), 702–712.

Nielssen, O., Westmore, B., Large, M., & Hayes, R. (2007). Homicide during psychotic illness in New South Wales between 1993 and 2002. *Medical Journal of Australia, 186*(6), 301–304.

Nu.nl. (2010, March 19). *Sander V. had zware psychische problemen*. Nu.nl. https://www.nu.nl/binnenland/2208347/sander-v-had-zware-psychische-problemen.html.

Pridemore, W. A. (2003). Recognizing homicide as a public health threat: Towards an integration of sociological and public health perspectives in the study of violence. *Homicide Studies, 7*(2), 182–205.

Putkonen, A., Kotilainen, I., Joyal, C. C., & Tiihonen, J. (2004). Comorbid personality disorders and substance abuse disorders of mentally ill homicide offenders: A structured clinical study on dual and triple diagnosis. *Schizophrenia Bulletin, 30*, 59–72.

Rodway, C., Flynn, S., While, D., Rahman, M. S., Kapur, N., & Appleby, L. (2014). Patients with mental illness as victims of homicide: A national consecutive case series. *The Lancet, 1*(2), 129–134.

Ruschena, D., Mullen, P. E., Burgess, P., Cordner, S. M., Barry-Walsh, J. H. D. O., & al., e. (1998). Sudden death in psychiatric patients. *British Journal of Psychiatry, 172*, 331–336.

Schanda, H., Knecht, G., Schreinzer, D., Stompe, T., Ortwein-Swoboda, G., & Waldhoer, T. (2006). Homicide and major mental disorders: A 25-year study. *Acta Psychiatrica Scandinavica, 110*, 98–107.

Shaw, J. (1999). Psychiatric aspects of homicide. *Current Opinion in Psychiatry, 12*(6), 673–676.

Shaw, J., Hunt, I. M., Flynn, S., Meehan, J., Robinson, J., Bickley, H., Parsons, R., McCann, K., Burns, J., Amos, T., Kapur, N., & Appleby, L. (2006). Rates of mental disorder in people convicted of homicide: National clinical survey. *British Journal of Psychiatry, 188*, 143–147.

Simpson, A. I. F., McKenna, B., Moskowitz, A., Skipworth, J., & Barry-Walsh, J. (2004). Homicide and mental illness in New Zealand, 1970–2000. *British Journal of Psychiatry, 185*, 394–398.

Swinson, N., Flynn, S. M., While, D., Roscoe, A., Kapur, N., Appleby, L., & Shaw, J. (2011). Trends in rates of mental illness in homicide perpetrators. *The British Journal of Psychiatry, 198*, 485–489.

Taylor, P. J., & Gunn, J. (1999). Homicides by people with mental illness: Myth and reality. *British Journal of Psychiatry, 174*, 9–14.

Thornicroft, G. (2020). People with severe mental illness as the perpetrators and victims of violence: Time for a new public health approach. *The Lancet, 5*(2), E72–E73.

Tuttle, J., McCall, P. L., & Land, K. C. (2018). Latent trajectories of cross-national homicide trends: Structural characteristics of underlying groups. *Homicide Studies*. https://doi.org/10.11771/1088767918774083

UNODC. (2019a). *Global study on homicide*.

UNODC. (2019b). *Statistics and data: Global study on homicide*. https://dataunodc.un.org/GSH_app

Weiss, D. B., Santos, M. R., Testa, A., & Kumar, S. (2016). The 1990s homicide decline: A western world or international phenomenon? *A Research Note. Homicide Studies, 20*(4), 321–334.

Wilcox, D. E. (1985). The relationship of mental illness to homicide. *American Journal of Forensic Psychiatry, 6*(1), 3–15.

Zinzow, H., Rheingold, A. A., Hawkins, A., Saunders, B. E., & Kilpatrick, D. G. (2009). Losing a loved one to homicide: Prevalence and mental health correlates in a national sample of young adults. *Journal of Traumatic Stress, 22*(1), 20–27.

Further Readings

To get more acquainted with the nature, causes and patterns of homicide, we recommend you take a closer look at the following handbooks:

Brookman, F., Maguire, E. R., & Maguire, M. (2017). *The handbook of homicide.* Wiley-Blackwell.

Liem, M. C. A., & Pridemore, W. A. (2012). *Handbook of European homicide research: Patterns, explanations, and country studies.* Springer.

A more detailed assessment of the relationship between mental disorders and homicides can be found in: Farrell, M. (2021). *Homicide and severe mental disorder. Understanding and prevention.* Routledge.

Domestic Violence: Intimate Partner Violence, Child maltreatment, and Co-Occurrence

24

Sara R. Nichols and Amy M. Smith Slep

Key points

- Worldwide prevalence rates for intimate partner violence and child maltreatment are extremely high.
- Lack of standardized definitions of abuse and neglect have had implications for establishing accurate prevalence, as well as assessment and treatment. New systems for standardization are promising and starting to take hold.
- Co-occurrence of types of maltreatment within families, and polyvictimization within individuals are common, and are more the rule than the exception.
- Risk factors that distinguish between individuals who perpetrate IPV versus child abuse have been identified.
- Efforts to mitigate or reduce occurrence of IPV and child abuse via risk factor-based prevention efforts have not always proved impactful and that area is in need of further advances.

Introduction

This chapter will review the prevalence of family maltreatment and describe the definitional challenges of maltreatment as they pertain to both clinical work

S. R. Nichols (✉)
New York University, New York, NY, USA
e-mail: sara.nichols@nyu.edu

A. M. S. Slep
New York University, New York, NY, USA
e-mail: amy.slep@nyu.edu

© The Author(s), under exclusive license to Springer Nature Switzerland AG 2022   461
C. Garofalo and J. J. Sijtsema (eds.), *Clinical Forensic Psychology*,
https://doi.org/10.1007/978-3-030-80882-2_24

and research. Research on the co-occurrence of maltreatment in families is discussed, along with proposed explanatory theories. We turn to the risk factor literature and overview risk factors for co-occurring and singly occurring patterns of maltreatment. Finally, the implications for prevention and intervention are discussed.

Prevalence

Family violence is a major public health concern, impacting millions of people across the globe each year. Only a small portion of family violence is reported to police or comes to the attention of child protective agencies (Negriff et al., 2017; Tjaden & Thoennes, 2000). U.S. lifetime prevalence rates estimate that 30.6% of women and 31.0% of men experience physical violence by an intimate partner (Smith et al., 2018). Worldwide estimates are similarly high (Devries et al., 2013). Worldwide child sexual abuse lifetime prevalence rates range from 8–31% for girls and 3–17% for boys while meta-analysis of self-report studies indicates a 36.3% child emotional abuse prevalence and a physical abuse prevalence of 22.6% (Barth et al., 2013; Stoltenborgh Bakermans-Kranenburg, Alink et al., 2012; Stoltenborgh Bakermans-Kranenburg van Ijzendoorn et al., 2013). Although not all sexual abuse is intra-familial, the vast majority of emotional and physical abuse are. Rates of abuse within the family verses that perpetrated by extra-familial individuals vary according to the type of abuse as well as the source of information. In the U.S., approximately, 80% of the reported child abuse and neglect is perpetrated by parents (Centers for Disease Control, 2014). While prevalence rates vary a great deal depending on the information source, one thing that does not vary is the staggeringly high percentage of adults and children, worldwide, who are exposed to abusive behavior in their homes or within their families.

Definitions

Definitions of the types of family maltreatment, including physical, sexual, and emotional intimate partner violence (IPV) and neglect as well as physical, sexual and emotional child abuse and neglect, are far from standardized. Interestingly, despite decades of attention and public concern about intimate partner and family maltreatment, definitions of these constructs have only recently begun to be standardized, and only in a very limited way. One rigorous approach to the creation and field-testing of definitions of partner and child physical, sexual and emotional abuse, as well as neglect resulted in the FAIR system (i.e., Field-tested Assessment, Intervention-planning, and Response; e.g., Heyman & Slep, 2006). This work has subsequently been modified for inclusion in the *Diagnostic Statistical Manual of Mental Disorders-Fifth Edition* (*DSM-5*) and *International Classification of Disease-11th Revision* (*ICD-11*), with evidence for validity of those revised definitions of psychological and physical partner and child abuse (Heyman, Snarr et al., 2020).

In survey research, operationalizations of family maltreatment often rest on a single purported assaultive act, without consideration of the impacts related to the act (Straus & Gelles, 1990). This traditional approach is behaviorally clear, but it has been criticized as potentially being too inclusive and failing to include context. All aggressive acts are operationalized as maltreatrment, regardless of risk of harm (Heyman & Slep, 2006). Clinically, significant acts (or omissions, in the case of neglect) should account for the impact or potential for impact to the victim (Heyman & Slep, 2006). The consideration of what comprises a clinically significant act of abuse and neglect is of extreme importance to policy and decision-makers and has obvious criminal justice implications. Is pushing your partner an act of abuse? What about calling him "stupid" in the heat of a fight? Certainly, these behaviors are not kind, but a consistent answer to whether they are abuse depends on the force and contextual circumstances of the initial act, as well as the impact or likely potential impacts on the victim (Foran et al., 2013). However, the vast preponderance of epidemiological and other research has other definitions. For example, one of the most widely utilized assessment tools of physical and emotional aggression in romantic couples, The Conflict Tactics Scale (CTS; Straus, 1979), uses the "any act" approach to defining aggression. It has highlighted physical aggression as falling into "severe" and mild or so-called common acts of aggression, with items falling into the mild factor including "pushing" and "slapping" while severe factor items include choking, beating up, and using weapons on a partner (Pan et al., 1994).

The other predominant source of definitions around abuse and neglect come from a body of literature conducted with "clinical" or severe samples. This research typically defines maltreatment through service involvement, focusing on victims residing in domestic violence shelters, children engaged with child protective services, or perpetrators mandated to treatment (e.g., Dixon & Graham-Kevan, 2011). Generally, these samples are considered more severely affected by family violence than those identified through anonymous surveys, however, this approach to defining maltreatment also confounds maltreatment with other factors that contribute to service involvement such as having limited access to resources.

Finally, definitions of child abuse are subject to controversy. Some definitions of child abuse include acts that some communities and individuals consider to be normative physical punishment; there is controversy within the field about which acts comprise "abuse" (Jouriles et al., 2008). This is challenging for the field. On the one hand, some communities may consider lashing a child with a switch or depriving them of food for a day as normative parenting; however, does that mean it is non-abusive? The United Nations Convention on the rights of children declared that all children had a right to be free from violence at all times (The United Nations, 1989, art. 15). This is consistent with the notion that even if a parenting technique might be normative, it is not necessarily acceptable. The FAIR system, which includes an impact threshold, is one approach to "drawing a line" between acceptable normative parenting and those that are not acceptable, even if normative: if the parental act harms or has significant potential to harm the child, it is considered abusive. This balancing of culture and child safety contributed to the incorporation of this approach into the *DSM-5* and *ICD-11*.

The movement toward standard definitions, with FAIR (see Foran et al., 2013) definitions in place in medical classification systems, is being used throughout the U.S. military services and in the child protection system in Alaska. A review field of trials suggests that reliable decision-making, preventative impacts, and rigorous research are supported by a more precisely operationalized approach to defining maltreatment (Foran et al., 2013).

The history of lack of standardization of definitions and measurement in the field makes it difficult to establish the true prevalence of these acts. Depending on measurement approach and definitions, prevalence can vary widely. In general, a small minority of victims receive official services, and a small minority of perpetrators are formally detected; thus, officially classified maltreatment can be considered a lower bound of prevalence estimates. In contrast, some representative surveys use methods that assess specific potentially maltreating acts (e.g., slapping) without assessing context or consequences. These surveys tend to obtain higher prevalence estimates and can be considered an upper bound (see Euser et al., 2013).

Co-occurrence

Importantly, these maltreatment statistics frequently co-occur within the family constellation, and this co-occurrence can be overlooked. Where one type of maltreatment is occurring, another may also be. Most notably, children who witness domestic violence are, often, also victims of direct maltreatment (Edleson, 1999;

Sousa et al., 2011; Wolfe et al., 2003). Likewise, physical and emotional abuse are likely to co-occur within a given family (Debowska et al., 2017; Kim et al., 2017). Sexual abuse also has a high co-occurrence with other forms of abuse (Bidarra et al., 2016). The explanations for this co-occurrence are complex, but the interconnections among forms of maltreatment have implications both for understanding risk and planning intervention.

Within a family, a child whose parents are aggressive with each other is likely to also be the victim of abuse—in the form of the psychological impacts of the parents' domestic violence, as well as direct physical violence that may be enacted by a parent. Depending on measurement and definitions, this type of violence co-occurrence may occur in as many as 60% of cases (Edleson, 1999). In a seminal review article on the topic, Appel and Holden (1998) found average co-occurrence rates of 40% in clinical populations. Of note, the average rate for co-occurrence was only 6% in "representative" community samples (Edleson, 1999). However, others have found much higher rates in the community. In a study that utilized random digit dialing of a community sample in the U.S., Slep and O'Leary (2005) found rates of aggression co-occurrence between both partners and children to occur at 22%, with 11.3% of families reporting instances of severe aggression of both partners toward each other and both toward their child. Aggression by either adult toward only one family member (partner or child only) was far less common (Slep & O'Leary, 2005). Thus, it is safe to say that in situations of intimate partner violence, children are at elevated risk for co-occurring violence. Reasons for the broad range in estimates of co-occurrence of intimate partner violence and physical child abuse are hard to be certain of, but it does appear that sample and definitions make a difference; co-occurrence is higher in "clinical" or help-seeking families, where intimate partner violence is usually more severe and intense than the acts found in community samples (Jouriles et al., 2008).

Of note, these studies examine rates of co-occurrence of physical aggression between partners and children. When children's exposure to intimate partner violence (IPV) is examined in and of itself as a form of potential child maltreatment, then the rates of exposure are even higher. In a United Kingdom nationally representative sample, Radford et al. (2018) found lifetime prevalence rates of exposure to parental IPV of almost 24% by the time children reached young adulthood; 12% of under 11-year-olds in their large sample reported exposure to parental IPV. Of course, some caution is needed in interpreting these numbers: not all exposure to IPV is necessarily an act of child maltreatment. Exposure can include witnessing or overhearing the incident itself, but can also include being exposed parents' distress or injuries, and other sequelae of the IPV. Issues that need to be considered in whether exposure to IPV comprises maltreatment include the frequency, the severity of what they are exposed to, the unique circumstances and perhaps most importantly, the child's own developmental age, resiliency factors and emotional response. The impact of witnessing a physical parental fight will likely be different for an infant than it would be for a five-year-old, than it would be for a teenager. The likelihood of the child becoming directly involved in a physical altercation would also change with age. Yet, while children's individual responses to IPV exposure may vary in terms of whether the exposure meets the criteria for child maltreatment or does not cross that threshold, across the population, impacts of such exposure have been well-documented. Exposure to IPV can have deleterious impacts on children including social skills impairments, feelings of shame, anxiety, and depression, and increased risk of substance use, suicidal ideation and delinquency (Gewirtz & Edleson, 2007).

Other types of abuse also co-occur, leading to "polyvictimization" (Finkelhor et al., 2007). In a clinical population, 96.8% of men who were court-ordered into batterer intervention programs after arrest for domestic assault reported perpetuating multiple types of abuse (physical violence, sexual violence, emotional abuse and stalking) (Basile & Hall, 2011). In less severe, population-based samples, co-occurrence of multiple types of intimate partner abuse have been robustly documented (Basile et al., 2004; Coker et al., 2000; Tjaden & Thoennes, 2000). In one large population-based study, 45.1% of women who reported experiencing abuse reported experiencing more than one type (Thompson et al., 2006). Indeed, this co-occurrence can manifest within fights, episodes or days: in a longitudinal microanalytic study examining co-occurrence of types of partner abuse in a community sample of women using substances, Sullivan and colleagues (2012) found that physical IPV was 64 times more likely to occur on days when psychological IPV also occurred.

Polyvictimization is also evident when IPV and child abuse within a family are examined. For example, a recent review shows discrepant figures (ranging from 12 to 70%) for the likelihood of co-occurring intimate partner violence and child sexual abuse, depending on whether the sample was representative or "clinical" and how the data were collected (Bidarra et al., 2016). These authors also point to likely issues around reporting bias and sources of data particularly about sexual abuse, where stigma is high (Bidarra et al., 2016). In a large, representative sample of Chinese families in Hong Kong, employing the CTS, IPV (physical and psychological) was found to be the risk factor most associated with child abuse and neglect; 37% of adults who reported maltreating their child also reported that they had a lifetime history of IPV (Chan, 2011).

In an examination of nationally representative data from United States, the National Survey of Children's Exposure to Violence, Hamby and colleagues (2010) widen the lens beyond the co-occurrence between witnessing acts of violence in the home and experiencing physical abuse; they examine the co-occurrence of witnessing violence and experiencing other forms of abuse. Their results, even after accounting for demographic variables and statistical corrections, show extremely high odds ratios for children who have witnessed partner violence to also experience neglect (Odds Ratio (OR) = 6.17), sexual abuse by a known adult (OR = 5.18), physical abuse (OR = 4.99), and psychological abuse (OR = 4.32) at some point in their life. The odds ratios for many of these acts to have occurred in the past year (since the report), is even higher for many types of abuse. Overall, 33.9% of children who had witnessed partner violence had also experienced abuse in the past year, and that number rose to 56.8% when lifetimes prevalence was examined. That number contrasts with only 8.6% of young people who had not witnessed abuse but had been abused in the prior year (Hamby et al., 2010). In other analyses of the same sample, Finkelhor and colleagues (2009) show that forms of victimization (including crime victimization) increase odds for other victimization in children. Clearly, shared risk factors likely contribute to this co-occurrence.

Risk Factors

What factors contribute to the phenomenon of multiple forms of abuse happening within the same family? One explanation, with roots in theories of crime, is that some individuals have a higher propensity to act aggressively (Jouriles et al., 2008). This explanation, situated within the individual perpetrator, offers that individual characteristics including personality traits such as hostility, impulsivity, reactivity, and individual psychological risk factors, such as depression of substance abuse, can interact with an individual's history (e.g., history of exposure and victimization of abuse; Jouriles et al., 2008). Of note, though, not all explanations lay within the individual characteristics of the actors; it may be the interaction between the involved individuals itself that contributes to co-occurrence. Several theoretical models account for ways in which the interactions between individuals may contribute to risk for abuse (Jouriles et al., 2008). One explanation is that some individuals have a propensity for aggressive behavior, which applies to co-occurring IPV and child abuse perpetrated by the same individual. This explanation is rooted in theories of crime (e.g., Donovan & Jessor,

1985; Gottfredson & Hirschi, 1990), that suggest that aggressive individuals do not tend to differentiate among different types of victims.

Individual-centered risk factors are the focus of such theories and include personality (e.g., impulsivity, hostility), biology (e.g., physiological reactivity to stress), psychological functioning (e.g., depression, substance dependence), and historical risk factors that set the stage for later aggression (e.g., exposure to violence in family of origin). An alternative explanation is that aggressive behavior is triggered by stressful events (e.g., financial stress, transition to parenthood). Another possible explanation is that one type of abuse causes the other. This explanation is most often presented as a variant of the "spillover hypothesis," wherein IPV spills over and increases the likelihood of the victim aggressing against a child. It is noteworthy that these notions are all consistent with at least some correlational literature (see Jouriles et al., 2008). One formulation of this is sequential co-occurrence, where the impact of the adult parent's own victimization results in changes to their own risk level (e.g., increased mental health problems), which in turn increases their risk of perpetration against their child (Sijtsema et al., 2020). It is quite possible, even probable, that multiple processes operate in concert and that co-occurring IPV and child maltreatment are not a function of a single underlying process.

Extending beyond merely identifying risk and protective factors, but identifying the processes and mechanisms through which they relate to maltreatment is critical, not just for the occurrence of abuse generally, but for particular subtypes of abuse, and has clear implications for both assessment and treatment: if particular profiles distinguish specific risk constellations, those could be used as markers for further assessment and/or targeted for potential change. Thus, research has been directed to the question of what risk factors distinguish between individuals who are "dually" versus "singly" aggressive, meaning those who aggress toward both a partner and a child, versus only one or the other. In an important study, data from the 1985 National Family Violence Survey showed a pattern of differences that suggested that dually aggressive individuals might be distinguishable from those who only aggress toward their children in various ways (they are younger, lower income, married for less time, report higher frequency of insulting partner, saying things in spite, and smashing things, and husbands are more likely to use drugs; Tajima, 2004). Overall, this study found that dually aggressive individuals have higher levels of depression and report stomping out of the room more often than those who are only aggressive toward one recipient. However, no risk factors emerged out of that particular study that distinguished individuals who aggress toward a partner versus those who aggress toward both a partner and child—the only factor that emerged empirically is that the study's target child was older in families with only partner violence (Tajima, 2004). A similar study with a smaller "clinical" sample of mothers and fathers who participated in forensic interviews after an allegation of child maltreatment in England found few differences between mothers who had engaged in both IPV and child maltreatment (Dixon et al., 2007). However, that study did identify factors that distinguished between fathers who were dually versus singly aggressive. Dually aggressive fathers had significantly higher prevalence of childhood abuse history, juvenile substance abuse, criminal convictions and offenses, adult substance dependency, relationship problems, personality disorder symptoms, and at-risk parenting scores compared to those fathers who perpetrated child maltreatment only (Dixon et al., 2007). Thus, some group differences in risk factor profiles were identified in men in a smaller, more severe sample.

A theoretically-driven approach to examining which risk factors distinguish between individuals who are dually versus singly aggressive has also been employed (Slep & O'Leary, 2009). In particular, based on earlier theoretical work (Slep & O'Leary, 2001), one study separated "role-independent" risk factors, such as depressive symptoms, childhood history of aggression and aggression in family of origin, perceived stress, age, education, occupational status, anger traits, and impulsivity, from "role-specific" factors that pertain to the specific role (parent or partner) where aggression may or may not occur. Role-specific risk factors include marital adjustment, power imbalance, emotional reactivity, emotional flooding and jealousy or dominance in your relationship (for partners) or parenting satisfaction, overreactive discipline, emotional reactivity to your child, or attributes that blame children or approve of parent aggression (for parents) (Slep & O'Leary, 2009). In the large community sample used for this research, the authors found that, as expected, dual aggressors were high in parent-specific risk factors, partner-specific risk factors, *and* role-independent risk factors such as depression, stress, and history of aggression. Single aggressors had more elevated risk factors for the relationship in which their aggression took place (e.g., partner-only aggressors were more elevated in the partner-specific risk factors while parent-only aggressors were more elevated in the parent-specific risk factors). Taken together with the more empirically derived work of Tajima, the findings here suggest that it is both possible to discern between risk profiles for individuals at risk for perpetrating abuse in different interpersonal contexts, and for prevention efforts, it may be important to do so. In particular, in treatment contexts, role-independent factors such as impulsivity, difficulty managing anger, depressive symptoms, and violence in family of origin might warrant further exploration of aggressive behavior in different types of relationships. In treatment contexts, aspects of the particular relationships and the individual's cognitive and emotional schema (Chapter 30) and reactions in that relationship context should be a target.

Research examining shared and unique risk factors for other types of dual abuse, aside from IPV and child physical abuse, is sparse. In a recent study conducted with men who perpetrate IPV, Snead and Babcock (2019) attempted to identify unique risk factors for sexual coercion versus physical assault against a partner. They found that controlling behavior, physical assault perpetration, and behavioral jealousy all predicted intimate partner sexual coercion. However, none of their identified risk factors were *unique* predictors of sexual coercion; none of the identified risk factors predicted sexual coercion more than they predicted physical assault perpetration, leading the authors to hypothesize that "sexual assault perpetration is another type and form of physical assault without unique predictors" (Snead & Babcock, 2019, p. 11). Thus, more study of predictors of sexual coercion is warranted, as clearly not all partners who perpetrate physical assault also sexually coerce their partners.

In the field of child abuse and neglect, far more work has been conducted differentiating between risks for types of abuse. In a meta-analysis of risk factors for child abuse versus neglect, Stith and colleagues (2009) reviewed 155 studies and reported large effect sizes for four risk factors for physical abuse, and six for child neglect. Two of these risk factors were overlapping: parent perceives child as a problem, and parental anger. Two additional robust risk factors for child physical abuse include poor family cohesion and family conflict. With respect to child neglect, parental stress and self-esteem, as well as child social competence and parent–child relationship quality, have emerged as robust risk factors (Stith et al., 2009). Thus, both parent and child characteristics have emerged in the area of child neglect, while family factors also play a role in risk for child physical abuse. Although unique risk factors for types of child abuse and neglect can be identified, it is also the case that shared risk factors such as economic disadvantage, parental mental health, and substance abuse and social instability are shared across types of maltreatment (Doidge et al., 2017).

In contrast with the child maltreatment area, within IPV research, risk factor research has focused more on determining if there are different risk profiles for different levels of severity of IPV. Research has sought to understand if risk for milder, or "situational" IPV can be distinguished from risk for more severe, or "intimate terrorism" IPV. Research has also sought to identify whether risk factors differ for male and female perpetrators of IPV. In general, this body of work suggests similarities in risk factors and finds very few differences for severity level of gender of perpetrator (e.g., Love et al., 2020; Slep et al., 2015). In part because physical IPV nearly never occurs without co-occurring psychological IPV, research has not focused on risk distinguishing types of IPV to the extent it has in the child maltreatment literature.

Implications of Co-occurrence for Assessment and Treatment

For many years, the assumption has been that taking a risk-factor-based approach can help to inform both assessment (Chapter 25) and treatment of abuse and neglect, impacting prevention approaches. In particular, known risk factors that are both shared for multiple types of maltreatment and unique risk factors for particular types of maltreatment can be assessed when families seek routine health and mental health care, which would allow for prevention and or identification of victims who have not sought help in other ways.

Moreover, distinguishing among constellations of maltreatment, driven by different risk profiles, may allow for interventions that are more effectively targeted to an individual's specific needs. Unfortunately, the challenge is significant: taking a preventative, risk-based approach is not always successful. In the Healthy Start Program, a large randomized controlled study aimed at reducing risk factors in families with a newborn who were at risk for child abuse, the intervention was largely unsuccessful at changing risk (Duggan et al., 2004). The authors attributed this failure to the intervention's home visitors being insufficiently trained to identify risks and to connecting families to community resources that might help. Regrettably, this pattern of failure to impact risk factors and or to mitigate actual occurrences of abuse has also been demonstrated in IPV prevention efforts (Heyman et al., 2019; Wood et al., 2010). In particular, relationship education programs aimed at high-risk couples have shown mixed findings, with weak effects for unmarried and impoverished individuals (Hawkins & Erikson, 2015). Some have even demonstrated paradoxical impacts with the target abuse increasing rather than decreasing after intervention (Heyman et al., 2019). Possible explanations for null and paradoxical effects include timing of the intervention (during the postnatal rather than perinatal period), difficulty with retention of participants, possible failure to retain active ingredients of the intervention, and other methodological constraints. Yet, those explanations fail to provide entirely satisfying explanations for why a well-designed and delivered intervention for high-risk couples should fail to reduce IPV.

Given those challenges to effective prevention for both child maltreatment and IPV, it might make sense to question whether a risk-factor based approach is, in fact, worth pursuing. However, many prevention efforts have targeted family with risk factors such as poverty, marriage status, and age, which are largely socially-driven, and not easily malleable. These are also shared risk factors for multiple types of maltreatment and abuse. Expecting increased communication skills to counter the impacts of instability around basic needs (sustenance, shelter, security) is a tall order. Efforts to reduce child maltreatment and IPV may be most impactful when efforts can be tailored to specific risk profiles, and layered throughout development, with "just in time" interventions in moments in which they are most relevant. Although the urge to develop a one-size-fits-all (or most) approach is clearly strong, it may be misguided. Instead, the field must move toward employing knowledge of co-occurrence and shared and unique risk factors to develop flexible and individually adapted interventions to work to mitigate the impacts of within-family and intimate relationship abuse and neglect.

References

Appel, A. E., & Holden, G. W. (1998). The co-occurrence of spouse and physical child abuse: A review and appraisal. *Journal of Family Psychology, 12,* 578–599.

Barth, J., Bermetz, L., Heim, E., Trelle, S., & Tonia, T. (2013). The current prevalence of child sexual abuse worldwide: A systematic review and meta-analysis. *International Journal of Public Health, 58*(3), 469–483. https://doi.org/10.1007/s00038-012-0426-1

Basile, K. C., Arias, I., Desai, S., & Thompson, M. P. (2004). The differential association of intimate partner physical, sexual, psychological, and stalking violence and posttraumatic stress symptoms in a nationally representative sample of women. *Journal of Traumatic Stress, 17,* 413–421. https://doi.org/10.1023/B:JOTS.0000048954.50232.d8

Basile, K. C., & Hall, J. E. (2011). Intimate partner violence perpetration by court-ordered men: Distinctions and intersections among physical violence, sexual violence, psychological abuse, and stalking. *Journal of Interpersonal Violence, 26*(2), 230–253. https://doi.org/10.1177/0886260510362896

Bidarra, Z. S., Lessard, G., & Dumont, A. (2016). Co-occurrence of intimate partner violence and child sexual abuse: Prevalence, risk factors and related issues. *Child Abuse & Neglect, 55,* 10–21.

Center for Disease Control. (2014). *Child maltreatment facts at a glance.* Retrieved from https://www.cdc.gov/violenceprevention/pdf/childmaltreatment-facts-at-a-glance.pdf

Chan, K. L. (2011). Co-occurrence of intimate partner violence and child abuse in Hong Kong Chinese families. *Journal of Interpersonal Violence, 26*(7), 1322–1342.

Coker, A. L., Smith, P. H., McKeown, R. E., & King, M. J. (2000). Frequency and correlates of intimate partner violence by type: Physical, sexual, and psychological battering. *American Journal of Public Health, 90*(4), 553–559. https://doi.org/10.2105/ajph.90.4.553

Debowska, A., Willmott, D., Boduszek, D., & Jones, A. D. (2017). What do we know about child abuse and neglect patterns of co-occurrence? A systematic review of profiling studies and recommendations for future research. *Child Abuse & Neglect, 70,* 100–111. https://doi.org/10.1016/j.chiabu.2017.06.014

Devries, K. M., Mak, J. Y., Garcia-Moreno, C., Petzold, M., Child, J. C., Falder, G., Lim, S., Bacchus, L. J., Engell, R. E., Rosenfeld, L., Pallitto, C., Vos, T., Abrahamas, N., & Warrs, C. H. (2013). The global prevalence of intimate partner violence against women. *Science, 340*(6140), 1527–1528. doi:10.1126/science.1240937

Dixon, L., & Graham-Kevan, N. (2011). Understanding the nature and etiology of intimate partner violence and implications for practice and policy. *Clinical Psychology Review, 31*(7), 1145–1155.

Dixon, L., Hamilton-Giachritsis, C., Browne, K., & Ostapuik, E. (2007). The co-occurrence of child and intimate partner maltreatment in the family: Characteristics of the violent perpetrators. *Journal of Family Violence, 22*(8), 675–689.

Doidge, J. C., Higgins, D. J., Delfabbro, P., & Segal, L. (2017). Risk factors for child maltreatment in an Australian population-based birth cohort. *Child Abuse & Neglect, 64*, 47–60. https://doi.org/10.1016/j.chiabu.2016.12.002

Donovan, J. E., & Jessor, R. (1985). Structure of problem behavior in adolescence and young adulthood. *Journal of Consulting and Clinical Psychology, 53*(6), 890.

Duggan, A., Fuddy, L., Burrell, L., Higman, S. M., Mcfarlane, E., Windham, A., & Sia, C. (2004). Randomized trial of a statewide home visiting program to prevent child abuse: Impact in reducing parental risk factors. *Child Abuse & Neglect, 28*(6), 623–643. https://doi.org/10.1016/j.chiabu.2003.08.008

Edleson, J. L. (1999). The overlap between child maltreatment and woman battering. *Violence Against Women, 5*(2), 134–154.

Euser, S., Alink, L. R., Pannebakker, F., Vogels, T., Bakermans-Kranenburg, M. J., & Van IJzendoorn, M. H. (2013). The prevalence of child maltreatment in the Netherlands across a 5-year period. *Child Abuse & Neglect, 37*(10), 841–851.

Finkelhor, D., Ormrod, R., & Turner, H. (2007). Poly-victimization: A neglected component in child victimization trauma. *Child Abuse & Neglect, 31*, 7–26.

Finkelhor, D., Turner, H., Ormrod, R., & Hamby, S. (2009). Violence, abuse and crime exposure in a national sample of children and youth. *Pediatrics, 124*(5), 1411–1423.

Foran, H. M., Beach, S. R. H., Slep, A. M. S., Heyman, R. E., & Wamboldt, M. Z. (Eds.). (2013). *Family problems and family violence: Reliable assessment and the ICD-11.* Springer.

Gewirtz, A. H., & Edleson, J. L. (2007). Young children's exposure to intimate partner violence: Towards a developmental risk and resilience framework for research and intervention. *Journal of Family Violence, 22*(3), 151–163.

Gottfredson, M. R., & Hirschi, T. (1990). *A general theory of crime.* Stanford University Press.

Hamby, S., Finkelhor, D., Turner, H., & Ormrod, R. (2010). The overlap of witnessing partner violence with child maltreatment and other victimizations in a nationally representative survey of youth. *Child Abuse & Neglect, 34*(10), 734–741.

Hawkins, A. J., & Erickson, S. E. (2015). Is couple and relationship education effective for low-income participants? A meta-analytic study. *Journal of Family Psychology, 29*, 59–68. https://doi.org/10.1037/fam0000045

Heyman, R. E., & Slep, A. M. S. (2006). Creating and field-testing diagnostic criteria for partner and child maltreatment. *Journal of Family Psychology, 20*(3), 397.

Heyman, R. E., Slep, A. M., Lorver, M. F., Mitnick, D. M., Xu, S., Baucom, K. J., Halford, W. K., & Niolan, P. H. (2019). A randomized, controlled trial of the impact of the couple

CARE for parents of newborns program on the prevention of intimate partner violence and relationship problems. *Prevention Science, 20*, 620–631. https://doi.org/10.1007/s11 121-018-0961-y

Heyman, R. E., Snarr, J. D., Slep, A. M. S., Baucom, K. J., & Linkh, D. J. (2020). Self-reporting DSM–5/ICD-11 clinically significant intimate partner violence and child abuse: Convergent and response process validity. *Journal of Family Psychology, 34(1)*, 101–111. https://doi.org/10.1037/fam0000560

Jouriles, E. N., McDonald, R., Slep, A. M. S., Heyman, R. E., & Garrido, E. (2008). Child abuse in the context of domestic violence: Prevalence, explanations, and practice implications. *Violence and Victims, 23*(2), 221–235.

Kim, K., Mennen, F. E., & Trickett, P. K. (2017). Patterns and correlates of co-occurrence among multiple types of child maltreatment. *Child & Family Social Work, 22*(1), 492–502. https://doi.org/10.1111/cfs.12268

Love, H. A., Spencer, C. M., May, S. A., Mendez, M., & Stith, S. M. (2020). Perpetrator risk markers for intimate terrorism and situational couple violence: A meta-analysis. *Trauma, Violence, & Abuse, 21*(5), 922–931.

Negriff, S., Schneiderman, J. U., & Trickett, P. K. (2017). Concordance between self-reported childhood maltreatment versus case record reviews for child welfare–affiliated adolescents: Prevalence rates and associations with outcomes. *Child Maltreatment, 22*(1), 34–44. https://doi.org/10.1177/1077559516674596

Pan, H. S., Neidig, P. H., & O'Leary, K. D. (1994). Predicting mild and severe husband to wife physical aggression. *Journal of Consulting and Clinical Psychology, 62*, 975–981.

Radford, L., Corral, S., Bradley, C., Fisher, H., & Bassett, C. (2018). *Child abuse and neglect in the UK today.* NSPCC.

Sijtsema, J., Stolz, E., & Bogaerts, S. (2020). Unique risk factors of the co-occurrence between child maltreatment and intimate partner violence perpetration. *European Psychologist, 25*, 122–133.

Slep, A. M. S., Foran, H. M., Heyman, R. E., & Snarr, J. D. (2015). Identifying unique and shared risk factors for physical intimate partner violence and clinically-significant physical intimate partner violence. *Aggressive Behavior, 41*(3), 227–241.

Slep, A. M. S., & O'Leary, S. G. (2001). Examining partner and child abuse: Are we ready for a more integrated approach to family violence? *Clinical Child and Family Psychology Review, 4*, 87–107.

Slep, A. M. S., & O'Leary, S. G. (2005). Parent and partner violence in families with young children: Rates, patterns, and connections. *Journal of Consulting and Clinical Psychology, 73*(3), 435.

Slep, A. M. S., & O'Leary, S. G. (2009). Distinguishing risk profiles among parent-only, partner-only, and dually perpetrating physical aggressors. *Journal of Family Psychology, 23*(5), 705.

Smith, S. G., Zhang, X., Basile, K. C., Merrick, M. T., Wang, J., Kresnow, M., & Chen, J. (2018). *The National Intimate Partner and Sexual Violence Survey (NISVS): 2015 Data Brief—Updated Release.* National Center for Injury Prevention and Control, Centers for Disease Control and Prevention.

Snead, A. L., & Babcock, J. C. (2019). Differential predictors of intimate partner sexual coercion versus physical assault perpetration. *The Journal of Sexual Aggression, 25*(2), 146–160. https://doi.org/10.1080/13552600.2019.1581282

Sousa, C., Herrenkohl, T. I., Moylan, C. A., Tajima, E. A., Klika, J. B., Herrenkohl, R. C., & Russo, M. J. (2011). Longitudinal study on the effects of child abuse and children's exposure to domestic violence, parent-child attachments, and antisocial behavior in adolescence. *Journal of Interpersonal Violence, 26*(1), 111–136. https://doi.org/10.1177/088 6260510362883

Stoltenborgh, M., Bakermans-Kranenburg, M. J., Alink, L. R., & van IJzendoorn. M. H. (2012) The universality of childhood emotional abuse: A meta-analysis of worldwide prevalence. *Journal of Aggression, Maltreatment & Trauma, 21*(8), 870–890, DOI: https://doi.org/10.1080/10926771.2012.708014

Stoltenborgh, M., Bakermans-Kranenburg, M. J., van Ijzendoorn, M. H., & Alink, L. R. (2013). Cultural-geographical differences in the occurrence of child physical abuse? A meta-analysis of global prevalence. *International Journal of Psychology : Journal International De Psychologie, 48*(2), 81–94. https://doi.org/10.1080/00207594.2012.697165

Straus, M. A. (1979). Measuring intrafamily conflict and violence: The conflict tactics (CT) scales. *Journal of Marriage and the Family, 41*(1), 75–88.

Straus, M. A., & Gelles, R. J. (1990). *Physical violence in American families: Risk factors and adaptations to violence in families.* Transaction.

Sullivan, T. P., McPartland, T. S., Armeli, S., Jaquier, V., & Tennen, H. (2012). Is it the exception or the rule? Daily co-occurrence of physical, sexual, and psychological partner violence in a 90-day study of substance-using, community women. *Psychology of Violence, 2*(2), 154. https://doi.org/10.1037/a0027106

Stith, S. M., Liu, T. L., Davies, C., Boykin, E. L., Alder, M. C., Harris, J. M., Som, A., McPherson, M., & Dees, J. (2009). Risk factors in child maltreatment: A meta-analytic review of the literature. *Aggression and Violent Behavior, 14*, 13–29.

Tajima, E. A. (2004). Correlates of the co-occurrence of wife abuse and child abuse among a representative sample. *Journal of Family Violence, 19*, 399–410.

Thompson, R. S., Bonomi, A. E., Anderson, M., Reid, R. J., Dimer, J. A., Carrell, D., & Rivara, F. P. (2006). Intimate partner violence: Prevalence, types, and chronicity in adult women. *American Journal of Preventive Medicine, 30*(6), 447–457. https://doi.org/10.1016/j.ame pre.2006.01.016

Tjaden, P., & Thoennes, N. (2000). Prevalence and consequences of male-to-female and female-to-male intimate partner violence as measured by the national violence against women survey. *Violence Against Women, 6*(2), 142–161.

The United Nations. (1989). Convention on the Rights of the Child. *Treaty Series, 1577,* 3

Wolfe, D. A., Crooks, C. V., Lee, V., McIntyre-Smith, A., & Jaffe, P. G. (2003). The effects of children's exposure to domestic violence: A meta-analysis and critique. *Clinical Child and Family Psychology Review, 6*(3), 171–187.

Wood, R. G., Moore, Q., Clarkwest, A., Hsueh, J., & McConnell, S. (2010). *Strengthening unmarried parents' relationships: The early impacts of building strong families (technical supplement).* Mathematica Policy Research.

Further Reading Suggestions

Appel, A. E., & Holden, G. W. (1998). The co-occurrence of spouse and physical child abuse: A review and appraisal. *Journal of Family Psychology, 12*, 578–599.

Hawkins, A. J., & Erickson, S. E. (2015). Is couple and relationship education effective for low-income participants? A meta-analytic study. *Journal of Family Psychology, 29*, 59–68. https://doi.org/10.1037/fam0000045

Heyman, R. E., & Slep, A. M. S. (2006). Creating and field-testing diagnostic criteria for partner and child maltreatment. *Journal of Family Psychology, 20*(3), 397.

Slep, A. M. S., & O'Leary, S. G. (2009). Distinguishing risk profiles among parent-only, partner-only, and dually perpetrating physical aggressors. *Journal of Family Psychology, 23*(5), 705.

Stith, S. M., Liu, T. L., Davies, C., Boykin, E. L., Alder, M. C., Harris, J. M., Som, A., McPherson, M., & Dees, J. (2009). Risk factors in child maltreatment: A meta-analytic review of the literature, *Aggression and Violent Behavior, 14*, 13–29.

Part IV

Risk Assessment and Treatment

Violence Risk Assessment: Research and Practice

25

Corine de Ruiter and Martin Hildebrand

Key points

- Structured risk assessment approaches have improved inter-evaluator agreement, predictive accuracy, and transparency, compared to unstructured approaches.
- Assessment of protective factors has been added to risk-only evaluations, resulting in more balance in risk assessment practice and research.
- Recidivism base rates need to be taken into account when conducting risk assessments in practice.
- We may not assume that risk assessment instruments that have proven validity in one population (e.g., male offenders), show the same validity in other populations (e.g., female offenders, ethnic minorities).

Introduction

Violence risk assessment refers to the practice of assessing the risk of future violent behavior, with the goal of determining the level of supervision, control, treatment, and victim safety planning that is needed to mitigate this risk. Mental health and criminal justice systems around the world have implemented evidence-based approaches to violence risk assessment to different degrees, and

C. de Ruiter (✉)
Maastricht University, Maastricht, The Netherlands
e-mail: corine.deruiter@maastrichtuniversity.nl

M. Hildebrand
Private Practice, De Bilt, The Netherlands
e-mail: info@martinhildebrand.nl

© The Author(s), under exclusive license to Springer Nature Switzerland AG 2022   479
C. Garofalo and J. J. Sijtsema (eds.), *Clinical Forensic Psychology*,
https://doi.org/10.1007/978-3-030-80882-2_25

the research literature in this field is growing exponentially. Risk assessment tools have been developed for adults, adolescents, and children (for an overview, see Douglas & Otto, 2021). For example, an international survey of more than 2100 mental health professionals reported the regular use of risk assessment instruments in 44 countries with more than 200 individual risk assessment tools (Singh et al., 2014).

In this chapter, we first describe the history of risk assessment research and practice: from unstructured clinical to actuarial to structured professional judgment (SPJ) approaches. The goals of risk assessment are described and the need to strike a balance between the need to keep society safe and the civil liberties of the individual. We explain important concepts in risk assessment research, such as sensitivity and specificity, positive and negative predictive power, and Area Under the Curve (AUC), so the reader will learn how to evaluate the research literature on different tools. Finally, we provide an overview of different risk assessment tools for different types of criminal and violent behavior, including tools that assess protective factors against violence risk.

The practical use of different risk assessment tools is illustrated with a case example that runs throughout the chapter. We compare unstructured clinical judgment with different risk assessment tools, that is, an actuarial and an SPJ instrument on the same case. We will also discuss the importance of recidivism base rates and apply base rate knowledge to the case at hand. In closing, we will discuss the future of risk assessment, and the inherent tension in risk assessment between the protection of society and the civil liberties of the individual.

Risk Assessment in Historical Perspective

In this section, we offer a discussion of the characteristics of three major approaches to risk assessment across the years: unstructured clinical judgment (UCJ), actuarial risk assessment, and structured professional judgment (SPJ). The strengths and weaknesses of these approaches are also outlined.

Unstructured Clinical Judgment

Historically, mental health professionals were expected to conduct violence risk assessments based upon their own professional opinion, experience, and intuition, with absolute discretion regarding the evaluation process and decision-making (e.g., Harris & Lurigio, 2007; Meehl, 1996; Murray & Thomson, 2010). Grove and Meehl (1996) described clinical prediction as an "informal, 'in the head', impressionistic, subjective conclusion, reached (somehow) by a human clinical judge" (p. 294). According to Ennis and Litwack (1974), the clinical prediction of violence is akin to "flipping coins in the courtroom" (p. 693).

Strengths and Weaknesses of the UCJ Approach. Using UCJ does have benefits, including its flexibility, its focus on the individual evaluee—tailoring the risk assessment process to a given individual using a variety of case-specific risk (and protective) factors—its low cost (no need for specific training or purchase of risk assessment tools). However, the UCJ approach also has some serious drawbacks, given the absence of guidance to risk assessors. A pre-eminent concern about UCJ is its inherent subjectivity, often resulting in poor rates of reliability and (predictive) validity (Hanson & Morton-Bourgon, 2009; Hart et al., 2007). Another major drawback of UCJ is the risk of human judgment biases[1] having a major impact on the risk assessment process (e.g., Dernevik et al., 2001; Neal & Grisso, 2014). For example, "clinicians may pay undue attention to factors that are not associated with violent behavior" or, conversely, "they may fail to attend to important factors that are indeed associated with violence" (Douglas, Hart, Groscup et al., 2014, p. 391; see also Hanson, 1998; Mullen & Ogloff, 2009). Furthermore, hindsight bias due to recent tragic events involving high-profile homicides by individuals diagnosed with a mental illness may result in the overestimation of violence risk in persons with quite low base rates of interpersonal aggression (Arkes, 1991; Large et al., 2011).

The first critical examination of the UCJ approach came in 1954 with Paul Meehl's seminal text, *Clinical vs. statistical prediction: A theoretical analysis and a review of the evidence* (Meehl, 1954). In this book on the pros and cons of human judgment versus actuarial integration of information as applied to a prediction problem, Meehl made the claim that clinicians could not predict offending better than actuarial formulae. As clinicians' assessments of dangerousness were used to influence many important decisions pertaining to individual liberty and access to therapeutic resources, Meehl's work started a major debate about the reliability and predictive validity of clinical judgment (e.g., Westen & Weinberger, 2004).

Perhaps the best-known critique of UCJ in (forensic) risk assessment is the influential monograph of John Monahan (1981; see also Monahan, 1984), entitled

---

[1] Bias is a systematic error in reasoning or logic that occurs as the result of the automaticity with which the human mind processes information based on expectations and experience (Tversky & Kahneman, 1974). Perhaps the most well-known example of this phenomenon is confirmation bias, which occurs when attention is drawn to evidence that supports a favored scenario or outcome, while evidence that weakens or contradicts the preferred hypothesis is discounted or ignored altogether (Nickerson, 1998).

The clinical prediction of violent behavior, in which he reviewed the research literature on the clinical prediction of violence published up to that date. Monahan reiterated Meehl's (1954) claim that clinicians were vastly overrated as predictors of violence and concluded that: "Psychiatrists and psychologists are accurate in no more than one out of three predictions of violent behavior over a several-year period among institutionalized populations that had both committed violence in the past (and thus had high base rates for it) and those who were diagnosed as mentally ill" (pp. 48–49). Based on his review, Monahan argued that clinicians should systematize their predictions. He also provided suggestions for structured risk assessment, for instance, he mentioned variables such as previous violence, which might have power as actuarial predictors. Furthermore, Monahan (1981, 1984, 1988) made a strong case for "second generation" research into risk assessment. Together with a number of colleagues, Monahan designed the MacArthur Risk Assessment Study, a multi-site longitudinal study conducted between 1992 and 1995 that followed civil psychiatric inpatients after discharge into the community with the goal to establish robust markers for violence risk (see Monahan et al., 2001; Steadman et al., 1993). The key findings were that most psychiatric patients admitted to an acute ward do not commit a violent act in the year after release, substance abuse is the strongest predictor of such violence, and most violence is directed at family members and not strangers (Torrey et al., 2008).

More recent studies into the predictive accuracy of UCJ have reported more favorable results compared to Monahan's review (1981). A meta-analysis by Mossman (1994) found that clinicians are able to distinguish violent from nonviolent patients with a modest, better-than-chance level of accuracy. However, UCJ is still liable to cognitive biases and less strongly related to violence than a structured approach (e.g., Aegisdóttir et al., 2006; Grove et al., 2000; Hanson & Morton-Bourgon, 2009). The meta-analysis of Guy (2008), for example, showed that unstructured judgment was significantly less strongly associated with violence than structured judgment (actuarial or SPJ).

Case Study 1
Thomas was a 51-year old man who had been admitted to a longstay forensic care facility in December 2005, after having spent 10 years (1995–2005) in two forensicForensic psychiatric hospitals in the Netherlands.2 Thomas disagreed with his longstay status, which basically entailed he was considered untreatable and a chronic danger to society. According to his file,

Thomas had been convicted in 1993 to four years imprisonment and involuntary treatment in a secure mental health facility,[2] because of deliberate firesetting in two residential dwellings and in a mobile home, i.e., an unlawful fire, started or allowed to spread in violation of the law. None of the arson offenses resulted in harm to persons, but there was some material damage in the two homes and the mobile home burned down completely. In the period prior to the arson, there were increasing tensions in Thomas' marriage and his business failed. Thomas himself believed that the main reason for his offenses was a nervous breakdown from years of stress and a failed attempt to cope with his frustrations. According to Thomas, he was burnt out, could not sleep, was very tense and anxious during this period.

In the pretrial mental health assessment (i.e., the expert report to the court), the experts concluded, based exclusively on professional opinion, that Thomas posed a high risk of firesetting recidivism: "There is no doubt that there is a risk of recidivism, since the personality structure and social network have not changed. [...] When he is again stuck in his inferiority he will only be able to restore his narcissistic balance by means of an analogous 'acting-out'." At the time Thomas was convicted, many psychoanalytically-oriented forensic experts in the Netherlands, but also abroad, believed that people who committed arson were very disturbed and sexually perverse individuals at very high risk to reoffend (Harris & Rice, 1984).

What would have been the outcome of the risk assessment if the experts had been able to use an actuarial risk assessment tool and based their judgment on it?

Actuarial Risk Assessment

Enjoying widespread popularity, Monahan's monograph announced the beginning of a "second generation" (Monahan, 1984, p. 141) of risk assessment instruments, where research into the predictive validity of UCJ was largely replaced by research into the development of actuarial risk assessment instruments (ARAIs).

---

[2] For a detailed description of the special legal provisions for mentally disordered individuals who are deemed guilty of a serious offense in the Netherlands, see de Ruiter and Hildebrand (2003) and van Marle (2002).

The actuarial judgment method is "a formal method" that "uses an equation, a formula, a graph, or an actuarial table to arrive at a probability, or expected value, of some outcome" (Grove & Meehl, 1996, p. 294). The risk factors in ARAIs are selected on the basis of their association with the outcome (e.g., violent or sexual recidivism) as found in empirical studies. The predictor variables are weighed and combined according to a fixed and explicit algorithm in order to reach a conclusion regarding the likelihood of violence over a chosen period of time (Grove & Meehl, 1996; Grove et al., 2000; Hart et al., 2007). Total scores are cross-referenced with a manual in which estimates of recidivism rates are provided for each score or range of scores (referred to as "risk bins" or "risk categories"). These estimates are derived from the actual rates of recidivism observed in groups with the same score or range of scores in the sample on which the tool was calibrated (i.e., the derivation sample or the group whose data were used to develop the instrument). Examples of commonly used actuarial risk assessment tools are the Violence Risk Appraisal Guide–Revised (VRAG–R; Harris et al., 2015) and the Ontario Domestic Assault Risk Assessment (ODARA; Hilton et al., 2004). For a sampling of (other) commonly used and investigated ARAIs, see Table 25.1.

Strengths and Weaknesses of ARAIs. The key benefit of actuarial prediction methods is that they facilitate standardization, objectivity, interrater reliability and predictive validity, especially in comparison with unstructured approaches. Because ARAIs use explicit rules for combining risk factors, they yield the same decision regardless of the person that uses them (high interrater reliability). Furthermore, they are transparent, which is a benefit in legal contexts (Douglas, Hart, Groscup et al., 2014) and relatively easy to score. Many ARAIs are statistically optimized because they weigh items according to the strength of their empirical association with the outcome (e.g., sexual violence, intimate partner violence). Hence, at least in the samples in which they were developed (Douglas, Hart, Groscup et al., 2014), they tend to have high predictive validity in comparison with UCJ. Other benefits include their time-efficiency and their basis in historical information (i.e., incorporating mostly static risk factors) that is routinely available in criminal/court/medical records.

Despite these evident advantages, particularly of enhanced interrater reliability and predictive validity of ARAIs, the actuarial approach has been criticized as well. For example, a serious drawback is that the predictive properties of most ARAIs tend to be optimized within the sample of development (derivation sample), with no guarantee that these properties generalize to other settings, samples, or jurisdictions. In fact, derivation predictive estimates tend to change upon cross-validation in new samples (Douglas, Hart, Groscup et al., 2014). Second, (some)

Table 25.1 Selection of commonly used actuarial violence risk assessment tools

Instrument	No. items	Intended application
BVC (Brøset Violence Checklist; Almvik et al., 2000)	6	Imminent violence among adult psychiatric inpatients
COVR (Classification of Violence Risk; Monahan et al., 2005)	Varies	Violence among acute psychiatric patients being discharged to the community
DASA (Dynamic Appraisal of Situational Aggression; Ogloff & Daffern, 2002)	7	Imminent (within the next 24 hours) aggression by patients in psychiatric hospitals and other secure settings
LS/CMI (Level of Service/Case Management Inventory; Andrews et al., 2004)	124	General an violent recidivism among adult offenders
ODARA (Ontario Domestic Assault Risk Assessment; Hilton et al., 2004)	13	Violent recidivism against female partners by adult males with a police record for domestic assault
RM 2000 (Risk Matrix 2000; Thornton et al., 2003)	9	Violent (including sexual) recidivism by adult male sex offenders
SIR–R1 (Statistical Information on Recidivism;Nafekh & Motiuk, 2002)	15	Reoffending within three years after release
SORAG (Sex Offender Risk Appraisal Guide; Quinsey et al., 2006)	14	Violent (including sexual) recidivism among sex offenders
Static–99/Static–2002 (Hanson & Thornton, 2000, 2003)	10/14	Violent (including sexual) recidivism among adult male sex offenders
VRAG–R (Violence Risk Appraisal Guide–Revised ; VRAG–R; Harris et al., 2015)	12	Violent recidivism among adult males from correctional and forensic psychiatric populations
VRS (Violence Risk Scale; Wong & Gordon, 2000)	26	Violent recidivism among adult male offenders

Note. The COVR has a varying number of items depending on answers given by the subject to previous items. Adapted from "Assessing violence risk," by Douglas, K. S., Hart, S. D., Groscup, J. L., & Litwack, T. R. (2014). In I. B. Weiner & R. K. Otto (Eds.), *The handbook of forensic psychology* (4th ed., p. 392). Copyright 2014 by John Wiley & Sons

ARAIs have been criticized for not being helpful in terms of planning of risk management strategies and evaluating change (Douglas & Skeem, 2005; Scott & Resnick, 2006). Most of the actuarial tools focus on static risk factors and do not include situational or dynamic (changeable) risk factors that may be better suited to treatment efforts. This can lead to pessimism in both mental health professionals and evaluees because it results in a lifetime risk judgment implying that the individual's risk of violence can never change for the better (de Ruiter & Nicholls, 2011; Douglas & Skeem, 2005). Third, most ARAIs include risk factors only and disregard protective factors (Rogers, 2000). Fourth, some ARAIs may have limited clinical applicability. That is, the assessment cannot be tailored to the individual. As Howe and colleagues (2016) noted, "risk factors receive the same empirical weight, and all risk factors are summed according to the same algorithm, regardless of potentially relevant differences in the individual being evaluated or the situation in which risk of violence is being assessed" (p. 399). Fifth, ARAIs have been criticized because they specifically aim at predicting the likelihood of future violence, thereby ignoring important other dimensions of risk, such as the nature, severity, frequency, and imminence of violence (Hart et al., 2007). Sixth, ARAIs are primarily statistically based and do not provide insight into the etiology and mechanisms that underlie the adverse behavior they predict (Grubin, 1997; Krauss et al., 2000), which would require further and more thorough psychological assessment. Finally, because of the highly variable nature of forensic cases and because it would be impossible to mathematically model every relevant risk factor, relying on an actuarial tool inevitably results in a limited range of predictor variables (Murray & Thomson, 2010). ARAIs could miss rare variables in individual cases that may be crucial to the prediction. Under the strictest actuarial approaches (i.e., the pure actuarial approach), it is not allowed to consider risk factors that are not contained in the ARAI (Douglas, Hart, Groscup et al., 2014).

Both clinicians and researchers have raised concerns about potentially necessary reasons to *adjust* an outcome of actuarial risk assessment. Hanson (1998), for example, argued that even the strongest proponents of mechanical methods of prediction (Grove & Meehl, 1996; Meehl, 1954) believed that adjustments to statistical predictions could be justified under certain circumstances. Grove and Meehl (1996) refer to this as the "broken leg case (p. 307)." In their argument, a broken leg is a clear objective fact with obvious implications, but individual cases with such variables are relatively infrequent. Actuarial tools do not acknowledge factors, which, though not likely to be common in large samples, could greatly influence risk at the individual level. It is arguments such as these that led clinicians and researchers to advocate the use of a method referred to as *adjusted* actuarial assessment. Such adjusted risk assessment "starts with an established actuarial score and then considers factors external to the actuarial instrument (i.e., the evaluator is allowed to judge the extent to which the predicted recidivism rates are a fair evaluation of the offender's risk)" (Hanson &

Morton-Bourgon, 2009, p. 3). Since this approach does not place restrictions on including, weighing, or combining factors, it still fits Grove and Meehl's (1996) definition of "subjective, impressionistic" decision-making to some extent (p. 293). Accordingly, some label the adjustment of an actuarially determined risk level as a clinical override (Andrews et al., 2004; Guay & Parent, 2018).[3] That is, the clinician is free to increase or decrease the risk level proposed by the instrument based on clinical judgment. According to Davis and Ogloff (2004), clinicians have very little knowledge about when to override actuarial assessment outcomes and replace them with clinical judgment. In recent years, the clinical override has been contested as to whether it is adding incremental validity to the risk assessment measure or if it is detracting from the actuarial measure's original predictive accuracy (DeClue & Zavodny, 2014; McCafferty, 2017; Wormith, Gendreau et al., 2012; Wormith, Hogg et al., 2012).

Case Study 2

What would have been the outcome of the risk assessment in Thomas' case if the experts had been able to use an actuarial risk assessment tool and based their judgment on it? In 1993, there was no specific actuarial risk assessment instrument for arsonists. Studies have shown that arsonists have risk factors in common with both violent and nonviolent offenders (Edwards & Grace, 2014; Rice & Harris, 1996). Using the same statistical approach that was used to develop the VRAG, Quinsey and colleagues (1998) found that seven risk factors ultimately led to an optimal prediction of future arson: young age at the time of the first firesetting behavior, total number of firesetting offenses, whether there was a childhood firesetting problem, low IQ, other criminal charges concurrent with the index firesetting, whether the offender had acted alone in setting the index fire, and a low aggression score.[4] Quinsey et al. reported that the total score on these seven risk factors significantly predicted firesetting recidivism (ROC AUC = .76, d = 1.1). However, Quinsey and colleagues did not develop a separate risk assessment tool for arsonists, but recommended using the VRAG instead. Coding of the VRAG in Thomas' case resulted in a total score of 0 (see below for the scores on the individual risk factors). Regarding the probability of violent recidivism at two different mean lengths of

---

[3] The widely used Level of Service/Case Management Inventory (LS/CMI; Andrews et al., 2004) is an example of an ARAI that relies on numeric cut-off scores for decision-making, but allows for clinical overrides.

opportunity as a function of nine equal-sized VRAG categories, this score is assigned to risk category 5 (= moderate risk). Among offenders in the development sample for the VRAG, 50% obtained a higher VRAG score, and approximately 35% in the assessed person's category reoffended violently within an average of 7 years (48% within an average of 10 years) after release.

VRAG coding for Thomas		
Risk factor		Score
1	Lived with both biological parents up to age 16	−2
2	No elementary school maladjustment	−1
3	No history of alcohol problems	−1
4	Marital status at time of index offense	−2
5	Criminal history score for convictions and charges for nonviolent offenses prior to the index offense	+3
6	Failure on prior conditional release	+3
7	Age at index offense (category 28–33 years)	−1
8	No victim injury index offense	+2
9	No victim	+1
10	No personality disorder	−2
11	No schizophrenia	+1
12	PCL-R score (10–14)	−1
Total score VRAG		0

What would have been the outcome of the risk assessment if the experts had been able to use a Structured Professional Judgment instrument and based their judgment on it?

---

[4] The last variable is of particular interest because of the negative relationship with fire-setting recidivism; more aggressive offenders were less likely to set future fires. A low aggression score seems counter-intuitive, but it appears that arsonists are often (extremely) inhibited, unassertive individuals, who have difficulty expressing (normal) anger in interpersonal relationships.

Structured Professional Judgment

Structured professional judgment (SPJ) risk assessment tools were developed since the early to mid-1990s (e.g., Douglas et al., 1999; Hanson, 1998; Webster et al., 1997), in part, to compensate for the perceived weaknesses of both the UCJ and actuarial approaches, but also to retain some of the strengths of both approaches (Douglas, Hart, Groscup et al., 2014). In other words, the SPJ approach represents an integration of UCJ and actuarial risk assessment.

SPJ instruments comprise risk and/or protective, static, and dynamic factors that are empirically associated with an increased risk of violence. Items of SPJ instruments are coded by a professional who uses a unit-weighing scheme with coding anchors provided in a manual. Total scores are not to be used as statistical estimates of risk but rather as an *aide-memoire*, guiding evaluators in making a final risk judgment as to whether an individual is at "low," "moderate," or "high" risk of future violence, when combined with case-specific information (Douglas et al., 2013). High risk indicates that the individual is considered by the evaluator as high priority for receiving risk management and reduction interventions, in line with the risk-need-responsivity (RNR) model (Andrews, 2012; Andrews & Bonta, 2010). Hence, risk is not presumed to be a simple linear function of the number of risk factors present—in fact, critical to the SPJ approach of assessing risk is the assumption that a single risk factor may play a disproportionate role in increasing an individual's risk level (e.g., Monahan et al., 2001)—although it is generally true that risk is greater when more risk factors are present. An example of this would be a patient with paranoid delusions who is in possession of a firearm, and who has recently revealed his plan to kill his father who he believes is the cause of all the difficulties in his life.

Unlike ARAIs, SPJ instruments do not aim to *predict* violence, but instead aim to *prevent* future violence (Douglas & Kropp, 2002; Hart, 2008a), by identifying the presence of relevant risk factors, to assess the individual's current level of risk, and to inform suitable interventions in order to best manage the presenting level of risk. Importantly, SPJ instruments consider risk as context-dependent and multi-dimensional. The same individual with a serious mental illness who poses a high violence risk when residing in the community without adequate psychiatric treatment and supervision may pose a low risk when he is receiving adequate community psychiatric treatment and monitoring while residing in supported housing. One of the first SPJ tools that was published and suggested to be "the leading instrument of the structured professional judgment approach" (Lamont & Brunero, 2009, p. 28) is the Historical, Clinical, Risk management-20 (HCR-20; Douglas et al., 2013; Webster et al., 1997) for the assessment of future violence risk. Table 25.2 provides a sampling of (other) commonly used and researched SPJ instruments.

Strengths and weaknesses of the SPJ approach

SPJ tools sought to address the weaknesses of ARAIs. Thus, the key strengths of SPJ instruments include a focus on the individual rather than groups and the ability to take into consideration risk-relevant information not included in the item content of specific tools. In addition, the flexibility of administration, scoring, and interpretation (discretion) of SPJ instruments is generally appreciated, particularly with practitioners (e.g., Murray & Thompson, 2010). Another benefit of the SPJ approach is the inclusion of dynamic risk factors that may assist in informing intervention planning, evaluating changes in risk level, and risk management strategies. Furthermore, SPJ instruments predict violent (including sexual) recidivism well. In fact, meta-analytic studies and systematic reviews found that the predictive validity of SPJ tools is similar to that of ARAIs (e.g., Campbell et al., 2009; Fazel et al., 2012; Singh et al., 2011; Tully et al., 2013).

Finally, a construct that has received considerable attention in the SPJ literature in the past several years is risk formulation (e.g., Hart & Logan, 2011; Hart et al., 2011, 2016; Lewis & Doyle, 2009; Logan & Johnstone, 2010). Risk formulation comprises two elements: (1) explaining the underlying mechanisms of risk in the individual case and (2) developing hypotheses about change. Risk formulation is recognized as a potentially important aspect of transferring a risk assessment into a risk management plan. Its basic function is the integration of case material (i.e., risk and protective factors) into an explanatory framework for a given individual under evaluation (Douglas, Hart, Webster et al., 2014).[5] In other words, the factors present in an individual case are entered into a holistic theory about the cause(s) of a violent outcome, in which different factors fulfill different roles (e.g., root cause, trigger, motivator, disinhibitor, reinforcer, mitigator, etc.; Douglas et al., 2013).

Critics of the SPJ approach have argued that the allowance of professional discretion at the weighing and integration phase of the final risk judgment lowers reliability and validity (e.g., Grove & Meehl, 1996; Quinsey et al., 2006). Although the less objective evaluation procedures, as well as the re-introduction of human judgment biases into risk assessment, are controversial aspects of the

---

[5] For an extensive discussion of desirable elements in a risk formulation, we refer to Hart and Logan (2011).

Table 25.2 Selection of commonly used SPJ violence risk assessment tools

Instrument	No. items	Intended application
B–SAFER (Brief Spousal Assault Form for the Evaluation of Risk; Kropp et al., 2005)	15	Violence against a current or former intimate partner by a man or a woman
CARE^{V2} (Child Abuse Risk Evaluation–Version 2; de Ruiter & Hildebrand, 2021)	22	Child abuse and neglect by parents/caregivers
EARL–20B/EARL–21G (Early Assessment Risk Lists for Boys (B) and Girls (G); Augimeri et al., 2001; Levene et al., 2001)	20(B)/21(G)	Antisocial and violent behavior in boys and girls under 12
ERASOR (Estimate of Risk of Adolescent Sexual Offence Recidivism Version 2.0; Worling & Curwen, 2001)	25	Sexual violence among adolescents with histories of sexual violence
HCR-20$^{(V3)}$ (Historical, Clinical, Risk Management–20; Webster et al., 1997) and Version 3 (Douglas et al., 2013)	20	Violence among adult males or females
HKT-R (Historical, Clinical, Future—Revision; Spreen et al., 2014)	33	Violent reoffending in male forensic psychiatric patients
RSVP (Risk for Sexual Violence Protocol; Hart et al., 2003)	22	Sexual violence among male adults with histories of sexual violence
SAVRY (Structured Assessment of Violence Risk Among Youth; Borum et al., 2006)	30	Violence among adolescents
START (Short-Term Assessment of Risk and Treatability; Webster et al., 2009)	20	Short-term violence by adult psychiatric inpatients
SVR-20 V2 (Sexual Violence Risk–20 Version 2; Boer et al., 2017)	20	Sexual violence among male adults with histories of sexual violence
V-RISK-10 (Violence Risk Screening-10; Hartvig et al., 2007)	10	Violence in acute and general psychiatry by adult patients

Note. Adapted from "Assessing violence risk," by Douglas, K. S., Hart, S. D., Groscup, J. L., & Litwack, T. R. (2014). In I. B. Weiner & R. K. Otto (Eds.), *The handbook of forensic psychology* (4th ed., p. 396). Copyright 2015 by John Wiley & Sons

SPJ approach (Hilton et al., 2006; Singh, 2016), research to date suggests that the reliability and predictive validity of SPJ instruments are at least comparable to the reliability and predictive validity of ARAIs. In addition, the SPJ approach has been criticized for the lack of guidelines about combining items to inform appraisals of overall risk (Olver, 2011). Other weaknesses of SPJ mentioned by Olver (2011) are that mechanisms for evaluating change on putatively dynamic items are not formulated, nor are there guidelines on how to translate such changes into the final risk judgment. Last, SPJ instruments are typically time-consuming which can be problematic in certain settings. For example, one study (Viljoen et al., 2010) found that a typical adult risk assessment in forensic psychiatry, including conducting interviews, obtaining and reviewing records, writing the report, consumes more than 16 person-hours.

Case Study 3

Because there is no specific SPJ instrument for arsonists (yet) when Thomas was assessed, the evaluator decided to use the HCR-20 as a structured professional guideline for the assessment of firesetting risk. The HCR-20 guideline includes arson as a "less clear" case of violence. When firesetting is motivated by anger and revenge or coupled with reckless regard for others' safety, it may be classified as violence, and this applies to Thomas' case.

Coding of the HCR-20 Version 2 at the time (see below) resulted in a maximum score of 2 on the Historical factors H4 (Employment problems) and H8 (Early maladjustment), which indicates that these risk factors are clearly present. A number of other Historical risk factors are present to a lesser extent: Previous violence, Instability in relationships, and Past violation of conditions. On the other four Historical factors (Problems with substance abuse, Mental disorder, Psychopathy ry>Psychopathy (PSY), and Personality disorder), Thomas receives a score of 0. On the five Clinical risk factors, which relate to functioning during the past 3–6 months, three are slightly elevated: Lack of insight, Impulsivity, and Unresponsive to treatment. There are no Active psychotic symptoms or Negative attitudes. The five Risk management factors are coded in view of the situation that Thomas would be rehabilitated and living in the community, because this is the crucial question in his case: Is a safe return to society feasible? Three of the five Risk management factors would not be present upon a return to society: Exposure to destabilizing factors (i.e., the factors leading up to the original arson, such as stress because of his failing business and relationship problems), Lack of personal support, and High level of experienced stress. Regarding social support, present conditions are favorable: Thomas has a good relationship with his sister; they have become more open with each other in recent years. He also has regular contact with his son. The Risk management factors R1 (Plans lack feasibility) and R4 (Noncompliance with remediation attempts) could not be coded, because to do this a detailed rehabilitation plan would need to be made.

When viewing the scoring of the HCR-20, we can conclude that the sum of the risk factors leads to a relatively low total score of 12. However, a SPJ based on the HCR-20 is more than a mere summation of risk factors. It is necessary to take into consideration whether there may be a certain combination or interaction of risk factors that could significantly increase the future risk of firesetting. This is not the case. From the empirical literature, we know that recidivism risk among arsonists of the vengeful type, as in Thomas' case, is particularly linked to two risk factors: substance abuse and antisocial personality disorder (Lindberg et al., 2005; Repo et al., 1997; see also Dickens et al., 2009). Both diagnoses are absent in Thomas' case. Therefore, based on the HCR-20, Thomas can be considered at low risk of firesetting recidivism. A low risk of recidivism implies that limited forms of supervision and support for return to society will suffice (Andrews & Bonta, 2010).

Historical items	Code (0, 1, 2)
HCR-20 coding for Thomas	
H1	Previous violence	1
H2	Young age at first violent incident	1
H3	Relationship instability	1
H4	Employment problems	2
H5	Substance use problems	0
H6	Major mental illness	0
H7	Psychopathy	0
H8	Early maladjustment (school dropout, theft, conflicts with father)	2
H9	Personality disorder	0
H10	Prior supervision failure (incident during treatment in secure mental hospital in 2004)	1
	Total Historical items:	8/20
Clinical items		Code (0, 1, 2)
C1	Lack of insight	1
C2	Negative attitudes	0
C3	Active symptoms of major mental illness	0
C4	Impulsivity	1
C5	Unresponsive to treatment (however, also did not receive appropriate treatment)	1
	Total clinical items:	3/10
Risk management items ☐ In☑ Out		Code (0, 1, 2)
R1	Plans lack feasibility (no plan available)	X
R2	Exposure to destabilizers	0
R3	Lack of personal support	0
R4	Noncompliance with remediation attempts	X
R5	Stress (the transfer to society would be stressful for anyone)	1
	Total risk management items:	1/10
	HCR-20 Total score	12/40
	Final Risk Judgment ☑ Low ☐ Moderate ☐ High	

Protective Factors

Numerous actuarial and SPJ tools have been developed over the past decades to assist clinicians in the assessment of violence risk and in making decisions regarding risk management and release for a wide range of violence types and populations. Researchers and clinicians have gradually embraced these risk assessment tools and have come to appreciate their usefulness for clinical practice and violence prevention. However, there is also growing concern about the field's overfocus on risk factors (de Ruiter & Nicholls, 2011; Hall et al., 2012; Miller, 2006). Rogers (2000), for example, warned scholars in the risk assessment field that the "overfocus on risk factors is likely to contribute to professional nega-tivism and result in client stigmatization" (p. 598). Others also argued that the overreliance on risk factors may lead to unbalanced and inaccurate predictions, such as overprediction of recidivism or stigmatization of offenders (de Vogel et al., 2011; Miller, 2006). Hart (2008b) noted similar drawbacks and pointed at the potential contribution to be made by protective factors or personal strengths: "All forms of risk assessment appear to share some problems or deficiencies. One is that they tend to focus on factors associated with increased risk, characteristics or features that are inherently negative, rather than personal strengths, resources, or 'buffer factors' [...] A comprehensive risk assessment designed to assist in the development of intervention strategies should take into account such positive features" (p. 6) (see also Chapter 27).

These critiques stimulated the development of SPJ tools for the assessment of protective factors for violence risk, such as the Structured Assessment of Protec-tive Factors for violence risk (SAPROF; de Vogel et al., 2009) and the Short-Term Assessment of Risk and Treatability (START; Webster et al., 2009), which in turn has facilitated research on protective factors for violent reoffending across differ-ent countries. Several studies have found that protective factors indeed provide a buffering effect: Individuals with moderate to high-risk levels, who also possess high levels of protective factors, show significantly lower recidivism rates than high and moderate risk cases without protective factors (de Vries Robbé et al., 2011, 2015; Kashiwagi et al., 2018). However, some studies did not find support for the incremental validity of the SAPROF beyond the accuracy of a risk-only focused instrument (e.g., Yoon et al., 2018).

Adolescence in particular is a period that can pose both obstacles and opportu-nities for psychological development (Chapters 2 and 20). Risk assessment tools for adolescents in particular should thus incorporate both risk and protective fac-tors. This was already acknowledged in one of the earliest risk assessment tools for adolescents: the Structured Assessment of Violence Risk in Youth (SAVRY;

Borum et al., 2006). The SAVRY includes 6 protective factors and 24 risk factors. Research in three different samples of adolescent violent offenders showed that the addition of protective factors yielded a significant increment in explained variance over the use of dynamic risk factors alone (Lodewijks et al., 2010). In medium to high-risk subgroups, the violent reoffending rate was significantly higher when protective factors were absent, compared to when protective factors were present (Lodewijks et al., 2010).

Although research on protective factors in forensic mental health is still in its infancy, it should alert forensic mental health evaluators to the importance of taking protective factors into consideration when performing risk assessments and when implementing risk management and rehabilitation interventions (de Ruiter, 2018). In addition, a stronger focus on protective factors inspires treatment motivation and the working alliance for both the professional and the offender/patient (Nyman et al., 2020).

Base Rates

An important part of conducting risk assessments is knowledge of recidivism base rates. The base rate is the prevalence of the defined behavior (e.g., violence) within a defined population over a defined period of time (Cunningham & Reid, 1998). The base rate depends on several factors, including the length of the observation period, the recidivism criterion (e.g., arrest, conviction, detention, self-reported recidivism), and the nature of the recidivism (e.g., non-sexual, with victim; sexual, with victim). The base rate level in a given population affects the possible improvement in predictive accuracy of a risk assessment instrument compared to chance level prediction (i.e., tossing a coin). If the base rate is very low (e.g., 5%) or very high (e.g., 95%), conducting a structured risk assessment (i.e., with the use of a risk assessment tool) makes little sense. If, for example, in a given population only 5% reoffend, we would already make an excellent "prediction" by saying—without using a risk assessment tool—that the likelihood of recidivism in the assessee, who is a member of that population, is very low. In the case of a very high base rate (e.g., 90%), we "predict" quite well when we state—again without the use of an instrument—that the assessee, as a member of the specific population, will have a high likelihood of reoffending. A risk assessment instrument would have to possess extremely high accuracy to be able to improve the chance-based prediction in both examples. However, if the base rate is close(r) to 50%, it does make sense to use a risk assessment instrument, because in these cases "flipping a coin" would not provide any guidance; in half of the tosses this would result in either a correct or incorrect prediction. In such cases, the use of a risk assessment tool can easily improve the accuracy of the risk assessment (e.g., Grubin & Wingate, 1996).

However, in actual risk assessment practice, the importance of the base rate is often insufficiently recognized. This phenomenon is referred to as the base rate fallacy or base rate neglect (Pennycook et al., 2014). Kahneman and Tversky (1985) attributed base rate neglect to the representativeness heuristic: Human cognition tends to assign cases to categories based on the degree to which the case is similar to a particular category, with little to no regard for the relative size of that category. Because of this, humans tend to over-predict low base rate behaviors (Miller & Brodsky, 2011; Neal & Grisso, 2014). In a study of 43 risk assessors who were members of two forensic psychology professional organizations, Walters and colleagues (2014) found that only 20% of the sample made effective use of base rate data that were provided along with 20 coded HCR-20 protocols. Just over half of the sample over-predicted high risk, and the level of experience of the professionals was unrelated to base rate neglect (Walters et al., 2014). In conclusion, knowledge of the base rate statistics of the category/population, to which the individual for whom the risk assessment is conducted belongs, is important, because clinicians tend to pay little attention to the base rates of specific violent behavior and are inclined to overprediction when estimating recidivism risk.

Case Study 4
What is the base rate of reoffending in firesetters/arsonists, more specifically, firesetters with revenge as the main motive, as in Thomas' case? We could not find any studies on recidivism rates for this particular category of firesetters, so we will briefly review a number of recent studies on firesetter recidivism, to obtain a general picture of recidivism in this offender population. In a review paper, Brett (2004) found that rates of firesetting recidivism varied from 4 to 40% depending on the sample used and the definition of recidivism employed. Studies of arson recidivism that have used non-psychiatric populations and only official records to follow-up result in much lower estimates of arson recidivism. Ducat et al. (2015) examined recidivism rates of 1052 firesetters convicted of arson between 2000 and 2009 in Victoria, Australia. The rate of firesetting recidivism, based on charges, was very low (5.3%) compared with the rate of general recidivism (55.4%) over an average follow-up period of 6.9 years. Thomson

et al. (2018) studied a consecutive sample of 113 Finnish pretrial male fire-setters who were evaluated at Helsinki University Hospital between 1990 and 1998. According to police register data, 18% of the sample committed a new firesetting offense over an average follow-up of 16.9 years. Simi-lar to the Ducat et al. (2015) study, the recidivism rate for any crime was much higher (74%), as was the violent reoffending rate (49%). Edwards and Grace (2014) studied individuals ($N = 1250$) who were convicted of an arson offense between 1985 and 1994 in New Zealand and were con-sidered criminally responsible for the offense. Over a 10-year follow-up, recidivism rates for arson, violent and general offending were 6.2, 48.5, and 79.3%, respectively.

In summary, base rates of firesetting recidivism tend to be much lower than those for other violent offenses. This finding should be taken into con-sideration when a structured risk assessment tool is used to judge recidivism risk.

Predictive Accuracy Performance Indicators

Researchers employ different types of statistics to communicate the accuracy of risk assessment tools. Given that risk assessment instruments are designed to maximize predictive accuracy, it is important to distinguish between two types of predictive accuracy: discrimination and calibration (Gutierrez et al., 2017; Hel-mus & Babchishin, 2017; Singh, 2013). Discrimination in risk assessment settings refers to the ability of a risk assessment tool to distinguish between recidivists and non-recidivists (e.g., differences between the risk scores of recidivists and non-recidivists). In contrast, calibration evaluates the correspondence between predicted recidivism rates per score (available in the norms of the risk assess-ment tool) and observed recidivism rates in a new sample (Helmus & Babchishin, 2017). If, for example, a risk assessment tool predicts that 25% of offenders with a certain score will recidivate, calibration assesses whether 25% of offenders with that particular score reoffend in new samples. Discrimination can be examined for any type of structured risk assessment tool (e.g., actuarial or SPJ), whereas calibration can only be examined for ARAIs because ARAIs are the only risk assessment method that includes empirically derived estimates of the probabil-ity of recidivism (Gutierrez et al., 2017). Singh (2013) states that measuring the accuracy of both discrimination and calibration is necessary and recommended to gain a more complete understanding of the utility of a risk assessment tool. However, the emphasis on calibration has only begun in recent years and there is no consensus on calibration statistics (Helmus & Babchishin, 2017).

In the following, we briefly discuss some of the performance indicators for measuring diagnostic accuracy that are widely used in the risk assessment literature. Each of these indicators captures a different dimension of predictive validity, and each has potential drawbacks.[6]

Receiver Operating Characteristics Analysis

Many researchers have recommended the use of Receiver Operating Characteristics (ROC) analysis[7] in the violence risk assessment field to examine diagnostic accuracy (i.e., discrimination)[8] (e.g., Mossman, 1994, 2013; Rice & Harris, 1995, 2005; Swets et al., 2000; see also Helmus & Babchishin, 2017; Singh, 2016). In fact, some experts consider ROC analysis the preferred measure of predictive accuracy (Swets et al., 2000), and most studies nowadays rely on ROC curves and the statistical significance of the area under the curve (AUC) as the evidential parameter that demonstrates a risk assessment tool is a valid predictor (or not) of future violence. ROC analysis yields a plot of the true positive rate (sensitivity) against the false positive rate (1 minus specificity) for every possible cut-off score of the risk assessment instrument (e.g., HCR-20, VRAG). Within the context of violence risk assessment research, the AUC of the ROC graph is an index of how well a risk assessment tool discriminates between offenders and non-offenders across all possible cut-offs of the risk assessment tool. The AUC score can range from 0 (*perfect negative prediction*) to 1 (*perfect positive prediction*); an AUC of .50 indicates that the tool is not able to predict any better than chance (Douglas

---

[6] A detailed description of all the (appropriate) statistics used to evaluate the accuracy of risk assessment tools is beyond the scope of this chapter. For excellent reviews of (calibration and discrimination) performance indicators that measure global performance, performance in identifying higher-risk groups, and performance in identifying lower-risk groups, and their pitfalls, we refer to Helmus and Babchishin (2017) and Singh (2013).

[7] ROC analysis originates from signal-detection theory in engineering and psychophysics (e.g., Green & Swets, 1966; Pepe, 2000; Swets, 1988).

[8] Other appropriate indicators, according to Helmus and Babchishin (2017), for indexing discrimination of risk schemes are Cohen's d (Cohen, 1988), regression coefficients from Cox regression (Allison, 1984) or logistic regression (Hosmer et al., 2013) and Harrell's C (Harrell et al., 1982).

et al., 2011). As a rule of thumb, AUCs between .65 and .70 are considered moderate, AUCs of .70 or above satisfactory, and AUCs above .75 typically indicate good predictive accuracy (e.g., Hosmer & Lemeshow, 2000; Quinsey et al., 1998). For example, if a tool used to predict reoffending has an associated AUC of .70, this means that there is a 70% likelihood that the score of a randomly selected recidivist will be higher than the score of a randomly selected non-recidivist.

Major benefits of this statistical method are its independence of cut-off thresholds and its insensitivity to (fluctuations in outcome) base rates (Douglas et al., 2012; Hanson, 2008). However, the use of the AUC as an indicator of predictive validity has also been criticized. The method is said to be difficult to understand for non-specialists (Munro, 2004), and the interpretation of its values is often too optimistic (Sjöstedt & Grann, 2002; see also Bengtson & Långström, 2007). Others have expressed concern that the ROC AUC is unable to differentiate between instruments that produce assessments that accurately identify high- versus low-risk groups (Singh et al., 2011). Moreover, ROC AUCs do not take into account very different numbers of false negative and false positive predictions resulting from different shapes of ROC curve that have the same ROC AUC (Mallett et al., 2012). That is, ROC AUCs of different risk assessment tools may found to be similar, but this may mask very different consequences of alternative tools due to different proportions and absolute numbers of false negative and false positive results, depending on prevalence of reoffending (Mallett et al., 2012; Mossman, 2013). Finally, the AUC provides an estimate of predictive validity that is independent of the base rate, but in the forensic field the clinical usefulness of an instrument *depends* on the base rate, as we explained above.

Positive Predictive Value and Negative Predictive Value

Two performance indicators that have been suggested as carrying more utility for the practice of risk assessment, as they emphasize the prospective prediction of violent outcomes, are positive predictive value (PPV) and negative predictive value (NPV) (Fazel et al., 2012; Mossman, 2013; Singh, 2013).[9] Both PPV and NPV are base rate-dependent and vary depending on the population, time at risk, and outcome of interest (Singh, 2013). PPV and NPV can be calculated using information available in a 2×2 contingency table, which organizes risk

---

[9] More generally, these authors advocate for applying diagnostic statistics (e.g., sensitivity/specificity trade-offs, PPV, NPV, number needed to detain (NND), number safely discharged (NSD)) when describing the predictive accuracy of risk assessment instruments.

assessment and outcome information into counts of true positives (TPs), false positives (FPs), true negatives (TNs), and false negatives (FNs) for a single cut-off threshold. The computation of these statistics is presented in Table 25.3. In the context of violence risk assessment, TPs are offenders judged to be at high risk who indeed committed a new offense, TNs are offenders judged to be at low risk who did not commit a new offense, FPs are offenders judged to be at high risk who did not commit a new offense, and FNs are individuals judged to be at low risk who did in fact commit a new offense. The PPV is the probability that offenders assessed as high risk of reoffending indeed commit a new offense (i.e., number of TPs divided by the total number of TPs and FPs), while the NPV refers to the probability that offenders assessed as low risk do indeed not reoffend (i.e., number of TNs divided by the total number of TNs and FNs). PPV and NPV are reciprocally influenced by base rates. A lower prevalence rate results in a loss of PPV and a gain in NPV (Elwood, 1993).

A systematic review and meta-analysis examining the predictive validity of violence risk assessment instruments from 73 samples involving almost 25,000 offenders in 13 countries showed that these tools appear to identify low-risk individuals with high levels of accuracy (i.e., high NPV), but have low to moderate PPVs (Fazel et al., 2012). In other words, many offenders who are assessed as

Table 25.3 Predictive accuracy parameters derived from a 2 × 2 contingency table

		Outcome		
		Violent	Not violent	Total
Risk assessment	Positive predictions	TP (Hits)	FP (False alarms)	TP + FP
	Negative predictions	FN (Misses)	TN	FN + TN
		TP + FN	FP + TN	

Note. TP = True positives. FP = False positives. FN = False negatives. TN = True negatives
Sensitivity (Se) = TP/TP + FN
Specificity (Sp) = TN/FP + TN
Positive predictive value (PPV) = TP/TP + FP
Negative predictive value (NPV) = TN/FN + TN
Positive likelihood ratio (PLR) = Se/1 − SP
Negative likelihood ratio (NLR) = 1 − Se/Sp
Number needed to detain (NND) = 1/PPV
Number safely discharged (NSD) = (1/1−NPV)−1
Diagnostic odds ratio = TP × TN/FP × FN

moderately or high risk with risk assessment tools actually have a low recidivism risk.

It should be noted that applying statistics intended for dichotomous diagnostic decisions, such as PPV and NPV, to assess the predictive accuracy of risk assessment instruments has also been criticized. Helmus and Babchishin (2017), for example, argue that risk tools provide *prognostic* information (i.e., probabilistic information about the likelihood of an event occurring in the future), and *not* *diagnostic* information (i.e., classifying offenders based on whether they have a condition), and statistics premised on a diagnostic classification are generally not useful for evaluating the accuracy of specific risk assessment instruments (Helmus & Babchishin, 2017).

The Future of Risk Assessment

In recent years, thoughtful criticisms have been voiced concerning established practices in both risk assessment research (e.g., Douglas et al., 2017; Singh, 2014) and risk assessment practice (e.g., DeClue & Zavodny, 2014; Silva, 2020, but see de Ruiter et al., 2020 for a response to Silva). Within the confines of this chapter, we will not be able to discuss all of these concerns and will thus mention only a few. Both Singh (2014) and Douglas et al. (2017) point at the need for more validation studies in different populations (e.g., women, ethnic minority groups), because it is not clear if predictive accuracy findings demonstrated in one population can be extrapolated to another one. Furthermore, the tradition of merely reporting AUC-values, without mention of PPV and NPV, is problematic because risk assessment tools with the same AUC-values may vary greatly in their ability to identify recidivists vs. non-recidivists (Singh, 2014).

The practice of risk assessment and the important role risk assessment reports play in legal decision-making about the assessee, call for caution and prudence. As an example, DeClue and Zavodny (2014) went so far as to argue that mental health professionals should only report the outcome of an ARAI (they use the Static-99 as an example) on a group level and not as applicable to the individual assessee, because the level of certainty of prediction at the individual level is quite low (see Fazel et al., 2012, for illustrations; Hart & Cooke, 2013). Research has also shown that even the subtle way probability estimates are framed impacts decision-making (Scurich & John, 2011). In a study with 303 university students who acted as mock judges, they found that risk framed as a 26% probability of violence generally led subjects to authorize civil commitment, whereas the same risk framed in the numerical complement, a 74% probability of no violence, generally led decision-makers to decide to release. The general tendency in violence risk assessment practice to frame estimates in terms of the probability of violence will skew decision-makers toward false positives. Perhaps forensic evaluators should become obliged to present both the probability estimate for the negative outcome and the positive outcome in their reports (Scurich & John, 2012).

Conclusion

Violence risk assessment research and practice has come of age during the past 40 years. A wealth of tools for specific violent outcomes have been developed and empirically tested. However, the field cannot rest on its laurels yet. The study of cognitive bias in violence risk assessment, including base rate neglect, is just beginning (e.g., Kamorowski et al., 2021). A structured risk assessment is evidently an improvement over an unstructured one, but there appears to be a ceiling to the predictive accuracy that can be attained (Heilbrun et al., 2021). We need to start conducting studies that link risk assessment to risk management strategies, to learn more about what works in risk reduction. Moreover, how we can most effectively communicate our risk assessment outcomes to legal decision-makers remains an understudied topic.

Real-world risk assessment evaluations can have dramatic and potentially harmful consequences for the assessee, but also for the general public. The competing values of individual liberties and public protection (Douglas et al., 2017; Petrila & de Ruiter, 2011) are at the heart of risk assessment practice. Structured risk assessment tools are by no means perfect, but they do offer a significant improvement over unstructured clinical judgment in terms of interrater agreement, predictive accuracy, and transparency.

References

Ægisdóttir, S., White, M. J., Spengler, P. M., Maugherman, A. S., Anderson, L. A., Cook, R. S., Nichols, C. N., Lampropoulos, G. K., Walker, B. S., Cohen, G., & Rush, J. D. (2006). The meta-analysis of clinical judgment project: Fifty-six years of accumulated research on clinical versus statistical prediction. *The Counseling Psychologist, 34*(3), 341–382. https://doi.org/10.1177/0011000005285875
Allison, P. D. (1984). *Event history analysis: Regression for longitudinal event data.* Sage.

Almvik, R., Woods, P., & Rasmussen, K. (2000). The Brøset Violence Checklist: Sensitivity, specificity, and interrater reliability. *Journal of Interpersonal Violence, 15*(12), 1284–1296. https://doi.org/10.1177/088626000015012003

Andrews, D. A. (2012). The risk-need-responsivity (RNR) model of correctional assessment and treatment. In J. A. Dvoskin, J. L. Skeem, R. W. Novaco, & K. S. Douglas (Eds.), *Using social science to reduce violent offending* (pp. 127–156). Oxford University Press.

Andrews, D. A., & Bonta, J. (2010). *The psychology of criminal conduct* (5th ed.). Anderson Publishing.

Andrews, D. A., Bonta, J., & Wormith, S. J. (2004). *The level of service/case management inventory (LS/CMI)*. Multi-Health Systems.

Arkes, H. R. (1991). Costs and benefits of judgment errors: Implications for debiasing. *Psychological Bulletin, 110*(3), 486–498. https://doi.org/10.1037/0033-2909.110.3.486

Augimeri, L. K., Koegl, C. J., Webster, C. D., & Levene, K. S. (2001). *Early assessment risk list for boys: EARL-20B, version 2*. Earlscourt Child and Family Centre.

Bengtson, S., & Långström, N. (2007). Unguided clinical and actuarial assessment of re-offending risk: A direct comparison with sex offenders in Denmark. *Sexual Abuse, 19*(2), 135–153. https://doi.org/10.1177/107906320701900205

Boer, D. P., Hart, S. D., Kropp, P. R., & Webster, C. D. (2017). *Manual for version 2 of the sexual violence risk-20: Structured professional guidelines for assessing and managing risk of sexual violence*. Protect International Risk and Safety Services Inc.

Borum, R., Bartel, P., & Forth, A. (2006). *Manual for the structured assessment for violence risk in youth (SAVRY)*. Psychological Assessment Resources.

Brett, A. (2004). 'Kindling theory' in arson: How dangerous are firesetters? *Australian and New Zealand Journal of Psychiatry, 38*(6), 419–425. https://doi.org/10.1111/j.1440-1614.2004.01378.x

Campbell, M. A., French, S., & Gendreau, P. (2009). The prediction of violence in adult offenders: A meta-analytic comparison of instruments and methods of assessment. *Criminal Justice and Behavior, 36*(6), 567–590. https://doi.org/10.1177/0093854809333610

Cohen, J. (1988). *Statistical power analysis for the behavioral sciences* (2nd ed.). Lawrence Erlbaum Associates.

Cunningham, M. D., & Reidy, T. J. (1998). Integrating base rate data in violence risk assessments at capital sentencing. *Behavioral Sciences & the Law, 16*(1), 71–95. https://doi.org/10.1002/(SICI)1099-0798(199824)16:1%3c71::AID-BSL294%3e3.0.CO;2-6

Davis, M., & Ogloff, J. R. P. (2004, June 6–9). *Broken leg countervailings and violence risk assessment: The views of practicing clinicians*. Paper presentation. International Association of Forensic Mental Health Services 4th annual meeting. Stockholm, Sweden.

DeClue, G., & Zavodny, D. L. (2014). Forensic use of the Static-99R: Part 4. Risk communication. *Journal of Threat Assessment and Management, 1*(3), 145–161. https://doi.org/10.1037/tam0000017

Dernevik, M., Falkheim, M., Holmqvist, R., & Sandell, R. (2001). Implementing risk assessment procedures in a forensic psychiatric setting: Clinical judgement revisited. In D. P. Farrington, C. R. Hollin, & M. McMurran (Eds.), *Sex and violence: The psychology of crime and risk assessment* (pp. 83–101). Routledge.

de Ruiter, C. (2015). A firesetter in longstay forensic care. In C. de Ruiter & N. Kaser-Boyd, *Forensic psychological assessment in practice: Case studies* (pp. 64–91). Routledge.

de Ruiter, C. (2018). Modifying risk factors—Building strengths. In A. R. Beech, A. J. Carter, R. E. Mann, & P. Rothstein (Eds.), *The Wiley-Blackwell handbook of forensic neuroscience* (Vol. 2, pp. 553–573). Wiley-Blackwell.

de Ruiter, C., & Hildebrand, M. (2003). The dual nature of forensic psychiatric practice: Risk assessment and management under the Dutch TBS-order. In P. J. van Koppen & S. D. Penrod (Eds.), *Adversarial vs. inquisitorial justice: Psychological perspectives on criminal justice systems* (pp. 91–106). Plenum Press.

de Ruiter, C., & Hildebrand, M. (2021). *Child Abuse Risk Evaluation—Version 2 (CARE^{V2}): Guideline for the structured assessment of the risk of child abuse and neglect*. C. de Ruiter.

de Ruiter, C., & Nicholls, T. L. (2011). Protective factors in forensic mental health: A new frontier. *International Journal of Forensic Mental Health, 10*(3), 160–170. https://doi.org/10.1080/14999013.2011.600602

de Ruiter, C., De Beuf, T., & de Vogel, V. (2020). A nuanced view on the HCR-20 and SPJ violence risk assessment: A response to Silva (2020). eLetter in response to 'The HCR-20 and violence risk assessment—Will a peak of inflated expectations turn to a trough of disillusionment?' *BJPsych Bulletin*. https://doi.org/10.1192/bjb.2020.14

de Vogel, V., de Ruiter, C., Bouman, Y., & de Vries Robbé, M. (2009). *SAPROF: Guidelines for the assessment of protective factors for violence risk*. [English version of the Dutch original]. Forum Educatief.

de Vogel, V., de Vries Robbé, M., de Ruiter, C., & Bouman, Y. H. A. (2011). Assessing protective factors in forensic psychiatric practice: Introducing the SAPROF. *International Journal of Forensic Mental Health, 10*(3), 171–177. https://doi.org/10.1080/14999013.2011.600230

de Vries Robbé, M., de Vogel, V., & de Spa, E. (2011). Protective factors for violence risk in forensic psychiatric patients. A retrospective validation study of the SAPROF. *International Journal of Forensic Mental Health, 10*(3), 178–186. https://doi.org/10.1080/14999013.2011.600232

de Vries Robbé, M., Mann, R. E., Maruna, S., & Thornton, D. (2015). An exploration of protective factors supporting desistance from sexual offending. *Sexual Abuse: A Journal of Research and Treatment, 27*(1), 16–33. https://doi.org/10.1177/1079063214547582

Dickens, G., Sugarman, P., Edgar, S., Hofberg, K., Tewari, S., & Ahmad, F. (2009). Recidivism and dangerousness in arsonists. *Journal of Forensic Psychiatry & Psychology, 20*(5), 621–639. https://doi.org/10.1080/14789940903174006

Douglas, K. S., Cox, D. N., & Webster, C. D. (1999). Violence risk assessment: Science and practice. *Legal and Criminological Psychology, 4*(2), 149–184. https://doi.org/10.1348/135532599167824

Douglas, K. S., Hart, S. D., Groscup, J. L., & Litwack, T. R. (2014). Assessing violence risk. In I. B. Weiner & R. K. Otto (Eds.), *The handbook of forensic psychology* (4th ed., pp. 385–441). Wiley.

Douglas, K. S., Hart, S. D., Webster, C. D., & Belfrage, H. (2013). *HCR-20^{V3}: Assessing risk of violence—User guide*. Mental Health, Law, and Policy Institute, Simon Fraser University.

Douglas, K. S., Hart, S. D., Webster, C. D., Belfrage, H., Guy, L. S., & Wilson, C. M. (2014). Historical-Clinical-Risk Management-20, Version 3 (HCR-20^{V3}): Development and overview. *International Journal of Forensic Mental Health, 13*(2), 93–108. https://doi.org/10.1080/14999013.2014.906519

Douglas, K. S., & Kropp, P. R. (2002). A prevention-based paradigm for violence risk assessment: Clinical and research applications. *Criminal Justice and Behavior, 29*(5), 617–658. https://doi.org/10.1177/009385402236735

Douglas, K. S., & Otto, R. K. (Eds.). (2021). *Handbook of violence risk assessment* (2nd ed.). Routledge.

Douglas, K. S., Otto, R. K., Desmarais, S. L., & Borum, R. (2012). Clinical forensic psychology. In I. B. Weiner, J. A. Schinka, & W. F. Velicer (Eds.), *Handbook of psychology, volume 2: Research methods in psychology* (pp. 213–244). Wiley.

Douglas, K. S., & Skeem, J. L. (2005). Violence risk assessment: Getting specific about being dynamic. *Psychology, Public Policy, and Law, 11*(3), 347–383. https://doi.org/10.1037/1076-8971.11.3.347

Douglas, K. S., Skeem, J. L., & Nicholson, E. (2011). Research methods in violence risk assessment. In B. Rosenfeld & S. D. Penrod (Eds.), *Research methods in forensic psychology* (pp. 325–346). Wiley.

Douglas, T., Pugh, J., Singh, I., Savulescu, J., & Fazel, S. (2017). Risk assessment tools in criminal justice and forensic psychiatry: The need for better data. *European Psychiatry, 42*, 134–137. https://doi.org/10.1016/j.eurpsy.2016.12.009

Ducat, L., McEwan, T., & Ogloff, J. R. P. (2015). An investigation of firesetting recidivism: Factors related to repeat offending. *Legal and Criminological Psychology, 20*(1), 1–18. https://doi.org/10.1111/lcrp.12052

Edwards, M. J., & Grace, R. C. (2014). The development of an actuarial model for arson recidivism. *Psychiatry, Psychology and Law, 21*(2), 218–230. https://doi.org/10.1080/13218719.2013.803277

Elwood, R. W. (1993). Clinical discrimination and neuropsychological tests: An appeal to Bayes' theorem. *Clinical Neuropsychologist, 7*(2), 224–233. https://doi.org/10.1080/13854049308401527

Ennis, B. J., & Litwack, T. T. (1974). Psychiatry and the presumption of expertise: Flipping coins in the courtroom. *California Law Review, 62*(3), 693–752. https://doi.org/10.2307/3479746

Fazel, S., Singh, J. P., Doll, H., & Grann, M. (2012). Use of risk assessment instruments to predict violence and antisocial behaviour in 73 samples involving 24827 people: Systematic review and meta-analysis. *British Medical Journal, 345*, Article e4692. https://doi.org/10.1136/bmj.e4692

Green, D. M., & Swets, J. A. (1966). *Signal detection theory and psychophysics*. Wiley.

Grove, W. M., & Meehl, P. E. (1996). Comparative efficiency of informal (subjective, impressionistic) and formal (mechanical, algorithmic) prediction procedures: The clinical–statistical controversy. *Psychology, Public Policy, and Law, 2*(2), 293–323. https://doi.org/10.1037/1076-8971.2.2.293

Grove, W. M., Zald, D. H., Lebow, B. S., Snitz, B. E., & Nelson, C. (2000). Clinical versus mechanical prediction: A meta-analysis. *Psychological Assessment, 12*(1), 19–30. https://doi.org/10.1037/1040-3590.12.1.19

Grubin, D. (1997). Predictors of risk in serious offenders. *British Journal of Psychiatry, 170*(32), 17–21. https://doi.org/10.1192/s000712500029867x

Grubin, D., & Wingate, S. (1996). Sexual offence recidivism: Prediction versus understanding. *Criminal Behaviour and Mental Health, 6*(4), 349–359. https://doi.org/10.1002/cbm.121

Guay, J.-P., & Parent, G. (2018). Broken legs, clinical overrides, and recidivism risk: An analysis of decisions to adjust risk levels with the LS/CMI. *Criminal Justice and Behavior, 45*(1), 82–100. https://doi.org/10.1177/0093854817719482

Gutierrez, L., Helmus, L. M., & Hanson, R. K. (2017). *What we know and don't know about risk assessment with offenders of indigenous heritage* (Research Report 2017–R009). https://www.publicsafety.gc.ca/cnt/rsrcs/pblctns/2017-r009/2017-r009-en.pdf

Guy, L. S. (2008). *Performance indicators of the structured professional judgement approach for assessing risk for violence to others: A meta-analytic survey.* (Unpublished doctoral dissertation). Simon Fraser University.

Hall, J. E., Simon, T. R., Lee, R. D., & Mercy, J. A. (2012). Implications of direct protective factors for public health research and prevention strategies to reduce youth violence. *American Journal of Preventive Medicine, 43*(2 Suppl 1), S76–S83. https://doi.org/10.1016/j.amepre.2012.04.019

Hanson, R. K. (1998). What do we know about sex offender risk assessment? *Psychology, Public Policy, and Law, 4*(1–2), 50–72. https://doi.org/10.1037/1076-8971.4.1-2.50

Hanson, R. K. (2008). What statistics should we use to report predictive accuracy? *Crime Scene, 15*(1), 15–17.

Hanson, R. K., & Morton-Bourgon, K. E. (2009). The accuracy of recidivism risk assessments for sexual offenders: A meta-analysis of 118 prediction studies. *Psychological Assessment, 21*(1), 1–21. https://doi.org/10.1037/a0014421

Hanson, R. K., & Thornton, D. (2000). Improving risk assessments for sex offenders: A comparison of three actuarial scales. *Law and Human Behavior, 24*(1), 119–136. https://doi.org/10.1023/A:1005482921333

Hanson, R. K., & Thornton, D. (2003). *Notes on the development of Static-2002* (User Report 2003–01). Department of the Solicitor General of Canada.

Harrell, F. E., Califf, R. M., Pryor, D. B., Lee, K. L., & Rosati, R. A. (1982). Evaluating the yield of medical tests. *Journal of the American Medical Association, 247*(18), 2543–2546. https://doi.org/10.1001/jama.1982.03320430047030

Harris, A., & Lurigio, A. J. (2007). Mental illness and violence: A brief review of the research and assessment strategies. *Aggression and Violent Behavior, 12*(5), 542–551. https://doi.org/10.1016/j.avb.2007.02.008

Harris, G. T., & Rice, M. E. (1984). Mentally disordered firesetters: Psychodynamic versus empirical approaches. *International Journal of Law and Psychiatry, 7*(1), 19–34. https://doi.org/10.1016/0160-2527(84)90004-9

Harris, G. T., Rice, M. E., Quinsey, V. L., & Cormier, C. A. (2015). *Violent offenders: Appraising and managing risk* (3rd ed.). American Psychological Association.

Hart, S. D. (2008a, July 14–16). *The structured professional judgement approach to violence risk assessment: Core principles of SPJ.* Paper presentation. International Association of Forensic Mental Health Services 8th annual meeting. Vienna, Austria.

Hart, S. D. (2008b). Preventing violence: The role of risk assessment and management. In A. C. Baldry & F. W. Winkel (Eds.), *Intimate partner violence prevention and intervention: The risk assessment and management approach* (pp. 7–18). Nova Science Publishers.

Hart, S. D., & Cooke, D. J. (2013). Another look at the (im)precision of individual risk estimates made using actuarial risk assessment instruments. *Behavioral Sciences & the Law, 31*, 81–102. https://doi.org/10.1002/bsl.2049

Hart, S. D., Douglas, K. S., & Guy, L. S. (2016). The structured professional judgment approach to violence risk assessment: Origins, nature, and advances. In D. P. Boer, A. R. Beech, T. Ward, L. A. Craig, M. Rettenberger, L. E. Marshall, & W. L. Marshall (Eds.), *The Wiley handbook on the theories, assessment, and treatment of sexual offending* (pp. 643–666). Wiley-Blackwell.

Hart, S. D., Kropp, P. R., Laws, D. R., Klaver, J., Logan, C., & Watt, K. A. (2003). *The Risk for Sexual Violence Protocol (RSVP): Structured professional guidelines for assessing risk of sexual violence.* Mental Health, Law and Policy Institute, Simon Fraser University.

Hart, S. D., & Logan, C. (2011). Formulation of violence risk using evidence-based assessments: The structured professional judgment approach. In P. Sturmey & M. McMurran (Eds.), *Forensic case formulation* (pp. 83–106). Wiley-Blackwell.

Hart, S. D., Michie, C., & Cooke, D. J. (2007). Precision of actuarial risk assessment instruments: Evaluating the 'margins of error' of group v. individual predictions of violence. *The British Journal of Psychiatry, 190*(Suppl 49), s60–s65. https://doi.org/10.1192/bjp.190.5.s60

Hart, S., Sturmey, P., Logan, C., & McMurran, M. (2011). Forensic case formulation. *International Journal of Forensic Mental Health, 10*(2), 118–126. https://doi.org/10.1080/14999013.2011.577137

Hartvig, P., Østberg, B., Alfarnes, S., Moger, T. A., Skjønberg, M., & Bjørkly, S. (2007). *Violence Risk Screening-10 (V-RISK-10).* Centre for Research and Education in Forensic Psychiatry.

Heilbrun, K., Yasuhara, K., Shah, S., & Locklair, B. (2021). Approaches to violence risk assessment: Overview, critical analysis, and future directions. In K. S. Douglas & R. K. Otto (Eds.), *Handbook of violence risk assessment* (2nd ed., pp. 3–27). Routledge.

Helmus, L. M., & Babchishin, K. L. (2017). Primer on risk assessment and the statistics used to evaluate its accuracy. *Criminal Justice and Behavior, 44*(1), 8–25. https://doi.org/10.1177/0093854816678898

Hilton, N. Z., Harris, G. T., & Rice, M. E. (2006). Sixty-six years of research on clinical versus actuarial prediction of violence. *The Counseling Psychologist, 34*(3), 400–409. https://doi.org/10.1177/0011000005285877

Hilton, N. Z., Harris, G. T., Rice, M. E., Lang, C., Cormier, C. A., & Lines, K. J. (2004). A brief actuarial assessment for the prediction of wife assault recidivism: The Ontario Domestic Assault Risk Assessment. *Psychological Assessment, 16*(3), 267–275. https://doi.org/10.1037/1040-3590.16.3.267

Hosmer, D. W., & Lemeshow, S. (2000). *Applied logistic regression* (2nd ed.). Wiley.

Hosmer, D. W., Jr., Lemeshow, S., & Sturdivant, R. X. (2013). *Applied logistic regression* (3rd ed.). Wiley.

Howe, J., Rosenfeld, B., Foellmi, M., Stern, S., & Rotter, M. (2016). Application of the HCR-20 version 3 in civil psychiatric patients. *Criminal Justice and Behavior, 43*(3), 398–412. https://doi.org/10.1177/0093854815605527

Kahneman, D., & Tversky, A. (1985). Evidential impact of base rates. In D. Kahneman, P. Slovic, & A. Tversky (Eds.), *Judgment under uncertainty: Heuristics and biases* (pp. 153–160). Cambridge University Press.

Kamorowski, J., de Ruiter, C., Schreuder, M., Jelicic, M., & Ask, K. (2021). Forensic mental health practitioners' use of structured risk assessment instruments: Views about bias in risk evaluations, and strategies to counteract it. *International Journal of Forensic Mental Health.* https://doi.org/10.1080/14999013.2021.1895377

Kashiwagi, H., Kikuchi, A., Koyama, M., Saito, D., & Hirabayashi, N. (2018). Strength-based assessment for future violence risk: A retrospective validation study of the Structured Assessment of PROtective Factors for violence risk (SAPROF) Japanese version in forensic psychiatric inpatients. *Annals of General Psychiatry, 17*, Article 5. https://doi.org/10.1186/s12991-018-0175-5

Krauss, D. A., Sales, B. D., Becker, J. V., & Figueredo, A. J. (2000). Beyond prediction to explanation in risk assessment research: A comparison of two explanatory theories of criminality and recidivism. *International Journal of Law and Psychiatry, 23*(2), 91–112. https://doi.org/10.1016/S0160-2527(99)00032-1

Kropp, P. R., Hart, S. D., & Belfrage, H. (2005). *The Brief Spousal Assault Form for the Evaluation of Risk (B-SAFER): User manual.* ProActive ReSolutions.

Lamont, S., & Brunero, S. (2009). Risk analysis: An integrated approach to the assessment and management of aggression/violence in mental health. *Journal of Psychiatric Intensive Care, 5*(1), 25–32. https://doi.org/10.1017/S1742646408001349

Large, M. M., Ryan, C. J., Singh, S. P., Paton, M. B., & Nielssen, O. B. (2011). The predictive value of risk categorization in schizophrenia. *Harvard Law Review, 19*(1), 25–33. https://doi.org/10.3109/10673229.2011.549770

Levene, K. S., Augimeri, L. K., Pepler, D., Walsh, M., Webster, C. D., & Koegl, C. J. (2001). *Early Assessment Risk List for Girls: EARL-21G, Version 1, Consultation edition.* Earlscourt Child and Family Centre.

Lewis, G., & Doyle, M. (2009). Risk formulation: What are we doing and why? *International Journal of Forensic Mental Health, 8*(4), 286–292. https://doi.org/10.1080/14999011003635696

Lindberg, N., Holi, M. M., Tani, P., & Virkkunen, M. (2005). Looking for pyromania: Characteristics of a consecutive sample of Finnish male criminals with histories of recidivist fire-setting between 1973 and 1993. *BMC Psychiatry, 5*, Article 47. https://doi.org/10.1186/1471-244X-5-47

Lodewijks, H. P. B., de Ruiter, C., & Doreleijers, T. A. H. (2010). The impact of protective factors in desistance from violent reoffending: A study in three samples of adolescent offenders. *Journal of Interpersonal Violence, 25*(3), 568–587. https://doi.org/10.1177/0886260509334403

Logan, C., & Johnstone, L. (2010). Personality disorder and violence: Making the link through risk formulation. *Journal of Personality Disorders, 24*(5), 610–633. https://doi.org/10.1521/pedi.2010.24.5.610

Mallett, S., Halligan, S., Thompson, M., Collins, G. S., & Altman, D. G. (2012). Interpreting diagnostic accuracy studies for patient care. *British Medical Journal, 345*, Article e3999. https://doi.org/10.1136/bmj.e3999

McCafferty, J. T. (2017). Professional discretion and the predictive validity of a juvenile risk assessment instrument: Exploring the overlooked principle of effective correctional classification. *Youth Violence and Juvenile Justice, 15*(2), 103–118. https://doi.org/10.1177/1541204015622255

Meehl, P. E. (1954). *Clinical versus statistical prediction: A theoretical analysis and review of the evidence.* University of Minnesota Press.

Meehl, P. E. (1996). *Clinical versus statistical prediction: A theoretical analysis and a review of the literature*. Jason Aronson (Original work published in 1954).

Miller, H. A. (2006). A dynamic assessment of offender risk, needs, and strengths in a sample of general offenders. *Behavioral Sciences and the Law, 24*(6), 767–782. https://doi.org/10.1002/bsl.728

Miller, S. L., & Brodsky, S. L. (2011). Risky business: Addressing the consequences of predicting violence. *Journal of the American Academy of Psychiatry and Law, 39*(3), 396–401.

Monahan, J. (1981). The clinical prediction of violent behavior. *Crime & Delinquency Issues: A Monograph Series, ADM, 81–921*, 134.

Monahan, J. (1984). The prediction of violent behavior: Toward a second generation of theory and policy. *American Journal of Psychiatry, 141*(1), 10–15. https://doi.org/10.1176/ajp.141.1.10

Monahan, J. (1988). Risk assessment of violence among the mentally disordered: Generating useful knowledge. *International Journal of Law and Psychiatry, 11*(3), 249–257. https://doi.org/10.1016/0160-2527(88)90012-X

Monahan, J., Steadman, H. J., Appelbaum, P. S., Grisso, T., Mulvey, E. P., Roth, L. H., Robbins, P. C., Banks, S., & Silver, E. (2005). *The Classification of Violence Risk (COVR)*. Psychological Assessment Resources.

Monahan, J., Steadman, H. J., Silver, E., Appelbaum, P. S., Robbins, P. C., Mulvey, E. P., Roth, L. H., Grisso, T., & Banks, S. (2001). *Rethinking risk assessment: The MacArthur study of mental disorder and violence*. Oxford University Press.

Mossman, D. (1994). Assessing predictions of violence: Being accurate about accuracy. *Journal of Consulting and Clinical Psychology, 62*(4), 783–792. https://doi.org/10.1037/0022-006X.62.4.783

Mossman, D. (2013). Evaluating risk assessments using receiver operating characteristic analysis: Rationale, advantages, insights, and limitations. *Behavioral Sciences & the Law, 31*(1), 23–39. https://doi.org/10.1002/bsl.2050

Mullen, P. E., & Ogloff, J. R. (2009). Assessing and managing the risks of violence towards others. In M. G. Gelder, N. C. Andreasen, J. J. Lopez-Ibor, & J. R. Geddes (Eds.), *New Oxford textbook of psychiatry* (Vol. 2, 2nd ed., pp. 1991–2002). Oxford University Press.

Munro, E. (2004). A simpler way to understand the results of risk assessment instruments. *Children & Youth Services Review, 26*(9), 873–883. https://doi.org/10.1016/j.childyouth.2004.02.026

Murray, J., & Thomson, M. (2010). Clinical judgement in violence risk assessment. *Europe's Journal of Psychology, 6*(1), 128–149. https://doi.org/10.5964/ejop.v6i1.175

Nafekh, M., & Motiuk, L. L. (2002). *The statistical information on recidivism—revised 1 (SIR-R1) scale: A psychometric evaluation* (Research Report No. R-126). Correctional Service of Canada.

Neal, T. M. S., & Grisso, T. (2014). The cognitive underpinnings of bias in forensic mental health evaluations. *Psychology, Public Policy, and Law, 20*(2), 200–211. https://doi.org/10.1037/a0035824

Nickerson, R. S. (1998). Confirmation bias: A ubiquitous phenomenon in many guises. *Review of General Psychology, 2*(2), 175–220. https://doi.org/10.1037/1089-2680.2.2.175

Nyman, M., Hofvander, B., Nilsson, T., & Wijk, H. (2020). Mental health nurses' experiences of risk assessments for care planning in forensic psychiatry. *International Journal of Forensic Mental Health, 19*(2), 103–113. https://doi.org/10.1080/14999013.2019.164 6356

Ogloff, J., & Daffern, M. (2002). *Dynamic appraisal of situational aggression: Inpatient version.* Monash University and Forensicare.

Olver, M. E. (2011, March 14). How to assess recidivism risk in sex offenders? A review of issues and approaches for assessing risk and evaluating change in sexual offenders. In K. Nunes & M. Seto (Chairs), *Advancing our understanding of treatment change among high risk sex offenders* [Symposium]. Carleton University.

Pennycook, G., Trippas, D., Handley, S. J., & Thompson, V. A. (2014). Base rates: Both neglected and intuitive. *Journal of Experimental Psychology: Learning, Memory, and Cognition, 40*(2), 544–554. https://doi.org/10.1037/a0034887

Pepe, M. S. (2000). Receiver operating characteristic methodology. *Journal of the American Statistical Association, 95*(449), 308–311. https://doi.org/10.2307/2669554

Petrila, J., & de Ruiter, C. (2011). The competing faces of mental health law: Recovery and access versus the expanding use of preventive confinement. *Amsterdam Law Forum, 3*(1), 72–83. https://doi.org/10.37974/ALF.163

Quinsey, V. L., Harris, G. T., Rice, M. E., & Cormier, C. A. (1998). *Violent offenders: Appraising and managing risk.* American Psychological Association.

Quinsey, V. L., Harris, G. T., Rice, M. E., & Cormier, C. A. (2006). *Violent offenders: Appraising and managing risk* (2nd ed.). American Psychological Association.

Repo, E., Virkkunen, M., Rawlings, R., & Linnoila, M. (1997). Criminal and psychiatric histories of Finnish arsonists. *Acta Psychiatrica Scandinavica, 95*(4), 318–323. https://doi.org/10.1111/j.1600-0447.1997.tb09638.x

Rice, M. E., & Harris, G. T. (1995). Violent recidivism: Assessing predictive validity. *Journal of Consulting and Clinical Psychology, 63*(5), 737–748. https://doi.org/10.1037//0022-006x.63.5.737

Rice, M. E., & Harris, G. T. (1996). Predicting the recidivism of mentally disordered firesetters. *Journal of Interpersonal Violence, 11*(3), 364–375. https://doi.org/10.1177/088626096011003004

Rice, M. E., & Harris, G. T. (2005). Comparing effect sizes in follow-up studies: ROC Area, Cohen's d, and r. *Law and Human Behavior, 29*(5), 615–620. https://doi.org/10.1007/s10979-005-6832-7

Rogers, R. (2000). The uncritical acceptance of risk assessment in forensic practice. *Law and Human Behavior, 24*(5), 595–605. https://doi.org/10.1023/A:1005575113507

Scott, C. L., & Resnick, P. J. (2006). Violence risk assessment in persons with mental illness. *Aggression and Violent Behavior, 11*(6), 598–611. https://doi.org/10.1016/j.avb.2005.12.003

Scurich, N., & John, R. S. (2011). The effect of framing actuarial risk probabilities on involuntary commitment decisions. *Law and Human Behavior, 35*, 83–91. https://doi.org/10.1007/s10979-010-9218-4

Scurich, N., & John, R. S. (2012). Prescriptive approaches to communicating the risk of violence in actuarial risk assessment. *Psychology, Public Policy, and Law, 18*(1), 50–78. https://doi.org/10.1037/a0024592

Silva, E. (2020). The HCR-20 and violence risk assessment—Will a peak of inflated expectations turn to a trough of disillusionment? *BJpsych Bulletin, 44*(6), 269–271. https://doi.org/10.1192/bjb.2020.14

Singh, J. P. (2013). Predictive validity performance indicators in violence risk assessment: A methodological primer. *Behavioral Sciences and the Law, 31*(1), 8–22. https://doi.org/10. 1002/bsl.2052

Singh, J. P. (2014). Five opportunities for innovation in violence risk assessment research. *Journal of Threat Assessment and Management, 1*(3), 179–184. https://doi.org/10.1037/ tam0000018

Singh, J. P. (2016). *International perspectives on forensic risk assessment: Measuring use, perceived utility, and research quality* [Doctoral dissertation]. University of Konstanz.

Singh, J. P., Desmarais, S. L., Hurducas, C., Arbach-Lucioni, K., Condemarin, C., Dean, K., Doyle, M., Folino, J. O., Godoy-Cervera, V., Grann, M., Ho, R. M. Y., Large, M. M., Nielsen, L. H., Pham, T. H., Rebocho, M. F., Reeves, K. A., Rettenberger, M., de Ruiter, C., Seewald, K., & Otto, R. K. (2014). International perspectives on the practical application of violence risk assessment: A global survey of 44 countries. *The International Journal of Forensic Mental Health, 13*(3), 193–206. https://doi.org/10.1080/14999013.2014.922141

Singh, J. P., Grann, M., & Fazel, S. (2011). A comparative study of violence risk assessment tools: A systematic review and metaregression analysis of 68 studies involving 25,980 participants. *Clinical Psychology Review, 31*(3), 499–513. https://doi.org/10.1016/j.cpr. 2010.11.009

Sjöstedt, G., & Långström, N. (2002). Assessment of risk for criminal recidivism among rapists: A comparison of four different measures. *Psychology, Crime & Law, 8*(1), 25–40. https://doi.org/10.1080/10683160208401807

Spreen, M., Brand, E., ter Horst, P., & Bogaerts, S. (2014). *Handleiding HKT-R. Historische, Klinische en Toekomstige – Revisie* [Manual HKT-R. Historical, Clinical and Future— Revision]. Stichting FPC Dr. S. van Mesdag.

Steadman, H. J., Monahan, J., Robbins, P. C., Appelbaum, P., Grisso, T., Klassen, D., Mulvey, E. P., & Roth, L. (1993). From dangerousness to risk assessment: Implications for appropriate research strategies. In S. Hodgins (Ed.), *Mental disorder and crime* (pp. 39–62). Sage.

Swets, J. A. (1988). Measuring the accuracy of diagnostic systems. *Science, 240*(4857), 1285– 1293. https://doi.org/10.1126/science.3287615

Swets, J. A., Dawes, R. M., & Monahan, J. (2000). Psychological science can improve diagnostic decisions. *Psychological Science in the Public Interest, 1*(1), 1–26. https://doi.org/ 10.1111/1529-1006.001

Thomson, A., Tiihonen, J., Miettunen, J., Virkkunen, M., & Lindberg, N. (2018). Firesetting and general criminal recidivism among a consecutive sample of Finnish pretrial male firesetters: A register-based follow-up study. *Psychiatry Research*, 259, 377–384. https:// doi.org/10.1016/j.psychres.2017.11.008

Thornton, D., Mann, R., Webster, S., Blud, L., Travers, R., Friendship, C., & Erikson, M. (2003). Distinguishing and combining risks for sexual and violent recidivism. In R. A. Prentky, E. S. Janus, & M. C. Seto (Eds.), *Sexually coercive behavior: Understanding and management* (pp. 225–235). New York Academy of Sciences.

Torrey, E. F., Stanley, J., Monahan, J., Steadman, H. J., & MacArthur Study Group. (2008). The MacArthur Violence Risk Assessment Study revisited: Two views ten years after its initial publication. *Psychiatric Services, 59*(2), 147–152. https://doi.org/10.1176/ps.2008. 59.2.147

Tully, R. J., Chou, S., & Browne, K. D. (2013). A systematic review on the effectiveness of sex offender risk assessment tools in predicting sexual recidivism of adult male sex offenders. *Clinical Psychology Review, 33*(2), 287–316. https://doi.org/10.1016/j.cpr.2012.12.002

Tversky, A., & Kahneman, D. (1974). Judgment under uncertainty: Heuristics and biases. *Science, 185*(4157), 1124–1131. https://doi.org/10.1126/science.185.4157.1124

van Marle, H. J. C. (2002). The Dutch Entrustment Act (TBS): Its principles and innovations. *International Journal of Forensic Mental Health, 1*(1), 83–92. https://doi.org/10.1080/149 99013.2002.10471163

Viljoen, J. L., McLachlan, K., & Vincent, G. M. (2010). Assessing violence risk and psychopathy in juvenile and adult offenders: A survey of clinical practices. *Assessment, 17*(3), 377–395. https://doi.org/10.1177/1073191109359587

Walters, G. D., Kroner, D. G., DeMatteo, D., & Locklair, B. R. (2014). The impact of base rate utilization and clinical experience on the accuracy of judgments made with the HCR-20. *Journal of Forensic Psychology Practice, 14*(4), 288–301. https://doi.org/10.1080/152 28932.2014.941726

Webster, C. D., Douglas, K. S., Eaves, D., & Hart, S. D. (1997). *HCR-20: Assessing risk for violence (Version 2)*. Simon Fraser University.

Webster, C. D., Martin, M. L., Brink, J., Nicholls, T. L., & Desmarais, S. (2009). *Manual for the Short-Term Assessment of Risk and Treatability (START)* (Version 1.1). Forensic Psychiatric Services Commission and St. Joseph's Healthcare.

Westen, D., & Weinberger, J. (2004). When clinical description becomes statistical prediction. *American Psychologist, 59*(7), 595–613. https://doi.org/10.1037/0003-066X.59.7.595

Wong, S., & Gordon, A. E. (1999–2003). *The violence risk scale*. University of Saskatchewan.

Worling, J. R., & Curwen, T. (2001). *Estimate of risk of adolescent sexual offense recidivism, version 2.0*. Ontario Ministry of Community and Social Services.

Wormith, J. S., Gendreau, P., & Bonta, J. (2012). Deferring to clarity, parsimony, and evidence in reply to Ward, Yates, and Willis. *Criminal Justice and Behavior, 39*(1), 111–120. https://doi.org/10.1177/0093854811426087

Wormith, J. S., Hogg, S., & Guzzo, L. (2012). The predictive validity of a general risk/needs assessment inventory on sexual offender recidivism and an exploration of the professional override. *Criminal Justice and Behavior, 39*(12), 1511–1538. https://doi.org/10.1177/009 3854812455741

Yoon, D., Turner, D., Klein, V., Rettenberger, M., Eher, R., & Briken, P. (2018). Factors predicting desistance from reoffending: A validation study of the SAPROF in sexual offenders. *International Journal of Offender Therapy and Comparative Criminology, 62*(3), 697–716. https://doi.org/10.1177/0306624X16664379

Further Reading Suggestions

de Ruiter, C., & Kaser-Boyd, N. (2015). *Forensic psychological assessment in practice: Case studies*. Routledge.

Douglas, K. S., & Otto, R. K. (Eds.). (2021). *Handbook of violence risk assessment* (2nd ed.). Routledge.

Logan, C., & Johnstone, L. (Eds.). (2012). *Managing clinical risk: A guide to effective practice*. Routledge.

Monahan, J., Steadman, H. J., Silver, E., Appelbaum, P. S., Robbins, P. C., Mulvey, E. P., Roth, L. H., Grisso, T., & Banks, S. (2001). *Rethinking risk assessment: The MacArthur study of mental disorder and violence.* Oxford University Press.

Using the MMPI-3 in Forensic Psychological Assessments

26

Martin Sellbom, Dustin B. Wygant, Anthony M. Tarescavage, and Yossef S. Ben-Porath

Key Points

- The MMPI-3 is the most recent version of the MMPI family of instruments with a new normative sample
- The MMPI-3 has 52 scales; 10 validity scales to assess response styles; 42 scales that measure a diverse range of substantive clinical content
- The MMPI-3 Technical Manual reports extensive reliability and validity data across a diverse range of settings

Yossef S. Ben-Porath is an author of the MMPI-3 and receives royalties from its sales. Yossef Ben-Porath, Martin Sellbom and Dustin Wygant are also paid consultants to the University of Minnesota Press, publisher of the MMPI instruments. All authors also receive research funding from the MMPI test publisher.

M. Sellbom (✉)
University of Otago, Dunedin, New Zealand
e-mail: martin.sellbom@otago.ac.nz

D. B. Wygant
Eastern Kentucky University, Richmond, KY, USA
e-mail: dustin.wygant@eku.edu

A. M. Tarescavage
John Carroll University, University Heights, OH, USA
e-mail: atarescavage@jcu.edu

Y. S. Ben-Porath
Kent State University, Kent, OH, USA
e-mail: ybenpora@kent.edu

- The MMPI-3 is well positioned to aid in forensic evaluations in light of this ability to detect various threats to response bias and capture a wide range of forensically-relevant clinical constructs.

Introduction

The Minnesota Multiphasic Personality Inventory-3 (MMPI-3; Ben-Porath & Tellegen, 2020a) is the most recent version of the MMPI instruments. Its 335 items are designed to provide comprehensive and efficient measurement of clinically relevant variables using revised, updated, and additional items, as well as new scales and a new normative sample. It is a broadband inventory intended for use with adults in the diverse range of settings in which the MMPI instruments have traditionally been applied.

The current chapter will focus on forensic applications of the MMPI-3 instrument. We start with a historical overview of the MMPI instruments, culminating in the development of the MMPI-3. We describe the scales of the test and general psychometric properties. The remainder of our chapter will focus on various common forensic applications and we also discuss how to address challenges to admissibility of MMPI-3 findings in court given its updated status. We end the chapter with conclusions and future directions for MMPI-3 research in forensic settings.

History and Evolution of the MMPI Instruments

Stark Hathaway and J. Charnley McKinley's development of the MMPI began in the 1930s in an effort to generate a self-report inventory to aid in differential diagnosis. The product, which was first labeled the Multiphasic Personality Schedule and later became formally known as the MMPI, was heavily influenced by the psychopathology nosology of that time. A candidate item pool they developed was guided by Kraepelin's (1921) descriptive nosology (Ben-Porath, 2012). Scale construction was purely empirical. Hathaway and McKinley identified eight of the most common mental disorders at the time and used an empirical keying method to select items that would differentiate a particular diagnostic group from a healthy comparison group. The items that statistically differentiated a particular disorder group from the controls were placed on a scale representing the targeted diagnosis (Hathaway & McKinley, 1940). This procedure yielded the eight original MMPI Clinical Scales. Within a decade it became clear that the clinical scales did not work as originally intended, as elevations typically occurred on multiple scales even among patients with only one mental disorder. Thus, research instead turned to examining empirical correlates associated with the Clinical Scales and various profile configurations (code types). This approach proved to be successful and the MMPI soared in clinical and research popularity (e.g., Lubin et al., 1971).

After decades of criticism by prominent personality scholars in the field (e.g., Norman, 1972; Loevinger, 1972; and even Hathaway himself in 1960 and 1972), the MMPI publisher made the decision to restandardize the test and introduce the MMPI-2 (Butcher et al., 1989). A large, nationally representative normative sample was collected in the 1980s. Although numerous changes were made to the item pool, allowing for the development of a new set of Content Scales, the original Clinical Scales were retained essentially unchanged, to preserve their research base and clinical familiarity (Ben-Porath, 2012).

The most significant contemporary development, which yielded the MMPI-2 Restructured Form (MMPI-2-RF; Ben-Porath & Tellegen, 2008), began with the introduction of the Restructured Clinical (RC) Scales (Tellegen et al., 2003). The primary rationale for the restructuring was that while the MMPI-2 item pool included rich clinical content, its aggregate scales were inefficient, and their development was outdated with respect to contemporary psychometric principles. The goal of the restructuring process was to capture the substantial clinical information accessible with the MMPI-2 item pool with more psychometrically sound, up-to-date, and efficient scales that also map onto the contemporary literature on psychopathology and personality (Tellegen & Ben-Porath, 2008). The MMPI-2 normative sample was retained with one modification. Nongendered norms were used instead of the traditional gender-based norms.

The MMPI-2-RF was a welcome development for the field as it was more efficient, associated with better psychometric properties, and was better linked to contemporary models of psychopathology and personality relative to previous MMPI versions (Ben-Porath, 2012; Sellbom, 2019). The MMPI-2-RF was also widely used in forensic settings (Sellbom & Wygant, 2018). The most recent version of the MMPI family, the MMPI-3, was designed to build on the foundations of the MMPI-2-RF.

Description of the MMPI-3

The MMPI-3 has 335 true/false items that aggregate onto 52 scales that are listed and briefly described in Table 26.1. Ten Validity Scales measure various forms of response styles that, when excessively present, could invalidate an MMPI-3 test protocol or indicate the need to qualify the interpretation. The other 42 scales measure substantive psychological constructs. Most are organized in a hierarchy that reflects both content-breadth and interpretive organization. More specifically, this hierarchy of scales includes three Higher-Order (H–O) Scales on the first tier, eight Restructured Clinical (RC) Scales at the mid-tier level, and twenty-six Specific Problems (SP) Scales at the bottom. The Personality Psychopathology Five (PSY-5) Scales, which are dimensional measures of personality pathology, appear in parallel to this hierarchy. Ben-Porath and Tellegen (2020a) provide a detailed discussion of the underlying psychological constructs assessed by the MMPI-3 substantive scales.

The ten Validity Scales can broadly be divided into three domains based on their response style measurement: non-content-based responding, over-reporting, and under-reporting (Ben-Porath, 2013). Non-content-based response bias refers to unintentional or intentional responding that manifests as unscorable, random/inconsistent/careless, or indiscriminant fixed (acquiescent or counter-acquiescent) responding. The over-reporting scales measure intentional or unintentional exaggeration or fabrication of psychopathology symptoms as well as non-credible somatic and cognitive complaints. The two under-reporting scales assess overly virtuous responding (or positive impression management) and a possibly non-credible avowal of good psychological adjustment and resilience.

The three H–O Scales, Emotional/Internalizing Dysfunction (EID), Thought Dysfunction (THD), and Behavioral/Externalizing Dysfunction (BXD) operationalize broadband psychopathology spectra of internalizing, thought disorder, and externalizing (respectively). They map onto broader level dimensions that have been identified in a wide range of psychopathology research (see, e.g., Kotov et al., 2017). At the top of the MMPI-2-RF interpretive hierarchy, they reflect general and pervasive dysfunction in their respective areas.

The eight RC Scales are slightly revised and shortened versions of their MMPI-2 and MMPI-2-RF counterparts. Unlike the original MMPI/MMPI-2 Clinical Scales, the RC Scales reflect transdiagnostic, dimensional psychological constructs rather than psychiatric syndromes. The 26 SP Scales, the most narrowband symptom and trait measures on the instrument, are organized into four thematic domains: somatic/cognitive, internalizing, externalizing,

Table 26.1 MMPI-3 scale labels, abbreviations, and brief descriptions

Scale	Abbreviation	General description
Validity scales		
Combined response inconsistency	CRIN	Combination of random and fixed indiscriminant responding
Variable response inconsistency	VRIN	Inconsistent Responding
True response inconsistency	TRIN	Indiscriminant fixed responding
Infrequent responses	F	Over-reporting validity scale based on rare responses in the general population
Infrequent psychopathology responses	Fp	Over-reporting validity scale based on rare responses in general and psychiatric populations
Infrequent somatic responses	Fs	Over-reporting validity scale based on rare somatic complaints in general and medical patient populations
Symptom validity	FBS	Over-reporting validity scale based on non-credible somatic and cognitive complaints
Response bias scale	RBS	Over-reporting validity scale associated with failure on performance validity tests
Unlikely virtues	L	Under-reporting validity scale based on rarely claimed moral attributes or activities
Adjustment validity	K	Under-reporting validity scale describing an avowal of good psychological adjustment
Higher-order scales		
Emotional/internalizing dysfunction	EID	Pervasive problems associated with mood and affect
Thought dysfunction	THD	Pervasive problems with disordered thinking

(continued)

Table 26.1 (continued)

Scale	Abbreviation	General description
Behavioral/externalizing dysfunction	BXD	Pervasive problems with under-controlled or acting out behavior
Restructured clinical scales		
Demoralization	RCd	General emotional distress; unhappiness and dissatisfaction
Somatic complaints	RC1	Pre-occupation with various types of health complaints
Low positive emotions	RC2	Attenuated positive emotional experiences; significant anhedonia; disengagement
Antisocial behavior	RC4	Antisocial proclivities, impulsivity, recklessness, and irresponsible behavior
Ideas of persecution	RC6	Self-referential beliefs that others pose a threat; persecutory delusions
Dysfunctional negative emotions	RC7	Dysfunctional anxiety, anger, irritability, fear, guilt
Aberrant experiences	RC8	Unusual thoughts or perceptions; dissociation
Hypomanic activation	RC9	Excessive activation, drive, aggression, and grandiosity
Specific problems scales		
Malaise	MLS	Overall feeling of physical debilitation and poor health
Neurological complaints	NUC	Complaints about faintness, weakness, bodily sensations, loss of balance, etc
Eating concerns	EAT	Difficulties with restrictive eating, binge-eating, and purging behaviors
Cognitive complaints	COG	Complaints about memory and difficulties concentrating
Suicidal/death ideation	SUI	Suicidal ideation and reports of suicide attempts; preoccupation with death
Helplessness/hopelessness	HLP	Belief that problems cannot be solved or goals be reached
Self-doubt	SFD	Lacking in confidence, feelings of worthlessness

(continued)

Table 26.1 (continued)

Scale	Abbreviation	General description
inefficacy	NFC	Perception that one is inefficacious; indecisiveness
Stress	STR	Poor stress tolerance; nervousness; difficulty with time pressure
Worry	WRY	Excessive worry and preoccupation; anxious apprehension
Compulsivity	CMP	Engagement in compulsive or ritualistic behaviors
Anxiety-related experiences	AXR	Intense anxiety; frights; panic; frequent nightmares;
Anger proneness	ANP	Poor anger control; frustration intolerance; impatient with others
Behavior-restricting fears	BRF	Fears that considerably inhibit everyday activities
Family problems	FML	Problematic family relationships; familial alienation
Juvenile conduct problems	JCP	Significant problems at school and at home; stealing as a youth
Substance abuse	SUB	Abuse of alcohol and drugs currently and/or in the past
Impulsivity	IMP	Poor impulse control and lack of planfulness
Activation	ACT	Increased excitation and energy level; euphoria; racing thoughts
Aggression	AGG	Aggressive behavior of both physical and verbal nature
Cynicism	CYN	Non self-referential beliefs expressing a generally low opinion and mistrust of others
Self-importance	SFI	Ideation regarding special qualities and abilities
Dominance	DOM	Being domineering and assertive in relationships with others

(continued)

Table 26.1 (continued)

Scale	Abbreviation	General description
Disaffiliativeness	DSF	Misanthropic attitudes about people; disliking being around others
Social avoidance	SAV	Eschewing or not deriving pleasure from social events
Shyness	SHY	Prone to feel inhibited and anxious around others; bashful
Personality psychopathology five scales		
Aggressiveness	AGGR	Proactive, goal-directed aggression; assertiveness; grandiosity
Psychoticism	PSYC	Proclivities toward poor reality testing
Disconstraint	DISC	Disinhibited behavior; impulsivity; sensation seeking; risk taking
Negative Emotionality/neuroticism	NEGE	Temperamental proclivity for anxiety, insecurity, worry, anger, and fear
Introversion/low positive Emotionality	INTR	Temperamental proclivity for anhedonia and social disengagement

and interpersonal, which also reflect the general interpretive organization of the instrument.

Finally, the five PSY-5 Scales are revised versions of their MMPI-2 and MMPI-2-RF counterparts. They are measures of the PSY-5 constructs originally articulated by Harkness and McNulty (1994) and represent dimensional personality traits with an abnormal range. They correspond well to a dimensional alternative to the categorical personality disorder framework that has dominated the DSM. Specifically, the PSY-5 constructs and associated MMPI-3 scales align well with the trait domains included in the Alternative Model for Personality Disorders (AMPD; American Psychiatric Association [APA], 2013) in Section III of the DSM-5. Research with the MMPI-2-RF versions have confirmed these associations empirically (Anderson et al., 2013, 2015; see Sellbom, 2019, for a review).

The MMPI-3 normative sample was collected between 2017 and 2018 with demographic targets to match 2020 US census projections for age, race/ethnicity, and education. These targets were generally met with good success. The MMPI-2-RF-EX was used for this purpose. The final sample consisted of 810 men and 810 women (60.3% White, 16.8 Latinx, 12.4% Black, 6.0% Asian American, 2.5% of other or mixed race/ethnicity), with the full span of age and education levels, and from different geographic areas representing all US regions. A Spanish translation of the MMPI-3 was developed as well, and a Spanish-language normative sample was collected, consisting of 275 men and 275 women tested in several locations throughout the USA. The Spanish norms are described in a separate MMPI-3 manual supplement (Ben-Porath et al., 2020). In both English and Spanish, the MMPI-3 utilizes non-gendered uniform T-scores for standardized score interpretation.

General Psychometric Properties of the MMPI-3

The MMPI-3 Technical Manual provides extensive information about psychometric properties of MMPI-3 scales, including (but not limited to) reliability, construct validity, and associations between MMPI-2-RF and MMPI-3 scales, as well as their relative associations with external criteria. The latter component has been critical, as it is demonstrated that MMPI-3 users can rely on the extensive peer-reviewed literature supporting the MMPI-2-RF with the exception of the five new scales. In other words, the construct validity data presented in the MMPI-2-RF Technical Manual (almost 54,000 correlations across a range of settings) as well as the extensive research base (> 500 publications) on the MMPI-2 RC and MMPI-2-RF scales can be applied to the use of the MMPI-3. This broader literature will not be reviewed here (however, see Sellbom, 2019, for an overview). The MMPI-3 applications across a number of forensic psychological evaluations covered next are informed by this literature.

Several recently published studies have focused on the MMPI-3. Two studies have examined the MMPI-3 Validity Scales. Using a simulation design, Whitman, Tylicki, and Ben-Porath (2021) investigated the utility of the MMPI-3 over-reporting and under-reporting scales as well as the impact of these response styles on substantive scale score validity. The authors found that all the over-reporting scales were very effective at identifying test takers who were simulating malingering in order to avoid prosecution for a serious crime, with Fp showing the strongest effect size (consistent with prior MMPI-2 and MMPI-2-RF research). The under-reporting scales were very effective at identifying participants simulating an effort to appear well-adjusted in the context of an employment-related evaluation. The need for assessing response styles was demonstrated by analyses showing significantly reduced validity of substantive scale scores for the simulation groups. Using a known groups design, Tylicki et al. (2020) examined the utility of the MMPI-3 Validity Scales in identifying over-reporting in a sample of forensic disability claimants. Consistent with prior MMPI-2-RF research, the

MMPI-3 RBS, Fs, F, and FBS effectively identified evaluees deemed malingering on the basis of established structured criteria for malingered neurocognitive dysfunction (Slick et al., 1999), with RBS showing the strongest effect size.

Turning to the substantive scales, Sellbom (2020) examined the criterion validity of the Self-Importance (SFI) scale in a large sample of university students. He found that SFI correlated, at large effect size magnitudes, with several other measures of grandiose narcissism. Marek et al. (2020) showed that the Eating Concerns (EAT) scale was correlated with other eating disorder measures as well as post-operative outcomes in a small sample of individuals undergoing bariatric surgery. Whitman, Tylicki, Mascioli et al. (2020) examined the psychometric properties of the MMPI-3 in a clinical neuropsychology setting using a sample of 197 independent practice outpatient examinees. Internal consistency coefficients and standard errors of measurement were generally consistent with findings reported in the MMPI-3 Technical Manual, and correlations with extra-test criteria—including presenting problems, psychological and behavioral dysfunction, and psychiatric diagnoses revealed a pattern of results that generally adhered to conceptual expectations.

Use of the MMPI-3 in Addressing Psycho-Legal Questions

Competency or Fitness to Stand Trial

Most countries throughout the world utilize an adversarial system of justice to adjudicate criminal culpability (Chapter 28). Intrinsic to this system is the notion that defendants understand the proceedings and possess sufficient rationality to participate in their defense. Rooted in English Common Law dating back to at least the seventeenth century (Zapf & Roesch, 2009), the concept of competency preserves the dignity and fairness of legal proceedings (Bonnie, 1992). Most courts throughout the world require the presence of a "mental condition", "defect", or "disease" as a threshold condition that forms the basis of incompetency (Zapf & Roesch, 2009). While the specific mental condition is typically not indicated, it must be severe and impact rational thought processes (e.g., Schizophrenia, Delusional Disorder, Dementia). The mental condition has to significantly interfere with the defendant understanding the nature and consequences of the proceedings or impact their rational participation in the defense.

Psychological testing such as the MMPI-3 can assist in competency evaluations to detect the presence of mental health symptoms that can impact rational decision making. Sellbom (2017) examined MMPI-2-RF scores in a large sample of criminal defendants being evaluated for competency to stand trial and criminal responsibility. Defendants opined incompetent to proceed to trial were significantly higher on RC6 and Psychoticism as well as significantly lower on several scales indicating internalizing dysfunction (EID), negative emotionality (RC7, NEGE-r, ANP), and externalizing tendencies (BXD, RC4, JCP, SUB, AGG, and DISC-r) than were defendants opined to be competent; such defendants were also less likely to overreport on the validity scales.

Sellbom and Wygant (2018) discussed ways in which the MMPI-2-RF can be used in competency evaluations. Their recommendations apply similarly for the MMPI-3. First, the MMPI-3's Validity Scales determine how the defendant approached the test and establish the validity of the resulting test protocol. These results can be useful in identifying defendants feigning psychological symptoms as a possible attempt to appear psychologically impaired and thus incompetent (i.e., malingering). Second, the MMPI-3 provides an overall assessment of the defendant's mental health functioning. Pirelli et al. (2011) found that defendants with a psychotic disorder were more likely to be found incompetent, and consistent with Sellbom's (2017) findings, the MMPI-3 includes scales that assess psychotic symptoms would be expected to be elevated. It is important for the evaluator to review item endorsements from these scales as they might reflect actual experiences (being part of adversarial proceedings rather than being paranoid; drug-induced hallucinations) that do not reflect psychosis. However, we do not recommend reviewing specific item responses with a defendant. Additionally, scales that measure hypomanic (and manic) symptoms, including Hypomanic Activation (RC9), Activation (ACT), Impulsivity (IMP), should be consulted. When these scales are elevated, along with the thought dysfunction measures (particularly RC8), this may indicate a Schizoaffective condition that can have a deleterious impact on competency.

Criminal Responsibility

Modern consideration of the insanity defense dates back to English Common law, with M'Naghten's case in 1843 (Goldstein et al., 2013). The construct of insanity relates to *mens rea*, which is the mental state of the defendant at the time of the offense (Chapter 8). The two general prongs for insanity pertain to the presence of a mental impairment at the time of the offense that affects the individual's ability to reason, understand the nature and quality of their actions, appreciate the wrongfulness of the conduct, and presence of volitional control over the behavior (Goldstein et al., 2013). Different jurisdictions differ in the exact manner in which the insanity defense is defined.

Criminal responsibility evaluations are challenging because they require a retrospective analysis of the defendant's behavior at the time of the offense. Evaluations of criminal responsibility (sometimes referred to as mental status at the time of the offense) can occur months (and even years) after the offense took place. Consequently, tests like the MMPI-3, which is focused on current mental health functioning, are more limited in an insanity evaluation (versus a competency evaluation). Nevertheless, the MMPI-3 can play an important role in an insanity evaluation. Similar to a competency evaluation, the issue of malingering and feigning of symptoms is paramount, particularly in light of a potential acquittal at stake. The MMPI-3 Validity Scales provide data on how the defendant approached the test, which can provide information about how the evaluation was approached. Sellbom (2017) found that criminal defendants opined to be criminally responsibility had significantly higher scores on MMPI-2-RF overreporting Validity Scales than defendants opined to be not criminally responsible. As noted earlier in the competency section, the MMPI-3 provides a thorough assessment of psychosis, which often serves as the foundation for an insanity defense (Packer, 2009). These conditions are often chronic in nature and therefore might be reflected in current MMPI-3 scores.

Risk Assessment (see Chapter 25)

The MMPI-3 is a useful adjunct in violence risk assessment, and in particular, the measurement of dynamic risk factors (Sellbom & Wygant, 2018). Tarescavage et al., (2016) introduced a conceptual model to integrate MMPI-2-RF scale scores into risk assessments completed with the HCR-20, Version 3 (Douglas et al., 2013). Given the comparability of MMPI-2-RF/-3 scale scores, this model is applicable for use with the MMPI-3. The MMPI-3 scales can cover so-called static (i.e., historical, unchangeable) risk factors to some degree. Juvenile Conduct Problems (JCP), which has items that are entirely worded in past tense, is one such example. Many of the externalizing scales (e.g., BXD, RC4, SUB, DISC) have items worded in both current and past tense; as such, any risk assessment should consider which items were endorsed on these scales. Moreover, because the MMPI-3 measures current functioning more so than historical problems, its scales will be better suited for the assessment of dynamic risk factors. Table 26.2 provides links between well-established dynamic risk factors and MMPI-3 scales based primarily on Tarescavage et al. (2016) model, but also Sellbom and Wygant

Table 26.2 MMPI-3 scales that measure dynamic risk factors

Risk factor	MMPI-3 scales
Poor insight	None specific; see L; BXD, RC1, RC4, DISC for indirect assessment
Pro-aggressive/violent attitudes	AGG, AGGR
Active symptoms of major mental illness	THD, RC6, RC8; RC9, ACT
Emotional instability	EID, RC7, NEGE, STR, WRY, AXR, ANP
Behavioral instability/impulsivity	BXD, RC4, JCP, IMP, DISC
Poor social support	FML, SAV, DSF
Treatment amenability	Motivation (EID, RCd); Rejection of psychological explanations (RC1); Mistrust/resentment (RC6, CYN, AGGR); Poor adherence (DISC)

Note Douglas and Skeem (2005), HCR-20, Version 3; see, e.g., Tarescavage et al. (2016), for a review

(2018), who provide extensive guidance (in the context of the MMPI-2-RF) on how to consider these factors in assessing for violence risk.

The research support for using the MMPI-3 for risk assessment comes from studies on the MMPI-2-RF. Tarescavage et al. (2016) examined associations between MMPI-2-RF scale scores and future institutional violence in a forensic psychiatric hospital. They found that the externalizing scales, as well as the internalizing scale Anger Proneness, were predictive of future violence. In a similar study with 128 forensic psychiatric inpatients, Grossi et al. (2015) found the thought dysfunction scales were the best predictors of institutional violence. These two studies when compared clearly reflected the need for setting context to be considered (Sellbom, 2019).

Tarescavage et al. (2019) conducted a similar examination of MMPI-2-RF predictors of institutional violence; however, they examined inpatients detained under sexually violent predator laws. In this case, indicators of mood dysfunction tended to be the strongest predictors (although, overall, the best predictor was the Aggression scale). Tarescavage, Cappo et al. (2018) also found that the MMPI-2-RF substantive scales (particularly the externalizing scales) demonstrated an expected pattern of association with the Level of Service-Inventory-Revised (Andrews & Bonta, 2000) and the STATIC-99 (Hanson & Thornton, 1999). Furthermore, other studies have supported use of the MMPI-2-RF in outpatient settings, including in the prediction of probation violations (Tarescavage et al.,

2014) as well as in recidivism after participation in a batterer's intervention program (Sellbom et al., 2008). Finally, a burgeoning research literature on use of the MMPI-2-RF in suicide risk assessment should remain applicable to the MMPI-3 (e.g., Anestis et al., 2018; Tarescavage, Glassmire et al. 2018).

Psychopathy is another important consideration in risk assessments, and the MMPI-2-RF can measure this construct with its standard scales (Klein Haneveld et al., 2017; Sellbom et al., 2007; Wygant & Sellbom, 2012) as well as experimental indices/scales (Kutchen et al., 2017; Phillips et al., 2014; Sellbom, Ben-Porath et al., 2012, 2016). We expect these MMPI-2-RF indices of psychopathy will be readily adaptable to the MMPI-3.

Civil Forensic Assessments

The MMPI-2-RF is commonly used in personal injury and disability evaluations. Forensic psychologists are often tasked with determining the presence of a mental injury that is causing dysfunction for which the individual being evaluated could be owed compensation. The MMPI-3 will be of value in such evaluations in which mental health problems are being claimed as it measures current functioning. Of course, the MMPI-3 is of limited value with respect to determining the cause of the mental injury, which is often a key question in these evaluations. However, there are two important ways in which the MMPI-3 can be useful in these evaluations. First, the MMPI-3 Validity Scales can assess the approach to the evaluation as many who undergo them have an external incentive to overreport problems (e.g., Mittenberg et al., 2002). Second, if the MMPI-3 profile is valid for interpretation, its scales can be informative about common claims in these evaluations, including depression, PTSD, anxiety, somatic symptom disorder, and substance use disorders.

In terms of validity scales, two meta-analyses have supported the utility of the MMPI-2-RF Validity Scales, including in civil litigation contexts (Ingram & Ternes, 2016; Sharf et al., 2017). Sharf et al. (2017), in particular, showed that the Infrequent Psychopathology Responses (Fp-r) was highly specific to overreporting of psychopathology across 25 different studies. The somatic and cognitive overreporting scales, Infrequent Somatic Responses (Fs), Symptom Validity (FBS-r), and Response Bias Scale (RBS), were good at detecting this manner of overreporting, which was typically evaluated in medico-legal contexts, though sensitivity at the higher cut-scores was somewhat low. More specifically, Gervais et al. (2007) developed the RBS, which is available on the MMPI-3 as a measure of non-credible cognitive complaints. Several articles have validated

RBS and other MMPI-2-RF over-reporting scales for use in disability examinations (e.g., Tarescavage et al., 2013; Wygant et al., 2010). In addition, Wygant et al. (2009) found large effect sizes for FBS-r, FS, F-r in both simulation samples (medical patients asked to overreport) and known group design (failure of performance validity tests) compared to genuine patients. Sellbom, Wygant et al. (2012) found that FBS-r was sensitive to non-credible report of somatic symptoms, but did not distinguish between somatic symptom disorders and deliberate feigning, whereas Fs and Fp-r did. Finally, Wygant et al. (2017) found that Fs was associated with number of Waddell signs in chronic pain disability evaluations. As reviewed earlier, similar findings have recently been reported for a sample of disability claimants assessed with the MMPI-3. Tylicki et al. (2020) found RBS to be the most effective indicator of malingered neurocognitive dysfunction in such a setting.

Several studies have also found support for using the MMPI-2-RF in disability samples. The somatic/cognitive scales have informative correlates in this setting (e.g., Gervais et al., 2009) and there is a model available for using the MMPI-2-RF in empirically guided case conceptualization of PTSD in disability evaluations (Sellbom & Wygant, 2018; Vines et al., 2012), which can be applied with the MMPI-3. Several studies have also found that MMPI-2-RF scale scores are associated with PTSD symptoms (Arbisi et al., 2011; Sellbom, Lee et al., 2012; Wolf et al., 2008). For instance, Sellbom, Lee et al. (2012) used structural equation modeling in a large sample of disability claimants that a set of hypothesized MMPI-2-RF scales (e.g., RCd, SFD, AXY, ANP, and SAV) predicted different types of PTSD symptoms, with the Anxiety scale (Anxiety-Related Experiences on MMPI-3) was the best predictor across the board.

Family Court Evaluations

Psychological evaluations for family courts generally focus on two separate issues, child custody and parental fitness (or capacity). Each type of evaluation has its own challenges, but both generally involve some consideration of how the parent's psychological functioning impacts their ability to provide a psychologically stable environment for the child. With respect to child custody, most jurisdictions use some version of the "best interests of the child" standard (Gould & Martindale, 2013) in making custodial decisions between parents. In parental fitness evaluations, which are generally focused on issues of child welfare (often following allegations of abuse or neglect), the issue is complicated by a lack of widely accepted standards for what constitutes minimally accepted parenting practices (Budd, 2001). It is important to note that any evaluation conducted for family court involves complex consideration of many variables, some of which are outside of the domain of psychological functioning. However, both types of evaluations do consider the mental health functioning of the parent, which is where tests like the MMPI-3 can provide assistance.

The MMPI and its subsequent editions have a longstanding history of use in custodial and parenting capacity evaluations. Archer and colleagues (2012) examined the MMPI-2-RF in a sample of 344 child custody litigants. They found that most evaluees produced within normal limits profiles. RC6 (Ideas of Persecution) was the most frequently elevated Restructured Clinical Scale, with 15% of male and 18% of females scoring above 65 T. Approximately one-fourth of their sample had at least one elevated RC Scale. Pinsoneault and Ezzo (2012) examined MMPI-2-RF profiles of 61 parents referred for a parental fitness evaluation and 168 child custody litigants. Over half of the child custody litigants had at least one clinical elevation on the test. Similar to Archer et al. (2012), RC6 was the most commonly elevated scale among child custody litigants. Parents undergoing parental capacity evaluations in neglect cases had higher scores on L-r, THD, RC3, RC6, and FML than the child custody litigants.

Given the nature of family court evaluations (where custodial rights are on the line), parents are often motivated to present a positive impression. Previous studies have shown the utility of the under-reporting Validity Scales of the MMPI-2 and MMPI-2-RF in capturing under-reporting in custodial evaluations (e.g., Sellbom & Bagby, 2008). Thus, the MMPI-3 Validity Scales (particularly L and K) can play an important role in determining how the parent approached the test, which can in turn inform the examiner about how the individual may have approached the entire evaluation.

It is important to note that the MMPI-3 (like previous versions of the test) does not directly measure parenting skills or ability. It cannot be used to predict future child neglect or abuse. Interestingly, Solomon and colleagues (2014) found that the EID scale was able to concurrently predict scores on the Child Abuse Potential Inventory (CAPI; Milner, 1986) in a sample of parental fitness evaluations. However, the test can still provide valuable collateral information about the parent's psychological functioning, which is relevant to forming impressions about their ability to provide a safe and nurturing environment for the child. Specifically, measures of internalizing symptoms (EID, RCd, RC2, RC7), behavioral issues such as aggression, impulsivity, and substance abuse (AGG, AGGR, IMP, SUB) are important considerations in family court evaluations. The MMPI-3 can also provide insight into maladaptive personality traits (e.g., passivity/dominance, affiliation, anger proneness), which can impact the ability of the parent to provide a safe and nurturing environment.

Conclusions and Recommendations for Future MMPI-3 Research

Release of the MMPI-3 represents the culmination of several years of development and validation, building on the foundations of the MMPI-2-RF. It continues to serve the objectives spelled out by its original developers, Hathaway and McKinley, as an aid in clinical and diagnostic assessments and formulations. The MMPI-3 builds on the psychometric improvements of the MMPI-2-RF while adding important contemporary advancements, most notably an updated normative sample, as well as expanded coverage of clinical constructs. Given its ability to assess various challenges to response bias, as well as capture a wide range of forensically-relevant clinical constructs, the MMPI-3 is well-positioned, like its predecessor, to aid in forensic psychological assessment.

As noted above, extensive data included in the Technical Manual for the instrument demonstrate the interchangeability of MMPI-2-RF and MMPI-3 empirical correlates. Thus, the research base of the MMPI-2-RF is largely applicable in guiding and supporting MMPI-3 interpretation in forensic assessments. There are, nevertheless, a number of new scales on the MMPI-3 that will require additional external validation beyond the extensive data that will be available in the MMPI-3 Technical Manual and recent publications. These scales, which provide expanded coverage of forensically-relevant areas of psychopathology (e.g., impulsivity, self-importance), will enhance the test's ability to capture psychopathy, personality disorder symptoms, and violence risk issues (e.g., Impulsivity).

Specific to its use in forensic assessment, future research should examine the degree to which the MMPI-3 contributes to decision making about psycho-legal issues (e.g., competency). For example, how well are MMPI-3 results associated with psychopathology ratings in various forensic evaluations? It would also be helpful to examine the degree to which the MMPI-3 scales add incrementally to these external criteria in predicting relevant forensic opinions. Additionally, in the area of risk assessment, research needs to address both the degree to which scores on the MMPI-3 can predict relevant risk outcomes (e.g., violence) as well as the degree to which it fits into structured professional judgment guides for violence risk assessment, in a manner similar to the MMPI-2-RF (Tarescavage, Glassmire et al., 2018).

References

American Psychiatric Association. (2013). *Diagnostic and statistical manual of mental disorders* (5th ed.). American Psychiatric Press.

Anderson, J. L., Sellbom, M., Ayearst, L., Quilty, L. C., Chmielewski, M., & Bagby, R. M. (2015). Associations between DSM-5 Section III personality traits and the Minnesota Multiphasic Personality Inventory 2-Restructured Form (MMPI-2-RF) scales in a psychiatric patient sample. *Psychological Assessment, 27*, 811–815.

Anderson, J. L., Sellbom, M., Bagby, R. M., Quilty, L. C., Veltri, C. O. C., Markon, K. E., & Krueger, R. F. (2013). On the convergence between PSY-5 domains and PID-5 domains and facets: Implications for assessment of DSM-5 personality traits. *Assessment, 20*, 286–294.

Andrews, D. A., & Bonta, J. (2000). *The level of service inventory-revised*. Multi-Health Systems.

Anestis, J. C., Finn, J. A., Gottfried, E. D., Hames, J. L., Bodell, L. P., Hagan, C. R., Arnau, R. C., Anestis, M. D., Arbisi, P. A., & Joiner, T. E. (2018). Burdensomeness, belongingness, and capability: Assessing the interpersonal-psychological theory of suicide with MMPI-2- RF scales. *Assessment, 25*, 415–431.

Arbisi, P. A., Polusny, M. A., Erbes, C. R., Thuras, P., & Reddy, M. K. (2011). The Minnesota Multiphasic Personality Inventory-2 Restructured Form in National Guard soldiers screening positive for posttraumatic stress disorder and mild traumatic brain injury. *Psychological Assessment, 23*, 203–214.

Archer, E. M., Hagan, L. D., Mason, J., Handel, R. W., & Archer, R. P. (2012). MMPI-2-RF characteristics of custody evaluation litigants. *Assessment, 19*, 14–20.

Ben-Porath, Y. S. (2012). *Interpreting the MMPI-2-RF*. University of Minnesota Press.

Ben-Porath, Y. S. (2013). Assessing personality and psychopathology with self-report inventories. In J.R. Graham & J.A. Naglieri (Eds.), *Handbook of psychology* (2nd ed., Vol. 10: Assessment). Wiley.

Ben-Porath Y. S., & Tellegen A. (2008/2011). *MMPI-2RF: Manual for administration, scoring, and interpretation*. University of Minnesota Press.

Ben-Porath, Y. S., & Tellegen, A. (2020). *Minnesota Multiphasic Personality Inventory-3 (MMPI-3): Manual for administration, scoring, and interpretation*. University of Minnesota Press.

Ben-Porath, Y. S., & Tellegen, A. (2020b). *Minnesota Multiphasic Personality Inventory-3 (MMPI-3):* Technical manual. University of Minnesota Press

Ben-Porath, Y. S., Tellegen, A., & Puente, A. (2020). *MMPI-3 Spanish manual supplement*. University of Minnesota Press.

Bonnie, R. (1992). The competence of criminal defendants: A theoretical reformulation. *Behavioral Sciences and the Law, 10*, 291–316.

Budd, K. S. (2001). Assessing parenting competence in child protection cases: A clinical practice model. *Clinical Child and Family Psychology Review, 4*, 1–18.

Butcher J. N., Dahlstrom, W. G., Graham, J. R., Tellegen, A., & Kaemmer, B. (1989). *Minnesota Multiphasic Personality Inventory-2 (MMPI-2): Manual for administration and scoring*. University of Minnesota Press.

Douglas, K., Hart, S., Webster, C., & Belfrage, H. (2013). *HCR-20 V3: Assessing risk for violence*. Mental Health, Law, and Policy Institute, Simon Fraser University.

Douglas, K. S., & Skeem, J. L. (2005). Violence risk assessment: Getting specific about being dynamic. *Psychology, Public Policy, and Law, 11*(3), 347–383.

Gervais, R. O., Ben-Porath, Y. S., & Wygant, D. B. (2009). Empirical correlates and interpretation of the MMPI-2-RF Cognitive Complaints Scale. *The Clinical Neuropsychologist, 23*, 996–1015.

Gervais, R. O., Ben-Porath, Y. S., Wygant, D. B., & Green, P. (2007). Development and validation of a Response Bias Scale (RBS) for the MMPI-2. *Assessment, 14*, 196–208.

Goldstein, A. M., Morse, S. J., & Packer, I. K. (2013). Evaluation of criminal responsibility. In R. K. Otto & I. B. Weiner (Eds.), *Handbook of psychology: Volume 11 forensic psychology* (2nd ed., pp. 440–472). Wiley.

Gould, J. W., & Martindale, D. A. (2013). Child custody evaluations: Current literature and practical applications (Chapter 6, pp. 101–138). In I. Weiner (series ed.) & R. K. Otto (Ed.), *Forensic psychology*, Vol. 11 of the Handbook of psychology (2nd ed.). Wiley.

Grossi, L. M., Green, D., Belfi, B., McGrath, R. E., Griswold, H., & Schreiber, J. (2015). Identifying aggression in forensic inpatients using the MMPI-2-RF: An examination of MMPI-2-RF scale scores and estimated psychopathy indices. *International Journal of Forensic Mental Health, 14*(4), 231–244.

Hanson, R. K., & Thornton, D. (1999). *Static 99: Improving actuarial risk assessments for sex offenders* (Vol. 2). Solicitor General Canada.

Harkness, A. R., & McNulty, J.L. (1994). The Personality Psychopathology Five (PSY-5): Issues from the pages of a diagnostic manual instead of a dictionary. In S. Strack & M. Lorr (Eds.), *Differentiating normal and abnormal personality* (pp. 291–315). Springer Publishing Co.

Hathaway, S. R. (1960). Foreword. In W. G. Dahlstrom & G. S. Welsh (Eds.), *An MMPI handbook: A guide to use in clinical practice and research* (pp. vii–xi). University of Minnesota Press.

Hathaway, S. R. (1972). Foreword. In G. S. Welsh & W. G. Dahlstrom (Eds.), *An MMPI handbook, Vol 1, Clinical interpretation* (pp. xiii–iv). University of Minnesota Press.

Hathaway, S. R., & McKinley, J. C. (1940). A multiphasic personality schedule (Minnesota): I. Construction of the schedule. *Journal of Psychology, 10*, 249–254.

Ingram, P. B., & Ternes, M. S. (2016). The detection of content-based invalid responding: A meta-analysis of the MMPI-2-Restructured Form's (MMPI-2-RF) over-reporting validity scales. *The Clinical Neuropsychologist, 30*, 473–496.

Klein Haneveld, E., Kamphuis, J. H., Smid, W., & Forbey, J. D. (2017). Using MMPI–2–RF correlates to elucidate the PCL-R and its four facets in a sample of male forensic psychiatric patients. *Journal of Personality Assessment, 99*(4), 398–407.

Kotov, R., Krueger, R.F., Watson, D., Achenbach, T.M., Althoff, R.R., Bagby, R.M., Brown, T. A., Carpenter, W. T., Caspi A., Anna Clark, L., Eaton, N. R., Forbes, M. K., Forbush, K. T., Goldberg, D., Hasin, D., Hyman, S. E., Ivanova, M. Y., Lynam, D. R., Markon, K., … Zimmerman, M. (2017). The Hierarchical Taxonomy of Psychopathology (HiTOP): A dimensional alternative to traditional nosologies. *Journal of Abnormal Psychology, 126*, 454–477.

Kraeplin, E. (1921). Ueber Entwurtzelung. *Zeitschrift Fur Die Gesamte Neurologie Und Psychiatrie, 63*, 1–8.

Kutchen, T. J., Wygant, D. B., Tylicki, J. L., Dieter, A. M., Veltri, C. O., & Sellbom, M. (2017). Construct validity of the MMPI–2–RF Triarchic Psychopathy Scales in correctional and collegiate samples. *Journal of Personality Assessment, 99*(4), 408–415.

Loevinger, J. (1972). Some limitations of objective personality tests. In J. N. Butcher (Ed.), *Objective personality assessment: Changing perspectives* (pp. 45–58). Academic Press.

Lubin, B., Wallis, R. R., & Paine, C. (1971). Patterns of psychological test usage in the United States: 1935–1969. *Professional Psychology, 2*, 70–74.

Marek, R. J., Martin-Fernandez, K., Heinberg, L. J., & Ben-Porath, Y. S. (2020). An investigation of the eating concerns scale of the Minnesota Multiphasic Personality Inventory–3 (MMPI-3) in a postoperative bariatric surgery sample. *Obesity Surgery, Advance Online Publication.* https://doi.org/10.1007/s11695-020-05113-y

Milner, J. S. (1986). *The child abuse potential inventory: Manual* (2nd ed.). Psytec Corporation.

Mittenberg, W., Patton, C., Canyock, E. M., & Condit, D. C. (2002). Base rates of malingering and symptom exaggeration. *Journal of Clinical and Experimental Neuropsychology, 24*(8), 1094–1102.

Norman, W. (1972). Psychometric considerations for a revision of the MMPI. In J. N. Butcher (Ed.), *Objective personality assessment: Changing perspectives* (pp. 59–83). Academic Press.

Packer, I. R. (2009). *Evaluation of criminal responsibility.* Oxford University Press.

Phillips, T. R., Sellbom, M., Ben-Porath, Y. S., & Patrick, C. J. (2014). Further development and construct validation of MMPI-2-RF indices of global psychopathy, fearlessdominance, and impulsive-antisociality in a sample of incarcerated women. *Law and Human Behavior, 38*(1), 34–46. https://doi.org/10.1037/lhb0000040.

Pinsoneault, T. B., & Ezzo, F. R. (2012). A comparison of MMPI-2-RF profiles between child maltreatment and non-maltreatment custody cases. *Journal of Forensic Psychology Practice, 12*, 227–237.

Pirelli, G., Gottdiener, W. H., & Zapf, P. A. (2011). A meta-analytic review of competency to stand trial research. *Psychology, Public Policy and Law, 17*, 1–53.

Sellbom, M. (2017). Using the MMPI-2-RF to characterize defendants evaluated for competency to stand trial and criminal responsibility. *International Journal of Forensic Mental Health, 16*, 304–312.

Sellbom, M. (2019). The MMPI-2 Restructured Form (MMPI-2-RF): Assessment of personality and psychopathology in the 21st century. *Annual Review of Clinical Psychology, 15*, 149–177.

Sellbom, M. (2020). Examining the criterion and incremental validity of the MMPI-3 Self-Importance scale. *Psychological Assessment.* Advance online publication. https://doi.org/10.1037/pas0000975

Sellbom, M., & Bagby, R. M. (2008). Validity of the MMPI-2-RF (restructured form) L-r and K-r Scales in detecting underreporting in clinical and nonclinical samples. *Psychological Assessment, 20*, 370–376.

Sellbom, M., Ben-Porath, Y. S., Baum, L. J., Erez, E., & Gregory, C. (2008). Predictive validity of the MMPI–2 Restructured Clinical (RC) scales in a batterers' intervention program. *Journal of Personality Assessment, 90*(2), 129–135.

Sellbom, M., Ben-Porath, Y. S., Patrick, C. J., Wygant, D. B., Gartland, D. M., & Stafford, K. P. (2012). Development and construct validation of MMPI-2-RF measures assessing global psychopathy, fearless-dominance, and impulsive-antisociality. *Personality Disorders: Theory, Research, and Treatment, 3*, 17–38.

Sellbom, M., Ben-Porath, Y. S., & Stafford, K. P. (2007). A comparison of MMPI–2 measures of psychopathic deviance in a forensic setting. *Psychological Assessment, 19*, 430.

Sellbom, M., Drislane, L. E., Johnson, A. K., Goodwin, B. E., Phillips, T. R., & Patrick, C. J. (2016). Development and validation of MMPI-2-RF scales for indexing triarchic psychopathy constructs. *Assessment, 23*, 527–543.

Sellbom, M., Lee, T. T. C., Ben-Porath, Y. S., Arbisi, P. A., & Gervais, R. O. (2012). Differentiating PTSD symptomatology with the MMPI-2-RF (restructured form) in a forensic disability sample. *Psychiatry Research, 197*, 172–179.

Sellbom, M., & Wygant, D. B. (2018). *Forensic applications of the MMPI-2 restructured form: A case book.* University of Minnesota Press.

Sellbom, M., Wygant, D. B., & Bagby, R. M. (2012). Utility of the MMPI-2-RF in detecting non-credible somatic complaints. *Psychiatry Research, 197*, 295–301.

Sharf, A. J., Rogers, R., Williams, M. M., & Henry, S. A. (2017). The effectiveness of the MMPI-2-RF in detecting feigned mental disorders and cognitive deficits: A meta-analysis. *Journal of Psychopathology and Behavioral Assessment, 39*, 441–455.

Slick, D. J., Sherman, E. M. S., & Iverson, G. L. (1999). Diagnostic criteria for malingered neurocognitive dysfunction: Proposed standards for clinical practice and research. *The Clinical Neuropsychologist, 13*(4), 545–561. https://doi.org/10.1076/1385-4046(199911)13:04;1-Y;FT545.

Solomon, D., Morgan, B., Asberg, K., & Achee, D. (2014). Treatment implications based on measures of child abuse potential and parental mental health: Are we missing an intervention opportunity. *Children and Youth Services Review, 43*, 153–159.

Tarescavage, A. M., Azizian, A., Broderick, C., & English, P. (2019). Associations between MMPI-2-RF Scale scores and institutional violence among patients detained under sexually violent predator laws. *Psychological Assessment, 31*(5), 707–713.

Tarescavage, A. M., Cappo, B. M., & Ben-Porath, Y. S. (2018). Assessment of sex offenders with the Minnesota Multiphasic Personality/Inventory–2–restructured form. *Sexual Abuse, 30*(4), 413–437.

Tarescavage, A. M., Glassmire, D. M., & Burchett, D. (2018). Minnesota Multiphasic Personality Inventory-2-restructured form markers of future suicidal behavior in a forensic psychiatric hospital. *Psychological Assessment, 30*, 170–178.

Tarescavage, A. M., Glassmire, D. M., & Burchett, D. (2016). Introduction of a conceptual model for integrating the MMPI-2-RF into HCR-20V3 violence risk assessments and associations between the MMPI-2-RF and institutional violence. *Law and Human Behavior, 40*, 626–637.

Tarescavage, A. M., Luna-Jones, L., & Ben-Porath, Y. S. (2014). Minnesota Multiphasic Personality Inventory-2–Restructured Form (MMPI-2-RF) predictors of violating probation after felonious crimes. *Psychological Assessment, 26*(4), 1375.

Tarescavage, A., Wygant, D. B., Gervais, R. O., & Ben-Porath, Y. S. (2013). Association between the MMPI-2 Restructured Form (MMPI-2-RF) and malingered neurocognitive dysfunction among non-head injury disability claimants. *The Clinical Neuropsychologist, 27*, 313–335.

Tellegen, A., & Ben-Porath, Y. S. (2008). *MMPI-2-RF (Minnesota Multiphasic Personality Inventory-2-Restructured Form): Technical manual.* University of Minnesota Press.

Tellegen, A., Ben-Porath, Y. S., McNulty, J. L., Arbisi, P. A., Graham, J. R., & Kaemmer, B. (2003). *MMPI-2 Restructured Clinical (RC) scales: Development, validation, and interpretation.* University of Minnesota Press.

Tylicki, J. L., Gervais, R. O., & Ben-Porath, Y. S. (2020). Examination of the MMPI-3 Over-reporting Scales in a Forensic Disability Sample. *The Clinical Neuropsychologist.* Advance online publication. https://doi.org/10.1080/13854046.2020.1856414.

Vines, L. M., Wygant, D. B., & Gervais, R. O. (2012). Empirically guided case conceptualization of posttraumatic stress disorder with the Minnesota Multiphasic Personality Inventory-2 Restructured Form (MMPI-2-RF) in a forensic disability evaluation. *Journal of Psychological Practice, 17,* 180–205.

Whitman, M. R., Tylicki, J. L., & Ben-Porath, Y. S. (2021). Utility of the MMPI-3 Validity Scales for detecting over-reporting and under-reporting and their effects on substantive scale validity: A simulation study. *Psychological Assessment, 33*(5), 411–426. https://doi.org/10.1037/pas0000988.

Whitman, M. R., Tylicki, J. L., Mascioli, R., Pickle, J., & Ben-Porath, Y. S. (2020). Psychometric properties of the Minnesota Multiphasic Personality Inventory-3 (MMPI-3) in a clinical neuropsychology setting. *Psychological Assessment.* Advance online publication. https://doi.org/10.1037/pas0000969

Wolf, E. J., Miller, M. W., Orazem, R. J., Weierich, M. R., Castillo, D. T., Milford, J., Kaloupek, D. G., & Keane, T. M. (2008). The MMPI-2 restructured clinical scales in the assessment of posttraumatic stress disorder and comorbid disorders. *Psychological Assessment, 20,* 327–340.

Wygant, D. B., Arbisi, P. A., Bianchini, K. J., & Umlauf, R. L. (2017). Waddell nonorganic signs: New evidence suggests somatic amplification among outpatient chronic pain patients. *The Spine Journal, 17*(4), 505–510.

Wygant, D. B., Ben-Porath, Y. S., Arbisi, P. A., Berry, D. T., Freeman, D. B., & Heilbronner, R. L. (2009). Examination of the MMPI-2 restructured form (MMPI-2-RF) validity scales in civil forensic settings: Findings from simulation and known group samples. *Archives of Clinical Neuropsychology, 24*(7), 671–680.

Wygant, D. B., & Sellbom, M. (2012). Viewing psychopathy from the perspective of the personality psychopathology five model: Implications for DSM-5. *Journal of Personality Disorders, 26*(5), 717–726.

Wygant, D. B., Sellbom, M., Gervais, R. O., Ben-Porath, Y. S., Stafford, K. S., Freeman, D. B., et al. (2010). Further validation of the MMPI-2 and MMPI-2-RF response bias scale: Findings from civil and criminal forensic settings. *Psychological Assessment, 22,* 745–756.

Zapf, P. A., & Roesch, R. (2009). *Evaluation of competence to stand trial.* Oxford University Press.

Further Reading Suggestions

Ben-Porath, Y. S., & Sellbom, M. (2021). *Interpreting the MMPI-3.* University of Minnesota Press.

Ben-Porath, Y. S., & Tellegen, A. (2020). *Minnesota Multiphasic Personality Inventory-3 (MMPI-3): Manual for administration, scoring, and interpretation.* University of Minnesota Press.

Ben-Porath, Y. S., & Tellegen, A. (2020b). *Minnesota Multiphasic Personality Inventory-3 (MMPI-3):* Technical manual. University of Minnesota Press.

Sellbom, M., & Wygant, D. B. (2018). *Forensic applications of the MMPI-2 restructured form: A case book.* University of Minnesota Press.

Tarescavage, A. M., Glassmire, D. M., & Burchett, D. (2016). Introduction of a conceptual model for integrating the MMPI-2-RF into HCR-20V3 violence risk assessments and associations between the MMPI-2-RF and institutional violence. *Law and Human Behavior, 40,* 626–637.

Wygant, D. B., Walls, B. D., Brothers, S. L., & Berry, D. T. R. (2018). Assessment of malingering and defensiveness on the MMPI-2 257 and MMPI-2-RF. In R. Rogers & S. D. Bender (Eds.), *Clinical assessment of malingering and deception* (pp. 257–279). The Guilford Press.

The Good Lives Model: A Strength-Based Approach to Rehabilitating Offenders

27

Mary Barnao

Key Points

- Risk management is a necessary but not sufficient component of offender rehabilitation
- Offenders have the same needs as other human beings
- Offending represents an attempt to meet universal human needs in socially unacceptable ways
- The best way to create a safer society is to equip offenders with the skills and resources to live fulfilling and socially connected lives
- The GLM aims to promote offenders' goals and reduce their risk of re-offending
- The core principles of the RNR model should be embedded in a good lives framework

Introduction

Over the past three decades, enormous strides have been made in our ability to help offenders become more prosocial. Much of this progress has been influenced by the development of the Risk Need Responsivity (RNR) model (Andrews & Bonta, 2010). This rehabilitation framework is concerned with decreasing the likelihood that offenders will engage in antisocial behavior. The assumption is

M. Barnao (✉)
School of Psychology, Victoria University of Wellington, Wellington, New Zealand
e-mail: mary.barnao@vuw.ac.nz

that by identifying and managing dynamic (i.e., changeable) risk factors, recidivism rates will reduce. First disseminated in 1990, and elaborated over time, the RNR has become the predominant framework in correctional services that adopt a scientific approach to offender rehabilitation. Importantly, it has been pivotal in the growing acceptance of offender rehabilitation throughout the world, largely because of its robust empirical support, relative simplicity of use, and flexibility in practice (Polaschek, 2012).

However, while the RNR has resulted in effective therapy and reduced recidivism rates (Andrews & Bonta, 1998; Hollin, 1999; McGuire, 2002), concerns have been raised about this approach to offender rehabilitation, particularly by Ward and colleagues (Laws & Ward, 2011; Ward & Stewart, 2003; Ward et al., 2007). These authors have criticized the RNR for primarily focusing on reducing risk rather than equipping offenders with the resources to live better kinds of lives.

The Good Lives Model (GLM; Ward & Maruna, 2007; Ward & Stewart, 2003; Ward et al., 2007) was developed to address the weaknesses of the RNR and provide an alternative, although complementary, framework for rehabilitating offenders. It is a strength-based rehabilitation framework that goes beyond a focus on risk and seeks to promote offenders' well-being and personal goals.

In this chapter, I suggest that the GLM can provide a more fertile framework for approaching offender rehabilitation. To provide a context for the subsequent discussion of the GLM, I first outline the RNR model and then summarize some of the main criticisms of it. Next, I describe the GLM in theory. I then consider the clinical implications of this innovative framework and, using a case study, illustrate how it can be applied in practice. Finally, I summarize the current state of play regarding the GLM.

The Risk-Need-Responsivity (RNR) Model

The RNR is based on a theory known as the Psychology of Criminal Conduct (PCC), developed by Andrews and Bonta in the 1980s, and refined over time. The PCC is grounded in the principles of social-learning theory which emphasizes that, in addition to traditional learning theories such as operant conditioning (Skinner, 1938), individuals can learn by observing other people engaged in that behavior, or modeling, without being explicitly reinforced themselves (Bandura, 1975). The PCC provides direction for effective correctional intervention (Andrews & Bonta, 2010), within which a wide range of interventions can be employed, and is embodied in three core principles—risk, need, and responsivity.

The risk principle holds that the intensity of intervention that individuals receive should be matched to their level of risk, as assessed by actuarial assessment instruments. Higher intensity intervention should be directed to individuals assessed to be at higher risk of re-offending. Conversely, lower risk offenders derive better outcomes from a less intensive level of intervention (Andrews & Bonta, 2003).

According to the RNR, the prediction of criminality requires the identification of empirically based social and psychological risk factors associated with subsequent offending. These can be categorized as static or dynamic risk factors. Static risk factors are historical indicators that are not amenable to intervention (e.g., criminal history, age at first offense) whereas dynamic risk factors are potentially changeable aspects of the person (e.g., distorted cognitions, substance abuse, antisocial peers, family problems) (see also Chapters 4, 9, 10, and 17).

The needs principle posits that, to reduce recidivism, interventions should address dynamic risk factors that have been found to be directly associated with risk for re-offending (e.g., antisocial attitudes, antisocial peers, substance abuse). These criminogenic needs can be differentiated from non-criminogenic needs (e.g., anxiety, low self-esteem, personal distress), which are factors that are not empirically associated with recidivism. Non-criminogenic needs should not be the focus of treatment except when they pertain to the third principle of the RNR, namely the Responsivity principle.

The responsivity principle is concerned with factors that may affect an individual's response to interventions and considers two types of factors: The general responsivity principle considers general techniques and processes, and states that effective interventions tend to be based on cognitive, behavioral, and social-learning theories, such as teaching skills or reinforcing prosocial behavior (Smith et al., 2009). The specific responsivity principle states that the treatment provided should be tailored to the cognitive, personality, and social characteristics of the individual, and should consider idiographic factors such as learning style, intellectual level, anxiety, and culture.

There is strong evidence that correctional programs that adhere to the principles of the RNR model lead to greater reductions in recidivism than those that do not, and that treatment effects are linearly related to the number of RNR principles adhered to. These results apply to general recidivism (Andrews et al., 1990), violent recidivism (Dowden & Andrews, 2000), sexual recidivism (Hanson et al., 2009), and to female offenders (Dowden & Andrews, 1999).

Criticisms of the RNR

There is no doubt that the RNR has made a substantial contribution to contemporary criminal justice knowledge and intervention. However, it has also attracted criticism (e.g., Laws & Ward, 2011; Ward & Stewart, 2003; Ward et al., 2007). Ward and colleagues have argued that the focus that the RNR places on risk factors (i.e., criminogenic needs) is a necessary but not sufficient aim of treatment (Ward & Stewart, 2003) and that treatment should help offenders achieve personally meaningful goals as well as manage their risk. The assumption is that helping offenders to meet their human needs in more adaptive ways will mean that they are less likely to harm others or themselves (Ward & Stewart, 2003).

Ward and colleagues argue that, by focusing on the identification and removal of risk factors in isolation, the RNR views offenders as "disembodied bearers of risk rather than as integrated agents" (Ward & Stewart, 2003, p. 354). This can lead to a simplistic approach to human behavior that disregards the crucial importance of human needs, such as agency, peace of mind, or relationships, and their influence on offending.

According to Ward and colleagues, the primary focus that RNR-based treatment programs place on an individual's risk of re-offending, and their emphasis on avoidant treatment goals (i.e., goals based on the avoidance or elimination of certain behaviors, thoughts, or situations) can create problems with motivation and engagement in treatment. For example, individuals may see little personal benefit in participating in a rehabilitation program that is designed to help them stop offending, especially when it is not linked to their important values and aspirations (Ward et al., 2007). Further, the focus on what is wrong with them and their lives may have a negative impact on the therapeutic relationship—a potentially serious problem given that the quality of the therapeutic relationship is strongly related to treatment outcomes (Ackerman & Hilsenroth, 2003; Leach, 2005).

It is true that the RNR concept of specific responsivity, which concerns factors that may impede an individual's response to interventions, can encompass matters such as the therapeutic alliance, motivational issues, and even human needs. Indeed, it has been argued that many of the ideas embodied in the GLM align with the concept of responsivity and that expansion of the latter would accomplish much of what the GLM purports to do (Ogloff & Davis, 2004). However, the responsivity principle, while central to the RNR, is theoretically underdeveloped and tends to act as a catch-all category (Polaschek, 2012), thereby limiting its practical utility. Further, while the responsivity principle potentially allows for consideration of a broad range of issues and interventions, this is in the service of addressing those factors which, if not addressed, would stop offender rehabilitation from proceeding. In other words, the focus is primarily on risk reduction through the targeting of criminogenic needs rather than on developing a more comprehensive understanding of the whole person.

Ward and colleagues argue that the RNR also neglects consideration of the role of human agency (Ward & Gannon, 2006; Ward et al., 2007). In their view, human beings are practical decision-makers who formulate plans to achieve goals. With this conception in mind, they argue that correctional rehabilitation should equip offenders with the skills and resources to carry out valued activities, such as developing an intimate relationship or obtaining meaningful work, rather than simply focusing on treating criminogenic needs (Laws & Ward, 2011).

The RNR has also been criticized for not addressing the important role of personal identity in the change process (Ward & Stewart, 2003) (Chapter 8). According to Ward and colleagues, change results from a "holistic reconstruction of the self" (Laws & Ward, 2011, p. 189), rather than the targeting of individual risk factors. In support of this, they note that individuals who desist from offending tend to adopt a personal identity inconsistent with offending (Laws & Ward, 2011).

Another concern is that the RNR perspective, and particularly the way that it is applied in practice (e.g. use of manuals), can result in a one-size-fits-all approach to treatment that downplays the critical role of contextual factors (Ward & Gannon, 2006; Ward et al., 2007). While contextual factors are considered in the RNR in so far as they relate to risk and criminogenic needs (e.g., antisocial peers, family & marital factors), the focus tends to be fairly narrow (e.g., broader issues such as poverty, racism, social exclusion, and the rehabilitation environment are not highlighted).

Other criticisms of the RNR relate to its insufficiency in providing clinicians with guidance on key aspects of correctional practice. For example, the RNR is relatively silent on the critical issues of establishing therapeutic relationships with offenders, therapist factors, and attitudes to offenders (Ward et al., 2007), and provides little scaffolding with respect to ethical decision-making (Robertson et al., 2011).

The GLM is intended to provide a rehabilitation framework that can incorporate empirically based, risk-management knowledge within a more holistic, person-centered approach, underpinned by a focus on human rights.

Overview of the GLM

The GLM is a contemporary theory of offender rehabilitation that aims to equip individuals with the skills and resources to live a "good life"—one that is personally fulfilling and that does not involve harming others (Ward & Maruna, 2007; Ward & Stewart, 2003; Ward et al., 2007). Firmly grounded in human rights, the GLM starts from the assumption that, while offenders have obligations to respect other peoples' entitlements to freedom and well-being, they are also entitled to the same rights. Two central treatment aims follow from this ethical principle: the promotion of offenders' well-being and the reduction of their risk of re-offending. According to the GLM, there is an inextricable link between these goals: helping offenders to achieve more satisfying, socially integrated lifestyles is the most effective way to create a safer society.

The GLM aims to equip offenders with the capabilities and resources to obtain primary goods in socially acceptable and personally meaningful ways. Primary goods are essentially activities, experiences, and/or situations that are sought for their own sake and that benefit individuals and increase their sense of fulfillment and happiness.

The psychological, social, biological, and anthropological research evidence provides support for the existence of at least eleven primary goods: (1) life (including healthy living and functioning); (2) knowledge; (3) excellence in play; (4) excellence in work (including mastery experiences); (5) agency (i.e., autonomy and self-directedness); (6) inner peace (i.e., freedom from emotional turmoil and stress); (7) friendship (including intimate, romantic, and family relationships); (8) community (connection to wider social groups); (9) spirituality (in the broad sense of finding meaning and purpose in life); (10) happiness (feeling good in the here and now); and (11) creativity (e.g., Purvis, 2010; Ward & Gannon, 2006). There is evidence from a wide range of literature that the attainment of primary human goods is associated with higher levels of well-being and their absence related to psychological problems of various kinds (Emmons, 1999; Ward & Maruna, 2007). The GLM posits that human beings are predisposed to seek out all the primary goods, but that they differ in the weightings they give to each of them, reflecting their values and priorities in life.

Individuals obtain primary goods using a variety of concrete means or secondary goods. Essentially, secondary goods are those activities that people carry out in the pursuit of primary goods. For example, a person may attempt to relax (i.e., satisfy the primary good of inner peace) by listening to music, meditating, or drinking alcohol, which are all secondary goods. From a GLM perspective, people use socially unacceptable secondary goods when they are unable to satisfy primary goods in other, more adaptive ways. Thus, offending represents an attempt to obtain primary goods within the context of personal limitations (e.g., lack of knowledge or skills) and/or environmental disadvantage (e.g., lack of opportunities or resources). In the GLM, these individual and environmental obstacles to the attainment of primary goods are conceptualized as criminogenic needs.

The GLM assumes that all human beings fashion their lives around the things that are most important to them, thus following some sort of (often implicit) good life plan (Ward & Gannon, 2006; Ward & Maruna, 2007). Theory and research suggest that there are four types of difficulties often evident in offenders' good lives plans and reflected in their lifestyles (Purvis, 2010; Ward & Maruna, 2007). First, offenders may have problems with the *means* (i.e., secondary goods) by which they secure primary goods and therefore engage in antisocial or maladaptive behavior. For example, an individual may seek to obtain a sense of power and control (i.e., primary good of agency) through rape. Second, their attainment of primary goods may be obstructed by problems with internal (i.e., personal) and external (i.e., environmental) capabilities (e.g., skills, attitudes, psychological characteristics, interpersonal, social, and cultural factors). For example, an individual may use rape as a means of satisfying agency needs due to a combination of poor interpersonal skills, misogynist attitudes, and low levels of social support. Third, they may not strive for or secure the full range of primary goods (e.g., focusing on work to the detriment of other goods such as relationships and interests), reflecting problems with scope. Finally, they may experience conflict between the goods being sought after (e.g., when a person's tendency to overwork conflicts with their need to have a close relationship with their wife), resulting in stress and unhappiness. These four flaws in individuals' good lives plans are not mutually exclusive but usually overlap (e.g., securing primary goods through inappropriate means may reflect problems with internal and external capabilities and can lead to conflict between the goods sought).

Recent research has demonstrated that there are two primary routes to offending: direct and indirect (Purvis, 2010). The direct pathway is implicated when offenders seek (often implicitly) to attain primary goods through their offending behavior. For example, an individual lacking the competencies and resources to take charge of his life might attempt to satisfy the need for agency through the use of violence. The indirect pathway is implicated when an individual does not have a direct intention to offend but problems occur in the pursuit of other goods, creating a ripple effect that culminates in an offense. For example, an individual who relies on alcohol to cope with work stress and feelings of inadequacy may, while out drinking, respond to a comment he interprets as disrespectful, in a physically aggressive manner.

The GLM is not a specific intervention but rather an overarching rehabilitation framework that can govern the integration of different theories, assessments, and treatments (e.g., CBT, mentalization-based treatment, schema therapy, EMDR, offending behavior programs) within a single rehabilitation plan. It provides a comprehensive, theoretically driven understanding of an individual's offending and core rehabilitation needs that can guide the selection of specific interventions and therapies. Consequently, use of the GLM can help practitioners to avoid the problem of theoretical incoherence that arises from trying to combine a variety of different approaches and interventions in an individual's rehabilitation plan without a superordinate conceptual framework to guide them (Barnao et al., 2016; Jones, 2019).

There are several other important ways in which the GLM can enhance offender rehabilitation. First, the focus on equipping offenders with the capabilities to achieve their goals is more likely to engage them in treatment, motivate them to change, and facilitate positive therapeutic relationships. Second, the GLM provides a richer, more integrated, etiological model of offending that emphasizes crucial aspects of human functioning such as human needs, agency, and identity. Third and relatedly, rehabilitation plans based on this much broader conceptualization of offending are comprehensive and positively keyed, focusing on an individuals' personal goals as well as their criminogenic needs. In the GLM, these goals of well-being enhancement and risk reduction are inextricably linked since the focus of rehabilitation is on equipping offenders with the personal and environmental resources to meet their needs in prosocial ways. Finally, the GLM has the conceptual resources to guide clinicians in all areas of practice, including the relational, motivational, ethical, and contextual aspects of rehabilitation (Barnao et al., 2016).

Implications of the GLM for Practice

Using the GLM as the framework for offender rehabilitation has several significant implications for correctional practice. One of these concerns the way in which offenders are viewed and how they should be treated. In the GLM, offenders are viewed as people who are trying to live a meaningful life in the best way possible in the specific circumstances that they face. Although they have committed harmful acts, they are not moral strangers but individuals acting from a common set of goals stemming from their human nature (Ward et al., 2007). In keeping with this conception of offenders, the GLM places a strong emphasis on collaboration, respect, and positive therapist characteristics (e.g., warmth, empathy, and encouragement). While these relational aspects of therapy are not unique to the GLM and should be prerequisites for all therapeutic approaches, they are explicitly addressed in the GLM as part of a broader set of ethical principles to guide practice.

As has previously been highlighted, the GLM does not just focus on decreasing the likelihood that an offender will harm others but, instead, takes a more holistic perspective, based on the core idea that the best way to reduce risk is to help offenders live more fulfilling lives. What this requires, in practice, is that practitioners carefully manage the delicate balance between promoting offenders' goals and reducing their risk of recidivism. Erring too far in the direction of either goal can have serious consequences. Thus, a disproportionate focus on an offender's goals may result in a happy but dangerous individual while giving insufficient attention to the person's core interests and values could lead to low levels of engagement in treatment (Ward et al., 2007).

In keeping with the positive orientation of the GLM, the language of treatment should be future-oriented and optimistic. Consequently, terminology associated with problems, deficits, and avoidance goals should be replaced with more positive language associated with approach goals (i.e., goals focused on obtaining a positive outcome). For example, "relapse prevention" could be labeled as "self-management" and "building emotional literacy skills" could be used in preference to "emotion regulation deficits."

As previously highlighted, the GLM is a theoretical framework that is complementary to the RNR, and that is intended to incorporate the core principles of the RNR within a more holistic, strength-based perspective. With this in mind, practitioners must assess risk, need, and responsivity issues throughout the evaluation process. In addition, they need to explore an offender's priorities in life. This usually involves asking a series of increasingly detailed questions about what matters most to the person in their lives and what they devote their energies to on a day-to-day basis. In exploring the individual's values (i.e., primary goods), an important task is to detect the goal(s) evident in the individual's offense progression to understand what gap the offense filled for the person.

Several issues are explored with the person with respect to each of the primary goods. They include: the relative importance of the good for the person; the ways in which the person has gone about satisfying the primary good in their life (i.e., secondary goods); the strategies that have worked the best for the person and those that have worked least well or turned out to be counter-productive; the obstacles that underpin an individual's maladaptive ways of satisfying primary goods; and the strengths that allow the person to fulfill primary goods in adaptive ways.

The assessment should also include an exploration of the problems with a person's way of living at the time of their offending. Enquiring about each of the primary goods in the manner outlined above will elucidate problems with the means by which an offender satisfies primary goods as well as problems with capacity (i.e., personal and environmental problems that impede a person from securing primary goods). Other questions that need to be considered are: Whether there are problems with restricted scope (e.g., the person is focusing on some goods to the detriment of others); and whether there is a clash or conflict between the goods sought.[1] Information generated from these questions, in conjunction with a systematic assessment of an offender's social and psychological functioning, forms the basis of a good lives oriented case formulation and treatment plan. The case formulation is essentially a narrative that explains why the person committed an offense. As such, it should describe the relationship between a person's offending, their criminogenic needs (i.e., the problems implicated in their offending), and the primary goods that are directly or indirectly linked to the offense. The offender's *overarching primary good* around which the other goods are oriented also needs to be identified because it informs practitioners about what is most important in a person's life and how the person sees himself or herself (i.e., their identity).

In addition to explaining why an individual committed an offense, a comprehensive GLM oriented case formulation will also specify his or her level of risk, identify the flaws in his or her good lives plan, ascertain whether there is a direct or indirect link between the pursuit of primary goods and offending, and highlight the person's strengths (See case study for an example of a GLM case formulation).

In the GLM, offenders' treatment plans are often centered around a specific goal that represents a concrete means of satisfying their overarching primary good. For example, if a person prioritizes the primary good of mastery (i.e., excellence in work), has studied accountancy, and enjoys working independently, his treatment plan could be designed around finding him work as a sole-charge accountant. A goal such as this will often provide the means of satisfying several primary goods simultaneously (e.g., excellence at work, relationships, community, life, agency, etc.). It is important that practitioners consider the environment that

---

[1] The recommended approach to obtaining this information is through a clinical interview. Incorporating information from other sources (e.g., interviews with family and staff) can be useful and is essential when working with certain groups of offenders (e.g., youth offenders, intellectually disabled offenders).

individuals are living in, or will be living in (if they are incarcerated), to ensure that goals are appropriate to their local contexts.

A GLM-oriented treatment plan also needs to specify the competencies, skills, and environmental resources that are required for individuals to put their plans into action. Since risk factors are conceptualized in the GLM as internal and external obstacles to satisfying goals in a socially acceptable manner, a major focus of rehabilitation is on equipping the person with the skills and resources needed to achieve a better kind of life. Linking a person's goal with a plan to address their criminogenic needs highlights to them that addressing risk is integral to achieving a good life.

GLM Developments

The GLM has undergone continued theoretical development since it was first formulated almost two decades ago. It has attracted interest internationally (Willis et al., 2013) and its popularity with correctional practitioners continues to grow. Although much of the earlier research on the GLM was conducted on sex offenders, subsequent literature has suggested that its clinical relevance extends to broader offending typologies including violent offenders (Whitehead et al., 2007), male perpetrators of domestic violence (Langlands et al., 2009), youth offenders (Fortune, 2018), and mentally disordered offenders (Barnao et al., 2016), as well as to probation case management (Purvis et al., 2013). The GLM has also been applied to non-offender populations such as individuals with substance abuse (Thakker & Ward, 2010) and medical patients (Siegert et al., 2007).

Research on the effectiveness of the GLM is still at an early stage and further research is urgently needed, including studies that examine the longer-term effects of the GLM and its impact on recidivism risk. The extant research suggests that GLM consistent programs are producing results consistent with RNR adherent programs (Fortune et al., 2015), with tentative evidence for improved treatment engagement (Mann et al., 2004), enhanced motivation (Mann et al., 2004; Simons et al., 2006), lower participant attrition (Simons et al., 2006; Ware & Bright, 2008), more positive outcomes (Simons et al., 2006), and increased therapist satisfaction (Harkins et al., 2012; Ware & Bright, 2008). It has been recommended that, pending strong empirical support, use of the good lives approach should be accompanied by practices with a demonstrated impact on recidivism (Netto et al., 2014).

Conclusions

Individuals who offend, like other human beings, want the chance to lead meaningful and fulfilling lives. Effective and ethical rehabilitation should aim to enhance their lives, not simply seek to reduce their risk factors. The Good Lives Model adopts a holistic approach to offender rehabilitation through its dual aims of promoting offenders' goals and well-being and reducing their risk of recidivism. These two foci of rehabilitation are linked: The assumption is that by equipping offenders with the skills and resources to satisfy their human needs in socially acceptable ways, they will be less likely to harm others. Underpinned by an understanding of human functioning and grounded in human rights, the GLM emphasizes offenders' shared humanity and inherent worth. As a strength-based, positive framework, the GLM has the conceptual resources to engage offenders in the difficult process of rehabilitation and to guide correctional practitioners in all aspects of their work.

Case Study

Graham is a 45-year-old married man who is an accountant by training but in recent years has worked as a senior manager for a multinational company. Graham's alcohol consumption increased following a period of stress at work, including some negative feedback from his manager. Graham's wife did not approve of his increased drinking and they started to argue. As the tension at home increased, Graham drank even more, struggled at work, and was eventually given a formal warning after making a series of serious errors. He was subsequently demoted at work and his wife moved out on account of his ongoing, heavy drinking. Following an office function, during which he had been drinking heavily, Graham followed a female colleague, whom he thought had insulted him, into a car park and raped her. He was given a medium length prison term.

Graham's risk level was assessed as medium and the criminogenic needs of substance abuse, problems with emotional regulation, demeaning attitudes toward women, a high need for power and control, and social isolation were identified.

Graham's overarching primary goods were excellence at work and autonomy. While he took pride in being good at his job, he tended to underestimate his performance. In addition, he was highly sensitive to perceived threats to his independence and resented it when he thought people were telling him what to do.

There were several flaws in Graham's lifestyle at the time of his offending. First, some means of obtaining primary goods were highly problematic, notably his use of violence, domination, and control to satisfy the primary good of autonomy, and his use of alcohol for tension release. Second, these maladaptive secondary goods were underpinned by a core set of problems that included: a lack of appropriate ways of asserting himself and exerting autonomy, a sense of inadequacy, misogynistic attitudes, poor emotional regulation skills, and social isolation (i.e., problems with internal and external capacity). Third, due to a tendency to overwork, his life was limited in scope. Graham had, in the past, been a good football player and had a few close friends whom he now rarely saw. Finally, there appeared to be a conflict between his desire to excel in his job and his need to have a close, loving relationship with his wife.

The pathway to Graham's offending was an indirect one whereby increased stress at work, coupled with poor emotion regulation skills, led him to rely on alcohol to relax. His increased alcohol consumption subsequently created a cascade of other stressors, including arguments with his wife and problems at work, leading to his demotion, which he dealt with by drinking even more. Outraged by his female colleague's perceived disrespect, which elicited feelings of inadequacy, he attempted to obtain a sense of power and control (i.e., primary good of agency) through the rape.

Graham's marriage remained intact, despite his offending, but he lost his job upon conviction. Work was a key focus of his rehabilitation plan and, through the local church, he obtained a voluntary position as a bookkeeper for a local charity, satisfying his need for mastery and autonomy. Graham's rehabilitation plan also gave a prominent role to his involvement in his friend's football team which helped him to increase his social contact and establish better community links. It was expected that these secondary goods (i.e., voluntary work and involvement in the football club) could also help to address a number of his other problems. For example, members of the church and football team could provide Graham with support, assist him to develop his communication skills, and help him learn to be become more sensitive to the needs of others. Further, his adversarial relationships with females and his tendency to overreact to perceived threats to his sense of masculinity and autonomy would be gently confronted by his football teammates. Graham was provided with some specialized therapy to help him build his emotional competence and relationship skills. He was an active participant in the construction and implementation of his rehabilitation plan and, while he struggled to accept full responsibility for his sexual offending, he was fully engaged in the reintegration process.

References

Ackerman, S. J., & Hilsenroth, M. J. (2003). A review of therapist characteristics and techniques positively impacting the therapeutic alliance. *Clinical Psychology Review, 23*(1), 1–33.

Andrews, D. A., Zinger, I., Hoge, R. D., Bonta, J., Gendreau, P., & Cullen, F. T. (1990). Does correctional treatment work? A clinically relevant and psychologically informed meta-analysis. *Criminology, 28*(3), 369–404.

Andrews, D. A., & Bonta, J. (1998). *The psychology of criminal conduct* (2nd ed.). Anderson.

Andrews, D. A., & Bonta, J. (2003). *The psychology of criminal conduct* (3rd ed.). Anderson.

Andrews, D. A., & Bonta, J. (2010). *The psychology of criminal conduct* (5th ed.). Mathew Bender.

Bandura, A. (1975). *Social learning and personality development.* Holt, Rinehart, & Winston.

Barnao, M., Ward, T., & Robertson, P. (2016). The Good Lives Model: A new paradigm for forensic mental health. *Psychiatry, Psychology and Law, 23*(2), 288–301.

Dowden, C., & Andrews, D. A. (1999). What works for female offenders: A meta-analytic review. *Crime and Delinquency, 45*(4), 438–452.

Dowden, C., & Andrews, D. A. (2000). Effective correctional treatment and violent reoffending: A meta-analysis. *Canadian Journal of Criminology, 42*(4), 449–468.

Emmons, R. A. (1999). *The psychology of ultimate concerns.* Guilford Press.

Fortune, C. (2018). The Good Lives Model: A strength-based approach for youth offenders. *Aggression & Violent Behavior, 38*, 21–30.

Fortune, C. A., Ward, T., & Mann, R. (2015). Good Lives & the rehabilitation of sex offenders: A positive treatment approach. In A. Linley & S. Joseph (Eds.), *Positive psychology in practice* (2nd ed.). Wiley.

Hanson, R. K., Bourgon, G., Helmus, L., & Hodgins, S. (2009). The principles of effective correctional treatment also apply to sexual offenders: A meta-analysis. *Criminal Justice and Behavior, 36*(9), 865–891.

Harkins, L., Flak, V. E., Beech, A., & Woodhams, J. (2012). Evaluation of a community-based sex offender treatment program using a Good Lives Model approach. *Sexual Abuse: A Journal of Research and Treatment, 24*(6), 519–543.

Hollin, C. R. (1999). Treatment programs for offenders: Meta-analysis, "what works" and beyond. *International Journal of Law and Psychiatry, 22*(3–4), 361–372.

Jones, L. (2019). New developments in interventions for working with offending behaviour. In D. Polaschek, A. Day, & C. Hollin (Eds.), *The Wiley international handbook of correctional psychology* (pp. 669–685). Wiley.

Langlands, R., Ward, T., & Gilchrist, L. (2009). Applying the Good Lives Model to male perpetrators of domestic violence. *Behaviour Change, 26*(2), 113–129.

Laws, D. R., & Ward, T. (2011). *Desistance from sex offending: Alternatives to throwing away the keys.* Guildford press.

Leach, M. J. (2005). Rapport: A key to treatment success. *Complementary Therapies in Clinical Practice, 11*(4), 262–265.

Mann, R. E., Webster, S. D., Schofield, C., & Marshall, W. L. (2004). Approach versus avoidance goals in relapse prevention with sexual offenders. *Sexual Abuse: A Journal of Research and Treatment, 16*(1), 65–75.

McGuire, J. (2002). Criminal sanctions versus psychologically-based interventions with offenders: A comparative empirical analysis. *Psychology, Crime & Law, 8*(2), 183–208.

Netto, N. R., Carter, J. M., & Bonell, C. (2014). A systematic review of interventions that adopt the "Good Lives" approach to offender rehabilitation. *Journal of Offender Rehabilitation, 53*(6), 403–432.

Ogloff, J. R., & Davis, M. R. (2004). Advances in Offender Assessment and Rehabilitation: Contributions of the risk-needs-responsivity approach. *Psychology Crime and Law, 10*(3), 229–242.

Polaschek, D. L. L. (2012). An appraisal of the risk-need-responsivity (RNR) model of offender rehabilitation and its application in correctional treatment. *Legal and Criminological Psychology, 17*(1), 1–17.

Purvis, M. (2010). *Seeking a Good Life: Human goods and sexual offending*. Lambert Academic Press.

Purvis, M., Ward, T., & Shaw, S. (2013). *Applying the Good Lives Model to the case management of sexual offenders: A practical guide for probation offices, parole officers, and case workers*. Safer Society Press.

Robertson, P., Barnao, M., & Ward, T. (2011). Rehabilitation frameworks in forensic mental health. *Aggression and Violent Behavior, 16*(6), 472–484.

Siegert, R., Ward, T., Levack, W., & Mcpherson, K. (2007). A Good Lives Model of clinical and community rehabilitation. *Disability and Rehabilitation, 29*(20–21), 1604–1615.

Simons, D. A., McCullar, B., & Tyler, C. (2006, September). *Evaluation of the Good Lives Model approach to treatment planning*. Paper presented at the 25th Annual Association for the Treatment of Sexual Abusers Research and Treatment Conference, Chicago, Illinois.

Skinner, B. F. (1938). *The behavior of organisms*. Appleton-Century-Crofts.

Smith, P., Gendreau, P., & Swartz, K. (2009). Validating the principles of effective intervention: A systematic review of the contributions of meta-analysis in the field of corrections. *Victims and Offenders, 4*(2), 148–169.

Thakker, J., & Ward, T. (2010). The Good Lives Model and the treatment of substance abusers. *Behaviour Change, 27*(3), 154–175.

Ward, T., & Gannon, T. A. (2006). Rehabilitation, etiology, and self-regulation: The comprehensive Good Lives Model of treatment for sexual offenders. *Aggression and Violent Behavior, 11*(1), 77–94.

Ward, T., Mann, R. E., & Gannon, T. A. (2007). The Good Lives Model of offender rehabilitation: Clinical implications. *Aggression and Violent Behaviour, 12*(1), 87–107.

Ward, T., & Maruna, S. (2007). *Rehabilitation: Beyond the risk paradigm*. Routledge.

Ward, T., & Stewart, C. A. (2003). The treatment of sex offenders: Risk management and Good Lives. *Professional Psychology: Research and Practice, 34*(4), 353–360.

Ware, J., & Bright, D. A. (2008). Evolution of a treatment program for sex offenders: Changes to the NSW Custody-based Intensive Treatment (CUBIT). *Psychiatry, Psychology and Law, 15*(2), 340–349.

Whitehead, P. R., Ward, T., & Collie, R. M. (2007). Time for a change: Applying the Good Lives Model of rehabilitation to a high-risk violent offender. *International Journal of Offender Therapy and Comparative Criminology, 51*(5), 578–598.

Willis, G. M., & Ward, T. (2011). Striving for a good life: The Good Lives Model applied to released child molesters. *Journal of Sexual Aggression, 17*(3), 290–303.

Willis, G., Yates, P., Gannon, T., & Ward, T. (2013). How to integrate the Good Lives Model into treatment programs for sexual offending: An introduction and overview. *Sexual Abuse: A Journal of Research and Treatment, 25*(2), 123–142.

Further Reading Suggestions

Barnao, M., Ward, T., & Robertson, P. (2016). The Goods Lives Model: A new paradigm for forensic mental health. *Psychiatry, Psychology and Law, 23*(2), 288–301.

Fortune, C.-A. (2018). The Good Lives Model: A strength-based approach for youth offenders. *Aggression and Violent Behavior, 38*, 21–30.

Ward, T., & Gannon, T. A. (2006). Rehabilitation, etiology, and self-regulation: The comprehensive Good Lives Model of treatment for sexual offenders. *Aggression and Violent Behavior, 11*(1), 77–94.

Ward, T., Mann, R. E., & Gannon, T. A. (2007). The Good Lives Model of offender rehabilitation: Clinical implications. *Aggression and Violent Behaviour, 12*(1), 87–107.

Ward, T., & Maruna, S. (2007). *Rehabilitation: Beyond the risk paradigm.* Routledge.

Culpability and Accountability: The Insanity Defense

28

Gerben Meynen and Johannes Bijlsma

Key Points

- The insanity defense is an element of many legal systems, but not of all.
- The insanity defense is a topic of much debate; central issues include: the criteria of legal insanity, the reliability of forensic psychiatric and psychological assessments, and the helpfulness of neuroscience data for insanity evaluations.
- Many insanity criteria include both a knowledge/appreciation component and a control component; in brief, the question is: did the defendant know that what he was doing was wrong and/or could he control his conduct?
- Legal insanity is a legal matter. Meanwhile, in order to arrive at a conclusion about the defendant's sanity, mental health experts are asked to provide information about the mental state—in terms of psychopathology and its impact on the behavior—of the defendant. In some legal systems, the behavioral expert is allowed and/or explicitly asked to formulate a conclusion regarding the matter of legal insanity as well.
- Neuroscience may be helpful to diagnose a disorder, in particular neurological disorders such as a brain tumor or dementia. If neuroimaging is being used, in

G. Meynen (✉) · J. Bijlsma
Willem Pompe Institute for Criminal Law and Criminology, Utrecht Centre for Accountability and Liability Law, Utrecht University, Utrecht, The Netherlands
e-mail: g.meynen@uu.nl

J. Bijlsma
e-mail: j.bijlsma@uu.nl

G. Meynen
Department of Philosophy, VU University Amsterdam, Amsterdam, The Netherlands

principle, it is advisable to also perform a neuropsychological evaluation in order to relate imaging findings to cognitive functioning. A neurological abnormality is not necessarily legally relevant.

Introduction

The insanity defense provides the possibility that a defendant who committed a crime is excused because of the presence of a mental illness at the time of the act (Meynen, 2016, 2021). Typically, it is not just the presence of a mental disorder, but its specific legally relevant influence that exculpates a defendant. Even though it may seem intuitive that, at least in some cases, a mental disorder excuses a person for his criminal conduct, the insanity defense is one of the most debated topics in criminal law.[1] In this chapter, we will consider the insanity defense by looking at some of the central issues under debate. The structure is as follows.

First, we address the legal framework of culpability and accountability as well as the ethical basis of the insanity defense. Next, we discuss the concept of mental disorder underpinning the insanity defense. Then we examine several influential legal criteria for insanity in the Western world. As we will see, these criteria often concern the defendant's lack of knowledge about the wrongfulness of the act and/or a lack of control over one's behavior. It will also become clear that there are many differences between legal systems regarding the insanity defense. Thereafter, we consider questions and concerns about the reliability and vulnerability of insanity assessments. Finally, we briefly discuss the role neuroscience and neuropsychology may play to increase the validity of insanity evaluations.

The Legal Framework of Culpability and Accountability

In Western criminal justice systems punishment is allowed only if a defendant is criminally responsible for an offense. Mental disorder can preclude criminal responsibility in most legal systems in at least two ways.

For most offenses it is not only required that the defendant committed a certain criminal act (*actus reus*—'wrongful act'), but also that he or she acted with a particular mental state (*mens rea*—'guilty mind'). The particular mental state

---

[1] Where we write he/his in this chapter, depending on the context, it also refers to she/her, and vice versa. On topics discussed in this chapter, see also Meynen (2016, 2021).

specified in the elements of the crime, for example 'recklessness' or 'intent', has to be proven beyond a reasonable doubt. It is possible that a mental disorder amounts to a so-called failure of proof defense, meaning that the required form of mens rea cannot be proven (Morse, 2011). An often-quoted, though a bit of an odd example, is the defendant who, under the influence of a psychotic delusion, believes that he is squeezing a lemon while actually choking somebody to death. This defendant does not act with the intent to kill, but merely with the (non-criminal) intent to squeeze a lemon. Mens rea for intentional homicide cannot be proven and the defendant will be acquitted.

More often, however, mental disorder is not an obstacle to prove the requisite mens rea. For example, a defendant under the influence of a persecutory delusion that police officers are plotting against her may act violently against a police officer. While this person has a severe mental disorder, she did act with the intention to harm the police officer. In this case, both actus reus and mens rea can be proven (e.g., intentional assault). However, due to the severe illness, the defendant may raise the insanity defense. The insanity defense is a so-called affirmative defense, meaning that the defendant does not deny the allegations (actus reus and mens rea), but offers a reason why he or she cannot be held responsible for this act (Morse, 2011). Most Western legal systems acknowledge insanity as an affirmative defense (Sinnot-Armstrong & Levy, 2011). However, Sweden and some states in the United States have abolished insanity as an affirmative defense. Mental disorders in these jurisdictions can only exculpate if the defendant did not act with mens rea due to the disorder (Morse & Bonnie, 2013).[2]

The chances of success of raising the insanity defense depend on the substance of the defense in the particular jurisdiction the defense is raised. For example, until recently, in Norway psychosis was a sufficient (and necessary) reason for legal insanity, but usually jurisdictions require that, in addition to the requirement of mental disorder, certain criteria for insanity are met. The formulation of these criteria varies across jurisdictions (see section "Legal Criteria for Insanity in the Western World"). Self-induced mental disorder due to, for example, the voluntary ingestion of illegal substances resulting in a psychosis usually precludes a successful insanity defense ('prior fault' or 'culpa in causa') (Dimock, 2011).

Typically, a successful defense of insanity does not lead to an outright acquittal. While *punishing* a defendant who is not responsible is precluded in Western criminal justice systems, usually some form of *preventive detention* is allowed

---

[2] This approach has received criticism for being unfair.

when the defendant is presumed dangerous due to mental disorder.[3] Treatment of the disorder should reduce the risk of recidivism to acceptable levels (Chapters 25 and 29). In a way, therefore, the mental illness constitutes a double-edged sword for defendants. On the one hand, they are exculpated for their crime, but on the other hand, they may be sentenced to (indefinite) treatment until risk levels have sufficiently decreased (the specific regulations vary across jurisdictions).

In order to support the fairness of the insanity defense, people tend not only to refer to legal matters, but also to ethical considerations (Chapter 31). For instance, Bonnie writes: "The insanity defense, in short, is essential to the moral integrity of the criminal law" (1983). This moral perspective highlights that it is not morally justified to blame and punish people if they do not *deserve* such blame and punishment because they were not actually responsible for their actions.

Mental Disorder

The insanity defense predates psychiatry as a medical specialty. Historically, various criteria for insanity have been used (Robinson, 1996). One well-known criterion in the Western world is the so-called wild beast test. According to this criterion, a defendant "must be a man that is totally deprived of his understanding and memory, and doth not know what he is doing, no more than an infant, than a brute, or a wild beast; such a one is never the object of punishment" (Robinson, 1996, p. 134). Notably, this criterion for insanity does not refer to any (specific) mental disorder or deficiency—so, to psychopathology. Rather, it refers to children and wild beasts as non-rational beings, but not to pathological categories. Nowadays, however, the standards for insanity tend to refer to some form of mental disorder or deficiency, though the formulations vary.

An important question—and issue of debate—is to which extent such a reference to mental disorder or deficiency refers to the medical domain or whether it is a legal notion. Until recently, in Norway, the 'medical principle' has been used (for instance in the Breivik case [Melle, 2013][4]): insanity was merely about the presence of a psychotic disorder at the time of the crime, and the psychotic disorder was considered to refer to the ICD-system, The International Classification

---

[3] The apparent assumption in various Western legal systems that there is a special connection between being not responsible due to mental disorder and being dangerous is, at least to some extent, challenged in Bijlsma et al. (2019).

[4] On 22 July 2011, in Norway, Anders Breivik killed 77 people, many of whom were youths attending a summer camp. Initially, psychiatrists considered him psychotic and legally insane, but eventually the court considered him sane.

of Diseases (currently, the 11th edition), which is a medical classification system (Syse, 2014; Gröning et al., 2020).[5] However, in the United States, according to Stephen Morse, the situation is different:

> The criminal law can, but need not, turn to scientific or clinical definitions of mental abnormality as legal criteria when promulgating mental health laws. The Supreme Court has reiterated on numerous occasions that there is substantial dispute within the mental health professions about diagnoses, that psychiatry is not an exact science, and that the law is not bound by extra-legal professional criteria. The law often uses technical terms, such as "mental disorder," or semi-technical qualifiers, such as "severe," but non-technical terms, such as "mental abnormality," have also been approved. Legal criteria are adopted to answer legal questions. As long as they plausibly do so, they will be approved even if they are not psychiatric or psychological criteria. (Morse, 2011, p. 894)

Apparently, the notion 'mental disorder' does not necessarily refer to medical criteria, at least not in the US context. Apart from this issue, it is good to realize that, ultimately, it is the court or jury that decides whether the criteria for insanity have been fulfilled. This is particularly relevant in cases where the experts disagree about the presence of a mental disorder, then the court or jury will take a prominent role in the decision.

Legal Criteria for Insanity in the Western World

Arguably, the most well-known criterion for legal insanity in the Western world is the M'Naghten rule. It was established in 1843, in the aftermath of the case of Daniel M'Naghten. He suffered, it is assumed, from a paranoid delusion for some time: he believed that the British political party of the Tories was behind the problems in his life. At some point he tried to assassinate the Tory Prime Minister, Sir Robert Peel. But, presumably because of a mistake, he shot—and killed—his secretary, Edward Drummond, instead. M'Naghten was acquitted by reason of insanity, but this result led to an uproar. It would not be the last insanity verdict that led to public upheaval. Judges were then asked to formulate the criteria for legal insanity. This was their response to this question:

> At the time of committing the act, the party accused was labouring under such a defect of reason, from disease of the mind, as not to know the nature and quality of the act

---

[5] See the English translation of the Breivik verdict Lovdata TOSLO-2011-188627-24E.

he was doing; or if he did know it, that he did not know what he was doing was wrong
(M'Naghten)[6]

So, if the defendant, due to a disease of the mind, did not know the nature, quality, or wrongfulness of the act, he is legally insane. The standard is currently
being used in England and Wales and in many states in the United States. However, there is debate about this standard. The standard is generally considered to
cover at least in part what people feel to be relevant for legal insanity. According to many scholars, if a person fulfills the criteria of the standard, the person
should be considered insane. Still, many are worried that the criterion for insanity
is too narrow (Meynen, 2016; Moratti & Patterson, 2016; Sinnot-Armstrong &
Levy, 2011; Slobogin, 2018). Mental illnesses may not only lead to insanity,
it is argued, because they affect a person's knowledge—the M'Naghten rule is
all about the defendant's knowledge—but also by affecting the person's behavioral control. For instance, a defendant may have been forced to do something
by an auditory command hallucination, which she could not but obey. She may
still have known the nature and quality of the act and she may even have felt
that the act was wrong, but she could not disobey the command. In a way, the
commanding voice 'hijacked' her behavioral control: she was 'made to do' what
she did by a psychopathological phenomenon. Still, this person cannot be found
legally insane under M'Naghten. Meanwhile, many may feel that this person
should also be a candidate for the insanity defense because her *behavior* was to
such a large degree determined by a psychopathological phenomenon (the voice).
Many countries and jurisdictions therefore have added a 'control element' to the
'knowledge' part. An example is the Model Penal Code insanity test, which is
used in a minority of US states. It reads as follows:

> a person is not responsible for criminal conduct if at the time of such conduct as a
> result of mental disease or defect he lacks substantial capacity either to appreciate the
> criminality (wrongfulness) of his conduct or to conform his conduct to the requirements
> of the law.[7]

In this standard we recognize the component of appreciating the wrongfulness
(echoing a part of M'Naghten), but there is a second element referring to one's
behavioral control. The Model Penal Code standard acknowledges that the effects
of mental illnesses may be such that, although the person recognizes that what he
is doing is wrong, the person could not control his behavior in accordance with

---

[6] M'Naghten's Case, 10 Cl. & Fin. 200, 8 Eng. Rep. 718 (H.L. 1843).
[7] Model Penal Code (American Law Institute 1985).

such knowledge. There are many more countries that have standards consisting of these two components—knowledge/appreciation and control—for instance Germany (German Penal Code (*Strafgesetzbuch*), section 20), Italy (Messina et al., 2019), and China (Zhao & Ferguson, 2013).

In Norway, until 2020, a very different insanity criterion was used. As, Løvlie writes, "The Norwegian Penal Code section 20, first paragraph letter b, has a specific reference: 'To be liable for punishment the offender must be accountable at the time of the act. The offender is not accountable if, at the time of the act, he/she is […] psychotic […]'" (Løvlie, 2019, p. 81). This criterion deviates from both standards we discussed—M'Naghten and the Model Penal Code test—in two ways. First, it does not stipulate a specific effect of the mental illness. While M'Naghten refers to effects on knowledge and the Model Penal Code test refers to effects on appreciation and control, the Norwegian standard merely mentions the illness. Second, while both earlier mentioned standards refer to mental disease *in general*, the Norwegian Penal Code specified a type of disorder: psychosis. Psychosis is central: if a person was psychotic at the time of the crime, the defendant will be considered legally insane—but if the defendant was not psychotic, the defendant will be considered sane (Melle, 2013). This is why in the Breivik case the central question was whether he suffered from a psychotic disorder. The first pair of psychiatrists who had evaluated Breivik concluded that he suffered from a psychotic illness, more specifically schizophrenia, paranoid type. Meanwhile, the second pair of psychiatrists concluded that even though there was some psychopathology, the defendant was not psychotic, and therefore, not legally insane. The court followed the second pair, providing a detailed argument explaining this decision (Syse, 2014).[8]

Yet another legal approach to defining insanity is found in The Netherlands. The criterion for legal insanity reads: "A person who commits an offence for which he cannot be held responsible by reason of the mental disorder, psychogeriatric illness and/or intellectual disability is not criminally liable."[9] This standard leaves both the nature and impact of the mental disorder open. This was, at the time, done deliberately: to leave as much room for both the expert and the court in deciding about a person's legal insanity. Research shows that judges apply a wide variety of criteria to decide on the insanity of the defendant (Bijlsma, 2016).

As said, ultimately, the judge or jury will decide whether the insanity criteria have been fulfilled. But in some jurisdictions, behavioral experts are allowed not

---

[8] See the English translation of the Breivik verdict Lovdata TOSLO-2011-188627-24E.

[9] Netherlands (1997). *The Dutch penal code.* Littleton, CO: F.B. Rothman. The American Series of Foreign Penal Codes. With adaptation because of a recent modification.

only to make statements about the presence of a mental disorder and its impact, but also regarding the ultimate question of the defendant's insanity, while in other legal systems, such statements are not allowed. Some scholars argue that as legal insanity is a legal matter it would be wise for behavioral experts not to make statements about it, and to restrict themselves to psychiatric and psychological concepts (Appelbaum, 2008).

In this section we have discussed four criteria for legal insanity, illustrating the variety of standards: the M'Naghten rule, the Model Penal Code test, psychosis as a criterion, and the 'open' criterion used in the Netherlands. Even though there is much variation, elements of the standards tend to be: a mental disorder resulting in problems with knowledge/appreciation and/or behavioral control.

Reliability of Insanity Assessments

Several concerns have been raised regarding the reliability of psychiatric and psychological insanity assessments, in this section we discuss two important topics. First, the evaluation of insanity concerns a moment in the *past*, and the past is gone. Typically, the crime has been committed weeks or months before the psychiatric evaluations take place. This entails that the mental state of the defendant may have changed considerably compared to the moment of the crime. For instance, the crime may have been committed under the influence of a psychotic state, induced by taking Mefloquine (Lariam), which is a medication against malaria which may sometimes induce a psychotic state. The defendant may have fully recovered by the time the evaluation is performed, so the psychosis will no longer manifest itself in the person's behavior. This means that, to a great extent, the psychiatrist will have to rely on the information the defendant can provide— as far as he remembers—about the events at the time of the crime. In addition, a relevant issue here may also be that our memory is not always reliable. If psychiatric diagnosis may be challenging in everyday clinical work, it will be extra challenging in retrospect.

Still, we should realize that both in psychiatry and in criminal law, retrospective assessments are not exceptional (Meynen, 2016). In fact, judgments about a defendant's intent, *mens rea*, or recklessness are also in retrospect; a criminal case always starts *after* the act, never during the act. In defense of retrospective assessments of mental illness in defendants, Morse and Bonnie write that the "severe mental disorder that is necessary for practical support of an insanity defense is in most cases easier to prove than ordinary mens rea" (2013, p. 493). In other words, the psychiatrist's task to retrospectively assess an illness may, in this respect, be easier than making a judgment about the crucial legal issue of mens rea. In addition, we should acknowledge that psychiatrists more often retrospectively diagnose a disorder, for instance in civil cases, in cases of people who have been traumatized, or in everyday clinical practice. For instance, if a patient is seen by a psychiatrist because of a depressive episode, the psychiatrist will try to determine whether there have been depressive episodes in the past.

A second point of concern regards the risk of faking a disease (malingering) or faking good (dissimulation, behaving as if one is healthy) (Gold & Frierson, 2018). To a considerable degree, psychiatrists have to rely on a patient's or defendant's own words in order to be able to establish the presence of a disorder. Psychiatry has a profound interest in 'subjective' phenomena, such as a person's mood, fears, anger, hopes, desires, obsessions, etcetera. Usually, people have to *tell* psychiatrists and psychologists about these phenomena, otherwise they will not know about them; 'objective' tests for establishing the presence of a mental illness are—apart from some neuropsychiatric disorders (see below)—not available. More specifically, there are currently no brain scans that could detect or visualize paranoid delusions, hallucinations, sexual desires, and so on. Yet, patients and defendants need not be truthful about the signs and symptoms they are experiencing. In fact, the risk of deception is often considered increased in the context of a criminal case. Defendants may try to behave as if they have a disorder if they feel that this will help to achieve a favorable legal outcome. Being considered insane may result in involuntary admission to a mental hospital but for some defendants this may be preferable to a long prison sentence. In other cases, a defendant may feel that he should hide his symptoms and try to convince the psychiatrist and psychologist that he is sane in order to avoid an insanity verdict. The risk of both scenarios is generally recognized in forensic psychiatry and psychology—and it entails a challenge (Meynen, 2017). This makes forensic psychiatric assessment (extra) vulnerable for malingering and faking good.

Surely, forensic evaluators are aware of this risk, and they will be on the alert regarding discrepancies between the things a defendant says or between the defendant's account and information from other sources, such as police files or, if available, medical information about earlier admissions to a mental hospital. For instance, the expert may obtain parts of a person's medical record, providing evidence of (previous) psychotic and/or manic episodes. Witness accounts may provide important information about the defendants' actions and their utterances at the time of the crime. In general, obtaining and corroborating evidence from different sources is crucial in forensic psychiatric assessments.

Neuroscience and Insanity Evaluations

Can neuroimaging be used to make psychiatric assessments of legal insanity more 'objective' (Meynen, 2020)? Brain scans have already been used in assessments of a defendant's sanity (de Kogel & Westgeest, 2015). Yet, concerns have been raised that showing brain scans in the courtroom may unduly impress the jury (Shniderman, 2014). In clinical and forensic practice, neuroimaging can be helpful to diagnose a neurological or neuropsychiatric disorder, such as Alzheimer's dementia or vascular dementia. Still, in the standard diagnostic process of psychiatric disorders such as bipolar disorder, autism, depression, and psychosis, brain scans are not routinely used, in spite of decades of neurobiological research on these disorders. Incidentally, brain scans may be used in psychiatric practice, but often to exclude the presence of a neurological disorder, such as a brain tumor or epilepsy (Linden, 2012; Meynen, 2020).

In a forensic setting, if some brain abnormality has been found, the relevance of that abnormality (e.g., a brain tumor) with respect to the legally relevant act has to be established. Some brain tumors may not influence a person's mental functioning at all, while others have disastrous consequences for a person's capacities. In order to get more insight into the impact of the neurological or neuropsychiatric disorder on the person's functioning, a neuropsychological evaluation may be performed (Meynen, 2019). In such an evaluation, a neuropsychologist examines specific neurocognitive functions—such as planning and impulse-control—and, if dysfunctions are observed, she tries to relate them to behavioral problems the person may encounter. This may also shed light on how the brain abnormality may have impacted on the person's behavior at the time of the crime. It is good to keep in mind that brain abnormalities per se do not have to be relevant for the question about a defendant's sanity: it is always about the relevance of the abnormalities for the legal question at hand. In fact, given the current state of neuroscience, the role of neuroimaging and measurements of biological parameters is very limited. Still, in some criminal cases, it provides relevant information. Therefore, it is important that forensic psychiatrists and psychologists recognize signs and symptoms of neurological disease and know when and how to consult a neurologist for further examination.

Conclusion

Legal insanity is an intriguing element of criminal law and it is often considered crucial for the fairness of the justice system. We have discussed some of the challenges it entails, both from a legal perspective and from a psychiatric and psychological perspective. Even though, eventually, the judge or jury decides about a defendant's sanity, it is of utmost importance that behavioral experts provide them with all the relevant information in order for justice to be done.

References

Appelbaum, P. S. (2008). Ethics and forensic psychiatry: Translating principles into practice. *Journal of the American Academy of Psychiatry and the Law, 36*(2), 195–200.

Bijlsma, J. (2016). *Stoornis en strafuitsluiting.* Wolf Legal Publishers.

Bijlsma, J., Kooijmans, T., de Jong, F., & Meynen, G. (2019). Legal insanity and risk: An international perspective on the justification of indeterminate preventive commitment. *International Journal of Law and Psychiatry, 66*, 101462. https://doi.org/10.1016/j.ijlp. 2019.101462

Bonnie, R. J. (1983). The moral basis of the insanity defense. *American Bar Association Journal, 69*(2), 194–197.

Dimock, S. (2011). What are Intoxicated Offenders Responsible for? The "Intoxication Defense" Reexamined. *Criminal Law and Philosophy, 5*, 1–20. https://doi.org/10.1007/s11572-010-9097-2

de Kogel, C. H., & Westgeest, E. J. (2015). Neuroscientific and behavioral genetic information in criminal cases in the Netherlands. *Journal of Law and the Biosciences, 2*(3), 580–605. https://doi.org/10.1093/jlb/lsv024

Gold, L. H., & Frierson, R. L. (Eds.). (2018). *The American Psychiatric Association publishing textbook of forensic psychiatry* (3rd ed.). American Psychiatric Association Publishing.

Gröning, L., Haukvik, U., Meynen, G., & Radovic, S. (2020). Constructing criminal insanity: The roles of Legislators, Judges and Experts in Norway, Sweden and the Netherlands. *New Journal of European Criminal Law, 11*(3), 390–410.

Linden, D. (2012). Overcoming self-report: Possibilities and limitations of brain imaging in psychiatry. In S. Richmond, G. Rees, & S. Edwards (Eds.), *I know what you're thinking: Brain imaging and mental privacy* (pp. 123–135). Oxford University Press.

Løvlie, A. (2019). Criminal Insanity: Concepts and Evidence. *Bergen Journal of Criminal Law and Criminal Justice, 7*(1), 78–96.

Melle, I. (2013). The Breivik case and what psychiatrists can learn from it. *World Psychiatry, 12*(1), 16–21. https://doi.org/10.1002/wps.20002

Messina, E., Ferracuti, S., Nicolò, G., Ruggeri, M., Kooijmans, T., & Meynen, G. (2019). Forensic psychiatric evaluations of defendants: Italy and the Netherlands compared. *International Journal of Law and Psychiatry, 66*(September–October), 101473.

Meynen, G. (2016). *Legal insanity. Explorations in Psychiatry, Law, and Ethics.* Springer.

Meynen, G. (2017). Brain-based mind reading in forensic psychiatry: Exploring possibilities and perils. *Journal of Law and the Biosciences, 4*(2), 311–329. https://doi.org/10.1093/jlb/lsx006

Meynen, G. (2019). Forensic psychiatry and neurolaw: Description, developments, and debates. *International Journal of Law and Psychiatry, 65*. https://doi.org/10.1016/j.ijlp. 2018.04.005

Meynen, G. (2020). Neuroscience-based psychiatric assessments of criminal responsibility: Beyond self-report? *Cambridge Quarterly of Healthcare Ethics, 29*(3), 446–458.

Meynen, G. (2021). The insanity defense. In B. Brożek, J. Hage, & N. A. Vincent (Eds.), *Law and mind: A survey of the law and the cognitive sciences.* Cambridge University Press.

Moratti, S., & Patterson, D. M. (Eds.). (2016). *Legal insanity and the brain: Science, law and European courts; with a foreword by Justice Andrâas Sajâo, Vice-President of the European Court of Human Rights.* Hart.

Morse, S. J. (2011). Mental disorder and criminal law. *Journal of Criminal Law and Criminology, 101*(3), 885–968.

Morse, S. J., & Bonnie, R. J. (2013). Abolition of the insanity defense violates due process. *Journal of the American Academy of Psychiatry and the Law, 41*(4), 488–495.

Robinson, D. N. (1996). *Wild beasts & idle humours: The insanity defense from antiquity to the present.* Harvard University Press.

Shniderman, A. B. (2014). The selective allure of neuroscience and its implications for the courtroom. *The Jury Expert, 26*(4), 1–3.

Sinnott-Armstrong, W., & Levy, K. (2011). Insanity defenses. In J. Deigh & D. Dolinko (Eds.), *The Oxford handbook of philosophy of criminal law.* Oxford University Press.

Slobogin, C. (2018). Introduction to this special issue: The characteristics of insanity and the insanity evaluation process. *Behavioral Sciences & the Law, 36*(3), 271–275. https://doi.org/10.1002/bsl.2342

Syse, A. (2014). Breivik - The Norwegian terrorist case. *Behavioral Sciences & the Law, 32*(3), 389–407. https://doi.org/10.1002/bsl.2121

Zhao, L., & Ferguson, G. (2013). Understanding China's mental illness defense. *The Journal of Forensic Psychiatry & Psychology, 24*(5), 634–657.

Further Reading Suggestions

Bijlsma, J. (2018). A new interpretation of the modern two-pronged tests for insanity. Why legal insanity should not be a 'status defense'. *Netherlands Journal of Legal Philosophy, 47*(1), 29–48.

Meynen, G. (2016). *Legal insanity: Explorations in psychiatry, law, and ethics.* Springer.

Meynen, G. (2020). Neuroscience-based Psychiatric Assessments of Criminal Responsibility: Beyond self-report? *Cambridge Quarterly of Healthcare Ethics, 29*(3), 446–458.

Moratti, S., & Patterson, D. (Eds.). (2016). *Legal insanity and the brain: Science, law and European Courts.* Hart.

Morse, S. J., & Bonnie, R. J. (2013). Abolition of the insanity defense violates due process. *Journal of the American Academy of Psychiatry and the Law, 4*(1), 488–495.

Sinnott-Armstrong, W., & Levy, K. (2011). Insanity defenses. In J. Deigh & D. Dolinko (Eds.), *The Oxford handbook of philosophy of criminal law.* Oxford University Press.

Common Psychological Treatments Used to Address Criminal Behavior

29

Michael Daffern, Nina Papalia, Emily Stevenson, and Stuart Thomas

Key Points

- Psychological treatments for people with a history of sexual and violent offences can have a positive impact on the risk of recidivism.
- Intensive programs delivered within a designated treatment unit that incorporated relapse prevention, role-play, homework, interpersonal skills, and anger control appeared to be associated with larger reductions in violent recidivism.
- Group-based cognitive-behavioral programs delivered in the community by expert practitioners appear to produce better outcomes for people with histories of sexual offending.

M. Daffern (✉) · N. Papalia · E. Stevenson
Swinburne University of Technology, Melbourne, VIC, Australia
e-mail: mdaffern@swin.edu.au

N. Papalia
e-mail: npapalia@swin.edu.au

E. Stevenson
e-mail: estevenson@swin.edu.au

S. Thomas
Criminology & Justice Studies, School of Global, Urban and Social Studies, RMIT University, Melbourne, VIC, Australia
e-mail: stuartdm.thomas@rmit.edu.au

© The Author(s), under exclusive license to Springer Nature Switzerland AG 2022   567
C. Garofalo and J. J. Sijtsema (eds.), *Clinical Forensic Psychology*,
https://doi.org/10.1007/978-3-030-80882-2_29

Introduction

Before proceeding with a discussion of contemporary psychological treatments and their impacts on criminal recidivism, it is worth considering how current treatment practices emerged and why they feature prominently in the rehabilitation strategies of many jurisdictions around the world. A critical point in the development of current correctional rehabilitation practice was Robert Martinson and colleagues (Martinson, 1974) review of the accumulated evidence concerning the effectiveness of "offender treatment"; the seminal report of this work is titled "What Works? Questions and Answers About Prison Reform". Martin's (1974) conclusion was pessimistic, noting "with few and isolated exceptions, the rehabilitative efforts that have been reported so far have had no appreciable effect on recidivism" (p. 25), and further, "our present strategies … cannot overcome, or even appreciably reduce, the powerful tendencies of offenders to continue in criminal behavior" (p. 49). Although Lipton and colleagues' ultimate report presented a more positive perspective, noting "the field of corrections *has not as yet* [emphasis added] found satisfactory ways to reduce recidivism by significant amounts" (p. 627) and Martinson (1979) later withdrew his earlier negative position, noting that "some treatment programs do have an appreciable effect on recidivism" (p. 244), the fundamental message, that "nothing works" prevailed and the relative emphasis on rehabilitation was dampened, with an emphasis instead placed on punishment and deterrence. It was not until the early 1990s, when Canadian scholars identified and promoted key principles of successful offender rehabilitation that the emphasis on rehabilitation within correctional services was renewed.

In 1990, Andrews, Bonta, and Hoge noted that "some service programs are working with at least some offenders under some circumstances, and we think that helpful linkages among case, service, and outcome are suggested by three principles" (p. 374), **risk, need and responsivity** (RNR). These three principles now underpin rehabilitation practices in many correctional settings around the world. The RNR framework has been expanded (Andrews & Bonta, 1994) and now includes a range of overarching, core, and organizational principles as well as key clinical issues. Other models, including Ward and colleagues Good Lives Model (GLM, see, e.g., Ward & Mann, 2004) (Chapter 27) have emerged and this approach, often integrated with RNR informed interventions, has contributed to new service provision and psychological treatment (see below), though the evidence-base for GLM is limited as compared with the RNR literature (Andrews et al., 2011; Mallion et al., 2020).

In general, and without pre-empting the main content of this chapter, treatment outcome evaluation research[1] suggests that psychological treatments can produce positive outcomes (McGuire, 2013), particularly for those treatments that adhere to RNR principles. For example, a recent review of 68 studies focusing on treatment outcomes for sexual, domestic violence, and general violence programs found offence-specific recidivism for treated individuals (13.4%) was lower than for untreated individuals (19.4%) (Gannon et al., 2019). Further meta-analyses of treatment outcomes for people who have committed sexual offences (Schmucker & Lösel, 2015) and violent offences (Papalia et al., 2019) suggest that treatment confers an advantage, in terms of reduced recidivism for those who complete treatment. We now turn to a review of treatments for people convicted of violent, and then sexually violent offences.

Treatments for People with a History of Violent Offending

This section summarizes key psychological treatments for violent offenders and examines their effectiveness in reducing recidivism. It begins with a description of the types of treatments delivered to violent offenders, with an emphasis on programs that demonstrate success in reducing reoffending. To assist with organizing the discussion, we group treatment types according to their primary focus, although we recognize there is often overlap: (1) cognitive skills and other CBT treatments; (2) anger management programs; (3) multi-modal programs; and (4) second/third-wave CBT treatments. While we do not exclude treatments for female violent offenders, the evidence-base overwhelmingly relates to men, so this is our emphasis. This section ends with a summary and an overview of findings from systematic reviews and meta-analyses.

Treatments for Violent Offenders and Their Effectiveness

Cognitive Skills and Other CBT Treatments

Cognitive skills and other cognitive-behavioral treatments emphasize the role of thinking errors and antisocial cognitions in contributing to violent behavior. A key aim of these treatments is to assist offenders to identify cognitive distortions

---

[1] Most offender treatment outcome research has focused on criminal recidivism as the primary outcome. We note that there is likely to be benefit in broadening outcomes so that they include wellbeing, engagement with social and family, education and employment, and other markers of successful reintegration.

and thought patterns that support crime and to learn new ways of thinking about and solving their problems (Ware et al., 2011). Treatments in this category are usually briefer (i.e., 15 to 32 hours); however, moderate (72 hours) and more intensive (300 hours) programs also exist.

Only three studies examined the impact of cognitive skills programs on violent recidivism, with none reporting significant effects. Henning and Frueh (1996) evaluated the cognitive self-change (CSC) program among 196 offenders, most of whom (84%) had adult convictions for violence. Participants were taught to recognize, monitor, manage, and alter criminogenic thinking. Group treatment sessions were delivered 3–5 times per week for 10 months on average, totaling around 300 hours. Program participants had fewer violent reconvictions at 24-months follow-up than untreated offenders (11% vs. 22%); however, differences were not statistically significant. Two other community-based CBT programs—"CBT for Antisocial Personality Disorder' and 'Choosing to Think, Thinking to Choose"—have undergone evaluation using randomized-controlled designs (Barnes et al., 2017; Davidson et al., 2009). Both programs involved weekly sessions, with Davidson et al. consisting of 15–30 hours of individual treatment and Barnes et al. involving 28 hours of group treatment. After 12 months, there were no significant differences in rates of violent reoffending for violent offenders allocated to the treatments and those allocated to treatment-as-usual.

Some studies have examined whether cognitive skills programs reduce violence in prisons and forensic mental health settings. Hogan et al. (2012), for example, found that the CHANGE program resulted in significantly fewer violent misconducts at 6-months follow-up among violent inmates. CHANGE taught the meaning of cognitive self-change and how cognitive distortions influence attitudes, beliefs, and thinking patterns. It consisted of 24–32 hours of individual and group-based treatment. Similarly, Cullen et al. (2012) evaluated the Reasoning and Rehabilitation (R&R) program on frequency of institutional incidents among 84 mentally disordered violent offenders. R&R is a well-known cognitive-skills offender program (Robinson & Porporino, 2001), however, evidence for its effectiveness with violent offenders is limited. The highly structured program involved 36 two-hour, group-based sessions encompassing eight core modules: problem-solving; assertiveness skills; social skills; negotiation skills; creative thinking; emotion management; values reasoning; and critical reasoning. During 12-months follow-up, R&R participants engaged in significantly fewer incidents of verbal aggression than treatment-as-usual participants. Incident rates for violence were also lower in R&R participants but differences were not statistically significant.

Anger Management Programs

Drawing on Novaco's adaptation of stress inoculation training (Meichenbaum, 1985; Novaco et al., 2001), anger management (AM) programs aim to increase offenders' awareness of anger and its triggers and teach a range of skills to reduce anger arousal and improve anger control (Ware et al., 2011); the underlying assumption being that dysregulated anger increases violence propensity. AM programs are usually delivered in groups and range in length from around 20 to 50 hours.

While some evidence suggests that AM programs reduce general recidivism (Bowes et al., 2014; Dowden et al., 1999), few studies have examined impacts on violent recidivism. Studies measuring violent reoffending show lower rates among offenders participating in AM relative to comparisons, but differences are rarely statistically significant (Bowes et al., 2014; Dowden et al., 1999; Hughes, 1993).[2] Dowden et al. (1999) evaluated Canada's Anger and Other Emotions Management Programme (AOEMP) with 220 violent offenders. Drawing on rational-emotive therapy and Meichenbaum's (1985) self-instructional training, AOEMP aimed to reduce aggression through emotion regulation skills development. Skills encompassed self-management and self-control skills, effective problem-solving, communication, identifying high-risk situations, and examining and correcting thinking errors underlying emotions-based aggression. AOEMP had an emphasis on staff involvement (e.g., modeling, role-play, providing feedback, and homework) and was longer (25 two-hour group sessions, 2–5 times per week) than other AM programs. After three years post-release, there were no significant differences between AOEMP offenders and matched comparisons in rates of violent recidivism, but time to violent reoffence was longer among AOEMP offenders. Further, when examined by offender risk level, AOEMP had a significant positive effect on violent recidivism for high-risk offenders only.

Other studies have evaluated AM outcomes on violent and general institutional misconducts, with no significant differences observed between treated and untreated violent offenders (Dowden & Serin, 2001; Watt & Howells, 1999; Wilson et al., 2013).

Multi-Modal Programs

Contemporary multi-modal treatment programs for violent offenders are generally more intensive and target a broader range of dynamic risk factors than

---

[2] However, when Papalia et al. (2019) pooled the effects for AM programs in their meta-analysis (three studies), the result was a statistically significant reduction in violent recidivism overall.

cognitive skills and AM programs. These programs are typically delivered over a series of modules that map onto areas of criminogenic need. Most multimodal violent offender treatments comprise up to 200 hours of intervention. However, residential multi-modal programs—that is, programs where participants reside in a designated therapeutic treatment unit/facility for the duration of the intervention—are longer, usually more than 250 hours.

Non-residential Programs

Non-residential multi-modal violence reduction programs comprise around 150–200 hours of group treatment; programs as brief as 40 hours and as long as 300 hours also exist. Violent offenders are often required to complete such programs before being eligible for release. Contemporary examples include: Persistently Violent Offender Programme (Serin et al., 2009), Violence Prevention Program (Cortoni et al., 2006; Higgs et al., 2018), and Aggressive Behavioural Control Program (Wong et al., 2012) in Canada; Violence Intervention Program in Australia (O'Brien & Daffern, 2016); the 300-hour Life Minus Violence–Enhanced Program developed in the UK (Daffern et al., 2017; Ireland, 2008); and the 40-hour Beyond Violence Trauma-Informed Program for women in the US (Covington, 2013; Kubiak et al., 2016).

Evidence for the impact of the above programs on violent recidivism has been mixed, with some evaluations showing no treatment effect or non-significant reductions in favor of treated offenders (Motiuk et al., 1996; O'Brien & Daffern, 2016; Serin et al., 2009; Wong et al., 2012). The Canadian Violence Prevention Program (VPP) has shown some promise. The VPP is a cognitive-behavioral reintegration program underpinned by social learning and social information-processing theories aimed at high-risk persistently violent male prisoners. It includes 10 modules delivered over 94 two-hour group sessions, at six sessions per week. Treatment targets include motivation enhancement, violence awareness, anger control, problem-solving, pro-social attitudes, positive relationships, conflict resolution, positive lifestyles, and self-control, with a broader emphasis on relapse prevention. An initial large-scale and rigorous evaluation of VPP found lower rates of general and violent recidivism among treated offenders relative to matched comparisons (Cortoni et al., 2006). A recent, similarly designed evaluation of VPP found a significant treatment effect for general recidivism at three-year follow-up, but effects for violent recidivism were only significant for Indigenous offenders (Higgs et al., 2018).

Residential Programs

Few evaluations of residential multi-modal violent offender treatments exist, but these generally show positive effects. Examples include the Violent Offender Treatment Program in Australia (Rahman et al., 2018), Montgomery-House Violence Prevention Program (Berry, 1998, 2003), and Violence Prevention Unit Program (VPUP) in New Zealand. The most compelling evidence for effectiveness comes from the VPUP; an intensive cognitive-behavioral intervention for high-risk violent offenders who are nearing the end of their custodial sentences. The intervention was delivered by a psychologist and rehabilitation worker to a group of 10 men who resided together in a 30-bed unit. Prisoners undertook 330 hours of highly structured treatment over 8 months, with 2- to 3- hour sessions four times per week. Program targets included identifying and presenting the offence chain, restructuring violence-supportive thinking, mood management, victim empathy, moral reasoning, problem-solving, relationship and communication skills, and relapse prevention planning. The program strongly emphasized active participant engagement in sessions, modeling and rehearsing learned skills in sessions, and practicing these skills out in the unit. An initial small-scale evaluation comparing VPUP completers to untreated offenders on violent recidivism at 2-years post-release showed a large positive treatment effect (Polaschek et al., 2005). An updated and more rigorous evaluation similarly demonstrated positive effects for violent recidivism, but only among high-risk violent offenders (Polaschek, 2011).

The VPUP was subsequently expanded, now comprising four purpose-built High-Risk Special Treatment Units (HRSTUs). The treatment framework is now a hybrid, combining the structured closed-group cognitive-behavioral approach described above with a hierarchical democratic therapeutic community model. Participants attend group sessions totaling around 250 hours over 25 weeks and remain in the therapeutic unit for 10–12 months. Alongside the treatment program, participants are involved in a range of other activities within the unit and are assisted to develop a comprehensive reintegration plan in preparation for their release from prison in the months following the program. A recent evaluation comparing HRSTU completers to comparable prisoners showed a significant positive treatment effect for violent reconvictions at 12-months follow-up (Polaschek et al., 2016). These findings were not explained by differences between groups on baseline risk-level and motivation to change.

Second/Third-Wave CBT Treatments

We could not locate any controlled evaluations of second and third-wave CBT programs that included violent recidivism outcomes. However, two studies examined the impact of these treatments on violent offenders' institutional behavior. Tarrier et al. (2010) evaluated Schema Modal Therapy (SMT) with male personality disordered forensic inpatients. SMT emphasizes Schema Modes, which are "sets of schemata with an associated state of emotional arousal and patterns of interpersonal behavior" (Tarrier et al., 2010, p. 3). SMT involves a set of techniques that allow the therapist to work with the rapidly changing emotional states and coping responses that are hallmark features of severe personality disorder. Treatment comprised 96 hours of individual sessions. Both the treatment and control groups showed a reduction in mean number of aggressive incidents from baseline (6.48 vs. 5.26) to 36 months (2.32 vs. 1.32).

Tomlinson and Hoaken (2017) undertook a small-scale ($n = 18$) controlled trial of Dialectical Behavior Therapy (DBT) with violent forensic inpatients. DBT was developed to treat highly emotionally dysregulated individuals and focuses on improving skills relating to mindfulness, interpersonal effectiveness, emotion regulation, and distress tolerance. It involved weekly 90-min group sessions over 6 months (32 hours) combined with individual skills coaching sessions. At six months follow-up, offenders participating in DBT had fewer violent incidents than a control group, but differences were not statistically significant.

Summary and Key Findings from Existing Reviews

The evidence-base for the impact of psychological treatments for violent offenders is surprisingly small, particularly when rigorous study quality criteria are applied. Although the aforementioned sections highlight some positive impacts of various types of programs, there remain only two meta-analyses exploring treatment outcomes for violent offenders (Jolliffe & Farrington, 2007; Papalia et al., 2019). In the first meta-analysis of violent offender treatments, Jolliffe and Farrington (2007) identified 11 studies of sufficient quality, ranging from small-scale evaluations of anger management programming comprising 12 weekly two-hour sessions, to a small ($n = 22$) but intensive (330 hours) multi-module intervention for high-risk violent offenders in a residential treatment program. Eight studies examined treatment outcomes for violent reoffending, two of which reported a statistically significant positive effect, four reported a reduction in violent reoffending that was not statistically significant, and two reported an increase in violent reoffending. The combined effect was a 7–8 percentage point reduction in violent reoffending for those receiving treatment (Jolliffe & Farrington, 2007). Further analyses revealed that treatment effects varied according to certain study characteristics, the content and delivery of the intervention, and methodological quality. For example, there was a positive relationship between treatment duration (overall and per session) and reductions in general and violent reoffending. Further, treatments that addressed cognitive skills, anger control, used role-play and relapse prevention, and had participants complete homework demonstrated larger reductions in reoffending (Jolliffe & Farrington, 2007).

Subsequently, Papalia et al. (2019) were only able to locate and meta-analyze the impact of 16 rigorous evaluations of violent offender treatments on violent recidivism. They found that treatments were effective overall, with a 10-percentage point reduction in violent recidivism in favor of those receiving treatment. Intensive multi-modal programs that incorporated relapse prevention, role-play, offender homework, interpersonal skills, and anger control appeared to be associated with larger reductions in violent recidivism than treatments not incorporating these components. Further, the authors found that treatments involving more frequent sessions per week and that were delivered within a designated treatment unit or therapeutic community-style unit also related to more positive effects on violent reoffending. Not surprisingly, study design predicted the size of the treatment effect, with studies rated as higher risk of bias (e.g., non-randomized and non-matched treatment and comparison groups) showing more positive effects. Collectively, the above two reviews suggest that psychological treatments for violent offenders have the capacity to reduce violent recidivism, but the effect is modest, highlighting the need to improve treatments.

Treatment for People with a History of Sexual Offending

This section examines the range of treatments available for sexual offenders and their effectiveness with respect to reducing criminal recidivism. It begins by considering the available international research evidence arising from published systematic reviews and meta-analyses, then moves on to a more nuanced consideration of different types of programs, focusing on those aspects which have shown most promise over time.

Key Findings from Existing Reviews

Despite populist perceptions to the contrary, robust international research has consistently shown that sexual offenders have relatively low rates of recidivism (generally operationalized as reconviction for a subsequent offence) when compared to other types of offenders (Goodman-Delahunty & O'Brien, 2014). Sexual offender treatment programs have also been offered in numerous correctional services around the world. While a good deal of the treatment outcome literature is comprised by modest samples and sub-optimal (if any) control groups, a series of published meta-analyses, pooling samples from research published across multiple jurisdictions and over time, have helped develop useful evidence pertaining to the efficacy of sex offender treatment.

An early meta-analysis reported by Hanson and Bussière (1998) found that, in a sample of 23,393 offenders followed up for an average of four to five years, 13.4% of sexual offenders went on to commit a further sexual offence, and that recidivism rates increased to 36.3% when recidivism was broadened to "any" type of criminal recidivism. A subsequent analysis by Hanson (2002), comparing 5,078 treated and 4,376 untreated sexual offenders, reported a sexual recidivism rate of 12.3 and 16.8%, respectively, using a range of follow-up periods from 2 up to 23 years. Other types of criminal recidivism were also found to be lower for treated offenders (27.9%) as compared to untreated offenders (39.2%). In 2009, Hanson and colleagues reported a sexual recidivism rate of 10.9% for treated offenders and 19.2% for non-treated comparisons, and similarly higher rates of general recidivism (31.8% for treated vs. 48.3% for untreated offenders) to those reported in an earlier paper (Hanson, 2002). A further review, this time more specifically focusing on randomized controlled trials evaluating psychological interventions for sex offenders (Dennis et al., 2012), reported no statistically significant differences between treatment and control groups.

More recently, Schmucker and Lösel (2015) reported on a meta-analysis that focused only on studies with a methodologically rigorous treatment design. Their analysis included a total of 28 studies published between 1980 and 2010; a minimum 12-month follow-up period was considered, with some studies providing follow-up periods exceeding 84 months. Overall, their results indicated a sexual recidivism rate of 10.1% in treated and 13.7% in untreated offenders. The most recently published meta-analysis, by Gannon and colleagues (2019), comprised 70 offence specific treatment studies for a range of adult offenders, including sexual offenders. Again, similar to prior studies, they found that, based on an average follow-up of 76.2 months, the rate of sexual recidivism for treated offenders was 9.5% compared to 14.1% for untreated offenders.

Research by Marshall and McGuire (2003) has demonstrated that not all sex offender treatments are equally effective, reporting effect sizes for sexual offender treatments ranging between 0.10 and 0.47. The Schmucker and Lösel (2005) meta-analysis concurred with these findings; while reporting a lower sexual recidivism rate of 11.5% for treated sex offenders compared to controls (17.5%), pooled across 69 studies, they noted a range of both positive and negative effect sizes, indicating both positives and negatives of treatment across individual studies. What these, and other, studies aptly demonstrate is that treatment does not have a uniformly positive effect for all sex offenders; there can be a positive effect, treatment can have no effect (e.g., Dennis et al., 2012), and it can even be deleterious (e.g., Mews et al., 2017). Although the factors that might contribute to these deleterious outcomes are not well known, Mews and colleagues (2017) have speculated that an exclusive reliance on group-based interventions may be a contributing factor. Group-based interventions may not adequately allow for tailoring of treatment and they may also create a normalizing of antisocial attitudes and behavior. In summary, despite occasional adverse outcomes, much of the available research suggests that somewhere between 12 and 30% of those who complete treatment going on to reoffend within five years of release (Watson et al., 2017).

Treatment for Sexual Offenders and Its Effectiveness

It has been shown that pharmacological treatments using anti-libidinal medications, and programs that adopt a cognitive-behavioral therapy (CBT) model, are associated with the most positive treatment outcomes for sex offenders. While the evidence suggests that pharmacological (and surgical) interventions are associated with much greater treatment effects than other psychosocial interventions, the intrusive nature of these interventions have been subject to much criticism (Mpofu et al., 2018). Indeed, more recent programs have focused on the delivery of programs that use a combination of group and individual therapy targeting criminogenic needs tailored to the specifics of an offender profile (Jennings et al., 2017). The majority of contemporary sexual offender treatments delivered are CBT based (Harrison et al., 2020). A recent review suggests that this type of approach is effective with medium and high-risk sexual offenders (Mpofu et al., 2018).

According to extant evidence, sex offender treatment programs should demonstrate a number of core criteria, including that they: (1) have a clear model of change; (2) target offending behavior; demonstrate effective risk management strategies; (3) take different learning styles (and capabilities) into account; maintain program integrity and quality of delivery over time. These map directly to the RNR model, which recommends that program intensity is matched with risk level, that criminogenic needs are targeted, and that treatment style and mode is matched to the offender's learning style (Andrews et al., 2011); greater adherence to these three principles in treatment is associated with better outcomes (Hanson et al., 2009).

More recently, authors have proposed GLM to help inform sex offender treatment programs. Willis et al. (2013) have offered some guidance about integrating GLM into programs that use RNR approaches and argue that it can complement treatment by improving client engagement in treatment (Gannon et al., 2019). Based on findings arising from long-term outcomes of the Rockwood program in Canada, a combination of these approaches have a strong potential to lead to improved treatment outcomes (Olver et al., 2020). While, to date, there are comparatively fewer published outcomes of GLM approaches, moving forward, some have argued that a combination of RNR and GLM approaches are likely to be used in conjunction to target behavioral and motivational change in offenders (Marshall, 2020).

One of the significant challenges facing those engaged in the treatment of sexual offenders is that the literature is not consistent regarding the specifics of the therapeutic content that is associated with moderating treatment outcomes (Day et al., 2019). In fact, a wide range of factors have been reported as impacting on treatment outcomes. For example, Gannon et al. (2019) found that group treatment resulted in greater reductions in sexual reoffending in comparison to individual or mixed individual and group treatment. In addition, Kim et al. (2017) note that, despite some research finding higher rates of drop-out, community-based treatments are more effective than institution-based treatments. Other authors have reported a significant reduction in recidivism when a qualified psychologist was involved in the treatment in comparison to when no psychologist was involved or had intermittent involvement, and when facilitators received supervision from a psychologist. Despite these encouraging findings, the evidence remains equivocal with these and a number of other key aspects of treatment, including treatment timing, length, frequency, and intensity (Day et al., 2019; Kim et al., 2017).

Summary

An established international evidence-base indicates that sexual offenders are criminally versatile; while rates of sexual recidivism have remained relatively low across time and place, general recidivism rates are much higher. The available evidence suggests that well-designed programs can lead to significant reductions in recidivism (Marshall, 2020). Despite considerable advances in the field of practice, there still remain challenges in the delivery of evidence-based sex offender treatment (Deming & Jennings, 2020). As such, for the time being, treatment continues to vary widely depending on where and how it is delivered (Marshall & Marshall, 2010).

Conclusion

This chapter reveals clear benefits, for correctional services who offer psychological treatment, and for participants who engage with and complete psychological treatments that focus on reducing the propensity for criminal behavior. However, the results of various outcome evaluations suggest the degree of benefit is modest and individual differences exist in terms of treatment responses; many people who complete treatment reoffend (Klepfisz et al., 2014). Some scholars note concerns with the elevated status of psychological treatment in the reform of offenders within correctional services. Day (2020) notes that treatment programs are often not powerful enough to produce systemic benefits, and that the focus of these treatments is typically too narrow to create meaningful and lasting change. As Papalia and colleagues (2019) note, more intensive and longer programs and those that build skills and that call on treatment clients to engage in between-session homework tasks tend to have better outcomes. Simply attending therapy in an isolated environment within the prison estate for a brief period each week before returning to the general prison environment is unlikely to enact change.

Day (2020) focuses on the context in which treatments are offered and notes that many prisons are not conducive to change. He writes of the experience of Sir Martin Narey, the former head of Her Majesty' s Prison Service, who oversaw the mass delivery of prisoner rehabilitation programs in England and Wales. Day (2020) reports on Narey's perception of poor outcomes of these programs, which "led Narey to form the view that prisons, by their very nature, served mainly to demoralize and institutionalize rather than to rehabilitate" (p. 1). Key to Narey's discontent was dissatisfaction with the prison environments where treatments were offered; "the best designed and delivered programs should not be expected to effect significant change on participants when they are provided in prisons where rehabilitative learnings are not reinforced outside of the programs room" (pp. 3–4). Consequently, it is important that these interventions occur within environments that support change. We cannot expect offenders to engage in a treatment and to change their behavior if the prison is unsafe and their well-being is undermined (Chapter 31).

It is important that we understand how treatment providers and the settings in which treatments are offered can be improved to enhance treatment practices and outcomes. Psychological treatment is neither necessary, nor is it suitable for every person with a history of offending. More work needs to be done to understand client preferences for treatment and delineate which treatments work best for which offenders and for whom psychological treatment is unhelpful. It is also important that we understand the stage during a person's sentence they might be most interested in, and responsive to treatment. Understanding the needs of offenders and tailoring treatment so that the treatment retains integrity yet is flexibly delivered to be relevant to each offender is important.

The process of change also requires attention. Although there is empirical support for the notion that change (in this context reducing the propensity for offending) occurs via reduction in the presence and impact of dynamic risk factors (Klepfisz et al., 2016) and possibly the enhancement of "protective factors" (Klepfisz et al., 2017), integrating other ideas about personal change derived from the desistance and recovery literatures may promote improved outcomes for psychological treatment. Accordingly, for offender change to occur, staff need to assist offenders to decide to end their offending and help them develop a coherent and plausible pro-social identity where the person no longer sees themselves as a criminal. It is important for this newly formed identity to comprise personally meaningful goals and it must meaningfully reconcile the past, including previous offending behavior (Chapter 8). According to McAlinden et al. (2012) *"the rehabilitation process involves at some level the need to develop a new story for oneself that can explain one's past and give a convincing account of why the person is no longer like that anymore"* (p. 16). This focus on identity change has substantial overlap with the concept of *personal recovery*, which is prominent within the field of mental health. Personal recovery *"involves the development of new meaning and purpose in one's life as one grows beyond the catastrophic effects of mental illness"* (Anthony, 1993, p. 527). Future treatment development work should consider how these concepts derived from the desistance and personal recovery literatures can be integrated into extant programs that are principally focused on ameliorating the presence and impact of dynamic risk factors so that the process of change is coherent, comprehensive, and personally meaningful for offenders. Finally, most attention has focused on the content of treatment, yet process variables, including treatment group cohesion and the therapeutic alliance between treatment providers and clients are likely to be important; these variables have been under-emphasized in research to date. More work in this area is necessary, and may well be enhanced by paying closer attention to offender perspectives with regard to rehabilitation preferences.

References

Andrews, D. A., & Bonta, J. (1994). The psychology of criminal conduct. Cincinnati, OH: Anderson.

Andrews, D. A., Bonta, J., & Wormith, J. S. (2011). The risk-need responsivity model: Does the Good Lives Model contribute to effective crime prevention? *Criminal Justice and Behavior, 38*, 735–755. https://doi.org/10.1177/0093854811406356

Anthony, W. (1993). Recovery from mental illness: The guiding vision of the mental health service system in the 1990s. *Psychosocial Rehabilitation Journal, 16*(4): 11–23.

Barnes, G. C., Hyatt, J. M., & Sherman, L. W. (2017). Even a little bit helps: An implementation and experimental evaluation of cognitive-behavioral therapy for high-risk probationers. *Criminal Justice and Behavior, 44*, 611–630. https://doi.org/10.1177/009385481 6673862

Berry, S. (1998). *The montgomery house violence prevention programme: An evaluation.* Department of Corrections Psychological Service.

Berry, S. (2003). Stopping violent offending in New Zealand: Is treatment an option? *New Zealand Journal of Psychology, 32*, 92–100.

Bowes, N., McMurran, M., Evans, C., Oatley, G., Williams, B., & David, S. (2014). Treating alcohol-related violence: A feasibility study of a randomized controlled trial in prisons. *Journal of Forensic Psychiatry & Psychology, 25*, 152–163.

Cortoni, F., Nunes, K., & Latendresse, M. (2006). *An examination of the effectiveness of the Violence Prevention Program.* Correctional Service of Canada.

Covington, S. (2013). *Beyond violence: A prevention program for women.* Wiley.

Cullen, A. E., Clarke, A. Y., Kuipers, E., Hodgins, S., Dean, K., & Fahy, T. (2012). A multisite randomized trial of a cognitive skills program for male mentally disordered offenders: Violence and antisocial behavior outcomes. *Journal of Consulting and Clinical Psychology, 80*, 1114–1120.

Daffern, M., Simpson, K., Ainslie, H., & Chu, S. (2017). The impact of an intensive inpatient violent offender treatment programme on intermediary treatment targets, violence risk and aggressive behaviour in a sample of mentally disordered offenders. *Journal of Forensic Psychiatry & Psychology.* https://doi.org/10.1080/14789949.2017.1352014

Day, A. (2020). At a crossroads? Offender rehabilitation in Australian prisons. *Psychiatry, Psychology and Law.* Advance online publication. https://doi.org/10.1080/13218719.2020.1751335

Day, A., Ross, S., Casey, S., Vess, J., Johns, D., & Hobbs, G. (2019). The intensity and timing of sex offender treatment. *Sexual Abuse, 3*(4), 397–409. https://doi.org/10.1177/107906 3217745069

Davidson, K. M., Tyrer, P., Tata, P., Cooke, D., Gumley, A., Ford, I., Walker, A., Bezlyak, V., Seivewright, H., Robertson, H., & Crawford, M. J. (2009). Cognitive behaviour therapy for violent men with antisocial personality disorder in the community: An exploratory randomized controlled trial. *Psychological Medicine, 39*(4), 569–577.

Deming, A., & Jennings, J. L. (2020). The absence of evidence-based practices (EBPs) in the treatment of sexual abusers: Recommendations for moving towards the use of a true EBP model. *Sexual Abuse, 32*(6), 679–705. https://doi.org/10.1177/1079063219843897

Dennis, J. A., Khan, O., Ferriter, M., Huband, N., Powney, M. J., & Duggan, C. (2012). Psychological interventions for adults who have sexually offended or are at risk of offending (review). *Cochrane Database of Systematic Reviews, 12.* https://doi.org/10.1002/146 51858.CD007507.pub2

Dowden, C., Blanchette, K., & Serin, R. (1999). *Anger management programming for federal male inmates: An effective intervention.* Canada: Research Branch, Correctional Service Canada.

Dowden, C., & Serin, R. C. (2001). *Anger management programming for offenders: The impact of program performance measures.* Correctional Service of Canada.

Gannon, T. A., Olver, M. E., Mallion, J. S., & James, M. (2019). Does specialized psychological treatment for offending reduce recidivism? A meta-analysis examining staff and program variables as predictors of treatment effectiveness. *Clinical Psychology Review.* Advanced online publication. https://doi.org/10.1016/j.cpr.2019.101752

Goodman-Delahunty, J., & O'Brien, K. (2014). Parental sexual offending: Managing risk through diversion. *Trends amp; Issues in Crime and Criminal Justice* (No. 482), 1–9. Retrieved from http://aic.gov.au/media_library/publications/tandi_pdf/tandi482.pdf

Hanson, R. K., & Bussie're, M. T. (1998). Predicting relapse: A metaanalysis of sexual offender recidivism studies. *Journal of Consulting and Clinical Psychology, 66,* 348–362.

Hanson, R. K. (2002). Recidivism and age: Follow-up data from 4,673 sexual offenders. *Journal of Interpersonal Violence, 17*(10), 1046–1062. https://doi.org/10.1177/088626 002236659

Hanson, R. K., Bourgon, G., Helmus, L., & Hodgson, S. (2009). The principles of effective correctional treatment also apply to sexual offenders: A meta-analysis. *Criminal Justice and Behaviour, 36*(9), 865–891. https://doi.org/10.1177/0093854809338545

Harrison, J. L., O'Toole, S. K., Ammen, S., Ahlmeyer, S., Harrell, S. N., & Hernandez, J. L. (2020). Sexual offender treatment effectiveness within cognitive-behavioral programs: A meta-analytic investigation of general, sexual, and violent recidivism. *Psychiatry, Psychology and Law, 27*(1), 1–25. https://doi.org/10.1080/13218719.2018.1485526

Henning, K. R., & Frueh, B. C. (1996). Cognitive-behavioral treatment of incarcerated offenders - An evaluation of the Vermont Department of Corrections' cognitive self-change program. *Criminal Justice and Behavior, 23,* 523–541. https://doi.org/10.1177/ 0093854896023004001

Higgs, T., Cortoni, F., & Nunes, K. (2018). Reducing violence risk? Some positive recidivism outcomes for Canadian treated high-risk offenders. *Criminal Justice and Behavior, 46*(3), 359–373. https://doi.org/10.1177/0093854818808830

Hogan, N. L., Lambert, E. G., & Barton-Bellessa, S. M. (2012). Evaluation of CHANGE, an involuntary cognitive program for high-risk inmates. *Journal of Offender Rehabilitation, 51,* 370–388. https://doi.org/10.1080/10509674.2012.664254

Hughes, G. V. (1993). Anger management program outcomes. *Forum on Correctional Research, 5,* 5–9.

Ireland, J. L. (2008). Treatment approaches for violence and aggression: Essential content components. In J. L. Ireland, C. A. Ireland, & P. Birch (Eds.), *The assessment, treatment and management of violent and sexual offenders* (pp. 153–178). Willan Publishing.

Jennings, J. L., & Deming, A. (2017). Review of the empirical and clinical support for group therapy specific to sexual abusers. *Sexual Abuse, 29*(8), 731–764. https://doi.org/10.1177/1079063215618376

Jolliffe, D., & Farrington, D. P. (2007). *A systematic review of the national and international evidence on the effectiveness of interventions with violent offenders.* Ministry of Justice.

Kim, H. Y. (2017). Statistical notes for clinical researchers: Chi-squared test and Fisher's exact test. *Restorative Dentistry and Endodontics, 42*(2), 152–155. https://doi.org/10.5395/rde.2017.42.2.152

Klepfisz, G., O'Brien, K., & Daffern, M. (2014). Violent offenders' within-treatment change in anger, criminal attitudes, and violence risk: Associations with violent recidivism. *International Journal of Forensic Mental Health, 13*(4), 348–362. https://doi.org/10.1080/14999013.2014.951107

Klepfisz, G., Daffern, M., & Day, A. (2016). Understanding dynamic risk factors for violence. *Psychology, Crime & Law, 22*(1–2), 124–137. https://doi.org/10.1080/1068316X.2015.1109091

Klepfisz, G., Day, A., & Daffern, M. (2017). Understanding protective factors for violent reoffending in adults. *Aggression and Violent Behavior, 32,* 80–87. https://doi.org/10.1016/j.avb.2016.12.001

Kubiak, S., Fedock, G., Kim, W. J., & Bybee, D. (2016). Long-term outcomes of a RCT intervention study for women with violent crimes. *Journal of the Society for Social Work and Research, 7,* 661–679. https://doi.org/10.1086/689356

Martinson, R. (1974). What works? Questions and answers about prison reform. *The Public Interest, 35,* 22–54.

Marshall, E. L., & McGuire, J. (2003). Effect sizes in the treatment of sexual offenders. *International Journal of Offender Therapy and Comparative Criminology, 47*(6), 653–663. https://doi.org/10.1177/0306624X03256663

Marshall, W. L., & Marshall, L. E. (2010). Attachment and intimacy in sexual offenders: An update. *Sexual and Relationship Therapy, 25*(1), 86–90. https://doi.org/10.1080/14681991003589568

Marshall, L. E. (2020). The utility of treatment for sexual offenders. In J. Proulx, F. Cortoni, L. A. Craig, & E. J. Letourneau (Eds.), The Wiley handbook of what works with sexual offenders: Contemporary perspectives in theory, assessment, treatment, and prevention. John Wiley & Sons.

Mallion, J. S., Wood, J. L., & Mallion, A. (2020). Systematic review of 'Good Lives' Assumptions and interventions. *Aggression and Violent Behavior, 55.* https://doi.org/10.1016/j.avb.2020.101510

McGuire, J. (2013). 'What works' to reduce re-offending: 18 years on. *In* L. A. Craig, L. Dixon, & T. A. Gannon (Eds.), *What works in offender rehabilitation: An evidence-based approach to assessment and treatment* (pp. 20–49). Wiley-Blackwell.

Meichenbaum, D. (1985). *Stress inoculation training.* Pergamon.

Mews, A., Di Bella, L., & Purver, M. (2017). Impact evaluation of the prison-based core sex offender treatment programme. Ministry of Justice. http://herzog-evans.com/wp-content/uploads/2017/07/UK-PROGRAMMES-STOPREPORT-NEGATIVE-FINDINGS.pdf

Motiuk, L., Smiley, C., & Blanchette, K. (1996). Intensive programming for violent offenders: A comparative investigation. *Forum on Correctional Research, 8*, 10–12.

Novaco, R. W., Ramm, M., & Black, L. (2001). Anger treatment with offenders. In C. R. Hollin (Ed.), *Handbook of offender assessment and treatment* (pp. 281–296). Wiley.

O'Brien, K., & Daffern, M. (2016). The impact of pre-treatment responsivity and treatment participation on violent recidivism in a violent offender sample. *Psychology, Crime & Law, 22*(8), 777–797. https://doi.org/10.1080/1068316X.2016.1181177

Olver, M. E., Marshall, L. E., Marshall, W. L., & Nicholaichuk, T. P. (2020). A long-term outcome assessment of the effects on subsequent reoffense rates of a prison-based CBT/RNR sex offender treatment program with strengthbased elements. *Sexual Abuse, 32*(2), 127–153. https://doi.org/10.1177/1079063218807486

Papalia, N., Spivak, B., Daffern, M., & Ogloff, J. R. P. (2019). A meta-analytic review of the efficacy of psychological treatments for violent offenders in correctional and forensic mental health settings. *Clinical Psychology: Science and Practice, 26*(2). https://doi.org/10.1111/cpsp.12282

Petrosino, A., Turpin-Petrosino, C., Hollis-Peel, M. E., & Lavenberg, J. G. (2013). 'Scared Straight' and other juvenile awareness programs for preventing juvenile delinquency. *Cochrane Database of Systematic Reviews*, Issue 4. https://doi.org/10.1002/14651858.CD002796.pub2

Polaschek, D. L. (2011). High-intensity rehabilitation for violent offenders in New Zealand: Reconviction outcomes for high- and medium-risk prisoners. *Journal of Interpersonal Violence, 26*, 664–682. https://doi.org/10.1177/0886260510365854

Polaschek, D. L., Yesberg, J. A., Bell, R. K., Casey, A. R., & Dickson, S. R. (2016). Intensive psychological treatment of high-risk violent offenders: Outcomes and pre-release mechanisms. *Psychology, Crime & Law, 22*(4), 344–365. https://doi.org/10.1080/1068316X.2015.1109088

Polaschek, D. L. L., Wilson, N. J., Townsend, M. R., & Daly, L. R. (2005). Cognitive-behavioral rehabilitation for high-risk violent offenders - An outcome evaluation of the violence prevention unit. *Journal of Interpersonal Violence, 20*, 1611–1627. https://doi.org/10.1177/0886260505280507

Rahman, S., Poynton, S., & Wan, W.-Y. (2018). The effect of the Violent Offender Treatment Program (VOTP) on offender outcomes. *Crime and Justice Bulletin: Contemporary Issues in Crime and Justice, 216*, 1–16.

Robinson, D., & Porporino, F. J. (2001). Programming in cognitive skills: The reasoning and rehabilitation programme. In C. R. Hollin (Ed.), *Handbook of offender assessment and treatment* (pp. 179–193). Wiley.

Serin, R. C., Gobeil, R., & Preston, D. L. (2009). Evaluation of the persistently violent offender treatment program. *International Journal of Offender Therapy and Comparative Criminology, 53*(1), 57–73.

Schmucker, M., & Lösel, F. (2015). The effects of sexual offender treatment on recidivism: An international meta-analysis of sound quality evaluations. *Journal of Experimental Criminology, 11*, 597–630. https://doi.org/10.1007/s11292-015-9241-z

Tarrier, N., Dolan, M., Doyle, M., Dunn, G., Shaw, J., & Blackburn, R. (2010). *Exploratory randomised control trial of schema modal therapy in the Personality Disorder Service at Ashworth Hospital*. Ministry of Justice.

Tomlinson, M. F., & Hoaken, P. N. S. (2017). The potential for a skills-based dialectical behavior therapy program to reduce aggression, anger, and hostility in a Canadian forensic psychiatric sample: A pilot study. *International Journal of Forensic Mental Health, 16*, 215–226. https://doi.org/10.1080/14999013.2017.1315469

Ward, T., & Mann. R. (2004). Good lives and the rehabilitation of offenders: A positive approach to treatment. In P. A. Linley, & S. Joseph (Eds.), *Positive psychology in practice*, Wiley, NY: New Jersey. pp. 598–616.

Ware, J., Cieplucha, C., & Matsuo, D. (2011). The Violent Offenders Therapeutic Programme (VOTP): Rationale and effectiveness. *Australasian Journal of Correctional Staff Development, 6*, 1–12.

Watt, B. D., & Howells, K. (1999). Skills training for aggression control: Evaluation of an anger management programme for violent offenders. *Legal and Criminological Psychology, 4*, 285–300. https://doi.org/10.1348/135532599167914

Wilson, C., Gandolfi, S., Dudley, A., Thomas, B., Tapp, J., & Moore, E. (2013). Evaluation of anger management groups in a high-security hospital. *Criminal Behaviour & Mental Health, 23*, 356–371. https://doi.org/10.1002/cbm.1873

Wong, S. C. P., Gordon, A., Gu, D., Lewis, K., & Olver, M. E. (2012). The effectiveness of violence reduction treatment for psychopathic offenders: Empirical evidence and a treatment model. *International Journal of Forensic Mental Health, 11*, 336–349. https://doi.org/10.1080/14999013.2012.746760

Further Readings

Gannon, T. A., Olver, M. E., Mallion, J. S., & James, M. (2019). Does specialized psychological treatment for offending reduce recidivism? A meta-analysis examining staff and program variables as predictors of treatment effectiveness. *Clinical Psychology Review*. Advanced online publication. https://doi.org/10.1016/j.cpr.2019.101752

McAlinden, A. (2012). "Grooming" and the sexual abuse of children: Institutional, Internet and familial dimensions. Oxford, UK: Oxford University Press.

McGuire, J. (2013). 'What works' to reduce re-offending: 18 years on. In L. A. Craig, L. Dixon, & T. A. Gannon (Eds.), *What works in offender rehabilitation: An evidence-based approach to assessment and treatment* (pp. 20–49). Wiley-Blackwell.

Mpofu, E., Athanasou, J. A., Rafe, C., & Belshaw, S. H. (2018). Cognitive-behavioral therapy efficacy for reducing recidivism rates of moderate-and high-risk sexual offenders: A scoping systematic literature review. *Current Sociology, 66*, 170. https://doi.org/10.1177/0306624X16644501

Papalia, N., Spivak, B., Daffern, M., & Ogloff, J. R. P. (2019). A meta-analytic review of the efficacy of psychological treatments for violent offenders in correctional and forensic mental health settings. *Clinical Psychology: Science and Practice, 26*(2). https://doi.org/10.1111/cpsp.12282

Polaschek, D. L. (2011). High-intensity rehabilitation for violent offenders in New Zealand: Reconviction outcomes for high- and medium-risk prisoners. *Journal of Interpersonal Violence, 26*, 664–682. https://doi.org/10.1177/0886260510365854

Schmucker, M., & Lösel, F. (2015). The effects of sexual offender treatment on recidivism: An international meta-analysis of sound quality evaluations. *Journal of Experimental Criminology, 11*, 597–630. https://doi.org/10.1007/s11292-015-9241-z

Watson, R., Thomas, S., & Daffern, M. (2017). The impact of interpersonal style on ruptures and repairs in the therapeutic alliance between offenders and therapists in sex offender treatment. *Sexual Abuse, 29*(7), 709–728. https://doi.org/10.1177/1079063215617514

Willis, G., & Ward, T. (2013). The Good Lives Model: Evidence that it works. In L. Craig, L. Dixon, & T. A. Gannon (Eds.), What works in offender rehabilitation: An evidence based approach to assessment and treatment (pp. 305–318). John Wiley & Sons.

Forensic Schema Therapy and SafePath: Individual- and Milieu-Therapy Approaches for Complex Personality Disorders and Externalizing Behavior Problems

30

David P. Bernstein, Marjolein F. van Wijk-Herbrink, and Truus Kersten

Key Points

- Forensic Schema Therapy is a specialized adaptation of Schema Therapy, developed out of the need for more effective treatment alternatives for forensic patients with severe personality disorders and a high risk of aggressive or sexual reoffending.
- An RCT conducted in Dutch forensic psychiatric hospitals shows that Forensic Schema Therapy outperforms TAU with respect to improvements in personality disorder symptoms, reduction in risks and improvements in strengths, reductions in early maladaptive schemas and schema modes, and speed of rehabilitation.
- Forensic Schema Therapy uses experiential, cognitive, and behavioral techniques to diminish dysfunctional modes linked to antisocial behavior and strengthen healthy modes.

D. P. Bernstein (✉)
Department of Clinical Psychological Science, Maastricht University, Maastricht, The Netherlands
e-mail: d.bernstein@maastrichtuniversity.nl

M. F. van Wijk-Herbrink
Pactum, VIGO Group, Zetten, The Netherlands
e-mail: m.vanwijk@ogheldring.nl

T. Kersten
Beuningen, The Netherlands
e-mail: info@akkerdistel.nl

- In Forensic Schema Therapy for adolescents, the therapist takes into account developmental issues and works with parents to recognize and modify dysfunctional interaction patterns.
- SafePath, a milieu-based intervention based on Schema Therapy principles, contributes to a better ward climate and less use of restrictive interventions (e.g., seclusion, physical restraint) by ward staff.

Introduction

Schema Therapy (Young et al., 2003) is a promising form of treatment for offenders with personality disorders (PDs). Schema Therapy is an integrative, evidence-based psychotherapy for PDs that combines cognitive, behavioral, experiential, and attachment-based approaches (Young et al., 2003). It is typically a moderate to long-term form of therapy, requiring about one year of weekly sessions in less complicated cases, and two to three years or sometimes more of therapy sessions, usually starting twice weekly, in severe PDs. In non-forensic settings, Schema Therapy has demonstrated effectiveness with Borderline PD (Giesen-Bloo et al., 2006; Nadort et al., 2009) and Cluster C PDs, Narcissistic, Histrionic, and Paranoid PDs (Bamelis et al., 2014).

Bernstein and colleagues (2007) developed Forensic Schema Therapy out of the need for more effective treatment for forensic patients with severe PDs, such as antisocial (Chapter 11), borderline (Chapter 12), narcissistic (Chapter 13), or paranoid PDs, and a high risk of aggressive or sexual reoffending. Although these individuals constitute the majority of patients in forensic settings, there are relatively few treatment alternatives for them (Berzins & Trestman, 2004; Chakhssi et al., 2014; Ware et al., 2016), and effect sizes are typically small, especially when treatments are legally mandated (i.e., coerced treatment) (Parhar et al., 2008).

The focus in Forensic Schema Therapy is on "schema modes," extreme emotional states such as those involving anger, impulsivity, manipulation, and aggression (Bernstein et al., 2007, 2019). Forensic Schema Therapy uses the mode approach to address patients' motivational difficulties; reduce modes that are risk factors for crime and violence; and strengthen healthy emotional states, which are seen as protective factors (Keulen-de Vos et al., 2016). In a recently completed randomized clinical trial, Forensic Schema Therapy showed good evidence of effectiveness with violent offenders with PDs, compared to patients who received usual treatment, in eight Dutch forensic hospitals (Bernstein et al., 2021).

In this chapter, we will review the theoretical model, treatment approach, and empirical evidence supporting Forensic Schema Therapy. We will further discuss its adaptation to two new and promising areas, namely adolescents with emerging personality disorders (van Wijk-Herbrink et al., 2017) and SafePath, a milieu-based form of Schema Therapy (van Wijk-Herbrink et al., 2019).

Theoretical Model

The Schema Therapy theoretical model (Young et al., 2003) distinguishes between strait concepts ("early maladaptive schemas") and state concepts ("schema modes"). Early maladaptive schemas are long-term propensities, repeating themes or patterns that play themselves out across a person's life (e.g., themes of abandonment, mistrust, or emotional deprivation). They stem from early childhood experiences in which basic emotional needs (e.g., safe attachment, autonomy, realistic limits, self-expression, and spontaneity) were insufficiently met.

Schema modes are state versions of early maladaptive schemas. They are the psychological states that occur when schemas, combined with dysfunctional forms of coping, are triggered (Lazarus et al., 2020). Schema modes consist of emotions, cognitions, and coping responses that dominate a person's functioning at a given moment. For example, an "Angry Child mode" involves the combination of angry feelings (e.g., anger, rage), thoughts (e.g., "It's unfair!", "You're mistreating me!"), and the open expression of anger (e.g., yelling, screaming, stomping feet, throwing things).

Schema modes can be of different types. "Child modes" represent basic emotions, such as sadness, fear, shame, and anger, which are triggered when basic emotional needs go unmet. "Inner critic modes" represent self-directed criticism or placing excessive demands on oneself. "Maladaptive coping modes" represent dysfunctional forms of coping, based on three broad coping styles. "Surrendering coping" is "taking the one-down position," in other words, compliant or submissive coping. "Avoidant coping" is coping by avoiding people, situations, or emotions. "Overcompensatory coping" is "taking the one-up position;" in other words, coping through the use of dominance, aggression, manipulation, or other overcompensatory strategies. Overcompensatory coping modes are quite prevalent in forensic populations (Keulen-de Vos et al., 2017; van Wijk-Herbrink et al., 2018b, 2020) and distinguish them from non-forensic patients, in which they usually appear less often (Bernstein et al., 2007). Finally, the "Healthy modes" involve the capacity of self-reflection, self-control, and healthy decision-making

("Healthy Adult mode"), and pleasure, spontaneity, and joy ("Happy, Playful Child mode).

Forensic Schema Therapy emphasizes schema modes, rather than early maladaptive schemas, because they are easier to observe and work with in forensic patients. Early maladaptive schemas consist mostly of themes involving vulnerability, such as feeling defective, abandoned, or emotionally deprived, which most forensic patients are not eager to reveal. They show little overt emotion, except, perhaps, for anger. Instead, they present an invulnerable exterior to the world. Only gradually over time is the therapist able to shift these patients into more vulnerable emotional states (see Therapeutic Approach, below).

In the Forensic Schema Therapy model (Bernstein et al., 2007, 2019), the relative balance of dysfunctional modes activated at a given moment and healthy modes representing the capacity for healthy attributions and coping (i.e., the Healthy Adult mode) determine the likelihood that antisocial behavior will occur. The focus in Forensic Schema Therapy is therefore on reducing the severity of dysfunctional modes that represent internal risk factors for reoffending, and strengthening healthy modes, or protective factors (Bernstein et al., 2007, 2019).

The Forensic Schema Therapy model shows many similarities with a widely adopted theory of aggression, the General Aggression Model (GAM; Anderson, & Bushman, 2002) (Chapter 19). Like the Forensic Schema Therapy model, the GAM also emphasizes the importance of emotional activation (e.g., anger arousal) combined with maladaptive cognitions (e.g., early maladaptive schemas, hostile attributional biases) and dysfunctional coping (e.g., poor self-control). In the GAM, aggression represents a person by situation interaction, involving the state activation of these enduring affective, cognitive, and behavioral propensities (e.g., in situations perceived as hostile or threatening). In the Forensic Schema Therapy model, schema modes also represent a person by situation interaction, occurring when early maladaptive schemas, combined with dysfunctional coping responses, are activated, increasing the risk for aggressive and other antisocial behavior. As such, schema modes can be likened to "knowledge scripts" in the GAM, representing habitual, overlearned forms of coping that guide behavior in certain situations (e.g., situations involving threats).

Empirical Support for the Forensic Schema Therapy Theoretical Model

In a study of schema modes and offending behavior, Keulen-de Vos and colleagues (2016) retrospectively assessed offenders' modes from descriptions of their index crimes. In about 75% of cases, the offense scenarios began with a vulnerable emotional state (Vulnerable Child mode), involving themes such as abandonment/loss, humiliation, mistrust, or shame. These sequences quickly escalated, as these states shifted from internalizing ones involving painful emotions to externalizing ones involving anger and impulsivity (Angry and Impulsive Child modes), substance abuse (Detached Self-Soother mode), and finally, reactive aggression (Bully and Attack mode) or cold, instrumental aggression (Predator mode). These findings suggest that aggressive behavior functioned as a form of dysfunctional coping in response to vulnerable emotional triggers. Moreover, Child modes and Overcompensatory Coping modes occurring during patients' index offenses (retrospectively assessed from reports in their case files) predicted later violence in institutional settings. Finally, retrospectively assessed schema modes also correlated with facet scores on the Psychopathy Checklist-Revised (PCL-R; Hare, 2003) (Chapter 15). These findings supported hypothesized relationships between schema modes and violent offending.

In studies of adolescents with emerging personality disorders and externalizing behavior, Van Wijk-Herbrink and colleagues investigated the relationship between early maladaptive schemas, schema modes, dysfunctional coping, and behavior problems. In one of these studies (Van Wijk-Herbrink et al., 2018b), they demonstrated that externalizing behaviors, such as oppositional-defiant and aggressive behaviors, resulted from overcompensatory coping responses and externalizing schema modes, which were themselves responses to schemas related to disconnection and rejection experiences. Another study showed that some early maladaptive schemas played a significant role in the relationships between perceived injustice, anger, and aggression (van Wijk-Herbrink et al., 2020). Adolescent boys, who were receiving court-mandated treatment in a closed residential youth care facility, displayed more state anger and aggression in response to perceived injustice when they had higher trait scores on the Abandonment schema (i.e., the expectation that significant others will abandon you) and Entitlement schema (i.e., the perception that one has special rights or is superior to others). These theoretical studies suggest that a treatment focus on early maladaptive schemas and schema modes could ameliorate antisocial and other disruptive behaviors.

Effectiveness Studies

Forensic Schema Therapy has been evaluated in a 3-year randomized clinical trial involving 8 forensic hospitals in the Netherlands (total $N = 103$), who were randomized to receive either Schema Therapy (ST) or treatment-as-usual (TAU) (Bernstein et al., 2021), which was usually cognitive-behavior therapy, systemic therapy, or a form of eclectic/integrative therapy (other than Schema Therapy). Results supported the effectiveness of both ST and TAU, but ST consistently outperformed TAU across a range of primary and secondary outcomes variables, with significant differences and small to moderate effect sizes (Bernstein et al., 2021). ST patients showed greater improvements in personality disorder symptoms; reductions in risks and improvements in strengths; reductions in early maladaptive schemas and schema modes; and moved more rapidly through the process of rehabilitation, involving gradual re-entry into the community. Although longer-term follow-up studies are needed to investigate recidivism, which was rare during treatment, these findings provide initial support for the effectiveness of Forensic Schema Therapy in violent forensic patients with severe personality disorders.

Research on the effectiveness of Forensic Schema Therapy for youth is still scarce, however, research supports the theoretic model of early maladaptive schemas, schema coping, and schema modes in adolescents with severe behavior problems (van Wijk-Herbrink et al., 2018b; 2018c). Moreover, a pilot study of Schema Therapy with adolescents with personality pathology and externalizing behavior problems (van Wijk-Herbrink et al., 2017) demonstrated reductions in schemas, schema modes, and behavior problems. We are currently awaiting results of a quasi-randomized controlled clinical trial comparing Schema Therapy to treatment as usual in a Dutch closed residential youth care facility (van Wijk-Herbrink et al., 2018a).

Therapeutic Approach in Forensic Schema Therapy

In forensic populations, schema modes are front and center in the patient's clinical presentation. Schema modes, such as those involving anger, impulsivity, deceit and manipulation, emotional detachment, indirect hostility, and overt aggression, often dominate patients' interactions with therapists and other personnel, as well as with other patients (Chakhssi et al., 2014). The therapist must learn to become adept in recognizing and working with these schema modes in the "here and now" of the therapy relationship.

In the beginning phase of Schema Therapy, we introduce the idea of schema modes with the patient. We explain what modes are, using simple and non-technical language. We use the term "a side of you" or "a part of you" to describe modes (e.g., "a side of you that detaches from your feelings," "a side of you that tries to take the one-up position"). In this way, the therapist and patient have a shared vocabulary to describe the patient's emotional states. This vocabulary is an emotionally neutral and non-judgmental one. It implies that we all have different sides of ourselves, and that we can understand even modes that involve harmful behaviors in terms of dysfunctional forms of coping.

Motivational problems are often central obstacles in therapy with forensic patients. In Forensic Schema Therapy, we conceptualize these problems in terms of the modes that are responsible for therapy-interfering behaviors (Bernstein et al., 2019). We view motivational issues as dynamic ones that fluctuate over the course of therapy, affecting the patient's ability to form an emotional bond with the therapist, and to make and keep agreements regarding the tasks and goals of therapy. The therapist uses a specialized form of schema mode work, which resembles motivational interviewing, to overcome these obstacles. In motivational interviewing, the therapist attempts to work in an evenhanded way that acknowledges the patient's reasons for and against making changes in his behavior (e.g., giving up addictions or aggressive behavior). In Forensic Schema Therapy, the therapist acknowledges that the patient's dysfunctional schema modes are also his "comfort zone"; they represent the dysfunctional forms of coping that keep the patient feeling safe and protected. The therapist works with the patient to explore his modes, the reasons for keeping them, and the reasons to give them up, an evenhanded approach that gradually increases the patient's motivation to change.

Compared to traditional forms of Cognitive-Behavior Therapy (CBT) (Chapter 29), Schema Therapy places a much stronger emphasis on the therapy relationship (Young et al., 2003) (see also Chapter 27). In light of these patients' histories of deficient attachment relationships (Chapter 9), Schema Therapy provides a corrective emotional experience in the therapy relationship known as "limited reparenting." The therapist provides, within appropriate limits, for some of the basic emotional and developmental needs the patient missed growing up. In forensic populations, these needs typically involve attachment needs such as warmth, attention, and stability, and the need for firm but fair and consequential limits (Bernstein et al., 2019). Thus, the therapist needs to work persistently to form an attachment relationship with their patients, who are often mistrustful and emotionally distant, while at the same time responding to the patient's boundary violations through limit setting. In addition, the therapist consistently calls the patient's attention to the various schema modes that manifest themselves in and outside of the therapy relationship, using a technique known as "empathic confrontation." The therapist confronts the patient in a clear but empathic way, bringing his attention to modes that represent responsivity factors in the Risk-Need-Responsivity model (Andrews et al., 2011) (Chapter 27)—the ones that interfere with the patient's ability to engage in treatment ("I see a side of you that is keeping me at a distance."). They use the same technique with the modes that represent risk factors for sexual and general aggression, including when offense paralleling behavior appears in the therapy relationship ("I see a side of you that acts like our relationship is more like boyfriend and girlfriend, rather than patient and therapist.").

Schema Therapy uses experiential, cognitive, and behavioral techniques to diminish dysfunctional schema modes and strengthen healthy modes (Young et al., 2003). In Forensic Schema Therapy, cognitive techniques such as chain analysis are often used to examine offense scenarios, as well as incidents that occur within the institution. This approach conceptualizes offense-related behavior as an unfolding sequence of schema modes, beginning with a trigger (i.e., situation) and escalating until its culmination in violent or other criminal behavior (Chakhssi et al., 2014; Keulen-de Vos et al., 2016).

Experiential techniques, such as role-playing methods (e.g., the multiple chairs technique) and imagery rescripting, play particularly important roles in Forensic Schema Therapy (Young et al., 2003). By activating emotions, these techniques help the therapist to overcome the "wall" of emotional distance behind which forensic patients often hide. In the early phase of the therapy, we often use variations on chair-work to explore and understand the patient's schema modes. Chair-work is a flexible technique in which patients move from chair to chair to play different roles. In Schema Therapy, the patient usually plays the roles of his different modes. When he does so, he experiences his different emotional states—the emotions, thoughts, and behavioral coping tendencies that accompany them—rather than merely talking about them in an abstract, or emotionally distant manner.

In later phases of the therapy, we often use imagery rescripting to explore and reprocess the early traumatic experiences that many of these patients endured as children—experiences that played a central role in the development of their early maladaptive schemas, such as Mistrust/Abuse, Abandonment, Defectiveness, and Emotional Deprivation. As noted above, we do not refer to early maladaptive schemas directly, preferring to work with modes. However, ameliorating schemas through techniques such as imagery should reduce the frequency and intensity of schema modes, the state forms of schemas. In imagery rescripting, we begin with a current, emotionally triggering situation, such as an incident that recently occurred on the ward. We ask the patient to close his eyes, vividly re-experience the current situation, and then "travel back to the past," retrieving an image of a situation from childhood that felt the same as the current one. The patient is often able to retrieve a childhood memory whose theme is strikingly similar to that in the current situation, reflecting the unmet emotional needs and early maladaptive schemas that connect them. The therapist then "enters" the image, providing for some of the needs in imagination that the patient missed in his real childhood, such as protection (e.g., in the case of abusive scenarios), nurturance (e.g., in scenarios involving neglect or abandonment), and so forth. Research shows that guided imagery produces emotional activation (Holmes & Matthew, 2005) and that imagery rescripting has beneficial therapeutic effects (Renner & Holmes, 2018). In our clinical experience, patients often experience profound feelings of relief following these exercises and appear less intensely triggered when they encounter similar, future situations.

Case Conceptualization and Risk Assessment

The case conceptualization is the starting point for treatment. In regular Schema Therapy, the case conceptualization includes (a) temperament of the patient, (b) the extent to which his basic emotional needs were met in childhood, (c) parent's modeling behaviors and family beliefs, (d) the patient's early maladaptive schemas, (e) life events or traumatic experiences in adulthood, (f) the patient's mode model, and (g) his psychological symptoms and strengths. All elements of the case conceptualization are related to each other to tell the life story of the patient and explain his psychological symptoms and strengths. The combination of childhood temperament and the extent to which basic emotional needs were met underlie the development of early maladaptive schemas, and temperament and parent's modeling behaviors contribute to the adoption of coping reactions to these schemas, resulting in schema modes. Linking psychological problems to the patient's schema modes and early maladaptive schemas, and their origins in childhood, provide the patient and therapist clear guidance in determining therapy objectives. As part of the case conceptualization, therapists may also think about how their own schemas and modes may be triggered by patients' schemas and modes, and how to activate their own Healthy Adult mode to cope with their own emotional reactions.

In Forensic Schema Therapy, the case conceptualization is supplemented with outcomes of risk assessment (Chapter 25) that is also linked to the patient's schema modes and their origins in childhood (Keulen-de Vos et al., 2017). Therapy objectives comprise the adaptation of the modes that play a role in the development or maintenance of risk behaviors. Risk assessment in forensic patients (e.g., HCR-20; Webster et al., 2004) is traditionally focused on patients' violent tendencies, including psychopathic or antisocial tendencies (e.g., PCL-R; Hare, 2003), but may also be extended to other domains relevant to forensic clinical practice, such as self-harm, suicide, unauthorized leave, self-neglect, substance abuse, and victimization (e.g., Webster et al., 2004).

Course of Treatment

Forensic Schema Therapy has three phases: (1) an *attachment phase*, (2) a *schema mode reprocessing phase*, and (3) a *reintegration phase* (Bernstein et al., 2019). In Box 30.1, we describe these phases for Stefan, a 35-year-old male who received Forensic Schema Therapy for five years at a forensic psychiatric hospital. For severe PDs (e.g., antisocial, borderline, narcissistic PDs) in forensic inpatient settings, each of these phases lasts for approximately one year, starting with twice-weekly sessions, and then gradually tapering the "dose" of therapy. Sometimes, an even longer course of a therapy is necessary for severe PDs with high risk of violence, to sufficiently lower recidivism risk. Although this intensity of treatment requires an investment of resources, we believe that it is justified in terms of risk-need-responsivity principles that recommend more intense treatments for higher-risk patients. In our RCT of forensic patients with severe PDs (Bernstein et al., 2020), we found that Schema Therapy speeded the process of re-entry into the community, raising the possibility that Schema Therapy is also cost-effective, compared to other treatments. In fact, Schema Therapy was found to be cost-effective in a study of (non-forensic) outpatients with Borderline PD (Giesen-Bloo et al., 2006). Schema Therapy is often shorter in less severe forensic patients and in ambulant settings, lasting one to two years.

The attachment phase is focused on forming a therapeutic bond, a process that only occurs gradually in patients with severe PDs and histories of insecure attachments. The goals in this phase are to motivate and engage the patient, make him aware of the schema modes that he uses to keep the therapist at a safe distance, overcome feelings of mistrust, and begin to make contact with his vulnerable sides. The therapist keeps a consistent focus on the patient's unmet emotional needs (i.e., limited reparenting) and confronts the patient's maladaptive modes empathically when they manifest themselves in the therapy relationship and outside of it. During this phase, the patient becomes more aware of his schema modes, which slowly play a less dominant role in the therapy, resulting in greater openness and engagement.

In the schema mode reprocessing phase, the therapist uses experiential techniques to deepen the therapy process. The therapist uses chair-work and imagery rescripting to explore the patient's reactions to current situations, and to retrieve and reprocess memories of early, traumatic experiences that played a role in the genesis of the patient's problems. Cognitive techniques may be used to explore pros and cons of dysfunctional coping modes, and to identify and change cognitive distortions. Flashcards (written or audio), for example, may help remind patients of the cons of their dysfunctional behaviors and support their Healthy Adult mode to choose for healthier, alternative (coping) behaviors.

In the reintegration phase, the therapist focuses on behavioral changes and relapse prevention. She uses chain analyses and other techniques to identify the triggers and escalating mode sequences that comprise the patient's typical crime scenarios, with the aim of breaking the chain (Chakhssi et al., 2014). The therapist prescribes behavioral experiments, where the patient can practice new, healthier coping behaviors, in situations where his schema modes might become activated. During this last phase, the patient has often attained leave and is busy spending time outside of the clinic for family visits and work activities. The therapist often reduces the frequency of the sessions for practical reasons, and also because patients become more interested in moving forward with their lives during this phase, and less invested in therapy. Nevertheless, when situations involving his risk behaviors occur during this phase, it provides important opportunities to intensify the therapeutic work. The patient is confronted with the ways his maladaptive modes can be triggered in real-life situations, and the genuine risks that they pose for relapse and recidivism. While episodes involving setbacks can be painful, they are often opportunities for further growth and learning.

Box 30.1: Case example: A 5-year Schema Therapy with a psychopathic patient

Stefan is a 35-year old Serbian national who was treated for several years at a forensic psychiatric hospital in the Netherlands, including receiving five years of Schema Therapy, beginning with twice per week sessions. His index offense was the murder of a female stranger whom he had met in a bar. He was heavily under the influence of polysubstances at the time of the offense, and undergoing a turbulent period in his life with feelings of rage, hopelessness, and depression. He had spent more than half of his life, beginning in his youth, in institutional settings. He had previously committed a wide range of offenses, including several contract murders. He was a member of the criminal underworld, known for his intelligence and toughness. He had a PCL-R score of 33 (in the highly psychopathic range) and DSM-IV diagnoses of antisocial, borderline, and narcissistic Personality Disorder, polysubstance dependence, and post-traumatic stress disorder (PTSD).

In his childhood, he had experienced physical, sexual, and emotional abuse, and multiple episodes of loss and abandonment, being sent back and forth from various institutions, interspersed with periods of living with his father and stepmother, who both physically abused and emotionally rejected him. He was an intelligent boy who got into frequent trouble at school for aggression. By the time that he was a teenager, he was abusing substances and committing serious, violent crimes.

Attachment phase. In the initial phase of Schema Therapy, Stefan exhibited a strong need to maintain control of the therapy sessions. He would speak in an intense and often non-stop manner, leaving his therapist little room to intervene. His emotional range was quite restricted, except for showing anger. His most prominent schema modes during these early sessions involved hyper-alertness (Paranoid Overcontroller mode), an obsessive need to tell highly detailed and elaborate stories (Obsessive-Compulsive Overcontroller mode), and the need to set the agenda for the meetings and dominate them with his physically imposing and intense manner (Self-Aggrandizer mode). In one of their first sessions, Stefan asked his therapist if she was strong enough to deal with him. When she replied that she was indeed strong enough to handle him and had worked with patients like him before, he seemed reassured. Issues around trust and mistrust seemed to be central for Stefan. Beneath his need to control, his therapist sensed a high degree of anxiety, an Abused Child side of the patient that never felt safe.

Despite his mistrust, Stefan seemed engaged in and motivated for therapy. He was willing to stop and reflect for a few moments when his therapist intervened with a remark or comment, though he quickly shifted back to his non-stop talking. His therapist's stance during this phase was one of warmth, interest, and attention, combined with reliability and predictably (e.g., starting and stopping the sessions on time, keeping any agreements that they had made), and firm, clear boundaries. This combination slowly helped Stefan to build trust, as he experienced her genuine interest and caring along with the safety of structure and limits, providing for some of the core emotional needs he had missed growing up (i.e., limited reparenting). His therapist slowly introduced the schema mode "language" and began to call his attention to his various schema modes, when they manifested during the therapy sessions and outside of them. Initially, his therapist made room for Stefan's need to dominate and control the sessions, self-protective forms of coping he had developed from the frightening and out of control experiences of his youth. However, several times per session she interrupted him by asking, "Which side of you is this right now?" (i.e., empathic confrontation). He would stop, think, and then say, for example, "My healthy adult mode" and resume talking. Within a few months of this combination of limited reparenting and empathic confrontation, Stefan's speech seemed less pressured. He spoke less and gave his therapist more room to talk, giving himself more time to take in what she said and engage in self-reflection. This was the first indication of a growing Healthy Adult mode capacity.

During this same period, Stefan began Art Therapy, in tandem with his Schema Therapy. Stefan was a talented artist. Under the Art Therapist's guidance, he began creating artistic renderings of his various schema modes in the form of paintings and sculptures. He found this process very rewarding, as it gave expression to his different modes and helped him to gain a deeper understanding of them, through the artistic media.

Schema mode reprocessing phase. Over time, his therapist introduced more difficult topics, such as the maltreatment Stefan had experienced as a child, and the crimes he had committed. Mostly, he would speak about these experiences in a distant, detached way, as if he was speaking of things that had happened to someone else (Detached Protector mode). However, from time to time, he would become genuinely vulnerable, even tearful, when discussing painful events (Vulnerable Child mode). One such occasion was when he discussed his index crime. He was shocked that he had committed such a horrible offense, murdering a female stranger whom he had met at a bar and lured outside with the intent to kill her. He had committed several murders before, but this one was different. The others were contract killings of other underworld figures, "just business." He felt no remorse for them. However, in this case, he became visibly upset when discussing what transpired that evening, when his emotional state was at a low point in his life, and how, after ingesting many substances, he had made the decision that, "If I am going to suffer, someone else is going to suffer, too. Someone is going to die tonight!" This degree of emotional vulnerability is unusual in a highly psychopathic patient, when the patient's hard shell—conceptualized as his maladaptive coping modes—keeps emotions under rigid control. In the case of Stefan, his clinical presentation was consistent with a picture of complex trauma and psychopathy (Dargis & Koenigs, 2018), including symptoms of borderline personality disorder (e.g., emotional lability, identity disturbance) and PTSD (e.g., nightmares, hypervigilence), but with an antisocial adaptation, where he assumed the role of predator, rather than victim (Bernstein et al., 2007).

During the second year of therapy, the therapist introduced experiential techniques. Because Stefan did not like doing chair-work ("It's weird, like you're trying to get me to make a fool of myself."), she used imagery rescripting to reprocess his traumatic experiences. Due to Stefan's mistrust and hypervigilance, he would not close his eyes to do imagery, but did agree to do the exercises with his eyes open, while staring at a fixed point on the desk in front of him. The therapist began by rescripting childhood experiences of neglect and abandonment, before turning to abusive experiences, which were more emotionally overwhelming. The therapist was careful to agree on measures to give Stefan a feeling of control and safety during these procedures, such as using a stop signal to end the exercise, if it became too intense. She took care to enter the image quickly whenever the memories involved experiences of abuse, so that she could protect the child in the image, providing the safety that he lacked when these experiences had actually occurred (i.e., rescripting). Although Stefan found these exercises intense, he felt that they were good for him, giving him some relief from painful memories, and over time, lessening his PTSD symptoms, such as nightmares and intrusive recollections.

Despite the growing trust between them, at times, Stefan became angry and agitated toward his therapist, when he perceived that she had let him down, or was just "part of the system." When he became verbally abusive toward her, or behaved in a way that she found threatening, she used limit setting to enforce boundaries (Bernstein et al., 2019). She would tell him to "Stop!" using his name, and telling him that he was making her feel unsafe, and that this was unacceptable. She emphasized the fact that the therapy needed to be a safe space for both of them. This limit-setting intervention helped to contain him, providing the safety that he had missed growing up. He would often apologize after these outbursts, genuinely regretful at frightening her.

Reintegration phase. In his third year of therapy, Stefan got permission to go on leave, first with supervision, and later without it. The process of reintegration was one of "fits and starts." He acknowledged his fear at the prospect of re-entering the outside world. He feared reprisals by former acquaintances in his criminal network and confessed to being clueless about how to behave in "normal" society. At times, his anxiety grew so great that he would withdraw his leave application, and stay mostly in his room, refusing to participate in daily activities, except for continuing to meet with his therapist. She used these setbacks as opportunities to explore his fears, including their realistic and unrealistic aspects, slowly encouraging him to face the challenges of re-integrating. The bond that they had formed helped him to feel that he was not alone in this process.

He would sometimes get into conflicts with ward staff, viewing them as deliberately provoking him or undermining him (Paranoid Overcontroller mode), leading to hostile standoffs when he would refuse contact, withdrawing to his room (Angry Protector mode). To resolve these impasses, the therapist assumed the role of coach for the ward staff, explaining Stefan's modes that underlay his reactions, including his vulnerable sides (Abused Child mode) that they could not observe. Eventually, she was able to arrange meetings where Stefan and the staff could resolve these situations in a constructive and non-threatening way, by discussing his reactions to staff, and vice versa, using the schema mode "language" as a means of communication. While Stefan still became angry at times, these episodes became less frequent and extreme, and he was able to talk about his reactions.

Termination of treatment and evaluation. Through this arduous process, Stefan was gradually able to re-enter the community, living first in a supervised residence, and then transitioning to his own apartment. He slowly reduced the frequency of sessions. Over time, he came to feel more relaxed and less guarded, more able to enjoy doing activities that he liked, and adapt to normal, daily activities like working. He had developed a strong bond with his therapist, whom he looked to as a maternal-figure, turning to her for guidance and support when he needed it.

After his first three years of therapy, he was assessed on a number of measures as part of a randomized clinical trial of Schema Therapy (Bernstein et al., 2021) in which he had participated. On the Historical and Clinical Risk Management-20 (HCR-20, Webster, 2004, his risk category had declined from high outside the clinic and medium inside, to medium outside the clinic, and low inside. There were statistically significant reductions in his dysfunctional schema modes, and improvements in his healthy modes, assessed by the self-report Schema Mode Inventory (SMI; Young et al., 2007), and by the Mode Observational Scale (MOS; Keulen-de Vos et al., 2011), in which videotapes of therapy sessions were scored by trained raters. Eventually, the Ministry of Security and Justice deemed him to be at sufficiently low risk, based on an independent evaluation, and his treatment sentence was terminated. He was free to live in the community. To the best of our knowledge, he has not recidivated in the approximately five years since he left the clinic.

Forensic Schema Therapy was developed as a form of individual psychotherapy for adult forensic patients. However, it has been further adapted in several ways: as a form of Creative Arts Therapy (e.g., drama, music, art, and movement therapies; van den Broek et al., 2011), an individual therapy for adolescents (van Wijk-Herbrink et al., 2017), and a milieu therapy for youth or adults (SafePath; van Wijk-Herbrink et al., 2019). In the remainder of this chapter, we briefly discuss the latter two of these developments.

Adaptations for Adolescents

Adolescence is a time of rapid physical, social-emotional, cognitive, and interpersonal changes (Chapter 2). With their development toward independence, adolescents struggle with rules, tend to argue with persons of authority, and experiment with risks. Their mood may change rapidly and their coping or problem-solving skills are still in development. Although some personality disorder traits may actually represent normal behaviors for this developmental stage, they may stand out because of their perseverance, impairment in the adolescent's life, or the suffering they cause to the adolescent or his environment. In that case, it is important to recognize these patterns as emerging personality disorders, so that it can be treated as such.

Moving to independence, adolescents typically show states of themselves in which they are impulsive and undisciplined (Impulsive and Undisciplined Child modes), sometimes combined into a state that may be called "Rebellious Child mode." These child modes need firm but fair limits, but the therapist should also take into account the adolescents' (developmental) need for autonomy and their developing problem-solving skills. For example, the therapist may set clear limits to problematic behavior, but also gives multiple options for desired behaviors to choose from. Additionally, the therapist avoids a debate with these child modes by giving the adolescent time and space to shift into a healthier mode.

The adaptive ability of adolescents to successfully move through the developmental stages of adolescence also depends on the skills and abilities of their parents to support them. This may be impeded by problematic behaviors of the adolescent, eliciting parental early maladaptive schemas, and corresponding (coping) reactions. Interactions between schema modes of the adolescent and schema modes of the parents may cause vicious cycles, maintaining problematic behaviors of the patient, or may cause rapid escalation of such behaviors. Mode collusions occur when modes of the adolescents and parental modes are congruent to each other. For example, an adolescent who refuses to obey the house rules (Rebellious Child mode) and a mother responding to this by letting him cross her boundaries and putting her own needs aside (Compliant Surrenderer mode). Mode clashes occur when modes of the adolescent and a parent collide. For example, an adolescent who is bragging and acting superior to others (Self-aggrandizer mode) and his father intimidating him to teach him a lesson (Bully and Attack mode). In Forensic Schema Therapy with adolescents, the therapist works with parents to recognize such patterns and teaches them to stay connected with their "healthy, good-enough-parent mode." This mode is able to meet the adolescent's needs, whether the emphasis is on attachment or on firm but fair limits with respect for autonomy.

SafePath

SafePath is a milieu-based approach that integrates elements of Schema Therapy, Mindfulness, and Positive Psychology. It is based on the idea that teams, such as the multidisciplinary team on a ward of a hospital or prison, can contribute to the rehabilitation process by creating a positive treatment climate. Research shows that climates that are supportive, rather than repressive, are associated with better outcomes (Schubert et al., 2012) and less institutional aggression (Ros et al., 2013).

In SafePath, we teach ward personnel to understand conflict situations and other incidents in terms of schema modes. We teach them a three-step process of working with modes during interactions with patients: (1) recognize the patient's schema modes as they occur in real time, (2) become mindfully aware of one's own schema modes, triggered by those of the patient, and recruit one's Healthy

Adult mode to restore equilibrium, and (3) return one's attention to the patient, and choose the intervention that matches the patient's schema mode. We introduce the language of "a side of you…" to describe the schema modes that staff observe in their patients and in themselves. Eventually, staff internalize this way of thinking and talking about emotional states and use it automatically.

Because ward staff often have primarily active and visual, as opposed to verbal, learning styles, we use the iModes cards (Bernstein et al., 2020) to facilitate the learning process. The cards have images of the modes on the front side, and the name and a short description of the modes on the reverse side. Through a series of exercises and "serious games" using the iModes, staff learns how to recognize schema modes, manage their own emotional reactions, and practice various basic Schema Therapy interventions (i.e., limited reparenting, empathic confrontation, and limit setting), which we have adapted to situations that occur on the ward. We also introduce the concept of schema modes to the patients residing on the wards, using the iModes as a visual medium to help them understand the role of their modes in their problematic behaviors. We have implemented SafePath in a variety of settings in the Netherlands, including adult forensic and addiction inpatient settings, and youth residential treatment and forensic inpatient facilities. Our impression is that the SafePath approach improves team functioning and communication among team members and creates a more supportive, therapeutic climate.

Research shows that SafePath positively affects ward climate and restrictive staff interventions, such as physical restraint and seclusion (van Wijk-Herbrink et al., 2019). In this study, SafePath was implemented on two wards of a Dutch secure residential treatment facility, where adolescents received court-mandated treatment for their externalizing behavior problems. Two other wards with a treatment milieu based on cognitive-behavioral theory served as a control group. Staff on the SafePath wards learned to translate problematic behaviors into schema modes, consider the function of these particular modes, and address the underlying basic emotional needs of the patient. In order to do so, staff learned to recognize and control their own dysfunctional responses to patients' externalizing behaviors. These skills led to a more safe and supportive group climate as assessed by patients, and less use of restrictive or repressive measures.

Conclusion

In this chapter, we discussed the theory and course of treatment of Forensic Schema Therapy, and how this may be adapted to adolescent patients in individual therapy, and integrated into milieu-therapy based on the same principles (SafePath) in forensic psychiatric care for adults or adolescents. As supported by research, these forms of treatment show good results, although further studies are still needed to replicate findings and conduct long-term follow-ups. The adaptation of Schema Therapy to forensic settings results in a long-term, intensive treatment, based on an attachment therapy relationship and incorporating multiple therapeutic modalities, that seems to be effective even for those patients who are often considered as untreatable.

References

Anderson, A., & Bushman, B. J. (2002). Human aggression. *Annual Review of Psychology, 53*, 27–51.

Andrews, D. A., Bonta, J., & Wormith, J. S. (2011). The Risk-Need-Responsivity (RNR) model: Does adding the good lives model contribute to effective crime prevention? *Criminal Justice and Behavior, 38*, 735–755.

Bamelis, L. L. M., Evers, S. M. A. A., Spinhoven, P., & Arntz, A. (2014). Results of a multicentered randomized controlled trial on the clinical effectiveness of schema therapy for personality disorders. *American Journal of Psychiatry, 171*(3), 305–322. https://doi.org/10.1176/appi.ajp.2013.12040518

Bernstein, D. P., Arntz, A., & de Vos, M. E. (2007). Schema-focused therapy in forensic settings: Theoretical model and recommendations for best clinical practice. *International Journal of Forensic Mental Health, 6*(2), 169–183. https://doi.org/10.1080/14999013.2007.1047126

Bernstein, D. P., Clercx, M., & Keulen-De Vos, M. (2019). Schema therapy in forensic settings. In *The Wiley international handbook of correctional psychology* (pp. 654–668). Wiley Blackwell. https://doi.org/10.1002/9781119139980.ch41

Bernstein, D. P., Keulen-de Vos, M., Clercx, M., de Vogel, V., Kersten, G. C. M., Lancel, M., Jonkers, P. P., Bogaerts, S., Slaats, M., Broers, N. J., Deenen, T. A. M., & Arntz, A. (2021). Schema therapy for violent PD offenders: A randomized clinical trial. *Psychological Medicine*. https://doi.org/10.1017/S0033291721001161

Bernstein, D. P., de Miquel Bleier, C., Broers, N., van der Steen, L., & Richter, M. (2020, submitted). *Initial validation of a pictorial icon based system of assessing personality states*.

Berzins, L. G., & Trestman, R. L. (2004). The development and implementation of dialectical behavior therapy in forensic settings. *International Journal of Forensic Mental Health, 3*(1), 93–103.

Chakhssi, F., Kersten, T., de Ruiter, C., & Bernstein, D. P. (2014). Treating the untreatable: A single case study of a psychopathic inpatient treated with schema therapy. *Psychotherapy, 51*(3), 447.

Dargis, M., & Koenigs, M. (2018). Two subtypes of psychopathic criminals differ in negative affect and history of childhood abuse. *Psychological Trauma: Theory, Research, Practice, and Policy, 10*(4), 444–451. https://doi.org/10.1037/tra0000328.supp (Supplemental).

Giesen-Bloo, J., Van Dyck, R., Spinhoven, P., Van Tilburg, W., Dirksen, C., Van Asselt, T., Kremers, I., Nadort, M., & Arntz, A. (2006). Outpatient psychotherapy for borderline personality disorder: Randomized trial of schema-focused therapy versus Transference-focused therapy. *Archives of General Psychiatry, 63*, 649–658.

Hare, R. D. (2003). *The Hare psychopathy checklist—Revised.* Multi-Health Systems.

Holmes, E. A., & Matthew, A. (2005). Mental imagery and emotion: A special relationship? *Emotion, 5*(4), 489–497. https://doi.org/10.1037/1528-3542.5.4.489

Lazarus, G., Sened, H., & Rafaeli, E. (2020). Subjectifying the personality state: Theoretical underpinnings and an empirical example. *European Journal of Personality.* https://doi.org/10.1002/per.2278

Keulen-de Vos, M. E., Bernstein, D. P., Vanstipelen, S., de Vogel, V., Lucker, T. P., Slaats, M., Hartkoorn, M., & Arntz, A. (2016). Schema modes in criminal and violent behaviour of forensic cluster BPD patients: A retrospective and prospective study. *Legal and Criminological Psychology, 21*(1), 56–76.

Keulen-de Vos, M., Bernstein, D. P., Clark, L. A., Arntz, A., Lucker, T. P., & de Spa, E. (2011). Patient versus informant reports of personality disorders in forensic patients. *The Journal of Forensic Psychiatry & Psychology, 22*(1), 52–71.

Keulen-de Vos, M., Bernstein, D. P., Clark, L. A., de Vogel, V., Bogaerts, S., Slaats, M., & Arntz, A. (2017). Validation of the schema mode concept in personality disordered offenders, *Legal and Criminological Psychology, 22*, 420–441.

Nadort, M., Arntz, A., Smit, J. H., Giesen-Bloo, J., Eikelenboom, M., Spinhoven, P., van Asselt, T., Wensing, M., & van Dyck, R. (2009). Implementation of outpatient schema therapy for borderline personality disorder with versus without crisis support by the therapist outside official hours: A randomized trial. *Behaviour Research and Therapy, 47*, 961–973. https://doi.org/10.1016/j.brat.2009.07.013.

Parhar, K. K., Wormith, J. S., Derkzen, D. M., & Beauregard, A. M. (2008). Offender coercion in treatment: A meta-analysis of effectiveness. *Criminal Justice and Behavior, 35*(9), 1109–1135.

Renner, F., & Holmes, E. A. (2018). Mental imagery in cognitive therapy: Research and examples of imagery-focused emotion, cognition, and behavior change. In R. L. Leahy (Ed.), *Science and practice in cognitive therapy: Foundations, mechanisms, and applications* (pp. 142–158). Guilford Press.

Ros, N., van der Helm, P., Wissink, I., Stams, G. J., & Schaftenaar, P. (2013). Institutional climate and aggression in a secure psychiatric setting. *The Journal of Forensic Psychiatry & Psychology, 24*(6), 713–727. https://doi.org/10.1080/14789949.2013.848460.

Schubert, C. A., Mulvey, E. P., Loughran, T. A., & Losoya, S. H. (2012). Perceptions of institutional experience and community outcomes for serious adolescent offenders. *Criminal Justice and Behaviour, 39*, 71–93. https://doi.org/10.1177/0093854811426710.

van den Broek, E., Bernstein, D.P., & Keulen-de Vos, M. (2011). Arts therapies and schema focused therapy; a pilot study. *The Arts in Psychotherapy, 38*, 325–332.

Van Wijk-Herbrink, M. F., Arntz, A.R., Roelofs, J., & Bernstein, D. P. (2018a). Study of a quasi-randomized controlled trial. In M. F. van Wijk-Herbrink (Ed.), *Schema therapy in adolescents with externalizing behavior problems: Bridging theory and practice* (dissertation). Maastricht, the Netherlands.

Van Wijk-Herbrink, M. F., Bernstein, D. P., Broers, N. J., Roelofs, J., Rijkeboer, M. M., & Arntz, A. (2018b). Internalizing and externalizing behaviors share a common predictor: The effects of early maladaptive schemas are mediated by coping responses and schema modes. *Journal of Abnormal Child Psychology, 46*(5), 907–920.

Van Wijk-Herbrink, M. F., Broers, N. J., Arntz, A., Roelofs, J., & Bernstein, D. P. (2019). A schema therapy based milieu in secure residential youth care: Effects on aggression, group climate, repressive staff interventions, and team functioning. *Residential Treatment for Children & Youth*. https://doi.org/10.1080/0886571X.2019.1692758

Van Wijk-Herbrink, M. F., Broers, N. J., Roelofs, J., & Bernstein, D. P. (2017). Schema therapy in adolescents with disruptive behavior disorders. *International Journal of Forensic Mental Health, 16*, 261–279. https://doi.org/10.1080/14999013.2017.1352053

Van Wijk-Herbrink, M. F., Lobbestael, J., Bernstein, D. P., Broers, N. J., Roelofs, J., & Arntz, A. R. (2020). *The influence of early maladaptive schemas on the causal links between perceived injustice, negative affect, and aggression* (Manuscript submitted for publication).

Van Wijk-Herbrink, M. F., Roelofs, J., Broers, N. J., Rijkeboer, M. M., Arntz, A., & Bernstein, D. P. (2018). Validation of schema coping inventory and schema mode inventory in adolescents. *Journal of Personality Disorders, 32*, 220–241. https://doi.org/10.1521/pedi_2017_31_295

Ware, A., Wilson, C., Tapp, J., & Moore, E. (2016). Mentalisation-based therapy (MBT) in a high-secure hospital setting: Expert by experience feedback on participation. *The Journal of Forensic Psychiatry & Psychology, 27*(5), 722–744.

Webster, C. D., Martin, M. L., Brink, J., Nicholls, T. L., & Middleton, C. (2004). Manual for the Short-Term Assessment of Risk and Treatability (START), Version 1.0 (consultation ed.). St. Joseph's Healthcare Hamilton: Ontario, Canada–Forensic Psychiatric Services Commission: Port Coquitlam, British Columbia, Canada.

Young, J., Arntz, A., Atkinson, T., Lobbestael, J., Weishaar, M., van Vreeswijk, M. F., & Klokman, J. (2007). *Schema Mode Inventory (SMI version 1)*. Schema Therapy Institute.

Young, Y. E., Klosko, J., & Weishaar, M. (2003). *Schema therapy: A practitioner's guide*. Guilford.

Further Suggested Reading

Bernstein, D. P., Arntz, A., & de Vos, M. E. (2007). Schema-focused therapy in forensic settings: Theoretical model and recommendations for best clinical practice. *International Journal of Forensic Mental Health, 6*(2), 169–183. https://doi.org/10.1080/14999013.2007.1047126

Chakhssi, F., Kersten, T., de Ruiter, C., & Bernstein, D. P. (2014). Treating the untreatable: A single case study of a psychopathic inpatient treated with schema therapy. *Psychotherapy, 51*(3), 447.

Van Wijk-Herbrink, M. F., Broers, N. J., Arntz, A., Roelofs, J., & Bernstein, D. P. (2019). A schema therapy based milieu in secure residential youth care: Effects on aggression, group climate, repressive staff interventions, and team functioning. *Residential Treatment for Children & Youth.* https://doi.org/10.1080/0886571X.2019.1692758

Van Wijk-Herbrink, M. F., Broers, N. J., Roelofs, J., & Bernstein, D. P. (2017). Schema therapy in adolescents with disruptive behavior disorders. *International Journal of Forensic Mental Health, 16,* 261–279. https://doi.org/10.1080/14999013.2017.1352053

Young, Y. E., Klosko, J., & Weishaar, M. (2003). *Schema therapy: A practitioner's guide.* Guilford.

Ethical Issues in Forensic Psychology

31

Estelle Moore and Gwen Adshead

Key Points

In this chapter, we cover the following:

- Morality and ethics in forensic psychology
- Conflicts between the interests of individuals who have harmed, and others who could be victims of harm
- The values underpinning professional tasks including risk assessment
- Methods of sponsoring justice and fairness in ethical decision-making.

Introduction

Human beings are social animals who live in complex relationships with others. Such complex relationships often throw up dilemmas about how to act if we want to be 'good' people (whether personally or professionally); such dilemmas also raise questions about what the 'right' course of action is and even whether there can be a single right course of action. Across history and cultures, moral philosophers have studied concepts like 'good' and 'right' and explored how we can develop competence in thinking about them. Ethics, in particular, is the study of how we put 'good' and 'right' into action; especially when it is not clear what the 'right' or 'good' outcome is, or when there are no good outcomes at all, only

E. Moore · G. Adshead (✉)
Broadmoor Hospital, Crowthorne, UK
e-mail: g.adshead@nhs.net

E. Moore
e-mail: estelle.moore@westlondon.nhs.uk

© The Author(s), under exclusive license to Springer Nature Switzerland AG 2022   609
C. Garofalo and J. J. Sijtsema (eds.), *Clinical Forensic Psychology*,
https://doi.org/10.1007/978-3-030-80882-2_31

a choice between 'bad' ones. Ethical concerns bring us face to face with values (or personal beliefs) that should be respected by all professionals but may yet conflict between individuals, families and communities.

In this chapter, we explore the principles underlying ethical decision-making, professional identity, the role of risk assessment in forensic psychology, and the value of reflective supervision and consultation practices to provide assurance that necessary and relevant codes of conduct are adhered to in complex cases.

Why Do We Need to Understand the Role of Ethics in Forensic Psychology?

The word 'ethics' comes from the Greek word 'ethos' which refers to a person's character or way that they engage with moral dilemmas. In ordinary life, people make ethical decisions every day, and our ethical reasoning skills develop in childhood, so that by the time we reach adulthood, we already have active ethical reasoning skills. As early as age 7/8, we start to use language such as 'fair' and 'right', and as we get older, we can recognise that that we are using ethical reasoning when we start to use words like 'ought' and 'should' about a course of action.

Adolescence is an especially important time for the development of ethical reasoning skills because this is a time when, for most, but not all teenagers, individual adult identity begins to emerge and evolve, especially with regard to gender, peer relationships and first erotic relationships. Inevitably there is also much variation, with juveniles referred to as delinquent' often displaying low levels of moral reasoning for their age (Stams et al., 2006). During late childhood and early adulthood, the *values* that are important to our personal identity become clear, and in turn they influence the story that we tell of who we are, and the groups to which we belong (Day & Tappan, 1996; Gilligan, 1977; Pratt et al., 2009; Tappan, 1989).

Ethical dilemmas are complex human interactions because they involve situations in social and community life where values conflict, or where there are many possible courses of action, none of which seem entirely good or right. Ethics lean towards decisions based upon individual character. In contrast, morals (systems of beliefs) tend to emphasise communal or societal shared norms. Dilemmas are both common and typically complex in health care, and especially in mental health care, because of the impact of mental health and disorder on identity, well-being, social relationships and functioning. These dilemmas become even more challenging and complex in forensic psychology and psychiatry because they often involve a clash between the values of biosciences (like psychology), the values of individual liberty and human rights, the values of the rule of law, and the process of justice. A common example of a dilemma for the forensic psychologist involves the prediction of risk: an offender with a history of serious interpersonal violence may report and demonstrate a sustained reduction in violence in an institutional setting. He may insist that he has no intentions of repeating his offending, and appears contrite in all interview scenarios. Actuarial analysis of his offending profile indicates a greater likelihood of risk recurrence than desistance in conditions of lower security. How might the psychologist balance the tensions of these two sources of information in relation to their recommendations as to the individual's future pathway? In another scenario, an offender with a mental disorder becomes highly disturbed and is brandishing a hand-made weapon. Emerging from his side room, he has removed all his clothes in preparation to attack staff and ensure that he is more difficult to manage using approved restraint techniques. As the situation is urgent, a team of staff decide to work together to escort him, despite the compromise to his dignity, to a safer room at the other end of the ward. In so doing, his nakedness is visible to those they pass on the unit. Ideally, it would be important to avoid this exposure but the staff felt that there was no time to act in any other way.

Forensic practitioners (whether forensic psychologists in prisons, the criminal justice system, secure hospitals, or in parole and probation services) regularly face ethical dilemmas, many of which will pit the welfare of offenders against the interests of others, including the state; the state to which we belong as citizens and with whose values we often identify. Practitioners may also be employed by the state in organisations whose primary task is to deliver justice and where the welfare of the individuals concerned is secondary (e.g. in prisons). Justice has been usefully be defined as: "a principle that describes the moral obligation to act on the basis of fair adjudication between competing claims" (Alzheimer Europe, 2010). It is not that the individual's welfare is irrelevant or unimportant; but it may not be the primary focus in some cases.

Balancing justice and welfare can raise real and difficult questions about professional identity and boundaries. Niveau and Welle (2018) distinguish the ethics of 'correctional' forensic 'clinical' practice (primarily deontological, in which the intention is 'good'), from the ethics of legal practice which are more consequentialist (based on the contribution made), with the goal of justice being achieved via objectivity and impartiality. The common ethical theme across both roles is the injunction not to collaborate in any activity that could lead to inhuman or degrading impacts. For example, in the case of the naked offender patient above, the management of a high risk situation with immediate impact (for the good of those at risk) by moving him, at the same time placed his dignity at risk in front of peers. While the team solved one problem, the solution generated another, as he now repeatedly recalls the incident as trauma-inducing for him. His expressed intention had been to evade 'hands on' restraint because this is a trigger for him to act violently, based on past experience.

The importance of ethical reflection in forensic psychology, and especially by those practitioners who assist justice and security services, has been recognised and discussed professionally for decades, from Kaslow (1980) to Forde (2017). There is no lack of guidance available for forensic psychologists or any other forensic practitioner facing an ethical dilemma in the course of their work. However, even with the best advice, attention to detail and reflection, the outcome in some scenarios may never feel 'right' or comfortable. In the most difficult dilemmas, it is important to record all discussions and reflections in order to illustrate that the process of ethical decision-making was rational, considered and fair, and would be what any person would want for themselves or a relative if their liberty or welfare was being subject to restraint, control or other forms of management. Where issues are long-standing (e.g. where mental disorder interacts with risk status) the process may need to be revisited many times to review and re-set the process of safe decision-making.

General Approaches to Ethics in Psychology and Mental Health Services

The 'Four Principles' (see Table 31.1) comprise a well-established approach to health care ethics (Beauchamp & Childress, 2009). Historically, it was clinicians who decided what was, and was not, an ethical dilemma, and they often took the view that they knew what was best for vulnerable people. The Four Principles approach became influential because it provided a practical framework for thinking about ethical decisions in health care, which included attention to principles (like respect for a patient's autonomy to make choices for themselves and always acting justly towards them), and to outcomes. When in doubt, ethical clinicians should act in ways that maximise welfare, good outcomes (beneficence), and do as little harm as possible (non-maleficence). Table 31.1 sets out these principles, the conditions required to make them viable, and the moral rules they imply.

This four principles model of health care ethics remains highly influential in general health care. However, it is not without problems when it comes to mental health care. First, mental disorders can compromise autonomy, which can make it more difficult for professionals to know how to 'respect' patient choices

Table 31.1 Four principles of health care ethics, the conditions that must exist for them to operate and moral obligations they require (Jahn, 2011)

Principle	Conditions to be met
Autonomy (covers intentionality, understanding and absence of controlling influences)	The person's right to retain control over his/her body. Professionals can suggest or advise but attempts to coerce or persuade the person into making a choice violate this principle. We are obliged to respect the self-determination of adults with decision-making capacity
Moral rules	Tell the truth; respect the privacy of others; protect confidential information and obtain consent for interventions
Beneficence	Providers must do all they can to benefit the patient in each situation. All recommendations must infer the most good for the patient, which requires an up-to-date knowledge base and a preparedness to consider individual differences (what works for one may not be best for another)
Moral rules	The edict to 'do n 'Do no harm'; the end goal for all decisions, including other people in society who could be harmed by a decision made
Non-maleficence	The edict to 'do no harm'; the end goal for all decisions, including other people in society who could be harmed by a decision made
Moral rules	Do not kill; do not cause pain of suffering; do no incapacitate and do not cause offence
Justice	References the element of fairness in all medical decisions, about burden and benefit, equal distribution of resources and treatments
Moral rules	Pivot on equitable distribution to each person according to need, effort, contribution, merit and equal share

(e.g. if they appear not to be in their best interests). Second, sometimes in order to benefit psychiatric patients, it is necessary to act in ways that the patient experiences as harmful (e.g. detention under the Mental Health Act legislation, which privileges beneficence over respect for autonomy, or the prescription and enforcement of medication that the patient prefers not to take). Most countries have some kind of mental health legislation that justifies professionals impos-ing treatment or assessment without consent (which is a breach of the duty to respect autonomy) because this will fulfil a duty to benefit the patient and pre-vents the harms of non-intervention where a condition is known to deteriorate in the absence of a potentially helpful treatment. States need to enact laws to do this because this is the best way to ensure that citizens who are mentally ill are treated justly; the Human Rights Act (HRA) (see Information Box 31.1) also provides a legal framework to protect citizens from detention without a properly constructed judicial process (Article 6).

Information Box 31.1: Human Rights Act 1998

The **Human Rights Act 1998** protects the rights of people in countries that belong to the Council of Europe. This includes the UK.

Human rights are based on principles, including dignity, fairness, respect and equality. Articles explaining these rights protect all citizens in daily life irrespective of who they are, where they live and how they chose to live their life.

Public authorities must follow this Act in everything they do. They must not interfere with rights and they must take positive steps to protect the rights of all in their care.

Examples of human rights include:

- the right to life
- the right to respect for private and family life
- the right to freedom of religion and belief.

And in particular for those with mental health disorders:

- the right not to be tortured or treated in an inhuman or degrading way
- the right to liberty
- the right not to be discriminated against.

Overall, the Four Principles is still a useful guide for mental health care pro-fessionals to use in relation to their patients. However, the approach may not apply so easily in those situations where the role of the professional is not as a clinician with a therapeutic aim, and where the person we interact with is not a 'patient' (i.e. a person with an assumed vulnerability/diagnosable impairment).

For example, a psychologist may be instructed to assess a male for the family court who is suspected of abusing and neglecting his child. The psychologist is asked to assess and report on the individual's mental health and psychological functioning and the purpose of the report is to assist the court in its deliberations about culpability. The report is 'for' the court and belongs to the court. It is not intended to improve the welfare of the person being assessed.

Ethical dilemmas in relation to respect for justice become most acute in locked and custodial environments where individuals' rights are over-ridden by law under specific circumstances. For example, Article 5 of the HRA gives everyone the right to liberty and security, but this right is trumped by international agreement that an institution has the right to remove liberty from those people who are risky to others, provided they have had access to a fair trial (Article 6). Decisions that deprive a citizen of liberty may increase that person's vulnerability both to further exploitation in detention and/or potentially stigmatising regimes (including unwanted treatment).

Psychologists in forensic settings have a collective responsibility to use their skills, abilities, and competences to enhance the effectiveness of law, and to demonstrate moral professional behaviour in all circumstances (Allan, 2018, 2019). In general, the ethical themes that challenge forensic psychologists fall into the following categories: (a) context and professional identity (b) welfare of evaluees and consent to assessment (c) honesty and integrity of risk assessment (d) duties to disclose and duties to protect confidentiality and (e) attention to professional codes.

Context and Professional Identity: What Is the Task and What Is My Role?

The ethical dilemma in Information Box 31.2 highlights the role question. The forensic psychologist needs to consider: whose agent am I? What is the purpose of this referral? What role am I fulfilling and for whom? Is there transparency about the way that I am working? For example, some forensic psychologists will be employed by prisons to prepare reports for parole hearings. In this role they are agents of the prisons who employ them (whether this is Her Majesty's Prison and Probation Service or a private prison), and therefore bound by professional contractual obligations to do the work that is asked of them. In relation to the Parole Board, they must provide reports that assist the Board with information about a prisoner's risk.

The most important ethical question is whether the *process* is transparent and honest; whether all prisoners understand that when the forensic psychologist meets with them, their own personal welfare is not the only issue under consideration. The psychologist needs to look at facts that relate to the welfare of others (see Information Box 31.2 for a brief case outline illustrating the implications of context).

Information Box 31.2: A complex case

A forensic psychologist is asked to work with a forensic psychiatrist to undertake an assessment of parenting skills for a mother and her temporary partner. Their 3-year-old daughter is presenting as insecure with some developmental delay and was observed to have a number of unexplained bruises by the GP during a session focused on the health needs of the parents.

The first thing the young mother says to the psychologist, before the purpose of the assessment has even been discussed, is: "If you take my baby away I will commit suicide myself, because I have been in care and I cannot let that happen to her".

Both forensic practitioners are legally required to make the child's welfare their priority but fulfilling this duty may mean that they cannot fulfil their duties to help a potential patient in distress. They may also have to act in a way that increases her distress if the evidence from the assessment convinces them that it is not safe for the child to be left in her care.

The context can be even more challenging for psychologists who get involved in interrogations; who advise security and intelligence agents about the best way to make a respondent anxious and likely to disclose information. In the USA, there have been concerns about forensic psychologists who have been employed to make sure that psychosocial pressures are sufficiently unpleasant to get a result, which might also be understood as assisting with torture (banned under Article 4 of the HRA; Patel & Elkin, 2015). This issue was raised in the USA in relation to prisoners detained in Guantanamo Bay detention unit, but has become 'live' in many countries who fear potential terrorist threats.

Welfare of Evaluees and Consent to Assessment

Is the role of the assessment clear to those who are being assessed? Prisoners or offenders awaiting trial may not understand that an interview with an apparently pleasant individual who seems so interested in them is actually designed to elicit information about potential risk factors and the probability of future offending. Prisoners are expected to comply with such assessments and must be informed that the outcome will be based on the assessment findings and that this may not be agreeable to them. Even if the opinion will be beneficial (in the assessor's view), the offenders may neither believe nor accept it as reasonable in their case. Respect for autonomy and human rights should require professionals to explain if any interview or assessment may not necessarily be in the subject's personal interests, and that they can (in theory) refuse to participate. Prisoners may point out that any refusal to engage in risk assessment may equally be held against them, and this is part of the ethical dilemma *they* face.

Even in secure psychiatric settings, where forensic psychologists are employed by health trusts to work with detained patients, there may still be times when the main purposes of any interview or assessment are not actually for the benefit of the person. In these circumstances, getting consent must be respectfully undertaken even if this leads to a refusal to participate. It is candid to acknowledge that there is clash of interests between institution and individual and the forensic professional is not going to be dishonest about this. Information Box 31.3 provides a brief case example.

Information Box 31.3: Welfare of prisoner and consent to risk assessment: whose rights must be prioritised here?

A (trained) forensic psychologist is asked to undertake a Penile Plethysmograph (PPG)* assessment with an inmate with a known history (determined by DNA) of sexual offending (against young women), who is over tariff. The parole board believe the inmate to be at high risk of re-offending. The psychologist explains the rational for the assessment. The inmate refuses to undertake the test citing the fact that his religion does not allow him to engage. A fair decision about the inmate's future has to be made in the absence of this form of current information about sexual aberration.

Phallometry* is a measure of blood flow to the penis which can give an indication of 'deviant' arousal which may be associated with increased risk of sexual assault. Meta-analytic research evidence has indicated that this form of assessment has the highest predictive accuracy in relation to future sex crimes (Hanson & Bussiere, 1998).

Honesty, Impartiality and Integrity of Risk Assessment

Information Box 31.3 highlights why risk assessment remains an ethically sensitive area for forensic psychologists. This is because the outcome of any risk assessment may have direct (and often negative) effects on another person's liberty, freedom and general public image. The evaluee's own view is treated as if it must be assumed to be unreliable and invalid, while the forensic psychologist's view is assumed to be honest and impartial. However, forensic psychologists may come under pressure to provide reports that support continuing detention if the prisoner whose parole is being considered is high profile. No professional is immune to influence: it is easy to be swayed by newspaper accounts of a prisoner's past crimes, especially if they involve acts of deliberate/planned cruelty towards others. It may be especially difficult not to rate risk as higher in cases where the victims were vulnerable and defenceless, such as children or older adults, despite the absence of evidence that victim vulnerability affects future risk.

Maintaining honesty and impartiality can be difficult in forensic settings for all kinds of practitioners. Any person may develop or acknowledge prejudice against different kinds of offenders, especially if the offender presents in a challenging or incomprehensible way. Yet, these understandable human responses should not be allowed to complicate the process of accurate assessment of risk. To obscure matters even further, the tools of the trade are not fail-safe: Forde (2017) has argued that many risk assessment tools used by forensic psychologists for parole hearings are not fit for this purpose because they are not evidenced based. He gives examples of occasions when he has challenged the prison's risk assessment with good quality evidence, which has had repercussions for his own professional standing (he himself being accused of bad practice). Forde also gives an account of evidence in relation to a state-supported intervention programme for sex offenders not only did not reduce risk, but may have increased it. The finding was initially suppressed and was later denied by the authorities who had commissioned the original research. Politically, this is contentious for prison services. Given that prisoners' detention is justified on the basis that they must complete a prison programme to reduce risk, it is hard to see how their right to be provided with effective interventions can be met, if there is no evidence that the intervention is effective. The state of the evidence on the effectiveness of these programmes is discussed by Lösel and colleagues (Lösel et al., 2020).

Duties to Disclose and Duties to Protect Confidentiality

All health care professionals are aware that personal information obtained in the course of their work is sensitive and cannot be disclosed without the individual's consent. This ethical principle ('no disclosure without consent') is also known as the principle of respect for confidentiality, and it has a long tradition in general health care as well as psychology. However, it is also recognised that there is no absolute right to complete confidentiality, and most discussions about confidentiality arise when professionals believe they must breach it, with or without consent. The commonest justification for breaching confidentiality is that disclosure will reduce the risk of serious harm or increase the welfare of another person.

If the individual consents to disclosure then there is no difficulty, and where psychologists have concerns about risk, the first step can always be to seek consent to disclose, explaining why and how, and providing reassurance about the purpose and scope of the disclosure. In most cases, the individual will consent to disclosure if the purpose and scope is explained.

For forensic psychologists, there may be a particular concern about the relationship between ethical duties and risk assessment. Forensic psychologists may be employed (e.g. by the Crown Prosecution Service or a state run prison) to assess an individual who is accused or convicted of a crime. In those circumstances, forensic psychologists may argue that they have a duty to the organisation that employs and instructs them, that they do not have a therapeutic relationship with the individual being assessed (i.e. the individual is not like a 'patient' in a health care setting), and the justice process needs information that assists the prosecution as much as the defence. In response, the individual being assessed may protest that they cannot tell between a psychologist who is there to help them as a therapist, and a psychologist who is instructed by the Criminal Justice system They may also say that the psychologist will use psychological skills to draw out information from the individual, which is then used against them in terms of the criminal justice process. This dilemma especially arises when forensic psychologists are asked to assess convicted offenders to determine their level of risk to other people, and where that assessment may then help a judge decide whether to impose a longer than normal sentence or a special order to manage risk (as happens in Scotland and the Netherlands).

The solution here is to get informed consent to risk assessment; even if that may mean that the person being assessed is non-cooperative or completely refuses to engage. The HRA provides protection against unfair trial processes, which includes being invited to self-incriminate without warning. People being evaluated for the state or the prison service must be informed about the nature and purposes of any assessment and the use to which the contents will be put.

There is another area of ethical concern that forensic psychologists experience, which is when they are working with an offender who then discloses information that makes the psychologist aware that a third party is at increased risk from the offender. If they are sure that the offender would not consent to disclosure of this risk information, then the forensic psychologist may perceive an ethical imperative to disclose the information in the face of an offender's flat refusal or even without the offenders' awareness of the disclosure. This kind of situation makes forensic professionals uneasy because it is potentially deceptive and dishonest in a way that sits uneasily with the prosocial values that underpin forensic mental health. Yet, if disclosure of this information would lead to reduction of risk of harm to others, especially the vulnerable, then arguably this is a reasonable justification for the disclosure.

There are some well-publicised cases where concerns about risk to others led mental health professionals to disclose personal information in order to reduce that risk. In the 1970s, an American case involving a counselling psychologist determined that psychological therapists had a duty to protect third parties from their patients, which could include breaching patient confidentiality. The English courts have been more cautious in their approach: while agreeing in principle that reducing the risk of serious harm to others could justify disclosure of confidential information, each case needs to be decided on its own merits and there is no specific duty to protect third parties (as there is in some states in the USA). The only exception to this is in relation to child protection where concern about a child at risk is generally held to justify disclosure of personal information, and professionals are expected to raise concerns about children at risk (safeguarding) as soon as they have cause. In a recent English case (ABC *vs* St George's health care), the court found that forensic professionals had discretion as to whether they disclosed risk information to third parties without consent, but they had a legal duty to carry out a balancing exercise, which examined the benefits of disclosure against the risks of breaching confidentiality.

Attention to Professional Codes

All professionals have codes of conduct and ethics that set standards of competence and performance as well as expectations of how they should relate to their clients. Martindale and Gould (2012) review the different kinds of codes that have been developed for forensic practitioners in the light of the context of their work and the ethical tensions described above.

In general, forensic practitioners' practice is regulated by their national licencing body. In the UK, forensic psychologists are regulated through the Health Care Professional Council (HCPC), which regulates all health care professionals (apart from doctors). Forensic practitioners may also be affiliated to the British Psychological Society (BPS) through the Division of Forensic Psychology. In the USA, forensic practitioners are regulated by the American Psychological Association (APA). The HCPC, the BPS and the APA have codes of ethics and conduct that act as standards for professional practice, and provide ethical guidance in relation to common dilemmas, such as issues of breaching confidentiality and consent to treatment and research participation. A summary is set out in Information Box 31.4.

Information Box 31.4: Professional Codes: Some examples
American Psychological Association, APA (2013) **Offers speciality guidelines for forensic psychology, covering:**

(1) Responsibilities
(2) Competence
(3) Diligence
(4) Relationships
(5) Fees
(6) Informed Consent, Notification and Assent
(7) Conflicts in Practice
(8) Privacy, Confidentiality and Privilege
(9) Methods and Procedures
(10) Assessment
(11) Professional and other public communications.

Health Care Professional Council (HCPC, 2016) **Standards of conduct**

(1) Promote and protect the interests of service users and carers
(2) Communicate appropriately and effectively
(3) Work within your knowledge and skills
(4) Delegate appropriately
(5) Respect confidentiality
(6) Manage risk
(7) Report concerns about safety
(8) Be honest and trustworthy
(9) Keep records of your work.

British Psychological Society Code of Ethics and Conduct (2018)
  Four principles of conduct described in a statement of values:

(1) Respect—for the dignity of persons and peoples
(2) Competence—the ability to provide specific services to a requisite standard
(3) Responsibility—must be accepted for what is within the power, control or management of the professional.
(4) Integrity—involving honest, truthful, accurate and consistent actions, words, decisions, methods and outcomes.

There is some degree of international consensus that forensic psychological practice generates particular issues in terms of professional codes. For example, Day and White (2008) comment on the utility of the Australian Psychologists Code of Ethics for forensic psychologists, useful for guiding practitioners, and thereby protecting the reputation of the individual practitioner and the profession. The UK BPS also offers ethical guidance for forensic practitioners, particularly in relation to applied psychological practice in the field of extremism and terrorism (BPS, 2018). The APA (2013) has developed specialist guidelines for forensic psychology, which set out eleven different responsibilities, including competence, diligence, relationships, fees, obtaining consent or assent and respect for confidentiality. These have been developed because of the complex relationship between forensic psychology and law, especially in the domain of giving expert testimony (Strasburger et al., 1997).

Ultimately, professional codes are guidelines that help regulators decide if professionals have met or failed to meet standards for fitness to practise. As such, they cannot give detailed ethical advice in every situation. It is always wise for psychologists to consult professional codes and guidelines as part of a more general ethical decision-making process, and record that they have done so. Documentation and the importance of careful, thorough note-taking is essential in forensic clinical practice; as is the noting of sources in forensic evaluation. The sharing of dilemmas via formal review with senior peers is another tool: ethics rounds (Schmitz et al., 2018) allow colleagues to explore the feelings that arise in complex case work that might otherwise cloud sound judgement. Ethics consultation services are not without their critics, but are commonplace in well-functioning hospitals in the USA (Fox et al., 2007) and Europe (Pfafflin et al., 2009). Vignette-based, shared case study examples between colleagues offer multiple opportunities to explore dilemmas within the safety of a learning space. Education on ethics has been shown to be effective in enhancing professional competence, and sponsoring resilience given the challenges to boundaries in modern life presented by social media (Knapp & VandeCreek, 2012).

Conclusion: Ethics as the Foundation for All Forensic Practice

Attention to ethical dilemmas is not optional in forensic settings and is arguably central to all levels of practice, from the individual practitioner to the forensic organisation in which they work (Metwally, 2019). For the public, ethical codes provide some assurance of trust in a profession, organise expectations and safeguard welfare. All forensic practitioners need to become skilled in ethical reasoning and recognise when a dilemma is an ethical, rather than a clinical, one.

For most people who work in forensic settings, ethical dilemmas are a daily occurrence, as the values of the state's right to protect the community from risky offenders clash with the offenders' right as human beings to be treated with dignity, and to be offered the chance to reduce their risk and contribute to the restoration of justice. Both rights need attention and neither should have priority over the other. Having time for review and reflection with trained peers improves the quality of ethical decision-making and also provides an opportunity to process the emotional demands of making ethical decisions in forensic settings. Anxieties will inevitably arise in the work (often a sign of role or other conflict), and sharing these in supervisory spaces can facilitate ideas for the resolution of conflicting concerns (Ward & Brigden, 2007). Holding the interests of all in mind when making any decision is the baseline for the additional review of what is ethical, right and fair.

References

Allan, A. (2019). Being ethical psychologists in correction settings. In *The Wiley international handbook of correctional psychology* (pp. 30–44).

Allan, A. (2018). Moral challenges for psychologists working in psychology and law. *Psychiatry, Psychology and Law, 25*(3), 485–499.

Alzheimer Europe. (2010, March 29). *Justice: The four common bioethical principles.* https://www.alzheimer-europe.org/Ethics/Definitions-and-approaches/The-four-common-bioethical-principles/Justice.

American Psychological Association. (2013). Specialty guidelines for forensic psychology. *The American Psychologist, 68*(1), 7–19. https://doi.org/10.1037/a0029889.

Beauchamp, T. L., & Childress, J. F. (2009). *Principles of biomedical ethics* (6th ed.). Oxford University Press.

British Psychological Society. (2018). *Code of ethics and conduct.* Retrieved November 15, 2020 from https://www.bps.org.uk/news-and-policy/bps-code-ethics-and-conduct.

British Psychological Society Division of Forensic Psychology Working party on extremism. (2018). *Ethical guidelines for applied psychological practice in the field of extremism, violent extremism and terrorism.* Retrieved November 15, 2020, from https://www.bps.org.uk/news-and-policy/ethical-guidelines-applied-psychological-practice-field-extremism-violent-extremism.

Day, A., & White, J. (2008). Ethical practice from the perspective of the forensic psychologist: Commentary on the uses and value of the Australian Psychological Society (2007) code of ethics. *Australian Psychologist, 43*(3), 186–193.

Day, J. M., & Tappan, M. B. (1996). The narrative approach to moral development: From the epistemic subject to dialogical selves. *Human Development, 39*(2), 67–82.

Forde, R. A. (2017). *Bad psychology: How forensic psychology left science behind.* Jessica Kingsley Publishers.

Fox, E., Myers, S, & Pearlman, R. A. (2007). Ethics consultation in United States hospital: A national survey. *The American Journal of Bioethics.* Taylor & Francis.

Gilligan, C. (1977). In a different voice: Women's conceptions of self and of morality. *Harvard Educational Review, 47*(4), 481–517.

Hanson, R. K., & Bussiere, M. T. (1998). Predicting relapse: A meta-analysis of sexual offender recidivism studies. *Journal of Consulting and Clinical Psychology., 66*(2), 348–362. https://doi.org/10.1037/0022-006x.66.2.348.

Health Care Professions Council. (2016). *Standards of conduct, performance and ethics.* Retrieved November 15, 2020, from https://www.hcpc-uk.org/standards/standards-of-conduct-performance-and-ethics/.

Human Rights Act 1998. Available at https://www.legislation.gov.uk/ukpga/1998/42/contents. Accessed 11 February 2021.

Jahn, W. T. (2011). The 4 basic ethical principles that apply to forensic activities are respect for autonomy, beneficence, non-maleficence, and justice. *Journal of Chiropractic Medicine, 10*(3), 225–226.

Kaslow, F. W. (1980). Ethical problems in prison psychology, 3–9.

Knapp, S. J., & VandeCreek, L. D. (2012). *Practical ethics for psychologists: A positive approach* (2nd ed.). American Psychological Association.

Lösel, F., Link, E., Schmucker, M., Bender, D., Breuer, M., Carl, L., Endres, J., & Lauchs, L. (2020). On the effectiveness of sexual offender treatment in prisons: A comparison of two different evaluation designs in routine practice. *Sexual Abuse, 32*(4), 452–475. https://doi.org/10.1177/1079063219871576.

Martindale, D. A., & Gould, J. W. (2012). Ethics in forensic practice. Chapter 3 (37–61), Volume 11, *Forensic psychology, of the handbook of psychology* (2nd ed.). I. Weiner, series editor; R. K. Otto, volume editor. Wiley.

Metwally, M. (2019). Forensic organizational psychology: Shedding light on the positive repercussions of ethical leadership in forensic medicine. *Egyptian Journal of Forensic Sciences, 9*(1), 32–40.

Niveau, G., & Welle, I. (2018). Forensic psychiatry, one subspeciality with two ethics? A systematic review. *BMC Medical Ethics, 19*(1), 25. https://doi.org/10.1186/s12910-018-0266-5.

Patel, N. A., & Elkin, G. D. (2015). Professionalism and conflicting interests: The American Psychological Association's involvement in torture. *AMA Journal of Ethics, 17*(10), 924–930.

Pfafflin, M., Robert, R., & Reiter-Theil, S. (2009). Evaluating clinical ethics consultation: A European perspective. *Healthcare Ethics*. HeinOnline.

Pratt, M. W., Arnold, M. L., & Lawford, H. (2009). Growing towards care: A narrative approach to prosocial moral identity and generativity of personality in emerging adulthood. In *Personality, identity, and character: Explorations in moral psychology* (pp. 295–315).

Schmitz, D., Gross, D., Frierson, C., Schubert, G. A., Schulze-Steinen, H., & Kersten, A. (2018). Ethics rounds: Affecting ethics quality at all organisational levels. *Journal of Medical Ethics, 44*(12). https://doi.org/10.1136/medethics-2018-104831.

Stams, G. J., Brugman, D., Dekovic, M., Van Rosmalen, L., Van Der Laan, P., & Gibbs, J. C. (2006). The moral judgment of juvenile delinquents: A meta-analysis. *Journal of Abnormal Child Psychology, 34*(5), 692–708.

Strasburger, L. H., Gutheil, T. G., & Brodsky, A. (1997). On wearing two hats: Role conflict in serving as both psychotherapist and expert witness. *American Journal of Psychiatry, 154*(4), 448–456.

Tappan, M. B. (1989). Stories lived and stories told: The narrative structure of late adolescent moral development. *Human Development, 32*(5), 300–315.

Ward, T., & Birgden, A. (2007). Human rights and correctional clinical practice. *Aggression and Violent Behavior, 12*, 628–643.

Suggested Reading

Bowers, L., & Friendship, C. (2017). Forensic psychological risk assessments for the Parole Board. In *Assessments in forensic practice: A handbook* (pp. 103–121).

Downing Hansen, N., & Goldberg, S. G. (1999). Navigating the nuances: A matrix of considerations for ethical-legal dilemmas. *Professional Psychology: Research and Practice, 30*(5), 495–503.

O'Donohue, W. T., & Ferguson, K. (Eds.). (2003). *Handbook of professional ethics for psychologists: Issues, questions, and controversies.* Sage.

Pirelle,G., Beattey, R. A., & Zapf, P. A. (2017). *The ethical practice of forensic psychology: A casebook*. Oxford University Press.

Weissman, H. N., & DeBow, D. M. (2003). Ethical principles and professional competencies. In I. B. Weiner (Series Ed.) & A. M. Goldstein (Vol. Ed.), Handbook of psychology (Vol. 11). Forensic psychology (pp. 33–53). Wiley.

Index

A

Accountability, 15, 68, 556
Actuarial, 175, 429, 480–487, 489, 495, 498, 611
Actuarial risk assessment instruments (ARAIs), 483–486, 489, 490, 492, 498, 502, 541
Adolescence, 35, 36, 39, 41, 53, 57, 69, 183, 184, 187–189, 191–193, 252, 289, 291–293, 308, 360, 361, 378, 386, 495, 602, 603, 610
Adolescents, 18, 68, 69, 71, 73, 75, 76, 129, 132, 165, 185, 187, 189, 192, 229, 288, 293, 305, 360, 364, 379, 380, 480, 495, 588, 589, 591, 592, 602–605
Adults, 33, 70, 110, 165, 185, 207, 208, 229, 276, 288, 293, 304, 305, 310–312, 345, 348, 362, 364, 398, 399, 401, 403–406, 417, 418, 423, 431, 462, 466, 480, 516, 570, 576, 602, 604, 605, 610, 613, 618
Adverse childhood experiences (ACEs), 207, 261
Affect dysregulation, 167
Affective empathy, 130, 131, 277, 278
Affect regulation, 208
Aggression, 36, 49, 54, 56, 59, 73, 87, 90–93, 95–100, 110, 112, 113, 119, 120, 133, 177, 184, 186, 188, 189, 205, 212, 227, 228, 232, 243, 246, 249, 252, 272, 288, 290, 294, 308, 323, 339, 346, 357–361, 364, 367, 369, 370, 383, 423, 463, 465, 469, 481, 487, 520, 521, 527, 530, 570, 571, 588–591, 594, 598, 603
Aggression and violence, 88, 94, 208, 227, 346
Aggression (proactive, reactive, relational), 51, 53, 55, 58, 91, 92, 98, 113, 119, 227, 272, 273, 277, 357, 359, 366, 591
Aggression subtypes, 359, 363, 365, 367
Alcohol-related crime, 348
Alliance, 177, 214, 331, 384, 496
Ambivalent, 164, 165, 167, 171, 175, 249
American Psychological Association, 6, 522, 621
American Psychology-Law Society, 5
Anger, 55, 88–94, 98–101, 157, 166, 176, 208, 226, 229, 230, 233, 243, 246, 252, 257, 259, 274, 290, 345–347, 349, 403, 405, 469, 492, 520–522, 563, 571, 575, 588–592, 598
Anger management, 100, 333, 569, 571, 574
Anger treatment, 345, 346, 348, 349
Antisocial, 11, 12, 14, 30, 34, 37, 50–59, 68, 71–73, 76, 77, 88, 92, 95, 97, 100, 110, 111, 120, 169, 185,

Printed in Great Britain
by Amazon

23917105R00368